JUDGING JUDGES

The Investigation of Rose Bird and the California Supreme Court

PREBLE STOLZ

THE FREE PRESS
A Division of Macmillan Publishing Co., Inc.
NEW YORK

Collier Macmillan Publishers
LONDON

The Free Press
A Division of Macmillan Publishing Co., Inc.
866 Third Avenue, New York, N. Y. 10022

Collier Macmillan Canada, Ltd.

Library of Congress Catalog Card Number: 81–67161

Printed in the United States of America

printing number
1 2 3 4 5 6 7 8 9 10

Library of Congress Cataloging in Publication Data

Stolz, Preble.
    Judging judges.

    Includes index.
        1. California. Supreme Court. 2. Bird, Rose
Elizabeth. 3. Judicial ethics—California. 4. Los
Angeles times. I. Title.
KFC960.S86   347.94073534   81–67161
ISBN 0-02-931670-7   AACR2

To Mary Jane

Contents

Contents

Foreword

by Anthony Lewis

This book tells a strange and disturbing tale: a true story about law and politics and journalism. It all happened in California, which makes it somewhat suspect for those of us who think of that state as far-out in more than a geographical sense. Moreover, I think the California setting may actually have affected what happened. The compulsive openness found there—the need to let everything hang out—seemed to move from the pages of fiction parodying life in Marin County to the reality of life in that usually most private institution, the judiciary. I wonder whether, in another state, participants in such an affair would have been so quick to go public with not just their actions but their emotions. And it was the public tangling of emotions that pushed these events along on their disturbing course.

But it is not just a California matter. This is a story for everyone who cares about the quality of law and the courts, and about the performance of the press. In American society those are subjects of fundamental importance, and here the reader is given a unique insight into them. Human and professional factors in the development of the law, usually concealed, are brought to light; and beyond those, the story raises large questions about the function of judges. The purpose of this Foreword is to give an outsider's appraisal. In writing it I find myself in an unusual position, for I differ with the author about some lessons to be drawn from the facts of his curious tale. But Professor Stolz says he does not desire conformity, and I proceed on that basis.

In stark outline, the story goes like this:

On Nov. 7, 1978, election day, the *Los Angeles Times* published a page one story saying that the California Supreme Court had "decided to overturn" a state law mandating a prison term for anyone using a gun in a serious crime, but that the court was delaying announcement of the decision. The piece had powerful political overtones. It said that the court's new Chief Justice, Rose Elizabeth Bird, was part of a four-to-three majority against the politically popular gun law. That very day the voters of California were deciding whether to confirm Bird in her position, and the implication of the *Times* story was that the court's decision was being delayed to help her election chances. In the event she won, very narrowly. Further charges and denials of the *Los Angeles Times* article followed, and demands for investigation by a state agency, the Commission on Judicial Performance—demands that Chief Justice Bird herself joined on November 24. On December 22 the court announced its decision in the gun law case, *People v. Tanner;* a four-judge majority, on diverse grounds, held that Tanner need not be sentenced to prison although he had used a gun in a robbery. In February, 1979, the court agreed to rehear the case, and in June it announced a contrary conclusion about the gun law; one judge had switched to produce a four–three majority the other way. The Commission on Judicial Performance then held open, highly-publicized hearings on whether there had been improper delay or leaks in the case. Five members of the Supreme Court testified, displaying bitter internal divisions. Then a sixth, Stanley Mosk, sued for the right to be questioned only in private. An ad hoc Supreme Court held that the open hearings violated a state constitutional requirement of confidentiality in the commission's proceedings, and the public circus came to an end. On November 5, 1979, the commission announced that it had found no basis for bringing formal charges against any member of the court.

Much ado about nothing, one may think: The delaying of a judicial decision is hardly a capital offense. Nor was there any convincing proof in all the Commission hearings and all the public slanging that anyone had improperly delayed the *Tanner* decision. How, then, did a court that was once one of the most respected state supreme courts get into such a pickle?

Professor Stolz believes that faults of character and discipline among the California justices were primarily responsible for bringing on the public imbroglio so damaging to the reputation of their court. He seems especially critical of Chief Justice Bird and of her strongest personal supporter on the court, Justice Mathew Tobriner—unfairly so, I think.

But before I come to the question of how the judges behaved, I have a deeper difference with Professor Stolz. He acquits the party that I think bears the heaviest responsibility: the *Los Angeles Times*.

It was the *Times* story of November 7, 1978, that precipitated events. Was it a fair story? Was it responsible? I think the answer to those questions is no.

The story, by William Endicott and Robert Fairbanks, began by saying that the court had "decided" the *Tanner* case but "not made the decision public." Well down in the piece it explained: "Technically, no Supreme Court decision is final until thirty days after it is announced. But as a practical matter, decisions become final when each justice has either drafted an opinion of his or her own, or signed one drafted by a colleague." These statements were untrue, betraying an ignorance of the way the California Supreme Court and many other appellate courts work. Individual members of those courts prepare opinions, and the opinions are circulated among their colleagues. They agree or disagree, comment and criticize; the opinions are then revised in light of what has been said. Intense bargaining may go on, and minds may change. In the process what began as majority opinions may become dissents; that has often happened in the United States Supreme Court. (The classic text on the subject is Alexander Bickel's *The Unpublished Opinions of Mr. Justice Brandeis.*) There is, therefore, no "decision" until the court has finally frozen the process by publishing its opinions. Endicott and Fairbanks, who are highly-regarded reporters in other areas, evidently did not understand the judicial process.

What of the story's statement that the announcement of the *Tanner* opinions had been "delayed?" In bare terms, the statement was true— but meaningless. The fact that courts are slow in deciding cases does not rise even to the dog-bites-man level of news interest. The point here was the suggested reason for the delay. The story implied, slyly but unmistakably, that it was a political reason. Announcement of the case, it said, was "being delayed by Associate Justice Mathew O. Tobriner, who has been one of Ms. Bird's strong supporters against a well-organized campaign to win voter disapproval of her appointment to the court." In case that hint was not clear enough, the story farther down recalled a month-old statement by the Republican candidate for Governor, speculating that the supreme court was holding up sensitive decisions until after the election for political reasons. That was the way the story was generally read in November, 1978. That was the accusation that aroused an outcry and that soon led to the demands for a formal investigation by the Commission on Judicial Performance. The commission, after exhaustively canvasing the evidence, decided not to bring charges against any member of the court for what would surely have deserved censure if it had happened: holding up a decision for political reasons. The commission, in short, found no persuasive evidence to support the real point of the *Los Angeles Times* story.

Newspapers cannot always be absolutely accurate. The Supreme Court of the United States has indeed said, in the great case of *New York Times v. Sullivan*, that the First Amendment does not allow libel judgments holding the press to a legal standard of absolute truth in comments on public officials. But when a newspaper prints what amounts to a grave charge, not least on election day, it should be held to a professional standard of fairness and responsibility.

What was the basis for the *Times* story? In the lead paragraph it referred to "well-placed court sources," naming no names. In the seventh paragraph it said two justices had "confirmed that individual decisions were signed some time ago by all members of the court. The justices could not explain why the outcome had not been announced." That passage, taken literally, did not mean much because, as explained above, an appellate judge may write an opinion and then change it in reaction to colleagues' views. But the passage was generally, and understandably, taken to mean more: to mean that two members of the court had confirmed an improper delay in the announcement of the *Tanner* decision. Who were those two justices, and had they confirmed the story? The commission's public hearings provided substantial answers to those questions.

The day before the election Justice William Clark of the California Supreme Court had a telephone call from a far-right member of the state senate, H. L. Richardson. Through an organization called the Law and Order Campaign Committee, Senator Richardson was campaigning for the defeat of Chief Justice Bird. The tone of his effort was indicated by a television commercial he had prepared; it showed an apparent assault on a woman and had a voice say: "Next May that rapist could be on the streets again because Rose Bird and the Supreme Court reversed an appellate decision. . . ." (For reasons explored by Professor Stolz, few viewers actually saw the ad.) Senator Richardson asked Justice Clark whether he would talk with reporters about the *Tanner* case. Clark replied, he told the commission, that he could not talk about a pending case but that "I customarily take press calls." Soon afterward Robert Fairbanks telephoned Justice Clark. He said, Clark testified, that he had a story about the justices' vote in *Tanner* and the fact that it was not being announced. Clark said he told Fairbanks that he did not want to discuss it. "I may have added, 'I don't understand why you are calling for confirmation if you think you have a story.'" Later that afternoon Fairbanks called again. He said, Clark testified, that he had talked in the meantime with Justice Mosk, who "responded that he wouldn't confirm their story . . . but stated that they certainly have interesting sources or good sources." Then, as Clark recalled, Fairbanks asked him: "If in the morning you should read the story that I have described to you, will you throw your coffee cup against the wall?" Clark said he responded only with a chuckle. That evening Fairbanks called a third time. He read to Clark the sentence in the story about confirmation by two justices. In the commission hearings, this exchange followed:

Q. Did it occur to you as you listened to him that you might well be one of the two justices he was referring to when he said two justices had confirmed that?
A. Yes, it did.
Q. Did you say anything at all to disabuse him of that possible idea?
A. No, I believe not.

There can be little doubt that Mosk and Clark were the two justices cited in the story as confirming sources. Were the reporters professionally justified in relying on what the two said, or did not say, as confirmation? In each case there had been what might have been a suggestive hint, but there was certainly nothing that in common English could be called a confirmation. Professor Stolz says this raises a large question: "Should a newspaper depend for important stories on the failure to deny as the equivalent of an affirmation?" He indicates that he has some doubts, asking whether the press should not stop trying to trick people into answers, but he concludes that "it would be quite wrong to fault the Times or Fairbanks for failing to live up to that ideal since the current generally accepted ethic of the press is clearly to the contrary."

There Professor Stolz and I part company. I do not believe it is the ethic of the responsible American press to rely on the sort of thing Justices Mosk and Clark said as "confirmation" for a sensitive story. In fact I am confident that most editors would reject any such notion. How, then, can one explain what was done here by reporters and editors of one of the country's best newspapers? My guess is that they were carried away by the lure of an exciting scoop—one whose significance would fade, moreover, if they did not rush the story into print the next morning. Just about every journalist knows that feeling of temptation. I have yielded to it myself, and later regretted what turned out to be a half-understood or inaccurate story. It is an explanation, not an excuse.

Of course there is the possibility that Justice Clark was not telling the truth in his testimony to the commission. Perhaps he really said to Fairbanks, in one of those conversations the day before the election, that the reporters had the story right. Perhaps Justice Mosk, who has not publicly explained his role, said more than we know to Fairbanks or Endicott. I doubt it. But if either of them did, or indeed on the scenario we have, another question arises: Was it fair for the *Los Angeles Times* to rely on those two members of the court as sources of a story damaging to Rose Bird without acknowledging, to itself and to its readers, how those two justices felt about Chief Justice Bird?

When Governor Jerry Brown picked Rose Bird, Stanley Mosk thought he should have been promoted to Chief Justice; his bitter disappointment was widely known. Beyond that, he gave public indications of animosity toward Bird. Shortly before the 1978 election the California Trial Lawyers' Association offered Justice Mosk its award as Appellate Judge of the Year. He turned it down, explaining—as the president of the association told his board in a letter—that "we had no business getting involved in the Rose Bird campaign or coming out in support of her without knowing all the facts." That letter was published in the newspapers a week before the election. On November 12, 1978, the *San Francisco Examiner* published an article by Justice Mosk ridiculing the use of such words as "chairperson" or "chair" instead of "chairman" as a gesture to women's rights. As one example, he said the chief justice of California had always been "chairman" of the State Judicial Council. "Since Rose Bird has been chief justice, however, a new designation of 'chairperson' has unceremoniously appeared." As to Justice Clark, his differences with Chief Justice Bird were well-known. Clark, a Reagan appointee, was the court's most conservative member, given to a sarcastic style in dissent. Bird was strongly in the liberal tradition.

The unfairness of failing to note that the judicial sources on whom the story relied were not exactly friends of Rose Bird was multiplied by the treatment given to Justice Tobriner. Describing him as a "strong supporter" of Bird, the story said Tobriner had hedged on whether he was delaying the *Tanner* decision, saying: "I'm utterly sealed. My oath is not to disclose anything that goes on in this court. I can say nothing, absolutely zero, zero, zero." That refusal to comment happened to be a proper response for a judge to make. But in the story it looked evasive, and harmful to Bird, particularly in contrast to the seeming (but nonexistent) candor of the two unidentified justices who were said to have confirmed the report.

Professor Stolz says that once Endicott and Fairbanks filed their story, the editors "had no realistic alternative" to printing it on election day. To postpone publication would have been seen "as a cover-up dictated by editorial policy." I think the editors had an alternative that was not only realistic but professionally required. That was to read such a story with a highly critical eye, question the reporters on the nature of the "confirmation" asserted and then, when they appreciated the flimsy basis for the story, hold the piece until it could be reported more fully and convincingly. Given these reporters' lack of acquaintance with the judicial process, the editors also might have discussed the story with a knowledgeable lawyer. If someone calls the refusal to rush into print with such a thin and inaccurate piece a "cover-up," the short answer is that editors are paid to keep such things out of the paper and to take any abuse that follows.

An outstanding lesson of the California Supreme Court inquiry for me, therefore, is how much damage a newspaper can do to a fragile institution when it writes without understanding or sensitivity in especially sensitive circumstances. And the courts are fragile. Professor Stolz quotes a superb statement of that truth by the counsel to the Commission on Judicial Performance in this proceeding, Seth Hufstedler. Hufstedler's message was that courts have to exercise a delicate kind of power that depends on public acceptance and also on a free and collaborative intellectual relationship among the judges. What happened to the California Supreme Court in the year starting November 7, 1978, threatened both those necessary conditions.

The fault did not by any means lie only with the *Los Angeles Times* story. As Professor Stolz says, the California Supreme Court itself bore much of the responsibility. It had lost touch to a troubling degree with its natural constituencies in the bar and at the law schools. Its procedures were archaic and discouraged a collaborative process among the justices. And personal relations were in some cases dismal. For the last, Professor Stolz blames several members of the court, criticizing them vigorously, but he seems to assign the heaviest responsibility to Chief Justice Bird. There again I reach a somewhat different conclusion on the facts he states.

The charges against Bird fall broadly into two categories: that she was a bad administrator, injuring the feelings of some people by her brusque ways when she became Chief Justice; and that she was oversensitive to disagreement or criticism, especially when it came from Justice Clark.

The first complaint has some basis. The Chief Justice has large administrative powers over the whole enormous California court system. When Rose Bird took office, she immediately and without consultation introduced changes that upset lower-court judges and caused the long-time chief staff administrator of the system to resign. So even assuming that she intended only to modernize and improve the system, she went about her work in ways that gave the staff and other judges reason for offense. But it is only fair to say also—and I think Professor Stolz understates this point—that there were some less worthy reasons for resentment of Rose Bird. She was only forty years old when appointed Chief Justice, she had never been a judge of any kind and she was the first woman on that court. In short, she was not part of the fraternity. Moreover, suspicion attached to her because of the Governor who had appointed her. Jerry Brown had treated the judges of the state with what looked like deliberate and ignorant disdain, as Professor Stolz brings out. If he had appointed Bird as an associate justice, there would have been less reaction. Making her chief justice may have struck some lawyers and judges as a move calculated to irritate and shake up people the governor considered old fogies. Looking at her record a year after the affair of the inquiry ended, my impression is that she has surmounted some of the suspicions and recovered from her over-abrupt beginnings. California lawyers tell me that she is at least performing conscientiously as a judicial administrator and doing more than her share of the court's opinions.

In discussing Rose Bird's personal characteristics, Professor Stolz calls her basically decent, diligent, intelligent, well-spoken, and highly-motivated. The fatal flaw that he sees is over-sensitivity: a tendency to retreat into a lonely, bruised privacy when human relations become difficult. Even her friends concede that she is too quick to take offense. But the question is whether she had reason to react with suspicion to the events of this affair. Consider, for example, some of the things done by her colleague Justice Clark.

First, Clark spoke with Senator Richardson, the leader of a brutal political campaign against Chief Justice Bird, the day before the election. He made clear to Richardson that he would take a telephone call from Fairbanks of the *Los Angeles Times*. (Why should Senator Richardson have been running interference for a reporter? What might that suggest to a minimally sensitive person about the possible thrust of the reporter's interest?) Then Clark spoke with Fairbanks not once but three times that day. Even when Clark knew he was being cited as a confirming source for a story whose crucial political implications he had not in fact confirmed, he did not object.

Second, Clark refused to sign a statement, circulated within the court by Justice Tobriner after the November 7 story, denying that the *Tanner* decision had been held up for improper reasons. He alone on the court refused to go along with any suggested form of denial. Professor Stolz excuses Clark by saying that for him "to join in a sweeping denial of any wrongdoing presented the risk of becoming a participant in a coverup, and in November of 1978 the lesson of Watergate was very fresh." The notion that Watergate was in Clark's mind is, to put it politely, imaginative. In any event Clark could have signed a less fulsome statement, as a colleague did.

Third, when the press reported that one member of the court had refused to sign such a statement, Clark gave an interview identifying himself as the nonsigner. Going farther, he told Lou Cannon of the *Washington Post*, in a story published November 23, 1978, that he had "decisive reasons" for not signing but did not want to say what they were because he expected to testify under oath about them in a commission inquiry. Professor Stolz correctly says: "In context, his answers to Cannon compelled the inference that Clark knew of wrongdoing. The only thing a reporter could make of his response was that Clark had proof of guilt but did not wish to reveal it at that time."

Fourth, just before the *Tanner* decision was finally announced in December, Clark sent a memorandum to Bird saying: "In conscience, it must be clear to all on the court that the *Tanner* case was signed up and ready for filing well in advance of November." Clark never offered the commission or anyone else a drop of evidence to support that sudden and intensely provocative statement—and that fact alone makes his action despicable. It was also demonstrably untrue. There were unexplained periods, from time to time during the months when the *Tanner* case was under consideration, when it rested in one justice's chambers or another without action. But the last of the various opinions had only been completed on October 24, hardly "well in advance of November," and by election day only one justice had finally signed off in light of all the other opinions.

As Professor Stolz sees it, Bird probably assumed that Clark's intention in doing these things was "to humiliate her" and force an investigation. "Although that is possible," Professor Stolz says, "Clark's testimony before the commission suggests more that Clark rather drifted into each of these incidents without any conscious design. . . ." The suspension of disbelief required for that view of Justice Clark's behavior is too much for me. If Rose Bird was sensitive about perceived attacks, this set of events was a good example of sensitivity with reason.

It seems to me that in general Professor Stolz is far more charitable to Justice Clark than to either Chief Justice Bird or Justice Tobriner. Thus Clark's slippery comment to Lou Cannon that he had "decisive" but undisclosed reasons for not signing the Tobriner statement denying wrongdoing is said by Professor Stolz possibly to reflect "nothing more than a kind of rigidity in his thinking." But Bird's action November 24 in joining public calls for a commission investigation, which Professor Stolz correctly says she should have left to the full court, he describes as not just a mistake of judgment by a person who with reason felt unfairly hounded, but an act showing that Bird "was prepared to sacrifice the core values of a collegial institution for transient benefits of her own design . . ., exposing an extraordinary indifference to the basic nature of the institution of which she was a member."

Similarly, Professor Stolz is critical of Justice Tobriner for not responding with more than his "zero, zero, zero" statement when Endicott of the *Los Angeles Times* asked him about the alleged delay in *Tanner* on election eve. He could at least have added, Stolz suggests, "but I can and do tell you that decision is not being withheld for any improper reason." That strikes me as bad advice on two counts. It would never satisfy the reporter; start down the slope of answering questions, and where does it end? And, second, judges should not be in the business of answering press questions of any kind on pending cases. The idea is simply outrageous to me, and I think should be to anyone concerned about the integrity of the judicial process. (Professor Stolz also criticizes Chief Justice Bird for "hiding" on election eve, that is, for not being available for press telephone calls. If it is now the received wisdom in California that supreme court justices must be available to the press at all times, I only hope that the disease does not spread.) Justice Tobriner also is reproached for initiating a joint court statement denying any improper delay in *Tanner*, and for testifying that he had not recognized the political impact of the case. Professor Stolz heard the testimony, and no doubt the proposed statement was tactically unwise. But surely those things may reflect nothing more than political naivete.

The judicial sin that I think was the gravest in the whole long story does not move Professor Stolz at all. That was the action of Justice Mosk in changing his position after the first decision in *Tanner*, thus switching the court's decision on rehearing, and never offering a word of explanation. Judges, like other people, are entitled to change their minds—even, in very rare instances, after they have formally announced their views. But to do so without explanation is an insult to the judicial process. To do so in the highly-charged circumstances of the *Tanner* case was to make that process seem a political mockery. Justice Mosk's performance was inexcusable.

Finally, I think Professor Stolz is a little harsh as a critic of judicial opinion-writing, even by the rightly elevated standards of law school judgment. The present California Supreme Court is not the first to decide cases on issues that counsel did not argue; Justice Brandeis did so, as Professor Stolz notes, in a great case called *Erie Railroad v. Tompkins*. It is not the only appellate court whose members write too many individual opinions; the practice is probably more egregious today on the Supreme Court of the United States. I do agree with Professor Stolz that Chief Justice Bird's opinion in the *Tanner* case was an example of judicial overreaching to avoid a harsh statutory result. She said the "Use a Gun, Go to Prison" law was an unconstitutional legislative intrusion on the discretion of judges. Hers was, incidentally, the only opinion that, in the incorrect words of the *Los Angeles Times* story's lead paragraph, sought to "overturn" the statute. The other justices in the original majority found as a matter of statutory construction that the legislation had not repealed an old provision, not mentioned in the new law, giving judges discretion to disregard aggravating factors in sentencing. Professor Stolz is critical of Justice Tobriner's opinion finding that that discretion still existed. But the court's final judgment on rehearing applied the mandatory prison rule to everyone except Tanner himself, letting him out as a matter of discretion because his case had been pending so long.

When the judges of the California court were called before the Commission on Judicial Performance and asked to explain themselves in public, justice in California and potentially elsewhere in this country faced a new and serious threat. Why that is so was explained by a San Francisco lawyer, William Bennett Turner, in the California State Bar Journal.

Few if any institutions in our society could have withstood this kind of exacting scrutiny of their decisional process. But the inquiry was doubly threatening to the judiciary. . . . It required the justices to disclose their thoughts and internal communications in the deliberative process; and it was the first time ever that judicial disciplinary proceedings were open to the public.

Turner noted the tension between judicial accountability and judicial independence: "A judge who must explain not just her conclusions but her motivations," he said, "a judge who is subject to interrogation on private conversations and the details of reaching an unpopular decision, is not independent." But having said that, Turner then concluded that nowadays some independence does have to be sacrificed for accountability. When judges pass on highly controversial issues, he said, the public is going to demand more and more open accountability. "Judicial secrecy is an idea whose time has passed. The public will no longer unquestioningly accept the courts' legitimacy simply because they publish reasoned decisions." Turner proposed that accountability be achieved by an improved Commission on Judicial Performance, operating at least partly in the open. Better that, he said, "than vigilantes." Perhaps there are vigilantes lying in wait for our courts these days. But if so, I still cannot believe that the way to avoid them is to undertake anything like the disastrous process that afflicted the California Supreme Court in 1978–79. And in the end I doubt that the American public really wants to strip the judiciary bare, demean it, injure its ability to function.

Preble Stolz, when he draws his conclusions from the California episode, shows a similar concern about public resentment of unpopular decisions by cloistered judges on social and political problems: abortion, affirmative action, and the like. But his answer is that judges should be more cautious in the use of their power. He sees what happened in California as one more skirmish resulting from the tension inherent in our curious system of having judges exercise great power in a democracy. The last great national battle occurred when the Nine Old Men of the United States Supreme Court tried to stop the New Deal in the 1930s. As the memory of that battle fades, Professor Stolz says, judges exercise their power more and more freely. He warns that they do so at peril. They will restrain themselves if they understand that "it is the highest duty of a judge to maintain for the future judicial power as part of our system of governance."

Ever since John Marshall, American judges have had to live with the incongruity of their position. Professor Stolz does not pretend that there is an escape from the dilemma of their power, but he says they can ease it by sticking to the ideal that they are "professionals who care deeply about impartiality" and by making clear that they have "no program beyond fair process." The only difficulty with that is that the Constitution is not limited to fair process; it also puts such substantive commands as freedom of speech and press into our fundamental law. It is no wonder, as this book reminds us, that Americans have a perennial fascination with law and the courts.

Acknowledgments

In 1978 I wrote several short pieces designed to alert Californians to what I thought was a serious problem concerning the election of judges, especially at the trial court level. Thereafter I maintained a clipping file on judicial elections, planning in a rather vague way to develop the subject more pretentiously in a law review article during a scheduled sabbatical leave for 1979–1980. The file included stories about the Bird election during the fall of 1978. Clippings began to accumulate rapidly on and following election day, 1978. Without a clear notion of why, I followed these developments closely, attending public events such as some of the meetings of the Judicial Council and nearly all of the hearings of the Commission on Judicial Performance. It occurred to others before it dawned on me that I could and perhaps should write a book for a nonprofessional audience that explained the background of what I had seen and what, if anything, I thought it all meant.

This book is the result. In large part it is built from my clipping file (limited, unfortunately, for the most part to stories from the *Los Angeles Times*, the *San Francisco Chronicle*, and the *San Francisco Examiner*), the transcript of the commission hearings, and relevant Supreme Court papers. But I have also been aided immeasurably by conversations with people knowledgeable about various aspects of the controversy. With hardly any exceptions, everyone I approached for help was extremely kind and forthcoming (within, of course, the bounds of confidentiality). There is scarcely a thought in this book that I have not borrowed (stolen?), although ultimate responsibility is, of course, entirely mine. In one way or another, each of the following people made an important contribution to this book: Evelyn Balderman, Donald Barrett, Carol Benfell, Gene Blake, Al Bowker, Jane Brady, Terry Bruniers, Julie Clarke, B. T. Collins, Douglas Cunningham, William Endicott, Robert Fairbanks, Jerome Falk, Hon. Gordon Files, Richard Frank, Jack Frankel, Burton Gindler, Hon. B. Abbott Goldberg, Hon. Joseph Grodin, Phillip Hager, Lola Harris, Hon. William Hogoboom, Thomas Houston, Seth Hufstedler, Jim Jensen, Lowell Jensen, Nancy Jewel, K. Connie Kang, Jack Kavenaugh, Peggie Kinney, David Kirp, Jonathan Kirsch, Ralph Kleps, Janice Kosel, Mary Ellen Leary, Jack Leavitt, Eugene Lee, Alexandra Leichter, Paul Li, Bishop Roger Mahoney, Sue Malone, Richard Morris, William K. Muir, Betty Nakashoji, John Oakes, Pierce O'Donnell, Hon. Marcel Poché, Joan Pomerleau, E. Lewis Reid, Donald Roeschke, Ed Salzman, Madeleine Sann, Hon. Gordon Schaber, Phillip Schrag, John Schulman, Murray Schwartz, I. J. Shain, Kit Stolz, Allen Sumner, Hon. Bruce Sumner, Brian Taugher, J. Michael Traynor, Wallace Turner, William Turner, Mike Ullman, Margaret Warner, Charles West, Natalie West, Arleigh Williams, Robert Williams, Sherrie Williams, Thomas Willoughby, Bernard Witkin, Joan Wolff, and Hon. Donald Wright.

Not included on this list are my colleagues at the law school at Berkeley, known as Boalt Hall. That is not because they did not help but rather because to include them would add another forty-five names. Suffice it to say that the support and encouragement I received from my colleagues surpasses my capacity for expression. A unique debt is owed to the dean of Boalt Hall, Sanford H. Kadish for his faith in me and in this project, and to Professors Paul Mishkin, Martin Shapiro, and Jan Vetter, each of whom showed me his remarkable talent as a teacher— the rare capacity to criticize sharply while motivating the student to try harder.

I enlisted the help of six students in assorted research projects and imposed on them to read preliminary drafts. Their skill and judgment belied their status as novices in the profession. Whatever merit this book has owes much to Ross Cheit, Martha Cunningham, Sandra Golze, Kathleen Gunn, Joe Ryshpan, and Kris Vaca. This book would not have been possible without the financial support of the University of California during a sabbatical leave and without the unstinting help of the secretarial staff of the law school.

Finally, for nearly two years Nancy and Melissa lived in the same house with a distracted husband and father who was totally preoccupied with matters they could only pretend to find interesting. Their uncomplaining support of me in my madness was crucial to the effort and far beyond what is normally asked of a wife or daughter. I thank them both.

ONE

Introduction

On June 26, 1979, Bertram Janes, chairman of the California Commission on Judicial Performance, stood to administer the oath to Rose Elizabeth Bird, chief justice of the California Supreme Court. The commission was investigating a charge that Bird and her colleagues had finished work on but had delayed until after election day the public release of an unpopular decision—an effort to protect the chief justice, whose name was on the ballot, from the wrath of the voters. If the commission found the charge to be true, Bird and any other justice implicated in the plot could and probably would be removed from office. A crowd of several hundred, including thirty-odd reporters, and a television camera watched as Bird began testifying about what had been going on inside the Supreme Court during the past year or more; testimony about what she and the other justices had said in their secret conferences, what she had discussed privately with her staff and other justices, and what she and others had written in confidential documents such as draft opinions. It was a bizarre moment, seemingly charged with the kind of tension the nation had not experienced since Watergate and rarely before then. In fact the hearings were second-rate theater: the leading roles were filled by public officials of mediocre talent whose evidence disclosed not venality but ineptitude and pettiness. Furthermore, the investigation fizzled out when the commission was forced by court order to stop taking evidence in public and prohibited from making any detailed report of its conclusions. Nonetheless the curtain of secrecy surrounding the highest court in the state had been parted, and the public had a unique chance to look inside a major appellate court. And the view was not through the eyes of either a scholar examining the dusty papers of a judge long dead or a journalist patching together hearsay from undisclosed sources; rather, the public could listen to living judges using their own words as they talked about recent events.

This book is an account of how the chief justice came to be taking the oath in public and what can be learned from the testimony she and her colleagues gave.

At one level the book is principally a story about people—mostly Chief Justice Bird and the six associate justices of the court—how they responded to events and how their personalities interacted. As such it is not an inspiring tale. Pride, distrust, arrogance, and ignorance often prevailed over better instincts, but the story is nevertheless interesting as an account of people in high places behaving on the whole rather badly. For a number of reasons, however, the book has a broader message. Quite apart from the commission's investigation, the published opinions of the California Supreme Court during 1978–1979 revealed a court badly divided along what may be loosely described as ideological lines, a situation characteristic of many other appellate courts at many times, including the U.S. Supreme Court, during those same years. The commission's hearings gave the public a look inside the court at a moment when it was in crisis. Though it would be unreasonable to extrapolate from this photograph of a court in stress an image of other appellate courts in ordinary times, recognizing that the specimen is pathological gives it special value as a demonstration of what happens to an appellate court when civility collapses. To carry the metaphor forward, what was exposed at the hearings was the next step in the progression of a disease the first symptoms of which can be seen in many courts at many times. The progress of the disease is probably not irreversible, but without self-conscious remedial efforts, what happened in California could happen anywhere.

The commission's investigation came at a time when nearly all American appellate courts were in a transition. Between the end of World War II and the late 1970s, the nation experienced an explosion of litigation that cannot be explained by population growth alone. The number of appeals took the largest leap; the number of state and federal judges doubled and tripled in size. In addition, under the pressure of workload, judges became more efficient so that each judge disposed of more cases. Because California was the largest state and also one of the fastest growing, the business of California's courts probably grew in absolute terms more than that in any other state, but the problem was nationwide.

The workload problem was particularly acute at the level of the highest court in each state and in the U.S. Supreme Court: unlike the lower courts, a supreme court cannot handle an increased workload by adding judges or by creating a new court. Because appellate courts traditionally work in confidence and perhaps also because the workload problem developed over time, the impact of a fourfold or fivefold increase in business at the supreme court level was seen only dimly by outsiders, both lay and professional; yet some consequences were of major importance—for example, the kinds of cases the high courts chose to decide and the way opinions were written. It also became plain that the public and perhaps much of the legal profession had a woefully out-of-date image of what an appellate court judge does. John Marshall scratched out his opinions with a quill pen; he drew on his own learning and research, but he also had to rely heavily on the work done by lawyers in the case and on consultation with fellow judges. A secretary with a typewriter was introduced generations ago, but the notion that appellate judges today do their own research and write their own opinions is almost as anachronistic as a quill pen. Judicial opinions are in substantial part written and researched by professional staff to the justices. The justices need not rely as Marshall did on the briefs written by counsel, nor do they depend anywhere near as much as Marshall did on the learning of their colleagues.

These shifts in the way justices do their work, and especially the growth and development of staff, involve issues worthy of public attention. Who are these faceless staff who help the justices? Are they usurping judicial decisionmaking power? There was some discussion of these problems in the professional literature in the late 1970s by judges and others with inside experience, but that treatment was abstract and colorless. The general public and most lawyers continued to assume that appellate judges write their own opinions in scholarly isolation. The testimony the commission heard both from the justices and from some of their research attorneys shattered this myth. The procedures of the California justices were of course peculiar to the California Supreme Court, but the picture of appellate judging that emerged from the hearings was true nationwide.

As a case study of a particular supreme court, this account can help correct two widespread misperceptions about courts and particularly the highest courts. First, every supreme court operates in a context with other institutions, both governmental and private, and many if not most decisions have a political dimension, especially if politics is defined to include the spectrum from mundane partisanship to high statesmanship. Only in the vaguest sense is the public aware of this political aspect to a supreme court's role. Even lawyers tend to view the decisions of an appellate court as if they were self-contained exemplars of pure deductive reasoning. The commission's investigation put the California court in a broader context because in order to understand the issues before the commission observers had to think about the justices in relationship to the governor, the legislature, and especially the press. The crisis that called for the commission's investigation was unique to California, but there was nothing special about the California court's functioning in a political context. Second, the book seeks to correct an imbalance in the public's view of the importance of state courts and state supreme courts in particular. Americans love the law and have long paid close attention to the U.S. Supreme Court, but they have tended to overlook the state supreme courts. The public erroneously assumes that state supreme courts are insignificant institutions of governance; indeed, most people probably assume (wrongly) that any major state supreme court judgment can readily be reviewed by the U.S. Supreme Court. Numbers alone suggest otherwise. There are about twice as many state court judges in California as there are federal judges in the entire United States. (There are also more judges in Los Angeles County than in the whole of England: we are a litigious people and nowhere more so than in California.) Something less than 3 percent of the nation's litigation is heard before federal judges. Unquestionably a disproportionate number of important matters are tried in the federal courts (hence the phrase "let's not make a federal case out of it"), but not all federal cases are important nor do state courts try only matters of relative insignificance. Furthermore, most issues decided by state courts are immune from review in the U.S. Supreme Court. The cry of the outraged litigant—"I will take this case all the way to the U.S. Supreme Court"—is often a hollow threat; that court can hear only those cases from state courts that involve a question of federal law. Most cases involve no possible claim under federal law because most of the law of crimes, torts, contracts, property, family law, corporations, workman's compensation, etc. is state law naked of any federal issues and thus quite beyond the reach of the U.S. Supreme Court.

Finally, without coming close to resolving them, this book deals with two sets of persistent problems about judges in America. First, as a nation we have never been entirely content with the way we select our judges, what the standards should be for an ideal judicial appointment, or what conditions should be imposed on the tenure of judges. The Founding Fathers took what has turned out to be an uncharacteristically extreme position on these issues. They provided for presidential selection of judges, checked only by the advice and consent of the Senate, and gave federal judges life tenure limited only by the possibility of impeachment. Politics perverted the original intent by vastly increasing the role of senators in the selection of federal judges, and impeachment over time withered into desuetude. In general, the states have rejected the federal model. More than half provide for some form of election of judges, and nearly all have fixed terms, often relatively brief, for judges. The California Commission on Judicial Performance was a pioneer institution, designed in 1960 to replace impeachment as a mechanism for judicial discipline and widely copied. This study of what happened in California in 1978 and 1979 does not answer such questions as what the standards for judicial appointments should be, whether judicial elections are a good idea or the utility of judicial disciplinary commissions, but the story does provide important data for future discussion of these seemingly eternal issues. Second, since the time of John Marshall American supreme courts have been a paradox in our governance. They are at once an elite institution with a professional obligation that is supposed to transcend the political issues of the moment and a governmental body required to settle political matters in a system committed to democratic principles. There is nothing original in the observation that judges often have a difficult time maintaining a proper balance between these conflicting forces. Though the California Supreme Court's problems in the late seventies were not new in this respect, the commission's investigation presents a unique opportunity to look inside a court as its justices struggled to stay upright.

I wrote this book with the nonprofessional reader in mind. I have tried to avoid jargon and unnecessary detail, but some of what follows is complicated. The book contains no secrets; it is not an exposé that discloses confidential information. Most of what follows was in the newspapers, in court records, or in testimony heard by the commission in public sessions.

I pass judgment with alarming frequency on nearly all the participants in the events described. The reader is, therefore, entitled to know something of my background and especially my past relationships with the principals. My father was a newspaperman, and I am predisposed to like reporters, to sympathize with their problems, and to think that what they write is important. On graduation from law school, I clerked for Walter Pope of the U.S. Court of Appeals in San Francisco and Harold Burton of the U.S. Supreme Court. Both judges were highly regarded for their dispassionate analysis of the cases that came before them and both were particularly valued by colleagues for their ability to stand above the personality quarrels that occasionally plague all human institutions. My experience with these men no doubt shaped my views as to how an appellate court judge ought to behave. I later worked for both Governors Brown of California: I served in a very junior capacity on the legislative staff of Edmund G. (Pat) Brown, Sr.; I was a senior advisor to

Edmund G. (Jerry) Brown, Jr., during the first two years of his administration. My feelings toward the senior Brown approach idolatry. Perhaps because I grew up some in the meantime, my feelings toward his son are a good deal less uncritical, but I left Jerry Brown's administration for personal reasons and over no policy difference. I was and remain fond of Governor Jerry Brown.

I have worked for or with four of the seven justices who sat on the California Supreme Court in 1978 and 1979. When Stanley Mosk was elected attorney general of California in 1958, I was a junior deputy in that office. Among my fellow deputies, somewhat my senior, was Wiley Manuel. When I left the attorney general's office to join the faculty at the University of California School of Law (Boalt Hall), Frank Newman was dean of Boalt Hall. Among my students in the following years was Rose Bird. Bird and I met again as fellow cabinet members in the early part of Jerry Brown's administration. Many others mentioned in this account are people I knew before the commission's investigation started: a few were good friends; most were not much more than acquaintances.

TWO

From the Primary to Election Day

The investigation of the justices of the California Supreme Court by the Commission on Judicial Performance was a by-product of the general election of 1978. A central figure in that election was Chief Justice Bird, who was on the ballot for confirmation by the voters following her appointment nearly two years earlier by Governor Jerry Brown (himself on the 1978 ballot for reelection). Bird and Brown were very closely linked. She was an important symbol of Brown's New Frontier: Bird was young (forty at the time of her appointment), female, inexperienced as a judge, and determined to challenge for the courts, as Brown had for state government generally, conventional wisdom and settled traditions. Whether behind the irreverent questioning of established values Bird had a vision of where she wished to move the system was uncertain.

Bird was unique in California history in two respects: she was the first woman appointed to the Supreme Court and she was the first justice who nearly lost a confirmation election. On election day the state's biggest newspaper, the *Los Angeles Times*, carried a front-page story by two of its most experienced reporters asserting that a controversial criminal case had been decided by the Supreme Court (by a 4–3 vote with Bird in the majority) adversely to a popular and well-publicized new statute, the so-called "use a gun, go to prison" law. Two justices, the story said,

7

had "confirmed that individual decisions were signed some time ago by all members of the Court" but the opinions had not yet been filed. The unmistakable implication was that the court had manipulated the release of the decision to help Bird get elected. Since Bird won confirmation by less than two percentage points, it seemed clear that if the *Los Angeles Times* story was correct the voters had been deprived of relevant information by a shoddy trick of timing. The accuracy of the *Times* account thus was critical, and probing this matter ultimately became the function of the commission.

The story of the commission's investigation, however, has to begin before election day because understanding the controversy behind the inquiry requires familiarity with political events that surrounded the election and, in particular, the campaigns for and against Bird.

THE POLITICAL CONTEXT

The roots of the campaign against Bird's confirmation were in the gubernatorial race of 1978 and particularly the Republican primary. Jerry Brown, the Democratic candidate for governor, had had no significant opposition in his bid for reelection, but the Republicans were in the state of disorder characteristic of a party out of power. The leading candidate, who ultimately won the primary, was Evelle Younger, the incumbent attorney general and former district attorney of Los Angeles. Younger was the only Republican candidate holding statewide office and he had an unblemished, if undistinguished, record of competence. The conservative wing of the Republicans never warmed to Younger, who was at bottom a practical, play-it-down-the-middle, essentially dull but straightforward politician. Ranged against him in the Republican primary were three principal candidates:

Ken Maddy, a young, energetic, and articulate assemblyman from Fresno, with a bit of a liberal record on issues relating to law enforcement from his time as chairman of the Assembly Criminal Justice Committee. Maddy hoped that financial support from agricultural interests in the Central Valley, bitterly opposed to Brown because of his support for Cesar Chavez's United Farm Workers, would permit him to get his name known statewide;

Pete Wilson, mayor of San Diego and the only Republican mayor of a major California city, with a liberal reputation on environmental issues because he claimed to have "managed" San Diego's growth; and

Ed Davis, recently retired police chief of Los Angeles, with a flair for dramatic overstatement (he described Evelle Younger as having all

Political Bird Dogs. © Dennis Renault, *Sacramento Bee.*

the excitement of a "mashed potato sandwich") and an attitude toward crime and criminals that was medieval in its severity.

An enormous amount of money was spent by the candidates, but public attention at the primary was stolen by Howard Jarvis and Paul Gann with their tax-cutting initiative, Proposition 13. Proposition 13 surprised all the candidates. None caught its importance until too late:

Brown campaigned against it, as did Maddy and Wilson; Younger hedged by saying little more than that he would vote for it; only Davis endorsed the proposal warmly, but he failed to make his endorsement a central part of the campaign.

The Republicans chose Younger as their candidate. His primary competition ultimately endorsed him and disappeared from view, but their supporters had a bit of a problem, especially the Davis and Maddy enthusiasts. Giving their all to support Younger was not especially attractive. For one thing, Younger was not likely to win and he made that apparent immediately by taking a week's vacation in Hawaii during the crisis caused by the passage of Proposition 13. Brown and the legislature worked out a responsible interim solution without the benefit of Younger's advice, giving Brown a substantive as well as a publicity victory that Younger could never match.

The Davis supporters, most notably state Senator H. L. (Bill) Richardson, were dedicated members of the right wing of the Republican party in California. To Democratic observers, this branch of the Republican party seems more concerned with ideological purity than winning elections or staying in office. From the right-wing point of view, however, a naked death wish is not a complete explanation. The right-wing's power is greatest at the primary because they have both money and a substantial segment of voters who will come out to the polls in the Republican primary. Repeatedly the right has felt itself the victim of apostasy as "their" candidate moderates his rhetoric during the general election campaign in an effort to attract Democratic voters. The right fears the victory of a moderate Republican almost as much as a Democratic victory. Once elected, the more successful a moderate Republican is, the less he requires money and support from the right and he need not, if he is skillful, pay too much heed to some of their more extreme positions. Thus, to the Davis people, Younger offered very little. If he won, which seemed unlikely, his game would be to pay just enough attention to them to keep them quiet; he would attempt to mute the differences among the branches of the Republican party while trying to attract people more interested in specific issues (e.g., the environment) than in party labels or ideology.

But the Davis supporters could not just walk away from the election. Their credibility depended upon their capacity to show that they could continue to make a difference in an election. They could do that by raising money from their own supporters primarily through direct mail solicitations and by generating issues of special interest to conservatives. Two propositions were on the November ballot of potential interest to the right wing. One was a death penalty initiative embellishing a death penalty statute already passed by the legislature over Governor Brown's veto; the second was a measure requiring the firing of homosexual public school teachers. Both measures were sponsored by state Senator John Briggs, a very right-wing Republican with evangelical Christian leanings whose concepts of social issues the *Los Angeles Times* described as "predating the Dark Ages."* Briggs had proposed the measures as a device to promote his own candidacy in the primary for the governorship (which had gone nowhere), and he was generally thought of as an ineffective extremist. The death penalty measure was a winner regardless of what Davis supporters did; it was therefore a poor vehicle for demonstrating political muscle. The proposition on firing homosexuals seemed to invite witch-hunts and as a device for demonstrating political power was not very promising.

As far as other candidates were concerned, conservative Republicans might help state Senator George (Duke) Deukmejian in his race for the attorney generalship. The best thing about that campaign, from the conservative viewpoint, was that his opponent, Yvonne Braithwaite Burke, a young, black congresswoman from Los Angeles, was a certified liberal (known to the nation for her skillful performance as presiding officer of the Democratic national convention that nominated George McGovern). Burke could easily be tagged as a free-spending supporter of welfare. She also had minimal experience with law enforcement whereas Deukmejian had supported a number of tough-on-crime measures as a legislator, including the death penalty bill Brown vetoed and a statute that came to be called the "use a gun, go to prison" law. Apart from money, however, Deukmejian was not asking for much help from the right. What he needed, in addition to simple voter identification, was public awareness of his position on issues that would attract support from the middle. The Davis supporters could not help him here and they could hurt him if they became too prominently identified with his campaign.

The only other possible issue on the statewide ballot was Rose Bird, the chief justice.†

The chances of defeating Bird could not have seemed very promising to the right. The power of incumbency is such that no appellate court justice had even come close to defeat since the confirmation election system was started in 1934. But as a rallying point, a campaign against Bird had some striking virtues. First, it would not be hard to

---

* Presumably invoking "the glory that was Greece and the grandeur that was Rome."

† Down toward the bottom of the ballot is a confirmation vote for justices of the California appellate courts. The state constitution calls for the initial selection of appellate justices by the governor. Nominees must then be confirmed by the Commission on Judicial Appointments—composed of the chief justice, the attorney general and the senior presiding justice of the Courts of Appeal, the intermediate appellate level. Once past that hurdle, the appointed justice takes a seat on the court, but his or her name appears on the ballot at the next gubernatorial election followed by the simple question: "Shall Justice X be elected for the term prescribed by law? Yes___. No___."

make the chief justice look like a mushy, soft-on-crime liberal, thus turning her confirmation into a liberal versus conservative battle. Maintaining a sharp conservative image is necessary for fundraising. The mailing lists could be used, kept current, and perhaps expanded. Second, there would be an almost certain measurable impact of an anti-Bird campaign. Unlike the race for the governor or the attorney general, the yes/no vote on the chief justice is more like a primary than a general election because many voters do not bother to mark the ballot if there is no opposition candidate. Conservatives in particular, Republicans in general, tend to be more conscientious about voting than Democrats: they come out to primaries and they are likely to vote on every issue on the ballot in both primaries and general elections. Third, statewide there was a strong antigovernment tide that was almost certain to affect the election results for the chief justice. Antijudge feeling had shown up at the primary for those who looked closely. Unlike appellate justices, trial court judges in California can be opposed; any lawyer can file to challenge the reelection of a trial judge. Historically few lawyers had tried and even fewer had succeeded in defeating an incumbent judge, but a trend against judges was beginning to manifest itself in June 1978: before 1976, no more than one incumbent superior court judge had lost in any single election; in 1976, five went down; five lost at the primary in 1978 (two more lost in November) and sixteen municipal court judges also lost their seats. Assuming that the voter attitudes underlying these results were broadly held—and there was no reason to suppose they were not —the same trend would predictably show up in the vote on Bird.

Finally, there was a chance to link up the conservative cause with the 65 percent yes vote on Proposition 13. Under California law, the Supreme Court does not normally pass on the constitutionality of ballot measures until after they have been voted on by the people. The court had not spoken on the constitutionality of Proposition 13 before the primary, but many legal divines had opined during the campaign that the initiative was legally questionable. Cases were filed challenging the constitutionality of Proposition 13 immediately after the primary, and it was likely that the court would hear argument and might well decide the case before the general election in November. If the court decided the Proposition 13 case before the election, and if it decided that 13 was unconstitutional, and if Bird were in the majority, her election was very uncertain.

In short, Bird was an attractive target for the Davis supporters, especially Senator Richardson. Richardson was a complex political phenomenon—a doctrinaire conservative, once both a member of and a fundraiser for the John Birch Society, and a shrewd backroom operator, twice elected by his colleagues in the state senate as Republican caucus chairman. He arrived in Sacramento in 1966 when Governor Ronald

Reagan was first elected, but by 1974 he and Reagan were quarreling publicly. In that year Richardson quit as caucus chairman because he was "disenchanted with the policies" of the Reagan administration; provided the critical vote to override a Reagan veto (the first override since 1946); and ran against a Reagan protégé, Earl Brian, for the U.S. Senate nomination. Richardson won the primary, but Senator Alan Cranston beat him in the election by a record vote of 62 percent.

Richardson, a passionate hunter and gun enthusiast, helped found Gun Owners of America and Gun Owners of California and served on the board of the National Rifle Association. His disastrous 1974 U.S. senatorial campaign was built largely around law and order, both in terms of the issues he discussed and because he used people from law enforcement—sheriffs, police chiefs and district attorneys—as his local contacts as much as possible. Since his 1974 defeat, Richardson invested much of his energy into developing a direct mail political money machine that could be used to support or defeat candidates or causes that engaged his interest.

In terms of raising money, Richardson was enormously successful. In 1976 he linked up with Richard Viguerie, credited with inventing the computerized, direct mail method of soliciting funds for politicians. In 1977 Richardson formed Computer Caging Corporation to provide direct mail service for Gun Owners and other organizations he sponsored. There is a certain irony in this. Richardson had vigorously opposed passage of the political reform initiative in 1974, but the reporting requirements of that act are what forced the use of a computer in direct mail solicitations. It was a small step from that to recognize that a list of contributors is itself useful in future fundraising. What works best are simple issues with emotional impact like the death penalty or gun control; they draw relatively modest contributions, $10 to $100, but from thousands. By 1978 Richardson had a list of about 65,000 people likely to contribute to conservative causes.

In 1976 Richardson formed the Law and Order Campaign Committee with Ed Davis as honorary chairman. The committee's first venture was a program to support candidates for the legislature who shared Richardson's views, especially on crime issues. This effort was not very successful, perhaps because the focus was too diffuse to inspire donors, but a second venture in 1977 did far better. Over $800,000 was raised in support of passing a death penalty bill and 200,000 letters were sent to Governor Brown to induce him to sign the bill and later to influence legislators to override his veto. In the 1978 primary, Richardson was a principal financial backer of Davis. His committees donated over $100,-000 to the Davis campaign.

Richardson denied a personal profit motive in creating Computer Caging Corporation, and any skimming would be caught by agencies such as the Fair Political Practices Commission or by the press, which monitored his activities closely. But Richardson undoubtedly benefited from the success of his ventures in terms of power and prestige. What was once a back office operation became a well-run organization with paid employees. During the campaign a member of the Brown administration was quoted as saying that Richardson's "purpose is not so much to defeat Rose Bird as to get names and addresses for his computer tapes. He trades in them, sells them to other people." Richardson of course denied this charge and pointed to his long record of concern with law enforcement. To be sure, Bird was a target of opportunity, but attacking her was also a way of influencing judges and legislators to be more sympathetic to what Richardson genuinely believed in: a hard line on law enforcement. Grass roots campaigns are perfectly appropriate, indeed constitutionally protected, techniques to influence governors and legislators. It is a closer question with judges who are supposed to blind themselves to the whims of the populace in their fidelity to the law. However, Mr. Dooley observed long ago that "the Supreme Coort follos th' iliction returns." Given that the California Constitution put the justices on the ballot, it is hard to conclude that Richardson's campaign against Bird was unprincipled political opportunism.

Moderate Republicans, the type who support a Mayor Wilson or an Assemblyman Maddy, generally have less interest in maintaining their identity between elections than does the right. In this instance, however, two people once very much involved in the Maddy campaign thought they could keep themselves and Russo/Watts Associates, a new public relations and political consulting firm, usefully employed by organizaing a campaign against Bird. To understand their decision it is necessary to look at the roots of Ken Maddy's campaign. Maddy's candidacy was partially an attempt to keep alive a resurgence of the political influence of agriculture in California. Agriculture's political effectiveness suffered a long-term decline as the coastal cities—Los Angeles, San Francisco, San Diego, and San Jose—and their urban areas grew. The U.S. Supreme Court's one-man, one-vote decision and the consequent reapportionment of the state senate had greatly weakened the strength of the "cow counties" in the legislature and thus in state government in general. Proof of the diminishing political potency of agriculture came in 1975 in the very early days of the Brown administration with passage of the Agricultural Labor Relations Act, which gave collective bargaining rights to farm workers.

Bringing "peace to the fields" by enacting this law was one of the governor's principal accomplishments, achieved over the bitter opposition of most of the agricultural interests in the state. However, creation of the Agricultural Labor Relations Board did not, in fact, bring peace to the fields or put to rest the political antagonisms aroused by passage of the law. Brown's initial appointments to the board were said to be over-whelmingly biased in favor of Cesar Chavez's United Farm Workers union. The UFW was both fighting for recognition as the collective bargaining agent with farmer-employers and competing with the Team-sters to organize farm workers. During its first year the board was buried in requests to conduct elections and in allegations of unfair labor prac-tices against both unions and employers, with the result that the board exhausted its appropriated budget little more than halfway through the fiscal year. Agriculture showed its political muscle by blocking what would normally have been a routine supplemental appropriation in spring 1976, demanding as ransom the resignation of several Brown ap-pointees to the board and passage of some weakening amendments to the act. The quarrel was bitter and it never came to a very clean closure. At one point, the board was obliged to let go most of its staff. Ultimately the entire board resigned, as did the general counsel. The act, however, survived without significant amendment, and a newly constituted board was adequately funded.

During the struggle over funding for the board, Chavez launched an initiative to put to the people the question of the creation of the Agricultural Labor Relations Board. Had this measure passed, it would have prevented legislative amendments to the act and provided an auto-matic appropriation for the support of the board. Floating an initiative measure as a bargaining chip in the midst of legislative negotiations is quite common; what was unusual about this one was that Cesar Chavez persisted in pushing what became Proposition 14 on the November 1976 ballot even after the legislative fight was over and he had, in some sense, won. Proposition 14 lost. The fight against Proposition 14 was the orga-nizing vehicle for the reemergence of agriculture as a political force in California. Maddy based his June 1978 campaign for governor on the "No on 14" effort of 1976. He hoped to tap the same financial sources, energy, and enthusiasm that had been generated in that struggle. As far as money went, he was reasonably successful but he was never able to generate much interest beyond the agricultural Central Valley.

Nevertheless, the Maddy supporters wanted to keep alive the politi-cal consciousness of agriculture. A "No on Bird" campaign was an ob-vious way to do so because Rose Bird had been Governor Brown's agriculture secretary and had received a great deal of the credit for draft-ing the Agricultural Labor Relations Act. As the cabinet official with administrative responsibility for the affairs of the board, Bird had been in the middle of the fight over the supplemental appropriation. More-over, she had campaigned for Proposition 14. If her name was known and disliked anywhere before her appointment as chief justice, that place was probably the Central Valley. How much the Maddy supporters hoped to accomplish is conjecture. They may not have expected much more than to give Russo/Watts some notoriety and to raise enough money to pay a few staffers. However, they clearly did not want to link arms with right-wingers such as Richardson. Agriculture's objection to the chief justice was not softness on crime or any theme from conservative ideology but Bird herself, her qualifications (or lack thereof), and her administrative abilities.

This outline of the political motivations of Bird's opponents sets the stage for a discussion of the campaigns for and against the chief justice. Before talking about the campaigns directly, however, it is necessary to examine some of the cases decided by the court after Bird's appointment that became issues in her confirmation effort.

THE CASES DISCUSSED IN THE CAMPAIGNS

Between her appointment in spring 1977 and the election in fall 1978, Bird participated in the decision of several hundred cases by the California Supreme Court. She herself wrote about thirty opinions in that period, not all of them for the court. Out of that considerable stock of both votes and opinions, only three cases were discussed in the campaigns over Bird's confirmation: the *Caudillo* rape case, the Proposition 13 case, and the Los Angeles school busing case. The selection of cases to discuss was made by her supporters and opponents, by the media, and, to the extent that she controlled which opinions to write and what to say in them, by Bird herself. There will be occasion later to discuss what might have been talked about in the campaigns, but as a starting point in understanding the campaigns it is necessary to know first something about the cases that were discussed.

Caudillo

On May 2, 1975, a young woman named Maria was subjected to a two-hour sexual assault in her apartment. She caught only a glimpse of her assailant before he blindfolded her, but she was able to identify him from photographs as a man who had been hanging around her apartment complex in the Los Angeles area. Daniel Caudillo, the man she identified, was tried and convicted of an astonishing array of crimes: kidnapping, forcible rape, sodomy, oral copulation, first-degree burglary, and first-degree robbery. In addition, the jury found that the defendant had been armed with a deadly weapon (a knife) and had inflicted great bodily injury on Maria. Caudillo also admitted that he had been found guilty of a prior felony.

At the trial the only real issue was identification: Did Maria have an adequate opportunity to see her assailant before he blindfolded her? The jury must have had difficulty with this question since they deliberated for three days, but they ultimately found Caudillo guilty of the offenses charged. The trial judge, E. Talbot Callister, was interested in sending Caudillo away for a long time. California law permits a judge to sentence an accused only once for a single course of criminal conduct even though more than one crime may have been committed. Thus, for example, Caudillo could not have been sentenced for both burglary (entering a structure with an intent to commit a felony) and rape, the felony he intended to commit. At the time Caudillo was sentenced it was unclear whether it would be proper to sentence him for sodomy and oral copulation consecutively with the rape charge.* But the robbery charge —taking $60 from Maria after Caudillo had completed his sexual assaults —could have merited a sentence consecutive to the sentence for either burglary or rape since, although the victim was the same, stealing $60 was a wholly independent act of criminal behavior. But Judge Callister did not have to worry about piling sentences on top of each other because the sentence for first-degree burglary, which normally carried a five-year sentence, could be enhanced to fifteen years to life with the jury's finding that great bodily injury had been inflicted on Maria. That meant Caudillo could be in prison for as long as the parole authorities thought it appropriate. Nothing would have been accomplished by adding an additional sentence for years to a life sentence.

Caudillo sought and obtained the assistance of the state public defender's office in conducting his appeal. Since he had been convicted in Los Angeles, his appeal was first heard in the Court of Appeal for the second appellate district. He drew division five and a panel composed of Justices Ashby, Kaus, and Stephens.† Justice Ashby wrote a crisp decision confronting the three issues Caudillo raised.‡

The first issue, and the most obvious one to any layman confronting the record, was the sufficiency of the evidence that Caudillo was the person who had committed the crime. Although this issue was hard for the jury, it was easy for the appellate court because a reviewing court has only to answer the question, viewing the evidence in the light most favorable to the prosecution, could a reasonable jury have found Caudillo guilty beyond a reasonable doubt? Clearly, a reasonable jury could have done so if the evidence were examined in that one-sided way. Ashby also summarily disposed of the second issue: could rape alone constitute

---

* Later, in *In re* Perez, 23 C.3d 545 (1979), the court sustained consecutive terms for assorted sex crimes committed on the same victim in a single episode.

† The California Court of Appeal sits as a court of three judges, but is subdivided into permanent divisions so that, for example, Justices Ashby, Kaus and Stephens routinely sit with each other. Some divisions have more than three judges, but in considering any particular case a division sits as a three-judge panel. In 1978 there were twenty Court of Appeal justices on the Los Angeles Court of Appeal, divided into five divisions.

‡ 134 Cal. Rptr. 176 (1976) (officially depublished).

great bodily injury for purposes of enhancing the sentence for burglary? Framing the issue that way may seem a little odd since Caudillo had done much more than simple rape. But in *People* v. *Cardenas*,* another division of the California Court of Appeal had said that rape alone was great bodily injury. If rape alone is enough, then multiple rapes plus multiple sodomies and multiple oral copulations would also plainly constitute great bodily injury. The intermediate appellate courts in California only infrequently reconsider issues decided by another division of the same court, especially where, as had happened with *Cardenas*, the losing party had been refused review by the California Supreme Court. Thus, it would have been extraordinary for Ashby to have decided anything other than that rape could constitute great bodily injury. The third issue was harder. Caudillo had been convicted of kidnapping: he moved his victim from an elevator to a storage room and then an unstated distance down the hall on the same floor to Maria's apartment. Was that enough movement to constitute kidnapping? In three 1974 cases the California Supreme Court had said that in kidnapping the movement must be "more than slight or trivial"; it must be "substantial." Ashby thought moving Maria from the elevator to a storage room and then down the hall to her apartment was substantial. Kaus agreed with him. Stephens did not and politely dissented on this point.

Ashby's decision was announced on November 19, 1976, about a year and a half after the crime. The final rung on the appellate ladder in California is to file a petition for hearing with the California Supreme Court. The justices of the Supreme Court must pick from among several thousand the roughly two hundred cases they decide annually with a formal opinion. A petition for hearing requests the court to hear oral argument and to decide with an opinion. Counsel for the petitioner must demonstrate that the case involves some point of importance to the law or to the public that would make it worthwhile for the Supreme Court to hear argument and write an opinion.

Counsel for Caudillo could not have been sanguine when Caudillo's petition was filed. The first issue, the sufficiency of the evidence on identification, had no lasting interest to anyone but Daniel Caudillo. The second question, could rape alone constitute great bodily injury, was also not very promising for two reasons: first, two years earlier the court had denied a hearing in the *Cardenas* case, which raised precisely that question; second, since Caudillo's conviction, the legislature had amended the "great bodily injury" statute as part of a general reform in the sentencing law so any decision construing the law as of 1975 would likely have little importance for the future. The third issue, how much movement is necessary for simple kidnapping, was the most likely to

* 48 C.A.3d 203 (1975).

justify a grant of a hearing, but the court had dealt with this problem only a few years earlier and it was hard to see how *Caudillo* would be a particularly useful vehicle for explaining the difference between trivial and substantial movements of a victim.

On January 27, 1977, the Supreme Court granted a hearing in *Caudillo*. Bird was not involved because she took office in March 1977. She was, however, on the court by the time the case was argued, as was Wiley Manuel, appointed by Brown at the same time as Bird. Frank Newman, the third Brown appointee, did not take his seat until July 1977; in what became Newman's place, the Chief Justice assigned Justice Bernard Jefferson of the Los Angeles Court of Appeal to sit temporarily, or pro tem. The California chief justice has the power to fill vacancies by assigning another judge (usually an appellate court justice or a retired Supreme Court justice) to sit temporarily so that the court almost always sits as a full bench of seven.

There was nothing unusual about Bird's naming Jefferson to sit pro tem in the *Caudillo* case. The case came from Los Angeles and was argued to the Supreme Court there; Jefferson was on the Los Angeles Court of Appeal and his division of the Court of Appeal had not participated in the case at the Court of Appeal level. His participation in the Los Angeles calendar of the Supreme Court, accordingly, involved a minimum of inconvenience to him or cost to the state. What was unusual was that Bird assigned the writing of the majority opinion in *Caudillo* to Jefferson. That was a departure from past practice, very rare in modern times. Pro tem justices occasionally write a dissent, although that too is unusual but that is in the control of the pro tem justice. Any justice who feels strongly about an issue is free to write a separate opinion and a pro tem justice has as much right to do that as a regular member of the court. But deciding who is to write the opinion expressing the views of the court is the prerogative of the chief justice when, as in *Caudillo*, she is in the majority.

There is no public indication why Bird assigned the writing of the *Caudillo* opinion to Jefferson. It may have been to spread the workload a bit, although that seems unlikely since she did not generally ask pro tem justices to write majority opinions. Perhaps Jefferson requested the assignment and Bird felt embarrassed to turn him down. Some discomfort in refusing Jefferson would be understandable since Jefferson, at that time the only black appellate judge in the state, had been prominently mentioned as a candidate for the chief justiceship before Bird's appointment. A third possibility is that Bird may have wanted to avoid personal responsibility for what she anticipated would be an unpopular decision, but that seems unlikely since she ultimately wrote a separate opinion concurring in Jefferson's majority view. Writing a separate concurrence contradicts a motivation on her part to duck political liability for an unpopular decision by assigning the writing of the opinion to someone else.

Asking Jefferson to write the *Caudillo* opinion was a mistake because the opinion was far from a model of the judicial craft. No particular purpose would be served by discussing here all the flaws in his opinion, but some of its shortcomings had immediate consequences in Bird's campaign. Beyond that, enough that was seriously questionable has to be exposed to show that none of the justices should have signed Jefferson's opinion.

The opinion was, among other things, much too long.* Jefferson took twenty-three pages to dispose of what Ashby had handled in five. Writing too much is a frequent if relatively minor judicial failing, but Jefferson went beyond that error to violate an established norm of judicial decorum by giving a full and detailed account of the sexual outrages committed by Caudillo. His pornographic summary of the evidence was unnecessary to his discussion of the legal issues. Justice Ashby in his opinion had said: "We need not recite the explicit details of the forcible rape or sodomy . . . or oral copulation." Sentences like that are common in sex cases because judges are reluctant to set forth the evidence at length unless there is a compelling reason to do so. Perhaps that tradition is no more than a matter of taste; most people recoil from writing sentences like: "Still not content, defendant again inserted his penis in Maria's mouth, wiping away his victim's vomit," but that graphic bit of irrelevant detail is now in the California Supreme Court reports. By transgressing a norm of good taste, Jefferson gave the case a publicity value it otherwise lacked. Holding that rape is not great bodily injury is an abstraction of some potential general interest; spelling out the details of a depraved sex orgy will hold the attention of a larger audience.

Jefferson's analysis of the legal issues opened with a needlessly long, but otherwise harmless, discussion concluding that there was enough evidence to identify Caudillo as the person who committed the crimes. He dealt next with the kidnapping problem: was moving Maria from an elevator to a storage room and then down the hall to her apartment a substantial or only a trivial or slight involuntary movement of the victim? These words are no more than labels for a conclusion; they are not reasons for the distinction. Earlier cases suggested only that two hundred feet is substantial but seventy-five feet is trivial. Jefferson's opinion yields not a clue beyond the bare result that in this case moving Maria an undisclosed distance down the hall was trivial. Although Jefferson's opinion was defective on this point, he was operating within a tradition of the Supreme Court; only a few years earlier, the court had similarly failed to explain the rationale behind the classifications of substantial and trivial.

* People v. Caudillo, 21 C.3d 562 (1978).

Well over half of Jefferson's opinion was devoted to the last issue: could rape alone constitute great bodily injury? Starting with that as the issue before the court was the most important mistake in Jefferson's opinion. Ashby could appropriately approach the case that way because if rape alone constituted great bodily injury, it follows that rape plus other sex crimes would also be great bodily injury. But Jefferson concluded that rape alone could not be great bodily injury and never got very far beyond that point. He did in one paragraph toward the end of his opinion consider whether the cumulative effect of the repeated rapes, sodomies, and oral copulations Caudillo inflicted on Maria might not have justified a jury verdict of great bodily injury (he said no), but the thrust of his opinion focused on the "rape alone" question.

The argument that rape alone could not constitute great bodily injury was simple. In 1967 the legislature had passed a three-bill package of amendments to the penal code escalating the penalty for rape, robbery, and burglary from a minimum of three to fifteen years if the accused intentionally inflicted "great bodily injury" on his victim. If a defendant charged with rape could be held to have inflicted great bodily injury on his victim because he raped her (without any additional abuse of the victim), the 1967 amendment would escalate the penalty for all rapes; there would, in short, be no distinction between rape and rape with great bodily injury. That result was not what the legislature wanted. Therefore, the argument ran, rape by itself does not constitute great bodily injury. Unfortunately, this argument would not dispose of Caudillo's case because he was charged not with rape with great bodily injury but rather with burglary with great bodily injury. However, Jefferson argued that the words "great bodily injury" should be given the same meaning in the three statutes enacted at the same time.*

Jefferson badly confused the issue by mingling this argument with a second contention more relevant to a related issue: if rape alone could not constitute great bodily injury, what about the sodomy and oral cop-

---

* Treating the words "great bodily injury" as words of art that must have the same meaning in all contexts was not obviously correct. It would have been possible to say, as Jefferson did, that the purpose of the statutes was to deter the commission of violence in addition to that necessarily involved in the commission of the crime. Starting from that premise, it would be possible to hold that rape could not be "great bodily injury" if the only crime committed was rape, but rape might still be great bodily injury if the charged crime were robbery. Jefferson did not discuss this argument. Another argument Jefferson might have used to buttress his conclusion could have been built out of the rules against multiple punishment. Burglary is entering a structure with an intent to commit a felony. Anyone who raped a victim after forcibly entering her home with the intention of committing rape would thus be guilty of burglary with great bodily injury. It is unlikely that the legislature intended that result and support for that conclusion could be found in the law against multiple punishment. Just as it is improper to sentence someone cumulatively for (1) burglary (entering with intent to commit rape) and (2) rape, so also ought it to be impermissible to escalate the punishment for burglary by making rape alone equal great bodily injury.

ulation convictions? Could either of these sex crimes be regarded as great bodily injury?

Jefferson's answer was no because, he concluded, great bodily injury requires serious or permanent physical injury. One way to reach this conclusion would be to argue that it does not matter which bodily orifice is penetrated if the only injury consists of the penetration. To phrase it differently, if rape is not great bodily injury, then neither is sodomy or oral copulation. Oddly, if he made this argument at all, Jefferson did not do so clearly. Rather, he chose to read "bodily injury" as meaning "physical injury" and from that premise to conclude that psychic trauma, no matter how severe, could never constitute great bodily injury. The words "physical injury," had the legislature used them, might well suggest an intent to exclude even severe emotional distress from statutory coverage; it is harder to reach the same result from the phrase "bodily injury." How Jefferson managed to convert "bodily injury" into "physical injury" deserves examination.

The problem was to determine what the legislature meant by the words "great bodily injury" in the package of bills passed in 1967. To answer that question Jefferson examined how the legislature amended the penal code in 1976 and 1977, ten years after the words were first used and, indeed, after Caudillo had committed his crime and been tried and convicted. A court will not often look at what today's legislature does to decide what an earlier legislature meant; if we take literally what is really a fiction, that the function of a court is to ascertain the intent of the legislature, it is absurd to suppose that the legislature of 1977 knew, or for that matter cared about, what the legislature of 1967 meant. But it is occasionally useful to look at what a later legislature has done if it is plain that the later legislature is doing nothing more than restating what it thought was existing law. Such was not the case in this instance. The 1976 law made any felony, not just rape, robbery, and burglary, subject to a substantial enhancement in sentencing if the defendant intentionally inflicted great bodily injury on the victim. Since the legislature was expanding the coverage of "great bodily injury" it would quite logically restrict the meaning of the phrase.

Jefferson noted that the 1976 legislature defined "great bodily injury" with precision:

[A] *serious impairment of physical condition, which includes any of the following:*
  (a) *Prolonged loss of consciousness,*
  (b) *Severe concussion,*
  (c) *Protracted loss of any bodily member, or organ,*
  (d) *Protracted impairment of function of any bodily member, organ or bone,*

(e) *Serious disfigurement,*
(f) *Severe physical pain inflicted by torture.*

In 1977, however, before the 1976 amendment went into effect, the legislature repealed this definition and substituted a broad, general definition: "[G]reat bodily injury means a significant or substantial physical injury." This language, Jefferson said in the text of his opinion, was the "exact language" used in the jury instruction in the *Caudillo* case. He was mistaken, as shown by his footnote in which he quoted the jury charge: the trial judge told the jury that great bodily injury "refers to significant or substantial bodily injury or damage; it does not refer to trivial or insignificant injury or moderate harm." The jury charge used the phrase "substantial *bodily* injury." The word "physical" was introduced for the first time by the legislature in 1976. After misquoting the relevant words, Jefferson added: "It is apparent, therefore, that the 1977 amendment to the Penal Code . . . was not intended to lessen the magnitude of bodily injury required by the 1976 detailed definition of great bodily injury." The effect of this sentence was to reenact what the legislature had repealed, a somewhat dubious maneuver under the best of circumstances but particularly questionable here since the 1976 law was repealed before it went into effect. But, passing that technicality, Jefferson discerned that the legislature in 1967 intended "bodily injury" to mean "physical injury"; therefore, the psychological and emotional trauma suffered by sex crime victims does not constitute great bodily injury.

What may politely be called Jefferson's reasoning led him to the conclusion that Judge Callister was wrong when he responded to a question from the jury—"Can rape, sodomy, or oral copulation be determined as inflicting great bodily injury?"—thus:

The answer to the question, ladies and gentlemen, is yes, that's a fact issue for you to determine. You have previously been given an instruction which defines great bodily injury. You are to take that instruction, apply it to the facts of the case and make your own determination as to whether it does or does not constitute great bodily injury.

As Jefferson considered rape (or sodomy or oral copulation) without additional physical consequences insufficient to constitute great bodily injury, this instruction was wrong and required reversal of the jury's verdict.

Jefferson's conclusion that the jury had been misinstructed required a reversal of the jury's determination that Maria had suffered great bodily injury. The next question was whether the physical injuries that Maria had suffered could be regarded by a properly instructed jury as substantial rather than trivial. If the injuries could be viewed as substantial, the case should be remanded for a new trial; if not, then the conviction should be reversed by the court at this point. Jefferson concluded that two minor knife wounds on the neck (neither requiring suturing) and the transitory distress of vomiting and diarrhea were legally insufficient to support a jury verdict of great bodily injury. Accordingly, Jefferson directed Judge Callister to strike the finding of great bodily injury. At the least, Jefferson should have remanded the case to the trial court for resentencing. That mistake came back to haunt the court later, just a few days before the election. Explanation of this point, however, can be postponed.

Four justices signed Jefferson's opinion (Bird, Tobriner, Mosk, and Manuel). We do not know why. Possibly they never read the opinion carefully. Jefferson certainly did not make a careful reading easy; his opinion was insufferably long and repetitive. Judges (and professors) are among the few who can indulge in the rhetorical device of boring their audience into agreement. Jefferson's opinion is a textbook example of this technique. Casual readers, and even those who have a professional responsibility to follow the decisions of the California Supreme Court with some care, may be pardoned if they failed to pay close attention to the *Caudillo* opinion.

The four justices who signed the opinion, however, had a responsibility to read and think about what they were approving. Perhaps they did not like the content of the opinion but thought the case did not matter very much. In one sense that was clearly right. What is sufficient movement of a victim to constitute kidnapping and whether rape and the other sex crimes were enough to constitute great bodily injury were not, compared with many other issues the Supreme Court had to deal with, weighty points of law. On the other hand, these points had been thought important enough to justify the grant of a hearing. On the kidnapping point, Jefferson's opinion neither advanced the law nor added to the confusion. However, Jefferson's result that significant physical as opposed to emotional harm to the victim is necessary to escalate the sentence for sex crimes, was new law and not unimportant.

It is hard to escape the sense that the four justices who signed the opinion cared more about this new rule than anything else. Certainly there is nothing to suggest an underlying concern that the lower courts had done an injustice to Daniel Caudillo. Jefferson's painful opening statement of the facts made sympathy for the accused impossible. More likely, the four justices wanted to further a policy preference for shorter prison terms—a defensible policy position that might be expected of "liberal" judges. Such policy preference would lead to a narrow reading of enhancement provisions such as the "great bodily injury" statutes. Jefferson's opinion did not speak in these terms, but his result as effectively implemented such a policy as an opinion that openly advocated shorter prison sentences.

Perhaps the four justices who signed the opinion did so reluctantly. Human frailty may explain part of their failure to insist upon a better opinion. For one thing it would take time and energy to write a good opinion coming to Jefferson's result and each of the four justices was very busy with other work of at least equal importance. Furthermore, it would be personally painful to reject the opinion. Jefferson was a nice man and had worked hard on *Caudillo*. Even the most graciously phrased concurrence would involve exposing some weaknesses in his opinion, which might be read by Jefferson's colleagues on the Courts of Appeal, as a bit of an insult.

Two justices did not sign Jefferson's opinion. Justice Richardson wrote a brief concurrence and dissent that Justice Clark joined. They concurred in the reversal on the kidnapping point but dissented from the conclusion that Caudillo's conduct was insufficient to constitute great bodily injury. Richardson explained:

[T]*he majority assumes that the term "great bodily injury" refers to more than the psychological or emotional distress experienced by rape victims generally. This . . . point is troublesome, however. It is certainly arguable that rape per se, without any aggravating circumstances whatever, involves a "substantial and significant" bodily injury [citing the* Cardenas *case from the Court of Appeal]. But even assuming that something more "substantial" than rape is required to constitute great bodily injury, surely that test is satisfied in the present case.*

Richardson apparently chose to part company with Jefferson not on how to construe the words "great bodily injury" but only on whether the case should be remanded for a new trial. On that assumption, his conclusion was plainly wrong. If substantial physical injury in addition to the sex crimes were required for great bodily injury, as Richardson seemed to concede, Judge Callister's answer to the jury's question was wrong and the jury's verdict had to be reversed. It is hard to avoid the conclusion that Richardson and Clark were as guilty as the four who signed it of not reading Jefferson's opinion or the record carefully.

Finally, there is Bird's concurrence. Because her opinion was short and its exact words became critical later, it deserves quotation in full:

I have given this case considerable thought, and I find I am compelled to sign the opinion of the majority since the legislative history of Penal Code section 461 indicates that the Legislature intended that rape per se could not be deemed "great bodily injury." This court must give full weight to

*that intent, whatever our personal views concerning this most serious
offense.*

*The offenses committed by appellant on the victim in this case were
"outrageous, shocking and despicable," as the majority state. It has been
noted that "[i]n the crime of rape, the victim is not only deprived of
autonomy and control, experiencing manipulation and often injury to
the envelope of the self, but also intrusion of inner space, the most sacred
and most private repository of the self. It does not matter which bodily
orifice is breached. Symbolically they are much the same and have, so far
as the victim is concerned, the asexual significance that forceful access
has been provided into the innermost source of ego." (Bard & Ellison,*
Crisis Intervention and Investigation of Forcible Rape, *The Police Chief
(May 1974) at pp. 68, 71.)*

*However, personal repugnance toward these crimes cannot be a legit-
imate basis for rewriting the statute as it was adopted by the Legislature.
It is precisely because emotions are so easily called into play in such
situations that extra precaution must be taken so that this court follows
the legislative intent and not our own predilections or beliefs. This court
has no choice in this matter. It must accept the Legislature's intent despite any personal feelings to the contrary. This court must accord the
words of statutes their plain meaning and has done so in this case. However, the Legislature is the proper governmental body to consider whether
rape per se is a basis for the enhancement of punishment and to so provide
if they deem it appropriate.*

The first thing to notice about Bird's opinion is what it did not do.
Nowhere did the chief justice attempt to correct or reformulate Justice
Jefferson's reasoning; if anything, she seemed to be saying that she
wanted to come to the opposite result but felt driven to his conclusion
by the remorseless force of his logic. Her concurrence thus did not dilute
the effect of her signature on Jefferson's opinion; to the contrary, by
concurring Bird endorsed its persuasiveness. At best this suggests that
Bird did not read Jefferson's opinion critically. Other alternatives are
more disquieting: she lacked the intellectual power to see the opinion's
flaws or she was being hypocritical.

Most puzzling, however, is why Bird bothered to write a separate
opinion. In retrospect it is easy to say that she should have anticipated
that writing any opinion would make her personally responsible for the
result far more than if she had been a silent member of the majority.
Writing an opinion would also focus attention on the case. The press
and others would almost certainly examine her opinions much more
closely than her votes. Thus, the case and its result would quite apart
from her opinion be far more likely to become a topic in the campaign
than if she had not written.

The most creditable motivation for her separate opinion was that Bird wanted the legislature to reconsider the issue. Though judges sometimes invite such reconsideration in their opinions, it is hard to take that motivation seriously here because of the flaws in Jefferson's opinion. Assuming that Bird did not read his opinion carefully, such may have been her purpose. In any case, the legislature did amend the penal code to "correct" the *Caudillo* result—indeed, before the election.

Perhaps Bird wrote a separate opinion because she thought that the *Caudillo* result—rape is not great bodily injury—was bound to become an issue in her campaign. The result would inevitably anger law and order advocates and the women's movement. Perhaps she intended to disarm the opposition with a few paragraphs. The content of Bird's opinion supports such a political purpose. Her single citation to the *Police Chief*, a journal rarely collected in law libraries, indicates a hope to gain the sympathy of an audience concerned with law enforcement. The quotation itself, however, employs the rhetoric of feminism and suggests concern for Bird's standing with the women's movement.*

If the chief justice's purpose was to deflect political heat, her separate concurrence was more than a failure; it was a disaster. Before considering how Bird's *Caudillo* opinion was received, however, notice must be taken of how painfully unnecessary the political consequences were because it would have been so easy to come to a result that affirmed Caudillo's prison sentence. First, all sides confused things by looking at the wrong issue. The focus should not have been on whether rape alone constitutes great bodily injury but rather on the cumulative effect of a two-hour combination of repeated rapes, sodomies, and oral copulations and whether that experience could constitute great bodily injury. At some point (if not two hours, what about a two-day gang rape?) the cumulative effect should be enough to warrant a jury's conclusion that great bodily injury had been inflicted. Second, even assuming that Judge Callister's answer to the jury's question was misleading, the case should have been remanded, at which point Callister could have arrived at the same result by sentencing Caudillo consecutively for robbery and rape. No one apparently considered the possibility of remanding Caudillo for resentencing.

Had Richardson (or anyone else) written an opinion along these lines it could rationally have gained the endorsement of those who believed that prison sentences in this country are generally inhumanly and uselessly long. It was entirely possible to say that rape alone is not great bodily injury while holding that what Caudillo did was worse. The failure

---

* Bird testified before the Commission: "I knew my position on the Caudillo case would not be popular at all, and I was well aware that it would be an instance where people who wanted to use it, could very easily use it against me. I was well aware of that when the decision came out."

of the majority members of the court to reach this result, as well as the failure of all the justices to consider the alternative of resentencing Caudillo, is evidence that the court was preoccupied with the policy result on sentencing generally, to the exclusion of any concern about justice for Daniel Caudillo. This charge certainly cannot be proven on the basis of the court's failure to do what no member may have considered. But the failure to adopt an apparent alternative course is troublesome. One of the great assets of an appellate court as a lawmaking institution is that a court is forced to consider policy issues in the context of the facts in particular cases. Justice to the individuals before the bench will thus shape a court's attitudes toward policy questions. In criminal cases, of course, justice can mean severe punishment in some instances as well as leniency in others. But if the court is not paying attention to the facts of the cases before it and instead is considering only broad policy questions, the court is denying itself its singular virtue as a lawmaking institution and throwing in doubt its legitimacy.

Proposition 13

Proposition 13 was a simpleminded proposal that dealt in an extraordinarily ham-handed fashion with a single aspect of the problems caused by inflation. Real estate prices in California, especially in suburban areas, had been going up in a dramatic fashion; stories about property values doubling in three or four years were common. With increased prices went increased real property tax assessments. Although the tax rate on real property did not increase (in terms of statewide average it declined), the tax bill for each homeowner had been going up as the assessed value of the home increased. Proposition 13 dealt with the problem in two ways: it imposed a 1 percent ceiling on the tax rate (reducing the rate from a cumulative statewide average of a little less than 3 percent) and provided that the assessed value would be rolled back to the 1975 level or the value at the date of acquisition for property acquired after 1975.

As in many states, local government in California, principally cities, counties, and school districts, historically had relied heavily upon the property tax for revenue. Increasingly, state subventions had been picking up a portion of the cost of local government, but the loss of property tax revenue to local government as a result of Proposition 13 was estimated at $6 billion statewide. This shortfall would have meant a drastic reduction in services had the state not come to the rescue. Inflation had, however, also caused a substantial increase in state revenue from the state sales and income taxes, and a very substantial surplus had accumulated in the state treasury. The governor and the legislature had not been indifferent to the plight of the homeowner-taxpayer. For several years they had been fighting over the method of distributing the surplus.

Speaking of Rape. . . . © Dennis Renault, *Sacramento Bee.*

Governor Brown wanted to concentrate property tax relief on people with relatively low incomes. Some legislators wished to provide relief to homeowners across the board. This and other policy differences prevented any legislative property tax relief until just before the deadline to put a measure before the voters in the June 1978 primary.

The passage of Proposition 13 on June 6 immediately caused a major crisis in Sacramento. As of July 1, the revenue prospects for local government were, without state relief, grim. Among other things, essential factual information was missing. No one knew what the real property tax base was (how much property had been sold since 1975?), how the 1 percent levy would be distributed among the local governments, or how much surplus was held by local governments that might be used to postpone the effects of Proposition 13.

In less than a month the legislature and the governor responded to this crisis by making available enough money from the state surplus so that local governments could continue functioning without serious disruptions in service. By July 1 things were reasonably stable for the 1979 fiscal year. How ultimately to resolve the problems created by Proposition 13 was uncertain; essentially the state surplus was used to buy time for careful study of the problem and possible solutions.

The successful creation and implementation of the "bail out," as this temporary solution was known, represented a remarkable political achievement for Governor Brown, Speaker Leo McCarthy, and the Republican legislative leadership. Much could easily have gone awry, especially since 1978 was a gubernatorial election year, when it might have seemed to the advantage of the Republicans to prolong the chaos.

In the background was the possibility of judicial invalidation of Proposition 13. As a piece of constitutional legislation, Proposition 13 was not well drafted, although its simplicity may have heightened the plan's appeal to voters. In any case, the proposition presented a number of constitutional issues under the state and federal constitutions and lawsuits were promptly filed. The California Supreme Court took the case on its original docket—thereby saving the time required for lower court consideration—and ordered briefs filed in July and scheduled the case for argument in early August, although the court normally does not hear arguments in August. There was speculation in the press that the court would not decide the case until after the election. Alternatively, it was assumed that if the court should decide the case before November and invalidate Proposition 13, those justices who voted to invalidate the measure would not be confirmed.

Public attention was riveted on Proposition 13 throughout this period. The tax revolt made the cover of national news magazines, and there was widespread speculation about 13's political significance nationwide. The bail out struggle in Sacramento was well publicized and in general the problem of soothing the taxpayer revolt was the preoccupation of candidates at state and local levels.

On August 11, gubernatorial candidate Younger, in his role as attorney general, chose to argue the Proposition 13 case to the court, a grandstand play of dubious taste considering that he had never before in his eight years as attorney general argued a case in the Supreme Court. In fact, he left the bulk of the argument to a deputy attorney general and made a rather weak impression on observers. But Younger did manage to get his face on the nightly news in the role of a supporter of Proposition 13. Newspaper reports on the argument, however, paid rather more attention to an opening statement the chief justice made:

Members of the Court have been subject to threats in this case of recall or defeat for confirmation at the polls and even an anonymous threat of physical harm to themselves and their families. All the threats in the world will not deter us from the important task before us.

Contrary to the cynical expectations of some, the court decided the case on September 22, well before the election. Frank Richardson, the only Reagan appointee to the Supreme Court on the ballot in November, wrote a thirty-page opinion sustaining Proposition 13 against all attacks although leaving for the future the resolution of some ambiguities in the measure.* The chief justice alone dissented on one ground: the measure violated the equal protection clause of the Fourteenth Amendment to the U.S. Constitution.

In general, the court deserved the good marks it got from the press for the handling of the Proposition 13 case. It is easy to imagine a different scenario. The legislature could well have failed to respond promptly with the bail out, thousands of local government employees would have been laid off and essential government services (fire, police and sanitation) drastically cut, with the court either coming to the rescue by holding the initiative unconstitutional or forcing the legislature to find a solution by sustaining Proposition 13. Either result would have provoked a genuine constitutional crisis. Most of the credit for averting that belongs with the governor and the legislature, but the court at least did not make matters worse, and it did act with commendable dispatch—little more than three months after the primary.

The chief justice's dissent is puzzling, however. We know from testimony before the commission that the chief justice's staff did not recommend to her the conclusion that Proposition 13 violated the equal protection clause. We also know that Tobriner prepared a lengthy memorandum on the point in an effort to dissuade Bird from taking this position. Why he "spent considerable time" doing so is obscure; the only explanation given at the hearings was that he "had hoped for a unanimous Court." Why this case, whose result would be popular, was worth an extra effort to achieve unanimity Tobriner was not asked. As a supporter of Bird's, he could have been worried about a possible adverse effect on her confirmation election.

Despite the opposition from Bird's own staff, Tobriner's memorandum, and public opinion, the chief justice chose to dissent, an action that seemed independent and courageous. Unfortunately, her argument was not very persuasive. It was spun out of a hypothetical concerning

* Amador Valley H.S. v. State Bd. of Equalization, 22 C.3d 208 (1978).

two identical homes of equal current value, one purchased in 1975, the other in 1977. The chief justice contended that the difference in tax paid by the two homeowners was a violation of equal protection. For the most part she relied on pre–New Deal cases of the U.S. Supreme Court that have been quite thoroughly repudiated if not squarely overruled. She had no effective rebuttal to Richardson's conclusion that acquisition as opposed to current value is a rational basis for property taxation. Bird ended her opinion with a curious paragraph:

This decision has not been an easy one. The issues are close and reasonable people may differ. Emotions run high on this question, but as judges we must follow the law and do what it requires. As Justice Story wrote in [the Dartmouth College *case], "It is not for judges to listen to the voice of persuasive eloquence, or popular appeal. We have nothing to do, but to pronounce the law as we find it; and, having done this, our justifications must be left to the impartial judgment of our country."*

It is hard to read this passage without thinking that Bird was speaking primarily to the voters who would be going to the polls in six weeks. But why, if she was worried about public reaction, dissent at all?

The answer to this question is not helped by Bird's failure to discuss the logical next point: supposing the rollback to 1975 values to be a violation of equal protection, what was to be done with Proposition 13? It could be invalidated in total; it could be partially saved by retaining the reduction in tax rate to 1 percent of current value; or it could be saved by making everyone pay 1 percent of the 1975 property value regardless of the acquisition date. The last option would have been more generous to taxpayers than Proposition 13 was; the second would have given tax-payers significant relief, although not as generous as that provided by 13. Only the first choice would have restored the status quo. Why did Bird not discuss the choices? Had she done so, and especially if she had elected the third option, the effect would have been to reduce signifi-cantly, if not to eliminate entirely, the potential adverse impact of her conclusion of unconstitutionality.

The answer to the enigma of Bird's separate opinion may be that at the time she thought she was going to lose the election. The private polls then being taken by the governor for the purposes of his campaign showed Bird losing. If she thought her defeat inevitable, she might have wished, perhaps unconsciously, to leave some trace that would explain her defeat; no one wants to be a martyr without a cause.

The press paid scant attention to the rationale of the majority opin-ion and even less to the chief justice's dissent. Editorials sighed with relief that one more possible disaster had been averted and dropped the subject. As things worked out, the Proposition 13 case had very little importance in the confirmation campaign. Its importance was negative; it could have been decisive if the court had followed the chief justice's dissent, but none of the other justices agreed with her and the case quickly vanished from public consciousness.

School Busing

Political pundits developed innumerable and often conflicting explanations for the overwhelming vote in favor of Proposition 13. One theory, as plausible as many others, was that 13's strong showing in Los Angeles, especially in the predominantly white San Fernando Valley, was an irrational lashing out by voters angered over the prospect of busing school children for integration that was to start in the fall of 1978. School busing was a major concern of many people in Los Angeles and a delicate problem for any politician apprehensive about arousing latent racial animosities. The four justices of the Supreme Court who were on the ballot in November played a minor role in the busing crisis of 1978, but even a walk-on in a show as big as busing has to be ranked as a major event, and it cost the justices votes in November.

The story of school desegregation in Los Angeles began when Bird was still a law student. In 1963 the American Civil Liberties Union (ACLU) filed a desegregation lawsuit against the school district on behalf of a black student named Mary Ellen Crawford. One unusual feature of *Crawford* v. *Board of Education* was that the suit was filed in state rather than federal court, a decision of the ACLU lawyers that reflected their belief that the California courts, especially the Supreme Court, would be more receptive to their position than the federal courts. In 1970 superior court Judge Alfred Gitelson ordered the school board to submit a desegregation plan. Gitelson's six-year term ended in 1970, and his efforts to be reelected were frustrated when he was forced into a runoff in the primary and defeated at the general election. That retributive vote by the people of Los Angeles shocked lawyers and judges throughout California accustomed to incumbent judges being reelected by overwhelming majorities. It was an unambiguous signal of the political potency of school desegregation.

Five years later, division three of the Los Angeles Court of Appeal reversed Judge Gitelson, relying mainly on U.S. Supreme Court decisions holding that a school board had no affirmative duty to integrate its schools in the absence of proof of an intention on the part of the public authorities to maintain a racially segregated system.* In 1976, the California Supreme Court vindicated the ACLU's strategy of using the state

---

* 120 Cal. Rptr. 334 (1975) (officially depublished).

courts by affirming Judge Gitelson's order requiring the school board to submit a plan to desegregate its schools. *

Justice Tobriner wrote a lengthy opinion for a unanimous court (including Richardson and Clark) that rested on the state rather than the federal constitution. The court held that the school board was obligated to take action to eliminate racial segregation in the schools whether or not the segregation was deliberately created. Tobriner's decision on this point made the California law of equal protection more aggressive than existing federal law. That Richardson and Clark concurred in the *Crawford* decision is notable because they had generally maintained that comparable concepts in the state and federal constitutions should be construed congruently. Perhaps their failure to protest this broader California interpretation of equal protection reflected their sense that on this highly charged issue it was essential for the court to be unanimous in order to maximize the decision's public acceptance. Tobriner ended his opinion by talking directly about busing. In essence he said that busing was one means of achieving integration but not necessarily required, and that it was important in considering a proposed desegregation plan to take into account the extent to which busing might cause the parents of white children to enroll them in private schools, thereby tending to defeat the objective of integration.

By 1977, the Los Angeles school board was in the somewhat tenuous control of people willing to do what the law required about integration, including board chairman Howard Miller, Kathleen Brown Rice, the governor's sister, and a prominent Chicano supporter of the governor, Julian Nava. Judge Paul Egly, to whom the case was ultimately assigned, rejected the first so-called voluntary plan the board of education submitted in March 1977, but he accepted a second plan in February 1978 as a "first step." This second plan, to be implemented in fall 1978, did a number of things, including sharply reducing class size in integrated schools, but its most controversial feature was to require busing of some students in the fourth through eighth grades.

The twists and turns in the development of these plans need not detain us. What is significant is that Judge Egly took a rather aggressive posture and the majority of the school board found itself caught between his requirements and an increasingly strident opposition both from within the board's membership and from politicians representing the San Fernando Valley in local government and in Sacramento. Strenuous efforts were made to prevent state funding of busing and to put an anti-busing proposition on the ballot in November. These attempts failed, but the fact that some of the state bail out funds going to the school district were to be used to pay for busing became an issue in the guber-

* 17 C.3d 280 (1976).

natorial contest. Some remembered that the education of children and their well-being after busing started was important. Many people and institutions (school administrators, teachers, churches, and newspapers) tried desperately throughout the summer of 1978 to promote acceptance of the busing plan by working with parents and community leaders. However, support for busing was spotty at best. The largest ethnic group, Hispanics (35 percent of the students), was on the whole against busing. And although busing was an important symbol to black leaders, it was not at all clear that the parents of black children destined for long bus rides were enthusiastic. Finally, at least in the perception of the majority of the board, everything possible was being done to whip up opposition in the already vaguely racist white sections of the valley. The only counterforce was the moral imperative of compliance with law, and on this point thoughtful people could reasonably conclude that Judge Egly had gone beyond the Tobriner ruling.

In spring 1977, an organization calling itself Bustop sought to intervene in the hearings before Judge Egly; on March 14, Judge Egly refused them permission. That was a close ruling: though several citizen groups were participating in the lawsuit most, like the ACLU, supported integration; Bustop's narrow perspective of opposition to busing was not otherwise clearly present. The importance of intervention was twofold: first it would give Bustop an additional platform for stimulating opposition, and second, it would enable Bustop to make motions and to appeal any adverse rulings.

On April 14, division two of the Los Angeles Court of Appeal overturned Egly and ordered that Bustop be permitted to intervene.* The unsigned opinion (presumably written by one of the court's four justices —Roth, Compton, Beach, or Fleming) ominously said twice that busing was not required by Tobriner's opinion and noted that "the history of [judicial] involvement with . . . schools . . . has too often been one of over-involvement rather than restraint," an injudicious attempt to tip the scales since the Court of Appeal had no factual evidence before it on the circumstances in the schools. The Supreme Court denied a hearing on the intervention issue, with only Mosk noting that he would have granted it (Bird and Manuel were on the court by then but Newman was not).

In mid-July 1978, Bustop used its status as a party in the lawsuit to ask Egly to suspend implementation of the plan he had accepted in early February. That plan called for busing to start in September. On August 3, little more than a month before school was to open, Judge Egly refused. Bustop appealed to the Court of Appeal on Friday, August 25. On the following Friday, September 1, division two (Justices Roth,

* Bustop v. Superior Court, 69 C.A. 3d 66 (1977).

Compton and Beach) ordered Egly to suspend implementation of the plan.*

The court order made banner headlines in the *Los Angeles Times* and caused consternation in the school district offices. It is not hard to understand why. The Los Angeles school district is huge. Its 1970 student body of well over half a million roughly equaled the total population of the State of Delaware; its territory of 711 square miles was about one-third of Delaware's. Enormous amounts of money and energy had gone into preparation for the beginning of school; for example, over 750 new buses had been purchased and a thousand drivers trained, not to speak of special training programs for thousands of teachers whose schools were in some way involved in the program. Given this context, the Court of Appeal's decision was outrageous. It was as if a court had ordered General Eisenhower to postpone the invasion on D-Day minus one pending a hearing on whether the draft notices from Trenton, New Jersey were legally defective. Nothing could have been better calculated to put the judicial system into disrepute. Judge Egly had gone far, possibly too far, and had pushed the school board into submitting a plan that was dangerously ambitious, but the time had passed for reconsideration of the factual premises underlying his decision. Possibly the justices wanted to put the Supreme Court, and especially the chief justice, in a difficult position; perhaps they wanted to embarrass the majority on the school board, which was vaguely linked to Governor Brown, although the governor himself successfully evaded taking a stand on the busing issue. We do not know.

The immediate problem was whether the Supreme Court might be persuaded to overturn the stay ordered by the Court of Appeal in time to prevent the chaos that would result if the school board attempted to undo its elaborately laid plans for mandatory busing. There was speculation that the Supreme Court would be reluctant to get into the case in view of the November election. Board member Julian Nava was quoted as saying: "It's uncertain because they're up for reelection and they might be affected by that fact," but then he added, "it would be a great disservice" if the court refused to act for political reasons. The *Los Angeles Times* urged the court to act "swiftly. The community needs to know where it stands as soon as possible." The ACLU filed a petition asking the Supreme Court to set aside the Court of Appeal's order on Tuesday morning (Monday was Labor Day); the school board on Tuesday, after what must have been heated debate in closed session, decided *not* to ask the court to overturn the stay order (in this divided vote Nava and Rice were in the majority). Attorney General Younger, whose office had up to this point stayed well away from the case, announced that he would

---

* Because the opinion was vacated the following week, it was nowhere printed in full; extracts were published in the *Los Angeles Times* on September 2, 1978.

file a brief in support of the suspension—in his capacity as attorney general, not as the Republican candidate for governor.

On Wednesday, the Supreme Court in a brief order without opinion vacated the suspension order. The Supreme Court's order was signed by five members of the court; Clark and Richardson neither signed nor dissented. The *Los Angeles Times* editorially praised the court for its promptness. The issue remained alive as Bustop sought last-minute stays from the federal courts, even applying to Justice Rehnquist in Washington, but the busing plan went into operation relatively smoothly.

Of the four justices on the ballot in November, only Richardson had participated in the original *Crawford* decision. The only significant involvement of Bird, Manuel, and Newman was in voting on the stay, which was scarcely substantive. It was not necessary to agree with Egly, or even with the original *Crawford* case, to believe that the time for seeking a stay had passed by late August 1978 or even mid-July when the motion was first made. There was ample room for criticism of the judicial system on the school busing issue: Tobriner's decision in 1976 was arguably extreme, Judge Egly's aggressive support for busing may well have been counterproductive because its effect may have been to reduce the number of Anglo students in the school system, and division two's decision to stay Judge Egly's action at the eleventh hour was inappropriate, but none of those actions could be laid at the feet of Bird, Manuel, or Newman. The only thing they could fairly be charged with was undoing the Court of Appeal's stay. That act was both legally correct and administratively sensible. It would have been almost impossible to unravel the busing plan and get the schools going by September 12.

The hostility to school busing in Los Angeles is hard to overestimate. Judge Gitelson was the first victim; a second immediate victim was Howard Miller, chairman of the board of education, who was recalled by the voters through a special election in spring 1979, an almost unprecedented action in a community as large as Los Angeles. Several local politicians, most notably state Senator Alan Robbins and Congresswoman Bobbi Fiedler, built successful political careers largely on opposition to busing. Given the high level of feeling about the issue, Bird's supporters generally skirted the matter, but some people who voted against the chief justice undoubtedly did so because they resented busing and thought that the justices on the ballot were in some sense responsible for it.

THE EARLY ARTICLES

Three justices were on the 1978 ballot with Bird: the two other Jerry Brown appointees, Wiley Manuel and Frank Newman, as well as Frank

"For our next assignment, children. . . . ." Cartoon by Paul Conrad. Copyright © 1979 *Los Angeles Times*. Reprinted with permission.

Richardson, a Reagan appointee whose appointment in September of 1974 came too late to make the general election ballot in that year. Traditionally, appellate justices have not campaigned for confirmation partly because no organized group usually opposes their confirmation. However, even before the June 1978 primary, Senator H. L. Richardson (no relation to Justice Richardson) announced that he would mount a $1 million effort against Bird. It was thus clear early on that 1978 would be an unusual year. Nothing much happened in the campaigns until September, but the press had been alerted to a coming problem and three articles were written in July and early August that were important in shaping future events.

—*Johathan Kirsch*—New West

On June 23, 1978, two weeks after the primary and a little more than three years after the crime had been committed, the Supreme Court's decision in *Caudillo* was handed down. Friday is not a good day for newspaper reporters covering the court. The Saturday morning papers are short on news columns and readership is relatively sparse. Events of Friday are also too late to make the Sunday columns that comment on the week's events. By Monday morning the story is stale.

No notice was taken of the *Caudillo* decision by any of the major newspapers in the state when it came down. That lack of coverage was not remarkable. Even the *Los Angeles Times* did not report on every decision of the Supreme Court; probably less than half of the court's decisions received any notice in the daily press. Most reporters and editors probably thought *Caudillo* was not newsworthy, a judgment that was doubtless helped by its Friday release and the exceptional length and obscurity of Jefferson's opinion.

The first media coverage of the *Caudillo* opinion came in *New West* in the July 31 issue. The four-page article was written by Jonathan Kirsch, a bright and energetic, but young and inexperienced, staff member. Kirsch came to *New West*, a regional magazine that mixes restaurant reviews, travel tips, and public affairs in a trendy format, after briefly clerking for a law firm. He specialized in articles on law, politics, and government.

Kirsch regularly read the *Los Angeles Daily Journal*, the local legal newspaper, which on June 26 ran a front-page story on the *Caudillo* decision. Kirsch had learned in law school that an attentive reader can usually anticipate a court's result on the legal issues in a case by studying the court's statement of the facts. Here the rhetoric of the facts as detailed by Jefferson and recounted by the *Journal* reporter suggested to Kirsch that Caudillo should be sent away for a very long time. But the result was to reduce Caudillo's sentence, and this conflict between the facts and the law puzzled Kirsch. He thought the court's decision would outrage feminists and he tested this idea by reading the *Journal* account to some women editors at *New West*. Not suprisingly, they confirmed his conjecture, and he decided to write a story on *Caudillo*. The focus would be politics and feminism: would *Caudillo* anger women voters and, if so, what impact would their reaction have on Bird's confirmation? Kirsch was working on a short deadline for a magazine; as he recalls it, he had to file by Friday, June 30. He called a number of people for their reactions to *Caudillo*. None of them had heard of the case, but Kirsch gave them an account of the facts and noted their reactions.

In the article, "Rose Bird and the Politics of Rape," Kirsch warned his readers that "an account of the rape . . . is not appropriate reading for the young or squeamish"; he then presented the facts with all of

Jefferson's needless detail. Kirsch claimed that the court's decision "scandalized both law-and-order hardliners and militant feminists" and speculated that *Caudillo* would cost Bird votes in her election. The story reported that Senator Richardson had "scoffed" at the conclusion that rape does not constitute great bodily injury, and Richardson predictably charged Bird with being "a wee bit contradictory." Kirsch had a little more trouble with Gloria Allred, a lawyer and local coordinator for the National Organization for Women, who would not criticize Bird but who was willing to say that it was outrageous to require broken bones or visible scars before a rape could be called great bodily injury. At no point did Kirsch attempt to state the legal argument that Jefferson had given to support his conclusion. Mostly the article talked about the chief justice's opinion and Richardson's dissent, focusing on the suggestion in Bird's opinion that legislature might change the law if it disapproved the *Caudillo* result.

The invitation to the legislature to respond to *Caudillo*, Kirsch implied, was hypocritical because Bird knew, or should have known, that the legislature would never pass such a bill. Indeed, Kirsch reported, three months before *Caudillo* was decided, the Assembly Criminal Justice Committee had killed a bill by Assemblyman Gene Gualco that would have included forcible rape and sodomy in the definition of great bodily injury.

Kirsch brought up the Assembly Criminal Justice Committee and quoted Senator Richardson as saying that the "[c]ommittee is structured for the killing of law enforcement-type bills" because he believed that knowledge of these facts would heighten the resentment of militant feminists at the chief justice's suggestion of a legislative solution. Although Kirsch quoted Ken Maddy, chairman of the Assembly Criminal Justice Committee, as saying that "[i]t's hard to stand up on the floor of the Senate or the Assembly and vote against a rape bill, so the committee has played a very important role in balancing civil rights and civil liberties," he did not adequately explain the committee's function.

The Assembly Criminal Justice Committee was one of those useful but vaguely fraudulent institutions in our government that permits politicians to maintain a public posture that differs from their genuine views. It was set up in 1961 and had been quite nonpartisan; Republicans, such as Maddy, frequently chaired it although committee assignments and chairmanships are made by the Speaker and there was a Democratic Speaker for almost all of the years since 1961. A clear majority of the membership had been both liberal and, more important, from safe districts. The committee's function was to hold in the committee hard-line crime bills, such as those providing for the death penalty or measures authorizing wire-tapping, that members with less-sure seats would be hesitant to vote against if the matter ever came to the floor. The existence of the committee permitted almost any law and order bill to pass in the Senate because it would be killed in the Assembly. Senators could vote "yes" for law and order; only a handful of Assemblymen had to vote "no." The California Peace Officers Association and Senator Richardson launched a major offensive against the Criminal Justice Committee in 1976 (which predictably failed) and they had been warring against it ever since.

Though the Gualco bill had been held in the committee earlier, Kirsch's confident assertion that the committee would pass no bill on the subject was wrong. Before the session ended, the committee passed out a bill that escalated the punishment for rape itself sufficiently so that in any repeat of the *Caudillo* facts a trial judge wishing to impose a severe sentence would opt for rape rather than burglary with great bodily injury as the sentencing vehicle. Assemblyman Maddy wrote a letter to the *Los Angeles Times* in mid-August explaining this point, and Assemblyman Gualco did what he could to make it known that he thought the purpose of his bill had been achieved although the bill itself had not been passed. Kirsch could not, of course, have predicted what would happen in the legislature after his article was written, but if he had dug a little deeper he might have realized that the committee was not unsympathetic to some solution to the *Caudillo* problem. His failure to do so and his glib repetition of the Richardson line against the Assembly Criminal Justice Committee was proof enough for those who wanted to believe it that Kirsch was nothing more than a publicity agent for what he called "law-and-order hardliners."

Kirsch was also wrong in his prediction that militant feminists would be angered over the *Caudillo* decision. March Fong Eu, the secretary of state, was quoted as saying that she thought Bird was "soft on rape," but other representatives of the women's movement maintained silence about *Caudillo* and were supportive of Bird.

Kirsch did not conceive of his article as a balanced review of the chief justice as she was approaching the election, but many people, and certainly the Bird partisans, read it against that standard. So viewed the article was patently unfair. It plucked a single case out from several hundred for discussion, omitted the reasons that explained the *Caudillo* result, and stated the facts—albeit straight out of Jefferson's opinion—in a slanted way that made the court seem terribly soft on a vicious criminal. Senator Richardson took full advantage of Kirsch's article by using it as campaign literature. Kirsch and his editors can fairly be faulted for not anticipating that the story might be used this way. Kirsch could have rounded out his portrait of Bird to make the article unattractive to partisans of either side, and *New West* was remiss in not running anything further about the chief justice before the election.

Certainly the Kirsch piece was not worth the attention it got in the campaign, but it was the only story apparently written from an anti-Bird point of view that surfaced in months before the election. As such it became obligatory for anyone else writing an article on the chief justice to mention *Caudillo* and discuss the case largely in terms of the Kirsch article: was Bird "soft on rape"? So framed it was a silly question that only a handful of people who read the *New West* article in July might be expected to have considered. Though far from the most important issue presented by *Caudillo*, this question became a focus, probably the main focus, of the confirmation battle.

—*Ed Salzman*—California Journal

Two articles were published early in August 1978 that were influential because they were consulted by nearly every reporter who later had occasion to write about the chief justice or the campaign. Perhaps the more important one appeared in the *California Journal*. It describes its content quite accurately, as: "non-partisan, non-ideological analysis of California government and politics established in 1970 and published monthly by the California Center for Research and Education in Government, a non-profit, tax-exempt corporation." The magazine's influence was far greater than its circulation of 17,000 would suggest. Reporters and editors read it avidly, as well as state politicians and bureaucrats, and its columns and articles are often reprinted in mass circulation newspapers.

Ed Salzman, editor and principal figure holding the magazine together, was an experienced journalist widely acquainted in Sacramento. He had known Rose Bird since 1964 and was pleased when Governor Brown appointed her to the court, partly because she was his friend and he thought she would do a good job but also because Salzman believed that women should play a larger role in government. Salzman was troubled about writing the piece on Bird because of his friendship with her. He tried to avoid using information he had obtained from informal conversations with her or otherwise to exploit their friendship. He wanted to be both analytical and impartial. Several aspects of his article, "Reviewing the Record of a Beleaguered Chief Justice," were unusual in the campaign coverage.

First, unlike almost every other reporter, Salzman drew a distinction between the chief justice's role as one member of a seven-judge court and her function as the administrative head of the California court system, and he paid some attention to the latter. He noted that Bird's twenty months of service was long enough to permit a fair evaluation of her work as an administrator. He got from Steven Buehl, the chief justice's executive assistant, a verbal checklist of her administrative accomplishments and printed the list with only a few changes. Salzman named twenty official actions and six less official actions (like selling the official limousine and bringing cookies to the formal Wednesday conferences of the court) that he considered Bird initiatives. He also noted certain controversies, as in the following passage:

Bird has assigned trial judges to the Supreme Court on a temporary basis. She said this is an effort to unify the court system and have judges understand what happens at other levels of the judiciary. She has also encouraged appellate judges to sit for short periods in trial courts. However, such procedures have been criticized by some lawyers and judges as an improper use of the appointive power to produce a measure of control over the judicial system.

For the most part, however, Salzman simply described what Bird claimed to have done and made no effort to determine either whether she deserved credit or whether there was opposition to her actions. It is a pity Salzman did not press harder: seven of the twenty official actions he listed were problematic on their merits but Salzman noted the presence of controversy on only two; eight others either were matters that had not in fact been accomplished or were not Bird's initiatives; two more were trivial. There will be occasion later to examine some of these administrative actions in detail; what is significant here is that although Salzman did well to look at Bird's administrative record, he did not look hard enough.

Salzman did a better job on Chief Justice Bird's record as a member of the court. He read all twenty-two of her opinions to that time and did a voting analysis of the entire court since she joined it showing how often Bird had agreed with each of the other justices in every case decided by a split vote. He concluded:

These statistics definitely would place her to the left of center. How far left is a matter of conjecture. Clark is generally considered the most conservative member of the Court and Tobriner the most liberal. Yet, on three occasions Clark and Bird were on one side and Tobriner on the other. One surprise is how often Bird disagreed with Newman, a liberal who was once her mentor at the University of California's Boalt Hall of Law. This suggests that Senator Richardson may be justified in calling her a liberal because of her record, but he will have a hard time backing up his contention that she is soft on crime.

This paragraph is important because it was the only effort anyone made to analyze Bird's votes. Many reporters looked at her opinions, or at least some of them (most often *Caudillo*), but no one else ever published an analysis of her voting record.*

Salzman next attempted a review of Bird's opinions (including the obligatory paragraph on *Caudillo*) but could extract only one theme that seemed to be common to a number of them: "[S]he relies heavily on what might be considered strict interpretation of statutes as the basis for many of her rulings"—a fair enough statement but not illuminating because most cases before the Supreme Court involve statutes and will turn on the meaning the court gives legislative language. Salzman was not a lawyer, and with one possible exception † the opinions Bird wrote up to June 1978 were in cases of at most middling importance. The truth was that little in Bird's opinions merited comment.

At the end of his piece Salzman noted that Bird's success in November would "hinge [not] upon her record, which is virtually unknown to those outside legal circles" but rather on politics—how much money Richardson could raise and how much attention the media would give to his attacks. Salzman concluded:

But the big unknown—and it could well be the deciding element—is how the public feels about a woman holding possibly the most important public office in the state. The campaigners won't be talking about it, but the feminine factor might well cause a great many Californians to vote either for or against a 12-year term for the Chief Justice.‡

—Gene Blake—Los Angeles Times

Gene Blake, whose by-line at the *Los Angeles Times* is legal affairs writer, wrote two articles about Bird: the first, a background piece at the time of her appointment on February 13, 1977; the second, a review of her work as chief justice at the threshold of her confirmation campaign on August 8, 1978.

The first piece traced Bird's career prior to her appointment as chief justice. Bird had grown up in the East, obtaining her undergraduate degree from Long Island University. She came to Berkeley first to do graduate work in political science and later as a student at the law school, from which she graduated in 1965. She clerked for a year for the Nevada Supreme Court and then took a position in the public defender's office in San Jose. She organized that office's first appellate division and in

---

* The testimony before the commission implied that the justices spent the majority of their time deciding how to vote and devoted relatively little effort to crafting their opinions, which were written in large part by staff. But the press, and presumably the public, evaluates justices on their opinions as if that were their only contribution to the decisionmaking process.

† *In re* Morrison , 20 C.3d 437 (1978).

‡ A technical error: the chief justice was up for confirmation for the remainder of her predecessor's term, not for a full twelve years. Bird's first term ends on January 1, 1987.

connection with this project taught a clinical course at the Stanford Law School, training students in the trial and appeal of criminal cases. In 1974 Bird left the public defender's office for private practice—just about the time Jerry Brown's campaign for the governorship began—and she became involved to some extent in his campaign. Bird had met Brown when they were both students in Berkeley. After Brown's election, he appointed Bird Secretary of Agriculture and Services.

Blake's first article consisted in large part of quotations from people Bird had worked for or with during each of these phases in her career. The quotes were overwhelmingly favorable, as the introductory paragraphs reveal:

Those who have been most intimately associated with Ms. Bird in her capacities as law clerk, public defender, law school teacher and Secretary of Agriculture and Services in Governor Brown's cabinet are enthusiastic in their praise.

The qualities these people repeatedly mention are intelligence, a solid background in criminal law at both the trial and appellate level, an analytical mind, organizational ability and a prodigious capacity for hard work.

But above all, they say, is her sensitivity to the problems of people as individual persons, particularly the underprivileged and the underdogs.

Blake met Bird at her confirmation hearings in March 1977. She thanked him for a positive account of her background. Not long thereafter, Ralph Gampell, the recently appointed director of the Administrative Office of the Courts, suggested to Blake that he do another story on Bird and Gampell promised to arrange an interview. Blake refused, thinking it would be better to wait a year or so, but he called in the promise when Bird began to look newsworthy.

Blake's August 8 article in the *Los Angeles Times* although longer than Salzman's was far less analytical. Like the February piece it was little more than a collection of quotes—these taken from a two-hour interview Blake had with the chief justice. "Rose Bird—Not One of the 'Good Old Boys' " featured what might be described as human interest items—the plants in her office, the cakes and cookies she baked for the Wednesday conferences and office birthday parties, the sale of the limousine, and Bird's decision to stay in a modest motel when the court sat in Los Angeles. The last, Blake said, "speaks volumes about Ms. Bird." Precisely what those volumes contained is obscure; clearly, this was a page taken straight out of Jerry Brown's book on public relations (Brown had scored major publicity triumphs by not using the governor's mansion built by Reagan and by using a Plymouth instead of a Cadillac). Blake's gaining a two-hour interview was a more subtle press relations trick Bird may also have learned from Jerry Brown. Many reporters who regularly covered the court had long-standing requests in for an interview; most had been denied or indefinitely postponed. Brown similarly held very few press conferences, although he did have frequent short press availabilities for reporters covering him in Sacramento. Extended interviews with the governor were vouchsafed primarily to out-of-town and especially out-of-state reporters who were, generally speaking, less well-informed about negative matters and more likely to focus their stories on the governor's style and broad vision than on specifics and issues. It infuriated the press corps covering the governor, but he mollified them by giving the local press some contact and a lot of genial camaraderie. An important difference between Brown and Bird was that the chief justice gave the press that covered the court virtually no contact. Phone calls were routinely referred to Stephen Buehl, her executive assistant. The court's press corps saw Bird only when she was on the bench or making a speech.

Blake's effort to confront the chief justice with issues that were irritating some lawyers and judges was largely frustrated by the unwillingness of judges and others to criticize the chief justice for attribution. Blake noted, "[S]ome members of the judiciary are critical of her performance in the job so far, although they refuse to be quoted by name." That reluctance of lawyers and judges to be openly critical continued throughout the campaign and made it difficult for any reporter to give a balanced picture. Specific factual allegations could be examined, for example, that the chief justice had written fewer than her share of opinions (Blake found this charge false), but general evaluations such as that Bird was a "miserable administrator" or that she only "superficially" attempted to build collegiality on the court were nearly meaningless without knowing their source. Blake attempted to overcome this problem with phrases such as "bitter former staffer" and "veteran jurist," but the tone of carping from malcontents was almost inevitable.

Blake's principal point in the story was that being a woman did not explain Bird's failure to qualify as "one of the boys." Although he tried to evaluate her performance independent of her sex, he did feed Bird a few loaded questions: "Is it difficult for [you] sometimes to get the six men on the court to get their work out?" Bird parried skillfully: "Well, it's a very heavy workload for anybody that is on this Court. And in everything that involves human beings, some people are quicker than others. Some are more thorough than others."

Finally, apart from one reference to the *Caudillo* case (not by name) and the *New West* article, Blake made no effort to analyze or discuss either the content of Bird's opinions or her votes.

"Sexism, hell! We did the same thing to Earl Warren!" Cartoon by Paul Conrad. Copyright © 1979 *Los Angeles Times*. Reprinted with permission.

THE CAMPAIGN AGAINST THE CHIEF JUSTICE

At the outset, reporters covering the chief justice's confirmation campaign assumed two facts: first, that the campaign against her would be well orchestrated and richly financed; and second, that she would not campaign in her own behalf. Neither proved correct. More was spent for the chief justice ($341,452) than against her ($301,156), and her supporters used their resources far more effectively than did her opponents. Bird very early said that she would not campaign and maintained that position throughout, but from the reporters' viewpoint, she or her supporters did nearly everything that a candidate for public office does to win an election except shake hands and kiss babies. By election day, reporters covering the campaign were aware that the efforts to defeat her had collapsed and thought her claim of not campaigning hypocritical, but neither conclusion penetrated the editorial offices of the papers or public consciousness.

The opening shot came from Senator H. L. Richardson, who announced on June 1 that his Law and Order Campaign Committee would raise $1 million to defeat Rose Bird and Frank Newman; he did not explain why he left out Wiley Manuel. Richardson intended to rely for funding on the 65,000 people included on his mailing lists.

Richardson explained his scenario to reporters as follows: "With the absence of Rose Bird and Frank Newman and a governor with a complexion other than Jerry Brown, we could have a law enforcement oriented Court for the first time in 30 years." This sentence is worth examination because it was characteristic of Richardson. First, it was unfair to Newman; Richardson was not assuming, he could not know, that Newman was not law enforcement oriented. On June 1 Newman had been on the court for less than a year, had written only one opinion in a criminal case (for a unanimous court), and had participated in only eight other criminal cases, none of importance, in which the court had announced the result. Second, Richardson was careless with the facts. The court of thirty years earlier was not law enforcement oriented; indeed, the same justices decided in 1955, before the U.S. Supreme Court imposed the rule as a matter of constitutional law on all states, that illegally obtained evidence would be excluded in criminal trials as a matter of judicial policy.* Finally, Richardson had not thought through what would happen if his effort succeeded. A defeated justice's term would run until the first of the year, as would Governor Brown's if he lost. If Bird, Newman, and Brown all lost on November 7, Bird and Newman would probably resign before January 1, in which event Brown, not Younger, would name their successors. Perhaps a loss of this nature would make Brown more responsive to law enforcement types in selecting replacements for Bird and Newman, but that is all Richardson could have accomplished.

Richardson had a record with reporters of being less than cautious with facts. Most reporters did not share his political persuasion and they approached his press conferences skeptically, checking factual assertions and noting errors and distortions. Mudslinging is a well-established and

* People v. Cahan, 44 C. 2d 434 (1955). In terms of long-range consequences, both practical and political, the *Cahan* decision was the most important anti–law enforcement decision the court made until it invalidated the death penalty in 1972.

sometimes successful campaign strategy; reporters and editorial writers suspected that Richardson would do that in his effort to defeat Bird. Nevertheless, one factual assertion Richardson made—that he was going to raise and spend $1 million to defeat the chief justice—went virtually unchallenged.

By mid-September, Richardson lowered his sights to $600,000 and dropped Newman as a target for defeat. He had by then less than a third of his target sum in hand.* Then, on September 22 the court sustained Proposition 13, thereby eliminating the most likely reason for widespread donations to a campaign against Bird.

Richardson planned to broaden his appeal beyond direct mail through television advertisements; on September 29 he showed two TV spots at a Sacramento news conference. The ads vindicated those who thought Richardson would run a simplistic, nasty, and unfair campaign against the chief justice. The first ad, based on *Caudillo,* showed a young woman pursued by a masked man into an elevator, the door closing, and then the same woman, bloody and sobbing on the floor with her clothes badly disheveled. The announcer's voice told viewers: "Next May that rapist could be on the streets again because Rose Bird and the Supreme Court reversed an appellate court decision and said they did not think the victim had experienced 'great bodily injury.' " The other ad showed a school bus picking up some Anglo children with what the *Los Angeles Times* described as "a low camera angle [that] makes the bus loom ominously on the screen." The voice said:

Last year our children were going to their neighborhood schools. Then the social engineers went to work, more interested in quotas and percentages than the education, safety and future of California's youth. The pleadings of parents and students alike were ignored when Rose Bird and the Supreme Court ruled that they knew what was best for our children. The buses will continue to roll until they get our message. On November 7th, vote "no" on Rose Bird.

Walter Cronkite used a clip from the *Caudillo* ad on the CBS evening news, as did many local news programs in California. Supporters of Bird immediately sent a telegram to all TV stations in the state urging them not to run the ads because they were "inflammatory and inaccurate." The telegram was followed by a five-page letter from Geoffrey Cowan on the stationery of the Center for Law in the Public Interest.

---

* Richardson could perhaps have diverted resources from some of his other organizations, such as the Gun Owner's of California, to the anti-Bird effort. People supporting Bird were always apprehensive that he would do that.

Cowan argued that this was an "issue" rather than a candidate campaign and that

[p]ublic issues are best developed in news and public affairs programs and spot announcements tend to distort the debate and to put undue influence in the hands of the affluent. . . . The nature of a judicial ratification election makes such spot advertising particularly unfair and inappropriate. Unlike candidates in contested elections, who are free to raise large amounts of money and who have an equal right to buy and respond to spot messages, Supreme Court Justices cannot adequately defend themselves since it is generally considered inappropriate for them to "campaign" for office. The Chief Justice, for example, has announced that she will not campaign for votes. Nor do the complexities of judicial rulings easily lend themselves to succinct advertising copy. Stations which sell time to groups such as Senator Richardson's therefore inevitably do a disservice to this unique electoral process, and we hope that as a matter of policy your station will reject all paid advertisements in judicial ratification campaigns.

This argument sounds hollow now since Bird's supporters outspent her opponents, a fact not clear when Cowan wrote the letter. Cowan went on to state that the ads were false and misleading and to assert that each station had an obligation under the Federal Communications Act to refuse material that the station had reason to believe was untrue. Finally, should any station choose to run the Richardson ads, Cowan requested an opportunity to run at no cost to the pro-Bird campaign rebuttal ads under the fairness doctrine of the FCC:

While we are fundamentally opposed to the use of spot messages in this election, we have concluded that the only effective way to answer such ads may be with messages of a similar length. Therefore we do intend to prepare some brief (but accurate) announcements which we will make available to stations which decide to air Senator Richardson's advertisements.

The telegram and letter worked. No station accepted the ads in either the Los Angeles basin or the Bay Area. The ads were carried briefly on one Sacramento station and a few stations in San Diego but obviously to a very limited audience. This episode effectively ended the Richardson campaign against Bird. He sent out some more mailings and tried to get some free newspaper publicity. His total expenditures were $254,000 of which about $50,000 was spent for the TV ads that were screened only once in partial clips on news programs in most of the major population centers of the state. Analysis of the Law and Order Campaign Committee reports filed with the Fair Political Practices Commission indicates that the remaining $200,000 was spent almost entirely on direct mail expenses which could not have reached very many of the more than 6 million people who ultimately voted for or against Rose Bird.

The success of Cowan's letter in stopping the Richardson commercials was noted in news stories but caused little comment. Phil Kerby, an editorial writer for the *Los Angeles Times*, wrote a signed column in the *Times* raising several questions that deserved more attention than they got. He confessed to some queasiness at the ads' suppression and wondered whether that "mythical fellow out there on the street would be . . . bamboozled" by such transparent appeals to emotion. Kerby thought there was a First Amendment issue present; he also wondered whether the underlying difficulty was in subjecting judges to the electoral process in the first place. He quoted the Century City Bar Association on judicial retention: "Although judicial philosophy is a factor for consideration, we believe that removal of a judge should be based primarily on factors such as incompetence, dishonesty or malfeasance, not the popularity of specific decisions." Kerby feared this standard would reduce the role of the people to rubber-stamping the governor's choice and he doubted whether such was the intent of the state constitution.

Every point Kerby raised was important, especially the last. What standard a conscientious voter should use in deciding whether to vote for or against a justice has never been clear. The Century City Bar's position, although widely held among lawyers and perhaps good policy, is not compelled by the history of California's constitution. The yes/no vote on appellate court justices was introduced in 1934 by an initiative measure supported by the League of Women Voters. The argument in the voter's pamphlet, about all that exists for purposes of legislative history, suggests that voters were free to second guess the governor's selection of a member of the court for any reason they deemed sufficient.* Although Richardson did not justify his anti-Bird project in these terms, his response to a reporters's question whether he was "tampering with judicial independence" was not unjustified:

Bull pucky—that's spelled b-u-l-l p-u-c-k-y. Judges don't like the judiciary being held accountable. They're upset that we're doing that. We have a constitutional privilege not to confirm her. We also have a First Amendment right to express our views.

---

* The pamphlet told voters that if this proposal was approved "the voter would have a power . . . of vetoing an appointment of the Governor, and of casting a vote for or against one particular candidate on the basis of his fitness for office."

The other organized group opposed to Chief Justice Bird thought it wrong to campaign against her because she was a liberal and tried hard to separate itself from Richardson. The agriculturally based "No on Bird" organization—led principally by Jerri Bigelow and Mary Nimmo—told the *Los Angeles Times:*

We started our campaign for completely different reasons from Richardson. He says she's soft on law-and-order issues. I don't think it is right to go after judges because of their philosophy, but I do think it is fair to challenge them on issues of judicial integrity, temperament, fairness and knowledge of the law. Rose Bird has said that herself.

Bigelow and Nimmo kept trying to distance themselves from Richardson, but it is doubtful that many people heard them or paid much attention because agriculture interests failed to fund this effort. The goal they announced in August of $500,000 to $750,000 for a media campaign was obviously unrealistic. The total spent by the agricultural "No on Bird" committee was $45,000 which included about $10,000 for radio spots. Nimmo and Bigelow spent a lot of time on radio and TV talk shows trying to get their message across, but in general they got minimal press coverage. For example, they mailed a ballot on the chief justice to all 1,114 judges in the state. Only 327 ballots were returned, but 221 were marked "no." The fact that one fifth of the state's judges returned a negative ballot to a committee opposed to the chief justice was a story worth probing, but few papers printed it and none in a prominent place. Unlike Richardson, some of the "No on Bird" charges were quite specific, for example, that Bird had appointed Steven Buehl, her executive assistant, to a position for which he was unqualified. The difficulty with that charge was that it was at best only partially accurate. Buehl was being paid at a rate comparable to a senior civil service attorney ($41,000) for which he was unqualified in terms of years as a licensed lawyer. However, the position of executive assistant to the chief justice was a new one (no previous chief justice had established such a position), and it is in the nature of such positions that the appointing authority should have considerable flexibility in selection. There was nothing illegal or especially unusual in Buehl's appointment. He was young and relatively inexperienced, but so was the chief justice.

Three anti-Bird stories got significant coverage during the campaign. The Republican party held a mid-campaign convention in September. The leadership of the convention planned to avoid the usual outpouring of resolutions because Republican conventions tend to be dominated by the party's conservative wing. Noises from that source are not what a minority party wants to trumpet when its candidates must attract Democratic voters. Unfortunately, the chairman's ruling that the meeting lacked a quorum not only prevented the adoption of resolutions, it also blocked adoption of the party platform. As a result the executive committee was authorized to act in the convention's stead, and it adopted both the platform and a resolution against the chief justice. The latter action got more coverage than the former.

The second anti-Bird story came out on October 25, when some deputy district attorneys held a press conference to release a statewide poll of prosecuting attorneys. The justices up for confirmation reportedly received the following votes:

	Yes	No
Bird	78	808
Newman	204	611
Manuel	334	483
Richardson	748	93

These figures, however, represented the opinions of only a fraction of the total population of prosecuting attorneys invited to vote and failed to reflect the difference in attitude toward the politics of law enforcement between elected district attorneys and their appointed deputies, who tend as a group to be considerably more hard-line than their bosses. Richardson and the "No on Bird" committee had been notably unsuccessful in getting elected district attorneys to come out against the chief justice, and some prominent elected prosecutors, like Joe Frietas, District Attorney of San Francisco, and Burt Pines, City Attorney of Los Angeles, endorsed her confirmation.

The third anti-Bird story was the most important since it came out just before the election. On November 2 some reporters got an anonymous tip that a letter (dated October 26) written by Ralph Drayton, president of the California Trial Lawyers Association, to his board recounted a conversation between Drayton and Justice Mosk that would be of interest to the public. After getting a copy and checking its genuineness with Drayton, reporters quoted the letter as follows:

I [Drayton] started the conversation by asking the Justice if he would do us the honor of accepting the award of the Appellate Judge of the Year.

He said, "I am not interested." He said, "I am very unhappy with your association getting involved with politics this year."

I asked him in what respect were we involved in politics that upset him. He said that we had no business getting involved in the Rose Bird campaign or coming out in support of her without knowing all the facts.

I explained to him that we felt it was an issue involving an attack upon the court in general rather than upon Rose Bird. He said that was "blatant nonsense."

At first Mosk declined to comment on the story but then issued a brief statement November 4:

The obvious fact that the California Trial Lawyers Association communications are politically controversial is the very reason I declined its award. I wrote no letter to the CTLA and did not authorize anyone to write on my behalf. I did not indicate to CTLA or to any other group how I intend to vote on any issue next Tuesday.

This statement, seemingly crafted to say nothing, served to keep the story alive for two days. Robert Fairbanks, in the *Los Angeles Times*, noted that Mosk "was known to have been dismayed when Gov. Brown appointed Ms. Bird as Chief Justice." Neither the *San Francisco Examiner* nor the *San Francisco Chronicle* made any effort to explain Mosk's motivations.

On October 6 the *San Francisco Examiner* ran a long story by K. Connie Kang that got less attention than it deserved because of the *Examiner's* relatively limited circulation. Kang was assigned to cover the San Francisco courts (both trial and appellate which, in San Francisco, includes the Supreme Court) in 1975, not too long before Bird was appointed. Other than law courses in journalism school, she had no training for the assignment, but she had worked for newspapers for over a decade including a period covering the Maryland legislature for a Baltimore paper. For a brief period she left the *Examiner* to work for the *San Francisco Chronicle* but returned to the *Examiner* because she "felt freer there to write about dull issues I thought were important." She found covering lawyers and judges difficult because they were so insistent about accuracy and unforgiving about what they called errors. She often thought her supposed mistakes were rather more differences of viewpoint then inaccuracies.*

Kang did better what only Salzman had attempted before: an assessment of Bird as an administrator. Kang had interviewed about seventy lawyers, judges, and court administrators, finding (as had Blake) that no one would say hostile things about the chief justice for attribution. Nevertheless, Kang became persuaded that more than grousing by malcontents was involved:

The criticism [of the Chief Justice], offered for the most part anonymously, is directed at Bird's management style, rather than her legal ability. The central theme is that the Chief Justice is trying to run the judiciary like the state Agricultural and Services Agency she once headed, managing abrasively and surrounding herself with a hand-picked, inexperienced and, in some cases, overpaid staff of loyal followers.

---

* Kang later won a bar association award for her coverage of the commission's proceedings.

Periodically Kang asked the chief justice's office for responses to certain questions but got no answers. Finally, in late July she dictated eight "charges" to the chief justice's secretary about the administration of the court system. Much to Kang's surprise, an answer came in the form of a letter from Justice Tobriner to the editor of the *Examiner*, Reg Murphy. Predictably that offended Kang because it seemed to her a tactic designed to demean her in the eyes of her employer and to cast doubt on her objectivity and professionalism. Tobriner's conclusion after stating that he, rather than the chief justice, was answering because "I have in mind the elimination of the possibility of anyone asserting that the Chief Justice was engaged in a self-serving response"—was: "I find no basis whatsoever for the assertions."

Kang quoted these remarks in the October 6 article, eliminating four of the eight original charges because she found Tobriner's responses more or less adequate. As to the remaining four, Kang led with the least important: the chief justice had overpaid her staff. This accusation was true only in the sense that Bird had departed briefly from past practice, whereby lawyers working for the courts received the same salaries as lawyers of comparable experience elsewhere in state service. Most of the people Kang mentioned by name were employed at the very beginning of Bird's tenure and had since left, as her story noted. The most important staff person remaining was Stephen Buehl; as to him, the charge was not maintainable.

Kang's second charge concerned the appointment of Court of Appeal Justice John Racanelli to the Commission on Judicial Performance. Rancanelli was an old friend of Bird's. He had been a judge of the superior court in Santa Clara County when she practiced there; Bird had abortively attempted to have Rancanelli named to the Agricultural Labor Relations Board, and Governor Brown had since appointed him to the Court of Appeal in San Francisco. Kang alleged that Racanelli had been appointed to the Commission on Judicial Performance by the chief justice alone although the Constitution gave the appointment to the whole court, and without first consulting the other members of the court. The charge was almost certainly true although it was also almost certainly inadvertent. Kang quoted Tobriner's response on this point:

No member of this Court may discuss what transpires in our conference sessions. Matters involving appointments to the Commission on Judicial Performance are discussed during our conferences. I will indicate to you that the allegation is false.

The difficulty with that bit of stonewalling was that other members of the court did not share Tobriner's view about the confidentiality of every subject discussed in conference, especially matters that were not in fact discussed. As Kang reported:

However, three justices, Frank Richardson, William Clark and Stanley Mosk, have confirmed that Bird did not put the Racanelli appointment for vote before she named him to the Commission. Justice Wiley Manuel said he could not remember and Justice Frank Newman was not on the Court when the Racanelli appointment came up. Bird's colleagues are understood to have expressed their displeasure at the method of the Racanelli appointment, and on April 6 of this year, it was the entire court that, through a split vote, appointed Los Angeles Superior Court Judge Jerry Pacht to another vacancy on the Commission.

The important thing about this was not that it happened, but the way Tobriner reacted to it. Bird's failure to consult her colleagues on the Racanelli appointment suggested bad staff work more than anything else. The unconsulted justices would normally accept an apology and ratify the Chief's action without much difficulty. But such mistakes happen and there is no good reason to attempt to cover them up.

Kang's last two charges related to the resignation and replacement of Ralph Kleps as director of the Administrative Office of the California Courts.* Kleps, the first incumbent of that office, was appointed by the Judicial Council in 1961. Kleps was an extraordinary man whose successful civil service career testified to competence and political impartiality. By the time Bird was appointed, Kleps was only a few years from retirement, and most people assumed that he would remain as head of the Administrative Office of the Courts until age forced him out. But Bird and Kleps clashed almost immediately for reasons that were not made public at the time. Six weeks after Bird's appointment, Kleps quit with a brief, uninformative announcement from him that he had resigned and from her that he had retired. Kleps's departure was noted in the press without speculation as to his reasons for leaving, but the cognoscenti suspected foul play. Kang charged that Bird had ordered Kleps to execute a contract for the Administrative Office of the Courts bringing in two people, Edgar Kerry and John Robbins (the first from the Fair Political Practices Commission and the second from the Department of Finance), to investigate the judiciary. As Kang explained:

Apparently, the idea of having two men from the executive branch to investigate the judiciary thrust upon him without prior discussion angered Kleps, who had an almost free rein under the three previous chief

---

* The Administrative Office of the Courts does the staff work for the Judicial Council. The Judicial Council is composed primarily of judges and acts as a kind of board of directors, determining policy for the court system as a whole.

justices. . . . Her action (in borrowing Kerry and Robbins) made it per-
fectly clear that she was thinking that "These people around me are all my
enemies, therefore, I must look for comfort of the executive branch from
whence I came," said a former Judicial Council employee.

Kang's last charge related to appointing a new director—the first major problem of Bird's administration. Technically the Judicial Council had the power to name Kleps's successor, and a large majority of the council had been appointed by the former chief justice, Donald Wright. Wright's appointees were widely respected judges, generally moderates, all of whom knew Kleps. Most were troubled by his abrupt resignation.

Ralph Gampell, then president of the state bar, was Bird's choice for director of the Administrative Office of the Courts. Gampell was born in England and trained there as a physician. He came to California in 1949 and ultimately took a law degree at Stanford University while practicing medicine full time. He abandoned his medical practice in favor of the law and involved himself heavily in bar association activities, which was unusual since he was essentially a solo practitioner specializing in tort litigation in Santa Clara county. He was an ebullient, happy man whose principal love was politics. He was elected president of the state bar and, once there, became something of a partisan of Governor Brown, warmly welcoming public members to the Board of Governors of the State Bar —foisted on the membership by Governor Brown by a bill—and trumpeting eagerly the cause of free representation of the indigent, although most members of the bar abhorred both causes.

Gampell's name, Kang charged, was submitted to the council with inappropriate haste and with accompanying information that sharply reduced the field of potential candidates. Kang claimed that Bird told her colleagues on the council that no judge currently sitting in California was eligible to serve as director and that the pay for the office was very low. If Bird said those things she was wrong, but even if she did it is unlikely that many members of the Judicial Council were misled since all of them were widely experienced in the system. Even so, Gampell's appointment was controversial and passed by a divided 14-4 vote.

One important twist in this story escaped Kang's notice. The dissenting minority on the council included William Hogoboom, presiding judge of the superior court in Los Angeles County, the biggest court in the state (then 171 judges). The presiding judge of that court is the most important administrative figure in the court system next to the chief justice. To appoint Gampell over the negative vote of the presiding judge of Los Angeles County superior court was as startling to the judiciary as if a Democratic president had appointed a secretary of labor over the objection of the president of the AFL-CIO.

Kang's October 6 article was slightly off target on many points but

overall it supported her thesis that Bird as an administrator was preoccupied with surrounding herself with people who would be personally
loyal. No other reporter saw that as a story worth exploring.

THE CAMPAIGN FOR THE CHIEF JUSTICE
AND AGAINST SENATOR RICHARDSON

Since confirmation of appellate justices was instituted in 1934, gubernatorial appointees generally have won by wide margins without campaigning. Assuming that Bird wanted to campaign, it was therefore hard
to know how she should do it. She would have no difficulty obtaining
invitations to speak, but what would she talk about? It would be improper
to discuss her views on any legal issue likely to come before the court or
even to defend decisions, such as *Caudillo,* already announced. Politicians in campaigns talk about the inadequacies of their opponents and
issues. Bird had no opponent and could speak in only the most vapid
generalities about her dedication to the law, not the most tempting topic
to take to the hustings. She made only two speeches in the summer and
fall of 1978, before the campaigning season was at its height, and she
canceled several speaking engagements to avoid the appearance of campaigning.

There is no reason to doubt the sincerity of Bird's statements that
she thought it inappropriate for the chief justice to campaign. Unlike
some of her predecessors, Bird enjoyed public speaking and was good at
it. From her point of view, she was doing less public speaking than
normal and much less than she wanted to.

The two speeches she made were quite different in character. In
August Bird spoke to a national convention of trial lawyers in Los Angeles. Most of her talk dealt with the tenuous position of the courts in
modern society and how courts are required to resolve fundamental
social tensions that the political branches of government sometimes
evade. Her remarks included the following passage, widely quoted in the
press:

*As you may be aware, there is a small group of extremists in this state
whose zeal for politicizing the bench to ensure ideological domination has
emboldened them to believe that the Chief Justiceship can be bought by
the expenditure of $1 million in a media-blitz campaign.*

She concluded with a string of rhetorical questions that to reporters
sounded like a politician's stump speech:

*Do we truly want a judicial system in which a person must pass a litmus
test in order to remain a judge? . . .*

Do we truly want a judiciary that decides issues not as an impartial arbiter but as a sycophant seeking to satisfy the wishes of a powerful few, a strident minority, or a momentary majority?

In contrast, her September speech to the state bar convention was almost dull and largely technical. A main point, for example, was why trial courts should be funded by the state government rather than the counties. However, Bird made one reference to her own problem:

A judge's integrity, fairness, temperament and knowledge of the law are all pertinent areas for public inquiry. The people have every right to express their views on these matters and engage in public dialogue about them. However, what is happening instead is that judges are being perceived as easy targets and are being portrayed in a manner calculated to create prejudice in the public mind and then play on it. This technique has met with increasing success as the distinctions between the judiciary and the executive and the legislative branches have blurred with the thrusting of more and more political issues on the courts. Those who attack for momentary political advantage have not hesitated to seize upon this opportunity.

Despite the relatively colorless content of her speech, Bird received a standing ovation from the delegates in San Francisco.

Even though the candidate would not make speeches or organize a publicity campaign in her own support, others had a strong interest in Bird's success. The most obvious was Governor Brown: the confirmation vote was in part a referendum on his selection and Bird's defeat would be a powerful blow to his prestige. Nevertheless, the governor maintained a low profile on Bird. He supported her, as he stated frequently —especially in the last weeks of the campaign—but he did not make her qualifications a major theme in his speeches or respond to Younger's attack on Bird and the Supreme Court. The governor never explained clearly his reticence on Bird and the subject of judicial independence. He was quoted in late October as saying: "I don't want to hurt her. [There] is a level of conservative voter that will vote for her that may not vote for me." Still, the governor helped Bird by giving some people in his administration leaves of absence to work in her behalf and encouraging his supporters and financial backers to help the chief justice.

Tom Houston, whom Bird had brought into state government when she was Secretary of Agriculture and Services and had remained with the agency after she left, was one of those given a leave of absence to work for the chief justice. Most people assumed that Bird had enlisted Houston, but in fact she had nothing to do with his involvement. Houston had seen polling data from the governor's campaign that showed Bird losing. He was also alarmed over the potential impact of Richardson's TV ads. Houston, a lawyer with some background in communications law, conceived the strategy of trying to block the Richardson commercials by asserting that any station that ran the ads could be required to give free time to opposing ads. He went to Los Angeles in late September to sell his concept to the pro-Bird campaign.

There he found various committees quarreling with each other and failing to accomplish much either in raising money or getting an effective message to the voters. One group interested in Bird's success was the women's movement: Bird was the most important woman in California government and quite visible nationally; her defeat would be a major setback to the movement. There was never any issue on the merits of her re-election, but who was to lead the campaign to support her, how it was to raise money, and what would be the message were all issues that tended to divide. Another group interested in a Bird victory were the Brahmins of the bar concerned about the independence of the judiciary. What was needed there was organization for fundraising purposes. The big-firm lawyers would contribute in reasonably generous amounts, but no one was doing very much to solicit money from them in a systematic way.

Houston decided to try to turn the situation around. He persuaded various people to let him act as coordinator, obtained a leave of absence for the month of October, and took over to the extent that he could. How he dealt with the Byzantine complexity of the various groups is not of importance here. It was enormously difficult because there was no candidate to make decisions and each group maintained a measure of autonomy by controlling the funds it raised. Houston sought to do three things: block the Richardson commercials, raise money, and cover the state first with radio spots in the last two weeks of the campaign and second with newspaper ads on election day.

Houston gave full credit to Richardson for making it easy to get people involved. The tone and nature of Richardson's campaign against Bird inspired support for the chief justice. Speaker Leo McCarthy early made it clear that the issue in the Bird campaign was not her qualifications or her competence but rather the nature of Senator Richardson's campaign against her. McCarthy told the state bar convention in September:

> There is occurring this year an extraordinary attack on the court system. There is an assumption that bare-faced ideological differences are enough to unseat members of the Supreme Court. . . . If we permit some group of yahoos to attack the court we are in deep trouble. I hope a sense of urgency is developing.

The loyalists gathered round, mostly Democrats like Mayor Tom Bradley of Los Angeles but also a few Republicans such as Congressman Pete McCloskey.

The Richardson commercials got the fountain of liberal support and money flowing. How to respond to the ads was a problem. Some Hollywood figures, especially Norman Lear, volunteered their help most usefully. Their answer was a TV spot featuring Carroll O'Connor. But as William Endicott of the *Los Angeles Times* noted:"An irony in the use of O'Connor for the pro-Bird spot is that he plays the quintessential conservative, Archie Bunker, in the popular television series, All in the Family." In fact, there was never any need to air the O'Connor spot on television because so few stations ran the Richardson ads, although the pro-Bird forces used O'Connor for a radio ad broadcast widely throughout the state. Given the continuing slippage in the polls (run weekly from October 1), it is not suprising that no one chose to remember that Geoffrey Cowan had earlier said on behalf of the pro-Bird forces, "[W]e are fundamentally opposed to the use of spot messages in this election. . . ."

Eastern columnists also helped Bird. David Broder, Anthony Lewis, Richard Reeves, and Tom Wicker all wrote articles reprinted in one or more California papers about the election. The Broder and Reeves columns came before the Richardson commercials, but even so they devoted as much space to tearing down Richardson as to building up Bird. Lewis and Wicker hardly glanced at Bird, focusing on the nature of the campaign against her.

The *Los Angeles Times* ran a very long editorial on Sunday, October 1, supporting Bird, much of the piece devoted to disparaging the motives of Richardson, the agriculturally based "No on Bird" people, and the executive committee of the Republican party. These themes were repeated four weeks later in a somewhat briefer lead editorial:

The malicious attempt to remove Chief Justice Rose Elizabeth Bird from the California Supreme Court threatens the integrity and independence of the state's judiciary. . . .

We urge our readers to vote Yes on Bird's confirmation Nov. 7. It will not only be a vote for a fair, able and energetic Chief Justice, it will also be a vote for a judiciary that has the courage to resist partisanship and intimidation.

The *Sacramento Bee* gave even more editorial space to supporting Bird. Five pro-Bird editorials were printed between September 7 and election day. The theme was the same as the *Times's*:

The longer the campaign against Chief Justice Rose Bird goes on, the less convincing it becomes. The anti-Bird forces have had plenty of time to come up with evidence of Bird's incompetence, yet they have presented none. They have not had to contend with any attempts by Bird to promote herself, since by tradition justices do not engage in electioneering, yet they have maintained their belligerent style. They have been warned by the legal community that the judicial confirmation process must not be politicized. Yet they have continued a partisan campaign, replete with scare tactics and distortions. The contrast with the dignified silence and the honorable records of Bird and the other three Supreme Court justices up for consideration is striking.

Other papers around the state were more restrained in their enthusiasm for the chief justice (or, more accurately, their distaste for Richardson), but all of the major papers endorsed her.

The statewide editorial support for the chief justice was not entirely spontaneous. In an addendum to a report she filed with the Fair Political Practices Commission, Bird said she had attended meetings of the editorial boards of the *Los Angeles Times*, the *San Diego Union*, and the *San Diego Tribune*. (She visited other papers as well, but listed those three because she felt it necessary to state that she paid her own expenses of her trip south.) In the addendum she said:

The meetings were at [the papers'] invitation, and the invitations were accepted only upon the following understanding: that I was neither seeking nor asking for their endorsements; that no stories would result from the meetings; that I would answer any question they might have regarding the judicial system.

Given the general collapse of the opposition and the breadth of her support, why was Bird doing so badly in the polls? Polling data on the chief justice were difficult to analyze: the undecided vote was large and it was never clear what percentage of voters would bother to cast a vote on Bird. Two major statewide polls, the California poll (run by Mervin Field) and the *Los Angeles Times* poll, showed the following results:

CALIFORNIA POLL

	Aug.	Sept.	Nov.
Yes	43	44	47
No	26	30	37
Undecided	31	26	16

TIMES POLL

	Aug.	Sept.	Nov.
Yes	39	33	39
No	26	31	34
Undecided	35	36	27

Cynical reporters thought her slippage in the polls explained Bird's decision to give the public television station in San Francisco (KQED) an interview and to submit to an interview for news programs broadcast on the commercial stations in Los Angeles. Bird was interviewed in her office by Belva Davis, one of KQED's regular reporters, and Bill Turner, a lawyer who covered legal affairs for the station. Davis asked Bird: "Up to now you've not talked to the press. . . . Why have you decided to talk to us today?" Bird answered:

I'm not campaigning for this office, and I'm not today asking anyone to vote for me. But a number of people wrote to me, and I also saw an article . . . by Bob Schmidt that appeared in the San Jose Mercury *which [said] that people perhaps had a difficult choice on very little information, and that perhaps they simply ought to have an opportunity to see the person, who they are, and listen to them speak. If I can do that for them, I thought perhaps I owed that to them.*

In terms of content, the KQED interview was a movie version of Blake's August article. The most memorable portions, emphasized in the press stories that followed, concerned cookies for conferences, meetings of the Judicial Council in state office buildings rather than posh resorts, and the problem of being the first woman on the court. Bird had laid down two conditions for the interview: that she not be asked about specific cases before the court and that she not be asked to respond directly to charges made against her. The first stipulation was dictated by the code of judicial conduct. Turner interpreted the second as formal rather than substantive. He could not ask, "Your opponents have charged you with being unqualified. What is your answer?" but he could ask, as he did, "Do you think you need any prior judicial experience in order to manage [the largest judicial system in the world]?" The questions were not pressed, however; they were posed as vehicles for Bird to present herself to the viewers.

Probably not many people saw the program, aired the Saturday before the election, but the KQED interview was widely covered in the press under gripping page-one column heads like "Justice Bird Speaks Out" and "Chief Justice Breaks Silence." Whether calculated as a campaign tactic or not, the interview worked very well. Bird got excellent press coverage on the weekend before the election, with more and better attention given to her message than her opposition had been able to get throughout the summer and fall. The message was made only a little murky by the simultaneous coverage of the Mosk conversation with Drayton, head of the California Trial Lawyers Association.

All that remained were the wrap-up stories for the weekend before the election. The *Los Angeles Times* ran a long analytical article by

Charles Maher, a legal affairs writer, that attempted a review of the chief justice's opinions. Maher started with *Caudillo* and gave enough of the background to make it clear that it was foolish to conclude from this case that Bird was soft on rape. Since Maher looked only at her opinions he encountered the same problem Salzman had faced earlier. As Maher phrased it, "The Chief Justice has yet to speak for the Court on a real cause celebre." But as a lawyer, Maher felt comfortable doing what Salzman had not, assessing her opinions for legal competence:

In terms of technical quality, as distinguished from philosophical orientation, Ms. Bird's opinions seem not to have attracted widespread criticism. They appear to reflect thorough research. She is not windbaggish, but some of her dissents run longer than the majority opinions from which they depart.

Endicott's wrap-up for the *Times* noted the collapse of the campaigns against Bird and questioned the fairness of the charge that Richardson was politicizing the judiciary:

That argument is vulnerable to countercharges that the very appointment by Brown, a fellow Democrat, was a political act. Her fortunes have been so inexorably linked with the political fortunes of the Governor that in that respect, at least, the Court was undisputably "politicized" from the day she assumed the job.

Kang raised two new points in the *San Francisco Examiner*. The first was that no one would have objected to Bird's appointment as an associate justice; the problem was that Brown made her chief justice. Undeniably, Bird was inexperienced, and Kang found Bird suspicious—in marked contrast to her predecessor, Donald Wright, who came to the court after years of judicial experience and "trusting everybody." Second, Kang suggested that Bird's sex should help, not hurt, her in the election.

California, the state that prides itself on being ahead of the rest of the nation, was ready to have a woman and member of a racial minority on its high court in February 1977 when Gov. Brown announced the appointments of Bird and Wiley Manuel, a black, to the court. The best evidence of this was the absence of opposition to Manuel, though he had barely a year's experience as an Alameda Superior Court judge and was not known as an exceptional legal mind. . . .

Kang then went on to list three prominent California women: Shirley Hufstedler, judge of the U.S. Court of Appeals (since appointed the first Secretary of Education), Dorothy Nelson, Dean of the University of Southern California law school (since appointed to the federal Court of Appeals), and Mildred Lillie, justice of the state Court of Appeal in Los Angeles.

It would [Kang thought] be difficult to imagine anyone daring to wage a campaign to unseat Nelson, Lillie or Hufstedler if any of those women were occupying Bird's seat. . . . The fact that [Bird] is a woman is an asset. Male lawyers and judges do not like to be accused of being sexists.

Though lawyers and judges may not like to be called sexist, the public might nevertheless vote against a candidate because she is a woman. No doubt Bird both won and lost votes on this ground alone; probably Bird's sex was most important in leading some voters to suspect that her opposition was at least partially sexist and to discount their arguments accordingly.

A FEW COMMENTS ON THE CAMPAIGNS

A complete evaluation of the campaigns and the media coverage requires looking at what might have been but was not discussed. That is the subject of the next chapter, but some observations can be made at this point.

First, partisans of both sides, columnists and editorial writers were notably patronizing of the voters. Issues were framed in the most simplistic fashion—law and order versus judicial independence—as if the voters were incapable of making balanced judgments on subtler points. Reporters, especially Endicott and Kang, credited their readers with more intelligence. Bird presented a tough problem. Her appointment was, as Endicott said, a political act by Brown that was properly deplored by people who thought the bench, especially the chief justiceship, should symbolize nonpartisan professionalism. Brown could have found some Democrat, even a woman (as Kang suggested), with established professional credentials. But does it follow that Bird should have been thrown out because Brown misbehaved? Certainly this result was not obvious; perhaps the Century City Bar Association correctly asserted that incumbent judges should be retained unless demonstrably incompetent. By this standard Bird was a sure winner.

Second, both Brown and Younger escaped criticism they deserved for failing to educate the voters about the differences between judges

"Come down here, Rose Bird, and fight like a man!" © Dennis Renault, *Sacramento Bee*.

and politicians like themselves. For nearly eight years Younger had been a quite professional attorney general; suddenly, apparently under the pressure of the campaign, he collapsed and began politicizing his office. His decision to argue the Proposition 13 case personally, his refusal to permit his office to represent the state Energy Commission in court (a pet agency of Brown's), his intervention in the school busing case, and his loose and inaccurate charges about death penalty cases being held by the court (discussed later) were the context for his announcement that he opposed Bird's confirmation. Younger deserved criticism for injecting partisanship into areas he had heretofore treated professionally. Brown, on the other hand, said too little too softly. He should have defended all the justices (including Reagan's appointee, Richardson) and made the argument that any judge deserves confirmation unless he or she is manifestly unfit. It was a perfect occasion to be a political leader educating the voters on a point they were apt to be confused about. Had Brown taken this step, he would have reassured people skeptical about his dedication to principle.

Why did Younger and Brown do so badly on Bird? The answer may lie in their instinct that any lesson about protecting judges was not something the voters wanted to hear. In 1978 California was going through an antigovernment phase, as shown by the overwhelming vote for Proposition 13, and thus it was not a good time to stand up and be counted in support of the judiciary. Senator Richardson thought attacking judges would be popular; the behavior of both Brown and Younger suggests that they agreed with Richardson's assessment of the public mood. Each trimmed his position accordingly.

CAUDILLO II

In his *New West* article, Jonathan Kirsch said that as a result of the Supreme Court's decision Daniel Caudillo could be out of prison as early as May 1979. He was wrong; Caudillo was paroled on September 22, 1978. He was rearrested October 24. On November 1, division one of the Los Angeles Court of Appeal ordered him released pending a hearing as to the lawfulness of his rearrest. This order was stayed two days later by Tobriner as acting chief justice.

No newspaper made a serious effort to unsnarl this tangle before the election, a noteworthy omission. Any editor wanting to embarrass the chief justice could have retold the *Caudillo* story much the way Kirsch had; the lurid facts of the crime would have both sold newspapers and damaged the chief justice. The press deserves credit for exercising restraint. Furthermore, the press cannot be faulted for failing to report what was in fact a newsworthy story: complex legal maneuvers were involved and many details were not available in time to be published before the election. However, some aspects of *Caudillo II* are relevant to what happened in the commission hearings and need to be discussed here.

Caudillo entered state prison in November 1975, after he had been sentenced by Judge Callister and while his case was on appeal. He had been sentenced under what was known as the indeterminate sentencing law for a term of fifteen years to life. As noted earlier, a minimum term of fifteen years did not mean fifteen years; the Adult Authority, the administrative agency that decided when prisoners would be paroled, had the authority to release him earlier (most people under such a sentence were released in five to eight years).

The indeterminate sentence was once hailed as a great improvement over the historic method of establishing a convict's term at the time of sentencing by the trial court. Starting from the premise that the function of prison was to rehabilitate the criminal, reformers of that day concluded that the length of the sentence was best determined by people who could observe how the incarcerated criminal was responding to the prison environment. Recently the rehabilitative ideal has come into serious question for a number of reasons, including a doubt that it is possible accurately to predict future criminality and a growing belief that it is terribly unfair, and debilitating to the prison environment, to hold people for widely disparate time periods for similar criminal behavior. As a consequence, the determinate sentence has come back into favor, governed by the concept that the legitimate function of prison is punishment and that the degree of punishment—the length of the prison term —should depend primarily on the nature of the crime rather than any factor as vague and difficult to establish as the likelihood that a particular prisoner will be dangerous if released.

With Governor Brown's strong support, the legislature incorporated the concept of the determinate sentence into a statute that went into effect on July 1, 1977. The new law was made applicable retroactively to those, like Caudillo, then in prison. Making the law retroactive was rational given the premise on which determinate sentencing rests: people should be punished equally for the same crime whenever the crime was committed.

Caudillo's case was pending in the Supreme Court when the determinate sentence law went into effect. The Community Release Board, the successor agency to the Adult Authority, was considering what Caudillo's determinate sentence should be (they fixed it at seven years) at the same time the Supreme Court was deciding that the enhancement of his sentence for great bodily injury was invalid. Indeed, the ultimate decisions of the court and board came down almost simultaneously in June and July 1978. The law involved in this matter was complicated and need not be explored in detail. Every government agency involved made a mistake: the Supreme Court by not remanding the case to the trial court for resentencing,* the attorney general by not noticing this error, the

---

* Later Jefferson wrote an opinion for the Court of Appeal that implicitly recognized his error in *Caudillo*. In People v. Ramirez, 93 C.A.3d 714 (1979), he remanded a case for resentencing after striking a great bodily injury enhancement for an erroneous instruction that rape alone could constitute great bodily injury.

Community Release Board by issuing a confusing rule, and the Department of Corrections (which operates the prisons) by not consulting the board before recalculating Caudillo's sentence as a result of the court's decision. The end result of this chain of errors was that Caudillo's term as fixed by the board was reduced by three years, which led mechanically to a release date of September 22, 1978. On that day, Caudillo walked out of prison on parole. He promptly returned to Santa Monica.

The Department or Corrections routinely advises the local police when a prisoner is paroled into their community. A police officer mentioned Caudillo's release to a reporter in Santa Monica and this remark prompted an inquiry to the *Sacramento Bee* whether it was true that Caudillo had been released. The *Bee* reporter on the court beat, Daniel O'Neill, was asked to check it out. Brian Taugher, head of the legal staff of the Community Release Board, at first denied the report because he knew the board had fixed Caudillo's sentence at seven years and in his view only the board had the power to reduce a sentence; when he checked out O'Neill's information, however, he quickly discovered that Caudillo had been released.

Taugher knew that *Caudillo* was politically sensitive, but what concerned him most was insuring that the Department of Corrections did not repeat the mistake of itself recalculating a sentence without consulting the board. Once assured that mistake would not be repeated, Taugher turned to the issue of what was to be done about Caudillo. The decision was made to rearrest him and schedule him for a prompt "serious offender" hearing on the theory that the department had the power to correct its own mistakes. This decision was taken not by Taugher but by two hearing officers after consulting with Gary Macomber, the executive officer of the Community Release Board, who was himself unaware of the possible political significance of Caudillo's rearrest.

Daniel Caudillo was rearrested and placed in the Los Angeles county jail on October 24. With the state public defender's help, Caudillo filed a petition for a writ of habeas corpus, first in the superior court, which promptly denied it, and then in the Los Angeles Court of Appeal on October 27. Division one's response (Justices Wood, Lillie, Thompson, and Hanson) to the writ was unusual. In the normal course of events (if a writ is not summarily denied), the court asks for a response from the attorney general and then, if any doubt remains, issues a brief order to show cause and schedules the matter for a hearing in the immediate future. Ten days for an "informal" response by the attorney general is more or less standard, although division one had a reputation for hard work and often demanded a quicker response from the attorney general. In this instance division one gave Deputy Attorney General Donald Roeschke Monday and Tuesday to prepare and file an informal response. Where the law and facts are unusually clear, the court can issue an order directing the immediate release of a prisoner.

It is hard to see how Caudillo's case was so compelling as to require an order for his immediate release without giving the attorney general a formal opportunity on more than two day's notice to be heard. Caudillo was not, after all, a wholly innocent member of the public taken at midnight from his domestic hearth by a jack-booted Gestapo. He was a convicted felon on parole who had been released from prison but a month earlier by what the prison authorities asserted was a mistake. It might be that the mistake was irretrievable, but Caudillo's claim for immediate release as opposed to a week or ten days later does not evoke much sympathy. But that is what division one did on November 1, the Wednesday following the Friday that Caudillo's petition was filed. Furthermore, the court released Caudillo not with a routine order that would be unlikely to catch the eye of any passing reporter but rather with a six-page opinion that opened with the following sentence:

Because we are merely messengers of bad news created by the actions of others, we preface this order to show cause why habeas corpus should not issue ordering the parole of Daniel Caudillo and order for his immediate release on parole pending hearing on the OSC [order to show cause] with an analysis of the circumstances leading to our order. *

This statement and another pious protestation toward the end of the opinion,

However repugnant Caudillo's conduct which led to his conviction may be to us, whatever our personal disagreement with the legislation and high court decision, whatever our personal outrage at the result, we cannot ignore our constitutional duty to insure that no one is illegally imprisoned.

cannot be read without creating some doubt about the justices' indifference to the election less than a week away. Why Wood, Lillie, or Thompson (we do not know which two of these three participated because the opinion was unsigned—Hanson dissented) seem purposely to have treated this case in a way designed to get attention is a question that has to be asked but cannot be answered.

The Supreme Court was hearing arguments in Los Angeles during the week of October 30–November 3. Donald Roeschke, the deputy attorney general involved, prepared and filed with the court an applica-

* The court's opinion was nowhere published but was included as an exhibit in the commission's proceedings.

tion for a stay of division one's order of immediate release.* In the normal course, this application would be given to the chief justice for action; she presumably saw the motion on Thursday, November 2. However, Bird apparently recognized Caudillo's name and disqualified herself. The matter then went to Tobriner, as the acting chief justice. He placed the papers in his briefcase and did not look at them until he returned to his office in San Francisco the next day, November 3.

Bird's decision not to participate merits comment. With rare exceptions, judges do not explain why they disqualify, or recuse, themselves from particular cases. There are legal standards for some obvious situations, for example, where the judge is related to a party or has a financial interest in the outcome of a pending lawsuit, but in general the law is uncertain on this problem. Bird, however, was consistently quick to disqualify herself from any case in which anyone might think her less than totally impartial.† *Caudillo II* is an example. The only apparent reason for disqualifying herself in Caudillo's case was the campaign issue of whether rape alone constitutes great bodily injury. The fact that *Caudillo II*, involving wholly different questions, was politically sensitive because it involved a man named Caudillo would not normally have been a ground for disqualification.

In any event, the papers in Caudillo's case went to one of the court's senior research attorneys, a law school classmate of Bird's who had worked for the Court for most of the years since graduation from law school in 1965. The text of the memorandum the research attorney prepared on the stay application was never made public, but both the attorney and Tobriner testified at the commission hearings that the conclusion was "deny, submit." That meant that in the attorney's thought the application for a stay was sufficiently meritorious to warrant consideration by the whole court in conference; however, his ultimate judgment was that the Court of Appeal was most likely correct in concluding that the Community Release Board did not have the power to rearrest Caudillo.

Testimony also disclosed a little-known procedural detail: the chief justice (or, in her absence, the acting chief justice) acting alone has the power to grant a stay to preserve the status quo, but a vote of four justices

---

* "Immediate" means days, not hours. Presumably, Caudillo would have been released by Monday if the Supreme Court had not acted on Friday, November 3.

† She announced during the campaign, for example, that she would participate in no cases involving the Agricultural Labor Relations Acts. Likewise, Bird withdrew from South Dakota v. Brown, 20 C.3d 765 (1978), a case involving Governor Brown's refusal to extradite a man who had fled to California after being convicted of rioting in connection with an Indian dispute in South Dakota. If Bird disqualified herself because she was identified with the governor and people might think her biased in his favor, this action could be described as either a manifestation of extraordinary delicacy or an evasion of responsibility to decide those cases that come before the court regardless of possible political repercussions.

is needed to deny a stay. This rule, not included in the published rules of court, is a well-understood practice within the court. The theory of the rule apparently is that the chief justice alone should have the power by issuing a stay to preserve the status quo so that the court as a whole can ultimately act on a case. Tobriner explained the rationale for the distinction between the power of the chief justice to grant a stay alone and the requirement of four votes to deny:

The reason is to preserve the status quo. The purpose is to see to it that at least the Court has a chance to pass on the matter, and therefore in order to prevent the Court from passing on it, there would have to be four votes to say there is nothing in it.

The application of this theory to Caudillo's case is unclear. First, what was the status quo? Caudillo had been released by the Department of Corrections on parole: was parole the status quo or was it his former state of imprisonment or his current position in the county jail? Furthermore, the court would have jurisdiction to consider the merits of Caudillo's rearrest whether he was in jail or on parole because in either event he would be technically in custody. So long as Caudillo remained in contact with his parole officer, granting a stay was not essential to the court's jurisdiction. Tobriner, however, testified that he was worried that Caudillo would disappear and in that event the court would lose jurisdiction; therefore, it was essential to keep him in custody by granting a stay of the order for immediate release. This reasoning was not as obvious as Tobriner's testimony would suggest. There was law to the effect that a court need not consider appeals or applications of prisoners who have escaped, but Caudillo was in custody when he filed his habeas corpus petition and if he chose to flee while his petition was pending his flight would not deprive the court of jurisdiction. At most, flight might justify the court's deciding that Caudillo had forfeited any right to attend a new "serious offender" hearing before the Community Release Board or to challenge any determination of the board to extend his sentence.

Discussing his reasons for granting the stay application in his testimony before the commission, Tobriner said: "[I]t was quite possible that Caudillo might leave the jurisdiction or might abscond *or might commit another crime* or might do anything." (Emphasis added.) His research attorney, Michael Willemsen, was more explicit: "My personal concern was less that [Caudillo] would flee than that he might commit another violent crime. But I did mention that I had no confidence that he would not flee." The political effect if Caudillo should commit another crime was transparently enormous. The chances were slight, but if he were caught after another vicious rape before the election, it would be front-page news and the end of any hope of Bird's confirmation by the voters. On the other hand, the legal relevance of the possibility of another violent crime by Caudillo was very cloudy. That Caudillo was a danger-ous man was something for the Community Release Board to consider, not the Supreme Court. The issue before the court was a technical one: did the board have authority to rearrest a prisoner once paroled? The viciousness of Caudillo was irrelevant to the answer.

Tobriner told the commission that he was aware of the political sensitivity of *Caudillo II* when he was considering the stay application:

I knew it was possible that [there] might be a political factor if he were released. I didn't know how much attention would be paid to it . . . or whether it would have any effect at all on the election.

But the thought came to my mind: This is the Caudillo who had been the subject of considerable political discussion and political conflict and so on. [But] my duty was to try to carry out my obligation as acting chief. And . . . I set aside the thinking, if any, about political consequences. As a judge we must do that very often. . . . We must recognize very often that there [are] political consequences with respect to an election when we are deciding a question. In deciding the question we may have that on our minds, but nevertheless we should still pursue our duty to decide the case or to dispose of the matter—in this case the stay—irrespective of those matters.

Tobriner's statement contrasts sharply with Bird's decision to disqualify herself. Tobriner thought he had a "duty to decide." What duty did Tobriner have that Bird did not have before him? True, she was on the ballot and he was not, but he was a supporter of hers and if the basis for her decision to recuse herself was to avoid the appearance of bias, this danger was also present if Tobriner acted on the stay. There may have been a difference but it was at most an exceedingly subtle question of degree.

As it turned out, the research attorney's legal analysis was not essen-tial because on Friday, November 3, there were not four members of the court present who could have voted to deny the stay. Thus, in the attor-ney's view, Tobriner had no choice but to grant the stay at least until four members of the court could consider the matter. Tobriner testified that he did not know that only two of his colleagues were available when he made the decision to grant the stay on November 3, but that was an alternative ground for his action. The full court (except for the chief justice) considered the *Caudillo* matter on November 29 and effectively ratified what Tobriner had done by retransferring the case to the Court of Appeal for a hearing on the merits of whether the Community Release Board had the power to order Caudillo's rearrest. Meanwhile, Caudillo was to remain in custody.*

---

* To complete the story: division one decided Caudillo's case early in February 1979. Thompson wrote a strong opinion reaffirming the division's initial conclusion that Caudillo's rearrest was illegal. Before Caudillo could be released, however, the Supreme Court, Bird again not participating, granted a petition for hearing and ultimately decided the case against him on March 24, 1980. Tobriner wrote the opinion, 26 C.3d 623 (1980). Clark concurred in a Mosk dissent, which, in addition to reprinting Thompson's opinion for the Court of Appeal, contained this language: "Caudillo's criminal conduct does not render him eligible for an outstanding citizenship award . . . but he is not guilty of seeking political notoriety, it was fortuitously thrust upon him. As a result, during and since 1978 the Caudillo case has been as sensitive as a lightning rod in an electrical storm. Thus Daniel Caudillo had been singled out for unusual attention; he was not given, and is not now being given, the objective and dispassionate treatment to which any person is entitled at the hands of administrative agencies and the judicial process. . . . The majority now misinterpret clear legislative language and reach a strained result designed to justify Caudillo's rearrest and continued confinement."

THREE

What Might Have Been Discussed in the Campaign

The most important thing the California Supreme Court does is decide cases. How well it performed this function from Bird's appointment to the election was hardly discussed during the campaigns over her confirmation. Apart from Senator Richardson's loose charges about Bird's attitude toward the death penalty and her allegedly anti–law enforcement bias based on *Caudillo* and her career as a public defender, no one asked whether Bird or the other justices on the ballot had in general contributed to an improvement or a decline in the quality of the court's decisions. Somewhat later, during the commission's hearings, it was frequently asserted that the court's reputation was in rapid decline from a high level of distinction achieved during the tenure of Bird's predecessors (Phil S. Gibson, 1940–1964; Roger J. Traynor, 1964–1970; and Donald R. Wright, 1970–1977). Institutional reputations tend to outlive the reality they are supposed to mirror. In this instance, the commission's investigation triggered an overdue reassessment of the court.

In truth, the California Supreme Court's performance during much of the seventies was open to considerable criticism; the downhill direction was established well before Bird's appointment. In addition to scholars increasingly skeptical about the quality of the court's decisions, a very broad spectrum of politicians were angry at the court.

Measuring the quality of a court's decisions is an enormously complex task with a technical dimension beyond the scope of this account. An impressionistic tour de horizon, however, can describe at least a part of the source of the court's rise to distinction as well as demonstrate why some elected political leaders turned against the California Supreme Court during the seventies.

HOW THE CALIFORNIA SUPREME COURT CAME TO BE GREAT

Governor Culbert Olson appointed in 1940 the two towering figures of California's modern judicial history: Chief Justice Phil S. Gibson and Associate Justice Roger J. Traynor (when Gibson retired in 1964, Pat Brown elevated Traynor to the chief justiceship). Gibson's fame was built largely on his skills as an administrator, and this aspect of his career will be discussed later; Traynor achieved distinction as a judge and scholar who, in addition to his judicial opinions, wrote prolifically in law reviews about the role of the state judiciary and the function of a state high court.

Traynor's vision of the role of the court was shaped by the thinking of Holmes and Cardozo and, more broadly, by what is loosely referred to as the school of legal realism. Holmes and Cardozo had each served on the high court of his state before joining the U.S. Supreme Court. The bulk of their extrajudicial writings concerned their views on the development of state as opposed to federal law. Traynor's chief concern also was the development and growth of nonconstitutional law—the law of torts, property law, criminal law, etc.—which by Traynor's time was a mix of statutory and court-made common law. In a sense Traynor outlived his time; by the end of his judicial career in 1970, the preoccupation of many of the more prestigious legal scholars and judges was constitutional law, expecially as developed by the U.S. Supreme Court.

Legal realists, like Cardozo and Traynor, thought it was the responsibility of a state supreme court to shape the law to fit modern conditions and they constantly struggled to test the rationality of rules of law as they were applied in different contexts. As Traynor observed:

The great mass of cases are decided within the confines of stare decisis. Yet there is steady evolution, for it is not quite true that there is nothing new under the sun; rarely is a case identical with the ones that went before. Courts have a creative job to do when they find that a rule has lost *its touch with reality and should be abandoned or reformulated to meet new conditions and new moral values.* *

The names of Holmes and Cardozo are great today; in their time, their conception of what judges should do was often rejected. The bulk of the bench was typically reluctant to reexamine established doctrine against reason and common sense. Traynor's willingness to entertain arguments of this nature did not distinguish him from Cardozo or some other leading judges. What made Traynor unique was his success during his thirty years on the California Supreme Court in persuading a majority of his colleagues and the bar to widen their vision of what was appropriate grist for argument and decision. In numerous instances Traynor's view on the ultimate issue in particular cases did not prevail. Nonetheless, Traynor's openness to a wide range of arguments based on reason and experience influenced his colleagues, lawyers, and the law schools. Pat Brown helped establish Traynor's vision as dominant: from 1959 to 1966 he made eight appointments to the Supreme Court—all of them men who shared in a general sense Traynor's (and Gibson's) conception of the proper role of the Supreme Court.† In sum, when Traynor retired in 1970 he left behind a court firmly committed to a creative role in state governance.

A few illustrations may help make the point clear. In 1944, Traynor wrote a concurring opinion in a case involving an exploding soft-drink bottle that helped start a revolution in tort law.‡ What was exciting about Traynor's opinion was less the result, which, after all, his colleagues had also reached, but the ground he took in his concurrence. Instead of expanding the liability of the manufacturer either through a presumption of negligence or by extension of doctrines of warranty derived from the law of sales, Traynor urged that the manufacturer should be held strictly liable (that is, regardless of negligence) in tort for accidents of this nature because the manufacturer was better able than the occasional victim to spread the risk of injury. The ideas in Traynor's opinion were not particularly new—they had been suggested in the academic literature—but his opinion was among the first to give these concepts the stamp of judicial respectability. As he had predicted, Traynor's route to the result proved far better than the alternatives, which sometimes produced inconsistent and arbitrary results. Eighteen years later (after intervening cases concerning broken beer and milk bottles), Traynor wrote a

* Traynor, *Law and Social Change in a Democratic Society*, 1956 U. Ill. L.F. 230, 232.

† Chronologically, Pat Brown's eight appointees were Raymond Peters, Thomas White, Maurice Dooling, Mathew Tobriner, Paul Peek, Stanley Mosk, Louis Burke, and Raymond Sullivan.

‡ Escola v. Coca Cola Bottling Co., 24 C.2d 453, 461 (1944).

unanimous opinion expressing his views on the manufacturer's liability in a case involving a defective power tool.* Thanks in large part to Traynor's receptivity to new ideas, the California Supreme Court gained a national reputation for pioneering developments in this area of the law.

Another tort case illustrates a different aspect of Traynor's leading the California court to distinction. This nation received into its common law from England a doctrine known as sovereign immunity, thought to have come from the maxim "the king can do no wrong." As applied on this side of the Atlantic, sovereign immunity meant that the government was not liable for the tortious acts of its servants—at least some of the time. Over the years the doctrine had been riddled with exceptions, some generated by court doctrine, others by statutes (for example, a statute making state and local governments liable for the negligent operation of motor vehicles by government employees). In the *Muskopf* case in 1961† the California court, in an opinion by Traynor, swept sovereign immunity into the dustbin, calling it "mistaken and unjust." Characteristically relying heavily on academic literature, Traynor's opinion asserted that the doctrine was founded on a dubious historical premise and described it as an "anachronism, without rational basis, [that] has existed only by the force of inertia."

The decision created major practical problems, for example, for some small units of local government that could not be expected to self-insure against this unexpected liability. Dissenters in *Muskopf* made this argument, urging that a revolutionary decision of this nature ought to come from the legislature rather than the courts. They argued that instances in which the legislature had imposed liability showed a legislative intention that governmental immunity from liability should prevail unless specifically overturned. Traynor's ingenious answer was that the multitude of specific impositions of liability by the legislature indicated a general disposition by the legislature to favor liability rather than immunity as the rule, noting that this legislative attitude was fully consistent with his conclusion.

Whether Traynor anticipated this development or not, the California legislature responded constructively to the *Muskopf* decision.‡ It first imposed a two-year moratorium on the decision's effect during which time the Law Revision Commission was assigned the task of developing a coherent body of law relating to the liability of state and local governments for allegedly tortious acts of their servants. Thereafter the legislature adopted with some modifications the commission's recommendations. As a result, California was among the first states to have

* Greenman v. Yuba Power Prod., Inc., 59 C.2d 57 (1963).
† Muskopf v. Corning Hosp. Dist., 55 C.2d 211 (1961).
‡ See Cobey, *The New California Governmental Tort Liability Statutes*, 1 HARV. J. LEGIS. 16 (1964).

an internally consistent and reasonable body of law on an important and complex set of questions. The legislature's effort spared the people of California generations of litigation on borderlines that the court would have taken years to develop case by case. This dialogue, as it were, between the court and the legislature over the *Muskopf* issue is perhaps as good an example as can be found of the kind of symbiotic relationship that can exist between a state's high court and legislature.

Traynor's approach to problems in the tort area was far more complex than a simple bias in favor of injured plaintiffs. He fought a generally losing battle within the court on the role of judge and jury in tort cases, seeking unsuccessfully to narrow the discretion of jurors with respect to the imposition of liability. At several points he tried, without much success, to bring into question the appropriateness of damages for pain and suffering, especially where liability was predicated on negligence rather than willful misconduct.* Although Traynor had led the way to recovery for the intentional infliction of emotional distress,† he made up part of the majority that rejected recovery for the unintentional infliction of emotional injury without physical harm in 1963‡ and was one of the dissenters when the court reversed itself five years later.**

A case of central importance from the criminal law area can serve as an introduction to another aspect of the California court's distinction —the relationship between it and the U.S. Supreme Court. For most of the nation's history, the protections afforded by the Fourth Amendment against arbitrary search and seizure as well as arrest were largely unrecognized because of the absence of any effective remedy against violations. At one point the U.S. Supreme Court held that evidence discovered as the result of an unconstitutional search or arrest was not, for this reason, inadmissible at a criminal trial; in 1914 it held that in federal criminal prosecutions illegally obtained evidence would be excluded, but only as a matter of judicial supervision of federal authorities.†† For many years, the California court permitted the introduction of illegally obtained evidence in criminal prosecutions despite increasing indications that, at least in some areas of the state, the police were routinely disregarding constitutional limitations.

In *People* v. *Cahan*,‡‡ Traynor and Gibson switched from the position they had taken thirteen years earlier. Traynor wrote the opinion

---

* See Malone, *Contrasting Images of Torts: The Judicial Personality of Justice Traynor*, 13 STAN. L. REV. 779 (1961); Kalven, *Torts: The Quest for Standards*, 53 CALIF. L. REV. 189 (1965).

† State Rubbish Collectors Ass'n v. Siliznoff, 38 C.2d 330 (1952).

‡ Amaya v. Home Ice, Fuel and Supply Co., 59 C.2d 295 (1963).

** Dillon v. Legg, 68 C.2d 728 (1968).

†† Weeks v. United States, 232 U.S. 383 (1914).

‡‡ 44 C.2d 434 (1955).

putting California among the relatively few states holding illegally obtained evidence inadmissible—the so-called exclusionary rule. The political response was heated, but contemporary observers found general support for the Supreme Court among the lower courts and from some important political leaders, notably Attorney General Pat Brown.* Six years later, the U.S. Supreme Court mandated the exclusionary rule on all the states as a matter of constitutional law in *Mapp* v. *Ohio.†*

Traynor's opinion in *Cahan* is often cited as one example of the California court's "leading" the U.S. Supreme Court to a conclusion on an open issue of law. In many ways, however, *Mapp* and the cases that followed from Washington repudiated Traynor's thought. In the six-year interval between *Cahan* and *Mapp,* the California court, largely through Traynor opinions, developed a California law of search and seizure that was in many ways more coherently focused on the issue of abusive police practices than the federal constitutional law that later emerged.‡ Furthermore, the California law, because it was premised on judicial supervision of police practices rather than the constitution, was subject to legislative revision, at least within broad limits. Finally, in Traynor's view the exclusionary rule was not to be applied retroactively through habeas corpus to people then in prison whose convictions depended on illegally obtained evidence.** On all these points, Traynor's views were rejected by the U.S. Supreme Court, which compelled all state courts to follow a uniform minimum law of search and seizure.

The California court was probably more influenced by the Warren Court than the other way around. The great decision of the Warren years, *Brown* v. *Board of Education,*†† overruled the doctrine of separate but equal in educational facilities. This decision, although bitterly resented in some areas of the country, was in general very well received as a long delayed vindication of what the Civil War had been all about. *Brown* was soon followed by *Baker* v. *Carr*‡‡ and its progeny, establishing the one-person, one-vote rule and requiring reapportionment of state legislatures and other elected bodies. Not since the depression years had the Supreme Court taken such a central position on divisive issues of social policy, but the Court's posture in the Warren era was profoundly different. In the thirties the Nine Old Men were obstructing the political arms of government; in the fifties and sixties the Court was forcing re-

---

* Note, 9 STAN. L. REV. 515 (1957).

† 367 U.S. 643 (1961).

‡ See Paulsen, *Criminal Law Administration: The Zero Hour Was Coming,* 53 CALIF. L. REV. 103 (1965).

** *In re* Harris, 56 C.2d 879, 880 (1961) (concurring opinion). The U.S. Supreme Court later returned to the Traynor view on this point in Stone v. Powell, 428 U.S. 465 (1976).

†† Brown v. Board of Educ., 347 U.S. 483 (1954).

‡‡ Baker v. Carr, 369 U.S. 186 (1962).

form on an unwilling Congress and state legislatures. Although the Court did not argue the cases in such terms, commentators claimed that this difference itself justified the Court's activism: if the democratic arms of government were so divided as to be unable to perform what was constitutionally required, the Court had to compel governmental response.

The perception that the court had a role to play as the leader on major issues, especially on behalf of those who were politically weak or unrepresented, added a new dimension to the Holmes-Cardozo-Traynor vision of a "creative" court. It may have encouraged the U.S. Supreme Court into two of its most unpopular decisions: the school prayer cases* and the abortion cases.† More important for present purposes, the same notion may have made the California court receptive to constitutional arguments that probably would have been rejected had they been presented in the fifties or sixties. Two cases were particularly troublesome to political leaders: *Serrano v. Priest*,‡ holding that the existing system of funding for elementary and secondary education violated the equal protection clause of the California constitution, and *People v. Anderson*,** holding that the death penalty violated the "cruel *or* unusual" punishment clause in the California constitution. The California court decided both cases shortly before the same issues were considered by the U.S. Supreme Court. In neither instance did Washington follow the California court.

Both cases profoundly disrupted the California legislature. A major portion of the state's budget was devoted to state subventions to local school districts. The *Serrano* decision mandated a restructuring of this system in ways that pitted legislators against each other in alignments that crossed all known partisan and regional lines. In this respect the decision had a political impact not unlike that of the earlier reapportionment decision that had come from Washington. In both instances a considerable amount of political capital was consumed in developing compromises on issues no legislator had chosen to fight about. The death penalty case was similarly disruptive. An initiative was put forward and passed almost immediately amending the California constitution to conform to the U.S. Constitution's prohibition on "cruel *and* unusual" punishments.†† The initiative, however, did not put the matter to rest because the U.S. Supreme Court issued a series of notably opaque decisions that forced the California legislature to repass a death penalty

---

* Engel v. Vitale, 370 U.S. 421 (1962).
† Roe v. Wade, 410 U.S. 113 (1973).
‡ Serrano v. Priest, 5 C.3d 584 (1971).
** People v. Anderson, 6 C.3d 628 (1972).
†† CAL. CONST. art. I, §27 (Approved by voters on Nov. 7, 1972).

measure twice (once over Jerry Brown's veto), not to speak of the unnecessary initiative in the November 1978 election.* In the process legislators were forced to take a public position on an agonizingly difficult moral issue. Vast quantities of energy were expended on what was, like abortion, a profoundly polarizing controversy that divided politicians in ways that were destructive of their capacity to compromise in other contexts. The effort left an indelible stain on numerous political leaders and gravely damaged the public credibility of the court.

Both decisions came early in Chief Justice Wright's tenure (1970–1977). The legislature is an institution that can resolve only a limited number of divisive issues at any one time. It is not surprising, therefore, that political leaders increasingly tended to resent the extent to which the courts were dominating their agendas during and following Wright's tenure. Together the U.S. and California Supreme Courts had put reapportionment, school desegregation, abortion, the death penalty, and school finance as priority items on the legislature's agenda, leaving hardly any room for political initiatives by elected leaders. Relations between the two arms of government became hostile. The point is well illustrated by the legislative response to *Li* v. *Yellow Cab Co.*,† a 1975 decision substituting the concept of comparative negligence for the historic defense of contributory negligence. The decision was not unlike the *Muskopf* decision fourteen years earlier in that it cried out for a thorough reexamination of the structure of tort law similar to what the Law Revision Commission had done in the wake of *Muskopf*. But behind *Li*, as with *Muskopf*, loomed politically divisive issues, and the legislative leadership decided that there was insufficient political energy and resources available to settle these problems. The result was to leave a mess for prolonged and expensive resolution by the courts.

The political rhetoric about the courts also underwent a subtle shift. In the fifties and beyond, controversial judicial decisions had been defended by a broad spectrum of politicians on the ground that what the courts ordered was the law and deserved support even if the substance of a decision were distasteful. As time went on, however, political leaders tended to defend particular decisions only if they agreed with the result. As a consequence, the California court became identified with the liberal side of the political spectrum, and attacking the court became easier for the extreme right as moderates tended to withdraw from the debate.

---

* Mosk discussed the California response to the U.S. Supreme Court's waffling on the death penalty in People v. Frierson, 25 C.3d 142, 188 (1980) (concurring opinion). For an eloquent and angry discussion of the U.S. Court's decisions, see Black, *Due Process for Death*, 26 CATH. U.L. REV. 1 (1976.)

† 13 C.3d 804 (1975).

THE DECISIONS OF THE BIRD COURT TO THE ELECTION

Three justices retired from the California Supreme Court early in 1977.* Because the four remaining justices were in large part evenly split, Governor Jerry Brown had the opportunity to reshape the court. Mathew Tobriner and Stanley Mosk, Pat Brown appointees, had been leaders over the past fifteen years in promoting an aggressive role for the court, particularly since Traynor's retirement. William Clark and Frank Richardson were Reagan appointees who had in general been reluctant followers and had often dissented. The three Jerry Brown appointees thus could, especially if they were cohesive, move the court in either direction.

The twenty months between Bird's appointment and her confirmation election was insufficient time for the new members to develop and articulate their own conception of the court's role. For those who looked closely, however, it soon became apparent that the new members of the court had no intention of slowing down the pace of judicial intervention; indeed, if anything, the Jerry Brown appointees, especially Bird and Newman, seemed impatient to expand the court's role in governance.

In one case Mosk wrote the opinion holding that peremptory challenges to jurors could not be exercised on a "group bias" basis,† although the U.S. Supreme Court had recently held to the contrary.‡ The decision was based on the California constitution. In another, Tobriner, writing for the court, rejected the historic *M'Naughten* test for criminal insanity and substituted the test proposed by the American Law Institute.** In a third case, Manuel held, on nonconstitutional grounds, that a routine clause in mortgages was unenforceable, with the effect that most purchasers of real estate could assume existing mortgage debt at the interest rate given to the seller, a decision of considerable significance at a time of rapidly rising interest rates.†† Finally, Richardson held in another case,‡‡ promptly overturned by the legislature, that a social host was liable for damages for injuries caused by a guest who had been served liquor when obviously intoxicated.

All of these cases involved controversial issues and most were the subject of bills before the legislature at the time the court acted. The insanity case was significant because the court had been reshaping the

* Chief Justice Wright and Associate Justices Raymond Sullivan and Marshall McComb.
† People v. Wheeler, 22 C.3d 258 (1978).
‡ Swain v. Albama, 380 U.S. 202 (1965).
** People v. Drew, 22 C.3d 333 (1978).
†† Wellenkamp v. Bank of America, 21 C.3d 943 (1978).
‡‡ Coulter v. Superior Court, 21 C.3d 144 (1978).

law of criminal responsibility since Traynor's time and in the view of many commentators had been steadily making it worse. This issue became politically sensitive when the assassin of Mayor George Moscone of San Francisco was given a relatively light sentence on the basis of one of the court's earlier "diminished responsibility" decisions.

Bird wrote none of the majority opinions in these cases, but she voted with the majority in all of them, as did Newman. Given the recent history of the court, there was nothing unusual about the decisions; to put it another way, Bird, Manuel, and Newman appeared to be carrying forward what the court had been doing at least since Traynor's retirement in 1970. However, the new members of the California Supreme Court were exposed, as their predecessors had not been, mainly because none of them had significant judicial experience. Given his liberal orientation, it would have been surprising for Jerry Brown to want his appointees to change the general direction of the court's decisions. But since the court was already under fire, why should Brown choose people, especially Bird, so vulnerable to attack?

WHY BROWN SELECTED BIRD

Brown announced his appointment of Bird and Manuel on Saturday, February 12, 1977, and made the Sunday headlines: "Brown Selects First Woman and Black to Serve on State Supreme Court." In his press conference Brown said that he was "looking for talent where others haven't looked before" and that Bird's sex and Manuel's race were "part of the chemistry" of his decisions. He also mentioned their relative youth and their experience in the executive branch as relevant selection factors. (Manuel's entire career as a lawyer had been spent as a civil servant in the California attorney general's office; he had spent one year as a superior court judge in Oakland.)

Brown hardly knew Manuel except by reputation. Bird, however, had been one of Brown's earliest cabinet appointees. She had served as secretary of agriculture and services for two years. There was speculation that Brown was appointing Bird to the court in part for her abilities as a "tough, hard-driving administrator." For anyone who had followed Brown's first two years as governor, administrative skills seemed an odd thing for him to care about: he saw himself as a symbolic leader, not a manager, and he drove his immediate staff crazy by his refusal to be scheduled, his capacity to let "things emerge" (which sometimes meant delaying decisions past the point of most effective implementation), and his penchant for calling knowledgeable civil servants at the operating level rather than taking their views as filtered through the administrative hierarchy.

Bird's record as administrator of the Agriculture and Services Agency is hard to evaluate. The success of a cabinet member is usually measured in large part by legislative responses to those portions of the administration's program that are his or her responsibility. This criterion tests political and lobbying skills more than management ability, but, measured in those terms, Bird proved quite successful. She received considerable credit from the governor for having guided the Agricultural Labor Relations Act through the legislature. In fact, she did not contribute that much. The basic concept of the act was a campaign pledge of the governor's and the bill itself was copied in large part from the National Labor Relations Act with some intricate modifications caused by the floating nature of a migrant work force. This is not to say that Bird did not assist its passage; she met with many people and worked hard but, to the astonishment of legislators and lobbyists accustomed to Reagan's remoteness, the final negotiations were conducted by Governor Brown himself, who insisted on getting involved with the most detailed issues of legislative drafting.

Bird deserved more credit for the "public members" bills. The whole array of occupational licensing boards, from dentists and doctors to contractors and barbers, was part of the Agriculture and Services Agency. Each regulatory board consisted of gubernatorial appointees, but the governor was required by law to appoint only licensed members of the regulated occupation. Reagan had vetoed bills putting public members on some of these boards to represent a larger vision of the public interest. Invariably the occupation targeted resisted public members, but opening up the boards and putting consumer representatives on them was a major piece of Governor Brown's program. Bird was the administration's chief spokesperson on these measures. Again, the bills were not difficult to draft or conceptually complex, but they were controversial.

Bird's most thorny administrative problem was probably the funding fight over the Agricultural Labor Relations Board. She was not responsible for grossly underestimating the budgetary needs of the new agency; the Department of Finance made the estimate on the basis of assumptions that were overwhelmed by events that could not have been anticipated. Bird's authority over the board was also somewhat unclear since it was an independent agency whose board members and general counsel were appointed by the governor. Nor was Bird at fault for the difficulties the administration had in getting the necessary supplemental appropriation; nevertheless, in the process she angered many people in and around the legislature.

Within the Brown administration, Bird was regarded by many as a person sometimes difficult to deal with. She brought with her as her immediate deputies some former students from Stanford Law School, including Tom Houston and Steven Buehl. These men, albeit able, were young and as inexperienced as she in state government. (Lack of experience was characteristic of the first years of the Brown administration.) Bird's relationship with her immediate deputies was unusual: she held them on a very short leash. She rarely attended meetings without one or more of them present (they came to be known as "Rose's ducks"), but they hardly ever spoke in her presence. Their authority to negotiate on her behalf in her absence was also very limited. Several of the departmental directors in the agency were appointed by the governor without Bird's direct participation and their relations with Bird were often tense; she seemed to them at times to be trying to block their access to the governor. In bureaucratic lingo, Bird was regarded as "turf-conscious" —jealous, that is, of her agency and her authority.

Bird was not active in the social life of the Brown administration. Her hours away from the office, which were relatively few, she kept to herself. She attended the obligatory parties but did not otherwise mingle with government people. She made no particular effort to get her name in the papers and resisted press efforts to pry into her private life. Sacramento, like any other government center, is preoccupied with gossip and inside information. It was characteristic of Bird's noninvolvement with gossip that hardly anyone knew she had gone into the hospital for a mastectomy until after the operation was over. She made no effort either to suppress or to publicize the story, and she handled solicitous inquiries with dignity. Her experience gave an emotional jolt to many members of the Brown administration, most of whom were her contemporaries, but few people who worked with Bird detected any changes in her behavior following the surgery in 1976.

The initial prognosis was reported to be good. Bird said after she had been appointed to the court that the doctors had "given her a clean bill of health." Later, however, Bird underwent a series of small operations and in May 1979, shortly before the commission hearings started, she told a couple of Associated Press reporters:

Under the statistics, I will be lucky if I am alive in five years. Nobody knows. You live with the sword of Damocles hanging over your head.

I feel fine, I work my full day and most weekends. I work very hard, but I'm realistic enough to appreciate that my days may be limited. I've made my peace. If it is soon, I can live with it.

An awful lot of the pettiness, the meanness and the cruelties that are part of public life are placed in perspective when you think . . . of your own mortality.

There were a number of good lawyers in the Brown administration whom the governor had known longer and better than Bird and whose judgment he relied on more than he did on hers. Brown later appointed several of them to the appellate bench. If his objective was to appoint someone who would represent his point of view on the court, they would have been more logical choices. Almost certainly the thing that drew Brown's attention to Bird was her sex. Appointing a woman would be a dramatic break with tradition and combined with the appointment of a black, as it was, it would be a very strong statement of Brown's commitment to break up the old boy network. When rumors of Bird's appointment became common, a number of people urged Brown not to name her. Bird herself probably did not promote her own candidacy; it would not have been like her to do so and she undoubtedly knew that such an effort would likely prove self-defeating. The outgoing chief justice, Donald Wright, was consulted by Brown and argued that Bird should be appointed at most to an associate justiceship, primarily on the grounds that naming Bird chief justice was simply a way for Brown to draw attention to himself and that the position needed an experienced judge.

THE COMMISSION ON JUDICIAL APPOINTMENTS

Before Bird and Manuel could take the oath of office their appointments had to be confirmed by the Commission on Judicial Appointments. The commission, composed of the chief justice, the attorney general, and the senior presiding justice of the Courts of Appeal (at that time Parker Wood of Los Angeles), had been created by a constitutional provision derived from the 1934 initiative that introduced the yes/no vote on appellate court judges. One obvious problem with this arrangement was having the chief justice vote on the qualifications of potential members of the Supreme Court. If the chief justice were the only commissioner to vote against a nominee, the chief would end up with a colleague whom he or she had publicly labeled unqualified (as happened when Chief Justice Wright voted against Clark in 1973).

Only once, in 1939, had the commission turned down an appointment, although in a few instances appointments had been withdrawn because of anticipated negative action by the commission. For the most part, the process had become a formality, so much so that the commission had no rules or procedure and virtually no experience with controversy. Brown anticipated a problem with Bird's appointment, and before going public with the decision he talked with Tobriner, the acting chief justice, Attorney General Younger, and Justice Wood. Wood probably gave Brown no comfort. Wood was known to be opposed to candidates who had no judicial experience and was likely to vote against Bird, as he in fact did. Tobriner was much easier. Tobriner had been appointed by Pat Brown, and Jerry Brown had clerked for him after law school. Tobriner was doubtless enthusiastic about the concept of a woman chief justice. Younger was in a difficult position. He could not impose a high standard for who was "qualified" to serve on the Supreme Court and be consistent since he had voted to confirm Reagan's appointment of Clark even though Clark had never graduated from either college or law school. Moreover, and this twist may have intrigued Brown, the appointment of Bird placed Younger in a delicate political position. Younger was planning to run against Brown in less than two years and a vote against the first woman appointed to the Supreme Court would not look good. On the other hand, to vote for Bird, whose legal experience was limited to the public defender's office, could easily embarrass Younger with right-wing Republicans, whose votes he needed to win the gubernatorial nomination. How much of a commitment Brown got from Younger is not known, but it may have influenced Younger's judgment that Bird's nomination was packaged with Manuel's. Wiley Manuel had been promoted by Younger to head the civil section of the attorney general's office. Younger respected Manuel and could well have been apprehensive that some other minority judge (the most likely seemed to be Bernard Jefferson) would be Brown's selection for the court.

If it was part of Brown's scheme to embarrass Younger, the Republicans promptly helped him achieve this goal. Nineteen of twenty-three Republican assemblymen and seven of fourteen Republican senators signed letters urging Younger to vote against Bird; they were joined by Ed Davis and Pete Wilson, Younger's most probable opponents in the Republican primary. This effort outraged the *Los Angeles Times* and the *Sacramento Bee*, which editorially deplored the injection of partisanship into the selection of judges. Two other groups, however, announced that they would not oppose Bird's confirmation: the California Peace Officers Association and the District Attorneys Association. Rod Blonien, spokesman for the CPOA, explained that they were very pleased with Manuel's appointment because they had feared and lobbied against Jefferson's appointment. While "[Bird is] not our favorite," Blonien was quoted as saying, "I think she's got some good things to offer."

Trouble with Bird's appointment developed from a wholly unexpected source. Roger Mahony, Roman Catholic auxiliary bishop of Fresno, was Brown's first chairman of the newly created Agricultural Labor Relations Board; he served in that capacity from July 1975 until December 1976. Mahony was upset over press speculation in the fall of 1976 that Bird might be the governor's choice for chief justice. He felt no capacity to judge her legal abilities and had no doubts about her intelligence, but he was gravely concerned about her personality in the "very important leadership" position of chief justice. Mahony talked to Brown about his reservations before he left state service, but it was clear to him that the governor was determined to appoint Bird. Mahony brooded over the matter for a bit and called Justice Tobriner, whom he knew slightly and respected greatly. Tobriner made it clear that he did not share Mahony's reservations about Bird but encouraged him to write a letter to the Commission on Judicial Appointments, which, Tobriner assured him, would be treated confidentially.

The bishop mailed his letter, addressed to Tobriner as chairman of the commission, on the day Brown publicly announced Bird's selection:

After careful reflection I am writing to offer my vigorous opposition to [Bird's] appointment as Chief Justice, and my qualified opposition to her appointment as a Justice of the Court. . . .

My opposition to her appointment as Chief Justice centers on her questionable emotional stability and her vindictive approach to dealing with all persons under her authority. I experienced personally her vindictiveness on many occasions when the ALRB, an independent state agency, chose to pursue a course other than that desired by Ms. Bird. She has a personal temperament which enables her to lash out at people who do not agree with her. Her normal approach is to become vindictive, then to transfer her feelings to a long phase of non-communication. She would refuse to take or return telephone calls or to acknowledge any attempts at communication.

I am gravely concerned that the future Chief Justice of our state Supreme Court be a person of balanced emotional stability, of judicial temperament, and of corresponsible [sic] collaboration with the other Justices. In my experience and opinion Ms. Bird fits none of those requirements. . . .

Because Ms. Bird is the Secretary of Agriculture and Services and has direct authority over her Department Directors, I am confident they will feel insecure about coming forward to offer the truth about her dealings with them. That is one of the principal reasons I have chosen to write to you at the Commission on Judicial Appointments.

The only other persons who may feel comfortable in coming forward to speak openly and honestly about her lack of qualifications might be former Department Directors or members of the Governor's staff who have resigned in the past several months.

. . . This was a difficult letter to write, but I feel an obligation in justice to the State to bring into the open the many shortcomings of Ms. Bird.

Mahony was upset when news of his letter, described as "devastating," appeared in the *Political Animal,* a political newsletter published in Los Angeles, and in the papers immediately thereafter. When interviewed by reporters, Mahony stated that his letter was a private communication to the commission and he had no intention of releasing it or of testifying before the commission. The text of Mahoney's letter became public on March 1, however, when Younger released it as an attachment to a letter he wrote to Bird.

Younger's letter told Bird that he thought answers to some questions were "essential" to resolving legitimate doubts about her qualifications and he invited Bird to respond either in writing or in testimony before the commission. Younger also enclosed and made public a letter he had written Tobriner, which read:

I received a copy of Bishop Mahony's letter dated February 12 concerning Rose Bird's nomination. I also received your letter concerning the Bishop's phone call to you wherein he stated that he didn't want his letter to be publicized; that he did not intend to make any appearance before the Commission; and that he just wanted to "share" his views with us.

I assume that both you and Justice Wood agree that when a person sends a signed letter to our Commission, obviously designed to influence our judgment with respect to a nomination, both law and logic demand that the communication be made a part of the public record.

In his letter to Tobriner, Younger said that an investigator from his office had sought to interview Mahony but Mahony "would not discuss the matter unless and until you [Tobriner] indicate to him that it is your personal wish that information be supplied." Tobriner was outraged at this public disclosure of what he had promised would be a confidential statement to the commission. Nevertheless, there were no formal rules regarding communications to the commission, and Younger was right in suggesting that it would be grossly unfair to any nominee if the commission found him or her unqualified on the basis of communications undisclosed to the nominee and never made public.*

The content of Mahony's letter got lost in the uproar over its disclosure. The press was full of Younger and the political problem he was in. What Younger needed to escape his political dilemma was some solid, nonpartisan group or person to recommend a negative vote. If the state bar, for example, found Bird unqualified, Younger could have hidden behind this opinion and turned his dilemma into a publicity defeat for Brown. Younger called Wright in hopes that the former chief justice would testify against Bird. Wright refused, telling Younger to vote *his* conscience.

Mahony's letter gave Younger some leads for people who might

---

* One of Bird's first acts as chief justice was to prepare a set of rules for the commission requiring that all communications received by the commission be shown to nominees and be made part of the public record.

support the allegation that Bird's personality ill suited her for the job,* but Younger's aides never pressed the investigation, and no one else volunteered to support Mahony. Why not? Bird war stories were commonplace within the Brown administration. But most of the people involved were Brown appointees, loyal to, fond of, and dependent on the governor. It would be treasonous to Brown to speak out against his nominee. Furthermore, Bird's tendency to withdraw, refusing to discuss a problem, often made people unsure what her problem was. That behavior was sometimes destructive of good government because issues would linger unconfronted while Bird sulked, but nothing dreadful happened as a result. Her unhelpful and confusing behavior was maddening but it was far from anything illegal or immoral that people might think would impose a duty on them to come forward to testify against her confirmation.

The state bar almost rescued Younger in a closed session held five days before the commission's first meeting on March 7. Ralph Gampell, the president of the bar, announced that "after considerable debate" the board of governors had found Bird qualified. The board defined "qualified" as meaning that the candidate possessed "qualities and attributes considered to be worthy of special note, as indicative of superior fitness to perform the judicial function with a high degree of skill and effectiveness." That phrase, known as the Hufstedler formula, had been thrashed out during Reagan's administration when Seth Hufstedler was president of the state bar. Some hint of tension within the board of governors emerged, however, when Gampell later announced that a special meeting of the board, held Saturday, March 5, had produced a divided vote: twelve members found Bird qualified, three found her not qualified, and five abstained.† He reported this result to the appointments commission on Monday, but two lawyer members of the board of governors, Joseph Cummins and Oliver Jamison, felt strongly enough about the matter to tell the commission that six of the votes in Bird's favor had been cast by the new public members of the board, all recently appointed by Brown. Cummins and Jamison were outraged that Gampell had not specified the public members' votes, a matter they thought critical. Gampell, equally outraged at what he regarded as a breach of confidentiality, supple-

---

* "Personality" in the sense that Mahony was using the word is not generally considered a qualification for the bench; "judicial temperament," an accepted criterion, refers to being fair and open-minded, not to the capacity to get along with fellow justices.

† No one disclosed the content or nature of the debate within the board of governors. What did emerge clearly was intense resentment by some of the lawyers on the board at the presence of, and bloc voting by, public members—all of whom were women or minorities appointed by Brown. They especially objected to the presumption that lay members were qualified to evaluate the professional capabilities of lawyers to be judges. The Bird appointment thus served to bring out resentment that had been developing since public members joined the board in September 1976.

mented his earlier testimony by stating that three of the five abstentions and one of the three negative votes had been based on "lack of information." The situation was not eased by the absence of Warren Christopher who was heir apparent to the presidency of the state bar until he resigned to join the Carter administration as Deputy Secretary of State. Not only were Christopher's judgment and considerable diplomatic skills missed, but his absence forced the board to confront a contested election for the next president and the role of the six public members of the board in that process was as yet untested.

Younger's refusal to disclose how he would vote turned the commission proceedings into passably good theater although little of substance emerged. KQED, the public television station in San Francisco, televised the sessions. Most of Monday's hearing consisted of Bird's first reading a long statement about her background and then fencing inconclusively with Younger. Former Chief Justice Gibson, then eighty-four years old, spoke in Bird's support under very tender questioning by Tobriner. His testimony raised a question no one asked: where did the other two living former chief justices, Traynor and Wright, stand on Bird's nomination? Roughly sixty people had signed up to testify in Bird's support with about fifteen in opposition. It was clear that the commission could not hear all the witnesses on Monday so the matter was continued until Friday. Some of Bird's supporters became nervous when Younger engineered Manuel's confirmation through on Monday. Was it possible that Younger, having gotten his man confirmed, would now feel free to vote against Bird? If so, it was clear that Tobriner had been too slow to block Younger's maneuver.

Whatever concern Bird's friends had was put to rest about halfway through Friday's proceedings when Younger asked whether any other witnesses wished to tesfity against Bird. When none appeared, Younger announced that he was prepared to vote in her favor:

I will [vote for her] reluctantly, because I believe there are many California judges better qualified by training and experience to assume this high office. But it is the Governor's opinion, not mine, that is significant. The law does not require that he appoint a judge or the best-qualified or even a well-qualified person. My limited responsibility requires only that I determine if Rose Bird is qualified. Absent any significant evidence to the contrary, I am compelled to find that she is.

The record clearly indicates that Rose Bird is intelligent and industrious. She was a good student and a good instructor. Criticism concerning her allegedly vindictive nature and her inability to get along with others has been overcome by overwhelming evidence to the contrary. In my opinion there has been no substantial question raised concerning her honesty and integrity.

Assuming, without deciding, that she is, in fact, extremely liberal, that is not a legal disqualification. A former deputy public defender is no less qualified to become a judge than is a deputy district attorney. . . . Had I the authority, I would have appointed someone other than Rose Bird, but having determined that she is qualified, I have no legal or moral right to substitute my judgment for the Governor's.

In the Governor's behalf, it should be noted that he deceived no one. During his campaign for Governor he described the kind of appointments he would make. Rose Bird fits the mold. The decision as to the kind of Chief Justice California would have was, in effect, made by our voters in November of 1974.

Younger deserved more praise than he got for this speech. To be sure, he took some political advantage by emphasizing that he did not think Bird was the best-qualified candidate, but he accurately and fairly stated that Bird was intelligent, industrious, and honest and that he had no right to substitute his judgment for that of the governor on appointments. He could have put more content into the constitutional meaning of "qualified," but that would have been inconsistent with his prior vote on Clark. Given Younger's narrow view of the commission's function, on the record before him Bird was qualified.

Two weeks later, Bird was sworn in by Governor Brown. Some dignitaries were noted for their absence, especially Mosk and Clark. The governor in his remarks said it was "a day of spring"; certainly, it was the start of something new but whether the appropriate metaphor was spring or fall was less clear.

JERRY BROWN AND THE JUDGES

The legal community was apprehensive about whom Brown would appoint when Wright announced in January his intention to resign on February 1, 1977. By then Brown had been governor for two years, and he seemed to be making a career out of doing the unexpected and disconcerting. Those who anticipated a return to the liberalism of Pat Brown were startled by Jerry Brown's frugality—he out-Reaganed Reagan at least in the rhetoric of cut, squeeze, and trim—and he warmly supported Republican sponsored bills to increase the punishment for various crimes, including Duekmejian's "use a gun, go to prison" measure.

The judiciary was not exempt from Brown's surprises. Perhaps the most important development was the governor's failure to appoint judges to vacancies as they occurred through death or resignation and his reluctance to sign bills creating new judgeships. This bizarre gubernatorial behavior went on for months with the number of unfilled vacancies steadily growing. Brown's "policy" of nonappointment had increasingly severe effects in localities already short of judges. No appointments were made despite urgent requests from people accustomed to respectful treatment—presiding judges, Ralph Kleps, the chief justice, and even the governor's father. Adverse comments about the governor's refusal to make judicial appointments began to appear in the press and were answered by rhetoric that judges found insulting and incomprehensible. Brown seemed to be saying that our society is too litigious; we have too many judges; judges are overpaid fat cats who should figure out ways to be more efficient; and until judges started making changes he would make no judicial appointments.

Part of Brown's message had merit: judges cannot be added endlessly to the system as the caseload grows without threatening other important values. But Brown offered no program to reduce the workload or improve the efficiency of the trial courts. (Much later he successfully sponsored legislation to divert relatively minor civil cases to arbitration.) Furthermore, his nonappointment remedy seemed wholly inappropriate since it was administered randomly, depending on where vacancies occurred, and was felt mostly by litigants whose cases would be delayed. Brown revealed no awareness of the hard work the Judicial Council and presiding judges had been doing to increase the efficiency of the trial courts. But most infuriating was Brown's apparent pleasure in dwelling on the judges' high pay with the implicit charge that judges are lazy. As a group, the California judiciary was probably as conscientious and hardworking as any. It was not, however, the unfairness of the charge that enraged many judges. Judges had persuaded themselves they were important and their role fundamental to maintaining the social fabric. In the largest sense, this is correct, but much of what judges do from day to day is not very difficult and of little lasting significance. Brown's assertion that judges were overpaid hit them at the point where their egos were most vulnerable.

Once Brown began making judicial appointments (he started slowly, about six months after his inaugural), it became clear that he was looking hard for minorities and women. The legal community could not attack this goal frontally and many, perhaps most, welcomed it, but Brown's unwritten policy added to the judiciary people who tended to be younger and less experienced and upset some lower court judges' expectations of promotion. Pat Brown and Reagan frequently promoted municipal court judges to superior court vacancies and superior court judges to the court of appeal. A lot of white male judges, especially appointees of Pat Brown who had been passed over during the Reagan years, began to wonder whether the fact that they were doing what they thought was a notably good job would make any difference in their chances of obtaining a promotion.

In any case, no one was surprised that Brown's first apointments to the Supreme Court were a woman and a black or that the appointments were made a little late, two weeks after Wright had resigned. Wright told Brown in October of 1976 that he planned to retire on February 1, 1977. Had Brown announced Wright's replacement before he stepped down, Bird could have been confirmed by the Commission on Judicial Appointments before Wright's retirement, which would have enabled her to participate in the selection of new members of the Judicial Council (the membership shifts on January 31) and to spend some time becoming acquainted with the judiciary and the Supreme Court staff before assuming her official responsibilities. Good appointment practice called for that kind of orchestrated transition, especially where the governor was making an appointment of someone outside of the judiciary.

Why was the governor tardy? One reason might have been because he knew or suspected that Wright as a member of the confirming commission would vote against Bird. If Brown waited until after Wright resigned, then someone else, presumably Tobriner, would be acting chief justice. Tobriner did play that role, but it happened in an odd way. Wright had intended to appoint Mosk acting chief justice before he retired, but when Wright announced his impending retirement from the bench Tobriner immediately began a speech of encomiums in which he implied that he would be the acting chief justice until Wright's successor was confirmed. Wright did not have the heart after that to embarrass Tobriner by appointing Mosk so he dropped the plan. The governor talked to Tobriner about appointing Bird and was assured that Tobriner would vote to confirm her, but whether Tobriner knew that Bird was the likely appointee (or that there was any thought of appointing someone other than himself as acting chief) when he leapt into the breach with his little speech is unknown. The chances are that nothing so Machiavellian took place. More likely the governor did not name Bird in December or January simply because he thought he had more important things to do than anticipate the transition problems of his appointee.

BIRD'S PREDECESSORS AS CHIEF JUSTICE

The hierarchical structure of the courts probably intensifies the sense lawyers and especially judges have that their own worth is somehow measured by the reputation of "their" chief justice. The human impulse to identify with a leader had been reinforced during the professional lifetimes of most California lawyers, who had basked in the glory of Chief Justices Gibson, Traynor, and Wright. Some account of these chief justices' careers is thus relevant to why the judges felt that they were diminished because Bird was not of her predecessors' stature.

Bird inherited what was generally regarded as the best state court system in the country, bigger and perhaps better than the federal courts. Taken as a group, the twelve hundred judges in the state were more than merely competent and there had been no hint of corruption in the system for generations.* The quality and honesty of the bench was attributable as much to the judges' good pay and generous retirement program as to anything else; indeed, when Bird took the oath of office California judges were better paid than their counterparts on the federal bench. There were no overlapping jurisdictions within the court system, and much of the technical procedural law was in the control of competent professional draftsmen rather than the legislature. The people involved in judicial administration were receptive to new ideas, focusing on incremental changes that would improve the efficiency of the system and the quality of the justice dispensed. This is not to say there were no problems, some of them major, but California's court system was in good shape overall.

The picture was far less bright when Phil S. Gibson became chief justice in 1940. Credit for the high quality of the California court system is due in large part to Gibson, who although honored locally never received the national recognition he deserved. This is not the place to correct that oversight, but some discussion of his stewardship, as well as that of his successors, Roger Traynor (1964–1970) and Donald Wright (1970–1977), is important.

Gibson was appointed by Governor Culbert Olson, the first Democratic governor since 1894. Gibson had been modestly active in politics in Los Angeles, where he had practiced law since 1923. Olson made Gibson his first director of finance in 1939, but it was understood at the time that Gibson was interested in a judicial appointment. Olson put him on the court as an associate justice in August 1939, elevating him to the chief justiceship in June 1940, after the death of Chief Justice Waste. In many ways Bird and Gibson were similar. Both were in their forties when appointed; both came to public attention when appointed to a high position in state government; apart from Gibson's less than a year as associate justice, neither had judicial experience; and both had been active in politics, although Gibson was more important in Olson's campaign than Bird had been in Brown's.

Gibson was an active man who enjoyed command and understood politics. The court system he confronted had some obvious targets for

---

* One superior court judge was convicted of bribery in 1970.

reform. The lower courts were chaotic, with 768 separate inferior courts of eight different types, often with overlapping jurisdictions, below the superior courts. Gibson saw that the system needed simplification and consolidation and a mechanism for centralized direction. The inherent tension in judicial administration between central control and local autonomy (judges are fiercely jealous of their prerogatives) went unnoticed in California at that time because no one was pulling from the center. Gibson started hauling and by the time he left almost twenty-five years later, trial judges and local officials were barely hanging onto vestiges of local control.

Gibson believed that success in reform depends on careful research and professionally competent draftsmanship; therefore, he put together a staff of highly skilled lawyers. His first move was to suggest that the Judicial Council be staffed to conduct a study of procedural reforms and reorganization needed in the courts. The council had been established in the 1920s with a rather vague constitutional charter "to improve the administration of justice." The judicial council movement was a nationwide fad that failed, however, and by 1940 California's Judicial Council, like most of the rest in other states, was essentially moribund. Gibson nevertheless recognized its potential as a tool for reform. The council was structurally perfectly suited to his purpose since it was composed entirely of judges appointed by the chief justice.

In 1941 the legislature passed a statute authorizing the Judicial Council to prepare and submit rules on appeal that, unless modified by the legislature, would supersede inconsistent statutes. The bill was not quite what Gibson had wanted because it did not give him a permanent staff, but Gibson maneuvered the court's reporter of decisions, Bernard E. Witkin, into a position where he could work on the rules.

Witkin did a magnificent job; the rules on appeal have survived to this day with relatively minor modifications. (Witkin later became a major figure in California law; his numerous books, found on every judge's desk, are the first, and often last, place lawyers look to find some point of law.)

Gibson supervised Witkin's work, forced extended consultation with committees of the state bar, and encouraged involvement of the law schools, all aimed at creating professional consensus so that when the rules were presented to the legislature there would be no controversy. A by-product was the creation of a permanent professional staff for the Judicial Council. Gibson used the new staff next by broadly reading a legislative resolution to study administrative law and brought in Ralph Kleps on the job. The Administrative Procedure Act, the end result, was a pioneering statute and a national model that succeeded because of the professional competence of its drafters and the efforts Gibson made to consult with the relevant publics.

Lower court reorganization was more difficult because it potentially threatened the jobs of minor court judges and the revenue of local government. (Lower courts, especially traffic courts, are moneymakers because of fines and forfeitures.) Gibson helped engineer a plan that grandfathered in most of the existing corps of minor court judges and protected the fine and forfeiture revenues of the cities. He was forced to yield to county government the power to define judicial districts so that the system ended up with more judges and courts than he preferred. But Gibson lobbied the matter through the legislature and campaigned vigorously for the necessary constitutional amendment, which passed easily in 1950.

Gibson was responsible for one other major reform of special relevance to this account: the creation of the Commission on Judicial Performance. Gibson regarded this as his most important accomplishment. Until 1960 judges who were incompetent could theoretically be removed by several methods: impeachment, concurrent resolution of the legislature, recall, and reelection defeat. In fact, none of these remedies had been used except for a rare defeat of a judge up for reelection. Gibson wanted to create a commission—composed of judges appointed by the Supreme Court, lawyers appointed by the state bar, and nonlawyers appointed by the governor—empowered to hold hearings and ultimately to recommend to the Supreme Court that the court remove a judge for proven misconduct. There will be occasion later to consider the standards and procedures of the commission in detail; for the moment it is enough to note that the commission's principal mandate was to get rid of senile and drunken judges on the trial courts. As might be expected, the proposal generated opposition from some judges. Gibson's prestige, however, was by 1960 sufficient to force an approving resolution through the Conference of California Judges (later called the California Judges Association) by an overwhelming vote of 364 to 34. From there the resolution went through the legislature and was approved by the voters as a constitutional amendment in 1960. The concept has been widely copied: forty-seven states now have comparable machinery to deal with judicial incompetence.

Gibson was chief justice for nearly twenty-five years. By the time he retired his reputation was, at least in California, colossal. He enjoyed good relations with each of the governors who followed Olson—Earl Warren, Goodwin Knight, and Pat Brown. He was a very strong chief justice, with his strength rooted in highly competent staff work, a clear vision of where he wanted to go, and a willingness to compromise in order to build consensus for reform. He was quite prepared to change things, indeed rather enjoyed basic structural reform, but he was also prepared to spend years developing support and understanding. Gibson was a commanding man held in awe if not fear by nearly everyone. He led the Judicial Council not by appointing its members but by the force of his personality. No one ever questioned Gibson's involvement in judicial selection because they knew that he would not abuse his influence for partisan or other improper purposes. Gibson was no saint. He was capable of being abrupt and impatient with nonsense, and some of his reforms never worked, but he avoided transferring differences on the merits into personality conflicts.

Roger Traynor, Gibson's successor, had a towering reputation by the time he became chief justice in 1964. He, too, was an appointee of Governor Olson's; he took Gibson's seat as an associate justice when Gibson became chief. As a law professor at the University of California Traynor had made something of a name for himself as the draftsman of an innovative tax code for the state. His lasting reputation, however, was made through his scholarly judicial opinions, which often pioneered doctrinal developments and were followed elsewhere in the country. By the time he became chief justice, Traynor was nationally known among lawyers as one of the great judges of his time, ranked with Learned Hand and perhaps a few others. He did not have Gibson's enthusiasm for either administration or reform through political action in the legislature. Traynor presided ably over the Judicial Council that Gibson had created, reacted to proposals others made, but he left the bulk of the innovative work to the council members and especially to Ralph Kleps, head of the Administrative Office of the Courts. *

It was a puzzle to many people why Traynor wanted to be chief justice. The burdens of administration would obviously distract him from what was seemingly his first love and greatest talent: writing scholarly judicial opinions and sweeping, sometimes almost poetic, law review articles. For whatever reason, Traynor wanted the appointment badly and lobbied Pat Brown rather clumsily for it. Brown was intensely proud of "his" Supreme Court, and on the basis of distinction as a judge Traynor was the obvious choice as Gibson's successor. As an administrator or effective political operator, however, Traynor was not the strongest candidate. It is unlikely that Traynor had much of an agenda of administrative reforms he wanted to accomplish as chief justice, and Brown appointed him probably in recognition of his notable record as a judge rather than for what he would do as an administrator.

---

* Increasingly, reform was achieved directly by the Judicial Council rather than accomplished through legislation. This development reflected both the delegation of rule-making power to the council from the legislature (as, for example, with family law rules) and the council's issuance of standards of judicial administration that might or might not be mandatory rules for the trial courts. During this period the federal government contributed to the autonomy of the Judicial Council by providing through the Law Enforcement Assistance Administration an alternate funding source for experimental programs and research. The Judicial Council continued to deal with the legislature, but most of this activity took the form of reacting to bills currently before the legislature rather than sponsoring legislation.

Reagan was governor when Traynor resigned in 1970. Reagan had elevated the traditional campaign pledge to take judicial appointments out of politics to a major part of his program and invested an enormous amount of energy in promotiong a "merit selection" proposal, which would have confined his choices for judicial vacancies to a list of candidates submitted by bar leaders, judges, and civic leaders. Reagan successfully lobbied the measure through the state bar association and he obtained Traynor's support for an endorsement "in principle" from the Judicial Council, but he ultimately failed to persuade the legislature. (Characteristically, Traynor did not involve himself in the drafting of the proposal. He waited until it arrived, weighed its merits and decided to endorse it. If Gibson had thought it a good idea—in fact he did not—he would have been involved much earlier in order to shape it to his liking.) In any case, Reagan was still talking seriously about his campaign pledge to depoliticize judicial appointments when Traynor stepped down. Whether or not Reagan paid much attention to political attitudes in screening candidates, he could not have chosen a more apolitical person than Donald Wright to succeed Traynor.

Wright was appointed by Warren to the municipal court in Pasadena in 1953. He won election to an open seat on the Los Angeles superior court in 1961 and his superior court colleagues later chose him to be their presiding judge. Reagan elevated him to the Court of Appeal in 1968. Wright was a judge's judge—professional, quiet, and undramatic in demeanor—who seemed to exude dignity, open-mindedness, fairness, and compassion. Unlike Gibson and Traynor, Wright was loved as well as admired by other judges. It was nearly impossible to get angry with him or to be jealous of his preferment. He led by gentle persuasion more than by force of will or the powers of his office.

Wright was also brave and he determined to take on a problem Traynor and his colleagues on the court had tried hard to avoid seeing. Marshall McComb, appointed an associate justice of the court by Goodwin Knight in 1955, had become senile but refused to retire. It was an increasing embarassment to the court. McComb often fell alseep on the bench and was writing hardly any opinions, but his vote must occasionally have been critical in important cases. The problem was complicated by McComb's consistently conservative voting record, especially on issues relating to criminal law. Any effort to remove him might thus have seemed a maneuver to get rid of him because of his politics rather than his condition, a danger vastly heightened when McComb leaked news that the court was about to invalidate the death penalty in 1972. (That decision, written by Wright, enraged Reagan and taught him a lesson about the appointment of judges.)

No appellate court justice had ever been removed from office by the Commission on Judicial Performance: it was not well suited to consider cases involving justices of the Supreme Court because the commission's power was limited to making recommendations to the Supreme Court. Nonetheless, Wright persuaded his colleagues that the problem had to be faced, and behind the scenes he helped engineer a constitutional amendment through the legislature that the voters approved in 1976. The amendment provided that if a justice of the Supreme Court were involved, the commission's recommendation would be referred to a special tribunal of seven randomly selected Court of Appeal justices.

The McComb matter had to go all the way through to a conclusion by a special tribunal that the justice should be retired for senility. Only in the final stages did the case attract public notice but at no point was any suggestion made that McComb's removal was politically inspired nor were the details of McComb's bizarre behavior stressed. Removing McComb was the most visible administrative accomplishment of Wright's tenure. For a liberal court to rid itself of a senile but also blatantly conservative justice without charges of political motivation and without public discussion of his newsworthy misbehavior was a triumph of administrative skill. It also showed the extraordinary confidence the press and others had in the good faith of Wright. No one could have conceived, Wright least of all, that he was laying some important groundwork for what was to happen to the court in 1979. The McComb affair made it clear that the commission's authority extended to justices of the Supreme Court and made it thinkable for the commission to discipline a member of the highest court. Four justices on the court in 1979 had testified under oath before the commission about the behavior of one of their colleagues in conference and elsewhere and had thus compromised their ability to claim in the 1979 commission hearings that judicial deliberations must be kept in strict confidence.

One additional administrative matter deserves discussion because it illustrates the mind set of the Judicial Council during the time of Traynor and Wright. The Courts of Appeal were in trouble; their workload had increased far faster than that of the trial courts. The traditional means of dealing with a growing backlog is to add judges. In this way the number of appellate court justices went from twenty-one in 1960 to forty-eight in 1969. But appointing more judges is ultimately self-defeating because as the number grows it becomes increasingly difficult to maintain the quality of appointments and uniformity among their decisions. One solution is to restrict in some fashion the right to appeal.

Various proposals to reduce the caseload received careful attention before they were rejected in favor of a wide-ranging effort to improve the productivity of appellate justices. The program of increasing the output of justices involved many facets, but the core concept was that judges could do more work faster if they had more people helping them. Bernard Witkin, as advisor to the Appellate Court Committee of the Judicial

Council, persuaded his colleagues, and ultimately the council and the justices, that a central staff could relieve the justices of some routine work and increase their productivity. The program was successful: in 1960 the average output of a justice on the Court of Appeal was about sixty-two opinions annually; by 1975 the number had risen to slightly over one hundred. As a result, despite increasing workload there was no need to add authorized positions to the Courts of Appeal for ten years.

The pattern of solution is revealing here. The council gave thoughtful consideration to structural reform but ultimately chose a much more conservative, less dramatic way of dealing with the problem. The result was accomplished by quiet persuasion, required no legislation (apart from a modest appropriation for an increase in staff), and got very little attention. Gibson would have been impatient with such a low visibility venture; although the program was conceived in Traynor's time, he let others carry the initiative; Wright was the one who saw it through, coaxing his fellow judges into acceptance.

CHIEF JUSTICE ROSE BIRD

For purposes of evaluating Bird's behavior as chief justice it is convenient to consider separately her conduct as one of the seven Supreme Court justices—her votes and opinions; her policies and practices as head of the California court system—mainly her exercise of the appointment and assignment powers; her behavior as administrator of the Supreme Court itself—staff appointments and reorganization of the court's internal processes; and, finally, her informal relations with judges and others, notably the press. The first has already been discussed and was by far the most public. The others were largely invisible to the public but very well known to judges throughout the state and more important in shaping their attitudes toward her than any case she had decided on the court.

Bird as Administrator of the California Court System

Bird's and Manuel's appointments symbolized the most obvious complaint that the governor had with the judiciary: it was overwhelmingly dominated by white males. The governor never explained, probably because nobody asked, why this situation was undesirable. One reason, perhaps the best, is because the clientele of the courts, especially the criminal courts, is disproportionately urban and minority and an overwhelmingly white bench tends to confirm the suspicion of some that the criminal justice system is racist. The presence of minority judges, jurors, and lawyers should allay this suspicion. Bird, however, read the governor's concern about the composition of the bench as meaning something more; she concluded that he wanted to break up an elite establishment within the judiciary that was dominating its councils and affairs and that the way to do so was to insure that minorities and women were well represented on all committees and the like. From the beginning, Bird used her power of appointment with this objective obviously in mind.

Before examining how she proceeded, it is worth asking whether there was an establishment that excluded anyone or needed to be "opened up." The judiciary is, of course, an exclusive club, albeit one that in California has about one thousand two hundred members. Unlike most club members, however, judges have no control over who joins them and the formal structure of the court system, with its Courts of Appeal and Supreme Court, precludes any informal in-group's effectively dominating the judiciary. Individual judges did have influence and reputations disproportionate to their position (Justice Jefferson, a black, and Judge Harry Low, an Asian who was president of the California Judges Association, for example), but they had achieved prominence for the most part by their activities prior to appointment to the bench, their willingness to take on extramural work, or their exceptional talents. The evidence for an elitist judicial establishment with a program that went beyond such mundane matters as judicial salaries and retirement benefits was very thin.

The chief justice of California appoints the judicial members of the Judicial Council, assigns three superior court judges to sit as the appellate department of the superior court in each county, and assigns individual judges to sit pro tem at all levels to fill vacancies and equalize workloads. Brown's tardiness in appointing Bird deprived her of the power of naming new members to the Judicial Council in 1977, but the single most important appointment within the judiciary came up when Kleps resigned as Director of the Administrative Office of the Courts six weeks after Bird took office. Why Kleps quit has already been discussed and will be returned to later; what is important here is how Bird obtained the consent of the Judicial Council to her selection of Ralph Gampell as Kleps's successor.

Gampell was not a particularly close friend of Bird, but he knew her from the time when they were both practicing in Santa Clara County, and as president of the state bar, Gampell had played a prominent role in getting the board of governors to approve her appointment as chief justice. Bird also knew that Gampell had been a strong supporter of the governor within the bar particularly on the issue of public members on the board of governors. As the president of the state bar and a man who was a good deal older than Bird, Gampell had some obvious credentials as a person of experience and presumed wisdom. But his record as an expert on the subject of court administration or on state government generally was at best limited.

The Judicial Council got short notice of Bird's desire that Gampell be appointed as Director of the Administrative Office of the Courts. The notice was followed by some heavy lobbying of some members of the council by Tobriner and Newman that pulled out all the stops. Their arguments included (1) that the appointment, although technically the council's, was really the chief justice's since it would be pointless to appoint a director who did not get along with the chief; (2) that Gampell was the ideal candidate and Bird needed all the help she could get; (3) that it would be pointless to conduct a search since no better candidate than Gampell could be found. This kind of pressure was offensive to some members of the council who saw no reason for haste. Perhaps it was true that Gampell was the best candidate, but why not conduct a search and see what other candidates were available? Furthermore, to some members of the council what seemed to be at issue was professionalism versus raw patronage. Kleps and others had been preaching the gospel that judicial administration was a quasi-science requiring study and special talents not necessarily evidenced by a law degree. Gampell, whatever his virtues, had no qualifications of that nature.

The Gampell episode was important, came early, and was not forgotten. For someone who was as concerned as Bird purported to be with breaking down old boy networks and opening up the processes, the affair proved her at least indifferent to the forms and process of affirmative action searches. It also showed that she was either getting very bad advice or disregarding good counsel. Not since Gibson's time had any chief justice pressured the council as hard as Bird did on the Gampell appointment. Traynor and Wright had been very quick to sense opposition and had never made a council issue a point of personal privilege. Furthermore, there was no need to press so hard to get Gampell appointed. A search would doubtless have produced some competitive names, but no other candidate would have had on his record the presidency of the state bar. In time Gampell would doubtless have emerged as the choice of the council if Bird wanted him. When the suggestion was made to conduct a search, Bird could and should have agreed to one. Her failure to do so showed her to be, at least at times, an inept politician who preferred to rely on the power of her position rather than her ability to persuade colleagues.

The appellate department of the superior court is not a particularly important branch of the California judiciary. One such court sits in each county as a three superior court-judge panel to hear appeals from the municipal courts in that county. With rare exceptions the decisions of the appellate department are not published. The selection of the three judges is vested in the chief justice, but as a practical matter Gibson, Traynor, and Wright had given this power to the presiding judge of the superior court in the larger counties as part of the latter's general responsibility to assign judges to various departments (criminal, probate, juvenile, etc). Wright modified the practice slightly: he met periodically with the presiding judges of the larger superior courts and at one point suggested to them that assignments to the appellate department be rotated with a new judge added each year who would serve for a total of three years and then return to other assignments. Before then in some counties assignment to the appellate department had, through the seniority system, become more or less permanent. This modest reform was thoroughly discussed among the presiding judges and accepted.

Bird went one step further. She asked for suggestions as to who should be assigned to the appellate department for the year starting in January 1978, but she surprised the presiding judges by rejecting their advice and appointing to the appellate department judges already assigned elsewhere. Her choices included a number of women and minorities and, insofar as there is any explanation for her action, that seems to have been her purpose. Of course, assigning a minority trial judge to the appellate bench takes that judge out of the trial court and puts him or her in a place where few litigants venture. But what most troubled the presiding judges was Bird's direct and untimely interference with their most difficult and important job: the assignment of judges to the various departments in the superior court. That is a complicated balancing act that has to take account of each judge's wishes and each of their strengths and weaknesses as well as seniority. Bird's action was the same kind of interference that baseball managers resent when the owner presumes to tell them who should play second base. It is hard to imagine a better example of the difference in management style between Wright and Bird. Wright had in fact broken up an old boy system, but he did so after consultation and in a way that was acceptable to the vast majority of judges (a few old-timers had resented losing what they regarded as a prestige assignment). Bird consulted no one, angered many, and relied entirely on naked legal authority for reasons that were obscure. If her purpose was, as some supposed, to make friends at the trial court level, her action was counterproductive: she made far more enemies than friends.

The California constitution gives the chief justice the power to assign judges, including retired judges (with their consent), to sit on any court. This power is probably the single most important tool of judicial administration since it enables the chief justice to redirect judicial resources as circumstances require. Originally the power had been used largely to keep judges with relatively light calendars busy helping others with clogged dockets. As the system grew, however, the assignment power had been used increasingly to relieve workload in places that were, for one reason or another, in trouble. By Wright's time, the selection of judges to be assigned to the trial courts had been substantially delegated to Kleps's office, where the task was managed with the single goal of getting the most work out. Heavy reliance was placed on retired judges primarily because they could be added to the system without weakening it some other place.

Bird withdrew what had been a formal delegation to Kleps and undertook to manage the assignment function herself. She also instituted some new policies that were to a certain extent inconsistent with the previous goal of using the assignment power to increase productivity. For example, she announced that retired judges would be assigned only to positions below that which they had previously held, for example, retired Supreme Court justices could sit only on the Courts of Appeal or below; this stipulation deprived the appellate courts of people who were familiar with the processes of the court and able to churn out cases without going through a period of learning. Second, Bird made assignments for relatively short periods—thirty days at the outset, later extended to sixty days. Before then, assignments had typically lasted six months or a year because it takes a week or so for a judge both to work into a calendar and then, at the end, to work out of it.

Bird explained that her purpose was to weaken the hierarchical structure of the courts and, with assignment of active trial judges to the appellate courts, to give trial judges exposure to the perspective of an appellate court. Some judges are foolishly conscious of their superior or inferior status as municipal or superior court judges. Bird made this kind of nonsense a major target in her administration and publicized symbolic steps such as assigning for the first time a municipal court judge to sit pro tem on the Supreme Court. The question has to be asked whether the problem was worth so much attention, especially if the price was a significant reduction in the productivity of the system. Furthermore, Bird's assignments to the appellate courts began to look suspiciously like patronage rewards to the faithful and possibly as a screening device to test judges for promotions. It is hard to prove this charge and it may well not be true, but the suspicion was widely held. In late 1979 Bird recognized the problem and sent a letter to every judge in the state inviting him or her to volunteer for pro tem assignments. Finally, some lawyers began to wonder whether ideology was not influencing pro tem assignments, with judges selected because they were likely to decide cases in a particular way.* That thought had never heretofore surfaced, largely because retired judges were the primary source for appellate court as-

---

* Comment, *Selection of Interim Justices*, 32 STAN. L. REV. 433 (1980).

signments and the appointments to the Courts of Appeal were for extended periods of time.

The last thing to be discussed about Bird's stewardship of the entire court system is something that did not happen but should have. The funding of the courts is unbelievably chaotic, with some costs of the trial courts paid by the county and others by the state. For example, the clerks, bailiffs, and court reporters who service the superior courts are county employees although they are in fact subject to the direction of the judges. Similarly, courtrooms are built and maintained by the county, and from time to time backlogs develop because local government is unwilling to purchase needed facilities. The administration of justice is among the clearest of state as opposed to local functions and ought in any rational system to be funded and to some extent controlled at the state level. It is an accident of history that courts are funded partially locally, but power once vested in local government is exceedingly difficult to dislodge, as Gibson learned when he reorganized the inferior courts in 1950. Gibson made no attempt then to centralize funding, although he doubtless would have liked to, and the state hobbled along with a badly divided funding system that frequently hampered efficiency.

The passage of Proposition 13 provided a unique opportunity for reform. Local government, including the counties, was in the helpless role of supplicant, and the state was prepared to assume a substantial share of the costs of local government. At the outset, many people were talking about state assumption of the counties' share of court maintenance costs. In terms of dollars state funding of the courts represented a trifle compared to state assumption of welfare or education costs, but in terms of potential for long-range reform this proposal had major possibilities.

Bird asked for state funding and should have been able to get it. Most important, she failed to win the governor's support. At the time of her appointment, the *Los Angeles Times* had editorialized that Bird "would have the support of the Governor—and his influence with the legislature—in effecting the reforms that she does believe are necessary." The governor never explained his decision to reject state funding of the courts, but the *Times* was correct in supposing that Bird ought to have had enough influence with Brown to accomplish this kind of structural reform, particularly since it was a nonpartisan proposal, not in context very costly, and a clear "good government" reform. Somehow between 1977 and 1979, Bird had dissipated her political capital with the governor.

She had also lost the support of what should have been a chief justice's natural constituency on the issue. Quite a number of trial judges were less than enthusiastic about being made that much more subject to central control and apprehensive that Bird's parsimonious ways would lead to less rather than more adequate facilities. A delegation from the Judicial Council failed to persuade the legislature to include state funding of the court system in the long-term bail out following Proposition 13 (the council selected Seth Hufstedler as its spokesman). The legislators realized that Bird had been unable to enlist either the governor's or the judiciary's support and ultimately did nothing to change the existing method of financing the court system.

Bird as Administrator of the Supreme Court

The California Supreme Court relies heavily on a permanent staff to assist the justices in deciding which cases to hear, in preparing for oral argument, and in writing opinions. The U.S. Supreme Court uses law clerks for the same functions, but its clerks are hired for one or at most two years, generally out of law school. The concept of a permanent clerk, or research attorney as they are called in California, is a California invention that antedated Gibson. Gibson, however, revolutionized the device by placing an enormous premium on selecting the ablest subordinates.

Being a research attorney is an unusual career for people as vain as lawyers tend to be. The job has its virtues—the work is interesting, intellectual, and obviously important, and Gibson saw to it that the pay was respectable (a practice regularized by Wright with guidelines that made their pay comparable to civil service lawyers of equal seniority)—but the position is totally hidden from public view. Research attorneys have no contact with lawyers appearing in the Supreme Court, and their work is labeled the product of a justice. Except among themselves, research attorneys cannot discuss what matters they are currently working on and they cannot point to an opinion or even a paragraph in an opinion and say, "That was my idea," or "I wrote that." Finding able people willing to accept this subordinate and anonymous role as a career is not easy, but over the years the court had been remarkably successful.

Each associate justice is authorized to have a staff of three professional employees—two are permanent and one is a "year" clerk comparable to law clerks on the U.S. Supreme Court. In Wright's time externs, law students who spend a semester working for a justice, were added. Gibson understood that in order to make the job attractive he and his colleagues would have to guarantee research attorneys some form of job security against the inevitable time when a justice retired. Fortunately there was very little turnover in the court in the first fifteen years of Gibson's tenure, and thereafter Gibson, Traynor, and Wright managed to protect research attorneys of justices who left by shifting personnel so that although research attorneys might change bosses they were never rotated out of a job altogether. By the time Bird was sworn in, the most senior people around the Supreme Court were the research attorneys.*

The chief justice has twelve professional assistants, a somewhat misleading number since seven of them work on the central staff. The central staff started in Traynor's time as a pool of lawyers who technically report to the chief justice but who work primarily on criminal matters for the entire court. The central staff gives the chief justice additional flexibility to insure the continued tenure of research attorneys who work for individual justices.

When Bird became chief justice the Supreme Court family of course also included the staff of the clerk's office, again filled with employees of impressive seniority, and secretaries to the justices, who were routinely handed on from one justice to another. None of these people had civil service status but they were protected by an inviolable informal understanding. As a group, the staff of the court was congenial and profoundly loyal to the institution they served.

Before Bird took office she passed the word that Virginia Marks, who had served as secretary and administrative aide for Chief Justices Gibson, Traynor, and Wright, as well as Diane McHenry, Wright's other secretary, should "return to the pool." It was an act of breathtaking insensitivity and was accompanied by an order to put four young lawyers, including Steven Buehl, on the payroll of the chief justice's staff, some of them at pay rates that exceeded Wright's guidelines. Suddenly a keystone in the foundation on which the loyalty of the Supreme Court family rested was gone and this loss affected not only the people who reported to the chief justice but everyone else as well. Furthermore, it was already a tense time for the staff: Bird and Manuel† were new, McComb was shortly to leave, and Tobriner was likely to resign soon.

In fact the worst apprehensions of the staff never came to pass, but Bird altered the atmosphere irretrievably. The chief justice had been a protector; she was now a threat. She also developed a pattern of remoteness from any staff other than her own, including the central staff, which technically reported to her. The contrast between Wright and Bird on this point was dramatic. Wright knew everybody, was accessible to anyone, and was thoughtful and attentive to people as people. One of Bird's first actions was to change the locks on her and her staff's offices and she

---

* The most senior, Donald Barrett, had been there since 1948 and had worked for Traynor for most of his thirty-year career as associate justice and chief justice. Richard Morris, who testified in 1979 as Justice Clark's research attorney, started working for Shenk in the fifties and since then had worked for Peek, Traynor, White, and Wright.

† Manuel took on as his staff those who wished to remain from Justice Sullivan's staff.

limited the keys to members of her own staff. This small act symbolized much to the family.*

After a brief transition period, during which she used a longtime research attorney, Richard Morris, to head up the central staff, Bird built a personal staff composed entirely of people who had not worked for the court before. These people were mostly relatively young and while they were able they lacked judgment based on experience. (Newman initially followed Bird's pattern of building a new staff but in time took on an experienced research attorney from the central staff.) Bird's decision not to use the experienced help available insulted and puzzled the court family but was entirely consistent with what they increasingly began to recognize as her suspiciousness. She apparently could not bring herself to trust people not of her own selection who might have lingering loyalties to others.

Bird may also have been influenced by an article written in 1977 by Phillip Johnson, a law professor at Berkeley. Johnson was highly critical of the way the California Supreme Court processed its cases and argued that the justices relied too heavily on each other's staff work, with the occasional result that a mistake by one staff person became the decision of seven justices without anyone's noticing it. Johnson contrasted California Supreme Court methodology with that of the U.S. Supreme Court, where each justice's chambers independently works up every case, thereby greatly reducing the possibility of error.† Building a staff of her own, encouraging it to maintain some distance from the staffs of other justices, and changing practice so that recommendations of the central staff were not even nominally her own were all actions consistent with Johnson's thesis that each justice should as independently as possible make each decision with help from only the justice's own staff. But Bird could not follow through with Johnson's idea without substantially augmenting the staffs of the other six justices, which she could not do and keep faith with the governor's passion for frugality.

There will be occasion later to examine in detail the way the court handles its work. For present purposes it is sufficient to note that Bird made no alterations of consequence. Nevertheless, some obvious things could have been done. The testimony before the commission revealed shocking anachronisms. The court, for example, had no modern word processing equipment: when opinions were altered, as they frequently

---

* Bird also changed the combination on the safe in her office. That struck Wright, the only one who could possibly have remembered the combination, as strange. The only thing he had ever kept in it was a bit of Watergate memorabilia: the original of Nixon's letter of resignation from the state bar. Wright put it in the safe because Mosk had told him that most of Lincoln's autographs had been stolen from publicly available legal documents in Illinois courthouses. Wright returned the original to the clerk's office when he retired.

† In 1972 Chief Justice Burger had reorganized the work of the Court's law clerks to pool some of their efforts; only five of the nine justices participated, however.

were, the secretaries had to retype at least a portion of the opinion and were still using "white out" to correct mistakes. Research attorneys had to do their own typing, and dictating equipment was largely unknown. Bird could not have been expected to know precisely how modern technology might improve productivity but the potential was obvious and professional advice was available elsewhere in state government. Showing interest in matters of this sort could have done much to improve staff morale.*

Bird's Relations with Judges and Others

Bird continued to protect her privacy and socialized little outside of ceremonial occasions. Very few people got to know her except in a working context. Judge Hogoboom, the presiding judge of the Los Angeles superior court, chanced to be in Sacramento after Bird's selection had been announced and called on her to introduce himself. He was startled to have Steven Buehl present taking notes during his conversation with Bird, and he found the whole atmosphere a little strange. Buehl's ubiquitous presence quickly became a source of resentment. Private meetings with the chief justice were rarely private; Buehl was usually on hand, taking notes but not otherwise participating. Telephone calls from judges to the chief justice were routinely directed to Buehl and messages through him only sometimes resulted in a returned telephone call from the chief. In contrast, Wright had always taken and returned telephone calls.

Stories about Bird's inaccessibility began circulating almost immediately. The departure of Ralph Kleps confirmed what rumors had been insinuating. Kleps himself kept silent but it quickly became gospel that Bird had barely spoken to him in the six weeks between her inaugural and his resignation. Jon Smock, Sacramento lobbyist for the Judicial Council, quit some months later with a tasteless blast at the chief justice that he circulated widely. Though he did not say so in his letter, the grapevine knew that Smock's desk had been moved into the hall and it had been made clear that he would be given no work to do.

Bird was not, of course, responsible for the governor's judicial appointments but her influence was obvious. Judges John Racanelli and Sidney Feinberg, both friends of Bird's from Santa Clara who had testified in her support before the appointments commission, were elevated to the Court of Appeal in San Francisco less than a year after her appointment. They were joined in 1979 by Joseph Grodin, who had been active in Bird's campaign in 1978. And Newman, who replaced McComb on the court in July 1977, was also a friend of Bird's who had advised her

---

* In 1980 the court began utilizing electronic word processing equipment and dictating machinery.

during the Agricultural Labor Relations Board funding fight. It was clear
to judges that their own promotions could depend on staying in the good
graces of the chief justice, who was influencing some gubernatorial appointments and almost certainly could block any appointment she disliked.

Bird missed an opportunity to improve relations with judges on the
matter of their pay. Some years earlier, during Pat Brown's administration, the judges had persuaded the legislature that it was demeaning to
them and to their independence to be forced annually to petition the
legislature for a cost of living increase. A formula was developed and
refined in Reagan's time that gave judges each year the previous year's
cost of living increase. With double-digit inflation, however, salaries
began to be alarmingly large, especially when contrasted with the pay of
federal judges, who were not then protected by a similar formula. The
problem came to a head with the passage of Proposition 13. The governor and legislature sought to deny pay increases to all public employees.
Suddenly, the judges stood out, virtually the only public servants in the
state to get an inflation adjustment, and a generous one at that. The
governor, not surprisingly, made the judges pay a major issue. Bird's
response was to write a letter advising judges that she was returning to
the state treasury the increase in her salary, a letter also signed by Tobriner. The pay matter was a tough issue: traditionally the chief justice and
the Judicial Council had left matters of pay and retirement benefits to
the Judges Association to negotiate with the legislature and the governor.
Bird's behavior was consistent with tradition—she basically kept her
hands off. On the other hand, to the judiciary Proposition 13 represented
a crisis and an opportunity for leadership that Gibson, for example,
might well have seized. Bird ought perhaps to have attempted to mute
the governor's rhetoric and to play a role in the negotiations. Had she
done so successfully (which would have been hard) she might have been
seen by the judges as sympathetic to their interests. Her symbolic refusal
of the cost of living increase was not so viewed.

Probably most important of Bird's informal relations was her handling of the press. In the sixties, partly in response to the public uproar
over the Proposition 14 fair housing decision, the court established a
public information office and began issuing press releases on certain
decisions. Wright insisted on putting out a release on every case. The
public information officer of the court drafted releases, which were reviewed by the justice who had prepared the opinion (and any dissenting
justices) and also by the chief justice before publication. In Wright's view
the only test for a press release was accuracy. The function of these
releases was solely information, not advocacy. For no reason stated at
the time, the flow of press releases slowed down after Bird's appointment
and almost stopped. The reason came out in testimony before the com-

mission. The justices, it appeared to Bird and others (including Clark), were using the releases as instruments of public advocacy. She accordingly authorized the issuance of decisions before the relevant press releases were ready.

Reporters had been used to talking with Wright and other members of the court. Wright would frequently decline to answer their questions (invariably explaining why if asked) but he would take and return their telephone calls. Calls to Bird were directed to Buehl; questions for the chief justice that Buehl could not answer were often not answered at all. In any case, this process made follow-up questions difficult. At one point Bird explained her reluctance to deal with the press on the ground that she was constantly besieged by requests for interviews, which she attributed in part to her sex. This argument had some merit, but distinctions could have been made between working reporters trying to understand what the court was doing and writers wanting to do magazine puff pieces on a new and different kind of public figure.

Other customs also vanished under Bird. In the past reporters had been warned when an important decision was about to be announced so that they could be present when the opinion was filed. That stopped. Moreover, the list of cases to be voted on at the regular Wednesday conferences was no longer released to help reporters prepare the usual Wednesday afternoon story. Finally, requests for certain kinds of information readily available from internal court records but elusive in the public records were refused, which made research difficult. As a result, reporters who regularly covered the court stopped using the public information office or talking with the chief justice's office until after they had developed a story from other sources and then only for confirmation or comment. The court beat became in part an adversarial game—what could a reporter develop that galled the chief justice—a destructive exercise but quite consistent with the post-Watergate passion for investigative reporting (to some extent, this situation was fed by the considerable number of judges and staff people increasingly disenchanted with Bird).

THE BIRD RECORD AND WHY THE KNOWLEDGEABLE WOULD NOT TALK ABOUT IT

This discussion of Bird as chief justice has emphasized negative factors because the purpose here is to expose what might have been but was not discussed in the campaign. That leaves an unfair picture because her faults formed a pattern that concealed her greatest virtue: exceptional conscientiousness and hard work. Bird was sensitive enough to see

that much of the judiciary was antagonistic toward her but she read that
as hostility toward her personally; in fact, most judges disliked Bird because of her connection to the governor. Her response was to demonstrate her merit by working incredibly hard, presumably hoping that in
time she would be seen as worthy of loyalty. Bird found direct commun-
ciation with "enemies" (more accurately, strangers) and confrontation
over issues personally painful, and she tended to withdraw and to limit
her contacts to known friends and formal events that kept her distant.
As chief justice she structured her relations with the Supreme Court
staff and the judiciary in ways that preserved her privacy, which in turn
enabled her to work even harder. At every turn of the screw Bird's response was both to become more isolated and to work more.

Unhappily, Bird's problems would not yield to conscientious solo
effort. The chief justice of California has too many decisions to make to
reach them alone. Bird needed to rely on subordinates, but her insecur-
ity generally led her to depend too much on staff less experienced than
she and on a very few senior people, especially Tobriner and Racanelli,
whose loyalty she trusted. Solving the leadership problem through hard
work was also precluded by Bird's native ability. Neither Gibson nor
Wright was a towering intellect with a clear and inspiring vision of the
appellate function. Traynor was exceptionally talented but even he relied
heavily on others. Very few judges in history have been able to command
as leaders because of the power of their vision. In the United States John
Marshall stands practically alone in this respect. Bird's failure to command through the strength of her mind and pen is neither surprising nor
reprehensible, but the effort was misguided.

Bird was also constrained by her loyalty to the governor and her
interpretation of his ideas. She may have overread Brown's egalitarian
anti-elitism. Perhaps he bent standards somewhat in his search for minorities and women to appoint to the bench, but he still professed a
concern for quality and his rhetoric often clashed with anti-intellectual-
ism. Bird's dedication to Brown's principle of frugality likewise got her
into trouble. The public cost of the administration of justice is a droplet
in the budget of state government. Obviously, Bird should not have
encouraged profligacy, but she might have expressed interest in ideas
that could significantly improve judicial administration at a modest cost.
At the outset Bird indicated her intention to veto any proposal with a
price tag, going beyond Jerry Brown's practice, although perhaps not
beyond his rhetoric.

Bird's record as one justice of seven on the Supreme Court was
undistinguished but not otherwise remarkable. She was rather liberal
and apparently untroubled by the self-confident tendency of the court
that preceded her to undertake ambitious reforms that consumed the
court's limited resources of good will in the legislature and among the

public. Her opinions reflected no new vision of the judicial role or the appellate function and were limited by a literary style that verged on the banal. But none of this distinguished her greatly from her colleagues, and her less than two years on the court was too little time to expect much more. Unless, like Senator Richardson, a voter believed that a liberal point of view constituted grounds for voting against her, there was nothing in Bird's record as a member of the court to justify a no vote.

On the other hand, as administrator of the Supreme Court and the court system, a case could be made against Bird. She had destroyed staff morale within the Supreme Court, alienated the trial bench, squandered her political capital with the governor by requesting the appointment of Bird loyalists,* lost the confidence of the press, and generally forfeited whatever capacity a chief justice might have for leadership. Most of these faults stemmed from the flaw in her character that Bishop Mahony identified in his letter to Tobriner. Bird's unwillingness to be accessible to and deal openly with people who were predisposed to be hostile to her because of her relationship with the governor confirmed the beliefs of those who were apprehensive about her and drove Bird to be even more remote. Yet nobody during the campaign remarked upon this destructive cycle.

Why no public discussion of her faults? Much of the responsibility belongs with Senator Richardson. His anti-Bird campaign rested on the wrong grounds and profoundly offended anyone who cared about accuracy or felt that judges should be encouraged to stand up to the public whim if their view of the law required it. Coming out publicly against Bird would put potential opponents in bed with Richardson and his misleading and inflammatory rhetoric. The absence of an opponent to Bird made this condition worse, as did Bird's sex since few wanted to risk being labeled sexist.

During the campaign some said that fear of retribution by Bird was holding the tongues of lawyers and judges. Subtler factors were probably more important. During Watergate, President Nixon kept invoking the Presidency as an institution, and the Supreme Court as an institution was an abstraction with real content for many lawyers and judges. Attacking the chief justice they feared would diminish the institution of the court. Lawyers and judges are trained to venerate justices of the Supreme Court, and talking against them is something decent lawyers and judges do not do, at least in public. In this age of total media exposure of public figures, this attitude may sound anachronistic, but it curtailed candid discussion during Bird's campaign.

Finally, personal charm has never been a qualification for judicial

---

* This was not obvious until after the election, when the governor refused to support her request for state funding of the court system.

office. Some great judges in history were notoriously ill-mannered, despised by the bar and hated by at least some of their colleagues. Perhaps they would have been more effective as judges had they been nicer; perhaps their irascibility was somehow crucial to the independence of their thought. Nothing in Bird's behavior was even hateful. She had not gone around smashing her opponents; she just disregarded people who disagreed with her and had a regrettable tendency to hold grudges.

THE ROLE OF THE PRESS IN JUDICIAL ELECTIONS

How well did the press cover Bird's confirmation election? Except for Kang, no reporter made a serious effort to lay before the voters the case against Bird as an administrator. Several factors besides the reticence of sources to talk for attribution may explain why reporters did not push to tell the whole Bird story.

First, confronted with the problem of exposing defects in public figures who are at bottom honest and moral, reporters understandably draw back and place a heavy value on presenting a balanced picture. Investigative reporters on the scent of corruption are indefatigable. The more successful ones seem to think that their righteous cause gives them license to probe with deceit and even to publish stolen documents. But no hint of moral corruption such as pervaded the Nixon White House could be attached to Bird. As contrasted with the corrupt, the worst that could be said about her was that she was not very smart, and even that depended on who she was compared with. Measured against the populace generally, or lawyers or even judges, Bird stood out as intelligent, well-spoken and highly motivated. And though she did not compare favorably with Gibson, Traynor, or Wright, very few people could. Furthermore, no one could say that she would not improve with experience.

Second, reporters accepted the conventional wisdom that the most common defect of judges is laziness. It is possible for nearly any judge to choose not to work very hard, and some of the judges most willing to complain about Bird were also judges who, reporters knew, had not for some time if ever seriously overtaxed themselves in the pursuit of justice. Measured on a scale of hard work, Bird was assiduous. She could perhaps be charged with working too hard and with having lost as a consequence some perspective and humor, but she surely deserved praise for setting a pace that few on the bench equaled.

Finally, and probably most important, no one knew the rules of the game in a close judicial election. How relevant was Bird's administrative ineptitude? Had she been serving in an executive position such as mayor or governor, the voters would by common consent be entirely justified in voting against her. But was the same standard applicable to a chief justice? True, Bird as chief justice had administrative responsibilities, but was it wise because of that to hold her to a standard inapplicable to the other justices on the ballot? Her performance as one of seven justices on the court was competent. Lawyers, obviously well-intentioned, assured reporters that judicial performance was the appropriate standard because it is of overriding importance to protect judges, who must from time to time take unpopular stands.

Electing judges is a peculiar American phenomenon with roots in nineteenth-century Jacksonian democracy; this practice may reflect a time when many judges were part-time officials, like justices of the peace, whose principal source of income was not judging but farming or lawyering or something else. The election of judges has lingered in California and many other states, an anachronism in a system that demands a career judiciary of full-time judges. So long as incumbent judges were routinely reelected by colossal majorities, the practice seemed harmless. However, in 1978 the vulnerability of the court to California's volatile public opinion thrust Bird forward as a possible victim of a long-delayed backfire of frontier egalitarianism. It is not surprising that the press and the bar, as well as political leaders, stood by openmouthed, for the most part unable to say anything helpful.

FOUR

From Election Day to the Opening of the Hearings

ROSE BIRD WINS CONFIRMATION

For present purposes, the most important thing that happened on November 7, 1978, was that Bird won confirmation as chief justice. But she did not win by much, and she did far worse than her colleagues on the court, as shown by this table:

Richardson	72.5%
Newman	65.3
Manuel	61.5
Bird	51.7

She also did much worse than the Court of Appeal justices whose names were on the ballot.

Why did Bird do so badly? An analysis of the vote and of polling data accumulated before the election points to three reasons: (1) voter antipathy toward the courts in general, (2) partisanship, and (3) hostility to Governor Brown. There is no evidence that Bird's sex hurt her with the voters; it may have helped.

The easiest of these to prove and measure is the overall negativism of the voters toward the judges. The vote on justices of the Courts of

Appeal is a good index of general attitude toward appellate courts: despite the fact that some Court of Appeal justices are quite liberal, others quite conservative, over the years the vote for or against them has been substantially uniform in each appellate district; since the voters for the most part know nothing about the candidates and they have no opponents, it is plausible to suppose that those who vote against Court of Appeal justices are expressing general hostility to appellate courts. During the 1970s that negative attitude grew substantially. From 1934 through 1964 Court of Appeal justices were winning by margins of about 90 percent. In 1970 the winning margin sank to 80 percent, in 1974 to 75 percent, and in 1978 to 70 percent. Whatever the explanation for this steady decline in voter approval of the judiciary, it is clear that about half of the no vote on Bird must be attributed to general antipathy toward the courts, for which Bird could scarcely be held personally responsible.

The following table separates out the antijudiciary vote and the anti-Bird vote in the major counties by subtracting the no vote on Court of Appeal justices from the no vote on Bird. The anti-Bird column thus

COUNTY	Total Vote for and against Bird[1]	Antijudiciary as % of Total Vote on Bird	Anti-Bird as % of Total Vote on Bird	Total % against Bird
Bay Area				
Alameda	309	20.9	19.6	40.5
Contra Costa	200	22.5	28.6	51.1
San Francisco	192	16.5	14.9	31.4
San Mateo	181	19.6	29.2	48.8
Santa Clara	339	15.8	26.7	42.5
Sonoma	96	27.7	23.6	51.3
Southern California				
Los Angeles	1,785	22.8	25.6	48.4
Orange	545	27.4	25.7	53.1
Riverside	164	25.4	25.3	50.7
San Bernardino	192	26.4	23.8	50.2
San Diego	469	18.8	26.3	45.1
Santa Barbara	90	19.4	21.7	41.3
Ventura	129	26.9	26.0	52.9
Central Valley				
Fresno	116	20.2	26.7	46.9
Kern	93	29.1	26.7	55.8
Sacramento	238	27.3	27.7	55.0

[1] In the thousands.

represents people who either voted for some other justice on the ballot or failed to vote on any other appellate court candidate. Some of the purely anti-Bird votes apparently were influenced by partisanship. The polling data assembled by the Field organization shortly before the election showed that only 34 percent of Republicans favored Bird whereas 53 percent of Democrats indicated they would vote for her. In general, Bird did best in counties with the highest percentage of registered Democrats and worst in Republican strongholds. However, except for three small counties (Mono, Sierra, and Tulare), Brown outdid Bird throughout the state, and Brown won six major counties that Bird lost. This suggests that there was a considerable number of disenchanted Democrats, most visible in the results from Sacramento and Contra Costa counties. Perhaps Bird served as a surrogate for Brown for some Democrats who wanted to express displeasure with the governor but found it impossible to vote for Younger.

Bird's sex apparently was not influential with the voters although without a male opponent it is impossible to assess this factor definitively. Polling data from the Field organization and the *Los Angeles Times* showed Bird supported by substantially the same percentages of men and women (Field: 49.1 percent of men and 47.8 percent of women supported Bird; *Times:* 42 percent of men and 44 percent of women supported Bird). There was, however, one interesting difference between men and women in the Field sample: Republican women were significantly more

Cartoon by Steve Greenberg, Editorial Cartoonist for the *Daily News of Los Angeles.* © *Daily News of Los Angeles.*

likely to be for Bird and less likely to be against her than were Republican men. Democratic men and women, on the other hand, reacted toward Bird in about the same way.

THE *LOS ANGELES TIMES* NOVEMBER 7 STORY

The second most important event on November 7 was a story in the *Los Angeles Times* that morning. Every paper in the state carried the story, as the *Times* did, on the front page. An indeterminate number of voters were no doubt influenced by the article to vote against Bird. Though political experts tend to discount the importance of last-minute events on voting behavior, the large number of undecided voters on Bird reflected in the final polls suggests that the *Times* article had more impact than eleventh-hour charges typically have. After the election, Senator Richardson said that if the story had come out even one day earlier Bird would have lost.

Since the *Los Angeles Times* article precipitated all the events that followed, it deserves quotation in full:

SUPREME COURT DECISION TO REVERSE GUN LAW REPORTED

But Sources Say Ruling, Completed by Justices Several Weeks Ago, Has Not Been Made Public

by William Endicott and Robert Fairbanks Times Staff Writers

SACRAMENTO—*The California Supreme Court has decided to overturn a 1976 law that required prison terms for persons who use a gun during a violent crime, but has not made the decision public, well-placed court sources said Monday.*

The decision, in People vs. Tanner, is certain to anger law enforcement officials around the state.

The court sources said the decision was reached on a 4–3 vote, with Chief Justice Rose Elizabeth Bird, whose name goes before voters today, among the majority.

The sources said that announcement of the decision is being delayed by Associate Justice Mathew O. Tobriner, who has been one of Ms. Bird's strong supporters against a well-organized campaign to win voter disapproval of her appointment to the court.

When asked whether he was delaying the decision, Tobriner replied: "I'm utterly sealed. My oath is not to disclose anything that goes on in this court.

"I can say nothing, absolutely zero, zero, zero."

However, two other justices confirmed that individual decisions were signed some time ago by all members of the Court. The justices could not explain why the outcome had not been announced.

Ms. Bird could not be reached for comment.

Nearly a month ago, Atty. Gen. Evelle J. Younger, the Republican candidate for Governor, suggested that some potentially controversial court decisions were being withheld because of their possible effect on the election. A spokesman for Ms. Bird denied Younger's claim.

The 1975 law in question is the keystone of an advertising campaign sponsored by law enforcement which has made the slogan "Use a gun, go to prison" well known around California.

Gov. Brown has frequently cited the statute as one of the law enforcement accomplishments of his Administration. In effect, the measure denies a judge the right to grant probation after a defendant has been convicted of using a gun during the commission of a violent crime (murder, rape, robbery, etc.).

In this case, the word "use" means either firing the weapon, or brandishing it in a menacing manner.

The Supreme Court decision upholds a San Mateo County Superior Court judge who placed convicted robber Harold E. Tanner on probation after ruling that the 1975 law unconstitutionally limited judicial discretion.

Asst. Atty. Gen. Michael V. Franchetti, a legislative representative for the state Department of Justice, predicted that law enforcement officials would "rise up in anger at the decision."

"This is really an important law, more than the death penalty," he said, "This is really working; people are going to prison. The death penalty is just sitting around."

Franchetti said that law enforcement officials probably would attempt to nullify the Court decision during the next session of the legislature, which begins Dec. 4.

If the Court acted on constitutional grounds, he said, then law enforcement would seek an amendment to the Constitution that would go before the voters in 1980.

Technically, no Supreme Court decision is final until 30 days after it is announced. But as a practical matter, decisions become final when each justice has either drafted an opinion of his or her own, or signed one drafted by a colleague.

In this case, the opinions and signatures were said to have been in place more than several weeks ago.

Talk of delayed announcements by the court is not new. Early last month, Younger said he was "speculating" that decisions in sensitive cases were being deliberately withheld until after the election.

Younger said then that the action was being taken because of the political effect the announcement might have upon Ms. Bird and Associate Justices Wiley Manuel, Frank Richardson and Frank Newman, whose names are also on the ballot.

All justices must face a yes-or-no vote of the people at the first general election after their appointment and thereafter every 12 years.

A spokesman for Ms. Bird, replying to Younger's speculations, said they were "unfounded."

"There are no cases, no opinions, in the court where all the justices have reached their final decisions and which have not been announced," he said.

Several aspects of this article require discussion: where did it come from; how did people on the court and elsewhere initially respond to Endicott and Fairbanks's disclosures?

THE STORY BEHIND THE *TIMES* ARTICLE

Long before November 7 there had been public speculation that the court was holding the *Tanner* case until after the election. On September 11 a Los Angeles legal newspaper, the *Daily Journal*, put out a special ninetieth anniversary issue that contained a long, highly critical article about the court's behavior toward law enforcement; the story was written by George Nicholson, Edwin Meese, and William James. Nicholson was head of the District Attorneys Association; Meese, a former deputy district attorney, had succeeded Clark as executive secretary to Reagan; and James was a career civil servant in the attorney general's office and one of the senior criminal appellate lawyers on Younger's staff. Their criticisms of the court ranged across the entire spectrum of the court's criminal law decisions. The article certainly did not feature the *Tanner* case, but at one point the case was mentioned by name:

While it is considered likely the state high court will hold Deukmejian's "use a gun, go to prison law" invalid . . . it is not at all clear what is holding the decision up. . . . [T]here has been a slowdown in the release of important decisions as the November elections draw nearer. . . . If indeed the "use a gun, go to prison law" is to be invalidated, it will be interesting, and surprising, if it, or any other controversial ruling, is released before the November election.

A month later, Younger charged in a campaign speech that the court was stalling on important cases. He made the charge at a fund-raising dinner at the end of the day in Los Angeles when it was too late to make the morning papers. "Has the Brown Supreme Court decided once again to strike down the death penalty?" he asked, and answered himself by saying that "several" death penalty cases had been decided. Younger went on, "I believe the Brown Court has reached many important decisions which have been written and have only to be released." Although he specifically referred to the *Tanner* case, reporters focused their stories on his charge regarding the death penalty cases. The next day Younger repeated his charges before the San Diego Lawyers Club, an association of women lawyers, which greeted his attack on the chief justice with something less than enthusiasm. By then reporters were ready for Younger with some hard and embarrassing questions. Assistant Attorney General James had told reporters that no death penalty case had even been argued before the court. Ultimately Younger backed down lamely: "The Court can calendar [three death penalty cases] any time it wants to. I do not claim that they have made up their minds on the death penalty. Whether they have informally discussed it, I don't know." But Younger did not retreat on *Tanner*. As Richard Bergholz and Gene Blake reported in the *Los Angeles Times:*

The mandatory sentence issue [i.e., Tanner] is what he is really talking about, Younger told reporters. "I have suggested certainly that the Court is deliberately withholding the decision until after the election." He declined to identify the source of his information, and then added "it's more of a question than a charge."

After noting the facts in *Tanner*, Bergholz and Blake reported that the case had been argued on February 6 but that it was not at "all unusual for a case to be pending for [eight months] or even longer, particularly if complex issues are involved and the Court is closely divided." At the top of the story Steven Buehl was quoted as authorized to call Younger's charges "unfounded" and to say that there "are no cases, no opinions, in the Court where all the justices have reached their final decisions and which have not been announced."

Younger had managed to do what might seem difficult: make a newsworthy charge at a time when it could not be publicized and then partially retract it in such a way that the retraction got far more attention than the accusation. In view of his embarrassment, it is not surprising that he did not speak again on the subject of court delays on sensitive decisions. Very few readers noticed that Younger had not, in fact, withdrawn his charge, or "question" as he preferred to call it, about the delay in *Tanner*.

Reporters who covered the court noticed, however, and what Younger had said was not news to them. They had been hearing for some time that *Tanner* was likely to be decided against the validity of the statute and that the vote was likely to be four–three. The difficulty was to pin this information down as something more than the prediction of someone, like Nicholson, Meese and James, who followed the court closely and could guess how the individual justices would vote on such an issue. Younger's allegation of deliberate delay was something more, but it was also common speculation among cynics and Younger had rather backed down with his "it's more of a question than a charge." Courthouse gossip, which reporters hear, was buzzing with rumors of heated controversy among the justices on the court, including particularly Bird and Clark. Although it is unlikely that anybody explicitly told reporters that the fight centered around *Tanner*, reporters may have been able to guess that *Tanner* was an issue.

The mandatory sentencing law had been promoted by the California Stop Crime Coalition, a loose network of associations and individuals connected to law enforcement. The coalition, following an idea that reportedly had had some success in Florida in reducing armed robberies, had launched an advertising program to make the public aware of the new law—whence the slogan "use a gun, go to prison." A significant amount of money had been raised and the cooperation of various groups such as the Association of Retail Liquor Dealers obtained. But so long as the validity of the statute remained in doubt, the campaign was stymied. As time passed the coalition leaders felt increasingly frustrated and angry.

Senator Richardson was one of those complaining about the *Tanner* case. Obviously, Richardson's interest was twofold: first, to embarrass Bird before the election; and second, to get the campaign on the "use a gun, go to prison" law moving. Much later, after the commission's public hearings had ended, Richardson was quoted as somewhat uncertain about the charge of delay in *Tanner*:

When it came to Tanner, *or any other decisions, my judgment very honestly, was a subjective judgment based on how Bird and Tobriner acted in the past. I never had any specific knowledge. I made a projection on her past behavior. I knew she was against the death penalty and that she'd probably be against* Tanner. *I made a projection. I wanted the press to pursue it.* *

---

* New West, Nov. 19, 1979, at 127.

To help reporters along, Richardson called Clark on the day before the election, asking whether Clark would talk with the press about *Tanner*. Clark testified before the commission that he told Richardson he would not discuss the case but did "customarily take press calls."

Not long thereafter, Robert Fairbanks, head of the Sacramento bureau of the *Los Angeles Times*, called. Clark told him, "Mr. Fairbanks, you can call me any time and you don't need an introduction from a senator." Clark testified about the conversation as follows:*

A. He said he wanted to ask me some questions about the Tanner *case. I told him the* Tanner *case was still pending and I could not discuss the* Tanner *case.*

Q. Then what if anything did he say?

A. He said something to the effect that he had the Tanner *story and proceeded to tell me that he was writing a story that he had understood that a decision had been reached by a four–three vote. And he gave other details concerning the story. I do not recall those details, however, as I sit here.*

Q. Do you remember whether or not he said that he had information that the case had been decided but was being withheld?

A. No, I don't think he discussed withholding. It was more to the effect that the case had been decided but not filed.

Q. What else did he say, if anything?

A. He then asked me if I would confirm that this was the case or the situation.

Q. Excuse me, but what does the "this" refer to? That it had been decided but hadn't been filed?

A. Yes, and whatever other description he had given me.

Q. All right.

A. He said he was looking for confirmation from a judge.

Q. As I listen to you, the description you have given us to date is that it was decided and not filed and that it was a four to three vote, and you believe there were some other details but you don't know what they are?

A. That's correct.

Q. Did he give you any names of justices?

A. He may have referred to the chief justice as being on the majority side, but I am unsure.

Q. What else, if anything, did he say?

A. He asked if I would confirm the story. I told him no. I may have

---

* Quotations from the transcript of the commission proceedings have been corrected for obvious errors. In addition, the transcript has been edited to omit phrases like "well" or "all right" that only slow down the reader. Brackets indicate editing to make meaningless text comprehensible. Unless otherwise noted, Seth Hufstedler questioned witnesses.

added, "I don't understand why you are calling for confirmation if you think you have a story."

Q. You say you may have told him that. Does that indicate you are not sure whether you said that?

A. No, I am confident that, as I work out the sequence, that I said that in response to his request for confirmation.

Q. But you are clear that you told him no, you would not confirm it? Did you tell him that?

A. No, I am not. I in effect told him I didn't want to discuss it further and I believe added the bit about if he had a story I didn't understand why he was calling us for confirmation.

Q. Let me be sure I am right. You didn't really respond to his question "Will you confirm it?" You said you didn't want to discuss it further?

A. Yes.

Q. What else was said by him or by you?

A. He had mentioned Justice Mosk. He assured me that I wasn't the only judge being called, that he had tried to reach Justice Mosk, who would not be in until after three o'clock. Then he said, "Well, if you won't discuss Tanner could I ask a few questions about how cases are processed?" I said, "Well, you can ask them but if they relate to Tanner I can't answer them." I think he did ask a question or two about the decison-making process, but I can't recall specifically what those questions were, nor whether I even answered them.

Q. Do you remember anything further that he said?

A. Yes. He continued questioning, and I stated that we had a canon on judicial ethics covering the matter of pending cases. And he answered "I know all about your canon, but can you use a canon," he said, "as a shield where it is conceivable that there may be some impropriety?"—or maybe he used the term "wrongdoing."

Q. Did you respond to that?

A. Yes. I told him that when he called me he told me he was trying to reach Justice Mosk and that if he wanted to talk about canons to call a more senior justice than myself. That ended the conversation.

This conversation was followed by a second telephone call later that afternoon from Fairbanks to Clark. As Clark testified:

A. He said he'd like to discuss Tanner further, that he had discussed the matter with Judge Mosk, and referred to Mr. Endicott as having spoken to Judge Mosk as well. He said they were—I think he used the term —"going with the story" but that their editor, city editor or someone in the Los Angeles office, would like further confirmation from members of the court if at all possible.

Q. What further did you or he say?

A. He said that Justice Mosk had responded that he wouldn't confirm their story, [or] answer [the] questions that they had asked me, but stated that they certainly have interesting sources or good sources—some reference to their sources.

Q. Let me interrupt a moment. He told you that Justice Mosk had told him that they had interesting sources or good sources?

A. Yes. Either that or that Justice Mosk had told Mr. Endicott that. I am not sure which. Mr. Endicott's name did come in at that point.

Q. What else, if anything, did he say in that second conversation?

A. I believe he asked that if I wouldn't confirm it, would I deny it?

Q. What did you say?

A. I believe I indicated or stated that the same problem in relation to the canon, that I could not, or no, or at least I gave him a negative on either confirming or denying.

Q. What else occurred?

A. He said, "Well, let me ask you another question. If in the morning you should read the story that I have described to you, will you throw your coffee cup against the wall?"

Q. What, if anything, did you say?

A. I don't think I responded, or if I did it was—I am certain—not a yes or a no but maybe a chuckle. I am uncertain.

Q. Do I understand from what you have said [that] you told him positively that you would not either confirm or deny in the course of that conversation? Is that correct?

A. I don't know how positive it was but that is my recall.

Q. But also that you do not recall any specific reply to his coffee cup question?

A. That is correct

In the early evening Fairbanks phoned Clark again. Clark testified:

A. As I recall, it was in the evening. I received a call from him, I believe, just as I was leaving my apartment to go back to the court.

Q. This would have been Monday evening before election day?

A. Yes.

Q. Will you tell me please what he said and what you said in that conversation?

A. If I recall, he said, "We have filed the story and I want to tell you what we have said about two justices on the court."

Q. Then did he read you something?

A. Yes. He read something that I later recognized in the article.

Q. I will point out in [the November 7 article] there is a paragraph which reads, "However, two other justices confirmed that the individual decisions were signed some time ago by all members of the Court. The justices could not explain why the outcome had not been announced." Is that the part he read to you?

A. Yes. *I am not sure that he read both sentences, but he read, certainly, the first sentence about the two justices' confirming that individual decisions were—I am reading it from your board—signed some time ago by all members of the court.*

Q. *Did you respond to that? What did you say when he read that to you?*

A. *I think after reading it he invited further comment on it.*

Q. *Did you comment on it?*

A. *I don't believe so.*

Q. *Did he ask you to confirm that statement?*

A. *No, I don't think he did. He asked, he invited, my comment on it. He may have asked if this should be expanded or would I add to it. But I did not.*

Q. *What did you say to him?*

A. *It was very short. I don't know that I said anything that I can recall.*

Q. *Did he say that you were one of the persons he was relying upon for confirmation of that statement?*

A. *He may have said something to that effect because that was the impression I was getting, or had gotten, I realized, both in the course of the conversation and later thinking about it.*

Q. *Did you have any intention of being one of the persons who confirmed that statement to him?*

A. *No.*

Q. *On the other hand, did it occur to you as you listened to him that you might well be one of the two justices he was referring to when he said two justices had confirmed that?*

A. *Yes, it did.*

Q. *Did you say anything at all to disabuse him of that possible idea?*

A. *No, I believe not.*

The commission heard testimony about one other conversation with reporters that was behind the *Times* story. Tobriner testified that he had spoken briefly with Endicott on November 6. Tobriner said that the November 7 story "substantially correctly quoted" his response to the question of whether he was delaying the release of *Tanner:* "I am utterly sealed. My oath is not to disclose anything that goes on in this court. I can say nothing, absolutely zero, zero, zero."

That is all we can learn from testimony under oath about the background for the November 7 story. Mosk never testified publicly and Hufstedler decided as a matter of policy that no useful purpose would be served by calling Endicott or Fairbanks because they would refuse to testify, probably even if ordered to do so by a court. Given these limitations and accepting Torbiner's and Clark's testimony as truthful,[*] was the *Los Angeles Times* justified in printing this story?

In defense of the *Times* one fact stands out with startling clarity: *no one denied that the decision was being delayed.* When Younger had made the same charges in October, however, Buehl had called the charge unfounded, and the chief justice's statement issued on election day said, in part, "There are no completed cases before this court where release has been delayed for political reasons or for any other reason extraneous to the decison-making process." Why did Clark, Mosk, and Tobriner refuse to deny that *Tanner* had been delayed? For Clark, if his testimony was accurate, the answer is simple: he was not asked whether the case was being held up for political reasons.[†] As to Mosk, we do not know precisely what was asked so it is impossible to say. But Tobriner testified:

Mr. Endicott called me to ask me what was the status of the Tanner *case and whether or not I delayed it or had taken, done, any action on it. And I think I very quickly said, "Bill, you know better than to ask me about a pending case." I think that's probably quoted in here that "my oath of office, the canons, prevent me from saying a word to you about it and my answer to you is zero, zero, zero."*

Directly asked whether he was holding up release of the *Tanner* case, why did Tobriner refuse to say no?

The reason Tobriner gave both Endicott and the commission, that the canons of judicial conduct prohibited him from making any comment on a pending case, is unsatisfactory. On this basis Tobriner should have criticized the chief justice for permitting Buehl to answer Younger and issuing her election day statement. Furthermore, Tobriner admitted that Kang had correctly quoted him in the *San Francisco Examiner* as saying, "All I can tell you about *Tanner* is that it was treated as any other case." Concerning this statement, Hufstedler asked Tobriner:

Q. Is that a statement that is prohibited by the canon on divulging anything about the status of a pending case?

A. I didn't think it was. Merely that the course of the court was regular conduct in all respects.

---

[*] There were some minor conflicts in their testimony. Tobriner's account of the discussion that took place at the court's November 9 conference had Clark saying then that he had talked with Endicott, not Fairbanks. Tobriner also reported that Mosk had said at the November 9 conference that he also had been asked the coffee cup question, which Clark did not recall.

[†] It is a little hard to credit Clark's testimony on this point. Certainly the implication of improper delay was in the air in the Fairbanks-Clark conversations and Clark could have reached out to deny this suggestion.

Q. Confirming regular conduct is not within the prohibition on commenting on pending cases?

A. I don't think so.

If the canons permit an assertion that the course of conduct is regular, it is difficult to see how a denial of wrongdoing would be improper.

In Tobriner's defense, the code of judicial conduct speaks in absolutes and does not recognize as a problem the question of what a court or judge should do when accused of wrongdoing. The canon Tobriner was relying on provides:

A judge should abstain from public comment about a pending or impending proceeding in any court, and should require similar abstention on the part of court personnel subject to his direction and control. This subsection does not prohibit judges from making public statements in the course of their official duties or from explaining for public information the procedures of the court. *

A denial of wrongdoing, although not explicitly excepted, is plausibly regarded as not within this prohibition since this kind of disclosure would hurt no one and presumably would further the broad objective of the canons "to promote public confidence in the integrity . . . of the judiciary."

Tobriner's failure to deny delay probably had more to do with his impatience with Endicott than with the canons. Tobriner admitted he was "rather abrupt" with Endicott and responded "very quickly" to his question. Undoubtedly, Endicott had in his question recited facts that Tobriner could not properly have commented on, for example, that the case was then on his desk. Tobriner could, however, have responded, "I cannot comment on the status of the case, whether I am writing an opinion or what the tentative vote is, but I can and do tell you that the decision is not being withheld for any improper reason." If he had done so or, to put it another way, if he had thought, as former Chief Justice Wright did, that being as helpful as possible to reporters is important, the November 7 *Times* story would have been quite different.

Clark's explanation for his failure to deny the implication in the *Times* story that *Tanner* was being delayed is also unsatisfactory. He said

---

* Canon 3(A)(6), code of judicial conduct. The legal status of the code of judicial conduct in California is cloudy. The code has not been adopted by statute or rule of court. The code was approved by the California Judges Association (a non-statutory private association) in 1975. Canons have been cited from time to time in judicial opinions and have been referred to by the Commission on Judicial Performance. The California form of the code is an adaptation of the code of judicial conduct proposed by the American Bar Association. Chief Justice Traynor, after his retirement as chief justice, served as Chairman of a special ABA committee that revised the code in 1972.

he was worried that anything he might say would turn into a story: "It's a little like saying 'no comment,' which someone suggested goes back to Mr. Capone. It's a story in itself, I have learned, among the press." Clark's observation is accurate, but it is not hard to disarm the coffee cup question. "I do not understand the question" is an unquotable response that leaves the reporter with nothing. The coffee cup gambit and games of its sort have developed into a high art since Watergate. The naive and unwary can easily be trapped, but Mosk and Clark had very little standing to claim that they were inadvertently caught saying something they did not mean to. Mosk had twice successfully run for attorney general and Clark had been Reagan's executive secretary. They were, or should have been, seasoned players in reporters' games.

Although he did not so testify, Clark's problem was probably not so much that he felt trapped by Fairbanks's question as that he was uncertain whether *Tanner* was being delayed for political reasons. Fairbanks in his first conversation with Clark had raised a genuine problem: is it proper to invoke the canons to conceal wrongdoing? Suppose, for example, that a justice reveals in conference that he has a financial interest in a case but refuses to disqualify himself. Are his colleagues prohibited by canon from disclosing such wrongdoing? Plainly justices ought not to be prohibited absolutely from making disclosure no matter what the circumstances; to the contrary, they have a duty to alert the appropriate authorities such as the Commission on Judicial Performance. Tobriner and Clark had in fact done just that when they testified before the commission about McComb's senile behavior in conference (and their testimony ultimately became public). Presumably, an implied exception permitting disclosure of wrongdoing to authorities would not normally justify disclosure to the press, but judicial elections complicate the problem. The California constitution gives the voters a role to play in judicial retention; it is arguable that the voters' right to make an informed decision weakens the requirement of confidentiality. In a dubious ruling based on relevance, the chairman of the commission cut off some hypothetical questioning of Tobriner designed to explore the issue of whether Clark would have violated the canons by disclosing publicly his good faith belief that *Tanner* was being withheld for political reasons.* An even harder problem, which may more accurately reflect Clark's state of mind, is whether Clark would have been wrong to disclose possible misbehavior if he were uncertain who was responsible for it or whether it was going on.

---

* Neither Clark nor anyone else ever argued this because Clark never admitted disclosing confidential material. Had the commission chosen to disbelieve his testimony on this point, however, the question would then have been before the commission of whether the disclosure was improper.

Clark undoubtedly had not thought all this through and perhaps it is unreasonable to expect him to have done so given that he was, as he testified, surprised by Fairbanks's call.* But his admission that he knew that Fairbanks was relying on him as one of the two confirming justices put him in a dilemma, albeit one of his own construction. He could have told Fairbanks not to consider him a source, but he probably was reluctant to do so because he suspected that *Tanner* had been held up for political reasons. Alternatively, he might have forthrightly told Fairbanks his doubts; his instinct about the canons held him in check there. Clark chose a middle course: to say nothing except perhaps to chuckle.

The refusal of anyone to deny that *Tanner* was being held up for political reasons was critical to the *Times*.† Probably Endicott and Fairbanks would not have "gone" with their story if either Tobriner or Bird had categorically denied the charge; certainly the story would have read quite differently if some responsible official had entered a denial. (The reporters tried to find Bird, but she had gone to some lengths to avoid the press on election eve.) The question remains whether the *Times* fairly had Mosk and Clark confirming deliberate delay. Narrowly, the story did not assert that any justice had confirmed that Tobriner was holding release of *Tanner* for political reasons. The justices were said to have confirmed "that individual decisions were signed some time ago by all members of the Court"—literally accurate but unmistakably implying deliberate delay, that implication reinforced by the following sentence, "The justices could not explain why the outcome had not been announced."

Should a newspaper depend for important stories on the failure to deny as the equivalent of affirmation? This approach puts reliance ultimately on some reporter's intuition that a particular informant's silence is laden with meaning. In this instance, Clark's testimony that he knew he was one of the two justices "confirming" the story vindicated Fairbanks's judgment—surely a slender reed to rest on. To put the point another way, ought not the press to stop trying to trick people into

---

* November 6 was not, however, the first time Clark had been questioned by a reporter about a delay in *Tanner*. About a month earlier, Clark had been asked the same question by a "woman reporter in San Diego." At that time he refused to speak "off the record" about a case "having seven signatures but not [being] filed." Nothing came of the conversation.

† Except for one point—that the decision was four–three when it was in fact three–one three—the article was literally accurate. (If quibbles are insisted upon, technically the first *Tanner* decision did not overturn the "use a gun, go to prison" statute if overturn is equated with holding the statute unconstitutional, and Bird was not in the majority in the sense that she wrote a separate opinion coming to the same result as Tobriner's lead opinion but for different reasons.)

disclosing things they would prefer not to discuss? Perhaps. But it would be wrong to fault the *Times* or Fairbanks for failing to live up to this ideal since the current ethic of the press is clearly to the contrary.

Neither Endicott nor Fairbanks regularly covered the court and neither was familiar with its process of decisionmaking, which, as shall be seen in detail, permits judges to delay reaching a final decision on any case until the last moment. Judges are technically and in practice totally free after an initial tentative vote to change their mind on a case until they have seen every opinion in final form. Endicott and Fairbanks routinely covered governmental institutions like the legislature, which operates under a wholly different ethic. A legislator's word to a colleague that he or she will support or oppose a proposal is an irrevocable commitment even though the understanding is made far in advance of any formal vote; breaking such an understanding is a serious offense with damaging consequences to any legislator's reputation and effectiveness. Endicott and Fairbanks wrongly exported to the judicial arena the political ethic they were familiar with: a position once taken on an issue is, for all intents and purposes, final. As a consequence, they failed to include in their November 7 story a paragraph such as Gene Blake had put in the *Times* story about Younger's charge that Tanner was being held up.

One of the seven justices is assigned by the Chief Justice to write what appears to be the majority opinion of the Court. This will be circulated to the other justices for comment. One or more of the other justices may decide to write a dissenting opinion. And one or more may write opinions concurring with either the majority or dissenting opinions, giving slightly different reasons. Those are circulated among the justices and may lead to modifications of the earlier draft opinions or even a switch in votes. Finally, when all the justices are satisfied they have reached a decision, the opinions are filed and made public.

The November 7 story misled readers by failing to note this elaborate process. Worse, one paragraph in the November 7 story suggested that tentative votes are only nominally tentative: "Technically, no Supreme Court decision is final until 30 days after it is announced. But as a practical matter, decisions become final when each justice has either drafted an opinion of his or her own, or signed one by a colleague."

In summary, no one was blameless with respect to the November 7 story. Tobriner (and presumably Mosk) should have said straight out that *Tanner* was not being delayed. Bird should not have been hiding. Endicott and Fairbanks should not have been so quick to assume that

they understood the appellate court process. Clark should have said
nothing or something, not hidden in ambiguous silence.

THE REACTION WITHIN THE COURT

The November 7 story made the front pages of the morning papers;
radio and television broadcast the story throughout most of election day.
The chief justice in the late afternoon issued a statement, too late to
make the early editions of the evening newspapers but in time to catch
the evening news for those who had yet to vote. Few news sources
quoted the statement in full, but the whole is worth repeating here
because it foreshadowed how much Tobriner's outrage at the attack on
his integrity distorted his and Bird's thinking:

A Statement to the People
of the State of California

*As Chief Justice of the State of California, I wish to make a statement to
the people of this State.*

*In election campaigns, it is healthy to have full discussion of the
abilities of those who hold public office. Criticism is a natural part of that
process. I accept that, and I further accept the fact that criticism sometimes gives way to the excesses of falsehood and personal vilification.*

*Up to this time, I have not responded to the political attacks upon
me and the court because the office of Chief Justice must be kept above
the rough-and-tumble of politics.*

*However, today these attacks have gone too far by impugning the
integrity of one of the most respected justices on this or any other court.
Justice Mathew Tobriner has been a member of this court for 16 years, and
his adherence to the oath of office and to the canons of ethics is beyond
reproach. Yet today, his refusal to answer any questions regarding a pending case is used to suggest that he is delaying release of that case until
after the election. Nothing could be further from the truth.*

*There are no completed cases before this court where release has been
delayed for political reasons or for any other reasons extraneous to the
decision-making process.*

*Moreover, Justice Tobriner's refusal to comment on a particular pend-
ing case was the only proper response. Canon 3(A)(6) of the Code of
Judicial Conduct requires a judge to "abstain from public comment about
a pending or impending proceeding in any court." This principle applies
not only to this court but also to courts throughout the land, including
the United States Supreme Court.*

*It is a curious coincidence that this story appears on the morning of
the day when the voters are going to the polls. Those involved in the*

campaign against me, knowing full well that neither Justice Tobriner nor I may properly comment on any pending case, seek to exploit the fact that we honor that ethical standard.

I will not permit Justice Tobriner's integrity to be maligned by those who seek momentary political advantage in their attacks against me. It is with a deep sense of sadness that I find it necessary to issue this statement today. However, I cannot stand by while an unprincipled attack is made on this Court and one of its most distinguished members, Justice Mathew O. Tobriner.

Issued too late, the statement was also too long to be effective; the fifth paragraph, not the first, was the one reporters quoted—the categorical denial of delay for political reasons, which probably would have killed the November 7 story had it been made the day before. The statement also reacted too much to something that was not, in context, central. The charge that Tobriner was holding the *Tanner* case was less important than the basic charge that the case was being held to help Bird win confirmation. However, the statement gives the impression that Bird thought it more important to protect Tobriner's reputation than to clear the court of an accusation that it was manipulating the release of decisions.

Tobriner and Bird, together with some of their staff members, met at the court on the morning of election day. The group obviously lost sight of the importance of speed and brevity. They also apparently never considered what would have been the most effective form of denial: prompt issuance of a denial signed by *all* members of the court. No one attempted to get the whole court together to discuss the subject. Bird and Tobriner spent time speculating on which of their colleagues had "confirmed" the *Times* story but, seemingly, they had sufficient confidence in the *Times* reporters not to question the accuracy of the story or to ask their colleagues immediately whether they thought they had confirmed the story.

Perhaps inadvertently, Bird's statement also converted what might have been a technical and somewhat ambiguous issue—is it improper to delay a decision until after an election—into a much simpler issue comprehensible to any layman: truthfulness. In testimony before the commission, the chief justice indicated that it was the view of an unnamed constitutional law expert "that courts frequently hold up cases in light of an election." In response to a hypothetical question, however, Bird said it "probably would" be improper conduct for a justice to hold up release of a decision "for the express purpose of seeking to prevent the filing of the case before the election."

Is it ever proper for a court to speed up or slow down its decision-making process for reasons extraneous to the merits of the case? Some situations are clear. There is general agreement, for example, that it is proper to accelerate the consideration of a case that carries strong public reasons for a prompt decision. The Proposition 13 case is an example of appropriate special consideration. In other situations delay is appropriate; certainly, trial courts from time to time indulge delaying tactics of counsel to let a community's passions cool before beginning the trial of a controversial case. There may occasionally be comparable reasons why the release of an appellate decision might properly be postponed; a court might think a decision would have a distorting impact on an election and therefore choose to delay the announcement briefly. No precedents are known,* but the argument is tenable. The *Tanner* case would not seem to fit the mold. The central issue did not divide the candidates; both Governor Brown and Attorney General Younger were strong supporters of the "use a gun, go to prison" statute. But more important, the people most likely to be hurt by a preelection release of *Tanner* would be the justices of the court on the ballot, especially the chief justice. Holding up release of a decision to benefit oneself (or one's colleagues) is different from delaying announcement of a decision in order to keep the court neutral in an election squabble.

Bird's election day statement, however, rendered these questions irrelevant because even if we assume that delaying the release of *Tanner* was legitimate, her assertion that the case had not been improperly delayed made the truth of her statement the overriding issue. If *Tanner* had been deliberately delayed, Bird was lying to the people of California

---

* According to Woodward and Armstrong, Justice Powell suggested that the Nixon tapes decision be withheld pending the imminent vote in the House Judiciary Committee to impeach President Nixon: "Brennan, Stewart and Douglas pounced hard on Powell. Many of the Court's decisions, perhaps all of them, had political repercussions of one kind or another. In the past they had always rejected suggestions that they delay cases for political reasons. The Court could not, it must not, ever get in the business of selecting which secondary effects it preferred and adjust its timetable to suit them." B. Woodward & S. Armstrong, The Brethren, at 345–6 (1979). Similarly, Woodward and Armstrong reported that Stewart and Brennan were outraged when they thought Chief Justice Burger was stalling release of the abortion decision until after Nixon's second inaugural. *Id.* at 236.

In his "House Divided" speech, Abraham Lincoln charged that the U.S. Supreme Court's decision to schedule reargument of the *Dred Scott* case was motivated by a desire to postpone release of the opinions until after the 1856 presidential campaign. Unquestionably it was convenient politically for the Democrats to have unresolved during that campaign the issue of the power of Congress to prohibit slavery in the territories, but modern scholars have been unable to substantiate Lincoln's allegation. There is, however, no question that conference debate among the justices about the *Dred Scott* case was leaked to the press, or, more startling, that two justices corresponded with President-elect James Buchanan, advising him of what the court's decision would be before the decision was handed down, in the end only two days after Buchanan's inauguration. The release of the *Dred Scott* decision led to some venomous correspondence between Justice Benjamin Curtis and Chief Justice Roger Taney concerning whether the chief justice had changed his opinion between its announcement and its publication in the official reports. Although the chief justice self-righteously denied making any changes of substance, he apparently added about eighteen pages to his opinion largely responsive to the Curtis dissent. Curtis shortly thereafter resigned from the court, probably in large part because of this incident. D.E. Fehrenbacher, The Dred Scott Case (1978) at 289–90, 309–21.

and lying to conceal wrongdoing is a simpler and more serious offense then delaying release of a decision for political reasons. The analogy to Watergate is obvious: the cover-up was far more serious than the burglary.

Because of the election on Tuesday, the normal Wednesday morning conference of the court had been postponed until Thursday. Early Thursday morning Tobriner met with one of his research attorneys, Hal Cohen. Cohen understood that Tobriner wanted him to prepare a memorandum outlining the chronology of the *Tanner* case for circulation to the other justices; Tobriner was considering issuing a statement exonerating himself to be signed by all the justices. Cohen's understanding was that the statement (but not the memorandum) would be given to the press, and Cohen immediately set about preparing what ultimately became a three-page memorandum that opened with the following paragraph:

As we are all aware, in the past few days there have been numerous reports in the news media suggesting that I have improperly delayed the court's decision in this matter for political purposes. There is absolutely no truth to these charges and the suggestion of impropriety on my part disturbs me deeply. In order to lay these charges to rest and to remove the cloud on both my own integrity and the integrity of the court, I believe it is essential for the justices to join me in a statement attesting to the falsity of the charges.

The memorandum proceeded to describe how the *Tanner* case had been handled within the court, focusing largely on the period between October 24 and election day—the period during which the *Tanner* file had in fact been in Tobriner's office.* The memorandum concluded:

By issuing a statement in which we all join, we may be able to remove that cloud and restore confidence in the integrity of our judicial process. I suggest the following statement for your consideration.

Cohen appended the following statement on Supreme Court letterhead for all the justices to sign:

As a Justice of the California Supreme Court, I hereby declare that as of November 9, 1978, the Court's decision-making process has not been com-

---

* Cohen's account of the travels of the *Tanner* file said that it had been with Manuel from August 25 to October 24, whereas in fact it had been in Tobriner's office for about half that time—from August 25 to September 21. This "error," Cohen testified, was inadvertent; it was not itself of consequence but was repeated in press accounts, proving that the Cohen memorandum was the source of the reporters' information.

pleted in the case of People v. Tanner *and that neither the final determination nor the filing of that decision has been delayed for a political or any other improper purpose.*

While Cohen was preparing the memo, Tobriner was meeting with the other justices in conference. We have slightly divergent accounts from Bird, Tobriner, Clark, and Richardson of what happened at that meeting.* Clark's version is the most vivid; he said Tobriner opened the discussion by reading the canon while pointing his finger and looking at Mosk and Clark. Clark thought Tobriner "was somewhat emotional," that "he was upset, and it would be highly prudent to say nothing." After Mosk and Clark recounted their conversations with Fairbanks and Endicott, Clark recalled Tobriner's saying, "I'm going to have a statement to clear my name in this matter." Tobriner, although not certain whether it was the November 9 meeting, did recall reading the canon at a conference. He was, by his own account, "very much disturbed" and "personally hurt." He testified that he told his colleagues:

"It's unbelievable members of our Court should in any way give any information to the press about pending cases or even what went on at our conferences. What goes on in the conference, to my mind, is sacred and should never be disclosed to anyone except perhaps to members of our staff who were informed of the confidential nature of it." And I said if anyone did any such thing, that it seems to me it would be a matter ultimately for the Commission on Judicial Performance. And I read the canon.

In their testimony Richardson and Bird did not mention the reading of the canon, Tobriner's suggestion of disciplinary action, or Tobriner's remark that he would need a statement to clear his name. Immediately after the conference Tobriner reviewed Cohen's work and proceeded up and down the hall with copies of the memorandum, soliciting signatures to his statement.

It would be interesting to know the precise order in which Tobriner asked his colleagues for their support because he ended up with five signatures on the statement, one on a slightly revised statement from Richardson, and a refusal to sign from Clark. With the benefit of hindsight, it is clear that Tobriner should have started with a full discussion of the idea and text of a statement at the conference. Had he done so, two ambiguities would likely never have arisen: Was the statement to be released to the public and on what grounds did Clark refuse to sign?

When he was preparing it, Cohen never had any doubt that the memorandum describing the chronology was intended to be an internal

* Clark was the last to testify, and some of the divergence between his testimony and that of the others may exist because he was asked questions that were not put to his colleagues.

document only, whereas the statement itself was to be given to the press. In his testimony before the commission, however, Cohen stated that he was not certain where this notion had come from and in particular whether Tobriner ever told him that a public release of the statement was contemplated. Tobriner himself was unclear about his intentions concerning public release of the statement. Commissioner Willoughby asked him:

Q. What did you intend to do with this statement after you had obtained the signatures of all of your colleagues?

A. At one point we thought possibly we could release it to the press. * But thinking further, we decided probably not, and I told all the justices that if any time we intended to release it to the press, we'd get their consents before we did that. The reason I got the statement was I wanted to make sure the justices knew that I had not engaged in any misconduct, and I wanted them at least to give me the feeling that they agreed there was no misconduct, that they themselves agreed with that position. And that's why I asked them to give me this reassurance upon a showing of the chronology of the case that nothing had been done that was out of order.*

Q. You felt that a verbal, face-to-face assurance wouldn't be sufficient?

A. Probably. But I felt better [with a written statement]. I said, "In case this is investigated later by the Commission on Judicial Performance, I'd like this on the record." That's what I said.

Tobriner testified that he started soliciting signatures with the chief justice, then approached Newman, Mosk, and Manuel. At some point he encountered Clark in the hall as Clark was leaving the office to catch a plane for a speech he was scheduled to make that evening in Los Angeles. Clark said he did not have time then to look at the statement and he wanted to think about it; he took along copies of both the memorandum and the statement. From this point on, Clark's and Tobriner's testimony differ somewhat.

According to Clark, he called Richardson from the airport and told him: "I have read this statement. I don't know what it is going to accomplish. I would hope that we could wait until Monday and confer on it." Clark reported that Richardson told him that Tobriner was at that moment in his office and that he understood what Clark was telling him. Clark testified that he called Tobriner over the weekend. Clark asked Tobriner what the purpose of the statement was and Tobriner responded, "I want to clear my name." Clark asked him whether he in-

---

* Tobriner later defined "we" as "chiefly myself" but thought he "may have" discussed the subject with Bird. Bird testified that she discussed preparing a memorandum and statement with Tobriner on election day.

tended to release the statement to the press and Tobriner responded that
he did. Clark then testified: "I told him I would like to discuss that aspect
of it when I returned on Monday, and I recall he responded, 'It won't be
necessary to confer, because I have five signatures.' " When he returned
to the court Clark visited Tobriner to discuss the subject further. The
conversation, according to Clark went as follows:

A. I told him, "I want to assure you first of all, Matt, that I am
unaware of any impropriety on your part. But I think that further statement is a demeaning thing to do. It's merely going to [attract] further
attention. And, secondly, I don't know why Tanner has not been filed."

Q. Did Justice Tobriner say anything?

A. Yes, he said in that regard, "Tanner has been treated like any
other case and I would therefore very much like your signature." He asked
me for my name, my signature.

Q. What did you say?

A. I said that at this point I didn't feel that I could give it.

Q. Did you have any further discussion?

A. Yes. He said, "Justice Clark, I'm telling you," or "I am warning
you," I forget which, "that unless you sign you may become the subject of
an investigation by the Commission on Judicial Performance."

Q. Did he accompany that statement with any kind of a gesture?

A. Yes, he did.

Q. And what gesture?

A. The index finger, not unlike the conference on Thursday, the
previous week.

Q. Do you presently have a vision of his waving his index finger at
you?

A. Yes.

Q. Did you say anything about the possibility of your being investigated by the commission?

A. No, I did not.

Q. Did you say anything more?

A. I just said, "Well, Matt, that pretty well seals it on my ability to
sign your statement."

Q. Anything else said by either of you?

A. Not that I recall.

Clark later expanded somewhat on his reasoning. He thought issuing a statement would be a "dumb thing to do" because it would "continue what we had read the previous week concerning Tanner." He also
thought that Tanner should have been filed before the election and that
the delay possibly had been caused by an impropriety by someone.

Tobriner recalled these conversations differently in some trivial as well as significant details. Tobriner thought the telephone call was placed by Clark on Thursday from the airport, rather than over the weekend, and Tobriner did not recall saying anything about five signatures. He also remembered the conversation with Clark in his office differently:

A. He said that it would be unwise, he thought, to do anything with the statement. First he said, "Is this going to be published or given to the media?" I said I didn't expect to give it to the media and didn't intend that it be published. And in any event, if there was any reason to give it to the media, I would get the consents of Justice Clark and all members of the court. He said, "However, I think it's unwise that this be done, that this statement be signed, because it's just a matter of blowing up the Tanner case again in the media." Well, it would blow it up again.

Q. Did you respond to that?

A. I said again, "Well, I don't intend to give it to the media." He said, "Well, there's no purpose in it then."

Q. Was there anything more that either you or he said at that meeting?

A. I said, "Bill, I'd feel better if you sign it because I'd know my integrity is not being questioned. I'm sure you don't join in that and I would feel more comfortable if I knew that you agreed that the Tanner case had not been improperly held up."

A. His reply was, "I have no question about the conduct or the statement particularly, but I just don't see any point in it."

Q. His reply was that he had no question about your conduct?

A. That is correct.

Q. Or your integrity?

A. That is correct.

Q. At any time during your conversations with Justice Clark about that document, was there any mention of the Commission on Judicial Performance?

A. My best recollection is that I mentioned that the possibility could arise that the commission might investigate the whole problem of the Tanner case and that was one reason I wanted a clear commitment or a clear statement that no one had withheld the Tanner case beyond the day of election.

Q. Did you tell him how or in what manner it might assist in the event of an investigation by the Commission on Judicial Performance if [the statement] was signed?

A. No, I didn't get into that detail.

Q. Did he respond at all with regard to your statements with regard to the signing of [the statement] and the Commission on Judicial Performance?

A. He did not discuss that.

Q. In the course of that discussion, that is, with regard to the signing and the relationship with any possible investigation, did you ever say to him in words, substance, or effect that if he did not sign that statement he might be investigated by the Commission on Judicial Performance?

A. I did not. I emphasize I did not.

The varying recollections of Tobriner and Clark suggest that neither was trying to understand what the other was saying. And both showed a remarkable unwillingness to search for a mutually satisfactory solution.

Clark had a legitimate grievance over not being consulted by the chief justice on her election day statement.* He thought another statement on *Tanner* would revive public interest in the issue, which could best be dealt with by silence. And he no doubt believed, probably correctly, that a majority of his colleagues would agree with him on this point. On its face the Tobriner statement appeared to be designed for public release, the accompanying memorandum said as much, and Clark never recalled Tobriner's saying that he had decided not to release the statement to the press. To Clark signing but not releasing the statement was incomprehensible. What was the point of a signed statement, especially if Clark were willing to say to Tobriner, as he did, that he knew of no impropriety on Tobriner's part? Tobriner's answer, whether explicitly so phrased or not, Clark read as a threat: proceedings before the Commission on Judicial Performance.

Clark was not a man endowed with a great deal of self-confidence, especially in dealing with his senior colleagues. His testimony before the commission revealed heavy reliance on staff, and his attitude toward Tobriner was one of deference, if not fear.† Standing firm in the face of threats may have been so important to Clark that he understood Tobriner to be threatening him when Tobriner intended no such thing.

Clark decided that he had to do something. According to his testimony, after consulting with his staff he raised the subject at the Wednesday conference of November 15. The chief justice was absent and Tobriner was presiding. As Clark testified:

A. [When] the conference opened, I stated that I wanted my colleagues to know that I had not signed Justice Tobriner's statement and that I wanted them to know why I had not.

---

* He was not the first to be concerned about public statements by Bird. According to Bird, Mosk had complained at the October 25 conference that Buehl had represented himself as "spokesman" for the court in denying Younger's charges. Bird assured him that Buehl's instructions "when he spoke to the press [was to speak] only in terms of answering or responding for the chief justice."

† Commissioner Chodos asked Clark: "When Justice Tobriner aimed the Canon at you, so to speak, did you retort that there were also ethical implications to delaying opinions past election day?" to which Clark responded: "Mr. Chodos, I don't think I have ever retorted to Justice Tobriner."

Q. And did you tell them?

A. Yes.

Q. What did you say?

A. As I recall, I gave the three reasons [why], and I think I referred, repeated, the word, I feel it's a dumb thing to do; secondly that I did not know why Tanner *had not been filed; and thirdly I mentioned my conversation with Justice Tobriner and his admonition as to what would occur if I did not sign it.*

Q. Perhaps it would be helpful if I ask you to tell us what you said. First of all, what if anything did you say about any impropriety by Justice Tobriner?

A. As I recall, I repeated what I had told Justice Tobriner . . . that I wanted to assure them on the one hand that I knew of no impropriety on his part.

Q. All right.

A. On the other hand, I did not know why the case had not been filed.

Q. And then you said something about his admonition. What did you say at the conference about his admonition?

A. As I recall, I repeated it as I had recalled it.

Q. Would you describe it, please?

A. "Justice Clark, I am warning you that unless you sign you may become the subject of an investigation by the Commission on Judicial Performance."

Q. After you finished your statement was there any response from anybody else there at the conference?

A. Yes. Justice Tobriner said, "We will not discuss this matter further until the Chief Justice returns."

Although several other justices testified about the November 15 conference, none referred to this intercharge. Clark was probably wrong on his dates; the chief justice was present at the November 15 conference but absent from the next conference (November 22). The dates make a difference because word of the Tobriner statement and one justice's refusal to sign had appeared in the newspapers by November 22. Clark deserves commendation for trying to get the conference to focus on the *Tanner* controversy, if he indeed did so, before the public learned of his not signing the Tobriner statement. But explaining himself to his colleagues after the matter was common knowledge merits no praise.

From Tobriner's perspective things looked quite different. He was, first of all, consumed with reestablishing his own integrity. He testified to feeling "terrifically upset" because of

[t]he effect of the [November 7 story] upon the court—how disastrous this was to the court. Indeed, how disastrous it was to my own reputation, to

my own integrity. I expressed myself in strong terms that after seventeen years on the court that I should be accused of holding a case up [was] to me disastrous, was a tragedy, at least in my life.

Tobriner wanted reassurance from his colleagues that they knew he had been guilty of no wrongdoing and this need for reassurance was apparently his dominant motive in seeking signatures on the statement. Bird's testimony confirmed Tobriner's motivation for his statement:

I think [the purpose of the Tobriner statement] was twofold. I think Justice Tobriner felt his integrity had been attacked, and I think he wanted to know if anyone on the court truly thought that he had done something improper. My own feeling was that perhaps a few people on the court actually thought that something improper had been done; they simply wouldn't sign the statement and it would be out and we could discuss it then.

The last sentence suggests that Chief Justice Bird wanted to smoke out the opposition because she thought some of her colleagues were against her. She apparently equated a refusal to sign with charging her and Tobriner with deliberately delaying *Tanner* without recognizing that there might be other reasons for not signing the statement. How much of her thinking was communicated to Tobriner and accepted by him is not clear, but it seems plausible that he internalized some notion that a refusal to sign equaled an accusation of wrongdoing. In any case, Tobriner was baffled by Clark's refusal to sign but willingness to state that he had no reason to believe Tobriner had done anything wrong.

Hufstedler carefully avoided asking either Bird or Tobriner about their election day speculations on the identity of Endicott and Fairbanks's sources. Clark's name, however, undoubtedly was the focus of their conjectures. The story's Sacramento dateline would be sufficient to suggest Clark or Richardson since Clark worked for Reagan in Sacramento and Richardson lived there. It was a plausible guess (although in fact untrue) that Clark and Fairbanks were friends from the time when Clark was working for Reagan. Their speculation must have led them to consider taking the offensive by charging Clark with a breach of the canon prohibiting disclosure of matters relating to pending cases. They almost certainly entertained the thought that Clark would be lying if he denied disclosure.

In retrospect, the sad thing is that Tobriner and Clark were not very far apart. If they had listened to each other more carefully, Tobriner could probably have gotten Clark's signature on a statement very much like the one he prepared. Richardson produced a formula that could have resolved the impasse when he returned to the court on Tuesday,

November 14. After the Tobriner-Clark conversation, Richardson showed both Tobriner and Clark a slight variation on the Tobriner statement: "As a justice of the California Supreme Court, I hereby declare that as of November 14, 1978, I have no reason to believe that the filing of the decision in *People* v. *Tanner* has been delayed for political or any other improper reason." Richardson said nothing about whether the decisionmaking process in *Tanner* was incomplete, confining his declaration to what he knew. As he explained to the commission:

I was satisfied then that I . . . had no reason to believe that there had been any improper reason for the delay of Tanner, as I do not now. But [my statement] didn't have quite the force of certainty that I thought was implicit in [Tobriner's]. I didn't know. And so I thought my expression that I have no reason to believe that it had been delayed more accurately reflected my state of mind.

Clark might well have been willing to sign Richardson's statement, particularly if there could have been discussion in conference on the subject of public statements and agreement on the strategy that the court was going to follow with respect to the *Tanner* controversy. Moreover, Tobriner testified that he was entirely satisfied with the Richardson statement.

The testimony before the commission included not the slightest recognition by anyone that an unsigned Tobriner statement was a bomb that if released to the public would explode with sufficient force to make some sort of inquiry into the court inevitable. Thus, no one tried to control circulation of the statement or warned against disclosure, even to staff. The story was in the newspapers on Thursday, November 16.

THE FOLLOW-UP STORIES

Two days after the election the Supreme Court compounded its problems by releasing the decisions in *Levins* and *Hawkins* (cases subsequently discussed in detail). The effect of *Hawkins*, the principal case, was to render the grand jury a substantially useless institution in the prosecution of criminal cases. The five–two decision (Richardson and Clark dissented) did not surprise experts in the field nor did it compel significant change in California criminal procedure. Nevertheless, the decisions predictably provoked hostile comment from law enforcement figures, who overstated the decision's impact. For the Supreme Court so soon after the election to "abolish" the historic institution of the grand jury was proof enough for many that the court had, as the November 7 story said, delayed announcement of unpopular anti–law enforcement decisions.

In another sense, however, the release of *Levins* and *Hawkins* only two days after the election came close to proving the court's innocence. Surely, if the court were playing games with the timing of decisions, the justices would wait longer before handing down the grand jury cases, especially once the charge of deliberate delay had been made.

On November 15, Endicott and Fairbanks had a follow-up story on *Tanner* of precisely the sort that might have been anticipated. The article, based on undisclosed court sources, added some facts about how the justices had handled the *Tanner* case, but the new details did not contribute to proof of the basic charge in the November 7 article that the case had been delayed to help Bird in the election. The lead was: "A strongly worded dissent by [Clark] critical of [Bird] may have been the reason . . . the Court delayed filing the [*Tanner*] decision, The *Times* has learned." The reporters had sniffed out the connection between *Tanner* and the *Caudillo* rape case: "Reportedly, the [Clark] dissent charges that the Chief Justice switched legal philosophies between the sentencing case and a well publicized rape decision of last June. In both cases, her vote was in favor of criminal defendants." The article, however, still wrongly assumed that Bird had signed Tobriner's opinion rather than reaching the same result for different reasons in a separate opinion.* In any event, only the *Times*, with special interest in the accuracy of its November 7 story, gave the November 15 article front-page treatment. Other than the obligatory coverage of the *Tanner* decision when it was filed, press interest in the whole episode probably would have ended here, but the next day, November 16, Endicott and Fairbanks wrote:

Associate Justice Mathew O. Tobriner of the state Supreme Court has taken the apparently unprecedented step of asking his colleagues to sign a statement that the Court has done nothing improper in its handling of California's "use a gun, go to prison" law. However, The Times learned Wednesday, not all of his colleagues will go along. At least one justice has refused to sign the statement and has said he will not do so. . . .

Tobriner refused to discuss the statement he is circulating including the reason for circulating it. "I will not tell you anything about what goes on within the Court. . . . Whatever goes on inside the Court is sacred to the Court," he said. He conceded that he is not forbidden by law to discuss the statement as he would be to discuss a case pending before the Court. But he said his personal rule is to "never comment on internal matters of the Court. I don't think it is ethical."

* Carol Benfell reported on November 8 in the Los Angeles legal newspaper, the *Daily Journal*, that Bird had written a separate opinion on constitutional grounds.

Kang also reported on the nonsigning of the Tobriner statement in the November 16 *San Francisco Examiner,* but her big story was printed on Sunday, November 19. She had obtained access to a copy of Cohen's memorandum and she quoted from it as well as summarized the contents. Based on the memorandum, her article gave a detailed account of the travels of the *Tanner* file within the court and disclosed for the first time in the popular press the existence of Bird's separate opinion. Since the memorandum had been written for Tobriner's colleagues, neither it nor Kang's article revealed the basis for Tobriner's or Bird's opinion. Most important, Kang reported that one justice had signed Tobriner's statement "only after adding the qualifying phrase, 'to the best of my knowledge and belief,' according to sources."—not an accurate quotation though it captured Richardson's meaning.

Once the fact that two justices had refused to sign the Tobriner statement became public, external investigation of the court was nearly inevitable. Months later, at the opening of her testimony before the commission, Bird complained bitterly that the court was being subjected to the rigors of the investigation solely because of faceless accusers and a powerful newspaper. Her rhetorical flourish omitted an indispensable link in the chain of causation that ended in the commission's hearings —the nonsigning of the Tobriner statement. This event, not the November 7 story, was what convinced people outside the court that there had to be an investigation into whether Bird had lied in her election day statement that *Tanner* was not being withheld for political reasons.

Who leaked the Cohen memorandum? Every justice who publicly testified denied being the source of the leak or having any knowledge of who was responsible. Assuming that the source was a supporter of someone on the court, possibly a staff member, what did he or she hope to achieve? Tobriner thought the memorandum conclusively proved his innocence by showing that the case was not ready for filing by election day. But as Kang noted: "The question that still remains to be answered is: If Manuel's dissent was completed and returned to Tobriner on October 24, why wasn't the opinion released shortly thereafter?" There were other questions that the Cohen chronology of *Tanner* suggested. Someone who wanted to keep the pressure on the court could easily see that to the public the memorandum would raise many possibilities of wrongdoing even though it disproved the implication in the November 7 story that *Tanner* was ready for filing on election day.

One of the questions surfaced publicly in the next big story, the first press account to contain assertions of facts that could have been known only to the justices and that were not confirmed by evidence introduced before the commission. Lou Cannon, West Coast correspondent for the *Washington Post,* wrote a long article on Thanksgiving Day that reported, for example:

One of the dissenting judges [Manuel, although Cannon did not report that] was persuaded, reportedly by Ms. Bird and Tobriner, to write a separate dissent, an action which under the Court rules requires recirculation of the opinion to everyone. It was this latter action, Court sources say, that gives Tobriner grounds for arguing that the Tanner opinion has not been completed. "Tobriner was technically right but morally wrong because the case was substantially decided and was held for artificial reasons," said one Court source. "This had never been done before. It was a cover-up, but one that was accomplished within the framework of Court procedures."

Manuel's public testimony never reached the issue, and no other public evidence produced before the commission supported the allegation that Manuel was induced by either Bird or Tobriner to write a separate dissent. But it was an obvious speculation from the chronology Kang had obtained that Manuel might have been encouraged to write a separate opinion so as to delay release of *Tanner*.

The Cannon article contained several other paragraphs of significance. Perhaps the most dramatic, although it did not add much except color, reported:

Ms. Bird accused Clark, a frequent conservative dissenter, of taking a political position and insisted he remove the footnote [citing Caudillo]. Clark responded to what he considered unfair pressure on her part by elevating the footnote to the body of the opinion. In the process, tempers frayed, Ms. Bird wept, Clark shouted and other justices expressed themselves emotionally. *

The major contributions of the Cannon article, however, were two: the naming of Clark as the person who refused to sign the Tobriner statement and the revelation that at least he and Tobriner expected an investigation of the court. Cannon's lead was that the court "will face a formal inquiry into whether it violated judicial ethics by withholding announcement of a sensitive decision." The article went on:

California Supreme Court Justice William Clark brought the Court's precarious position into the open Tuesday. In an interview with The Washington Post, he acknowledged that he had refused to sign a statement saying that in a key case "neither the final determination nor the filing of that decision has been delayed for political or any other improper reason." Clark said he had "decisive reasons," for not signing the statement circulated by Justice Mathew O. Tobriner, the reputed author of the unannounced 4–3 decision. . . . But Clark said he did not want to go into his

---

* As will appear, there was factual support for the movement of a footnote to the text, but no testimony before the commission supported weeping or shouting.

reasons because he expected to be called to testify under oath about them in the future.

Clark told the commission that he gave Cannon an interview on November 21 and admitted disclosing that he was one of the two justices who had refused to sign the Tobriner statement.* When Hufstedler asked whether he was concerned that disclosure might breach confidentiality, Clark responded that he was not because the matter was "factual." This unsatisfying answer was followed by an admission that Clark never had thought about whether disclosure would violate the canons of judicial conduct. But admitting that he had refused to sign the Tobriner statement invited the next question: why did he refuse? Clark's explanation to the commission is perplexing:

Q. You will note at the top of the second column appears a passage which reads, "Clark said he had 'decisive reasons' for not signing the statement circulated by Justice Mathew O. Tobriner, the reputed author of the unannounced 4–3 decision to strike down the law requiring a prison sentence for persons using a gun in commission of a robbery." Do you recall discussing with [Cannon], first of all, why it was that you did not sign the statement beyond what you have told us?

A. I recall I gave him no reason for not signing the statement.

Q. Did you say to him that you did have decisive reasons for not doing so?

A. I know he has "decisive reasons" quoted. I do not recall using that term, though . . . I have no reason to believe that he would quote something if I hadn't said it. But I don't recall specifically.

Q. The next paragraph says you did not want to go into your reasons because you expected to be called to testify under oath about them in the future. Did you make some such statement to him?

A. That's not in quotes. My recall would be that I said that I dealt in probabilities. I recall that he had brought up that he had spent the previous week in Sacramento discussing this case with press people because he was interested in that aspect more than he was in what occurred in the court itself. He felt that the emphasis would be on that part of the story. I recall that he said that it was speculated that there would be more action either by the commission or through the legislature. . . . I felt [that] was a good reason for not giving those reasons. And I at that time felt that could occur in light of the reference to the commission by Justice Tobriner in two conversations. So I did tell him that. Yes.

Clark waffled but at bottom conceded that he told Cannon he had "decisive reasons" for not signing the statement and that his refusal to

---

* Clark denied being the source of the report that Bird wept, he shouted, or that Manuel had been induced by Bird or Tobriner to dissent.

disclose those reasons related to the prospect of proceedings before the commission. He later explained that his conduct was related to a peculiar rule he invented for himself in the commission proceedings against Justice McComb. When the commission was considering whether to retire McComb for senility, Clark refused to answer whether he thought McComb was incompetent because that was the ultimate question to be decided by the commission. He similarly shied away from testifying in 1979 whether he thought any of his colleagues had deliberately withheld release of Tanner for political reasons. If true, it is perfectly proper to say, "I do not know," but "I refuse to answer on the ground that it is not for me to decide" makes very little sense. In context, his answers to Cannon compelled the inference that Clark knew of wrongdoing. The only thing a reporter could make of his response was that Clark had proof of guilt but did not wish to reveal it at that time.

Undoubtedly Bird and others thought Clark's "decisive reasons" statement a calculated maneuver to keep attention on the court and the question of the chief justice's truthfulness. It is equally possible, however, that Clark's responses to Cannon reflected nothing more than a rigidity in his thinking. Clark had rationalized his behavior with Fairbanks. Having thought the matter through to a conclusion, he would behave the same way with all other reporters. He acted toward Cannon just as he had with Fairbanks. Similarly, he had earlier invented a theory for refusing to answer questions in the McComb hearings and he trotted it out again for Cannon and the commission.

Cannon's article contained one other item of consequence. Cannon sought to verify the possibility of a formal investigation and called Tobriner. Tobriner told him that he would "welcome" an investigation by the "appropriate body," namely the Commission on Judicial Performance.

THE CHIEF JUSTICE'S PREEMPTIVE STRIKE

On the Friday after Thanksgiving, the day following publication of the Cannon article, the chief justice publicly released the following letter to Justice Bertram Janes, chairman of the Commission on Judicial Performance:

As you know, there have been a number of accounts in the press charging that the Supreme Court deferred announcing a decision in People v. Tanner, Crim. 20075, *until after the November 7th election even though, allegedly, the process of deliberation and opinion preparation had been completed before that date.*

This charge is totally false. It has, however, posed a serious dilemma. The deliberations of this court are confidential. Each justice, and each member of the staff, is compelled by settled principles of judicial ethics to hold inviolate the contents of draft opinions, the exchange of views among the justices, and the tentative votes taken. Thus, although the deliberative process in Tanner was without question incomplete prior to November 7th, and indeed remains incomplete to this day, the incontrovertible evidence of these facts is found in internal court records and draft opinions which cannot be made public.

It has been my intention for some time to request, once the Tanner decision was announced, an impartial and complete investigation by the Commission on Judicial Performance into this charge. I noted over the Thanksgiving Holiday that there has been some speculation in the press over the possibility that the Commission might undertake such an investigation. Although Tanner has not yet been decided, I now believe that all such speculation as to whether the Commission will inquire into the matter should be laid to rest. Such an inquiry should be made.

I therefore request that the Commission undertake an investigation of the charge that the Supreme Court improperly deferred announcing a decision in the Tanner case. Its authority to conduct the investigation is established by article VI, section[s] 8 and 18 of the California Constitution and by Rule 904(a) of the California Rules of Court. I further request that if, after investigation, the Commission finds that circumstances warrant, it consider the issuance of a public report under the authority of Rule 902(b)(2), describing the Commission's factual findings and conclusions in sufficient detail to address all issues which have been raised.

You will have my full cooperation and assistance, and that of my office, in conducting your investigation. I am confident that each of the other justices of the Court will also provide all cooperation and assistance. As soon as the decision in the Tanner case is announced and has become final, you will be provided all necessary access to the internal records of the Supreme Court relevant to your inquiry. I have previously transmitted to you a 12-page description of the decision-making process entitled, "Description of California Supreme Court Procedures."

It is my firm conviction that in this way the false allegations which have been made against this Court and its justices can be fully and completely examined. If the charges were true, they would be grave. I know that they are not. But that is not enough. The people of California are also entitled to be assured that their judges are conducting themselves properly. A full and fair examination of the charges by your Commission can clear the air, and thereby restore the public confidence in the judiciary which has been damaged by these false accusations. I am today releasing to the public a copy of this letter and the description of the Court's procedure.

Why did Bird write this letter when she did, whom did she consult before sending it, and how aware was she of the difficulties her request would necessarily create?

One reason for writing the letter was a fear that if the judiciary did not do something in response to the *Tanner* controversy, the legislature might. Gibson's 1960 proposal that led to creation of the Commission on Judicial Performance did not repeal the historic method of legislative impeachment contained in the state constitution. Impeachment had not been used in modern memory in California, but Watergate made this remedy seem a possibility. Many well-intentioned people were apprehensive over the prospect of a legislative investigation of the court, whatever the form, because they foresaw politicization of the judiciary and grandstanding by legislators. The best way to forestall legislative involvement would be to invite some other agency, such as the commission, to undertake an investigation.

A second probable reason for sending the letter was to improve Bird's and Tobriner's public images. The person who demands a thorough investigation obviously cannot be guilty of wrongdoing, or so he would like the public to think. That explains Tobriner's saying he would welcome an investigation. Unhappily, this public relations ploy has lost its effectiveness through overuse.

A third possible reason was to define the issue so narrowly that the investigation would be limited to whether the "process of deliberation and opinion preparation [in *Tanner*] had been completed before [election day]." With the aid of a little explanation of the court's internal processes, documents alone could disprove this charge. However, the crucial question implicit in all the press stories was broader: had some justice knowingly slowed up his or her processing of *Tanner* to help Bird by delaying release of the decision until after the election? In retrospect, it is hard to believe that Bird could have hoped to deflect inquiry away from motive or intent by her phrasing of the issue, but such may have been a purpose.

None of these reasons demanded an immediate response to Cannon's article; releasing the letter somewhat later would not have significantly diminished its effectiveness. That Bird did not take a few days to consult with her colleagues suggests that some other, perhaps less rational, reason was motivating her. It is plausible to hypothesize that as of Thanksgiving, Bird felt herself the victim of the press and opponents within the court (probably including Clark). It is natural in that situation to want to take the offensive and thereby at least to have the sense of being in control of events. Pushing the controversy into the commission would be doing something, and if the controversy were in the hands of the commission the issues would be broadened to include violations of the canon on confidentiality, where Bird thought Clark and possibly Mosk were vulnerable.

Whatever her reasons, Bird acted alone on November 24; she consulted, if anyone, only Tobriner among her colleagues. Issuing the letter without discussing the subject with the other members of the court was an astounding exercise of power by a member of a collegial body. Hierarchical institutions vest ultimate power in a single person at the top of the pyramid; the president is expected to seek the counsel of his cabinet on major decisions, but he is free to disregard the advice offered because he alone is elected. An appellate court is a wholly different institution. The chief justice presides at oral argument and conference but has no power to act for the court. The court decides only by majority vote, and the chief justice's vote is but one of seven. Calling for a commission investigation of the court did not technically require a vote of the justices, but such a proceeding would profoundly affect each justice personally and the reputation of the court as a whole. Bird's letter thus constituted a usurpation of power. And though Bird had spoken publicly several times about the importance of colleagueship in the successful administration of the court, her unilateral action on November 24 showed that under pressure she was prepared to sacrifice the core values of a collegial body for transient benefits of her own design.

The November 24 letter also in effect waived legal rights that were not Bird's to yield. As her letter noted, draft opinions, conversations between justices about pending cases, tentative votes in conference, and the like are confidential communications. Although the law is far from clear, there undoubtedly exists a judicial privilege comparable to the executive privilege President Nixon asserted in the Nixon tapes case. Among the people most plausibly entitled to assert the judicial privilege were the justices who were parties to the confidential communications. Bird's unilateral offer to throw open the court's internal records after *Tanner* was decided irretrievably forfeited the right of the other members of the court to protest this disclosure.*

Any or all of her colleagues could, of course, have repudiated the chief justice by filing a lawsuit to enjoin disclosure. Such a suit would have presented some interesting and open questions of law, but as a practical matter that tactic was unthinkable. The public, conditioned by Watergate, would have charged a cover-up.

Likewise, no one questioned Bird's offer to make the records avail-

---

* Before the December 13 conference of the court, Bird circulated a proposed exculpatory statement to be issued with the *Tanner* opinions when they were announced. Her statement implicitly recognized that she should have obtained her colleagues' consent before she opened up the court records.

able *as soon as* the decision in *Tanner* was announced. She probably never entertained the possibility of making the records available with her letter, but there was, in fact, no good reason to wait if the files were going to be opened eventually. The purpose of judicial privilege is two-fold: first, to encourage the utmost candor and directness in communications among members of the court; and second, to protect against premature disclosure of information that might be used by litigants or others. The second seems inapplicable to a criminal case such as *Tanner*,* but encouraging open discourse within the court applies to any case. However, once Bird announced that the internal records would be delivered to the commission, further communications among the justices would be constrained whether the records were released before or after the decision became public. †

Although Bird did not send the records in *Tanner* with her letter, she did send and make public a twelve-page document, "Description of California Supreme Court Procedures," explaining how the court handled its work. The content will be covered in detail later; here we need to ask why Bird made the essay public on November 24.

The genesis of the document is obscure. Bird asked her staff to prepare it sometime after the election and copies were submitted to her colleagues for review. Without consulting the other justices, however, she had sent the description to Chairman Janes on November 19— whether on her own initiative or in response to a request is unknown. Testimony and news accounts revealed that the document was not discussed in conference before its public release. Buehl was quoted in the press as saying that the document had been circulating for a week and that the chief justice interpreted her colleagues' silence as approval.

The document, carefully avoiding *Tanner*, showed in painful detail how the records and opinions in a hypothetical case would move from one justice to another. If combined with Cohen's memorandum in support of the Tobriner statement (made public by Kang on November 19), the description made it possible to see how *Tanner* was not ready for filing on election day even though, as the *Los Angeles Times* November 7 story had claimed, every justice had by then signed an opinion. ‡

Reporters read the description carefully and with a very suspicious eye but could not determine Bird's purpose. Few articles paid much

---

* For people not in custody, like Tanner, advance knowledge of the certainty of imprisonment might increase the risk of flight. Tanner, however, was a first-time offender and not the type likely to flee.

† In fact, the commission received the internal court records before the *Tanner* decision was final since the court granted a rehearing in *Tanner* and did not finally decide the case until after the commission's hearings started.

‡ The description was mildly misleading because it did not mention that a copy of each draft of an opinion goes to every justice's chambers as soon as it is issued even though the file with the originals can be with only one justice at a time.

attention to the document, but Benfell, in the *Los Angeles Daily Journal*, used the occasion to quote a "highly placed source" who said its release "seriously damaged collegial feeling on the Court."

Bird may or may not have anticipated other problems posed by the November 24 letter. Undoubtedly the most important was how public the commission's investigation ought to be. Bird had addressed this problem in her letter:

I further request that if, after investigation, the Commission finds that circumstances warrant, it consider the issuance of a public report under the authority of Rule 902(b) (2), describing the Commission's factual findings and conclusions in sufficient detail to address all the issues which have been raised.

Rule 902 requires that "all papers filed with and proceedings before the Commission" be confidential,* with a few limited exceptions including (b)(2):

If a judge is publicly associated with having engaged in serious reprehensible conduct or having committed a major offense, and after a preliminary investigation or formal hearing it is determined there is no basis for further proceedings or recommendation of discipline, the Commission may issue a short *explanatory statement. [Emphasis added.]*

Bird's desire for a release of the commission's findings and conclusions "in sufficient detail to address all the issues" would not fit comfortably within the compass of a "short explanatory statement." Furthermore, it is doubtful that a private inquiry by the commission would have met what she announced was her overall purpose:

The people of California are also entitled to be assured that their judges are conducting themselves properly. A full and fair examination of the charges by your Commission can clear the air, and thereby restore the public confidence in the judiciary which has been damaged by these false accusations.

The Commission on Judicial Performance was not a well-known institution with a long record of public achievement like the grand jury. None of its members had more than local fame (compare the Warren Commission, which investigated President Kennedy's assassination), and

---

* A rule Bird arguably violated when she made public both her letter and the essay describing the court's process of preparing opinions. Had the commission released her letter, it would clearly have violated the rule, but whether the prohibition includes disclosure by the person communicating to the commission is less certain.

most of the commissioners were judges. The commission was an arm of the judiciary, and as such it lacked the independence from the Supreme Court that might give its findings and conclusions public credibility. If Bird's objective was to clear the air of false accusations, it is hard to see how a secret, internal investigation by judges of their own superiors, with only a conclusory report of no wrongdoing at the end, would allay concern about the integrity of the Supreme Court.

The entanglement between the court and the commission was bound to produce other problems. Although Bird may not have known it, as she was writing Chairman Janes on November 24 he was announcing to the press his intention to retire from the bench, and therefore the commission, at the end of the calendar year. Janes ultimately postponed his retirement; if he had not, the Supreme Court would have had to appoint one of the commissioners charged with reviewing the justices' behavior. As it happened, two members of the commission had been appointed since Bird's inaugural. One of them, Justice John Racanelli, was widely known to be a close friend of Bird's whose appointment to the commission had been something of an issue in her campaign. Finally, and perhaps most important, procedural rules for the commission were made by the Judicial Council. The council of November 1978 was composed of Wright appointees but after January 1979 all the judicial members of the council—the overwhelming majority—would be Bird appointees.

THE COMMISSION ACCEPTS

Editorial writers and columnists took about a week to decide that they thought the chief justice's proposal a sound idea. They were helped to their conclusion by a Republican, Bruce Nestande, minority whip of the assembly, who made public on November 27 a letter he had written Bird asking questions about *Tanner* and announcing that if her responses were unsatisfactory he would introduce an impeachment resolution. In view of the proposed investigation, however, Nestande said he would await the results of the commission's probe. Nestande's conclusion that Bird's call for an investigation was "what any smart person would do" was echoed by the *Los Angeles Times*, which assumed that the commission's investigation would not be a "star chamber" proceeding. Some writers were troubled by the close connection between the commission and the court and the secrecy with which the commission was required to work. The *San Francisco Examiner*, for example, observed:

The problem is, however, that a majority of the Commission, which holds sessions in secret, was appointed by the Supreme Court. Whether its de-

Cartoon by Steve Greenberg, Editorial Cartoonist for the *Daily News of Los Angeles.* © *Daily News of Los Angeles.*

termination in this case would be accepted as final revelation by an increasing skeptical public is far from certain.

The *Examiner* and Abe Mellinkoff, a columnist for the *San Francisco Chronicle*, both suggested as an alternative to the commission that an outside group, perhaps of law school experts, be convened to examine the controversy.

Chairman Janes announced that the commission would hold a special meeting on December 1 to consider the chief justice's request. A number of difficult problems had to be considered and the commission took all day before its executive officer, Jack Frankel, issued the following press release:

The Commission on Judicial Performance commenced a full inquiry into the charges that have been made concerning alleged improprieties in the processing of cases—and related matters—by the Supreme Court of California.

The Commission is considering what procedures should appropriately be employed in this unusual case, including the extent to which any aspects of the inquiry should be public.

The commission's first task was to determine whether it had power to investigate the "charge that the Supreme Court improperly deferred announcing a decision in *Tanner*." In fact, the commission's authority was limited to disciplining individual judges, not courts, for misconduct; of course misconduct by a court could be translated into misconduct by individual judges (for example, if Bird had encouraged Tobriner to delay filing *Tanner* for political reasons), but the core of the wrongdoing discussed in the press was improprieties by the Supreme Court. Furthermore, investigating individual wrongdoing of the sort alleged in the *Tanner* controversy would require the commission to decide issues of intent or mental state that were beyond its experience. Up to this point, the cases which the commission had considered involved individual misbehavior and many of those related to incompetence attributable to sickness, age, or alcoholism. There were also some cases of abusive use of power by judges against either litigants or lawyers, but no previous case involved comparable allegations of conspiratorial wrongdoing among judges. Drawing inferences about competence from objective behavior in sickness, alcoholism, or senility cases is an exercise different in degree if not in kind from deciding whether or not a judge did something otherwise lawful for an impermissible purpose.

Investigating leaks to the press also involved some formidable jurisdictional problems. Disclosure of confidential matter by a judge constituted misconduct within the commission's competence, but the commission had no authority to discipline court staff and it could investigate staff disclosures only on a theory that staff leaks had been made with the knowledge and consent of a justice, which was neither necessary nor likely. Furthermore, the commission could expect unyielding resistance from reporters if it attempted to get them to reveal sources. The press and the bench throughout the country were at loggerheads over the confidentiality of a reporter's notes and sources.

Finally, the procedural rules the Judicial Council had promulgated to regulate the commission's proceedings were ill suited to handling an investigation of the sort the chief justice apparently wanted. They provided for a four-stage process: complaint, preliminary investigation, formal hearing, and recommendation of discipline by the commission to the Supreme Court (or a special tribunal of Court of Appeal justices if a Supreme Court justice were involved).

The commission was required to undertake a preliminary investigation upon receipt of a sworn statement showing facts constituting misconduct. Most cases were settled without a preliminary investigation: the commission's executive officer would determine that even if the facts asserted were true, no ground for discipline had been shown (sometimes the commission reviewed this finding). The chief justice's letter did not allege misconduct—to the contrary Bird denied wrongdoing—but the commission under the rules had power to initiate a preliminary investigation on its own motion, which Bird was requesting.

The preliminary investigation was normally conducted by the commission's executive officer and involved principally an exchange of correspondence. The commission was required to notify the judge involved of the charges against him, and the rules gave him the opportunity to respond. Evidence in the sense of oral testimony was not taken at this stage; occasionally witnesses were interviewed and statements taken but primary reliance was placed on the written statement of the complainant and the written response from the judge. On the basis of this material, the commission would decide whether there was sufficient cause either to issue a "private admonishment" (more on this later) or to issue a "notice of formal proceedings." Or the commission might dismiss the case on the ground that there was insufficient cause to believe misconduct had occurred.

Bird's letter referred to Rule 904(a), which describes the preliminary investigation. She obviously expected a preliminary investigation that would result in an exoneration; however, such a proceeding was far too informal to meet her objective of a full and fair examination of the allegations that would clear the air of the false accusations, especially if the case involved questions about the mental state of the justices. To be full and fair an inquiry into intent would have to include oral testimony.

The commission could perhaps escape this problem by going immediately to the formal hearing stage without a preliminary determination of sufficient cause to justify a formal hearing. The rules for formal hearings require a statement of charges in a notice of formal proceedings to be given to the respondent judge, followed by an answer from the judge and then an evidentiary hearing before either the commission or a master or masters selected by the Supreme Court. Masters must be judges (if three masters are used, two can be retired). Evidence in support of the charges is presented by an examiner selected by the commission; the respondent judge is entitled to be represented by counsel, who can cross-examine and introduce evidence on behalf of the judge.

The commission, a part-time body, normally met for a day or two each month. Not surprisingly, it usually chose to use masters to take testimony at the sometimes prolonged evidentiary hearings. The master or masters would ultimately report findings of fact and conclusions to the commission for review. Masters could not easily be used in this instance since the Supreme Court could scarcely be asked to select the people who would initially decide whether any of the justices had been guilty of misconduct. Likewise, the commission normally used a deputy attorney general as an examiner, which would not do in this case because the attorney general was a party to *Tanner* and Deukmejian, who was soon to be sworn in as attorney general, had as state senator sponsored the "use a gun, go to prison" law at issue in *Tanner*. Accordingly, the commission would have to engage outside counsel to serve as examiner, an expensive and potentially complicated process since few lawyers of stature would be willing to compromise their clients' cases in the Supreme Court.

At the conclusion of the formal hearing, the commission had five courses of action open to it: dismiss the matter; privately admonish the judge; recommend to the Supreme Court (or, in this instance, a special tribunal) public censure, removal, or involuntary retirement of the judge. Private admonishment and public censure were refinements on Gibson's 1960 plan added by constitutional amendment in 1966 (censure) and 1976 (private admonishment). The theory was that certain forms of judicial misbehavior worthy of discipline do not merit removal from office; having at its disposal lesser sanctions, the commission could regulate a wider range of misbehavior.

Private admonishment was wholly inconsistent with what the chief justice had requested because it required that the commission's proceedings be entirely secret. Accordingly, to accept Bird's request for an investigation required an advance determination by the commission that it would under no circumstances issue a private admonishment at the end. The commission's authority to make this determination was, to say the least, unclear, particularly in the context of a proceeding against a justice of the Supreme Court. Public censure of a Supreme Court justice is not, realistically, a lesser sanction than removal because if the commission should censure a justice he or she would be under enormous, probably irresistible, pressure to resign. Thus, as a practical matter, eliminating the sanction of private admonishment forced the commission into defining misconduct in terms of behavior sufficiently grave to justify removal from office (one of the features the 1976 amendment was designed to change).

How seriously the commissioners considered the possibility of refusing the chief justice's request on the ground either that they were legally incompetent to perform the function or that it would be unwise for them to undertake the investigation is not known. And it is easy to sympathize with their decision on December 1 to announce a full inquiry: every commissioner took his or her responsibilities seriously; the court was in trouble; and the chief justice had asked them to help. Although hindsight suggests they were wrong, only the most far-seeing and self-confident could be expected to respond to the Chief Justice's request with a polite but firm refusal.

Whatever happened at the December 1 meeting of the commission, Justice John Racanelli did not influence its deliberations. He delivered to the commission the following letter:

As a result of my close personal relationship with some of the Supreme Court justices, I have decided it would be inappropriate for me to partic-

ipate in the Commission's deliberations concerning the subject matter and inquiry disclosed in the communications forwarded to us by the Chairman earlier this week.

While I might personally believe that such existing relationships would not interfere with my ability to participate objectively and impartially in any required deliberations, I nevertheless concede that such participation could possibly result in an appearance of impropriety.

Under these circumstances I am convinced that any conceivable doubt should be resolved in favor of upholding the unquestioned objectivity of Commission proceedings thus assuring continued public confidence in the integrity of the Commission's performance of its constitutionally prescribed duties.

Accordingly, I deem myself disqualified from participating in the so-called Tanner matter and any related subject-matter.

The most notable feature of Racanelli's action was his choice to disqualify himself rather than to resign. That may have been simply from habit as a judge. If a judge disqualifies himself from a case, another judge can be assigned to take his place. But no such replacement process was available to the commission, and Racanelli's recusal meant that the commission would have to act with eight rather than nine members. His action did more than create the relatively remote risk of an eventual four–four split. The commission's rules required the affirmative vote of five commissioners to recommend either dismissal or any form of discipline. Racanelli's disqualification changed the odds to five out of eight. When two other commissioners later left, the odds were shifted to five out of six.* Racanelli, of course, could not have known that two more commissioners would leave before the matter was over and he could well have thought his course least compromised the court, which would have had to appoint a replacement to hear the case against the justices.

At least one other commissioner had a problem about possible bias. By mid-December, Kang disclosed in the *San Francisco Examiner* that public member Thomas Willoughby had contributed to Bird's campaign and had written a letter in her support at the time of the confirmation hearings in which he described Bird as a "valued friend." Willoughby was appointed to the commission by Brown after Bird joined the court, in all likelihood at Bird's suggestion. Despite the pressure of Racanelli's letter, however, Willoughby decided not to resign from the commission, telling Kang, "It sounds corny, but I did take an oath and that means a great deal to me." He also said that he could come to an "unbiased decision based on the inquiry."

* Actually, five out of five because one commissioner was out of the country at the time of the commission's final meeting on the *Tanner* controversy.

THE COMMISSION PROPOSES A REVISION OF THE RULES

The commission's December 1 announcement that it was undertaking a full inquiry noted that the commission was considering "the extent to which any aspects of the inquiry should be public." Whether calculated to do so or not, that provoked a number of public comments. Attorney general–elect Duekmejian said that if the investigation was "to be meaningful, it ought to be made available to the press and public," and a spokesman for the California Chamber of Commerce challenged the impartiality of the commission; "A closed investigation by this Commission would be worthless."

On December 5 Chairman Janes announced that he would postpone his intended retirement. He also gave a long interview to the *Los Angeles Daily Journal*, in which he carefully avoided discussing the *Tanner* controversy, but in connection with describing the usual procedures of the commission Janes observed that he favored a public hearing in all commission proceedings that went to formal charges against a judge.

The commission met in closed session for two days at the end of the week of December 15, and on the following Monday, December 18, Chairman Janes released to the press a three-page letter he had sent to the chief justice and all members of the Judicial Council requesting a change in the rules to permit some public awareness of the commission's activities in the *Tanner* matter. In his letter, Chairman Janes asked the council to accept the following amended Rule 902(b)(3):

In a proceeding in which the Commission finds that:

1. *the subject matter is generally known to the public;*
2. *there is broad public interest;*
3. *confidence in the administration of justice is threatened due to lack of public information concerning the status and conduct of the proceeding; and*
4. *the public interest in maintaining confidence in the judicial office and the integrity of the administration of justice requires that some or all aspects of such proceeding should be publicly conducted or otherwise reported or disclosed to the public,*

the requirement of confidentiality may, to the extent determined by the Commission, be modified with respect to said proceeding; and, after completion of the preliminary investigation, said proceeding may be publicly conducted, disclosed or reported, in whole or in part, having due regard for the personal reputations and other legitimate interests of the judge or judges involved and their right to due process.

Such determination to modify may be at any time after the Commis-

sion undertakes to conduct an inquiry or investigation, or otherwise to institute such proceeding with respect to the subject matter, but only after affording notice and an opportunity to be heard on the issue to any judge whose conduct may be called into question in such proceeding.

Several things were wrong with this proposal, ranging from the cosmetic to the jurisprudential. The most obvious was that the commission did not intend to eliminate the existing Rule 902(b)(3) but rather to add a new section (ultimately the commission's proposal became Rule 902.5). The first three numbered points in the proposal derived from existing Rule 902(b)(3). Following the findings, the proposal also gave the commission discretion to open up the proceedings as much as it wished. Since the commission could not know how its investigation would develop, a desire to have some flexibility was understandable, perhaps even wise, but such sweeping discretion was bound to alarm people, especially judges, who looked beyond the immediate *Tanner* controversy. Once adopted, the proposal would permit the commission to make public as much of its work in any case as it wished provided the press gave some publicity to the fact of a disciplinary proceeding against a judge.

A close reading of Chairman Janes's accompanying letter suggests that the commission did not need such broad discretion. The commission had two scenarios in mind for what would follow a confidential preliminary investigation. The commission might conclude on the basis of the material developed in its investigation that there was insufficient cause to believe judicial misconduct had occurred; the commissioners would then issue a public report disclosing in considerable detail the evidence that led them to their conclusion. This statement would be much more elaborate than the short explanatory statement provided for in Rule 902(b)(2), which the chief justice had referred to in her November 24 letter, and might be analogized to the Warren Commission report. If, alternatively, the commission found sufficient cause to believe misconduct had occurred, it would file a notice of formal proceedings against one or more of the justices. In that event the commission wanted to conduct the formal hearings in public, much like a trial.

Both scenarios presented legal and policy questions. A Warren Commission type report precluded the possibility of private admonishment. It also was unlikely to satisfy the public if the case involved questions concerning the intent or mental state of the justices as they had processed *Tanner.* Janes's letter said that "the only effective way to dispel [the appearance of a whitewash] is by public disclosure of our proceedings in this matter to the maximum possible extent." Many took this sentence to mean that oral testimony would be heard in public, certainly on issues of intent, because no matter how detailed a report was it could not otherwise avoid the appearance of a whitewash.

A detailed report explaining a no sufficient cause decision raised another problem. One reason for confidentiality in commission proceedings is to protect informants, especially lawyers and court personnel, who could be subject to retribution by a judge if they gave evidence of possible wrongdoing. The danger of retribution is greatest if the judge is ultimately exonerated. The prospect of a detailed public report could well discourage people on the staff of the Supreme Court, the individuals most likely to have proof of wrongdoing, from coming forward. Neither Janes's letter nor the commission's proposed rule showed any sensitivity to this risk.

The scenario of a public formal hearing following a commission determination of sufficient cause presented principally legal issues. The most obvious was whether the Judicial Council had authority to permit public formal hearings. A number of states in their judicial disciplinary schemes had done what Chairman Janes thought California should do: require formal proceedings to be conducted publicly. But it was uncertain whether the Judicial Council had authority to permit public formal hearings since the California constitution requires the council to promulgate rules "providing for confidentiality of [commission] proceedings." The merits of this question were ultimately decided in Justice Mosk's suit against the commission, which brought the *Tanner* proceedings to an end.

The final paragraph of the proposed rule—requiring the commission to hear any justice on the issue of whether the new rule departing from confidentiality should be followed—was bizarre given Janes's statement in his letter that "the Commission has determined that the public should be fully informed and is presently considering when and how that determination should be implemented." The commission's proposed rule thus required it to go through the hollow formality of hearing argument on an issue that it had already publicly decided.

How could a commission, dominated by competent, well-meaning lawyers and judges, produce such a sloppy piece of legal work? The answer is pressure of time that was not compensated for by imaginative staff work. The ablest lawyers have trouble drafting statutes or rules if they start from scratch in committee. The solution is to leave drafting to a single person or a committee whose product can later be reviewed by the full body. The commission, however, could not easily do that because it met infrequently and members came from all over the state at considerable state expense and personal sacrifice. Furthermore, the commission was under severe time pressure. The Judicial Council normally gives public notice of proposed rule changes and invites public comment for at least sixty to ninety days after publication. This proposed change had to be heard by the council and disposed of before the council's membership shifted on January 31, about six weeks away. Under these circumstances, no one seriously considered postponing submission of the proposed rule until it had been carefully drafted. The commission thus produced a camel, the only animal in the bestiary said to have been designed not by God but by a committee of angels.

THE PUBLIC DEMANDS OPEN HEARINGS

When the chief justice received the commission's letter she immediately scheduled a meeting of the Judicial Council for January 16 and ordered prompt public circulation of the proposed rule. She simultaneously announced that neither she nor Tobriner would participate in the council meeting. Her disqualification, however, did not reach so far as to prevent Buehl from telling reporters that Bird "personally is in favor" of opening the commission proceedings.* The *Los Angeles Times*, the *San Francisco Chronicle*, the *Sacramento Bee*, and the *San Francisco Examiner* immediately endorsed "open" or "public" hearings without recognizing that the commission was not contemplating this course. Predictably, editorial writers assumed the commission intended something analogous to a congressional investigation. Janes's letter to the council invited this misunderstanding, especially his statement of the commission's objective of "public disclosure . . . to the maximum possible extent." That, and the sweeping discretion given to the commission under its proposed rule, totally obscured the commission's intention of issuing a detailed report without conducting the preliminary investigation in public.

The proposal was favorably received by most lawyers and judges—only some of whom could have known what the commission planned. The chairman of the California Judges Association, Harry Low of San Francisco, was troubled by the future impact of the commission's proposal. His remedy was simple: limit the applicability of the new rule to the Supreme Court controversy over *Tanner*. As he phrased it, this solution amounted to a suspension of the confidentiality rule for this case. Judge Low successfully urged his position to the executive committee of his own association and later, as ex officio member, to the Judicial Council. How the council's power to promulgate rules included a power to

---

* On December 20, Bird explained herself in a memo to Clark as follows: "You state that there is an inconsistency between my disqualifying myself from Judicial Council consideration of the proposed rule change and my personal opinion as to the desirability of open hearings. There is none. I have said that I favor open hearings in the forthcoming investigation regarding the *Tanner* case, but I have taken no position as to the merits of the specific rule change, which would also apply to other cases in the future. They are two completely distinct questions."

suspend one rule for one particular case, Judge Low managed to avoid discussing. The board of governors of the state bar debated the new rule at length at a meeting in January and by a vote of sixteen–three endorsed the commission's proposal, with Robert Raven of San Francisco protesting that open sessions would have a "very chilling effect on the Commission, which has been too chilled in the past." Both houses of the legislature joined the chorus, passing resolutions calling on the council to permit open hearings.

Leaks. © Dennis Renault, *Sacramento Bee*.

THE COLLAPSE OF THE JUDICIAL COUNCIL

Leadership of the council devolved on Justice Thomas Caldecott of the San Francisco Court of Appeal after Bird and Tobriner announced that they would not participate in the council's January 16 deliberations. Caldecott decided to refer the matter to the council's executive committee, composed of himself, Justice George Brown of the Court of Appeal in Fresno, and superior court judges Spurgeon Avakian of Oakland and Bruce Sumner of Orange County—an unusually able group of experienced judges, none of whom had any particular connection to Bird or any other figure in the Supreme Court controversy.

Sumner, as chairman of the California Constitutional Revision Commission, had overseen the rehaul of Gibson's plan creating the Commission on Judicial Performance. The requirement that the commission do its work entirely in secret was replaced by a single phrase authorizing the Judicial Council to make rules "providing for confidentiality" of the commission's proceedings. Sumner had no doubt that this rule-making power did not include authority to abandon confidentiality altogether. He was reinforced in this conclusion by a memorandum he asked Kleps to prepare. Kleps had played a central role in the revision of the judiciary article of the constitution and his position was unequivocal:

Thus, the Judicial Council cannot constitutionally adopt the rule change that is proposed by the Commission . . . Neither can it create a different rule designed to enable the Commission to conduct a public inquiry into "improprieties" that have not resulted in any specific charges against a specific judge. And, finally, it cannot dispense with confidentiality in the traditional disciplinary cases in which charges have been filed.

Sumner was baffled by the chief justice's endorsement (through Buehl) of what he and the other members of the executive committee considered a plainly unconstitutional proposal. In fact, Sumner thought Bird fully expected and desired the council to reject the commission's proposal, in which case the public would be left with the impression that Bird had demanded a thorough public investigation of alleged misbehavior on the court but some force beyond her control had frustrated her effort. This gambit deeply offended Sumner, who credited Bird with more Machiavellian capacities than she probably possessed. Having sowed the whirlwind, Bird probably never considered whether the council would reject the commission's proposal.

Sumner's three colleagues on the executive committee decided to recommend a polite rejection of the commission's proposal, including an explanation of their reasoning, and Avakian undertook to draft the explanatory statement. Although he thought the commission's proposal unconstitutional, Avakian decided not to rest the argument on legality but rather on policy grounds.* As a result, when the full council came to consider the matter, the members never focused on the legal question of giving carte blanche to the commission to open up the proceedings.

Avakian's analysis of the commission's proposal was a remarkably prescient document. His six-page statement opened by placing the commission's proposal in context and concluded:

Once the Commission embarks on a course of public hearings in some cases, it would have difficulty in resisting insistent demands in other cases. The alleged need to satisfy the skeptics of the thoroughness and integrity of its investigation would put pressure on the Commission to question the judge publicly in an adversary manner, challenging the accuracy of his memory as to what he did and what he said and when and for what reason. The judges would almost be compelled by public opinion to join in the request for public hearings, lest they be suspected of having something to hide. What would evolve would be something quite different from what was contemplated in the adoption of Article VI, Section 18, and the repercussions might seriously affect the process by which judges do their daily work and decide cases. . . . It would expose the court and judges to the very public political pressures the judicial process must at all costs resist and would have a chilling effect upon, if not entirely freeze, open and candid exchange of views inherent in and necessary to the collegial decision-making process. The function of the Commission on Judicial Performance . . . is to investigate allegations of impropriety quietly and fairly and recommend discipline when it finds serious misconduct. It is not the function of the Commission to provide a public forum for airing of charges so that the public can form its own opinion as to the validity of accusations.

Sumner dissented from his colleagues on the executive committee. His mind was riveted on the publicity that the chief justice had solicited in giving the press her November 24 letter to the commission and in endorsing through Buehl the commission's request for public hearings. Bird's behavior and the failure of any justice to object to the proposed public investigation astounded Sumner. Why should the council save the justices and the commission from their own folly? Sumner's not very satisfactory solution was to treat the matter as if the commission were

* Avakian was concerned primarily with persuading the ultimate audience, the public, rather than with influencing his colleagues on the council. The public would find a constitutional argument legalistic and technical. Second, calling the commission's proposal illegal would tell the world that some elements within the judiciary either did not know how to read the constitution or did not care about living within its limits.

acting as a private group of citizens. As citizens, not commissioners, they would be outside the framework of the constitution and the rules; thus, there would be no need for action by the council. On January 9 Sumner submitted a motion (by mail) to the members of the full council:

I move that the request of the Chief Justice that there be "an investigation of the charge that the Supreme Court improperly deferred announcing a decision in the Tanner case" be acknowledged as action taken by her in her capacity as Chief Justice.

Further, that the designation of the members of the Commission on Judicial Performance as the body to conduct that investigation does not require Judicial Council approval or confirmation.

Further, that the method or procedure announced by Justice Janes in response to the request of the Chief Justice need not be approved or authorized by the Judicial Council of California.

Further, that if it is determined by the Commission on Judicial Performance at any time in the future that a change in the California Rules of Court is needed for the proper performance of its constitutional duties while sitting as the Commission, the Judicial Council will consider its proposals as it has done in the past.

The problems with this solution were boundless, not the least being who was to pay the costs of the investigation. Sumner eventually retreated but not from his determination to prevent the chief justice from maneuvering the council into the role of the heavy who cut off Bird's opportunity publicly to prove her innocence.

The seventeen members of the Judicial Council who gathered in San Francisco on January 16 found themselves in an unusual situation. A typical meeting was covered, if at all, only by the legal press; yet television cameras were present on the morning of January 16. The usual agenda for a council meeting was long, accompanied by numerous supporting documents from staff, consultants, and state bar and council committees. Here the agenda was short and the staff work thin. Gampell's office prepared a short memorandum concluding that the state constitution did permit some relaxation of confidentiality but made no effort to analyze the commission's proposal in any detail.* The executive committee's recommendation to reject the commission's request was, of course, simple, containing no analysis or alternative drafts of the commission's proposal. Finally, the legislative members of the council,

---

* Hufstedler's office had also hastily prepared a legal memo to the same effect (Hufstedler had been employed as the commission's special counsel on December 28, after the commission's proposed rule had been submitted to the council). Sumner earlier had sent all members of the council copies of an article Kleps had written in the *Los Angeles Daily Journal* coming to the opposite conclusion.

Senator Jerry Smith and Assemblyman Jack Fenton, who attended council meetings irregularly, were present and possessed of very strong views.

The meeting lasted four hours. At the outset, Justice Bernard Jefferson established a tone of acrimony by challenging unsuccessfully the acting chairman's reference of the commission's proposal to the executive committee. After Avakian moved the recommendation and statement of the executive committee, Sumner produced a substitute motion (an altered version of the one he had mailed the members earlier). Sumner's motion opened with three new clauses:

WHEREAS, *a public inquiry into the actions of the Supreme Court in reaching a decision in the Tanner case has been requested and widely supported, and*
WHEREAS, *no opposition to such an inquiry has been expressed by the members of that Court and*
WHEREAS, *the office of the Chief Justice has publicly expressed support of a public inquiry. . . .*

Sumner also altered the third paragraph. His earlier draft had said that the commission's proposal "need not be approved or authorized by the Judicial Council"; he totally reversed field, saying that the proposal was "approved" by the council. Senator Smith asked whether that meant the commission's proposed rule was being adopted, and Sumner accepted Assemblyman Fenton's suggestion of an amendment that included the text of the commission's proposal as a part of the resolution. Sumner also accepted Judge Low's suggestion that a sentence be added to make it clear that the new rule was applicable only to the current controversy. The council was well on the way to producing another camel.

Justice Janes was present and invited to comment. He opened by disagreeing with Avakian that the short explanatory statement permitted under the existing rule would be satisfactory to the public. He then let the cat out of the bag by disclosing that the commisson did "not propose to hold a preliminary investigation in public." Probably only a few council members up to that point understood that the commission intended to hold a public evidentiary hearing only if the matter went as far as filing formal charges. In the event the commission concluded that there was insufficient cause to file formal charges, it planned only to submit a report explaining the reasons for this conclusion. Once it became clear that public hearings were not a necessary or even likely result of approving the commission's proposal, the atmosphere of the meeting changed. A number of council members agreed with Assemblyman Fenton that a detailed report would not satisfy "those people . . . who are clamoring for a public hearing." If Sumner's motion did not presage a public hearing, Fenton and Smith were against it. Jefferson agreed with them, calling for a substitute for the substitute that would require the commission to conduct its preliminary hearing in public. The acting chairman proposed a set of straw votes followed by a reference to a drafting committee, but Sumner insisted on a vote on his substitute motion.

After prolonged discussion, the council got around to voting. The members first rejected the Jefferson proposal by a vote of seven–nine (Justice Caldecott, the acting chairman, consistently abstained) presumably largely because Janes said the solution was unworkable. They then turned down Sumner's proposal by the same vote, which left only the original executive committee motion, also rejected.

At this point Sumner proposed a revision of his motion that would require, not just permit, the commission to hold a public hearing after completing an investigation. He accepted an additional hump on the camel from Assemblyman Fenton providing that the "Commission's determination shall be based solely on evidence taken at the hearing." The tired council passed this package by a vote of eleven–six, with Jefferson and Avakian in the minority. The January 16 resolution follows, with the revision of Sumner's original motion emphasized:

WHEREAS, *a public inquiry into the actions of the Supreme Court in reaching a decision in the* Tanner *case has been requested and widely supported, and*

WHEREAS, *no opposition to such an inquiry has been expressed by the members of that Court, and*

WHEREAS, *the office of the Chief Justice has publicly expressed support of a public inquiry,*

RESOLVED, *that the request of the Chief Justice that there be "an investigation of the charges that the Supreme Court improperly deferred announcing a decision in the* Tanner *case" by the Commission on Judicial Performance be acknowledged as action taken by her in her capacity as Chief Justice.*

Further, that the designation of the Commission on Judicial Performance as the body to conduct that investigation be approved.

Further, that the proposed rule 902.5 which states:
In a proceeding in which the Commission finds that:

1. *The subject matter is generally known to the public;*
2. *There is broad public interest;*
3. *Confidence in the administration of justice is threatened due to lack of public information concerning the status and conduct of the proceeding; and*
4. *The public interest in maintaining confidence in the judicial of-*

*fice and the integrity of the administration of justice requires that
some or all aspects of such proceeding should be publicly conducted or otherwise reported or disclosed to the public,*

the requirement of confidentiality may, to the extent determined by the
Commission, be modified with respect to said proceeding; and, after completion of the investigation, a public hearing shall be held and shall be
publicly conducted.

The Commission's determination shall be based solely on evidence
taken at the hearing.

*Such determination to modify may be made at any time after the
Commission undertakes to conduct an inquiry or investigation, or otherwise to institute such proceeding with respect to the subject matter, but
only after affording notice and an opportunity to be heard on the issue to
any judge whose conduct may be called into question in such proceeding.*

*be approved and authorized by the Judicial Council of California for this
investigation only.*

*Further, that the Judicial Council does not otherwise repeal or amend
any rule of the California Rules of Court as they presently exist.*

WHY THE COUNCIL COLLAPSED

Months later, during the hearings, commissioners and Bird all took
the position that the Judicial Council, not they, was responsible for the
public hearings required by Rule 902.5. It is possible to come to the
conclusion that neither the chief justice nor the commission requested
public hearings only by paying close attention to what they meant rather
than what they said. In public documents both used language calculated
to give the impression that each favored as much openness as necessary
to dispel any possible charge of whitewash, which patently required taking testimony under oath in public.

In one sense the council deserves credit for having exposed the
equivocation in the commission's proposal and resolved the ambiguity in
the only straightforward way possible. However, in a larger sense the
council failed abysmally. The council was ideally equipped to stand up
to public clamor and do what was right despite pressure from important
public figures: the judges on the council of January 1979 were among the
best and most experienced in California; they were constitutionally well
insulated from public pressure; and an article by Ralph Kleps,* sent by
Sumner to all council members, and Avakian's statement laid before
them with some eloquence good arguments against public hearings by

---

* Judicial Discipline and Confidentiality, Los Angeles Daily Journal, Jan. 2, 1979, p. 3.

the commission. But nonetheless the council approved what was both illegal and bad policy.

This failure was as much a default of imagination as a mistake of judgment. Avakian and others suggested at the January 16 meeting the alternative of some form of legislative investigation, which Assemblyman Fenton derisively rejected. Most members of the council were terrified of a politicized legislative inquiry, but impeachment and the participation of politicians was not the only possible format for a legislatively authorized investigation. The legislature could also create an ad hoc investigatory panel that excluded legislators; such a body could by statute be given subpoena power and other procedural powers deemed necessary. Ample precedent existed: for example, the Warren Commission or a commission on organized crime that Earl Warren had sponsored when he was governor of California.

Such a body would have had several advantages over the Commission on Judicial Performance. First, its legislative creation would have avoided the inherent incestuous relationship between the commission and the Supreme Court. Independence from the California Supreme Court could have been buttressed by the appointment of people of statewide and even national stature. Second, an ad hoc body external to the judiciary would be in better position than the commission to give due weight to the confidentiality problems inherent in the controversy.* Finally, and perhaps most important, a new panel could be given a mandate to consider matters broader than potential judicial misconduct (for a mundane example, court-press relations, which were troubled not so much by leaks as by day-to-day working difficulties). In any case, the council never considered the possibility of a legislatively authorized investigation not involving politicians or others with an axe to grind. That failure was partly because the council was long out of the habit of participating aggressively in public issues. The council also lacked a structure of leadership since the chief justice had disqualified herself. Had Kleps still been head of the Administrative Office of the Courts he might have filled the vacuum, but Gampell could not play that role because he was too closely connected to Bird to be credible. The most important cause of the council's collapse, however, was the presence of too much emotion and too little time for detached reflection. Senator Smith was quoted after the meeting as saying, "I think it was a good decision; one that everyone is mad at." He was wrong that it was a good decision but right that everyone was mad. Council members were angry about the rapid decline in the prestige of the Supreme Court and many, like Sumner, felt that they were being used as players in the court's tragedy. To expect

---

* Bird's ill-considered waiver of judicial privilege made the commission impotent to deal sensibly with the confidentiality problem.

an innovative and constructive response under all these circumstances would be asking too much.

THE COUNCIL REPAIRS RULE 902.5

On December 29 the commission announced its decision to retain Seth Hufstedler as special counsel for the Supreme Court investigation. Hufstedler was a member of the Judicial Council in 1978, one of the four members appointed by the state bar. He resigned before the council meeting on January 16, and on January 22 he wrote his former colleagues on behalf of his new client requesting a clarifying amendment to Rule 902.5:

As you know, the rule now provides that it shall apply "for this investigation only." I have assumed that the word "investigation" as used there means all of the proceedings relating to the subject matter of the resolution. However, the subject matter of the resolution is nowhere defined in the rule. There are references to the subject matter in the first "Whereas" clause, and in the paragraph beginning "Resolved." In one case there is a reference to "the actions of the Supreme Court in reaching a decision in the Tanner case," and in the other, a reference to "an investigation of the charge that the Supreme Court improperly deferred announcing a decision in the Tanner case." Not only is there some variance between the language of those two references, but neither of them is said to be a definition of the scope of the rule. Furthermore, the charges which have been referred to and the discussion of the Judicial Council itself in adopting the rule, are not limited precisely to the Tanner case, but rather to various charges regarding the processing of cases, and delay in the processing of cases in the period preceding the last general election. Since the scope of the rule has immense practical and legal effects upon any proceedings of the Commission which might fall within the rule, it seemed to me imperative that the scope of the rule be clarified.

Hufstedler accompanied this letter with a proposed amendment, which the council adopted with only one minor change:

This rule shall apply to any investigation or proceeding of the Commission on Judicial Performance relating to any possible improper conduct of any Justice of the Supreme Court of California arising out of (1) any irregularities or delays in handling the Tanner case; (2) any irregularities or delays in handling any other case prior to the election of November 7,

1978, *caused or instituted for the purpose of delaying the filing of the Court's decision in any such case until after the date of the election; and/ or (3) any unauthorized disclosure of confidential information regarding any of the above pending cases prior to the public release of the decision.*

This was the first time the commission publicly defined the issues it planned to investigate. In his oral presentation to the council at a special meeting on January 29, Hufstedler mentioned the *Fox* case and "two or three other cases" as having been referred to in the press in addition to *Tanner*. In urging his proposal Hufstedler noted that it would be impractical for the commission simultaneously to investigate delay in *Tanner* publicly while confidentially probing delay in *Fox* and other cases. The argument was persuasive, but Hufstedler's amendment solved only a piece of the problem the new rule created. What if the public investigation suggested wrongdoing other than delay for political reasons or improper disclosure of confidential information? In that event the commission would have to refer the matter to itself for confidential treatment. The revised Rule 902.5 built, as it were, a jurisdictional box within a box. The commission's power was limited to wrongdoing by justices; in its public hearings the commission was further limited to specific kinds of wrongdoing by justices in certain cases.

Limiting a case to specific charges is appropriate, indeed required by due process, when proceedings are at the formal hearing stage. But the commission's public hearings were to be at the investigatory stage, which precedes the drafting of charges. A grand jury investigating a suspected embezzler does not blind itself to evidence that the suspect may also have been guilty of extortion, which is what the modified rule required the commission to do in its public hearings for any form of misconduct not mentioned in Rule 902.5.

In January Hufstedler had only begun his factual investigation. It would have been better to wait until he had completed his own investigation before attempting to state the issues to be explored in the public hearings. But waiting was impossible because on February 1 the membership of the Judicial Council would shift and the fourteen judicial members selected by Chief Justice Wright would be replaced by Bird appointees. Hufstedler had less than a week to get his proposal approved by the commission and before the council.

At the January 29 meeting the council, on its own motion, added one sentence to Rule 902.5. Assemblyman Fenton, supported by Justice Jefferson, insisted upon including a definition of a public hearing: "A public hearing shall include the right of all segments of the news media to be present and report the proceedings." The issue was television. No one argued that dignity might suggest the inappropriateness of television coverage; rather, debate in the council was limited to whether the commission should be given discretion to regulate the form of television coverage. A motion to add the phrase "under such reasonable conditions as the Commission in its discretion shall prescribe for purposes of securing order and decorum" failed after a heated colloquy between Assemblyman Fenton and Judge Hogoboom. Their conversation ended with this exchange:

> *Hogoboom: It's absolutely asinine to think that [the commission] is going to get together and say nobody can televise, nobody can record, nobody can do anything. All I know is that if you don't have trust in [the five] judges and two representatives of the Governor's office [on the commission], who are you going to have faith in?*
> *Fenton: That's two representatives of where? (Laughter.)*
> *Hogoboom: I pass.*

The Judicial Council was divided on many things but unanimous in feeling that Governor Jerry Brown was the real villain behind the court's problems.

THE SELECTION OF SPECIAL COUNSEL

Seth Hufstedler embodied all the values Governor Brown had overlooked in appointing Bird. At fifty-six, Hufstedler was probably the most highly regarded lawyer in the state. Hufstedler had been everything: president of the Los Angeles County bar, president of the state bar, and chairman of some of the county and state bar's most important committees. He was a very active trial lawyer whose practice consisted almost entirely of major business and commercial litigation referred to his firm by other lawyers. Hufstedler was very much a creature of the Los Angeles legal establishment, but that was an unusual establishment during the 1950s and 1960s. Perhaps because of the phenomenal growth of California, leadership in the bar was very open and talent was eagerly welcomed and promoted. Noblesse oblige was a part of the bar's ethic, but conservatism was not. Despite some strong disagreements among leaders, government reform and the promotion of civil liberties were the dominant values.

Naming a California lawyer special counsel was not an obviously wise choice by the commission. Almost any active California lawyer would be hesitant to undertake the job for fear that it might compromise his or her ability to represent clients before the Supreme Court: a lawyer has a duty to avoid extracurricular activities that might damage clients' interests. California lawyers would also tend to have ties to the justices that an out-of-state lawyer would not. There were some big, out-of-state names that could possibly have been prevailed upon, for example, Archibald Cox or Leon Jaworski of Watergate fame, or Edward Levi, President Ford's Attorney General. Trading on an established national reputation would lend weight to the commission's conclusions. On the other hand, and perhaps more important to the commissioners, this was a California problem and the commissioners probably wanted Californians to solve it by themselves.

It is a mark of Hufstedler's extraordinary reputation that the commission selected him because he was more than a little involved personally with some of the justices. He had known Mosk and Tobriner for years, and although neither was a close friend their contacts had been more than casual or professional. At the time of Clark's appointment, Chief Justice Wright had asked the state bar to prepare a report on Clark for the Commission on Judicial Appointments. Hufstedler had been one of three members of a special committee appointed to prepare that report; the report made no recommendation but contained a considerable amount of unfavorable information about Clark. Hufstedler had been told, although not by Clark himself, that Clark deeply resented the committee's report. Furthermore, and most obvious to the public, Shirley Hufstedler, the special counsel's wife, was believed to have been a competitive candidate for the chief justiceship at the time of Bird's appointment.

Hufstedler had no illusion that becoming special counsel for the commission, however flattering the appointment, would enhance his reputation. He had little hope that the proceedings would improve the Supreme Court's public image. He believed the court was blocked from performing its function with a reasonable degree of public acceptance by the charge that release of its decisions had been manipulated for political purposes. The commission's function was to get the court off dead center, and his role was very much like that of a ship's damage control officer who assumes a catastrophe and tries to limit its impact. Hufstedler took the job out of a sense of duty.

Hufstedler's belief that the court was stuck in the mire of the *Tanner* controversy very much shaped his conception of how he and the commission should proceed. The object was to resolve the dispute as quickly as possible so that the justices could put the matter behind them. Hufstedler tried to limit the issues as much as possible and resisted the temptation to be diverted into collateral matters. Although the legal issues were fascinating and important, Hufstedler declined the opportunity to litigate such matters as the scope of judicial privilege and the right of reporters to conceal their sources. He also very much hoped the commission could finesse dealing with the constitutional issue of its power to hold public hearings.

FROM *TANNER I* TO THE HEARINGS

The Court

The November 7 story in the *Los Angeles Times* noted that "technically, no Supreme Court decision is final until 30 days after it is announced." This interval permits the parties to file a petition for rehearing in which the losing side can point out errors in the court's opinion. Rehearing petitions are rarely granted, although the court not infrequently makes minor changes in its opinions in response to a petition; occasionally the result changes because one or more justices switches his or her vote from one side to the other. Although a change in result is very rare, rehearing petitions are nonetheless frequently filed either because the losing lawyers want to express their displeasure or because, especially if some form of legislative relief is a possibility, the petitioner wants to use the occasion for a press release exposing the reasons why a particular decision should be overturned.

A petition for rehearing of the latter sort was filed in *Tanner* by Attorney General Duekmejian's office shortly after *Tanner I* was released on December 22. The brief's principal contention was rather more a debater's point than a legal argument. With heavy-handed irony, the brief suggested that in its haste to get the decision in *Tanner* filed, the court may have "neglected to count the votes" because four justices (the three dissenters and Bird) all agreed that the legislature intended the "use a gun, go to prison" law to abolish the trial court's power to put a defendant on probation.* Although true, this claim overlooked Bird's holding that such a statutory objective was unconstitutional. For purposes of the result in the case her opinion inevitably led to the same result as the lead opinion of Tobriner, Mosk, and Newman.

Over half of California's 120 legislators filed an amicus curiae brief in support of the attorney general's petition for rehearing. No one at the time commented on the legislators' intervention, but it deserved notice and condemnation. A more brazen attempt to pressure the court would be hard to imagine. The Supreme Court, whatever its faults, was the head of a co-equal branch of government with a serious public relations problem that should have worried any responsible public official. To abuse the court then for personal (and marginal) political gain must be described as a cheap shot. That so many legislators willingly forgot their pretensions as statesmen speaks volumes about the depth of feeling in the capitol towards the court in general and probably Bird in particular.

On February 8 the court surprised everyone by granting a rehearing in *Tanner* and scheduling the case for argument in early March. Mosk joined the dissenters to make up the necessary four votes. It was the

---

* Clark had made the same point in his *Tanner* dissent.

second time within a month that the court had granted a rehearing in a criminal case. The press called these grants the first of their kind in fifteen years, probably an exaggeration, although re-argument of a criminal case was unusual.

The grant of a rehearing in *Tanner* had two obvious effects: first, it kept the case and the controversy about the court before the public; second, it had the potential of obstructing Hufstedler's investigation and thus the start of the commission's hearings until after *Tanner II* was released. Hufstedler publicly expressed concern that the court might as a consequence of the rehearing be unwilling to release the documentary evidence essential to his investigation while the rehearing was pending. In fact that did not happen. Although no public statement was made, apparently an agreement was reached between Hufstedler and the justices that the issue before the commission was the alleged delay in the release of *Tanner I* and that whatever happened at the rehearing stage was not relevant to any matter under investigation. The grant of the rehearing, however, may more subtly have inhibited the investigation. Because the case was still pending, Hufstedler was anxious to avoid in any way influencing the final decision in *Tanner*. As a consequence he shied away from questions based on the substance of any of the justices' various opinions. As shall be seen, Bird took in *Tanner* an extreme, arguably outlandish position that gained no support from any of her colleagues. If the characterization of outlandish be accepted (and it is obviously arguable), her taking such a position was itself evidence that something out of the ordinary was going on in *Tanner*. But Hufstedler (and the commission following his lead) never got close to considering this a relevant piece of evidence. Bird's opinion in *Fox*, although not outlandish, was also largely pointless. No one noticed that either, perhaps because everyone was so sensitive not to reargue the merits of *Tanner* and *Fox* that everyone overlooked the obvious, albeit inconclusive, relevance of the substance of those opinions to the issue of deliberate delay.

The Press

On the morning of the day *Tanner I* was released, December 22, the *Los Angeles Times* had a front-page story by Robert Fairbanks and Phillip Hager under the head "Varied Opinions Reportedly Delayed Gun-Case Ruling." The lead was:

The fact that four justices wrote four separate opinions in a controversial gun-law case is what prevented the California Supreme Court from issuing a decision before the election, Court sources said Thursday. The sources said one dissenting opinion was not completed until October 24, causing Justice Mathew O. Tobriner to take additional time to modify a majority opinion he originally prepared for the Court last March. A series of dates tracing the Court's handling of the case was cited by these sources in defense of Tobriner against claims that a decision overturning the law had been purposely delayed beyond the election to try to insure voter approval of Chief Justice Bird on the November 7 ballot.

The article then described chronologically how the various justices had processed the *Tanner* case. The source was said to be a "secret memo" printed the day before in the *Metropolitan News*, a Los Angeles legal newspaper.

The secret memo was Cohen's supporting memorandum for the Tobriner statement, which had been summarized (and quoted) by Kang in the *San Francisco Examiner* on November 19. With one exception, the *Times* December 22 story said nothing that was not in Kang's earlier *Examiner* article. The exception was the difference in reasoning between Tobriner's opinion and Bird's. The *Times* article described the substance of their opinions as follows: "Court sources said that [Bird] said that the legislature had no right to infringe upon a judge's power to grant probation. Tobriner's opinion reportedly said only that the gun law was improperly written to accomplish its goal." Cohen's memorandum did not contain any hint as to the content of the opinions since (as noted previously) the memo was intended for confidential circulation among the justices, all of whom knew what the various opinions said. Neither the *Metropolitan News* nor Kang's *Examiner* article described the substance of the opinions since both were based on the Cohen memorandum. Unfortunately, the significance of this disclosure was lost because it was news for such a brief period of time. In the afternoon of December 22, the court filed the opinions in *Tanner I*, which simultaneously preempted and confirmed the Fairbanks-Hager story of that morning.

But the disclosure of the basis for Tobriner's and Bird's opinions indicated a breach of confidentiality and there is little doubt that Tobriner proponents were the source. The December 22 article did not say so, noting only that "well-placed Court sources verified the dates Thursday [December 21]." Later, Endicott in a *Times* article on January 10 (relating primarily to Rule 902.5, then pending before the Judicial Council) said in some background paragraphs:

The Chief Justice and Tobriner subsequently denied any impropriety in the handling of the case, and sources defending Tobriner, who wrote the lead opinion and thus had control over when it would be filed and made public, outlined a timetable which they said prevented him from filing the decision earlier. They said one dissenting opinion was not completed until Oct. 24, which did not permit Tobriner sufficient time before the election to rewrite his own opinion to take the dissent into account.

Other sources said, however, that the dissent by Associate Justice Wiley W. Manuel was so brief that it would have necessitated little if any adjustment in Tobriner's lead opinion. [Emphasis added.]

The emphasized passage and the last paragraph were an attempt to repair a defect in the December 22 story. Although the December 22 story had made the same points, they were not presented clearly, causing some dispute about what the story meant. The *Los Angeles Herald Examiner* in an editorial on December 26 charged its competitor with a "total repudiation" of the November 7 story, and Peter Schrag, associate editor of the *Sacramento Bee*, wrote a long column on January 8 coming to essentially the same conclusion:

The Times *[on December 22] made no mention of the fact that the "claims" to which it referred [that Tanner had been purposely delayed] were originally made by the same newspaper—and one of the same reporters—who now appeared to be undercutting them. Nor did it ever indicate whether the "sources" cited in the second article were the same as the first or, if not, whether the sources for the first story still stuck to their allegations.*

Fairbanks later insisted that the purpose on December 22 was not to repudiate or retract the November 7 article but to supply more details from Tobriner's side of the controversy.

Unfortunately, this particular leak was overlooked by Hufstedler and the commission. Although "well-placed sources" "defending Tobriner" were not necessarily Tobriner himself or anyone acting with his knowledge, these are code words usually taken to mean just that.* Furthermore, confirming the dates in the Cohen memorandum was no more than a technical breach of confidentiality because, although the *Times* apparently did not know it, people within the court were well aware that these dates had been public information since Kang's story on November 19. Anyone could also be forgiven for having forgotten that Kang's earlier article did not disclose the content of the opinions, especially since the content would become public information so soon.

The importance of the December 22 story was not so much its disclosures as its effect on the press. The November 7 article raised eyebrows in editorial offices throughout the state; the December 22 article heightened the professional interest of reporters and editors in the hearings. Their concern was as much whether and how the *Times* would

---

* Tobriner was not asked about the December 22 story but one of his research attorneys, Michael Willemsen, was. Willemsen told the commission that he had "no knowledge or information that Justice Tobriner himself, either directly or indirectly, provided any of the information contained in [the December 22] article."

be vindicated as whether any justice was guilty of misconduct. As a consequence, some very good reporters were assigned to cover the hearings and they were given ample column inches for their stories, probably more talent and space than the general public's interest in the court's problems warranted.

Between the announcement of *Tanner I* (December 22) and the start of the commission hearings (June 11) the press had a number of stories about comments and events of notable shallowness that reporters let pass without criticism, a sort of holiday for cheap shots. Perhaps the low point was the immediate reaction to the decision. Law enforcement figures were quoted saying such things as "the Court with one swoop [sic] of the pen has given renewed hope to the armed robbers of this state" (California Peace Officers Association) and "the Supreme Court votes in favor of violence" (Los Angeles County sheriff, Peter Pitchess). The press charitably paid less attention to a statement Tobriner issued when *Tanner I* was filed:

As I have repeatedly stated, neither the Court nor I delayed the filing of the Tanner *case for a political or any other improper reason; the case was handled no differently than any other case and proceeded in its regular course through the Court. The entire matter is now before the Commission on Judicial Performance, the appropriate constitutional body to investigate such matters, and I do not believe it would be proper to discuss the matter.*

As with the inflated rhetoric of law enforcement figures, the inconsistency between the first and second sentences of Tobriner's release passed without comment.

Legislators, including Speaker Leo McCarthy, who had not heretofore been a supporter of mandatory sentencing, quickly introduced corrective legislation. By suspending the rules, the senate within a week unanimously passed a bill to overturn the decision. The governor, although he did not criticize the court, said he would "promptly seek whatever statutory and constitutional changes are necessary." The Assembly Criminal Justice Committee slowed things down a bit in early January by agreeing to a delay in view of some unexpected technical difficulties, and legislative activity stopped when the court granted a rehearing on February 8. At about the same time, editorial writers on the *Los Angeles Times* woke up to the fact that the wisdom of the "use a gun, go to prison" measure was not as plain as some had supposed. In two editorials, one in mid-January and the other shortly after the court granted a rehearing in *Tanner*, the *Times* concluded that some flexibility in sentencing was justified in extraordinary cases.

The court's decision to grant a rehearing of course forced a rehash in news columns of the whole controversy. Although some speculated that the court's purpose in granting the rehearing may have been to obstruct the commission's investigation, no one noticed that the court had scheduled the rehearing for March 7, less than a month away. On the weekend before the argument, the *Los Angeles Times* ran two long articles on *Tanner*—one by Attorney General Duekmejian and the other by Tom Nolan, Tanner's counsel. The questionable propriety of lawyers' arguing their cases in the newspapers apparently never crossed the mind of anyone involved, including the editors of the *Times*.*

On March 6, the day before the re-argument of *Tanner*, the *Los Angeles Times* published a very long article by Fairbanks titled "Anatomy of a Duel: A Court amid Turmoil." It was a very good article that pulled together all of the strands in the *Tanner* controversy. Though the story contained little that was new, Fairbanks spelled out much more fully than anyone had before the link between *Caudillo* and *Tanner* and the extent to which the protagonists were Bird and Clark. He also gave credit to the *Washington Post* for identifying as an issue why and when Manuel decided to write a separate dissent. (Fairbanks also noted that the Cohen memorandum "was reported in the San Francisco *Examiner* [on November 19] and was covered in the *Times* on December 22" but did not explain why the *Times* printed as fresh news something public for nearly a month.)

The oral argument on March 7 was yet another occasion for a retelling of the controversy. Oral arguments are not good media events because they lack a conclusion or even any direct interchange between adversaries. It is traditional for justices to shield their tentative decision in their questioning so that reporters make no effort to infer a justice's final decision. The argument was held before a packed house, with Attorney General Duekmejian himself arguing the case for the people.

From this point until just before the hearings started, the *Tanner* controversy largely disappeared from the press. However, there was a brief flurry of articles in April, when the commission announced its rules, and some reporters became alarmed when they learned that Hufstedler's investigation included interviewing reporters. They should have been reassured, however, when Hufstedler was reported as saying: "No-

---

* Edward Lascher in his column in the monthly State Bar Journal commented as follows: "Good grief! Since when do lawyers take to the Sunday morning press to discuss the merits of cases they're going to argue on Wednesday? Since when (doubled) does the state's chief legal officer do so? I have felt for a long time that there's been too much leaking to the press regarding pending cases. . . . But this was a leak turned into a torrent. If we are going to treat the judicial process as merely a specialized branch of the political game, then we can't complain when people insist we play according to the politician's rules. But if we want to stick to the idea that the courtroom is not necessarily the market place, then we've got to treat it that way. I think we have here an ethical question . . . but I don't suppose we'll hear a murmur about this cynical adventure in pamphleteering. It's enough to make you want to drop out, if there were only some place to drop to." 54 Cal. St. Bar J. 172 (1979).

body's going to be thrown in jail. That is not going to happen . . . It's very doubtful anybody will help me; if they do I will be pleasantly surprised. The reporters I have talked to were essentially not cooperative."

Kang had three stories of consequence that others missed. She interviewed Hufstedler in March and he told her that the grant of a rehearing had delayed his investigation. He refused to say whether so far he had received the full cooperation of the justices. Nonetheless, he was "very optimistic" that he would get the cooperation "you would expect" from the court. Early in April, Kang reported that Bird had approved an allocation of $250,000 for legal expenses for the commission and that Hufstedler and one of his partners (Burt Gindler) were being paid $100 an hour (Hufstedler's normal fee ranged from $150 to over $200 an hour); Evelyn Balderman and Pierce O'Donnell were billing the commission at $55–90 an hour. Kang also reported that Bird, Tobriner, Manuel, and Newman had retained counsel to represent them. Kang's third story, published in May shortly before the hearings started, reported that Newman had filed a claim through the Administrative Office of the Courts for $1,495 for legal fees he had paid counsel for services from December through March. Kang's story did not editorialize on Newman's indifference to the public reaction to his behavior, an attitude akin to arrogance that reappeared even more spectacularly later. But Kang did put a needle in Ralph Gampell who, she said, "refused to talk about the claim other than to say that the judge making it was not Chief Justice Bird."

The Commission

Hufstedler and his associates conducted an elaborate investigation before the hearings started. He described the effort in general terms:

[The] *five-month pre-hearing investigation has involved four lawyers and has taken over 2,000 attorney hours. This inquiry has entailed, among other things, conducting nearly sixty interviews, examining about 1,300 pages of documentary material (most of it from the records of the Court and the justices) and ultimately taking sixty-two depositions under oath. We interrogated all of the justices, almost the entire staff of the Court, and many persons outside of the Court who seemed to have relevant information.*

Any investigation of such scope was bound to generate a number of procedural issues especially if, as in this instance, there were no obviously applicable rules to follow. For example, should counsel for the justices be permitted to attend, participate in, or review the product of Hufstedler's interviews and depositions? Treating the justices as if they were litigants in a civil lawsuit would give counsel for the justices access to whatever evidence Hufstedler developed. However, Hufstedler chose in general to treat the justices as if they had only the rights of witnesses before a grand jury or in an administrative investigatory proceeding. That kept confidential most of what Hufstedler found until he chose to introduce it is as evidence at the public hearings.

Although there were extended debate and exchanges of legal memorandums between Hufstedler and counsel for the justices on this and many other issues, most of the controversy remains shrouded in secrecy and presumably will remain so until the *Tanner* affair becomes a matter of archival interest only. That is unfortunate because, as everyone recognized, Hufstedler and counsel for the justices were breaking new ground, and regardless of the correctness of their decisions the fact that certain positions were taken and some decisions made had precedential as well as historical significance.

A little was learned about some of these controversies during the course of the commission's hearings. For example, it was revealed that each justice had a copy of his or her deposition, which Hufstedler had taken, and that all, except Clark, had exchanged copies of their depositions before the hearings.* However, what emerged during the hearings was so fragmentary that any account of the competing positions would almost certainly be misleading. For the moment it will have to suffice to note that procedural controversy was very much present during Hufstedler's investigation, that sharply divergent positions were sometimes taken, and that hard feelings came perilously close to the surface from time to time.

On April 25, the commission announced that the hearings would start on June 11 and publicly released three resolutions it had adopted in closed session on April 20.

The first resolution reported the commission's solemn, but ridiculous, act of holding a hearing after notice to the justices on the issue of whether the hearings should be public. The commission dutifully found, as required by Rule 902.5, that the *Tanner* controversy was a subject "generally known to the public," that there was "broad public interest," and that "confidence" in the judiciary required public hearings, thus triggering the rule's requirement that there be a public hearing. The commission also authorized the chairman to make public reports

on the status of the investigation, but not its substance, and on the timing of the oncoming hearings, including any matter or problem that may develop that affects the timing of the hearings. Such status reports may include . . . the progress of the investigation including the reasons

---

* A deposition is testimony taken under oath and recorded by a court reporter. It differs from testimony in court only by the place where it is taken (usually a lawyer's office) and, especially in an investigatory proceeding such as this, in the range of questioning because some of the rules of evidence, including relevance, are considerably relaxed.

for any delays, and any enforcement proceedings needed to procure the production of documents or the attendance of witnesses.

The commission was determined not to be charged with foot-dragging and went out of its way to warn the justices that it was prepared to focus public attention on them should any or all engage in dilatory tactics.

The second resolution announced the adoption by the commission of rules of procedure for the public hearing. Precisely where the commission found the authority to adopt rules of this nature is unclear. As noted earlier, the state constitution vests procedural rule-making power for the commission in the Judicial Council. Within the framework of the rules adopted by the council, the commission has some authority to regulate the conduct of any particular proceeding, but whether the resolution adopted on April 20 fitted comfortably within that implied authority is debatable. For a number of reasons, the commission was reluctant to request additional rule changes from the council. By April, of course, a new Judicial Council composed overwhelmingly of Bird appointees was in existence, and the commission had no desire to subject itself to a possible repetition of the Rule 902.5 fiasco. The commission's understandable wish to avoid further involvement of the Judicial Council thus led it to stretch to the maximum its procedural authority.

The basic decision reflected in the commission's rules was to "bifurcate" the proceedings into a preliminary investigation hearing to be followed, if necessary, by a formal hearing. The bulk of the commission's rules related to the procedures for the preliminary investigation hearing. Charitably viewed, these provisions were no more than an elaboration of the Judicial Council's Rule 904, describing the normal, confidential preliminary investigation conducted mainly by the commission's executive officer but inadequate here because of the requirement of a public investigatory hearing. The commission's new rules provided that the preliminary investigation hearing was to include a description by special counsel of his investigation, a delineation of the issues on which he would present evidence, and as much undisputed factual background material as necessary to clarify the issues. The proceedings would then adjourn for a week for the commissioners and counsel for the justices to become familiar with the background material, after which period the commission would reconvene and special counsel would commence the introduction of evidence through witnesses. The rules then provided that "each justice, in person or by counsel, shall have a reasonable opportunity to present to the Commission evidence relevant to the issues. The method of presentation shall be within the sound discretion of the Commission." Significantly, this provision did not give counsel for the justices a right of cross-examination. At the conclusion of the public hearing and after briefing and argument, the commission would determine whether "sufficient cause exists for further proceedings as to each justice." If no sufficient cause were found, the commission would issue a final report as to each justice so exonerated. If it found sufficient cause, the commission would then formulate formal charges and schedule the second stage, a formal hearing. At the formal hearing the existing procedural rules of the Judicial Council would be fully applicable, including the right of cross-examination, except that the hearing would be conducted in public. Finally, the rules provided: "The evidence produced at [the preliminary investigation hearing] shall not be considered as evidence in [the formal hearing], unless appropriately admitted therein as evidence."

This last provision reflected a basic problem in the bifurcation scheme. Evidence was bound to be admitted at the investigation stage that would be inadmissible at the formal hearing. An illustration would be newspaper articles. Presumably, they would be introduced at the investigation stage, especially on the issue of leaks, but in formal hearings newspaper articles would be unvarnished hearsay from largely undisclosed sources and wholly inadmissible as proof as to whether any justice had delayed a decision for political reasons. How were the commissioners to forget at the formal hearing stage what they had learned during the preliminary investigation hearing? To a limited extent courts ask jurors or trial judges to disregard items of improperly introduced evidence. But the bifurcation of the hearings was doomed to produce an unmanageable volume of unforgettable but inadmissible factual material. Even more than the commissioners, the public could not possibly be expected to forget evidence introduced in the investigatory stage simply because it was, for example, inadmissible hearsay. If the purpose of the public hearings was to persuade the press and public that the commission's conclusions were not the result of a whitewash, bifurcation of the hearings was bound to create a credibility problem if the commission should decide that formal hearings were necessary.

One way to limit this risk would have been to restrict the scope of the preliminary investigation to particular issues, narrowly defined. To some extent the commission followed this route with the third resolution it adopted on April 20, to be discussed shortly. But the commission was inhibited in doing so by its belief that if the investigation were too circumscribed the public would fail to be persuaded by the commission's conclusions.

One way to avoid the problem altogether would have been to skip the preliminary investigation stage and go straight to a formal hearing, or, to put it another way, not to attempt a bifurcation of the hearings. That would have put Hufstedler in an adversary role which was probably repugnant to him. It would also have given counsel for the justices a full right to cross-examine and thus create a potentially very cumbersome hearing with seven justices as respondents, only some of whom were centrally involved. It also would have put the commission in the role of adjudicator with very minimal control over the nature of the issues explored or the way in which the interrogation of witnesses proceeded.

The only way the bifurcation scheme could have worked well would have been if everyone—justices, their counsel, and the commissioners —had let Hufstedler control the scope of the examination of witnesses. Under the best of circumstances that would have been a delicate line for him to walk, but if he and the witnesses were disciplined perhaps enough public testimony could have been produced to persuade observers that Hufstedler's investigation was thorough without irretrievably cluttering the record with material that would be inadmissible in a formal hearing. It may be unreasonable to expect the justices and their counsel to have had so much confidence in Hufstedler; he was, after all, their potential adversary. But the commissioners had selected Hufstedler, and if they had supported him vigorously, the dangers of an unduly cluttered record could have been minimized. But, as will appear, commissioners, the justices as witnesses, and their counsel could not resist broadening Hufstedler's intended scope of the examination. Thus any hope Hufstedler may have had of an implicit understanding that he would run the show vanished once the hearings started.

The third resolution adopted by the commission on April 20 defined the issues to be explored. In fact, this step had earlier been taken when the Judicial Council accepted Hufstedler's amendment to Rule 902.5 on January 29. The commission on April 20 approved a memorandum prepared by Hufstedler that noted he "had found no credible evidence to present to the Commission relating to issues beyond those defined below":

1. *Was there any delay or irregularity in the handling of the* Tanner *case caused or instituted for any improper purpose? (In that connection, how, if at all, does the handling of the petition for stay in the case* People *v.* Court of Appeal (Caudillo) *reflect upon any such irregularity or delay?)*
2. *Was there any delay or irregularity in the handling of the* Fox *case or the* Levins *and* Hawkins *cases caused or instituted for the purpose of delaying the filing of the decision in either of these cases until after the date of the election of November 7, 1978?*
3. *Did any justice improperly disclose confidential information about the* Fox *or* Tanner *case prior to the release of the decisions therein?*

Although the commission purported to reserve the right to modify this statement of issues, it probably could not have done so very broadly for purposes of the public hearings since Rule 902.5 defined the subject matter of the public hearings. Hufstedler, indeed, rather stretched the commission's authority by including the *Caudillo* stay matter as a "delay or irregularity in the handling of the Tanner case."

The remaining problems of the commission were largely logistical. Each commissioner had a personal problem of arranging his or her calendar so as to have two weeks free in June for the hearings. The commission's executive officer, Jack Frankel, had to cope with a host of unfamiliar tasks. The most pressing was where to hold the hearings. He dealt at length with the federal courts in San Francisco in hopes of finding a suitable courtroom the commission could use, but the federal judges refused permission to lend any of their facilities. Ultimately the auditorium of Golden Gate Law School in downtown San Francisco was selected. Problems about television coverage were initially resolved when the educational TV station in San Francisco (KQED) agreed to provide live, gavel-to-gavel coverage and to tape the proceedings so that commercial stations could use clips for their news programs.* Press cards and kits were prepared and a press room provided for reporters in addition to office space for special counsel and the commissioners. Given that the commission and Frankel had no experience as impresarios of a major public event, things worked out surprisingly well for the start of the show on June 11.

---

* KQED, however, pulled out after one day and was replaced by KNBC, which did not broadcast the hearings live but made tapes available on a pooling basis; KQED continued to cover the proceedings live on its radio affiliate.

FIVE

The Cases: *Tanner, Fox, Levins,* and *Hawkins*

Before the commission's hearings started on June 11, the court had released the decisions in the four cases that Hufstedler indicated would be the focus of the testimony. What was not known until the evidence was introduced were the internal documents, draft opinions and the like, that lay behind the filed opinions. Hufstedler presented a substantially complete set of the internal documents behind *Tanner I,* a few critical confidential documents behind *Fox,* and hardly anything with respect to *Hawkins* and *Levins.* This chapter analyzes the opinions in these cases, beginning with the internal documents and tracing step by step how the final opinions emerged. Commissioners and observers of the proceedings saw the process the other way around; they were reading the book, as it were, after they had seen the movie version.

The evidence laid before the commission presents a unique opportunity to do this sort of literary history of judicial opinions. Never before has an appellate court made public substantially all of the internal memorandums about any of its cases. In the context of the court's total output, the internal documents Hufstedler presented were obviously fragmentary and any large conclusions about the court's internal processes drawn from these shards of evidence can only be tentative. Nonetheless, the material made public by the commission reveals a great deal about some of the justices and raises important questions about how the court was doing its work. Recognizing that the evidence is incomplete, it is fair to ask: did the memorandums and draft opinions revealed at the commission hearings generally facilitate or obstruct the appropriate processing of these cases?

HOW THE COURT HANDLES ITS WORKLOAD

Before looking at this material it is necessary to understand in a general way how the California Supreme Court has organized its work and something about its workload. The business of the California Supreme Court is basically divided between two kinds of decisions: first, determining which two hundred of the roughly three thousand cases that annually come before the court to hear and decide with a formal opinion; and second, deciding and writing opinions in these cases.* In this respect the California Supreme Court is quite similar to the U.S. Supreme Court; both courts have substantially complete control over which cases they will decide. Both courts also have experienced a steady growth since World War II in the number of petitions for hearing, although the number of formal opinions filed annually has remained reasonably constant.

The volume of petitions for hearing in the California Supreme Court (mostly petitions for certiorari in the U.S. Supreme Court) was staggering by 1978. Testimony before the commission indicated that the average Wednesday morning conference of the California court in 1978 considered roughly eighty matters, the bulk of which were petitions for hearing (in contrast, when Traynor became chief justice in 1964 there were about forty matters per week and early in Gibson's tenure [1945] the number was about twenty). In most cases there was an opinion in the Court of Appeal plus a brief from the petitioner and sometimes from the respondent arguing why the court should or should not hear this particular case. Although lawyers persist in believing that each justice carefully reads every word in their briefs, that is plainly false. It would be physically impossible for each justice to plow weekly through what amounts to a shelf full of opinions and briefs composed of dense legal prose. The U.S. Supreme Court has a precisely comparable problem although the volume is differently distributed over the year because that

* The "three thousand" figure refers only to petitions for hearing, substantially understating the court's total workload. The court must also dispose of a multitude of miscellaneous items ranging from administrative matters to death penalty cases, where appeal is directly to the Supreme Court. In 1978 the total items of business transacted by the court numbered 6,168, of which about half were petitions for hearing.

court meets in annual terms and does not hold conferences for roughly three months in the summer.

CONFERENCE MEMOS

How do the two courts deal with this volume? Both rely heavily on digests prepared by staff, but the two courts deploy their staffs quite differently. Until recently in the U.S. Supreme Court, petitions for certiorari were reviewed independently in each justice's chambers so that for each case nine summary memorandums were prepared on the issue of whether a particular case should be selected for decision on the merits. In 1972, some justices of the U.S. Supreme Court decided to form a "cert pool" whereby the petitions for certiorari would be parceled out in rotation to the chambers of those who participated so that only one memorandum would be prepared in each case. Only five justices, however, chose to join the pool. Thus, five memorandums are prepared in each case, an expensive way to use staff but also a mechanism that reduces the chance that any case worthy of close attention will slip by undetected. The California court, in contrast, conserves staff resources by preparing only one memorandum in each case and circulating it (the "conference memo") to all the justices. In criminal cases the conference memos are prepared by the central staff; in civil cases they are parceled out to the six associate justices' chambers in rotation.

Historic accident may explain the different methods the two courts use to handle requests that a case be heard on the merits, but the California system of using career research attorneys may also be a part of the explanation. As noted earlier, the U.S. Supreme Court uses law clerks who stay with their justice for no more than a year or two, whereas the California court uses career research attorneys many of whom have been with the court longer than the justice for whom they work.

Although lawyers are notably ignorant of the standard, the decision whether or not to hear a particular case is usually quite obvious. Only relatively few cases present an unresolved question of law worthy of the attention of either Supreme Court. This is evidenced by the practice in both courts of dividing the conference list and discussing only some of the cases. The California court calls the two lists the A and B lists, with cases on the B list not discussed unless a justice so requests; the U.S. Supreme Court calls the B list more vividly the "dead" list. In modern times the dead, or B, list contains half or more of the cases to be decided in any one week, and the A, or "discuss," list contains some cases that are as obvious for granting a hearing as cases on the B list are obvious denials.

After a few months on the job a U.S. Supreme Court law clerk can predict with remarkable accuracy which cases the court will grant certiorari; it is a little harder to predict how the California court will act. One reason for this difference is worth a moment's notice. Both courts assert that a denial of a hearing is not to be taken as an approval of the opinion of the court below, but nonetheless there is a practical difference between the federal and California systems because of the way the lower courts behave. A decision on some point of federal law by one federal Court of Appeals is regarded as a binding precedent within that circuit, but it is not so regarded in any of the other ten federal circuits or by any state supreme court. In other words, decisions from other circuits are authoritative only to the extent that they are persuasive. As a result, two cases presenting the identical issue can quite properly be decided differently by federal trial courts sitting in New York and San Francisco. (This kind of conflict between circuits is one of the reasons for the U.S. Supreme Court to grant certiorari.) By contrast, the California Courts of Appeal generally regard the decisions of other Courts of Appeal as binding authority. Conflicts occasionally emerge but infrequently simply because the Courts of Appeal justices happen to disagree on a point of law. The result is that if the California Supreme Court denies a hearing, the law becomes fixed on that point and the issue may well not appear again for some time, if ever, in another petition for hearing to the California Supreme Court. There is, thus, rather more pressure on the California court to grant a hearing whenever it sees what it thinks is error in the opinion of a Court of Appeal than there is in a similar situation confronting the U.S. Supreme Court. This circumstance not only makes it harder to predict which cases the California Supreme Court will hear but also puts a premium on having an experienced person widely familiar with details in the court's past decisions writing or at least reviewing the conference memorandums on petitions for hearing because such a person is more likely to recognize error, especially of a technical nature, than a fresh law school graduate.

CALENDAR MEMOS

The California Supreme Court hears oral argument in the cases in which a petition for hearing has been granted for one week each month, ten months of the year—four times each in San Francisco and Los Angeles and twice in Sacramento. In preparation for oral argument each case is assigned to one of the seven justices to prepare a "calendar memorandum," which states in much greater detail than the conference memo the facts and issues presented and the contentions of the parties. These calendar memos are supposed to be circulated within the court ten days before argument and, together with the briefs of counsel and the opinion, if any, of the Court of Appeal, the calendar memos provide the background for the oral argument and for voting at the posthearing conference that follows oral argument. In civil cases the justice who prepared the conference memo often prepares the calendar memo unless that justice recommended that the case not be heard and was outvoted by his or her colleagues. In this event, the preparation of the calendar memo is assigned to one of the justices who voted to grant a hearing. Similarly, in criminal cases, where the conference memo is prepared by the central staff, the calendar memo is assigned by the chief justice to someone who voted to grant a hearing.

The calendar memo is initially prepared by staff and reviewed by the justice in whose name it circulates. Here also there is a sharp difference between U.S. Supreme Court and California Supreme Court use of staff. In the U.S. Supreme Court, a "bench memo," comparable to the calendar memo, is prepared separately in each justice's chambers. A bench memo for an individual justice will concentrate on the points and arguments most likely to be of interest to and difficult for that justice in light of his past decisions. Usually a law clerk to a justice of the U.S. Court will have discussed the case with the justice when certiorari was granted and will know in a general way what points were of special concern to that justice. Writing a calendar memo for the entire California court presents a different problem. The staff member of a single justice can at best have only hearsay knowledge of the points troubling other members of the court and an ideal calendar memo presumably would discuss fully all points of possible concern to any member of the court.

Immediately or very soon after oral argument, the California Supreme Court convenes in a "posthearing conference." The justice who prepared the calendar memorandum states the case for his or her colleagues, and after discussion a tentative vote is taken (in order of seniority except for the chief justice, who votes last). If a majority of the court agrees with the author of the calendar memorandum, the case is normally assigned to that justice for preparation of the opinion. The assignment of justices to write opinions is another place where the U.S. Supreme Court and the California Court differ. In the U.S. Supreme Court this task is performed by the chief justice (or the senior associate justice in the majority if the chief justice is in the minority) after the tentative vote following argument.

There are several subtle consequences of this difference in the way cases are assigned for opinion preparation. One is that no justice on the U.S. Supreme Court can know that he will not be assigned to write the opinion in a case until, after the postargument conference, someone else is given the task of preparing an opinion. In contrast, a justice of the California court who has not prepared the calendar memorandum can be reasonably confident that unless he or she chooses to write a separate opinion or dissent, the monkey of writing an opinion will never be on his or her back. Obviously, no justice should think less carefully about a case because he or she will not have to write an opinion, but it must from time to time be tempting to slack off a little, especially in complex technical cases of no intrinsic interest. Second, the chief justice of the United States can use the assignment power to build consensus by assigning troublesome cases to justices who represent a middling view and who have a talent for writing opinions that bridge differences. Furthermore, this aptitude can be rewarded by assignments of important and difficult cases to justices who are successful in building large majorities. Finally, although there is little evidence of this practice in modern times, it is possible to use the assignment power to develop specialties, so that most labor cases go to one justice, tax cases to another, etc. The rotation system of assigning civil cases for the preparation of conference memorandums diminishes these powers of the California chief justice. Even in criminal cases, where the conference memorandum is produced by central staff, the individual associate justices can influence their opinion writing destiny by preparing supplemental conference memorandums, as Tobriner did in *Tanner*, which will normally result, if they succeed, in having the opinion writing assigned to the justice who first wrote on the case.

As shall be seen shortly, calendar memorandums are only sometimes, and relatively rarely, attempts to set forth impartially all the competing contentions presented by a case. Typically, calendar memos are first drafts of opinions. In testifying before the commission about their votes at the posthearing conference, the justices spoke of voting for or against the calendar, that is, the draft opinion that circulated as the calendar memo. How did this practice develop?

From 1945 to 1955 the court had no change in membership and over those years the justices must have come to know each other and their staffs very well. Accordingly, it must have seemed wasteful to canvass every point in a case when everyone could predict what the critical issues were and how all the justices were likely to react. Time and energy could be conserved by beginning at the earliest opportunity to draft an opinion that focused on the issues most likely to be troublesome and presented a resolution of difficult points in the strongest way possible. As of 1959 the court experienced a considerable turnover in membership but, except for Mosk, every justice who joined the court had been on a Court of Appeal, where the same process was used. It must have seemed natural for each of the newcomers to follow the existing practice, especially since they built their staffs around people familiar with court tradition.

For this system to work adequately two things are necessary: first, the justices have to know each other's positions in general quite well; and

The Supreme Court of California, 1978-1979. Standing, left to right: Justice Wiley Manuel, Justice William Clark, Justice Frank Richardson, and Justice Frank Newman. Sitting, left to right: Justice Mathew Tobriner, Chief Justice Rose Bird, and Justice Stanley Mosk.

The Commission in Session. The Commissioners are, from left to right: Thomas Willoughby, Howard Schwartz, Kathryn Gehrels, Thomas Kongsgaard, Chairman Bertram Janes, Hillel Chodos, Margaret Ann Shaw (absent), Jerry Pacht, and Executive Officer Jack Frankel. Special Counsel Seth Hufstedler (standing at left) is questioning Justice Clark (seated at witness table). Television camera is at center. Photograph by Paul Glines. Copyright © *San Francisco Examiner.*

The Justices as They Testified

Justice Frank Richardson.
Photograph by Paul Glines.
Copyright © *San Francisco Examiner.*

Justice Mathew Tobriner.
Photograph by Paul Glines.
Copyright © *San Francisco Examiner.*

The Justices as They Testified

Chief Justice Rose Bird. Photographs by Paul Glines. Copyright © *San Francisco Examiner.*

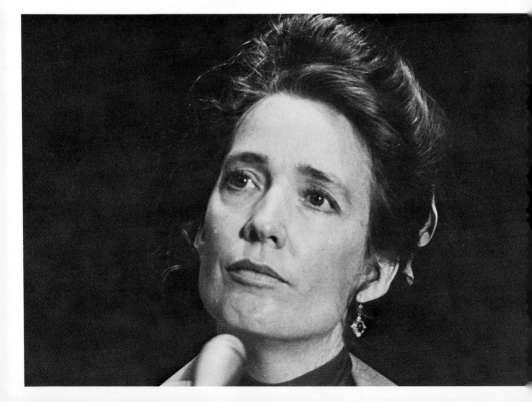

The Justices as They Testified

Justice William Clark. Photograph by Paul Glines. Copyright © *San Francisco Examiner.*

Justice Wiley Manuel. Photograph by Paul Glines. Copyright © *San Francisco Examiner.*

The Justices Who Did Not Testify

Justice Frank Newman.

Justice Stanley Mosk.

Special Counsel Seth Hufstedler. (Document on easel is Clark's "green sheet" in *Tanner*.) Photograph by Paul Glines. Copyright © *San Francisco Examiner*.

Chairman Bertram Janes. Photograph by Paul Glines. Copyright © *San Francisco Examiner*.

Chief Justice Phil Gibson (1940-1964).

Chief Justice Roger Traynor (1964-1970).

Chief Justice Donald Wright (1970-1977).

second, the justices have to trust each other not to present a case so as to hide a point that may be troublesome to a colleague. The process of drafting an opinion as a calendar memo in the first instance is economical only if the other justices do not have to go back and read carefully the briefs and record to make sure that the facts and contentions are fairly stated. The first of these conditions was not present in 1977 because Bird, Manuel, and Newman were still in the process of developing their views on a wide array of legal issues. But, in addition, as shall be seen shortly, the conference and calendar memorandums prepared in *Tanner* by Clark and Tobriner were so argumentative and so pointed toward a particular result that they failed objectively to present the issues. A conscientious justice would have had no choice but to read the briefs and record and think through for himself or herself every question in *Tanner,* an obligation that was realistically impossible to meet because of the court's heavy workload.

For some years the California Supreme Court had been coping reasonably successfully with a remorselessly increasing workload. Bird surely did not create this problem, but very shortly after her arrival it assumed crisis proportions. Her explanation for the sudden and sharp decline in the court's productivity was the presence of three inexperienced newcomers. Some observers were skeptical, however, and the evidence produced before the commission suggested powerfully that Bird's character was not only contributing to the problem but also was blocking its eventual solution. The thesis, briefly stated, was that the court's method of operation had been conceived and implemented during a period when the workload was much lighter and the justices had an uncommon degree of confidence in each other and in the entire staff of the court. As the caseload grew, justices increasingly relied on the work done in each other's chambers. Clark's arrival may have threatened this mode of absorbing workload increases and McComb's disability could not have helped, but both justices at least used known and respected staff, as did Manuel when he came on. But Newman (at first) and Bird did not, and Bird's instinctive distrust of people was in total conflict with the way the court had been coping with its steadily enlarging workload.

If this thesis is right, and even with the testimony presented to the commission we cannot be certain, it would be easy to fault Bird for having undermined the court's solution to the workload problem. However, Bird may well have been correct in suspecting that each justice was depending too much on his colleagues and could be better employed critically reviewing each other's conclusions. But this problem could not be solved in isolation because the justices simply did not have time to examine each other's work more closely; somehow the court's total process would have to be reorganized to free the needed judicial time and energy. With this background it is now possible to turn to the cases themselves.

TANNER'S CRIME AND TRIAL

In 1976, Harold Emory Tanner was twenty-seven years old, a high school graduate whose most successful years came in his teens, when he was promoted into a management training program in retail merchandising. Tanner lost his job when he was drafted into the army in 1968 and served nearly two years in Korea. After his honorable discharge he married, but the marriage shortly ended in divorce; the trial judge, Gerald Regan, thought the experience may have emotionally unsettled Tanner. He had been living for the last three years with a new girl friend, Melanie. Sometime in 1975 Tanner got a job as a clerk in a 7-11 convenience store in the southern Bay Area. The owner of the store, a man named Dyer, had developed a sideline "security" business servicing other 7-11 stores in the Bay Area. Precisely what this security service was supposed to do was not made altogether clear in the testimony. A person employed by Dyer would make periodic unannounced shopping visits to the stores subscribing to the service and report to their owners on such things as whether the floors were clean, the shelves properly stocked, and the clerks courteous.

Tanner began working as a shopper for the security service, devoting an increasing portion of his time to this job. The employee Dyer had in charge of the security service was cutting down on his hours and Tanner hoped he could replace him. Tanner's testimony emphasized, probably exaggerated, the security aspects of the service. He saw his role as primarily checking the honesty of clerks, their alertness to shoplifters, and their attention to possible illegal conduct going on in or around the store. He liked to call his shopping visits "surveillance"; he would "stake out" a store for as long as twelve hours, hiding in the bushes, visiting the store occasionally in assorted disguises. According to his testimony, he was once detected in this activity by some drug dealers and since then had kept a 22-caliber pistol in his car, although Dyer had specifically forbidden Tanner to carry a gun. Tanner also admitted shoplifting at clients' stores. He was unclear about what he did with the lifted merchandise beyond reporting his theft to the store owners. Dyer testified that it was not part of Tanner's duties to shoplift.

On the night of January 8, Tanner took Melanie along on one of his "shopping" tours. They had with them a tape recorder, apparently used for making notes for the reports Tanner was to prepare on the various visits. In the small hours of the morning they stopped at a 7-11 store in East Palo Alto that had once been a client of the security service but had

canceled a few months earlier. Tanner had tried unsuccessfully to re-
enroll the owner. Melanie went into the store to ask for matches when
other shoppers were present. According to Tanner's testimony, he sent
her into the store to find out which clerk was on duty, and her description was sufficient for him to identify the clerk as a "sensible" person
who had not panicked when he had been robbed.

Sometime later, at about three o'clock in the morning of January 9,
Tanner and Melanie returned to the 7-11. Tanner reached into the back
seat of the car, took his unloaded and, he thought, inoperable gun, and
went into the store. (The gun was later fired successfully by the police.)
He attempted to enter the store by jumping over the warning light but
the clerk saw him. There were no customers present. Tanner went behind the counter, showed his gun to the clerk, and made him open both
cash registers. Tanner carefully avoided triggering a silent alarm,
cleaned out the bills in the register, and made the clerk open the floor
safe, from which he took at least one roll of quarters. During the course
of the robbery, which netted $41.05, Tanner made some odd remarks to
the clerk, telling him not to worry, that he (Tanner) also worked for a 7-
11, and instructing the clerk to "play it straight" and turn in an alarm
when Tanner left.

What Tanner apparently did not think about or know was that there
was a sheriff's substation a few blocks away and that he was committing
the crime just about the time of a shift change. Consequently, there
were twice as many officers in the area as usual for early morning. Within
moments of his leaving the 7-11, sheriff's officers converged on the site
and two officers in one car almost immediately saw Tanner's vehicle run
a stop sign. They stopped the car and Tanner got out and approached
the sheriff's car. When one officer was patting Tanner down he felt the
roll of quarters and saw the loose bills in Tanner's pocket. Meanwhile
the second officer was getting reports on the car radio from officers at
the 7-11 store, and it quickly became obvious that Tanner was the likely
robber. At that point the second officer went over to the car and asked
Melanie to get out. She did so screaming, "What do you expect people
to do when you tax them so high? They have got to rob." Meanwhile
Tanner was trying to persuade the officers to call Dyer, who would
"explain everything." Tanner also told Melanie not to say anything. The
officer looked in the car, saw a briefcase, which he opened, and found
the gun. He also saw some empty beer and wine bottles and the tape
recorder, which he took. Within an hour both Melanie and Tanner were
identified by the clerk in the 7-11 store.

Tanner testified at the trial to the effect that he conceived the plan
of a "mock" robbery that night (without communicating this scheme to
Melanie) as a way of persuading the owner of the 7-11 to resubscribe to
the security service. He said that not until he left the store did he realize

that he had a problem with disposing of the money he had stolen. When he got back in the car he gave the gun to Melanie, who put it in the briefcase, and Tanner drove off looking for a phone booth to call the owner of the store. (Precisely how that gentleman would be persuaded to buy the security service by a telephone call from Tanner, the robber, at 3:30 in the morning was another problem Tanner had apparently not anticipated.) Alarmed when he saw a sheriff's car with siren on and lights flashing, Tanner inadvertently ran a stop sign and knew he was in trouble.

The crime took place in San Mateo County, whose elected district attorney, Keith Sorenson, had been in office since the early 1950s. Sorenson was an old-line district attorney whose general policy was to play it by the book; his deputy district attorneys customarily charged the use of a gun when the evidence warranted it. Furthermore, the county had been experiencing a spate of what the local law enforcement people called "7-11, 2-11's" (penal code §211 is robbery). San Mateo is a suburban county on the peninsula between San Francisco and San Jose and quite a number of people had been dropping off the freeway, robbing a 7-11 late at night, and vanishing. Under the circumstances there was no question in the mind of John Oakes, the deputy district attorney assigned to handle the case, that Tanner should be charged with robbery with the use of a gun and Melanie with robbery as his accomplice. Later it was asserted by a supporter of Bird's that Oakes had offered to drop the gun use charge against Tanner if both Tanner and Melanie would plead guilty to robbery, the implication being that Oakes had employed the gun use charge to extort a guilty plea from Melanie, whom he knew to be innocent.* That seems unlikely since the evidence of use against Tanner was overwhelming and there was significant evidence of Melanie's complicity. Oakes did not recall making such an offer. It is entirely possible that the subject was discussed by Oakes and counsel for Tanner and Melanie, but the claim of extortionate overcharging by the district attorney was unwarranted.

Oakes (a law school classmate of Bird's) anticipated three evidentiary problems in prosecuting Tanner and Melanie. One was the gun. The officer had found the gun when he took the briefcase out of the car and opened it. Tanner's counsel could have objected that the search was illegal since it had been made without a search warrant and without Tanner's consent.† The gun was put in evidence in this instance because counsel for Tanner made no objection. Presumably Tanner's counsel

---

* Portman, L.A. Daily J., June 21, 1979, at 4.

† The law of search and seizure is tangled and nowhere more confusing than with respect to an officer's right to open and examine closed containers found in automobiles. In 1976 a case could have been made for the legality of such a search; by 1979 the court had decided such a search was illegal.

did not object because nothing substantial would have been gained by keeping the gun out of evidence. Proof of the gun's use did not depend on showing the gun itself. The clerk would testify that Tanner had used a gun and the defense of Tanner and Melanie depended on their testifying; they could scarcely afford to contradict the clerk's testimony that Tanner had had a gun with him.

A second evidentiary problem was whether there was sufficient evidence to convict Melanie as an accomplice. She made a motion to dismiss the information against her on the ground that the evidence produced at the preliminary hearing was insufficient to show probable cause of her guilt. The issue was whether she knew what Tanner was planning when he got out of the car to go into the store; if she did, she was guilty. The superior court denied her motion to dismiss the information. She had entered the store earlier, which looked like a casing visit, and her statement when the officers asked her to leave the car was ample to satisfy the probable cause standard. But whether these facts alone were sufficient to persuade a jury of Melanie's guilt beyond a reasonable doubt was a closer matter. The best evidence Oakes had of her complicity was what was on the tape recorder, and that raised his third evidentiary problem. The tape sounded like the voices of Tanner and Melanie talking an odd mixture of fantasy and reality in which they described the shopping visits and some obviously imagined exploits. It was perfectly clear from the tape that Melanie knew that Tanner had engaged in more than a little shoplifting, largely of perishable food, beer, and wine. Given the tape it was unlikely that Melanie did not know that Tanner was planning the robbery. Oakes realized, however, that he would have a hard time proving a foundation for the tape because he had no way of showing that the voices were Tanner's and Melanie's, or when the recording was made, or distinguishing between fantasy and reality on the tape. Oakes also knew that the trial judge was strict on evidence issues and was unlikely to admit the tape in evidence. Oakes decided not to attempt it.

The case was tried before Judge Gerald Regan May 17–18, 1976. Tanner and Melanie were represented by private counsel, Thomas Nolan and Maurice Kemp, because San Mateo County uses private counsel rather than a public defender office to represent indigents. Nolan initially tried to show that Tanner had been too drunk to form the specific intent to rob, but that effort was undercut by his client who testified that although he had had something to drink he was not intoxicated. Nolan also failed to persuade Judge Regan to permit him to argue to the jury that the effect of finding Tanner guilty of using a gun would be to send Tanner to prison for a minimum of three years. He was left with arguing that Tanner had had no real intent to rob. Kemp had a better case on the issue of whether there was proof beyond a reasonable doubt that Melanie knew what was going on. Tanner loyally testified that he did not tell her what he was going to do, and she denied making the statement the officers had reported when she came out of the car.

After two days of deliberation, the jury returned a guilty verdict against Tanner with a finding that he had used a gun in the commission of the robbery. The jury acquitted Melanie.

Tanner Sentenced by Judge Regan

From the outset of the trial, all counsel and Judge Regan were very much aware of penal code §1203.06, the "use a gun, go to prison" law enacted in 1975, which appeared to prevent the trial judge from putting a defendant on probation who had been charged and found to have used a gun in the commission of a robbery. Regan refused to allow Tanner's counsel, Nolan, to argue the impact of this provision to the jury, but after the jury returned its verdict, Regan instructed the probation department to consider whether Tanner should be placed on probation. Such an instruction was necessary because otherwise the probation department would have assumed that a prison term was required and would not have considered probation as a possible disposition.

The probation department prepared a full and detailed report on Tanner. The report noted that the investigating detective did not think a prison term appropriate for Tanner and that Tanner had managed to obtain new employment. The department recommended that Tanner be placed on probation for three years on condition that he serve six months in the county jail and undertake a program of psychiatric therapy. Judge Regan was impressed with some elements of emotional and mental instability in Tanner. Some years earlier Tanner and his brother had come to the attention of the police when they put on a display of Batman and Robin by doing rooftop gymnastic stunts in costume for neighborhood children. Testimony on this incident was heard at the trial; Tanner was bizarrely concerned about the misleading image that the TV program had projected of the real Batman and Robin.

On July 1, 1976, Judge Regan announced that he thought §1203.06 was unconstitutional if it prohibited his exercising discretion to place Tanner on probation (he cited one case, *Tenorio*, to be discussed shortly), and he placed Tanner on five years' probation on condition that he serve one year in the county jail and receive psychiatric treatment. Regan also encouraged Tanner's counsel to attempt to have the sheriff place Tanner in a work furlough program. Regan was perfectly aware that what he was doing was legally questionable; at one point he said to counsel that he felt as though he were being "set up" for an appeal.

The legal ritual Judge Regan had to go through to give Tanner a year in jail instead of three years in prison was complicated. He first struck the jury's finding that Tanner had used a gun in the commission of the robbery, then committed Tanner to the California Department of Corrections (that is, prison) for the term prescribed by law, but immediately suspended execution of this sentence by placing Tanner on probation for five years on condition that he spend one year in the county jail. Regan did not enter an order in the minutes of the court explaining why he was striking the use of a gun finding.* His failure was clear error and the attorney general raised the point in his first brief on appeal. After the brief was filed, Judge Regan, presumably at the request of Tanner's counsel, filed a *nunc pro tunc* (now for then) order formally reciting for the minutes the reasons he had given orally for thinking a prison term for Tanner inappropriate. Technically Regan may not have had power to correct the record in this way, but the Court of Appeal paid no attention to the issue, and the Supreme Court chose to regard the attorney general's failure to protest the issuance of the *nunc pro tunc* order as a waiver of any objection to its entry.

This chain of events illustrates two features of the modern law of criminal procedure that seem to be of growing importance. The first is that the criminal procedure in general (and the law of sentencing in particular) has become increasingly ritualistic, with the consequence that trial judges have to go through a minuet of formulas that are often meaningless. Some formal requirements are mandated by statute, others by court developed doctrine. The current excess of formalism is a revival of a phenomenon from the distant past: grand jury indictments were once read with the utmost technicality to evade the indiscriminate use of the death penalty. A second consequence of the growth of formalism is that whenever the law imposes a regimen of technicality, the courts must develop a cognate body of law dealing with inadvertent failures to comply with the elaborate detail. Typically such law is fuzzy; in one case the court will insist on compliance, in the next the court will overlook a seemingly identical default without explaining how the cases differ. That is exactly what happened in *Tanner.* Either the Court of Appeal or the Supreme Court could have said that Judge Regan's attempt to strike the use of a gun charge was fatally flawed by his failure to record in the minutes his reasons for making such a determination. Such a decision would have made it unnecessary to decide whether Regan had the power to strike the use charge. But both courts wanted to decide the question of the authority to strike, so each finessed the procedural issue, the Court of Appeal by pretending it was not there, the Supreme Court by charac-

---

* Entering an order in the minutes (the clerk's formal record of a case) would seem unnecessary in this instance since the judge had explained himself quite fully in open court, but penal code §1385 requires that "the reasons for the dismissal must be set forth in an order entered upon the minutes." A good technical lawyer would have made the argument that Judge Regan's failure to enter an order in the minutes was proof that he had no intention of relying on §1385 but rather was relying on some inherent (but debatable) constitutional power of the court to dismiss.

Legal Process. Cartoon by Steve Greenberg, Editorial Cartoonist for the *Daily News of Los Angeles.* © *Daily News of Los Angeles.*

terizing the attorney general's position as a waiver although he had raised the point as ground for appeal.* Both solutions verged on lawlessness (especially that of the Court of Appeal) but neither court could be said to have broken with tradition. To sum up, as procedural law proliferates technicalities, the courts become relaxed about enforcing them because so many rules seem pointless; the end result is an immense area of discretion in the appellate courts, far greater than often appears on the face of opinions.

The Court of Appeal Decides Tanner

The period between Tanner's sentencing (July 1, 1976) and oral argument in the Court of Appeal (April 12, 1977) was taken up with preparation of the court reporter's transcript and briefs by counsel for Tanner and the attorney general. The issue of the power of a trial judge to strike the use of a gun charge for purposes of putting a defendant on probation was sufficiently important to attract the filing of amicus curiae briefs by the Los Angeles district attorney and the state public defender. Justice Robert Kane wrote an eight-page opinion for division two of the San Francisco Court of Appeal deciding that the "use a gun, go to prison" statute (penal code §1203.06) prohibited Judge Regan from put-

---

* Implicitly the court created a new formalistic procedural rule: in order to preserve a point on appeal, the attorney general must insist upon it at every opportunity.

ting Tanner on probation.* Kane's opinion was filed May 2, 1977, a little more than two weeks after the oral argument and sixteen months after commission of the crime. Tanner had by then completed his county jail term. Had Kane's opinion survived, Tanner eventually would have been sentenced to prison for three years and he would have served—with credit for good behavior and time spent in the county jail, about fifteen months in state prison. †

No point would be served by reviewing Kane's opinion in detail. One argument made on behalf of Tanner depended on the relationship among penal code §§12022.5, 1203.06, and 1385. Section 12022.5 is an enhancement provision, comparable to that involved in *Caudillo*, which adds two years to the prison term of anyone convicted of a felony "who use[d] a firearm" in the commission of the crime. Another Court of Appeal had held that the trial court had the power to strike the use of a gun charge with the effect of avoiding the enhancement provided by §12022.5 on the theory that the power to dismiss a use charge was included within the §1385 power of a trial court to dismiss a case altogether "in furtherance of justice." It was argued in *Tanner* that if the gun use charge could be stricken to avoid the enhancement of the sentence, it could also be stricken for purposes of putting the defendant on probation despite the prohibition of the "use a gun, go to prison" statute.

The first half of this argument, that §1385 permits disregarding the enhancement, was possibly raised in another case, *People* v. *Hunt*, then before the Supreme Court. The Supreme Court had granted a hearing in *Hunt* in May 1975 but the case had not been decided by June 1977, when Tanner's petition for a hearing was filed in the Supreme Court. On July 21 the court granted a hearing in *Tanner*. Although no information available to the public so indicated, the grant was, in fact, a "grant and hold," an internal court concept that in this instance meant the court recognized that there was an issue of law presented in *Tanner*

---

* People v. Tanner, 139 Cal. Rptr. 167 (1977) (officially depublished).

† It is interesting to contrast the fate of Daniel Caudillo and Harold Tanner while their cases were being litigated in the Supreme Court. Had Tanner gone to prison as the Court of Appeal thought he should have, he would have been out by about September 1978, before the Supreme Court decided his case. While the issue was pending, however, he was at large in the community. In contrast, Caudillo spent nearly two years in prison while the validity of his incarceration was being decided in the appellate courts although the Court of Appeal thought he should be at large. What was at stake in the two cases was identical: the validity of a three-year term in state prison. The difference in treatment, however, had nothing to do with what a layman would regard as the most significant difference between the cases—Caudillo was a violent and dangerous man whereas Tanner was more dumb than vicious. Tanner was never imprisoned because the Court of Appeal decision in his case was vacated by the Supreme Court's grant of a hearing. Caudillo, apart from a brief interval, was never released because the Court of Appeal decision so ordering was similarly vacated by the grant of hearing by the Supreme Court. The only time any court explicitly considered the issue of whether either should be at large pending final decision was when Caudillo made a motion to be released, denied by the Supreme Court in June 1979.

that might possibly be resolved by the court's pending opinion in *Hunt*. To prevent the decision in *Tanner* from becoming final until the court had a result in *Hunt* it was necessary to grant a hearing in *Tanner*. *Hunt* was decided on August 14, with an opinion by Justice Clark for a unanimous court. The decision was wholly unhelpful to resolving any issue in *Tanner*; Clark determined that the trial judge in *Hunt* had not intended to strike the use of a gun charge, thereby making it unnecessary to decide what the effect of striking the gun use charge would have been.

The Memos behind the Supreme Court Decision to Hear Argument

Because Clark wrote the opinion in *Hunt* it fell to him to prepare a memorandum for his colleagues suggesting a disposition of the grant and hold cases awaiting decision in *Hunt*, including *Tanner*. He circulated an eight-page memorandum on *Tanner* shortly before the conference scheduled for September 11, 1977. Either at that conference or earlier Tobriner indicated that he wished to write a supplemental memorandum to the conference on *Tanner* and he did so in time for the October 19 conference, but it was not until November 2 that the court actually decided to hear argument in *Tanner*. These memorandums were the first of the normally secret, internal court documents made public by the commission's investigation.*

Anyone reading the Clark and Tobriner memos cannot escape the impression that neither expected his readers—the other justices and perhaps their staffs—to look at anything other than his memorandum before coming to a decision. Clark quoted the relevant statutory language and summarized with quotations Kane's opinion for the Court of Appeal, the latter much more fully than necessary if he expected his colleagues to read the opinion for themselves. Clark stated two of Tanner's contentions but without indicating where in Tanner's brief these arguments were made and only obliquely referred to the constitutional argument Judge Regan had relied on when he put Tanner on probation. Neither memorandum made any reference to the attorney general's brief or to any of the amicus curiae briefs. This self-contained quality was equally true of Tobriner's supplemental memorandum, which did not even build on Clark's. Tobriner stated the facts of Tanner's crime (Clark had not)

---

* The Clark and Tobriner memorandums were not the first internal documents in the *Tanner* case; they had been preceded by a conference memorandum prepared by the central staff which circulated before the decision was made to "grant and hold" *Tanner*. Hufstedler presumably saw that memorandum but chose not to introduce it in evidence before the commission. The absence of the central staff memorandum is unfortunate because possibly it covered adequately points Clark and Tobriner left wholly undiscussed. It is probable, however, that most of the central staff's memorandum was concerned with showing the connection between *Tanner* and *Hunt* since that was the primary issue to be decided at that moment.

and emphasized Regan's conclusion that Tanner was more pathetic than dangerous. These two documents are strong evidence that the justices do not read the briefs in petitions for hearing or even the opinion of the lower court. Perhaps the justice responsible for preparing the conference memorandum reads them (he or she need not since conference memorandums are drafted by staff) but apparently no one expects the other justices to dip more deeply into the file than the conference memo. There is nothing wrong with this practice in simple cases with obvious issues, particularly if the author of the conference memorandum carefully states the contentions of the parties. The fact that the court split in *Tanner I* by a closely divided vote and reversed itself in *Tanner II* proves *Tanner* was not a simple case, but neither Clark nor Tobriner stated the issues in a neutral and detached way.*

Clark's memorandum opened with a totally abstract statement of the legal issue and moved immediately into language that was pure argumentative rhetoric: "the clear, unequivocal language of section 1203.06," "defendant's second argument is unpersuasive," and "section 1203.06 on its face explicitly and unequivocally lends itself to but one interpretation." Tobriner was somewhat less blatantly conclusory. He relied on two cases, *Burke* and *Dorsey*, which he argued were "analogous" to *Tanner* and which he said stood for the proposition that "absent explicit denial" by the legislature of the power to dismiss, trial courts "arguably" retain authority to put a defendant on probation. Whether *Burke* and *Dorsey* could fairly be read as supporting this proposition will be discussed shortly; what is revealing is that both the memorandums go straight to the merits of the *Tanner* case as if the only factor to be considered in deciding whether to hear argument in *Tanner* was whether Kane's opinion for the Court of Appeal was correct.

Rule 29(a) of the California Rules of court states that "a hearing will be ordered [by the Supreme Court] where it appears necessary to secure uniformity of decision or the settlement of important question of law." The importance of questions of law does not depend upon whether the Court of Appeal decided the issue correctly but rather on such things as whether the issue is likely to recur and whether people are likely to rely to their detriment on what may be a misstatement of the law by the

---

* A caveat may be needed here. There were several references during the commission's hearings to the asserted fact that the issue in *Tanner* was well known to the court and had been extensively discussed by the justices and their staffs although the question had obviously not been decided. If true, there was perhaps less need for either Clark or Tobriner to state fully or neutrally generally well-understood contentions. However, it is hard to see how the issue in *Tanner* could have been discussed earlier since the statute in *Tanner* was very new and how *Tanner* should be decided depended upon the particular language and legislative history of the new law. The broad issue of the validity of legislative restrictions on sentencing could have been presented in other cases, such as *Hunt*, but only Bird chose to deal with *Tanner* as presenting such a constitutional question and constitutionality was not the focus of either Tobriner's or Clark's conference memorandum.

Court of Appeal. So viewed, *Tanner* was a reasonably obvious case for granting a hearing. Tanner must have been one of the first defendants to be convicted of robbery with the use of a gun after the statute went into effect (his crime was committed little more than a week after the effective date of the "use a gun, go to prison" law), but he certainly was not going to be the last. Although Tanner was, as Kane's opinion noted, "something less than the usual armed robber" there would doubtless be many occasions in which defense attorneys would like to argue to a trial court that their client was more suited to probation than prison. District attorneys, defense counsel, and judges all needed to know whether this disposition were available, a resolution only the Supreme Court could provide.

The only possible reason not to hear and decide *Tanner* was that the issue was so clear that it would be a waste of time to consider it. That, of course, was Clark's conclusion but his conference memorandum did not approach the case as if that were the problem. Clark was obviously disposed to be supportive of rather than hostile to the "use a gun, go to prison" statute, but he could have stated Tanner's contentions as sympathetically as possible, perhaps concluding with a statement to the effect that although he found Tanner's arguments unpersuasive if several of his colleagues thought otherwise then the case should be set for hearing. Possibly Clark was trying to sneak one past his colleagues. If the Supreme Court sent *Tanner* back to the Court of Appeal with instructions to refile its opinion, as Clark urged, the law would become fixed in the Courts of Appeal that probation was not an available alternative. Under such circumstances it would be hard, although not impossible, to get a trial court to cooperate in making a record that would present the issue again as squarely as it was presented in *Tanner*.

If that was Clark's game, Tobriner caught him in it, but the content of Tobriner's memorandum suggests not so much that Clark was cheating but that the court, perhaps without much conscious thought, was operating under a different conception of the rules of the game. Apparently, the grant of a hearing (or, in this instance, the decision not to send a grant and hold case back) turned on how the justices individually thought a case should be decided rather than whether it was important for the Supreme Court to decide the legal issue presented—arguably a serious misapprehension of the purposes of the grant of discretionary jurisdiction to the Supreme Court. This practice also vastly increased the workload problem, because the justices had to consider with some care the merits of every Court of Appeal decision in which a petition for hearing was filed and apparently could not rely on their colleagues to summarize the issues neutrally.

The conference memorandums in *Tanner* do not prove that the court had slipped into the practice of going straight to the merits on all petitions for hearing. Unfortunately Hufstedler introduced in evidence no other conference memorandums. Although not conclusive, the Clark and Tobriner memos in *Tanner* point to this situation, and the same conclusion is to some extent supported by the fact that usually the justices who vote to grant a hearing also ultimately vote to reverse the Court of Appeal decision.*

Clark's and Tobriner's Substantive Contentions

Thus far the discussion has focused on the form and argumentative style of the Clark and Tobriner memorandums. It is now necessary to look at the substantive content of their positions in order to evaluate the calendar memorandum that Tobriner later circulated before oral argument in *Tanner.*

Clark's conference memorandum treated the case as presenting a single issue of statutory construction: what was the meaning of §1203.06? In relevant part the "use a gun, go to prison" law provides: "Notwithstanding the provision of section 1203: (a) Probation shall not be granted to . . . (1) any person who uses a firearm during the commission . . . of any of the following crimes . . . (iii) robbery, in violation of section 211." Clark's memo stated two of Tanner's contentions: first, because the trial court was permitted to strike a gun use charge for purposes of eliminating the enhancement of the prison term provided for in §12022.5 (the issue not decided in *Hunt*), the trial court also had the power to strike the use finding for the purpose of putting the defendant on probation despite the language of 1203.06. Clark's answer to this point repeated Kane's opinion for the Court of Appeal: "It is axiomatic that the striking of a prior or use allegation for one purpose does not render [the striking] valid and effective for another." Axiomatic is one of those words lawyers and judges use to paper over gaps in logic. Judge Regan's striking of the gun use charge did not mean that Regan thought Tanner was unarmed when he went into the 7-11. But if the law permits a trial judge to disregard truth and strike the use of a gun charge for purposes of reducing the prison term, is there any reason why it should not also permit the use charge to be stricken for the purpose of putting the defendant on probation? Perhaps there is an answer, but "axiomatic" does not supply it.

Clark's statement of and answer to Tanner's second contention, again quoting Kane's opinion, are worth setting forth in full:

Defendant's second argument . . . is predicated on the premise that because the legislature failed to clearly express its intent to exclude a use finding from dismissal under section 1385, such finding may be dismissed. . . .

Read together [§1203 and 1203.06] give "rise to the irrefutable infer-

* Richard Neuhoff, one of Bird's two permanent research attorneys, testified similarly: "I'd say the Supreme Court wouldn't grant [a petition for hearing] if the Court of Appeal weren't wrong. That isn't always true."

ence that the legislature did consider whether or not probation may be granted in the interest of justice, as provided by section 1385, in the event the offender uses a deadly weapon and/or a firearm in the commission of the enumerated felonies, and by deliberate choice determined that while criminal offenders using a deadly weapon other than a firearm may be excepted from the mandatory prison term and be released in unusual cases where the interest of justice is furthered thereby, those who use a firearm, an especially dangerous type of deadly weapon, are precluded from the privilege of probation without any exception and regardless of the circumstances of the offense and offender."

There is meaning in this one-sentence quotation from Kane's opinion, but only those unusually diligent and alert could be expected to find it on first reading. The argument can be recast less abstractly. Before the 1975 "use a gun, go to prison" law was passed, a trial court could "in the interests of justice," pursuant to §1203, in unusual cases put on probation a robber found to have used a gun or other deadly weapon. The 1975 law drew a distinction between guns and other deadly weapons, permitting probation in the interests of justice for robbers who used deadly weapons such as knives but not for robbers who used guns. That suggests a legislative intent to limit the trial courts' §1385 power to strike a gun use charge "in furtherance of justice." Otherwise the gun law was meaningless. This argument answered, as axiomatic did not, Tanner's first contention. Undeniably the argument was contained in both Clark's conference memorandum and Kane's opinion for the Court of Appeal, but could a justice reading the quoted passage in a summary memorandum grasp it quickly or at all?

Tobriner's supplemental conference memorandum made no attempt either to state the argument in more digestible form or to answer it. Rather, Tobriner concluded that the Court of Appeal had "rejected judicial authority to strike a use finding absent explicit statutory prohibition against such exercise of discretion [and] failed to put into effect the rationale behind our decision in *People* v. *Burke* and the Court of Appeal's decision in *People* v. *Dorsey*." In order to evaluate Tobriner's position it is necessary to look at these two cases (the only ones he cited) in some detail.

Burke *and* Dorsey

Justice B. Rey Schauer wrote the opinion in *Burke*, a 1956 Supreme Court unanimous decision.* Burke had been tried and convicted of possessing a small amount of marijuana in 1955; five years earlier he had been convicted of possession of marijuana and he admitted the prior

---

* People v. Burke, 47 C.2d 45 (1956).

conviction. Burke's principal contention on appeal related to the validity
of the search of his apartment; Schauer disposed of this claim by holding
that Burke had consented to the search. In addition, the attorney general
for the prosecution protested the trial court's striking of the charge that
Burke had previously been convicted of a narcotics offense. The short
answer to this contention was that the district attorney had not protested
the striking at the time it was done, nor had the prosecution appealed
the sentence so that, in Schauer's view, the point had been waived.
Schauer's decision rested on waiver but before reaching his conclusion
he took a little excursion into dicta to discuss the law concerning striking
of priors. Clark and Tobriner divided over how to interpret that dicta.

The relevant statute at that time (§11712 of the health and safety
code) provided:

*Any person convicted [of] . . . possession of any narcotic . . . shall be
punished by imprisonment in the county jail for not more than one year,
or in the state prison for not more than ten years. If such person has been
previously convicted of any [narcotic] offense . . . the previous conviction
shall be charged in the indictment or information and if found to be true
. . . the defendant . . . shall be imprisoned in the state prison for not less
than two or more than twenty years.*

The core of the attorney general's argument was that the second "shall"
required a prison sentence, and since Burke had admitted a prior narcotics conviction, the trial court had no discretion—Burke had to be sentenced to a minimum of two years in state prison.

The five critical paragraphs of Schauer's opinion began by noting
that the procedure of striking a penalty enhancing factor such as a prior
conviction or the use of a deadly weapon was not expressly authorized
by statute but was common in trial courts not only because proof of the
enhancing factor may be insufficient but also because in the interests of
justice the trial court may consider a longer sentence inappropriate.
Although not expressly authorized, the practice of striking a prior was,
Schauer said in the next paragraph, within the power of the judge provided for in penal code §1385: "The court may, either of its own motion
or upon the application of the prosecuting attorney, and in furtherance
of justice, order an action dismissed." "The authority to dismiss the
whole," Schauer said, "includes, of course, the power to dismiss or 'strike
out' a part" (the "of course" concealed a considerable chasm of logic).
But such a striking, Schauer went on to say, is "for the purpose of
sentencing only" and does not mean that the court found that Burke had
not committed a prior narcotics offense.

Up to this point, Schauer's purpose can be readily understood. The
problem of criminal recidivism had preoccupied the legislature, and over

the years a number of laws had been passed providing for more severe punishment for second- and third-time offenders. Legislators tend to think about this sort of problem in terms of gross classes or types of people—professional burglars, hardened criminals—and are apt to overlook the fact that the class description will always include some people as to whom a severe punishment is excessive. California trial courts had evolved the technique of striking priors as a way of dealing with defendants who did not seem to be hardened criminals. The courts' authority to do so was a little cloudy and in *Burke* Schauer was legitimating a long-established practice.

The remaining paragraphs of Schauer's opinion are harder to understand. After stating the attorney general's contention that a prison sentence for narcotics recidivists was mandatory, Schauer put aside language in several earlier cases using the word "mandatory" by noting that in all the cases the trial court had found the penalty enhancing factor to be present. He went on:

The cited cases—and the statutes referred to—do not purport to divest the trial court (or to hold that the court constitutionally could be divested) of the power to control the proceedings before it insofar as the essentials of the judicial process are concerned; i.e., to find the defendant guilty or not guilty of any offense charged, or of a lesser included offense, or to dismiss the action in toto or to strike or dismiss as to any or all of multiple counts or charges prior to conviction. The statutes in question do validly—and in respect to constitutionally vested judicial power they neither purport to nor validly could do more than—prescribe the sentence which must be imposed upon the appropriate adjudication of guilt of the substantive crime and judicial determination of the factor which results in increased punishment. Such adjudication and judicial determination are inherently and essentially the province of the court even as the punishment which may or must follow the offense adjudicated, either with or without a punishment augmentation factor, is essentially for the Legislature except as it may vest an area of discretion in the court or an administrative agency.

It is not altogether clear what Schauer was trying to say here, particularly in his elliptical references to a constitutionally exclusive judicial power. The legislature cannot punish a person by passing a statute that X shall be sent to prison—that would violate the bill of attainder clause; from that it is easy to develop a rule that punishment has to follow a judicial determination that the accused committed a previously defined crime. Schauer was correct that the "essentials of the judicial process" include an exclusive power to "find the defendant guilty or not guilty" but it was less clear that there is exclusive judicial authority to find "a lesser in-

cluded offense," or "to dismiss the action *in toto*," or especially "to strike
. . . multiple counts or charges prior to conviction." If Schauer meant
only that the power to punish rests on finding the underlying facts true
beyond a reasonable doubt through a judicial process, he was correct.
That would appear to be the most likely interpretation because in the
next paragraph he rejected the attorney general's argument that as Burke
had admitted a prior narcotics conviction, the trial court had no authority to strike the prior. Schauer disposed of this contention by saying:

*Whether [striking a prior] constitutes error must be resolved in any partic-
ular case upon the record in that case. The admission, conceivably, could
have been inadvertent, mistaken, or deliberately false; it is, at most, evidence which must be considered in the judicial process.*

And then Schauer held, as noted earlier, that the prosecution by failing
to object had waived any opportunity for appellate review of the striking
of the prior in Burke's case.

In order to sustain Judge Regan's striking of the use of a gun charge
in *Tanner*, Tobriner extracted from *Burke* a judicial rationale or premise
that mandatory statutory language is insufficient to deprive the trial
court of power to strike an allegation; the legislature must do so explicitly. *Burke* certainly did not hold that; it may be doubted that Schauer
even said so in dicta. In many ways *Burke* and *Tanner* were quite different. As Clark later pointed out, the prosecution protested striking the
use charge in *Tanner* and properly appealed the issue as had not been
done in *Burke*. Furthermore, there was no ambiguity in the evidence
that Tanner had used a gun; he admitted it in testimony and the jury so
found. The sole reason given by Regan for striking the use of a gun
charge in *Tanner* was that he thought not doing so would result in an
inappropriately harsh sentence; the record in *Burke* was silent as to why
the trial judge had stricken the charge of a prior conviction and it could
have been that the judge considered the evidence of a prior conviction
insufficient. Probably the trial judge in *Burke* had a purpose similar to
Judge Regan's in *Tanner*, but Schauer could, albeit somewhat disingen-
uously, assume a different purpose since the record was silent on the
point and, in general, a trial court will be presumed to have acted properly if any lawful reason can be imagined that would sustain its result.

The other case Tobriner relied on, *People v. Dorsey*, was a 1972 case
from the San Diego–San Bernardino Court of Appeal.* Dorsey shot and
killed a member of his family as part of a family quarrel; he was convicted
of second-degree murder and the jury found that he had used a firearm
in the commission of the crime. Presiding Justice Robert Gardner gave

* People v. Dorsey, 28 C.A. 3d 15 (1972).

only these facts in his opinion, but it is plausible that the conclusion of second-degree murder resulted because the killing was done in the heat of passion. The trial judge, J. Steve Williams, at the time of sentencing indicated that he would, if he could, strike the allegation that a gun had been used because of Dorsey's clean background, but he thought penal code §12022.5 prohibited him from doing so. Section 12022.5 provided:

Any person who uses a firearm in the commission or attempted commission of . . . murder . . . upon conviction of such crime, shall, in addition to the punishment prescribed for the crime of which he has been convicted, be punished by imprisonment in the state prison for a period of not less than five years.

In Gardner's view, the issue in *Dorsey* was whether the "shall" in §12022.5 overrode the authority of the trial court in §1385 to strike a use charge in furtherance of justice.

Gardner's discussion of this issue is not long, and unlike Kane, Clark and Tobriner, Gardner wrote clearly. If for no other reason than to prove that judges can write coherently on this subject, his opinion is worth quoting:

Thus we have had approval of the striking of an admitted prior for sentencing purposes (Burke), of an entire charge after a guilty verdict (Howard), of an entire charge to avoid an unnecessary trial which would presumably result in a concurrent sentence (Mowry), and the complete avoidance of the provisions of Penal Code §12022.5 in a plea bargain situation (Flores). The distinction between those situations and the instant one in which the court desires, as part of its sentencing responsibility, to dismiss a use of a firearm allegation strikes us as a distinction without a difference. . . .

Mandatory, arbitrary or rigid sentencing procedures invariably lead to unjust results. Society receives maximum protection when the penalty, treatment or disposition of the offender is tailored to the individual case. Only the trial judge has the knowledge, ability and tools at hand to properly individualize the treatment of the offender. Subject always to legislative control and appellate review, trial courts should be afforded maximum leeway in fitting the punishment to the offender.

Our holding in this case means simply that if the trial judge after hearing the case and reading the probation report feels that society needs the protection of the mandatory additional five years incarceration provided for under Penal Code §12022.5, that court may allow the finding to stand. If, however, the trial court finds that allowing such a finding to stand would be counter-productive to the eventual rehabilitation of the defendant and that such additional incarceration is neither necessary nor desirable in the handling of that particular offender, that court can strike the finding. We can see no social, moral or legal impediment in the striking of such an allegation in a proper case.

If the legislature intends that the provisions of Penal Code §12022.5 not be subject to dismissal, it could and should so indicate.

Tobriner seized on the last paragraph and exalted it to a principle that the legislature had to use explicit language if it wished to deny trial courts the power to strike the use of a gun charge—a questionable extension of Gardner's rationale. Gardner had argued that sound policy and long tradition encouraged individualized punishment and he was not going to assume a legislative intention to depart from that practice without clearer evidence than the single word "shall" in §12022.5. But the "use a gun, go to prison" law could easily be shown to be an intentional departure from the tradition of tailoring punishment to the offender. The governor, for example, when he signed the bill issued a statement that said:

By signing this bill, I want to send a clear message to every person in this state that using a gun in the commission of a serious crime means a stiff prison sentence. Whatever the circumstances, however eloquent the lawyer, judges will no longer have discretion to grant probation even to first offenders. This may not rehabilitate nor get at the underlying causes but it will punish those who deserve it. The philosophy of this bill is based not on sociology or Freudian theory, but on simple justice. Recent events underscore the appropriateness of swift and sure punishment for those who use guns to commit crimes.

Mandatory sentencing may be unwise but rehabilitation of the offender as the overriding objective of incarceration had, as noted earlier, been coming under increasing question. When Gardner wrote his *Dorsey* opinion in 1972 the rehabilitative ideal was still dominant in California law; in 1976 the legislature passed the determinate sentencing law. The 1975 "use a gun, go to prison" statute could be seen as the initial movement of the pendulum toward punishment rather than rehabilitation as the legislature's conception of the principal objective of imprisonment. Gardner could well have deplored the new thinking, but it is hard to believe that he would have ignored it or regarded it as unworthy of discussion.

Tobriner's supplemental conference memorandum spoke only in the narrowest technical terms. Unlike Gardner he made no effort to relate the issue to other stages in the criminal process or to the underlying policies of the legislature. Tobriner's only point was that the legislature had not used explicit language, a formula he said *Burke* and *Dorsey* required—a very broad reading of *Burke* and almost certainly a misinterpretation of *Dorsey*. It was not, in short, a very good argument, but taken as argument it was unexceptionable. But was that appropriate for a summary conference memorandum on the issue of whether the Supreme Court should hear argument in *Tanner*? It is hard to answer yes unless Tobriner viewed the court's mission as reviewing the wisdom of legislative enactments. If Tobriner started from the premise that the "use a gun, go to prison" law was bad policy (and thought a majority of his colleagues would agree) then the task was to develop a plausible argument to reach that result. Only in this way is Tobriner's seemingly perverse reading of *Burke* and *Dorsey* in his supplemental conference memorandum comprehensible.

But even assuming that Tobriner's objective was only to show that he could write a superficially plausible opinion evading the effect of the "use a gun, go to prison" law, he was imposing mightily on his colleagues. No one on the court in 1977 had been there when *Burke* was decided and few, if any, could have been familiar with the Court of Appeal decision in *Dorsey*. To make a balanced judgment on his premises his colleagues would have had to read those opinions or take Tobriner's statement of *Burke* and *Dorsey* on faith. At the least, a fuller and more neutral exposition of these cases was called for.

Tobriner's Calendar Memorandum

With the aid of the Clark and Tobriner conference memorandums, the *Tanner* case was discussed by the justices at the Wednesday conference of November 2, 1977. There is no public record but Clark testified that all but he and Richardson voted to hear *Tanner*. Following the court's usual practice, since Tobriner had prepared a prevailing supplemental conference memorandum, he was given responsibility for writing the calendar memorandum due to be circulated to his colleagues at least ten days before oral argument. Tobriner was a little tardy: his calendar memo was dated January 31 though oral argument in *Tanner* took place on February 6.

Tobriner's calendar memorandum opened, "In this case we must determine whether . . ."; up to the last paragraph ("Accordingly, I tentatively conclude that the [trial court's] judgment should be affirmed"), the memo took the form and tone of a judicial opinion. As will be seen, some changes were made after oral argument but they were relatively minor—a sentence here and there in the text, some new and enlarged footnotes. That California justices routinely prepare opinions before oral argument was known prior to the commission proceedings, but lawyers had never before seen a conference memorandum and they were told that calendars were just tentative first drafts of opinions. To call Tobriner's calendar memorandum a draft opinion would be misleading: it was a finished document with no awkward phrases, incomplete citations, or other rough spots normally associated with first or even second drafts.

Many lawyers are offended by the court's practice of writing opinions before argument, which seems to reduce oral argument to a meaningless gesture. What is the point of arguing to a court that has already written a final opinion and has psychologically committed itself by that act? Of course, only one of the seven justices on the court has gone that far, but the presence of a proposed opinion must influence all the justices to some extent.*

Justice Robert Thompson of the Los Angeles Court of Appeal in an article in the State Bar Journal urged that the calendar memo should be made routinely available to counsel before oral argument.† By so doing, he argued, the oral argument would be given a new and revitalized function by giving counsel an opportunity to shoot at the tentative conclusions reached by at least one member of the court, rather than speaking about the case at large without any knowledge of what issues were of central concern to the judges. Although he was speaking of his court, rather than the Supreme Court, Thompson's concept could be employed at the Supreme Court level as well. The idea was favorably received by many lawyers, but not by many appellate judges. The opposing position was that exposing the calendar memorandum to public view would constrain and inhibit the candid expression of doubts and questions—much the same kind of arguments that underlie the concept of a judicial privilege. That argument is badly undercut if all calendar memorandum are like Tobriner's in *Tanner.* Tobriner was writing a final opinion for public consumption from the very beginning, and an ideal calendar memorandum of that nature would be one that survived oral argument and posthearing conference without a single change as the opinion of the court. If the calendar memorandum was intended to be made public from the outset, there is no reason why it should not be released as tentative before oral argument.

In terms of content, although Tobriner's calendar memorandum was much longer than his conference memo it added very little in the way of new argument. The core was the same:

In the absence of an explicit statutory directive that the legislature had intended to eliminate or restrict the trial court's general power to strike under section 1385, the Burke *Court concluded that the statute should not be so construed.*

He repeated this assertion eight times, seven times using the word "explicit." About half of the memorandum was a statement of the facts and

* For one thing, if only four justices voted to grant a hearing, it would be hard on those who so voted to desert their colleague who has prepared what amounts to a final opinion. Switching sides after argument would make work for a badly overburdened court. The system thus subtly pressures the justices to vote "correctly" on the merits at the petition for hearing stage.
† Thompson, One Judge and No Judge Opinions, 50 Cal. St. Bar J. 476 (1975).

a largely irrelevant exposition of various uses that had been made of the §1385 power to dismiss before the "use a gun, go to prison" law was passed.

Tobriner did pay more attention to the statute and rules about statutory interpretation than he had in his conference memorandum. For example, the triumvirate of *Burke, Dorsey,* and *Howard* * decisions, Tobriner said,

had made it quite clear that no matter how "mandatory" the terms of a sentencing provision appear, such a provision would not be interpreted to curtail a trial court's section 1385 power to strike in the absence of explicit statutory language specifically and unambiguously restricting such power. It is a cardinal principle of statutory interpretation, of course, that in adopting legislation the legislature is presumed to have had knowledge of existing domestic judicial decisions and to have enacted and amended statutes in the light of such decisions as have a direct bearing on them.

The "cardinal principle" Tobriner invoked here is properly used only where it is plausible that the legislature had been aware of the judicial doctrines at issue. To suppose that anyone could have known the "explicit" rule that Tobriner found in *Burke* and *Dorsey* was absurd.

Tobriner acknowledged that the legislative history seemed to point to a conclusion different from his. He quoted a portion of the governor's statement (in a footnote) and commented:

The legislative history upon which the People rely unquestionably indicates—as indeed, does the explicit language of section 1203.06 itself— that one of the main purposes of the enactment of section 1203.06 was to curtail, in the specific instances enumerated in section 1203.06, the discretion to grant probation which had previously been accorded trial courts under section 1203. None of the legislative materials to which the People refer, however, makes any mention of the specific question presented by this case, namely whether the provisions of section 1203.06 additionally purported to eliminate a trial court's section 1385 power to strike priors or use allegations.

In this extraordinary passage Tobriner seemingly conceded that the legislature wanted to prohibit the granting of probation to all robbers found

---

* Tobriner took out of context the following passage from People v. Superior Court, (*Howard*), 69 Cal. 2d 491 (1969): "[T]he discretion of the judge [under § 1385] is absolute except where the legislature has specifically curtailed it." That was said to support his reading of *Burke* and *Dorsey*. Narrowly the issue in *Howard* involved the availability of an extraordinary writ to review a §1385 dismissal since no appeal by the prosecution was otherwise permitted. More broadly, the *Howard* opinion discussed the history of §1385, which originally was far less a grant of power to the trial court than a restriction on the power of prosecutors.

to have used a gun. But the legislative failure to conform to a formal judicial rule of construction resulted in Tobriner's approval of an evasive judicial maneuver that rendered the "use a gun, go to prison" law meaningless.

The Posthearing Conference and Tobriner's First Opinion

Shortly after the argument, probably on the same day, the court met in conference to consider and vote on *Tanner.* Again, only the somewhat conflicting recollections of the justices tell us how the vote came out. Tobriner, Mosk, and possibly Bird voted for Tobriner's calendar. Clark and Richardson were opposed and Newman and Manuel were somewhat uncertain.

Tobriner, in any event, was responsible for circulating the first opinion in the case. On March 3, less than a month after oral argument, he sent his colleagues a proposed opinion. In the Supreme Court an introductory memorandum from the author of the opinion on a "green sheet" indicates whatever changes have been made in prior circulations. The green sheet accompanying the first opinion in *Tanner* opened : "Although this opinion largely follows the calendar memorandum, I have made a number of additions" and Tobriner listed seven points of divergence.

Two items merit discussion. The green sheet said: "At Justice Newman's suggestion, I have included a new footnote . . . to distinguish the discussion of section 1385 in *Rockwell* v. *Superior Court.*" * The new footnote read:

In Rockwell . . . *we held that the legislature had not intended to permit trial courts to exercise discretion under section 1385 in sentencing defendants under a death penalty statute enacted subsequent to the United States Supreme Court decision in* Furman v. Georgia . . . *but in reaching that conclusion we relied heavily on pervasive indications that the legislature had believed that any such sentencing discretion would have rendered the statute unconstitutional under* Furman. *No similar evidence suggests that in enacting section 1203.06 the legislature thought that removal of* all *discretion from the trial courts was necessary to sustain the constitutionality of the enactment.*

Rockwell, a 1976 Supreme Court decision, ought to have been more of an embarrassment to Tobriner than the footnote suggests. The relevant issue in *Rockwell* was whether the trial court had power under §1385 to strike allegations of "special circumstances" required for imposition of the death penalty. In view of the detailed penal code provisions relating to how special circumstances were to be alleged and tried, Chief Justice

* Rockwell v. Superior Court, 18 C.3d 420 (1976).

Wright had no difficulty concluding that these provisions implicitly superseded any general §1385 power to strike "in furtherance of justice." This was true even though there was no "explicit" reference to §1385. *Rockwell* (1976) was thus inconsistent with what Tobriner said was the rule of *Burke* (1956), *Howard* (1969), and *Dorsey* (1972).

What is important here is that the change proves that Newman (or someone he was listening to) was reading materials outside the court generated conference and calendar memorandums circulated in *Tanner*. *Rockwell* was not mentioned in the Clark or Tobriner memos nor was it featured in the attorney general's brief.

Tobriner also added this sentence to the text of his opinion:

Thus . . . some legislators may well have been willing to accede to the seemingly inflexible provisions of section 1203.06 precisely because of their awareness that the section did not purport to remove all "safety valves" to further the ends of justice in a particular case, either through a trial court's exercise of the section 1385 power or by virtue of a prosecutor's exercise of his traditional discretion.

The green sheet did not indicate where this thought came from, but it was potentially a better argument than any Tobriner had made before. Sometimes a legislature knowingly passes laws that are intended to be no more than a gesture; traces of such a purpose, however, can usually be found. What starts out as a major effort is weakened through amendments until what is finally passed is a hollow shell of its former self. No such indications were present here. The various amendments made to the "use a gun, go to prison" law from the time it was introduced neither weakened the statute nor suggested any intention of gutting its original purpose. Most important, Tobriner cited nothing in the legislative history of the gun law that suggested any awareness of the possibility of evading the new law through continued use of §1385. In the absence of any such evidence in the legislative history, to conclude, as Tobriner did, that the legislature did not mean what it said because sometimes a legislature speaks hypocritically arrogated to the Supreme Court the power to ignore at will any attempt to change the law by statute.

Clark's First Dissent

A copy of the green sheet and Tobriner's first opinion went to every justice on March 3. The original of his opinion went into the court file —called the "box—in *Tanner* along with the only copy of the trial record and the original of the briefs of the parties and amicus curiae. The box acquired an inflated, almost mystical significance, during the course of the hearings. (At one point, passing down the aisle, Hufstedler dropped a piece of paper carefully folded into a small box on Connie Kang's lap labeled "Connie's box.") The circulation of the box is controlled by the secretary of the court, a deputy clerk, who physically moves the box from one chamber to another and keeps a record of every box's location at any time. The justices who testified before the commission said that they generally did not read opinions when they were circulated but waited until the box came to them before looking at any circulating opinion closely. That sounds wasteful but in fact it may be more efficient because of a quirk in California appellate practice: the California Supreme Court does not require or even ask for new briefs on the merits. The parties write full briefs on the merits of cases in the Court of Appeal. They also usually write a brief in support of or in opposition to a petition for hearing but that brief is supposed to focus on why the Supreme Court should hear the case rather more than on the merits of the Court of Appeal's decision. If a hearing is granted, no party has to file any other brief (although some do). If no other briefs are filed, and they frequently are not, the Supreme Court may well have only one or two copies of the full briefs on the merits which were filed in the Court of Appeals. If so, a justice will have in his or her chambers only copies of the briefs on petition for hearing, the conference and calendar memorandums and such notes as the justice may have made during oral argument. Reading the proposed opinion without being able to check points against the briefs or record may thus be more frustrating than useful.

If any justice at the posthearing conference indicates a disposition to dissent, the secretary of the court is instructed to send the box (with the proposed majority opinion in it) first to the likely dissenter. Under the court's internal rules he or she has forty-five days in which to prepare a dissenting opinion. The purpose of the forty-five-day rule is to give the remaining five justices the benefit of both opinions when the box gets to their chambers. Accordingly, the secretary delivered the *Tanner* box to Clark's chambers on March 3. Clark did not make the 45-day deadline and on April 17 he "passed" the box to Richardson. This loan of the box, which to an outsider seems a pointless formality, apparently had no purpose other than to evade the forty-five-day rule. Two weeks later, on May 2, Clark circulated his first proposed dissent, the effect of which was to take the box away from Richardson and send it back to Tobriner.

In terms of content, Clark's eleven-page dissent was not a particularly effective document. He opened with a screech:

I have before expressed concern when this Court, based on philosophical differences with legislative expression, has effectively modified or repealed a legislative enactment by judicial fiat. However, in no other instance has the majority so flagrantly disregarded legislative prerogative and the separation of powers doctrines as in this case.

By repetition judges have so debased phrases like "judicial fiat" and "flagrant disregard" that lawyers, at least, read them as meaning little more than "I disagree." As Manuel later showed, Clark could have written a quiet opinion in *Tanner* that made his points more powerfully than the extreme rhetoric he used.

Clark also could not let a debater's point pass without making it. His handling of *Burke* was typical. He made much of the fact that in *Burke* the trial court had struck a prior conviction whereas in *Tanner* Judge Regan had struck the finding that a gun had been used. Though one case did involve striking a prior, the other a use, that was not the important distinction between them. The central difference got lost: the single word "shall" in *Burke* was, in context, ambiguously mandatory, whereas in *Tanner*, as Tobriner admitted, no comparable ambiguity surrounded the legislature's purpose.

Clark's vision of relevant data was quite limited. He purported to give a brief history of probation in California, but his history began in 1923 and cited no sources other than California statutes and cases. Clark showed that probation was a legislative creation and that sometimes in the past, as with the "use a gun, go to prison" law, probation had been prohibited for certain classes of offenders. His argument would have been more forceful if it had been put in a larger framework of time and space. Theories of criminal punishments and how to implement them have undergone several waves of reform. Until very recently, they were the product in large part of legislative rather than judicial creativity. Three points could be drawn from such a historical overview: (1) penological policy has shifted dramatically and therefore what is today thought best will not likely be so regarded in the future; (2) the legislature has been attentive to this subject and has for the most part been the institutional leader of reform; and (3) only the legislature is capable of comprehensively implementing shifting policies. The logical conclusion: the court should be especially alert to follow, not obstruct, legislative policy as it emerges.

Clark's opinion concluded with a brief recitation of some items of legislative history—the legislative counsel's summary of the gun use bill, a similar summary prepared by the staff of the Senate Judiciary Committee, a letter from Deukmejian (then a senator) to the governor urging him to sign the bill, and the governor's statement on signing the bill—that Clark considered relevant and unambiguous indications of legislative intent. Summoning these sources was not unusual, but their use and proper interpretation later became the focus of Newman's opinion on rehearing.

In summary, Clark's dissent was unimaginative and undistinguished. It was ineffective as a piece of argumentation largely because of its shrillness. Given that when he wrote it Clark had some reason to hope that he might get a majority of the court since Newman and Manuel were, so far as he knew, still somewhat uncertain, Clark might plausibly have aimed his opinion at persuading his colleagues rather than speaking, as he appeared to, primarily to an audience outside the court—the press and the public.

Bird's Separate Opinion

When Clark's dissent was circulated on May 2, the box returned to Tobriner, as was normal under the court's practice, on the theory that he might wish to modify his opinion in response to the dissent. Tobriner held the box for three days but made no changes in his opinion and okayed what he had earlier written. The box then moved to Richardson, who signed Clark's dissent on May 10. Mosk signed Tobriner's opinion in a day. Manuel approved Clark's dissent after two weeks on May 24. Newman signed Tobriner's opinion on May 30. At that point each opinion had three signatures. If Bird spent, as her colleagues had, about a week to decide which opinion to sign, the case would have been ready for filing during the first week in June, roughly four months after the case was argued and five months before the election. Had Bird signed Tobriner's opinion then, there would have been a brief howl from law enforcement figures and the legislature might well have amended section 1203.06 to reverse the result before they adjourned. In any event, the *Tanner* case would have been at most a blip in California history.

Instead, Bird chose to write a separate opinion, which she circulated to her colleagues on July 11. Undoubtedly it did not take Bird six weeks to produce five pages; she and her staff must have been working on other matters for much of that time. Arguably *Tanner* should have been pushed toward the top of her priority list since as of May 30 she alone was holding up the filing of *Tanner*. But without knowing what else was on Bird's agenda during those six weeks, it is impossible to fault her on this point.

The extraordinary thing about the chief justice's opinion was the ground she took. In the California constitution a separation of powers clause (article III, section 3) provides that the executive, legislative, and judicial powers of the government are separately vested in the governor, the legislature, and the courts and that "persons charged with the exercise of one power may not exercise either of the others except as permitted by this Constitution." Analytically that says nothing without a definition of legislative or judicial powers, which courts in general have been most reluctant to do. Bird's separate opinion, however, said that the decision on whether to put Tanner on probation was a judicial power that could not be restricted by the legislature. She relied principally on a 1970 California Supreme Court case, *People v. Tenorio*, for this conclusion. In order to understand *Tenorio* it is necessary to look first at *People v. Sidener*, a Supreme Court decision that *Tenorio* overruled.

Both cases involved a statute enacted as part of a nationwide reaction to the growing traffic in illegal drugs. Throughout the nation extraordinarily severe punishments were imposed on drug offenders, especially repeating offenders. California did not escape the public clamor for legislation of this nature and one California bill passed at the time, in addition to imposing harsh minimum prison terms on narcotics recidivists, also prohibited a trial court from striking allegations of prior narcotics convictions unless the district attorney made a motion to that effect. The validity of this statute requiring the prosecutor's consent first came before the court in 1962 in *Sidener*, and Traynor, then an associate justice, wrote an opinion for the majority of the court sustaining the statute.* Traynor's opinion is worth attention since in many ways it epitomizes the California court at the height of its powers and contrasts sharply with *Tenorio*, decided only eight years later.

Traynor opened his opinion in *Sidener* by putting the particular statute in broad context—this was only one statute dealing with the problems of criminal recidivism—and putting the question first in historical terms. He noted that since the organization of the state the power of a trial court to strike criminal charges had been regarded as derivative from the prosecutor's common law power to enter a *nolle prosequi* plea, the effect of which is to abort a criminal prosecution once started. He cited cases from England and more than a half dozen of the early states before concluding:

The phrase "judicial power" cannot reasonably be given a meaning that it has never before been thought to have in this or any other state to invalidate an act of the legislature. Courts are not the only public agencies constitutionally empowered to determine the punitive consequences of recidivism.

But Traynor did not stop with this conclusion. "History alone," he wrote, should not control modern problems of governance and he went on to consider whether treating the power to strike as an exclusively judicial power would make sense in the general context of criminal procedure:

A court may feel that the punishment prescribed by the legislature for a recidivist narcotics offender is too severe or that by dismissing one or more charges punishment can be imposed that would better serve to rehabilitate him. . . . The fact that prior convictions are now given greater weight than they once were does not distinguish them from the host of other considerations of penology that are not given greater or lesser weight than they once were or compel the conclusion that their punitive effect is for

* People v. Sidener, 58 C.2d 645 (1962).

the courts alone. Like premeditation or malice aforethought in homicide or bodily harm in kidnapping, prior convictions have been made operative facts for the determination of punishment. Every day prosecuting attorneys exercise broad powers in this respect. It is they who decide what crime is to be charged or if any crime is to be charged. . . . It would exalt form over substance to hold that broad constitutional principles of separation of powers . . . permit vesting complete discretion in the prosecutor before the case begins, but deny him all such discretion once the information is filed.

There are innumerable facts other than commission of the crime itself that may have far more bearing on the punishment imposed than prior convictions. If not only their existence but their effect must be determined solely by courts, the indeterminate sentence law and the legislative restrictions on probation must fall. The indeterminate sentence law has been sustained, however, on the theory that a conviction carries with it judicially determined liability for the maximum sentence and that any remission from that maximum may be determined by an administrative agency . . . subject only to limited judicial review.

Sidener was not a great Traynor opinion. No new ground was broken and his opinion contained no insights or analysis of startling originality. But *Sidener* was typical in its approach. Traynor looked outside California for historical sources and recognized that accepting the invitation to invalidate this statute would have radiating implications inconsistent with existing law—notably the indeterminate sentence—and obstructive of future legislative reform. Finally, Traynor was characteristically reluctant to use the constitution to vindicate his view of wise policy even though it is safe to assume that he deplored the harsh effect of the new law.

Justice Schauer dissented in *Sidener* and there is little doubt that his view of the law's constitutionality was driven by his intense dislike of the draconian penalties the legislature had imposed on narcotics recidivists. He was profoundly offended by the statute's failure to distinguish between the "culpability of a non-addict possessor-pusher on the one hand, and on the other, that of the sick and impoverished addict, who, desperate for the drug, pushes it in order to possess it." He could not resist describing the obvious horror:

Under section [11532] a youth—exactly 21 years old (with one prior charged and found true)—who shared a marijuana cigarette with another youth one day younger, would be absolutely required to actually serve 10 years in prison. With the prior struck the youth . . . might be paroled after a minimum of five years served. In its application to a situation of this kind [the recidivist] statute, aside from being unconstitutional, is a throwback toward an abandoned concept of penology. It works at cross-purposes with the indeterminate sentence plan and objectives.

The narcotics recidivist statute was, as Schauer said, a return to terrorism as a deterrent strategy, and his basic argument was that punishments so severe could not be made to depend on the unreviewable discretion of the prosecutor without violating the due process clause of the federal Constitution. As an alternative ground, Schauer was prepared to hold that giving the prosecutor what amounted to a veto over a judge's power to strike a prior conviction represented an invasion of exclusive judicial power by the executive.

The same statute came before the court eight years later in *Tenorio,* and this time Justice Peters for a unanimous court overruled Traynor's opinion by adopting Schauer's alternative ground that the statute violated exclusive judicial power.* The core of his decision appeared in these sentences:

The judicial power is compromised when a judge, who believes that a charge should be dismissed in the interests of justice, wishes to exercise the power to dismiss but finds that before he may do so he must bargain with the prosecutor. The judicial power must be independent, and a judge should never be required to pay for its exercise.

That is good rhetoric if analytical nonsense. Judges have no roving commission to do right; they decide issues that for the most part are framed for them by the parties. Nonetheless it is easy to understand the pull on the court. By 1970 the strategy of terror was an obvious failure and productive of much injustice, especially in connection with marijuana, by then considered to be no more addictive than alcohol. *Tenorio* was just such a case. Eight years earlier Tenorio had been convicted of possession of a small quantity of marijuana; he was up this time on a second charge of possession of marijuana and if his prior conviction were not stricken he would spend a minimum of two years in prison. The true basis for the *Tenorio* decision was revealed a few years later in a law review article by Chief Justice Wright:

Now, only eleven years after [the narcotics recidivist statute] was adopted, numerous blue ribbon commissions have recommended that drug abuse be treated as a medical rather than a penal problem, and the President's special commission has reported that 24 million Americans have experimented with marijuana. The possibility that long prison terms would be mandated for great numbers of individuals convicted of drug offenses was

* People v. Tenorio, 3 C.3d 89 (1970).

not even considered at the time of the adoption of the statute embracing
the increased penalty.*

Judge Regan had mentioned *Tenorio* at the time of sentencing Tanner, and *Tenorio* was the principal basis for Bird's separate opinion in
Tanner. The cases obviously differed in one important respect: the "use
a gun, go to prison" law absolutely prohibited probation if a robber used
a gun and did not condition the availability of this option on the prosecutor's consent. Nonetheless, Bird pulled language out of Peters's opinion to support her conclusion that the power to strike the charge of a
prior conviction (or, in *Tanner,* the use of a gun) was a judicial power
that could not be restricted by legislative action.

This Court held [in Tenorio] *that "the power to strike priors is an essential
part of the judicial power" vested by the Constitution in the courts. Therefore, the exercise of that power could not be overruled or curtailed by a
representative of another branch of government. The basic premise of* Tenorio *was necessarily broad: "When the decision to prosecute has been
made, the process which leads to acquittal or sentencing is fundamentally
judicial in nature."*

Only a first-year law student could so wrench a case out of context.
Schauer in *Sidener* had conceded:

*Certainly the legislature could absolutely prohibit the granting of proba-
tion or parole to anyone convicted of a narcotics (or any other) offense; it
could order any minimum and maximum terms it sees fit, or a mandatory
life term without parole or even a nondiscriminatory death penalty for
such offense.*

In *Tenorio,* along the same lines, Peters had said:

*Even if the legislature could constitutionally remove the power to strike
priors from the courts, it has not done so, but rather has purported to vest
in the prosecutor the power to foreclose the exercise of an admittedly
judicial power by an appropriate judicial officer.*

Bird also relied on two cases, *Cortez* and *Ruiz,* that followed *Tenorio.*
The only issue discussed in the opinion in *Cortez* was the procedural
rights of Cortez, who had been convicted in the interval between *Sidener*
and *Tenorio* without the trial court's having considered, since it thought

* Wright, *The Role of the Judiciary,* 60 CALIF. L. REV. 1262, 1266 (1972).

it could not, the possibility of striking a prior narcotics conviction.* The effect of striking the prior would have been at least to reduce Cortez's minimum term and, the court assumed, also possibly to make him eligible for probation. Drawing an analogy to the rights of criminal defendants at a probation hearing, the court decided that Cortez was entitled when he appeared for the second time before the court for sentencing to be present and to have the aid of counsel. Bird noted that the applicable statute at the time prohibited probation where a prior narcotics conviction had been found, just as the "use a gun, go to prison" law prohibited probation to robbers who used a gun. Reading backward, as it were, she inferred that the court in *Cortez* had held that there was an inherent and constitutionally based judicial power to strike a prior narcotics conviction thereby making a person eligible for probation. Although technically different, *Ruiz* involved the same problem in another context.†

Bird's reading of *Cortez* and *Ruiz* was extreme; essentially what the court thought it was doing in these cases was jerry-building a process to accommodate its own "mistake" in *Sidener*, which would give to prisoners the same possibility of shorter prison terms or probation that it had given to Tenorio. The attorney general made no argument that probation was unavailable, though a good response could have been made to such an argument, as Clark later did, that §1203 in its form at the time authorized striking the prior for purposes of putting a defendant on probation.

Although difficult to explain, there is a chasm between Traynor's opinion in *Sidener* and Peters's opinion in *Tenorio*. Traynor did not consider it unconstitutional for the legislature to be unwise or even stupid; to put it another way, he thought judges had only a very limited capacity to correct injustice. Peters in *Tenorio* and Schauer in dissent in *Sidener* knew they were reaching for their result but felt compelled to do so because they thought the statute outrageously harsh. Still, they clearly explained why they thought the law dreadful and tried to limit their opinions to the narrowest grounds possible.

There is yet another gulf between Bird's first *Tanner* opinion and what Peters and Schauer did. There is no hint in Bird's opinion that she recognized that she was stretching already overextended case law. Nor did she bother to argue that the "use a gun, go to prison" law was inherently unfair. On the surface her approach was purely mechanical: here is constitutional doctrine; here is the statute; without reference to policy or history or anything else, the result of unconstitutionality followed remorselessly. Bird professed to be as policy neutral as a Holmes or Traynor while manipulating case authority in ways that would have

---

* In re Cortez, 6 C.3d 78 (1971).
† People v. Ruiz, 14 C.3d 163 (1975).

made Peters or Schauer blanch, and she did so without their or Wright's redeeming sense of proportion. Perhaps judges can be forgiven for reaching to overturn ten years of legislatively mandated harsh sentences for marijuana offenses; it does not follow that robbers using guns, even emotionally disturbed ones, deserve similar judicial gymnastics.

Clark Twice Revises His Dissent

Bird's first *Tanner* opinion circulated on July 11. The box accordingly returned to Tobriner, who took two weeks before okaying his first majority opinion without change. Normally the box would have gone to Clark next, but he was attending a European seminar at the time, so it passed instead in four days through the chambers of Mosk, Richardson, Manuel, and Newman. None signed Bird's opinion; all adhered to their former positions although they probably expected to see the case at least once more since Clark was likely to revise his dissent in response to Bird.

Having nowhere else to go, the box moved to Clark's chambers on July 28; he turned to *Tanner* when he got back to the office on Sunday, August 6. A week later, on August 15, Clark circulated what he called a new dissenting opinion, but he noted on the cover sheet that his first opinion had "been changed only to the extent necessary to address issues raised in the recently filed concurring opinion of the Chief Justice." He toned down his first paragraph somewhat and inserted five new pages responding to Bird's opinion.

The new material opened by making the obvious point that *Tenorio, Cortez,* and *Ruiz* were insubstantial support for the chief justice's proposition that the power to put someone on probation was an inherent judicial power that could not be restricted by legislative action. Clark then tried to establish a distinction:

The concurring opinion relies further only on statements in Burke *and* Tenorio *that it is the judiciary which is constitutionally vested with power to adjudicate and determine penalty enhancing factors. There has never been any doubt that the courts are exclusively vested under the separation of powers doctrine to make adjudication of any issue affecting the penalty to be imposed in a criminal proceeding. But that is not the issue here. Our concern is with the penalty to be imposed once the adjudication has been made by the court. "[S]ubject to the constitutonal prohibition against cruel and unusual punishment, the power to define crimes and fix penalties is vested exclusively in the legislative branch" [quoting a 1970 California Supreme Court decision]. "[T]he legislative branch of the government has the power to declare that in certain . . . cases, probation may not be granted. The exercise of such power in no way impinges upon the jurisdiction of the judicial branch of government. It does not impair, restrict nor enlarge upon the jurisdiction of the courts. The function of the courts is to determine the guilt or innocence of an accused. What disposition may thereafter be made by way of penalty is for the legislature to determine"* [quoting a 1951 Court of Appeal opinion].

Clark cited only California cases, all since 1950. The distinction he was making was scarcely a modern California invention; John Marshall said it nearly 150 years earlier, "It is the legislature, not the court, which is to define a crime and ordain its punishment." *

At the end of the quoted paragraph Clark added a footnote of major importance to this account:

Surely it must be understood that if the concurring opinion is correct, then large portions of the Penal Code—those fixing penalties for the crimes defined—constitute acts in excess of constitutional limitations and would be void. However, the Chief Justice herself has in another recent expression [Caudillo I] *acknowledged that it is the legislature in which the Constitution vests authority to prescribe criminal penalties.*

Bird thought Clark's citation of *Caudillo* was designed to embarrass her in the coming election, and this belief was a major cause of the ensuing breakdown in working relations between Clark and Bird. As will be seen, the "political" charge was communicated through staff to Clark, who responded quickly. Ten days after his first revised opinion he produced a second revision. The cover sheet said:

The staff to the Chief Justice has requested that our citation to People v. Caudillo in footnote 8 of the dissenting opinion be deleted. The reasons given for deletion are that Caudillo *is inapposite and that its use is "politically motivated."*

I reject both the request and the unfortunate reasoning. Rather, I now expand the discussion of Caudillo to show that it is clearly apposite* moving it from footnote to body.

* "However, the Legislature is the proper governmental body to consider whether rape per se is a basis for the enhancement of punishment and to so provide if they deem it appropriate." (People v. Caudillo . . . , conc. opn., Bird, C.J.).

In the text of his opinion Clark added his footnote and the following:

In determining the existence of great bodily injury as a penalty enhancing factor in rape, the Chief Justice stated: "[P]ersonal repugnance toward these crimes cannot be a legitimate basis for rewriting the statute as it was adopted by the legislature. It is precisely because emotions are so easily called into play in such situations that extra precaution must be taken so that this Court follows the legislative intent and not our own

---

* United States v. Wiltberger, 18 U.S. (5 Wheat.) 76, 95 (1820).

predilections or beliefs. This Court has no choice in this matter. It must accept the legislature's intent despite any personal feelings to the contrary. . . . [T]he legislature is the proper governmental body to consider whether rape per se is a basis for the enhancement of punishment and to so provide if they deem it appropriate."

How the controversy over the citation of *Caudillo* exploded became a major focus of the testimony before the commission and will be covered in chapter six. Underlying Bird's belief that Clark's purpose was political, however, was the premise that his citation of her *Caudillo* opinion was irrelevant to the issue Clark was discussing in *Tanner.* This is a fairly easy question of law or logic since the issue was not correctness or even persuasiveness but simple relevance. Was Clark's citation of Bird's opinion in *Caudillo* fair argument for the point he was making? The answer has to be yes, although Clark did not make his point as explicitly as he might have. Bird conceded in *Caudillo* that the legislature alone had the power to define criminal behavior. Clark thought the power to define criminal behavior included specifying the punishment for the proscribed conduct. There was nothing Humpty-Dumptyish about Clark's usage on this point and his understanding, although not explicit, could easily be inferred from his reference to the penal code sections "fixing penalties for the crimes defined." Given his understanding that the legislative power to define criminal conduct included the power to prescribe the punishment, Clark's citation of Bird's opinion was appropriate. Her *Caudillo* opinion was scarcely the best citation he could have found, but its logical connection to the point he was making was indisputable.

Manuel's Separate Dissent

The hullabaloo that arose over Clark's citation of *Caudillo* was a principal cause of delay after circulation of Clark's second revised *Tanner* dissent. The box returned to Tobriner on August 25 and stayed there until September 21, when, without either okaying or changing his opinion, Tobriner passed the box to Manuel. On October 24 Manuel issued a separate dissent. His opinion was short and almost elegant in its simplicity and directness, so much so that it, like Gardner's opinion in *Dorsey,* deserves to be quoted at length:

I dissent.

Penal Code section 1203 generally provides procedures for the grant of probation. Subdivision (d) of section 1203 sets a limit on those eligible for probation: "[E]xcept in unusual cases where the interests of justice would best be served if the person is granted probation, probation shall not be granted to any of the following persons: . . ." Subdivision (e) pro-

vides that "[w]hen probation is granted in a case which comes within the provisions of subdivision (d), the court shall specify the circumstances indicating that the interests of justice would best be served by such a disposition."

Section 1203.06, by contrast, provides that "[n]otwithstanding the provisions of Section 1203: (a) Probation shall not be granted to, nor shall the execution or imposition of sentence be suspended for, any of the following persons: . . ."

A comparison of sections 1203 and 1203.06 makes two things very clear: (1) The legislature knows how to use language giving the trial court the power to grant probation in the interest of justice to otherwise ineligible defendants; and (2) the legislature does not wish those who come within the classification of section 1203.06 to be placed on probation at all.

It is a fundamental rule of statutory construction that courts should ascertain the intent of the legislature so as to effectuate the purpose of the law. . . . The lead opinion seeks to escape the reach of section 1203.06 and the rule of construction here noted by stating that because section 1203.06 does not in explicit terms restrict a trial court's power to strike under section 1385, the provision cannot be interpreted to preclude a trial court's exercise of such power in light of People v. Burke. . . . I find this approach to be entirely too mechanical. In enacting section 1203.06 the Legislature intended to bar probation as a sentencing alternative to defendants within its scope. The failure to mention section 1385 obviously was not intended by the Legislature to allow use of that section to negate the clear purpose of section 1203.06.

If Cortez is correct in stating that "one of the paramount purposes of a motion to strike priors is to make the defendant eligible for probation" . . . the Legislature must have intended to bar the striking of a use finding as a means to circumvent the operation of section 1203.06. Only that interpretation gives effect to the purpose of the statute.

The net result of the lead opinion is that section 1203.06 accomplishes nothing. If People v. Burke presents an impediment to the implementation of the legislative purpose, as evidenced by the plain language of the statute and its legislative history, then to that extent Burke should be overruled.

I find it clearly within the power of the Legislature to restrict the granting of probation . . . and I conclude that the Legislature has done so in section 1203.06.

Why Manuel wrote this opinion, and in particular whether he was induced to do so by Bird or Tobriner, was a major issue before the commission. Had Manuel simply signed Clark's opinion, as he had done twice before, the only remaining task would have been for Tobriner and

Bird to revise their opinions. Ultimately that took Bird and Tobriner about six weeks (four of them after the election). Six weeks from when Tobriner passed the box to Manuel would have had the *Tanner* case filed during the week before the election. It follows in a mechanical sense that Manuel's decision to write a separate dissent was one reason why the *Tanner* decision was not filed until after the election. It thus becomes important to ask whether Manuel added anything to the debate: did he take a distinguishably different position from Clark's that justified writing his opinion?

Manuel did not add much but he made a few points beyond avoiding the use of intemperate language. First, he said clearly, as Clark had not, that the "net result of [Tobriner's] opinion is that section 1203.06 accomplishes nothing." Second, without attempting to penetrate Schauer's opaque language in *Burke,* Manuel simply overruled the decision to the extent that it was inconsistent with his view.* Third, he disposed of the chief justice with a single sentence; citing a case, Manuel noted that the legislature could prohibit the use of probation if it so wished. These are not inconsequential, but the difference in tone between his opinion and Clark's alone justified Manuel's separate effort.

Tobriner's Postelection Revisions

Manuel's opinion circulated two weeks before the election. Two weeks after the election Tobriner circulated a revised lead opinion in *Tanner.* By then, of course, the fact that the opinions in *Tanner* would be studied with unusual care by the press and others was obvious, and all postelection revisions undoubtedly were made with the notoriety of *Tanner* very much in mind.† The green sheet Tobriner wrote explaining his changes to his colleagues is thus worth quoting in full:

> At our conference of October 25, 1978, our Court denied a hearing in two cases which raised issues related to those presented by this case. . . . Those cases suggested to me the desirability of including in the Tanner opinion a new discussion of the application of this decision to other cases now pending on appeal which may arise in a significantly different context than the Tanner case itself. I have added a footnote . . . to address the question.

---

* Traynor had, as a matter of fact, already done the same thing in his opinion for the court in *Sidener.* Whether the overturning of *Sidener* in *Tenorio* revived the disapproved language in *Burke* is debatable.

† Michael Willemsen, Tobriner's research attorney, so testified about the revisions he drafted for Tobriner's opinion after election day: "I wanted to also write something in the opinion that would be easier to comprehend to the lay public because this was now after the election [day] articles and I thought the *Tanner* opinion might have a wider audience than it did before."

I have also added an important paragraph to footnote 18 responding to Justice Manuel's dissent. Finally, I have taken this opportunity to make a few minor additions. . . . I have likewise changed the language but not the substance of the introduction.

The last sentence was less than candid.

First, Tobriner added a paragraph to the introduction that could scarcely be called nonsubstantive:

Although we confirm the trial court's power to strike a charge of the use of a gun, the courts should use this power most carefully. The public has a compelling interest in deterring illegal use of guns, and the threat of certain punishment is an important deterrent. Thus the trial court should employ its power to strike a use of a gun charge only in extraordinary cases.

Clearly, this paragraph was designed to make the decision more palatable to the public and legislators, but where did Tobriner find statutory warrant for this restriction on the trial court's §1385 power to strike the use of a gun charge? The authority certainly could not have been the "use a gun, go to prison" law because Tobriner's whole opinion was based on his conclusion that without explicit amendment to §1385 there could be no implied revision.

Second, Tobriner added a couple of sentences to his introductory paragraphs that were obviously responsive to Bird's separate opinion:

Finally, we do not preclude further legislative action. If the legislature believes that the compelling importance of deterring illegal use of guns can be promoted only by denying trial courts the power to strike charges of the use of guns under section 1385, it has the power specifically to enact such legislation.

Arguably this dictum was implicit in his earlier opinion. Making the point directly would improve the opinion's chances of being accepted by the public (or at least by editorial writers); it also had the effect of isolating Bird as the only justice contending that trial courts had a constitutionally uncontrollable power to place criminal defendants on probation.

The footnotes Tobriner added need not detain us. He did, however, add a new paragraph to his conclusion that became the theme of Newman's opinion in *Tanner II:* "A myriad of interpretations of section 1203.06 cannot substitute for a single legislative statement that [§1203.06] should overcome [§1385]." Whether Tobriner previously had made this argument is not wholly clear.

Bird's Postelection Revisions

Tobriner's revised opinion circulated on November 21; in a day Clark revised his opinion, making only those changes necessary to correct quotations and cross-references to the lead opinion. The box went through all the other justices, reaching Bird on November 29. By then, of course, Bird had called for an investigation and had offered to open up the court files in *Tanner* to the commission. She thus knew that she was writing not only for her colleagues but also for the commission.

On December 15 she circulated a new opinion, sixteen typed pages, as opposed to her original five. The cover sheet noted:

Since I have not had the box since July 11th to permit me to respond to the points raised in the new dissent and the two revisions thereof by Justice Clark, the dissent by Justice Manuel, and the revisions in the plurality opinion by Justice Tobriner, I am now for the first time responding to all these opinions.

After restating the homilies she had earlier made in the Proposition 13 case, Bird asserted that the slogan "use a gun, go to prison" was a myth for three reasons. First, probation was not prohibited for some crimes not included in §1203.06. Most of the crimes listed, however, such as lynching and mayhem, carried more serious penalties than robbery with a gun and the perpetrators of these crimes were unlikely candidates for probation. Second, in a footnote, Bird noted that some youthful criminals, narcotics addicts, and mentally disordered sex offenders might be sent to institutions other than the state prisons—at best a quibble. Her third reason was more substantial but less clear than her assertion that the prosecutor has complete discretion to charge or not to charge the use of a gun. Section 1203.06(b)(1) states: "The existence of any fact which would make a person ineligible for probation under subdivision (a) *shall be alleged* in the information or indictment." Comparable language in statutes relating to allegations or prior convictions had been said to be mandatory and the California District Attorneys Association urged that all special allegations be utilized at the charging stage.* Nonetheless, a district attorney could fail to allege the use of a gun, the effect of which failure would be to make probation available to the convicted offender. Not charging use of a gun where the evidence indicated that a gun had been used would not necessarily be lawful, but no one would be in a position to object. Bird's remaining point was correct: the prosecutor either could accept as part of a plea bargain a striking of the use of a gun allegation or could move after trial to strike a charge found true if the attorney general had been correct in his concession at oral

---

* Uniform Crime Charging Standards, II(c) (1974).

argument of *Tanner*.* This review sought to prove the irrelevant fact that the "so-called mandatory gun law is not mandatory at all."

Part two of Bird's opinion repeated her earlier opinion with some amplification and revision. However, she added a few paragraphs and footnotes at the end directly responsive to Clark that seemingly shifted her ground somewhat. Bird now seemed to be saying that everything that preceded the entry of judgment was constitutionally "adjudication" and therefore immune from legislative control. Given that the penal code consists in large part of sections purporting to regulate criminal procedure, her proposition, although often repeated, lacked credibility.

The polite thing to do with Bird's *Tanner* opinion is to look the other way and change the subject. The propositions of law she asserted cannot be taken seriously and it is hard to believe that in less tense times she would not have backed down. It does not follow that she wrote her separate opinion for the purpose of delaying the release of the *Tanner* decision until after the election; indeed, the fact that she issued her opinion in July would support the opposite conclusion. But something was seriously wrong with her judgment and something more serious was amiss if Bird had become so isolated that neither her colleagues nor anyone on the court staff could protect her from foolishness.

Bird's redrafted opinion circulated to the other justices on December 15 and the case was publicly released on December 22, the Friday before the Christmas weekend.† Cynical reporters assumed the timing was designed to give the release the minimum possible public exposure in the press. No evidence supports this charge, and considering the complexities of the process, it would have been hard for Bird or anyone else to maintain the level of control necessary to insure press coverage of *Tanner* on the worst news day of the year—the Saturday before Christmas.

The publicly known circumstances surrounding the grant of a rehearing and the oral argument have already been discussed. Unfortunately for present purposes, Hufstedler introduced no internal memorandums concerning the grant of a rehearing or the preparation of the *Tanner II* opinions, which were filed four days before the commission began hearing testimony on June 18. The commission, of course, was interested only in the narrow issue of whether the release of *Tanner I* had been delayed past election day for political or other improper

---

* Neither Bird nor Tobriner used this fact to analogize *Tanner* to *Tenorio*. The attorney general's concession made the situations quite parallel since under his view of §1203.06 only if the prosecutor moved to strike the use allegation could the trial court strike a finding that a gun had been used. Such a conclusion would lead to the suggestion that the statute be saved by denying the prosecutor the power to move to dismiss after trial, with the result that the "use a gun, go to prison" law would be even more rigid in application. Perhaps for this reason Bird and Tobriner left this can of worms closed.

† People v. Tanner, 151 Cal. Rptr. 299 (1978) (rehearing granted).

reasons. The purpose here is somewhat broader: to learn as much as possible about how the California court functioned as a collegial institution resolving particular cases. To that end, even without the confidential internal documents, something can be learned from the opinions in *Tanner II.**

The factor that precipitated most of the changes in the opinions was Mosk's turnabout. As a consequence, Clark wrote a majority opinion rather than a dissent. Mosk and Richardson joined him without writing separately, as did Manuel, so that the latter's former brief dissent was eliminated. Tobriner substantially revised his *Tanner I* majority opinion as a dissent; Bird added an introduction to her former dissent but did not otherwise change it. Newman wrote the only wholly new opinion, an opinion that was longer than any but Tobriner's opinion in *Tanner I.*

The Opinions in Tanner II: *Clark*

Clark's opinion for the majority in *Tanner II* was a toned down and reorganized version of his dissent in *Tanner I* that borrowed somewhat from Manuel's earlier opinion. In particular, Clark stated more clearly than he had originally his (and Manuel's) best point: unless the new law restricted the 1385 power to put a defendant on probation, the "use a gun, go to prison" law was a "nullity." Clark supported this conclusion, as he had earlier, with references to the legislative history, including the governor's statement.

One thing in his opinion was new and surprising: Clark did not compel Harold Tanner to serve a prison term, as his interpretation of the "use a gun, go to prison" law seemed to require. Clark explained:

[T]*he uncertainty arising from the rule of law, resulting in the trial court's erroneous disposition, has created an unusual burden on defendant and a dilemma for this Court. Simply put, is it not unfair to require Mr. Tanner to now serve a second term for his criminal act?*

Tobriner, Bird, and Newman all cited this disposition as being inconsistent with Clark's holding and asserted that the majority was finding an authority to dispense a prison term for itself that it had denied Judge Regan—a charge not altogether fair or accurate. Regan thought a prison term for Tanner excessive in view of his crime and character; Clark held that Regan had no authority on such grounds to put Tanner on probation. It does not follow that Regan or anyone else lacked power to eliminate the prison term for other reasons, especially reasons that were, as Clark noted, the product of the judicial system's own indecision and confusion. Forcing Harold Tanner to go to prison when he had completed a jail sentence more than two years earlier would be unreasonably

* People v. Tanner, 24 C.3d 514 (1979).

harsh, especially since it was the prosecutor's appeal not Tanner's and nothing Tanner had done had contributed to the two-year delay.

Newman was "saddened" that "four colleagues have not felt impelled to explain fully their reasons" for not agreeing with him. (Apparently, Newman regarded Clark's opinion as so conclusory as to be a nonexplanation, which is a little odd since Newman's opinion was also somewhat elliptical.) The only justice in the majority who might have needed to explain himself was Mosk. Why did Mosk switch sides? One possible reason, of course, was further to embarrass Bird by keeping public attention on the *Tanner* case. That is hard to credit since the court's and Mosk's reputations also were at stake. More nobly, perhaps Mosk thought it was time to beat a strategic retreat else the court lose all credibility with the public and especially with the legislature. If such was his purpose, Mosk can fairly be criticized for being a little late. What few people noticed was that Mosk persuaded Clark, Richardson, and Manuel to change sufficiently to rescue about all that could be salvaged from the *Tanner* mess. The legislature was going to amend the "use a gun, go to prison" law to modify "explicitly" §1385 very soon; the senate had already done so and the Assembly Criminal Justice Committee could drag its feet for only so long. Thus, robbers who used guns were destined shortly for a mandatory prison term no matter which way Mosk voted in *Tanner*. In the meantime, however, Harold Tanner at least would stay out and there would be an opening for some others whose cases were on appeal to continue on probation. Thus, in a coldly realistic sense, Mosk won all that could be achieved by persuading Clark, Richardson, and Manuel to accept what was presumably his suggestion that Tanner be allowed to remain at large though the "use a gun, go to prison" law was affirmed.

The Opinions in Tanner II: Newman

The only new opinion in *Tanner II* was Newman's. The press picked up and stressed a few sentences:

The politicization of this proceeding after the summer of 1978 became phantasmagoric. A shrill, clamorous campaign—inspired and nurtured by experienced, well-financed and posse-like "hard on crime" advocates— has had a still incalculable but dismal impact on the judicial process in California.

The use of arcane words like "phantasmagoric" is a stunt not without judicial precedent: Justice Felix Frankfurter similarly enjoyed displaying his erudition. At best this practice is in dubious taste in judicial opinions, dissenting or majority. It does, however, prove that Newman's opinion was written at least in part by him and not by a law clerk or research attorney.

In addition to dropping off some snappish footnotes obviously addressed to the commission,* Newman made several points worth mentioning.† First, he was properly offended at the irresponsible use of legislative history, most notably in the amicus brief filed on behalf of sixty-five legislators asserting in 1979 what their intention had been in 1975.‡The clerk of the court, probably at Newman's insistance,had written to all counsel in advance of oral argument asking for discussion of the "advisability of utilizing post hoc legislative declarations in litigation generally." The responses of counsel, however, were so thin that Newman thought it inappropriate to discuss the general problem.

Second, Newman performed the same function for Tobriner that Manuel had earlier fulfilled for Clark: he focused attention on Tobriner's best argument, which Tobriner had not made very clearly. To Newman, the critical language in the "use a gun, go to prison" law started with the phrase "notwithstanding the provisions of Penal Code Section 1203." Tobriner did not quote these words in his conference memorandum and, although he quoted them in his calendar memo and thereafter he apparently failed to recognize earlier that the phrase literally led to his result; that is, §1203.06 did not amend 1385. Newman pointed that out and also noted that since the "use a gun, go to prison" law had been passed the legislature had added sections following §1203.06 that opened with a more inclusive phrase: "notwithstanding any other provision of law." Furthermore, he cited instances predating the 1975 act in which the legislature had used comprehensive language that literally encompassed §1385. His argument was thus quite simple: the legislature knew how to accomplish the result the prosecutor contended for; it chose not to; therefore, it intended no change in the authority of trial courts, pursuant to §1385, to strike a use charge.

As Manuel said, the difficulty with this argument was that it rendered the "use a gun, go to prison" meaningless; if 1385 gave the trial court the power to strike a gun use finding "in furtherance of justice," then the prohibition against placing robbers who used guns on probation "in the interests of justice" was pointless. There was a way to harmonize the statutes and give some effect to both. The court could have said that

---

* Footnotes 4, 5, and 6.

† One of Newman's points was rather more clever than persuasive. Newman avoided the force of the Legislative Counsel's summary and the Senate Judiciary Staff summary of the bill by pointing out that the phrase "Notwithstanding the provisions of Penal Code Section 1203" was added by amendment *after* those summaries had been prepared. Although true, Newman slid over the fact that what became Section 1203.06 was, as introduced, part of Section 1203 itself. There was thus no need to say "Notwithstanding etc." if the restriction on probation was part of the same section and the interpretative problem would be identical: how to give some effect to the prohibition on probation without implying a modification of 1385?

‡ Many of those who signed the brief had not even been in the legislature that passed the "use a gun, go to prison" law.

the "use a gun, go to prison" law modified §1385 to the extent that the trial court was deprived of authority to place on probation an offender who used a gun because the trial court thought the offender's rehabilitation would be better achieved by probation than incarceration. Section 1385 would still have vitality in other contexts; for example, where the trial court thought the evidence that the accused had used a gun was insufficient, or where the plea bargaining process so demanded, and, possibly, as the attorney general had argued, where the prosecutor after trial moved to dismiss the use of a gun finding. The last paragraph of Newman's opinion suggests strongly that he saw this possible resolution, but he rejected it for reasons undisclosed and with inexcusable crypticness:

At first glance [§1203's] stress on "the interests of justice" seems like [§1385's] requirement that trial court action be "in furtherance of justice." Analysis of the legislative and judicial histories helps prove, though, that the aims as well as the applications of the two sections have differed significantly.

The Opinions in Tanner II: *Tobriner*

The bulk of Tobriner's opinion repeated his *Tanner I* opinion with some additions borrowed from Newman on legislative history. In place of the statement of facts, however, Tobriner substituted an ill-tempered attack on Clark's opinion during the course of which he finally got around to answering explicitly the Manuel-Clark argument that an implied retrenchment of §1385 was necessary to avoid nullifying the "use a gun, go to prison" law:

Prior to 1975, section 1203—the general probation statute—included a provision specifically giving courts power to grant probation in an "unusual" gun case; trial courts apparently accorded the "unusual case" provision of section 1203 a more expansive interpretation than the legislature thought appropriate and in 1975 the legislature eliminated the "unusual case" provision of section 1203 for such cases. That legislative action unquestionably evinced an intent to reduce the granting of probation in gun use cases, a legislative policy decision that certainly has not been lost on trial courts and that has been and will continue to be reflected in a sharp decrease in the granting of probation in such cases. The legislative disapproval of the trial courts' pre-1975 probation practice, however, is by no means irreconcilable with a legislative decision to leave the trial courts' section 1385 power intact; the legislature may well have desired to disapprove the trial courts' quite liberal pre-1975 probation practice without completely stripping such courts of their traditional power to strike allegations or findings in the truly extraordinary or exceptional case.

This passage expanded and clarified the paragraph Tobriner added to his opinion after the election. But Tobriner was now saying, as he had not earlier, that the "use a gun, go to prison" law would accomplish something. Had his pre-election day opinion survived, there was no reason to suppose that trial courts would change their practices, and it is doubtful that much would have happened as a consequence of his opinion in *Tanner I*. With this paragraph, the gap between Tobriner and Clark sharply narrowed, and they possibly could have agreed on some formula defining the extent to which the "use a gun, go to prison" law implicitly restricted the trial courts' §1385 power to strike the use of a gun charge. If anyone tried to bridge that gap he failed; more likely no one made the effort since by then positions had become quite hardened.

The Opinions in Tanner II: *Bird*

Bird reprinted her *Tanner I* opinion in *Tanner II*, adding only a few disparaging paragraphs at the beginning. Her new language was cliché-ridden—"carve a compromise of expediency," "made the defendant a pawn in this process," "the majority give short shrift"—and she included a passage, perhaps aimed at Mosk, that did little to encourage public esteem for the court:

Have we forgotten that justice is not a matter of expediency? It is not a cloak in which we can wrap ourselves when we find its protection most convenient. It is, rather, a matter of principle, plain and simple. If we hope to maintain a legal system characterized by justice, we cannot defer its application as to even a single case that comes before us. *

She also added a few paragraphs that were in effect a gloss on her earlier opinion, making it clear that her conception of exclusive judicial power related to steps in the judicial process before the judgment. Apparently, in Bird's view the legislature had no power to regulate some aspects of criminal procedure although she never explained which powers of a trial court were immune from legislative interference, why, or how.

The Lessons of Tanner

The opinions of Tobriner and Clark were improved by the collegial process: Manuel helped Clark, Newman helped Tobriner, and as a con-

---

* This passage Bird took from her own speech delivered to the Association of Trial Lawyers in August, 1978.

sequence the difference between Clark and Tobriner was narrowed. Seemingly, Clark and Tobriner made very little effort to understand what the other was saying and it was not until Manuel and Newman sharpened the statement of the issue that the gap between them began to close. By the end Clark and Tobriner were within hailing distance of each other, and if circumstances had been different or if they had been different kinds of people, perhaps a substantially unanimous opinion for the court might have emerged.

One reason why that did not happen may be simply a matter of expectations—no one anticipated agreement and therefore neither looked for avenues of reconciliation. Certainly Clark and Tobriner started out in an adversarial posture; their conference memorandums were unabashed arguments for different conclusions and their first exchange of opinions was mainly a volley of debater's points that tended to obscure rather than clarify the real areas of difference.

The power of quiet statement as a mechanism for resolving differences is well illustrated by Manuel's dissent. It is tempting to wonder what would have happened in *Tanner* if Manuel had been asked to prepare a calendar memorandum that neutrally stated the contentions of both sides. Quite possibly, a unanimous opinion might well have followed.

For the justices to achieve unanimity presupposes that they do not conceive their role to be reviewers of legislative policy or, to put it another way, that a policy result is not the beginning point of analysis. The adversary nature of the court's internal process may exaggerate rather than mute the importance of the result on the deliberative process. It is natural for judges to look for arguments that will support the result they would wish to reach as a matter of policy. If, as seemingly Tobriner and Clark did, a justice thinks of his role as that of an advocate, he is likely to get psychologically committed to a result before he has carefully weighed the competing contentions. It turns into a game: "Can I get the votes for my side?" rather than "What is the best solution for this dispute after giving full consideration to all arguments?"

The adversary nature of the court's internal process also encourages the development of coalitions. Richardson and Clark tend to vote together, as do Bird, Tobriner, Mosk, and Newman, with Manuel tending toward Richardson and Clark much of the time. Such divisions are a natural consequence of starting with results and working backward toward legal arguments. If the justices started with the assumption that their task in preparing a calendar memorandum is to come to a conclusion acceptable to all, rather than just a majority, the contentious tone of their memorandums would be substantially muted. Both Clark and Tobriner, however, seemed to view their opinions as negotiating documents in which positions were stated at the extreme with the expectation or hope of winning the minimum number of votes necessary to prevail.

Although exchanging written memorandums is not the only way justices can communicate with each other, the paper record that makes up the literary history of the *Tanner* case strongly supports the hypothesis that the justices worked in substantial isolation from each other. Aside from one mention of a suggestion from Newman to Tobriner, there is scarcely a trace of collaborative effort. Bird's separate opinion embodied the most extreme form of isolation, but none of the justices showed much interest in cooperative efforts. The workload problem may encourage this tendency: each justice confronts a mountain of work to be done in his or her chambers, and constructive criticism of the work of others must sometimes seem a wasteful indulgence. If so, something of considerable importance has been lost.

Jefferson's opinion in *Caudillo* and Bird's separate opinion in *Tanner* are examples of what can happen when justices stop thinking they have a responsibility for the work of their colleagues. Multimember appellate courts reflect the belief that a collective decision is apt to be better than a solo performance. The California Supreme Court appears to have altered, probably unintentionally, the concept of collective decisionmaking. Instead of thrashing out the best possible joint product with the give-and-take necessary to such a process, the justices work together principally by voting up or down the recommendations or opinions produced by a solitary justice. The collective work within the court is done not among the justices but rather between each justice and his or her staff in a context where ultimate authority of course rests with the justice. It is easy to see how Bird and perhaps Clark found working with their staffs more congenial than negotiating with their colleagues, but the institutional product of the court as a whole was thereby substantially diminished.

THE FACTS IN *FOX*

The *Fox* case arrived at the Supreme Court with a very thin record. For roughly thirty years the Los Angeles city hall had been illuminated on Christmas Eve, Christmas Day, and Easter with a cross made by an arrangement of lighted windows. In the 1970s it was similarly illuminated on Eastern Orthodox Easter and it had also sometimes been lit up with the symbols of the Heart Fund and the Easter Seal Fund during the contribution drives of those organizations. On December 23, 1975, Dorothy Fox brought suit against the city seeking an injunction to prohibit displaying the cross on the ground that doing so violated the freedom of religion clauses of both the federal and California constitutions.

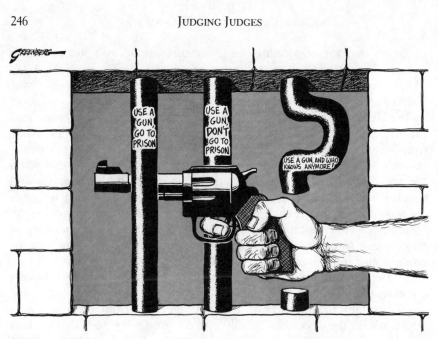

Cartoon by Steve Greenberg, Editorial Cartoonist for the *Daily News of Los Angeles*. © *Daily News of Los Angeles*.

Fox was represented by Alexandra Leichter, a woman of Hungarian descent, who passionately believed in the separation of church and state. The city council annually passed resolutions shortly before Christmas and Easter to permit the display of the cross, and Leichter thought these resolutions showed clearly that the council's purpose was religious. She was confident of winning when she moved for a temporary restraining order in the Los Angeles superior court. Leichter was wrong; the trial court denied her motion. She also had not anticipated a blast of adverse publicity touched off by the *Los Angeles Herald Examiner*, which asked in headlines on Christmas Day, "Is the Cross Too Much to Bear?" Leichter received hundreds of letters on the case, most of them hostile, some of them vicious.

After the motion for a temporary restraining order was denied, the matter was set for hearing on Leichter's alternative motion for a preliminary injunction that would prohibit the display of the cross while the case was pending. That motion, heard after Christmas, was decided on the basis of Fox's affidavit and some responsive declarations from city officials. The standards for granting a preliminary injunction are variously stated but come down to a weighing of several factors: how likely is the plaintiff to prevail after a full evidentiary trial; will the plaintiff or others suffer irreparable harm if the injunction is denied; and how serious will the adverse effects be on the defendant or others if the injunction is granted? Frequently the parties are content to let the hearing on the preliminary injunction suffice for purposes of making a record; here it was unclear whether either Fox or the city was satisfied with the record they had made.

Typically, trial courts in California dispose of motions for a preliminary injunction with a brief order supported by findings of fact that are often initially drafted by prevailing counsel. Sometimes the trial judge will write a brief opinion in lieu of findings explaining his or her reasoning. Superior court Judge Norman Dowds did more than that in *Fox;* he wrote a careful opinion discussing at length both the factual inferences he was drawing from the declarations and the law on the subject. He was moved to this effort because he recognized that the law concerning governmental display of religious symbols was fragmentary and unclear. The thrust of his decision was that the city council's purpose in displaying the cross was religious rather than secular and he thought that impermissible.

Unlike most intermediate steps in litigation, the issuance of a preliminary injunction is an appealable order. The city appealed Judge Dowds's order to the Los Angeles Court of Appeal and the case landed in division five before a panel composed of Justices Kaus, Ashby, and Stephens (the same panel that decided *Caudillo I*). On June 1, 1977, Stephens filed an opinion for himself and Ashby reversing Dowds. Kaus dissented, adopting as his own Judge Dowds's opinion for the trial court.*

Both opinions treated the case as if the issue presented were to be resolved by analysis of U.S. Supreme Court cases interpreting the federal Constitution and specifically the establishment clause of the First Amendment prohibiting government from "making any law respecting an establishment of religion." A series of cases in the U.S. Supreme Court in the 1970s involved in one form or another state aid to parochial schools; the opinions in these cases drew some exceedingly subtle lines. For example, the loan of textbooks to students in parochial schools was held permissible,† but funding for instruction in secular subjects in religious schools was prohibited.‡ On the other hand, funding for construction of buildings on the campuses of church sponsored institutions of higher edcuation was constitutional.** A "three-pronged test" had emerged from these cases: first, the government activity must have a

---

* 139 Cal. Rptr. 180 (1977) (officially depublished).
† Board of Educ. v. Allen, 392 U.S. 236 (1968).
‡ Lemon v. Kurtzman, 403 U.S. 602 (1971).
** Tilton v. Richardson, 403 U.S. 672 (1971).

secular as opposed to a religious purpose; second, it must have a primary effect than neither benefits nor inhibits religion; and third, the activity must not result in excessive "entanglement" of government with religious affairs.

Dowds and Stephens agreed about the test; they disagreed as to its application. Dowds thought the purpose of displaying the cross was religious and discounted as "self-serving" the resolutions adopted by the council, which claimed that the display was a celebration of the holiday season and, with respect to Eastern Orthodox Easter, a "symbol of peace and good fellowship toward all mankind on an interfaith basis, particularly towards the eastern nations in Europe." Stephens was disposed to take these statements as truthful particularly since he could find no evidence that displaying the cross benefited religion as a practical matter. The lack of benefit, Stephens thought, was shown by the failure of anyone (other than Fox) to protest the display in thirty years. Stephens could see no essential difference between the display of the cross and the motto "In God We Trust" on currency. Dowds, on the other hand, drew the opposite inference from the request by an Eastern Orthodox priest for a display of the cross on Eastern Orthodox Easter, a request the city council had granted. Dowds also thought that reviewing requests of this nature necessarily involved an excessive entanglement of government in religious matters.

Both Dowds and Stephens discussed each prong of the three-pronged test. Technically, Dowds need not have done so since if the display violated any of the prongs it was unconstitutional. Nonetheless, it was sound practice for a trial judge in Dowds's position to make a finding on each prong because making an adverse finding on only one might result in a reversal that would require a remand for the trial court's determination on the other prongs. In order to sustain the display, Stephens had to discuss all three, as he did. Both Dowds and Stephens recognized that government sponsored display of religious symbols was different from financial aid to religious schools. However, there had been a few cases in other states involving display of religious symbols that had used the three-pronged test. Early in Stephens's opinion he acknowledged the novelty of the issue in California, saying that it was "one of first impression in this jurisdiction."

No doubt the openness of the issue influenced the California Supreme Court to hear the case, a decision announced on August 18, 1977. Newman had joined the court only a month earlier, and if he wrote the conference memorandum in Fox, it must have been one of the first he prepared. (Hufstedler did not introduce the conference memorandum in Fox before the commission and it is possible that someone other than Newman wrote it.) Newman prepared the calendar memorandum in Fox.

Newman's Calendar Memorandum

In tone and content Newman's calendar memorandum in *Fox* differed entirely from Tobriner's in *Tanner.* It was not a draft opinion and it raised questions rather than resolved them, as the following passage indicates:

The case is complicated for us because the Court of Appeal disagreed with the trial court as to exactly what the facts are. As a result the issues, I believe, are: (1) Might the plaintiff succeed were there a trial; (2) Was there justification for the preliminary injunction?

Newman quoted extensively from both Dowds's and Stephens's opinions to demonstrate their conflicting resolution of the facts and noted that Stephens's conclusion—the display did not violate the establishment clause—necessarily precluded the plaintiff's introducing additional evidence on "(1) the practical effect of the illumination, (2) the benefits that may have been conferred, and (3) possible danger of divisiveness." It is not clear that Leichter wanted to introduce evidence on these points; she thought she had a winning case on prong one because the religious purpose of the city council seemed obvious in the resolutions it had adopted. If her view was correct, an improper religious purpose was a great deal easier to prove than such ephemeral concepts as a primary effect or benefit to religion. As a volunteer donating her time and effort to what she considered a worthy cause, Leichter understandably wanted to prove her case as economically as possible. On the other hand, Newman's desire for a full understanding of the facts was in a well-established tradition; novel constitutional issues should be decided only on as full a record as possible. As Newman said in his memorandum: "Are not more facts and fewer guesses needed? . . . When the facts have been found properly, after trial, then we and other courts can decide the exact impact of the state Constitution's new words."

Finally, Newman doubted that a preliminary injunction was justified even if it was "reasonably probable that the plaintiff would prevail"; though technically "irreparable," the injury to the plaintiff was not very serious. As Newman phrased it: "It seems fair to inquire whether and how the trial court here balanced the equities of numberless people whom the cross irritated against the equities of numberless others who may have regarded it as glorious." Accordingly, Newman concluded: "It is recommended that we reverse the order granting a preliminary injunction and remand the case to the trial court for further proceedings consistent with the views expressed herein."

Newman's calendar memorandum can fairly be faulted for being a little thin in its discussion of the law on the establishment clause. On the other hand, unlike Tobriner in his calendar memorandum, Newman apparently expected his colleagues to study the opinions of Stephens and Dowds in addition to reading his memorandum. Those opinions set forth adequately the relevant U.S. Supreme Court cases, as well as the few cases from other jurisdictions involving displays of religious symbols. A few sentences in Newman's memorandum suggested that perhaps the case should be decided on the basis of the California constitution rather than the federal. Newman noted that the establishment clause in the California constitution had been added in 1974 (as part of the constitutional revision process) and "when we interpret [the California establishment clause] we should of course seek guidance from decisions that interpret the same words in Amendment I of the United States Constitution."

"Guidance" is not the same as taking the U.S. Supreme Court's decisions as binding authorities, and the California court could give words in the California constitution a more expansive definition than the U.S. Supreme Court had given the same words in the U.S. Constitution. That Newman was leaning in this direction is suggested by his mocking quotation of the syllabus of a recent U.S. Supreme Court case reflecting the difficulty faced by that Court in applying the three-pronged test.*

Newman did not discuss explicitly either in his calendar memorandum or in his later opinion the relative merits of resting a decision on the state constitution, but he doubtless had pondered this subject at length since he had been an active member of the California Constitutional Revision Commission. Resting a decision on the state constitution has one virtue as a matter of judicial administration: because the U.S. Supreme Court's jurisdiction is limited to federal questions, a decision based on the state constitution could not be reviewed in Washington and, as a consequence, the litigants would be spared the delay and expense of a possible appeal to the U.S. Supreme Court. On the other hand, resting a decision on the state constitution has a ratchet effect that appears somewhat unfair because an appeal to Washington is cut off only if the state constitution is construed to be more protective than the U.S. Constitution. To put it another way, the city of Los Angeles could not win the *Fox* case on a state constitutional ground; it could only lose.

Newman's Opinion

The possible significance of the state constitution emerged at oral argument. Not surprisingly, counsel were not very well prepared to argue on the state constitution since every judge they had confronted to that point had been interested only in U.S. Supreme Court decisions. One

* Wolman v. Walter, 433 U.S. 229 (1977).

question in particular was raised that Newman had not mentioned in his calendar memorandum but which became the turning point of his opinion. The California declaration of rights, in addition to the establishment clause added in 1974, had from 1849 provided that "free exercise and enjoyment of religion without discrimination or preference are guaranteed." The First Amendment has a free exercise clause but there is no parallel language in the federal Constitution concerning discrimination or preference. United States Supreme Court decisions had put a gloss on the free exercise clause requiring governmental neutrality and particularly protecting against discrimination against religion or a particular sect, but, as Newman stated in his opinion, "preference is thus forbidden [in the California constitution] even where there is no discrimination. The current interpretations of the United States Constitution may not be that comprehensive."

Newman's opinion held that the display of the cross on city hall was an illegal preference under the California constitution. He circulated his opinion on December 2, 1977, sixty days after the argument. What persuaded Newman to alter his conclusion from the time of preparing the calendar memorandum is unknown. Possibly oral argument convinced him that a remand for a full trial was unlikely to be productive because Leichter did not want a retrial. Perhaps discussion at the posthearing conference or the process of preparing the opinion persuaded Newman that his position in the calendar memorandum was untenable. Regardless of the reason, it is notable that he reversed himself; this turnabout suggests that the tentative tone of his calendar memorandum accurately reflected genuine uncertainty.

Newman's opinion had four sections. The first section dealt with facts and quoted Dowds on three points: first, Dowds's finding that the cross was a symbol of the Christian religion and not, like Christmas trees or Santa Claus, a secular symbol of the holiday season; second, his finding that the cross displayed on city hall was visible for many miles in many directions; and third, Dowds's finding that the city council's purpose was religious despite disclaimers in some of its resolutions, particularly in connection with the display of the cross on Eastern Orthodox Easter.

The second section of Newman's opinion noted that the U.S. Supreme Court "has treated the Establishment and Free Exercise Clauses under various factual situations with perplexing diversity of views" and he cited a half dozen cases involving religious symbols, noting that they "reflect remarkably variant views." He concluded the section by stating: "Our case is marked by the location, size, and visibility of the Los Angeles cross, and also by the additional facts we discuss below."

The third section first observed that the California constitution prohibited a preference on behalf of religion and then asked: "Was there a preference here?" Newman went on:

The city hall is not an immense bulletin board whereon symbols of all faiths could be thumbtacked or otherwise displayed. . . . In the California Constitution there is no requirement that each religion always be represented. To illuminate only the Latin cross, however, does seem preferential when comparable recognition of other religious symbols is impractical. [A 1924 California case] declared re the Bible of King James, "If the Douai version and these other books (the Talmud, Koran, and teachings of Confucius) are not already in the library, we have no right to assume that they will not be added in the future." Librarians quite easily can offset a potential for preference, but a city hall tower is much less tractable than are shelves of a school library.

This passage appears to present the core of Newman's opinion.

The remainder of the third section and all of the fourth dealt with arguments presented by the city in defense of displaying the cross. Newman first disposed of the contention that thirty years of silence indicated no religious benefit on the ground that there "may be complex and troubling reasons why residents who are non-Christians have chosen not to" object to the display of the cross. "Easter crosses differ from Easter bunnies, just as Christmas crosses differ from Christmas trees and Santa Claus" was Newman's answer to the claim that the display had a secular purpose. The penultimate paragraph of his opinion is a little puzzling because Newman retreated somewhat from resting the case entirely on the California constitution:

On December 18, 1975, the council adopted a report that stated, "Your Committee has considered this and feels upon advice of the City Attorney's representative that the use of the cross is symbolic of the Christmas season and as such is not a religious service." Mere display of the cross is clearly not a religious service. By no means, though, should we infer that it is not action respecting an establishment of religion. Governments must commit themselves to "a position of neutrality" whenever "the relationship between man and religion" is affected [citing a U.S. Supreme Court decision]. To be neutral surely means to honor the beliefs of the silent as well as the vocal minorities.

Perhaps Newman was merely saying that his holding that display of the cross was an illegal preference was consistent with establishment clause cases. Indeed, his "preference" analysis and the second prong of the U.S. Supreme Court's three-pronged test differed little. Newman could have relied entirely on U.S. Supreme Court decisions and written an opinion coming to the same conclusion by holding that the primary effect of the display benefited the Christian religion. His opinion can be faulted for not discussing why he did not take this approach, and a sentence or two explaining why he had not might have deflected some of the criticism which followed.

Newman's concluding paragraph, "The case is remanded for appropriate further proceedings," was ambiguous only in the context of his calendar memorandum. His opinion held that it was not only probable that the plaintiff would prevail; it was certain. Therefore, no further trial was necessary. What remained was for the trial court to recast its preliminary order in permanent form and perhaps to award Leichter attorney's fees.

Richardson's Dissent

Newman's opinion circulated first to Manuel who signed it in a week, and then to Mosk, who approved it in a day. The box then moved to Richardson, who decided to prepare a dissent. Why it did not go first to Richardson, as *Tanner* went first to Clark, was never explained. It may have been because the secretary of the court was unaware of the intention of anyone to dissent. Perhaps Newman had so shifted his ground after conference that no one could be expected to know how his colleagues would react. Richardson passed the box after thirty-eight days, presumably to avoid the forty-five-day rule, and the box moved on to Tobriner who signed Newman's opinion in a day. The box moved next to Clark, who held it from January 17 until Richardson issued his dissent on February 9. Clark knew that Richardson was preparing a dissent and he may not have looked at Newman's opinion when the box first came to his chambers. Although the box was not with Richardson for the entire period, Richardson in fact took about as long to prepare his dissent as Newman had in writing his opinion.

Richardson's opinion was more than twice as long as Newman's.* For the most part, Richardson followed the reasoning of Stephens for the Court of Appeal. He dealt with Newman's state constitutional argument only briefly:

The majority, citing a "panoply of views" expressed in various opinions of the United States Supreme Court interpreting both the establishment and the free exercise clauses of the First Amendment of the United States

---

* Unfortunately for present purposes Hufstedler did not present to the commission the draft opinions in *Fox*, as he had with *Tanner*. He did note that Richardson's opinion was revised twice after it was first issued (as was Bird's later opinion). No change was made in Newman's opinion after its first circulation. Probably Hufstedler would have produced the initial drafts of Richardson's and Bird's opinions if significant substantive changes were made in any of them.

Constitution, elects to place its holding upon the substantially identical provisions of the California Constitution. . . . Given the similarity in language between the state and federal provisions, the same general standards should apply [citing a case called Mandel v. Hodges].*

The *Mandel* citation did not support Richardson's assertion. *Mandel* involved the validity of a traditional three-hour holiday for state employees on Good Friday. The San Francisco Court of Appeal said in that case that the establishment clauses in the two constitutions should be construed congruently, but it also specifically held that the holiday was in addition an illegal "preference or discrimination" under the California declaration of rights. Apart from misreading *Mandel*, Richardson did not otherwise comment on Newman's preference argument and devoted the remainder of his opinion to dealing with the U.S. Supreme Court's three-pronged test. Although his opinion was unresponsive to Newman's, it was unusually eloquent and evidently deeply felt.

The Chief Justice's Memorandum to Newman

With Richardson's dissent, the box returned to Newman on February 9. He okayed his opinion on the next day and in a week it passed through the chambers of Manuel, Mosk, and Tobriner, all of whom renewed their approval of Newman's opinion. The box went to the chief justice on February 16. At that point Newman had four signatures on his opinion and Richardson had dissented. Bird kept the box for a month before passing it to Clark; she signed neither opinion but sent the following memorandum to Newman to explain her position:

I agree with the conclusions reached in your opinion but I have some problems with the opinion itself.

First, the opinion does not set forth clear standards to be followed in these types of cases. This is especially critical when this court departs from a standard developed by the United States Supreme Court. Without something to take the old standard's place, a vacuum is created.

It is partly true that the courts have gone all over the map on these questions. However, as the dissent points out, there is a reasonably clear federal standard. The disagreement is in its application. Therefore, this court needs to be clear about the fact that it is using a state standard, why it is doing so, and most importantly, what the standard is. There is no clear statement phrased in terms of conduct that outlines what is and is not proscribed. In fact, there is no clear holding at all except that the trial court is affirmed.

I think your "preference" argument is a good one, but it needs to be clearer, since this case may spawn future litigation. In order to avoid the

* 54 C.A.3d 596 (1976).

result forecast by the dissent, of total separation of state and religion, there needs to be some statement why colored lights and trees and Santas are all right and crosses are not. State agencies need to know how far they can go in celebrating Christmas and Easter.

The opinion also fails to clarify the procedural problems raised by this case. The preliminary injunction is affirmed but it is not clear why. The trial court only said that plaintiff was reasonably likely to win or that the cross was probably unconstitutional. The opinion does not clarify who has the burden of proof on what point, and whether a finding of unconstitutionality is necessary before an injunction can issue. I think the court here has reviewed the evidence independently and concluded that the cross was unconstitutional on state grounds, but I'm not sure. The trial court used the language of the federal test and did not speak of preferences. Therefore, in view of the lack of a clear holding, I'm not sure what the court is doing. Was the trial court correct because the cross was unconstitutional? Or was it correct because plaintiff was likely to win? This could be inferred from the tentative nature of the opinion. If the case is remanded does the permanent injunction issue because the cross is unconstitutional? Or is there to be a hearing with more evidence? Can the City try to rebut the tentative conclusions of the majority or has it lost?

I am sorry but I must pass the box back to you, since I am unable to sign the opinion with these issues left dangling.

Newman wrote a response to Bird's memorandum but, consistent with his view that internal communications are privileged, he refused to disclose it to the commission, and the issue of whether the reply could be kept from the public was never resolved because Mosk's suit closed the hearings before Newman testified publicly.*

Bird's memorandum is worth attention even though we lack Newman's reply. Her tone of superiority was scarcely calculated to inspire a sympathetic response; it had all the warmth and helpfulness of a professor's caustic comments in the margin of a freshman term paper. But, apart from tone, were her comments otherwise warranted?

Her first point included several related items: she thought the standard should be clear "in these types of cases"; clarity was especially important when the state standard differed from the federal, particularly since "this case may spawn future litigation" and "state agencies need to know how far they can go in celebrating Christmas and Easter." These remarks suggest a remarkable conception of the function of an appellate

---

* Bird, presumably respecting Newman's claim of privilege, refused to disclose her copy of his memorandum, a consideration for Newman's rights not shown when she opened the court's records to the commission. Bird also successfully resisted disclosing a memorandum to her from one of her staff concerning Newman's opinion in *Fox.* Her counsel represented to the commission that the staff memorandum contained nothing bearing on the issue of delay.

court confronting a new and close issue of constitutional law. The traditional view is that courts should approach such matters gingerly and holdings should be stated as narrowly as possible lest the court's words be construed to foreclose in other circumstances lawful and appropriate conduct. Few cases better illustrate the dangers of loose language than some free exercise and establishment clause decisions of the U.S. Supreme Court in the 1940s. The academic literature had been savagely hard on the court for its careless language, and when the court finally got around to sustaining the legality of tax exemptions for church property, Chief Justice Burger had noted the "hazards of placing too much weight on a few words or phrases of the Court." Newman's opinion, whatever its faults, was very tightly tied to the facts of *Fox*. He held that a cross on the Los Angeles city hall represented an illegal preference and that was all. Newman's opinion carefully did not deal with religious symbols in general and quite clearly distinguished celebrations of holidays from governmental approval of the holy days of a particular religion or sect. Bird apparently wanted Newman to put up signposts all over the landscape indicating what was and was not permissible with respect to display of religious symbols if not church and state in general. Furthermore, Bird apparently assumed that Newman's preference standard was different from the federal, which Newman had not said. Underlying Bird's memorandum was a false belief that federal law was clear on the display of religious symbols. The "reasonably clear federal standard" Bird mentioned had been generated in cases involving financial aid to religious schools, and the U.S. Supreme Court might well reformulate its test in this different context.

Bird's second point, that it was unclear from Newman's opinion what the trial court should do after remand, was comprehensible in view of the procedural issues Newman had raised in his calendar memorandum, but no one unaware of his argument in that memorandum would be confused. There was authority for finally resolving constitutional issues at the preliminary injunction stage if it was impossible for the losing party to prevail after a full trial. Newman had referred to this in his calendar memorandum, and that such was now his view of *Fox* clearly emerged from his opinion.

Clark's Dissent

Bird sent her memorandum to Newman on March 16 and passed the box to Clark, the only justice up to that point other than Bird who had not signed either opinion. On April 10, Clark circulated an unusual, brief dissent. He concurred in Richardson's dissent but he did not discuss the substance of Newman's opinion, instead criticizing Newman's "failure to state either a definitive holding or a rationale."

Although similar to Bird's memorandum in its subject, Clark's dissent did not call for generous dicta on issues not presented. Clark was bothered by the tentativeness of Newman's holding that "to illuminate only the Latin cross . . . does seem preferential." Clark also protested Newman's failure to distinguish "displaying" the cross from "promoting" religion since Newman conceded that display alone was not necessarily improper. Finally, with Bird, Clark wanted to know what would happen on remand.

Clark testified before the commission that his dissent was not of the ordinary variety. Although its tone was sharp, it was not brutal and Clark reported that Newman had assured him that he was not offended by the dissent. What is odd is that Clark felt obliged to dissent. Why did not Clark write a private memorandum to Newman or perhaps talk to him rather than force the court to suffer the indignity of one justice's stating for public consumption that a colleague did not know how to write an opinion? Given Clark's concurrence in Richardson's dissent, Clark could not offer to trade his vote for some changes in Newman's opinion, but nothing prevented his suggesting changes even if he had no expectation of signing the opinion. By April, Newman had been on the court for six months; thus, he was still relatively new on the job and helpful criticism from an experienced colleague would not, to an outsider, have seemed untoward. Possibly Clark had tried to talk with Newman earlier but had failed to accomplish anything so that he now thought his only recourse was to humiliate Newman into altering his opinion.

Newman changed not a word in response to either Bird or Clark and his rigidity is equally troublesome. Bird and Clark were both wrong that the opinion was ambiguous as to what would happen on remand, but a sentence or two added to his opinion would have made it clear that Newman was holding that under no circumstances could the city win on retrial. That two of his colleagues found his opinion ambiguous should have induced Newman to make his meaning clearer. Furthermore, there was no obvious reason why Newman said "does seem preferential" rather than "is preferential." He might also have added a sentence or two, as Bird later did, explaining more fully why display of the cross on city hall was preferential.

Bird's Opinion

On April 10, the same day Clark circulated his dissent, Newman wrote a memorandum to Bird about *Fox* the content of which, as noted earlier, was never made public. Bird testified that Newman's memorandum convinced her that Newman "was from Missouri," by which she presumably meant he was not going to change his opinion to suit her wishes. Accordingly, Bird decided she would write an opinion of her own in *Fox*; pursuant to this plan, one of Bird's research attorneys, John Schulz, borrowed the record from the box in Newman's office on April

10. When Schulz returned the record on May 17, Newman passed the box, indicating that he was waiting for Bird's response to his memorandum. The box traveled quickly through the chambers of Manuel and Mosk and came to Tobriner on May 22. Bird testified that she asked Tobriner to hold the box as a subtle way of pressuring Newman to change his opinion, her theory apparently being that he would be apprehensive about losing Tobriner's vote and thus his majority. Tobriner held the box for almost three months before passing it to Bird on August 16, again without okaying Newman's opinion. On October 3, Bird circulated a proposed concurring opinion. Although the box was not with her for much of the time, Bird or her staff worked on her *Fox* opinion for about six months, roughly three times as long as either Newman or Richardson had taken for their opinions.

As might have been anticipated from her memorandum to Newman, Bird rested her opinion on every available ground and her opinion was quite long. Her first ground depended on article XVI, section 5, of the California constitution, which had not been invoked by Leichter in her pleadings or briefed thereafter by any of the parties. This section provides:

Neither the Legislature, nor any county, city and county, township, school district or other municipal corporation, shall ever make an appropriation, or pay from any public fund whatever, or grant anything to or in aid of any religious sect, church, creed, or sect, purpose, or help to support or sustain any school, college, university, hospital or other institution, controlled by any religious creed, church or sectarian denomination whatever.

That was a very tough provision that had, for better or worse, spared California some experiments with "secular" aid to parochial schools that had tormented the U.S. Supreme Court.* The obvious answer to any argument based on article XVI, section 5, in the context of *Fox* was that the amount expended was so small as to be inconsequential. As Richardson had observed: "While the record does not reflect the size of the annual budget of Los Angeles, I believe it fair to conclude that the ratio of $103 to the budget may sink from minimal to infinitesimal." Furthermore, no money flowed from the public coffers to any religious organization as a result of lighting the cross on city hall. Bird disposed of these arguments by saying that article XVI, section 5, "admits of no de mini-

---

* Some years earlier a California Court of Appeal had read the section broadly to prohibit public financing of reconstruction of the San Diego mission despite the obvious historical purpose of the project. More recently, the state Supreme Court in a Mosk opinion had read article XVI, section 5, narrowly to permit public agency loans to institutions of higher education affiliated with a church; the court reasoned that there was no public expense in a loan.

mus exception [and] the prohibitions would come into play even if no funds were expended [as] the ban is on aid to religion in *any* form." On this theory it is hard to see how fire or police protection can constitutionally be afforded church property, particularly since Bird also said that "the fact that a statute has some secular objective will not immunize it" from this prohibition. The short of the matter is that Bird's opinion on this point was a textbook example of needlessly broad language on an unargued and unnecessary point that will almost certainly come back to haunt Bird and the court in future cases.

Bird's second ground was Newman's preference argument and, although lengthy and needlessly elaborate, Bird's statement can fairly be said to have improved Newman's delineation of the argument. One paragraph (out of nine) might usefully have been incorporated in Newman's opinion:

The city argues that no preference was given to any religion, since the purpose of displaying the cross was the wholly secular one of promoting "peace and good fellowship toward all mankind." Whatever the city's subjective purpose, an impermissible religious preference has objectively resulted. Had the City delivered its message by simply lighting the words "Peace on Earth" on City Hall, no constitutional questions would have been raised. Instead, the city chose to deliver its "secular" message through a religious vehicle. The medium was the message. Once the cross blazed from the top stories of City Hall, some individuals obtained the satisfaction of knowing their faith was officially approved. Others had to pursue their faith knowing that beliefs they did not share had received official blessing. (Emphasis in original.)

Having decided the case on two separate state constitutional grounds, Bird went on to decide that display of the cross violated two of the three prongs in the U.S. Supreme Court's establishment clause test. Dismissing the question of purpose, she held that the effect of the display advanced religion and that the process of deciding whether or not to show the cross constituted an excessive entanglement of government and religion. The first conclusion substantially repeated what she had earlier said about preference and implicitly raised the issue, which she did not address, of whether there was a difference between the state prohibition on preferences and the federal ban on benefiting a religion. The entanglement issue was a wholly independent and fourth ground for her decision. The concept of entanglement was new: it first emerged in U.S. Supreme Court cases in 1971 and the contours of the concept were uncertain. Thus talking about it was good example of what a court should avoid discussing unless necessary to decision since almost anything said was certain to be debatable. There was no reason for Bird to reach the entanglement question in *Fox* and her dicta that the decision to display the cross on Eastern Orthodox Easter illustrated excessive entanglement was doubtful.

The Concluding Travels of the Box in Fox

Bird's concurring opinion was issued on October 3, whereupon the box returned to Newman. He held it past election day until November 13 before okaying his signature. The box passed to Tobriner, who held it until November 17, when Bird recalled it to make modifications in her opinion, whether or not at Tobriner's request is unknown. After Manuel and Mosk again okayed Newman's opinion, the box returned to Tobriner, who signed both Newman's and Bird's opinions. From then on there were some modest delays probably occasioned by minor modifications in Richardson's and Bird's opinions; the decision was issued on December 15, again a Friday.*

Newman and Richardson both took a long time to write their opinions in Fox, about two months each. Newman's slowness can be explained on two grounds: first, he was a new and inexperienced member of the court; second, unlike Tobriner in Tanner, Newman changed his view sharply from his calendar memorandum to his opinion. Richardson's two months can also be explained: he had to consider each prong of the three-pronged test, and his opinion shows unusual labor to produce a polished statement on a subject he apparently felt especially important.

It is considerably harder to forgive Bird's six months. She told the commission that the "new" state constitutional issue and the complexity of the problem as a matter of federal law required her and her staff to do much original research. Yet all that work was unnecessary as well as unwise since it resulted in unauthoritative (and probably wrong) dicta. As with Tanner, however, it does not follow that because Bird wrote a foolish opinion that occasioned much of the delay in Fox she did so for the purpose of delaying release of the decision until after the election. To the contrary, the fact that she committed herself to prepare an opinion as early as April suggests no such purpose.

One question about Fox was never answered since Newman did not testify publicly: why did Newman take from October 4 to November 15 to okay his opinion? There may have been reasons unrelated to the election and they may have been good ones, but the public never heard them.

Some Lessons from Fox

The same lack of collaborative effort observed in Tanner was visible in Fox. Newman's opinion would have been improved by borrowing

---

* Fox v. City of Los Angeles, 22 C.3d 794 (1978).

some sentences from Bird. Had Bird tactfully suggested certain improvements it is hard to see how Newman could have turned her down; he might also have made changes in response to Clark had Clark approached him in a less challenging way. But Bird's memorandum to Newman gave Newman hardly any room to respond without completely rewriting his opinion in ways that he presumably thought quite wrong, and Clark's dissent was rather more of a taunt than a suggestion for improvement. Again, it is hard to escape the inference that the justices were not trying to achieve consensus because they had stopped expecting it.

Unlike *Tanner*, there was no way to bridge the gap in *Fox* between Newman and Richardson on the substance of the question that divided them unless the case were turned off on some procedural issue that finessed their substantive differences. Newman's calendar memorandum suggested such a solution—possibly Newman, aware of Richardson's strong feelings, cast his calendar memorandum to suggest such a solution. Under what circumstances appellate courts should use evasive manuevers of this sort to avoid divisive substantive issues is a complex question about which there is no consensus among scholars or judges. A remand for a full trial would probably not have produced a significantly better record but it might have so discouraged Leichter as to make her withdraw. Alternatively, the city might have decided that the cross was not worth the candle. In any event, a remand would make the problem go away for a while, and in the meantime perhaps the U. S. Supreme Court would decide a religious symbol case that would be plainly controlling. On the other hand, Newman had a clear majority (five votes), could establish a precedent for a mode of decisionmaking he felt deeply about (using the state, rather than the federal, constitution), and could attempt to write an opinion so tied to the special facts of *Fox* as to avoid unduly disturbing Richardson. Whether Newman went through any calculus of this sort is unknown, but the possibility of such an analysis makes it difficult to fault his decision not to attempt to accommodate Richardson.

HAWKINS AND *LEVINS* AND THE NINETY-DAY RULE

Carol Benfell reported in the *Los Angeles Daily Journal* on November 8, 1978, the day after the election, that "As many as six other cases, including *Fox v. City of Los Angeles,* are sitting on Justice Mathew Tobriner's desk along with the *Tanner* decision, [court] sources said."*

* The box in the *Fox* case was not with Tobriner on election day; it had been with Newman since October 4. The box moved to Tobriner on November 13.

That was the first mention of the *Fox* case in the press. *Hawkins** and *Levins,*† the cases "abolishing" the grand jury, were not listed by Benfell by name then but she read the opinions closely when they were filed on November 9. On November 17, she wrote an article pointing out that some citations in Mosk's opinions were "open"; that is, page references had not been filled in although the full citations were available on November 9 and had been for some months. This lapse suggested that the opinions had been written and the cases presumably ready to file months before they were released. Like the lipstick-stained cigarette butt forgotten at the scene of the crime, the open citations seemed to outsiders to be just the sort of oversight that would prove the deliberate withholding of opinions past election day. Benfell pressed Buehl on the point and reported his rather lame excuse that "final proofing is not a perfect process."

Hufstedler and his associates spent hours developing evidence on the issue of whether the citation errors were more than proofreading mistakes. Hufstedler was never able to close the circle completely with public testimony because the *Mosk* suit prevented him from asking Mosk, the author of the opinions in *Hawkins* and *Levins*, a few final questions. Nonetheless, it is clear that Buehl's explanation, however inadequate it may have sounded to the suspicious on November 17, was correct. The open citations were only an oversight. (No useful purpose would be served here by repeating Hufstedler's demonstration of the complex chain of circumstances that established this fact.)

In the process of exploring the details of the final steps in the process of issuing an opinion, Hufstedler fell over a blunder in Bird's chambers that drew public attention to a matter that was not generally known by the public or probably many lawyers. The judicial article of the California constitution provides: "A judge of a court of record may not receive the salary for the judicial office held by the judge while any cause before the judge is pending and undetermined for 90 days after it has been submitted for decision." This provision had been in the constitution since 1879. It was a typically unsophisticated nineteenth-century mechanical solution to a complex and intractable problem: delay in the court system. The ninety-day rule made a crude sort of sense with trial judges and had been enforced by requiring every judge to certify monthly that he or she had no cases pending for more than ninety days after submission or not receive a paycheck. The rule made much less sense for the multimember appellate courts, first because the process of obtaining agreement among three or seven judges is potentially more

---

* Hawkins v. Superior Court, 22 C.3d 584 (1978).
† People v. Levins, 22 C.3d 620 (1978).

time-consuming and second because the remedy was inappropriate (three or seven justices would go without pay any time one justice held up the filing of a decision).

Mechanical rules invite mechanical evasions, and the courts developed a simple device for escaping the ninety-day rule: they "vacated" a submission and ordered the case "resubmitted" whenever it had been pending for ninety days. In some instances this tactic was entirely justified; for example, when a case presenting the same or a similar issue was pending in a higher court, the lower court would often be wise to await the upper court's decision.

Gibson became convinced that the ninety-day rule was interfering excessively with the production of quality opinions, and he established the pattern of not signing an order submitting a case at the conclusion of oral argument, instead waiting until the opinions were ready to be filed and then ordering the case submitted simultaneously with the filing of the opinion. This practice continued unchanged through Traynor, Wright, and Bird. Hufstedler described the problem with exquisite tact:

There is in California a provision in the Constitution which provides that a judge may not receive his or her compensation if that judge has had submitted before it a case which has not been decided for 90 days. . . . [F]or generations the Supreme Court has worked its way around that rule . . . by having an internal Court rule which says a case is not submitted until a submittal order is signed and the submittal order is not signed until the case is ready for filing. . . . I do want to emphasize that the practice of the Supreme Court in this regard is one that has continued and is of long-standing. It has been followed by the Court for many years and was not created by the present Court. Nonetheless, it does appear that it is not a clear recognition of the spirit of the obligation of the 90-day rule.

The court's historic evasion of the ninety-day rule was a persistent low-level embarrassment to the judiciary. Some effort was made to take the ninety-day rule out of the constitution during the constitutional revision process. That failed, although the members of the Constitutional Revision Commission and many legislators were quite aware that the rule was being honored in form only. In 1978, a repeal of the ninety-day rule was added to a proposal to establish a commission to fix the salaries of all elected officials, including judges. The voters defeated the measure in the June 1978 primary because of voter hostility to the commission proposal, not, presumably, because they favored the ninety-day rule.

During the fall of 1978 the Judicial Council adopted a rule that gave some reality to the ninety-day rule for the Courts of Appeal:

Rule 22.5. (a) A cause pending in a Court of Appeal is submitted when the court has heard oral argument, or has approved a waiver of oral argument, and the time has passed for filing all briefs and papers, including any supplementary brief permitted by the court. (b) Submission may be vacated only by an order stating the reasons therefor. The order shall provide for the resubmission of the cause.

The council's adoption of this rule caused something of a flap within the judiciary. The Judicial Council of 1978 was still composed primarily of Wright appointees but the sensitive issue, the new rule's inapplicability to the Supreme Court, undoubtedly reflected the views of Bird and Tobriner, the two justices who sat on the council. Court of Appeal justices could not help but resent this exemption.

This controversy came out in connection with *Hawkins* and *Levins* because of an error in the chief justice's chambers. *Hawkins* and *Levins* were related cases. In *Hawkins* the criminal defendants had been indicted by a grand jury and had requested, but been denied, a preliminary hearing before a magistrate in which they could cross-examine the prosecution's witnesses and present exculpatory evidence of their own. *Levins* presented the same problem in reverse. The defendant had been charged by an information and a preliminary hearing scheduled. Before the preliminary hearing was held, however, the accused was indicted by a grand jury for the same crime. When the preliminary hearing started, the district attorney moved to dismiss the information because of the later indictment. The magistrate (a municipal court judge) refused to dismiss, and the district attorney sought an order to prevent the holding of a preliminary hearing for an accused who had been indicted for the same crime by grand jury.

Levins got to the Supreme Court first. A hearing was granted on May 12, 1977, and the case was argued on August 31, 1977. Mosk was assigned to write the opinion, but he circulated nothing until March 13, 1978, more than six months later. The explanation for this extraordinary delay was the intervention of another case, *People* v. *Peters*, in which hearing was granted on November 10, 1977, and argument heard on January 13, 1978. Newman ultimately wrote the opinion in *Peters*, filed July 31, 1978, which decided on very technical grounds that a "magistrate" did not have the power to dismiss an information even though the magistrate was in fact a municipal court judge.* This ruling made the decision in *Levins* simple, and Mosk circulated on July 14 what was

---

* People v. Peters, 21 C.3d 749 (1978).

probably a totally different opinion in *Levins* from what he had circulated four months earlier. Although four brief opinions were written, the new *Levins* opinions went through the court quite promptly and the decision was ready for filing on August 15, 1978.

Meanwhile, however, the court had granted a hearing in *Hawkins* on September 22, 1977, and heard argument on the case February 7, 1978. Mosk circulated a proposed opinion on March 2, which held that denying a person indicted by a grand jury the benefits of a preliminary hearing violated the equal protection clause. Mosk used the occasion to develop a "three-tier" equal protection analysis, admittedly in advance of the U.S. Supreme Court. His opinion at first gained the adherence of Tobriner, Manuel, and Newman, a majority. Bird concurred in his result but not in his three-tier analysis. After she circulated a concurrence and dissent on August 22, Manuel decided to withdraw his signature on Mosk's opinion and instead to sign Bird's.* Mosk, no longer having a majority, decided to revise his opinion, adopting the traditional two-tier equal protection analysis, although he also wrote a separate opinion concurring in his own majority opinion. Mosk's revision required Bird and Richardson in dissent to revise their opinions and the case was filed on November 9.

While this negotiating was going on over the opinions in *Hawkins*, the *Levins* case was ready to be filed but waiting for *Hawkins*. The commission's hearings revealed that Bird had signed a submittal order in *Levins* on August 15. That was a mistake: *Levins* was not ready for filing until its companion, *Hawkins*, was also ready. Although signed and the date noted, the submittal order was not filed with the clerk, and Bird signed probably without much thought as to what she was doing or whether it would make any difference. In her testimony before the commission she indicated that she was unaware that her order had not been filed. Ultimately her action made no difference; *Levins* was filed eighty-seven days after Bird signed the submittal order.

Levins took 435 days from argument to the filing of the opinion. In terms of the difficulty of the point ultimately decided this delay was wholly unjustified. However, *Levins* also illustrates the inability of a mechanical ninety-day rule to work efficiently in the Supreme Court. It would have been wasteful and confusing to decide *Levins* before *Peters* or *Hawkins*, neither of which was even on the court's docket at the time of oral argument in *Levins*. As things finally worked out, *Levins* was a minor piece in a matrix of cases, but there was no way the justices could

---

* Manuel's action is noteworthy for two reasons. First, it shows a justice changing his vote after the posthearing conference and indeed after signing an opinion. Second, it is the one instance known in which a separate opinion by Bird made a difference. Bird also wrote separately in *Caudillo I*, *Proposition 13*, *Tanner I* and *II*, and *Fox*, but only in *Hawkins* did her separate opinion in any way alter the court's decision.

have known that when they granted a hearing in *Levins* or when *Levins* was first assigned to Mosk for an opinion.

The commission's evidence about the *Hawkins* and *Levins* cases made a broader public aware of the ninety-day rule and to the extent she was responsible for it, Bird's poor judgment in urging that Rule 22.5 be made inapplicable to the Supreme Court. Very little can be said in favor of Gibson's practice of signing submittal orders only when opinions were ready to be filed. The ninety-day rule is a stupid rule as applied to the appellate courts, particularly the Supreme Court, but it was in the constitution. Like Caesar's wife, judges have a special duty to be law-abiding, especially with rules that govern their own behavior, and the ninety-day rule deserved more from the Supreme Court than technical compliance that totally evaded the spirit and purpose of the rule. Rule 22.5 was a sensible interpretation of the constitution that gave the Courts of Appeal some flexibility but also held judges accountable for delays; the rule could have been applied to the Supreme Court (although its effective date might well have been postponed for six months or a year to permit the court to adjust its work to come closer to compliance). Making the rule applicable to the Courts of Appeal but not to the Supreme Court was certain to irritate some justices on the Courts of Appeal and it was defensible as a policy matter only because Gibson had started evading the rule years earlier. The decision to make the rule inapplicable to the Supreme Court was poor as a matter of judicial politics, and no better as a matter of policy. However, had it not been for *Levins* and *Hawkins*, the general public might well have remained quite unaware of the problem.

SIX

The Hearings

The Commission on Judicial Performance convened on June 11 in the auditorium of Golden Gate Law School in downtown San Francisco. The hearings lacked some essential elements of good theater: there was no protagonist, no single tragic flaw, and no conclusion. There was also notably little good humor because the actors were preoccupied with the deadly seriousness of their enterprise. Nonetheless, as Hufstedler promised at the opening, the hearings gave the public "an opportunity for the first time to become acquainted on an intimate basis with its Supreme Court"—that meant not only the justices but also the heretofore anonymous court staff.

Although theatrically aimless, there was ample character development. The public, if it paid attention, could have learned a great deal about the personalities of Richardson, Tobriner, Bird, and Clark, who completed their initial testimony before the hearings were closed by Mosk's suit. Much was later exposed about Mosk and Newman in connection with Mosk's suit. When it was all over, Manuel alone among the justices remained a relatively undefined figure. What was learned about the justices is one point of emphasis in this account of the hearings.

Another theme is the role of staff. All told, two of Tobriner's staff, two of Clark's, and four of Bird's staff testified, as well as one member of the central staff. Although far from a complete roster of the court staff, and probably not a representative sample, these nine witnesses gave testimony sufficient to support some generalizations about the character and importance of staff—something that before the hearings was almost unknown and unknowable.

A third major concern is the press. At the beginning press attendance was high; it began to slip after the first few weeks. How did reporters cover the proceedings, what did they choose to emphasize, and what did they neglect? A related issue is how the participants, especially the justices but also the commissioners, reacted to the presence of the press and what they presumed was widespread public attention to the hearings.

The hearings produced no clear winners. It is important, however to recall that the players had different objectives. Hufstedler's goal was the most modest and realistic. He sought to put to rest the allegation of deliberate delay of decisions so that the court could begin to reestablish public confidence in the judicial system. Tobriner saw the hearings as an opportunity to vindicate himself. Bird shared Tobriner's goal but also sought to defend herself against generalized charges of incompetent performance as chief justice. As a defensive tactic she chose to attack Clark and, to some extent, enlisted Tobriner in her effort. Their counterattack in large part defined Clark's objective of defending himself. Commissioners and the press had a hard time grappling with this mélange of goals; it is hard to keep score when you can't be sure whether the game is tennis, football, or golf.

HUFSTEDLER'S OPENING

The procedural rules the commission issued in April required Hufstedler to make an opening presentation to accompany his report and provided that the commission would then adjourn for a week before beginning to receive testimony from witnesses. In truth, other than to stage a media event, there was very little reason for the commission to hear Hufstedler at this point. His eighty-three-page background report was self-explanatory and considerably more detailed than a few hours' oral summary could justly indicate, and even his written report did little more than provide a road map for the documents in the two volumes of exhibits in the appendices that accompanied the report.

Chairman Janes opened with a brief statement emphasizing that the proceedings constituted a preliminary investigation that at most could result in the preparation of formal charges against a justice, which would then require a formal hearing. Janes struck a theme that was to recur throughout: these proceedings were a unique event in history; never before in California and "perhaps never before anywhere else in the country" had an appellate court been investigated in public. Everyone —commissioners, lawyers, and justices—had the sense that they were participating in a historic event and there were frequent allusions to Watergate, as if these hearings had comparable importance. In fact, despite extensive press coverage, few people paid close attention.

When Janes turned the floor over to him, Hufstedler spoke for about two hours, calmly and quietly summarizing efficiently the content of his report. For the TV audience, his talk must have been a colossal bore. He explained that his function that day was to summarize background facts, which meant mainly matters that were indisputable and provable by documents and therefore inherently unexciting. Hufstedler took one flight into high-minded rhetoric, remarkable because it was apparently extemporaneous:

We are dealing with a powerful institution, but a fragile institution. That institution is based upon the interrelationships of its seven justices, seven human beings with their own backgrounds, their own qualifications, their own interests, and must operate in an atmosphere in which those seven individuals can have the trust and confidence of the public in the decisions which they render and hand down. Any functioning appellate court requires a collegial atmosphere in which the justices can work freely. It requires an atmosphere in which they can have a free exchange of ideas regardless of whether they be initially sound or not, so they can explore them, test them out on each other to eventually come to a conclusion. It requires a high quality of scholarship so they may do this in a background of care and fairness and of justice and integrity. And the court does not have an army to support its determinations. Its determinations rest certainly upon the force of law of the state of California but also largely upon social acceptance and respect. A court cannot be an effective, functioning court unless it has the acceptance and the respect of the people of the jurisdiction. So we are dealing with delicate relationships and interpersonal relationships on the court itself, the external relationships with regard to the public and the commission. Special counsel have been alert to these problems of this institution in such a way that we do not impair those fragile relationships.

Hufstedler also spoke of his own role, explaining that he was neither a prosecutor nor a defense counsel but both. His obligation was "to present all of the relevant evidence," whether favorable or unfavorable to the justices. That is a hard role for a lawyer trained in the Anglo-American legal tradition. Trial lawyers, like Hufstedler, are advocates first and foremost; they are committed to the adversarial process, which presumes that the truth will emerge from the clash of competing viewpoints, each represented by a lawyer dedicated to expressing only his or her client's cause. At times during the proceedings one could almost see Hufstedler taking off his prosecuting hat and going back over the same evidence as counsel for a justice to develop an innocent explanation for what he had just shown to be damaging. But Hufstedler occasionally slipped by referring to himself as "special prosecutor" rather than special counsel. The presence of lawyers for some of the justices heightened the problem of his equivocal role. So long as Hufstedler was developing both sides of the evidence, his neutral role was manageable; once counsel for a justice entered an objection or otherwise sought to intervene, Hufstedler was almost driven into presenting the prosecutorial position else that viewpoint not be represented. Understandably, counsel for the justices thought of Hufstedler as the opposition, and they found it hard to accept his presentation of evidence favorable to their clients as adequate.

Shortly before the morning recess, Hufstedler indicated his intention to distribute copies of his report, with its appendices, to the commission, counsel, and the press and to devote the remainder of his presentation to a summary statement. The appendices contained a number of documents that Hufstedler knew Newman regarded as privileged, most notably draft opinions, conference memorandums, and Bird's memorandum to him on *Fox*. Immediately after recess, Newman's counsel, Richard Johnston, objected

to the release to the public or future introduction in evidence of any evidence relating to confidential communications between justices and members of their staffs relating to the substance of any case under consideration by the Supreme Court.

Chairman Janes disposed of Johnston's objection by stating that the report had been filed but "not received in evidence," implying that Johnston would be given an opportunity to renew his objection before any documents were received in evidence—an unsatisfactory solution since Johnston was protesting public disclosure (but by then it was too late: the appendices were already in the hands of the press).

However insubstantial, Newman's claim of privilege deserved to be heard and resolved on its merits rather than finessed out of existence by inattention. The chairman's apparent misunderstanding of the objection to public disclosure suggested that he was a little slow in grasping a point, which left a bad taste. In truth, however, the blame belongs with Hufstedler rather more than with Janes because Hufstedler alone knew what was in the appendices. He could easily have limited distribution of the appendices to counsel for the justices and given the press and commissioners only his report. That would have given Johnston a meaningful opportunity to object to public disclosure of the assertedly confidential documents in the appendices. On the other hand, Hufstedler was simply continuing something that had been started by the chief justice when she offered to make the internal records of the court available to the commission.

Bird's proposal, supported by the actions of the commission and the Judicial Council and resolutions by both houses of the legislature, rested on the ground that public confidence in the judiciary required an investigation of the claim that the court had delayed release of decisions for improper reasons—a charge that could not practically be investigated without disclosure of the internal and normally confidential documents. Newman's claim that something more substantial than unattributed claims of wrongdoing in newspapers was necessary to overcome confidentiality was, in this context, quite insubstantial. It was also, as Newman and Johnston must have known, most unlikely to prevail before the commission. If Johnston and Newman wanted to assert Newman's privilege claim and win, their only hope was to initiate a suit in superior court to enjoin disclosure. Newman's failure to file suit strongly indicated that he was more interested in asserting a principle than in seeing the principle vindicated. Hufstedler, if he thought at all about it, probably saw no special purpose in protecting Newman's right to claim a privilege that Newman was unwilling to assert in the only place he had a possible chance of winning.

Immediately after the proceedings adjourned, reporters and television crews clustered around the lawyers for the justices looking for a comment or story. Harry Delizonna, one of Bird's two lawyers, provided them with the copy they wanted. He protested bitterly that he was being denied the right to make an opening statement: "We're not being accorded the rights anyone is entitled to in a regular court proceeding. We've even been denied the right to know what witnesses the commission will be calling." Delizonna's outburst was certain to annoy commissioners and Hufstedler. Lawyers occasionally attack in the press the tribunal they are appearing before when they are confident of losing and are trying to build public support for their client. It is a high-risk strategy employed only in extreme situations. Did Delizonna think Bird was going to lose? Or did he perhaps think that the commission was less important than the media audience, who must be told, as Delizonna did, that "the hearings will vindicate [the chief justice] entirely."

PRELIMINARY MOTIONS

The hearings resumed a week later. In the meantime, the Supreme Court announced the decision in *Tanner II* and received, in general, a good response from editorial writers. KQED withdrew from providing gavel-to-gavel television coverage of the hearings, largely because the ratings system indicated that there was "no measurable audience" for their broadcast of opening day. As noted previously, KNBC (Burbank) agreed to videotape the entire proceedings and make the tapes available to other stations on a pooling basis for news programs; somewhat later KCET, the Los Angeles public television station, began broadcasting the day's proceedings, gavel-to-gavel, starting at 11:30 P.M. Only night watchmen and dedicated insomniacs could have seen much of this show.

Chairman Janes opened the June 18 hearings by reading a prepared statement that was partially responsive to Delizonna's outburst. Lawyers for the justices, Janes said, would have the following rights:

1. To object to questions or to the entry in evidence of documents offered by special counsel.

2. To request permission to cross-examine witnesses presented by special counsel if they could show good cause for doing so and provided that the cross-examination was not repetitive or argumentative. Good cause was not defined.

3. When the presentation of special counsel was completed, counsel for each justice would be permitted to offer noncumulative, relevant evidence preceded by an opening statement (a direct response to Delizonna) and followed by a concluding statement.

4. The justices' right to present evidence would be supported by the commission's subpoena power.

This statement fleshed out the procedural rule issued by the commission in April, which provided that "each Justice, in person or by counsel, shall have a reasonable opportunity to present to the Commission evidence relevant to the issues. The method of presentation shall be within the sound discretion of the Commission." This amplification of the rule was more generous than might have been expected, especially with respect to cross-examination. To some extent, it weakened Hufstedler's capacity to control the proceedings. Counsel for the justices could easily have been restricted to offering questions to Hufstedler, which he might or might not ask, rather than being given the possibility of themselves asking questions.

RICHARDSON

Hufstedler's first witness was Justice Richardson, Reagan's third and last appointment to the court. Three years before elevating him to the Supreme Court, Reagan had appointed Richardson to the Sacramento Court of Appeal, where he had served as presiding justice of the court on which Janes sat. Richardson previously had been in private solo practice in Sacramento for about twenty-five years; reasonably active in bar association activities, he had stayed away from politics. Richardson had a reputation among lawyers of being a solid, rather unimaginative, and conservative judge. Hufstedler's choice of Richardson as leadoff witness was dictated by the justice's relative lack of involvement in the controversy. Hufstedler used him to explain how the court organized its work —the way the court considered petitions for hearing, how cases were assigned for the preparation of opinions, the movement of the box, and so on.

One aspect of Richardson's testimony surprised Hufstedler:

Q: In a case which has been appealed to the Court of Appeal and the Court of Appeal has decided it and then the parties ask you for a hearing by means of a written petition, is it ordinarily necessary that the parties write a new set of briefs for the hearing in your court?

A: Yes. We have a rule that requires that there be original briefs filed with us in the cases in which we invite the briefs. We do not always get briefs. Sometimes the briefs we get [do not] come from parties or litigants. Sometimes application is filed with the court for the filing of what we call amicus curiae, or friend of the court, briefs.

This response was wrong: no rule requires new briefs after a petition for hearing has been granted in the Supreme Court. Hufstedler, assuming that Richardson had misunderstood the question, rephrased the query:

Q: Let's take a usual case where there has been a judgment in the trial court. It has been appealed to the Court of Appeal. Two parties, the plaintiff and defendant, each have filed a brief in the Court of Appeal. A decision is then made in the Court of Appeal and one of them petitions for hearing to your court and your court grants a hearing.

A: Yes.

Q: Do you use the briefs which were prepared for the Court of Appeal?

A: No. We anticipate the case will be presented to the Supreme Court on the basis of briefs filed originally with the Supreme Court.

Hufstedler may have been on the way toward asking the same question a third time when Commissioner Chodos, a lawyer with an active practice that included appearances before the Supreme Court, interrupted to give Richardson yet another chance to correct himself:

Q: Excuse me, Justice Richardson. To go over the point Mr. Hufstedler covered a moment ago: is it the rule that the Supreme Court in ruling for petitions for hearing [does not] consider the briefs filed in the Court of Appeal at all?

A: No, we may consider them. But we anticipate that they will not simply shift to us the Court of Appeal briefs. We would like to have the issues presented to us on the basis of Supreme Court briefs presented to us.

Chodos's question was a little ambiguous—it could have been understood as referring to the petition for hearing process rather than the briefing on the merits—but Richardson's answer indicated that he was thinking of briefs on the merits.

Richardson also seemingly tried to hide the fact that the conference list was divided into A and B lists. Hufstedler's first question invited a narrative response by asking Richardson what work he would routinely do in preparation for a Wednesday conference. Richardson's answer slid past the A and B list, so Hufstedler interrupted him:

Q: I apologize for interrupting your train of thought. We had mentioned earlier that you average something like eighty cases per week at your conference. Are all eighty of those cases discussed?

A: They are considered.

Q: All right.

A: And they are in effect voted upon.

Q: Are they divided into two different groups for consideration, however?

A: Yes.

Q: What are the groups they are divided into?

A: There is the A list cases, which have on them a recommendation of more active evaluation and treatment as a possible grant. Other cases on which a recommendation of denial has been made [are on the B list]. All of them, however, get the examination and evaluation of the judges and staffs and are voted upon whether they're on one list or the other.

Again, Commissioner Chodos tried to clarify the record:

Q: It occurs to me that it would be impractical to expect that every justice reads the whole set of briefs in eighty cases every single week. In your experience, do the justices actually read all the briefs [or do they] instead rely on a staff memorandum or a calendar memorandum from one of the others?

A: The court relies very heavily upon staff. We feel we have an invaluable staff. These are outstanding professional people. We wouldn't be able to function without them. [In] those cases . . . in which the judge has had his interest piqued or there are troublesome matters or he had either had experience or he feels he had some insight or he's picked up a signal, he not only will read the briefs, he will independently research the authorities, and this is routinely done. I must not represent to this com-

mission that in every conference, every judge reads every brief and every authority cited in every brief. It's really a physical impossibility, so there is a balance. There is a melding here, if I can use that term.

It is not hard to read Richardson's answer backward: only where a justice has some special interest does he or she read the briefs; otherwise he or she depends upon staff and colleagues.

Chodos let Richardson get away with a third instance of mild deception. He asked Richardson whether the first opinion "usually followed the pattern of the calendar memorandum?" and got this answer:

Not necessarily, Mr. Chodos. Often there will be a parallel or tracking of theory and maybe even of subject matter. But it is a rarity in my observation that the final majority opinion circulating the court would resemble too closely the calendar memorandum. There is major editorial work. This is the fruit of the conference, the postcalendar conference discussions, of additional insights from other judges or staff, from research and law review articles or other treatises, new decisions, federal or state. And so, in general, I would say that great help has been given by preparation of that calendar memorandum. But there are usually major changes in content and tone.

Richardson's replies on each of these points put Hufstedler in a bit of a dilemma. With a little pushing, Richardson could have been forced to give more accurate answers, as on the A and B list matter. But none of these issues was crucial to the charge of delay. On the other hand, Hufstedler knew that Richardson's answers were less than forthright and may well have been worried that the press would sense Richardson's dissembling and get their suspicions confirmed by knowledgeable people in the audience. Hufstedler, probably concerned most with pursuing the issue of delay, took the chance that the press would not pursue these details.

Hufstedler's decision evidently bothered some of the commissioners, especially Chodos. The trial lawyer's instinct makes any misstatement of fact by a witness a point to be pursued if for no other reason than to cast doubt on the witness's credibility. The format of the proceedings made it easy for Chodos and the other commissioners to indulge momentary enthusiasms of this sort. They rarely hesitated to interrupt Hufstedler's questioning throughout the hearings; in retrospect, it might have been better if they had held their questions until after Hufstedler had concluded his examination of each witness.

Richardson's reluctance to be fully candid about the court's internal processes was consistent with long tradition. The U.S. Supreme Court, for example, managed to keep hidden for years the fact that it used a dead list on certiorari petitions. Judges historically have clung to the myth that each of them works alone, reading with painstaking care every paper that is filed with the court. It should have been obvious to Richardson, however, that this fiction could not survive the commission's investigation and that he would better serve the court by being forthcoming.

The press did not pick up on these points in their stories about Richardson's testimony, but reporters have a trained nose for the less than complete answer and were aware that Richardson was fudging even if some did not know precisely what he was trying to hide. That made them skeptical of his testimony that he was largely unaware of the *Tanner* controversy in the court, that he could not recall discussing the problem with any of his colleagues or staff, and that he had only a vague recollection of the issue's coming up at several conferences. Richardson attributed his failure of memory in part to his preoccupation during much of the critical period with writing the Proposition 13 opinion. In addition, Richardson at several points said that he thought it inappropriate to press his colleagues on getting opinions out:

These are professional areas. I value my colleagues highly. They are a group of able, hard-working people. And I have never felt in this case or any other that I should push an individual who is working on a case, because I don't want to point a finger, but I have my own faults and they are numerous. This is a sensitive area for a justice.

Put in its most unfavorable light, Richardson's testimony indicated that he was willfully blind to much that was going on around him. He worked on matters in his office and kept apart from his colleagues, expecting them to treat him similarly. Later testimony, especially from Clark, makes it hard to credit fully Richardson's self-imposed distance from internal controversy. Clark indicated that he was in and out of Richardson's office frequently, and it is difficult to believe that Clark would not have mentioned his problems with the chief justice, which were a major concern to Clark.

The press stories about Richardson's testimony focused on exhibits not contained in the appendices to Hufstedler's report, which he distributed to counsel and the press before Richardson began testifying. There were two sets of exhibits. The first contained the Cohen memorandum in support of Tobriner's statement, Tobriner's statement, and the Richardson modification of the Tobriner statement—all written shortly after the election day story. Although most reporters had not seen these documents before, they were familiar with them from the Fairbanks-Endicott stories and the Kang story. The second set of exhibits, however, was new to the press and very newsworthy. On December 20, just before the

Tanner I opinions were released, the chief justice had circulated a proposed statement to be issued with *Tanner*. Clark had responded to this memorandum and Tobriner and the chief justice had each responded to Clark; all the memos were distributed to every member of the court.

Hufstedler's purpose in distributing these exhibits was to ask Richardson about them—he got very little of value—but the second set telegraphed much of what Hufstedler would later introduce.

Clark's memorandum contained this paragraph:

The Tanner *case apparently is now in Justice Newman's chambers and hopefully may soon be filed. I reiterate my position expressed at last week's conference that your "Proposed statement by the Court" not be released either in the name of the Court or by an individual justice. Again, not unlike Justice Tobriner's statement of 9 November and your own Court procedures statement of 24 November, the statement you propose to file concurrently with the filing of the* Tanner *opinion is inaccurate and unreasonably self-serving. In conscience, it must be clear to all on the Court that the* Tanner *case was signed up and ready for filing well in advance of November. The question remaining appears to be why was it not filed? That question must be resolved by the Commission and we should not attempt to influence it by conclusionary statements.*

Bird responded the same day:

You state that "it must be clear to all on the Court that the Tanner *case was signed up and ready for filing well in advance of November."*

I am appalled at this statement. It is untrue. Moreover, as Justice Tobriner told all of us in conference today, it is directly contrary to your own statements to him and to Hal Cohen on November 28th, in which you assured Justice Tobriner that you had never stated or suggested that he had acted for political reasons in the Tanner *case and that you in fact believed that the court had followed the normal procedures in that case. Moreover, when Justice Tobriner reminded you at conference of your earlier statement to him, you did not deny its inconsistency with your December 20th memorandum but merely said you did not wish to pursue the matter.*

Obviously, it was not "clear to all on the Court" that Tanner *was ready in advance of November. All of your colleagues signed statements declaring precisely the contrary. Your present statements, which repudiate those solemn declarations as well as your own representations to Justice Tobriner, are an affront to your colleagues and to the truth.*

As proof of what happened before election day these two memorandums (as well as Tobriner's, which echoed Bird's), written after the fact and in contemplation of the commission's investigation, were substantially worthless. They did, however, serve to define the issue and provide obvious clues as to some of the evidence that Hufstedler would later introduce. As such they became the subject of the lead paragraph in all the press stories. No reporter did much more than summarize the substance of Richardson's testimony; no one subjected his testimony to critical analysis.

TOBRINER

Tobriner was the second justice to testify. He was on the stand for the equivalent of three full days (half a day Wednesday, all day Thursday and Friday, and half a day the following Monday). Tobriner had been in the audience earlier, and many noticed that he was not looking well. By 1979, Tobriner was seventy-five years old; he appeared bent and frail. At no point during his testimony was any reference made to his age, but it was an ambient circumstance very much in the consciousness of all. It had been assumed that Tobriner would resign when he reached seventy. When that date passed, people thought he was waiting out Reagan so that a Democratic governor could name his successor. That day came and went when his former clerk, Jerry Brown, was elected. At the time of the hearings, it was widely supposed that Tobriner had postponed retirement because he was under attack and that he would step down soon after the commission proceedings closed. He did not.

Tobriner had an undergraduate degree from Harvard, a law degree from Stanford, and an advanced law degree from Berkeley. He began practicing in 1928 in San Francisco, worked for a while during the depression as regional attorney for the AAA, and thereafter became one of the leading labor lawyers in the area, representing principally unions. Early in Pat Brown's administration Brown appointed him to the Court of Appeal in San Francisco, one of the relatively few appointments the elder Brown made to an appellate court of someone who had not had experience as a trial judge. Tobriner served on the Court of Appeal for three years before Brown elevated him to the Supreme Court in 1962. Gibson was then chief justice; Tobriner had thus been with the court throughout Traynor's and Wright's tenures as chief justice.

Tobriner was an unabashedly liberal judge, and he was perhaps a little vain about his scholarship and writing style. He probably conceived of himself as Traynor's heir on the court as spokesman for advanced judicial thought. However, his reputation was not that good; Tobriner's opinions tended to be very long and sometimes failed, as in *Tanner*, to confront candidly difficult points in the way of his conclusions. But it was hard after meeting Tobriner to dislike him; he inspired deep and genuine loyalty in his clerks. His enthusiasm for his work, his passion for justice, and his joie de vivre were irresistible.

Tobriner was a terrible witness, which is not to say that he proved himself guilty of any wrongdoing but rather that he exposed himself as rigidly self-righteous, so much so as to raise a doubt as to his credibility. More than anything else, his performance was painfully embarrassing. The audience's discomfort was heightened by Tobriner's desire to vindicate himself before the public and his delusion that he was scoring points in his testimony. Neither Hufstedler nor any of the commissioners wanted to smash Tobriner, but there he was in the witness chair, pathetically undressing himself in public and quite unaware that he was damaging the very reputation he sought to restore.

Tobriner's testimony opened with some general questions about confidentiality. Tobriner announced that "I have always felt that the canons should be scrupulously observed, and in all my years on the court they have been so observed. Only recently we have come to a situation . . . these hearings, where apparently that has not been observed." Tobriner's language kept escalating: "Anything about a pending case is highly confidential and should be in the sacred wisdom of the Court"; "Whatever we say in the conference room, I think, would be sacred. I don't think that should ever be disclosed to the public." Every time he made such remarks he was in effect pressing a button questioning the commission's power to investigate allegations of improper delay. Nearly always, Chodos responded by challenging Tobriner; for example:

Q: I'm mindful of the fact that under various decisions of the courts of this state or of the United States, newspaper people, media people, lawyers, doctors, almost everyone is sometimes called upon to expose his mental processes discreetly, where the public interest requires that it be examined. Is there some reason in your mind why you believe that deliberations of judges or Supreme Court justices in particular should be exempt from that scrutiny as distinguished from all others in society?

A: I think the danger is that the process of decision in the appellate court in particular, indeed, in the superior courts, too, should not be exposed prior to the time of the conclusion of that thinking. [Confidentiality in] the thought processes of a judge is surely something that is essential to his reaching a fair conclusion. That [a judge] might at one point have one view and at another [point] another view [made public] would make it very difficult for him to really think it through.

The next day the same controversy recurred.

Q: Only this week in the advance sheets of the Supreme Court of the United States there is published an opinion, Herbert v. Lando. *In that*

*case the Supreme Court held that the editorial staff of the CBS program
60 Minutes could properly and lawfully be interrogated about their mental processes and state of mind because the litigation in which they were
embroiled and the forum in which they were presenting their contention
was a proper occasion to inquire into that issue. . . . Do you believe there
is some distinction between the reasoning I have exemplified by* Herbert
v. Lando *and the problem here before us today?*

*A: Yes, I do. I think the distinction is that [that] case involved not
judges or judicial process and therefore it is irrelevant to this point.*

Little would be accomplished by pursuing the controversy because
Tobriner, though protesting, answered the questions. The debate, however, caught the attention of reporters. For years the press had been
protesting judicial decisions requiring them to disclose their sources and
their thought processes. In general, the courts had rejected the argument that freedom of the press requires giving the media a special status;
some courts had gone so far as to override legislative shield laws that
purported to create an exemption for the press. Reporters understood
Tobriner to be claiming for judges the very kind of special status that
courts had refused to give the press. By exposing what reporters considered a hypocritical inconsistency, Chodos was, deliberately or not,
ingratiating himself with the press just as Tobriner was doing the opposite.

Tobriner testified that he had rented a vacation home for August
1978 and had expected to spend much of the month away from the
court. The Proposition 13 cases interfered with his plan, but he spent as
much time as he could on vacation. Tobriner was thus only occasionally
in the office during the period when Clark circulated on August 15 and
25 his new and reissued dissents in *Tanner*, which cited *Caudillo*, first in
a footnote and then elevated to the text. It will be recalled that the green
sheet accompanying the revised dissent said:

The staff to the Chief Justice has requested that our citation to People v.
Caudillo *in footnote 8 be deleted. The reasons given for deletion are that*
Caudillo *is inapposite and that its use is "politically motivated."*

*I reject both the request and the unfortunate reasoning. Rather, I now
expand discussion of* Caudillo *to show that it is clearly apposite, moving
it from footnote to body.*

Tobriner testified that he saw this green sheet first during the week
of September 11 and had a brief conversation about it with his reseach
attorney, Hal Cohen, when they were planning which of the boxes then
in his office Tobriner would next work on. Hufstedler asked:

Q: Didn't you say when you saw that, "Well, Hal, it looks like we are in for some stormy weather," or something to that effect?

A: No, we didn't take it very seriously because, if you read it, it says the staff to the chief justice has requested that our citation to Caudillo from footnote 8 be deleted. This seemed nothing more than the staff of the chief justice was supposed to be representing that to somebody on the staff of Justice Clark. I didn't know whether Justice Clark had written that or whether the staff of Justice Clark had written that. I did not consider that to be a very important point one way or the other. This didn't strike me as a great issue between the justices because it did not express that. And, in any event, I did not take that as a very important point.

Several commissioners jumped on the proposition that the contretemps was not between Bird and Clark but only between their staffs. Tobriner, however, stubbornly insisted that he did not think Clark was personally involved. The questioning got rather harsh:

Mr. Chodos: Justice Tobriner, to use plain English, are you telling us now that you thought this memo may actually have been from the hand of, say, Mr. Morris [a research attorney of Clark's]?

A: Yes.

Q: Rather than Justice Clark?

A: It could . . . very well have been.

Chairman Janes [takes over the questioning]: Do you authorize your staff to write memos for you in first person?

A: They have done it.

Q: The answer was unresponsive. Do you authorize it?

A: I would permit it. I would authorize it.

Tobriner reported that "The *Caudillo* case was purely a question of statutory interpretation as to whether a rape was great bodily injury. So neither Mr. Cohen nor myself could see the relevance of the reference to *Caudillo* in the *Tanner* case." Tobriner was never challenged on this statement, although he repeated it many times, but his credibility began to disintegrate when he said: "Frankly, I didn't know exactly what was intended by that 'politically motivated.' I never thought it had anything to do with any election. It never once entered my mind that it had anything to do with an election." The "never once" was hard to credit. Did he not know in September that two groups had been organized to defeat Bird's confirmation? "I don't know that I knew two groups were organized by that time to defeat her. Now, I didn't take the election too seriously at that point." However, Tobriner acknowledged that he was by then aware of the *New West* article and that the *Caudillo* case was a part of the campaign against Bird. Tobriner also admitted awareness in October of the anti-Bird commercials that were built around *Caudillo*.

Q: Did it not then occur to you that the Tanner *case might be politically sensitive within the court?*

A: I must say I never connected up the Caudillo *case as such with the election particularly. It did not cross my mind as such. I wasn't paying too much attention to that aspect of the* Caudillo *case or the* Tanner *case. The* Tanner *case looked to me like another case that we had to dispose of.*

Attorney General Younger's charges that the court was delaying release of death penalty decisions and the *Tanner* case were briefly discussed at a Wednesday conference in October. Tobriner "considered this assertion as carried by the press as to Mr. Younger as completely false and misleading. I didn't think anybody could be influenced by that, because it was so strange and ridiculous."

Q: So after you had read the article about the attorney general's conduct and his statements and charges, you still did not believe that Tanner *would be a politically sensitive case within the court?*

A: No, I did not think so.

Q: And by that time, did you still believe that the green sheet was not a matter of significance and that it simply represented some possible controversy among the staff?

A: It could have been a possible confrontation among the staff and, of course, it could have been between the chief justice and Justice Clark. I just didn't know.

Q: Yes, it could have been. My question is, Did you consider it only that by the time you had heard of the attorney general's charges?

A: I considered it unimportant and only that.

Tobriner recollected a "passing conversation" with the chief justice, sometime between September and November, about *Tanner* and the elevation of the *Caudillo* citation in Clark's dissent from the footnote to the text. Tobriner recalled the conversation:

A: She said, "I can't see the relevance of it." And I said I didn't see the legal relevance of it whatsoever. "It has nothing to do with the Tanner *case, and to claim that because you wrote this concurring opinion as to the constitutionality of the* Tanner *case . . . the* Caudillo *case has something to do with that," I said, "to me, it's completely legally irrelevant. It has no point whatsoever."*

Q: What, if anything, did she say to that?

A: She agreed.

Q: Did you ask her if this business about political motivation was just some kind of a controversy between the staffs?

A: I did not ask her. I thought it was beneath even a question. . . . As I said, we did not discuss any political ramifications. There wasn't a word said about political ramifications in my conversation with the chief. She did not raise it. I did not raise it.*

Some commissioners were having a hard time accepting this testimony. Chodos pursued the point:

Q: It is but a tiny step logically to say that since Clark didn't have a legitimate legal reason, he must have some other reason. And maybe he is politically motivated. Are you saying to us that, A, you were oblivious to these political motivations and, B, you and the chief didn't talk about them at all?

A: We did not discuss that Justice Clark had a political motivation that I can at this moment describe to you. I do not know. I do not know what the reason for that was. I surmised in a brief appraisal that it was perhaps argument in the staffs or perhaps even conceivably with the chief. But I did not attach that thought to the campaign.

Perhaps the most troublesome colloquy came over the extent of Tobriner's involvement with Bird's campaign. He admitted that his wife had given $1,000 to Californians for the Court, a group supporting the four justices on the ballot, but Tobriner claimed to have done nothing himself to further Bird's election. Chodos asked:

Q: Justice Tobriner, it was reported frequently in the press before the election that you were giving Chief Justice Bird comfort and support in her hour of trial. And based on your long experience in the court and before that in politics, there is no question that that advice would be valuable to anyone in her position. Is it fair to say that she did seek comfort and advice from you about her political fortunes?

A: I realize that [it] was stated in the press that I was her special kind of comfort or whatnot, as you express, Mr. Chodos. That was absolutely false, because I did support the chief when I thought she was right on legal issues. I disagreed with her, as you just saw, in the Tanner *case on one issue. I did not involve myself at all in any political activities. And I was no particular person on that court for her to discuss political affairs [with].*

Although he may not have thought about it, Tobriner crossed a line here: he was now discussing a subject some reporters in the audience—Kang, Endicott, and Benfell, for example—knew about from covering the campaign. They had been told, as Hufstedler may not have been, that Tobriner had been involved in arranging the meetings between Bird and the editorial boards of major newspapers. Hufstedler, however, did have a copy of Kang's October 6 story, which was based in part on Tobriner's answer to Kang's questions to Bird about her conduct as the administrative head of the court system. There was a bit of a row about the relevance of the article, which ultimately resulted in a production of Tobriner's copy of the letter to Reg Murphy, the editor of the *Examiner.* The letter, it turned out, had been written not in June, as Tobriner first thought, but on July 28; nonetheless, the early date gave a bit of color to Tobriner's claim that his reply had had nothing to do with any election. But Tobriner would not admit that he wrote the letter to help the chief justice:

A: *I prepared as the vice-chairman of the Judicial Council some an-swers to questions that had been sent in by Connie Kang.*

Q: *Are you telling me that you prepared the letter in your capacity as vice-chairman of the Judicial Council?*

A: *I felt that as vice-chairman some of these questions could be an-swered by me because of my familiarity with what was going on.*

Q: *I think that is a somewhat different point. Did anyone on the Judicial Council other than perhaps the chief justice ask you to prepare the letter?*

A: *No.*

Q: *Did the chief justice ask you [in her capacity] as chairman of the Judicial Council to prepare that letter?*

A: *I don't think she asked me to prepare the letter as such.*

Q: *Isn't it true, Justice Tobriner, that you prepared that letter in your capacity as a citizen, as an individual?*

A: *Chiefly.*

Q: *And did you or did you not do it because you thought it would aid the chief justice in her public image with regard to these questions which had been asked?*

A: *I felt it was more appropriate for me to answer them than for her to answer them.*

Q: *I understand that you felt it was appropriate for you. My question is, You prepared the letter and sent it in order to aid the chief justice, did you not?*

A: *I don't think I had to aid the chief justice. I wanted to answer the questions for the court. I felt that it was proper that the questions should be answered.*

Q: *One of your purposes in preparing that letter was to aid the chief justice in her public image in responding to those questions, wasn't it?*

A: *When you say "to aid her public image," I wanted to answer the questions for the purpose of making it clear as to the administration of the court itself. It wasn't particularly for her, although I suppose in passing it would be, too. But it would be in aid of all the members of the court that those questions be answered.*

Q: And does it follow from what you said that it was not your state of mind at all that your responding to the questions would be in aid to the chief justice?

A: It was not in my mind to aid the chief justice . . . in the election or anything of that kind, because it was not a matter of the election in June [actually late July].

This was one of the many times Hufstedler found himself pursuing an issue he originally had no intention of exploring. There was nothing wrong or shameful about Tobriner's supporting Bird; it certainly did not prove that he had delayed the release of *Tanner* or done anything else improper but it was relevant that Tobriner cared whether she won and, as evidence of that hope, that he did what he could to help her. Tobriner's refusal to admit that he did anything at all on Bird's behalf made an issue out of something that was not there before and forced Hufstedler to explore issues quite marginal to the inquiry.

The audience was squirming in their seats over this colloquy. Why was Tobriner insisting on portraying himself as a totally uninvolved, apolitical figure when he obviously cared deeply about Bird's fortunes? The most charitable explanation is that Tobriner simply forgot the extent of his involvement in his desire to appear as a nonparticipant who stood aside from politics and cared not a whit about Jerry Brown or Rose Bird or anyone else in his single-minded dedication to the law.* Many reporters were less charitable. The episode led them to discount heavily Tobriner's later claim that he never thought about the possibility that the release of the *Tanner* opinion before November 7 might adversely affect Bird's chances in the election.

Another example of how Tobriner's volunteered answers broadened the issues came in the same line of questioning. Hufstedler quoted Kang's October 6 article as a prelude to a question:

Q: "Speaking for Bird, Tobriner said . . ." Were you in any way, Justice Tobriner, speaking for the chief justice when you wrote that letter to the Examiner?

A: I would have to look at the original document. I haven't seen this for a year, Mr. Hufstedler.

---

* Tobriner returned to the point later: "Let me make that absolutely clear. I was never her political advisor nor did I participate one iota in her campaign. I'm a justice of the court. I don't think I have anything to do with political campaigns. I did not participate in her campaign. I didn't advise her. I hardly talked to her about it."

Q: And you don't recall in your letter whether you were speaking for the chief justice?

A: I wouldn't necessarily believe that because this is stated by Connie Kang that it is correct. Because we have known that a great many things signed by her have not been sustained by the truth.

Q: I am not asking you to sustain either the accuracy or inaccuracy of Ms. Kang's general picture, although you must admit that many of the things she has reported about the court have been accurate.

A: A great many have not been, Mr. Hufstedler. *

Tobriner's gratuitous answers defamed Kang in her professional capacity in circumstances that made it impossible for her to respond. It was one time when Hufstedler's instincts as a trial lawyer failed him; he should have requested that the answer be stricken as unresponsive and the witness instructed to avoid irrelevant and inappropriate remarks. Instead, probably because he was understandably angry, Hufstedler sought to dispel the canard with testimony of his own. Reporters found it hard thereafter to respect the legitimacy of Tobriner's concern for his own reputation when he was willing to reach out to smear the professionalism of one of their own.

Tobriner on the Issues

The foregoing, which took about half of Tobriner's time on the stand, provided the context for Tobriner's testimony about his participation in the *Tanner* case. One critical issue, raised first by Cannon's article, was whether Tobriner had encouraged Manuel to write a separate dissent, thereby—whether intending the result or not—postponing release of *Tanner*. Tobriner's testimony on the point was clear: he said he had not talked to Manuel about *Tanner* before September 21, when the box moved from his chambers to Manuel's. There was some uncertainty as to how and why Tobriner returned the box to the secretary of the court with instructions to send it to Manuel; Tobriner thought Bird had told him that Manuel wanted to write separately, but he was uncertain and Bird had no recollection of such a conversation. Tobriner testified

---

* "Speaking for Bird. . . ." was accurate. Tobriner's letter to Murphy read: "On a related matter, Ms. Connie Kang of your newspaper called the Chief Justice's secretary yesterday and made eight very serious allegations concerning the Chief's administration of the Court and the Judicial Council. . . . I have undertaken the task of answering them." Tobriner later returned to attack Kang by volunteering: "In that regard, may I point out to you that Miss Kang is inaccurate in her statement here that this was sent to editor Reg Murphy and not been sent a copy to her. This, I think, corroborates my statement to you that many things in the Kang articles are incorrect, omit various important matters, and are not to be relied upon." Kang's story said, "Justice Tobriner's responses were contained in a letter to Examiner Editor Reg Murphy, rather than to the reporter who had posed the questions." Kang nowhere asserted that she had not been sent a copy. Tobriner's letter was addressed, "Dear Reg: . . ." Although he must have been tempted, Hufstedler let it pass.

Cartoon by Steve Greenberg, Editorial Cartoonist for the *Daily News of Los Angeles*. © *Daily News of Los Angeles*.

that he had an impressive array of work to do at that time, which made plausible his claim that he did not look at Clark's dissents in *Tanner* until the day before the election.

Tobriner also reported that Clark visited him in his chambers sometime in late September or October (Clark placed the conversation before September 21) and Clark told Tobriner that he was disturbed over the charge that his citation of *Caudillo* was politically motivated. Tobriner recounted the conversation as follows:

In essence [Clark] said that if there was any question about the Tanner *case and its political aspects, that it could be held until after the election. He may also have added that the chief had the power to do that. And I objected. I said, "No, you can't do that, Bill." I said, "What you should do is delete the portion of your dissent which alludes to* Caudillo *because it has no place there. It's legally illogical and improper." And I urged that as strongly as I could. I said, "Bill, you should delete it." And he said, "Well, I don't think I should. . . . Why doesn't the chief pull out her concurring opinion and sign [Tobriner's] opinion in* Tanner?*" I said, "I can't convince the chief to drop her opinion. That's not my function, and I shouldn't ask her to do that, and I can't ask her to do that."*

Tobriner admitted that Clark saw a connection between the *Tanner* case and Bird's confirmation election, but Tobriner insisted that aspect of the conversation made no impression on him because he was so shocked at Clark's "highly improper" suggestion that the case might be held until after the election. Tobriner continued to assert that not until November 6 (when a reporter called) did he connect in his own mind the *Tanner* case and Clark's citation of *Caudillo* with the election.

This preelection conversation between Clark and Tobriner was another instance of people talking together without hearing each other. The explanation for Tobriner's failure to hear may lie in this statement. "I listened to what [Clark] said, and I must say I was not necessarily convinced." Precisely what Tobriner did not believe was never clarified: it may have been Clark's claim to feeling disturbed over the charge that he was politically motivated; it may have been that Tobriner thought Clark was in fact politically motivated. Tobriner's awareness of a controversy between Bird and Clark was suggested by his response to the question of whether or not he reported to anyone the "highly improper" suggestion of Clark's to delay filing *Tanner:*

I felt that it would only harm the situation, that it wasn't up to me to blow the matter up any further. And it occurred. I felt that I didn't want to create any more tension on the court. It was not my function to circulate that information to other justices. It was told to me by Justice Clark not necessarily that I should talk to others about that.

Later, Tobriner amended his answer, saying that on reflection he thought he had reported Clark's improper suggestion to the chief, although he was confident she would never delay the filing of a case for such a reason.

The most dramatic evidence of the deterioration in the relations between Tobriner and Clark came after the election. Clark visited Tobriner on November 28 and Tobriner arranged to have his research attorney, Hal Cohen, present during the discussion to take notes. As Tobriner said, he hardly ever did that in conversations among people who "have confidence in each other." Of course, by then an investigation of the court was an obvious possibility. Nonetheless, that one justice would want to have a witness to and a record of any conversation with another justice was breathtaking evidence of Tobriner's distrust of Clark. Both Tobriner and Cohen made a contemporary memorandum of the conversation. Cohen's notes were much fuller, and according to his memo Clark's visit was prompted by two things: the recent assassination of San Francisco Mayor George Moscone, a good friend of Tobriner's and an acquaintance of Clark's; and the recent publication in the *Washington Post* of Cannon's interview with Clark containing the "decisive reasons" quotation. According to Cohen's notes:

Justice Clark recalled that he had told all of his colleagues that the reason he did not want to sign the statement was because he believed the statement would only blow the situation up [all] over again and it would be a "dumb" thing to do for that reason.

Justice Clark said that he realized that he did not say the same thing to the reporter but instead had told the reporter that he (Clark) felt it was inappropriate to sign the statement about matters that might ultimately be brought before a commission. Justice Clark stated that he wanted to assure Justice Tobriner, as he had stated earlier, that he (Justice Clark) had never stated or suggested that Justice Tobriner had acted for political purposes in the Tanner *case and that he did not believe that Justice Tobriner had acted in any such improper manner. Justice Clark then said that he was glad that I (Hal Cohen) was present so that his (Justice Clark's) position on Justice Tobriner's conduct could be clear. Justice Tobriner said that it was clear that the court had followed normal procedures in the* Tanner *case, and Justice Clark said that was true.*

Clark then referred to his refusal during the McComb proceedings to testify on the ultimate issue before the commission, McComb's competence. Similarly here, Clark thought it inappropriate for him, as Cohen's notes had it, to "speculate as to the motivations of other judges' actions."

Tobriner could not grasp how Clark could simultaneously say that he knew of no wrongdoing by Tobriner and refuse to state publicly that there was no impropriety in the processing of *Tanner*. Clark's reasoning may have been foolish, but his theory was plain enough. He was unwilling to say that the case either had or had not been properly handled because he could not testify as to the private motivations of others. Tobriner's inability to see Clark's point is at least as baffling as Clark's wooden insistence upon it. Clark later made another effort to make himself clear to Tobriner, this time by sending an emissary, Clark's research attorney Richard Morris, to see Tobriner following Clark's response to Bird's suggestion of an exculpatory statement to be issued when *Tanner I* was filed. It will be recalled that Clark sent a memo to Bird, with a copy to the other members of the court, saying, among other things, "In conscience, it must be clear to all on the Court that *Tanner* was signed up and ready for filing well in advance of November. The question remaining appears to be why was it not filed? That question must be resolved by the Commission." Morris was dispatched, according to Tobriner, to tell him, "Please don't get the impression that Justice Clark is trying to impugn your handling of the case or to take exception to what you have done."

Not surprisingly, Hufstedler's effort to explain Clark to Tobriner at the hearings was also unsuccessful. Hufstedler emphasized that Clark "wasn't able to determine what the motivation was for the steps that took place along the way," but Tobriner could not square that with Clark's willingness to say he knew of no wrongdoing by Tobriner (or anyone else).

Hufstedler concluded his questioning of Tobriner on *Tanner* with a summary string of questions short enough to justify quotation:

Q: Did you take any step deliberately to delay the processing of the Tanner *case?*

A: I did not.

Q: Did you take any step to hold up the Tanner *case in connection with any political consideration?*

A: I did not, emphatically.

Q: Did you take any step at any time during the Tanner *case to aid the chief justice's chance of [election]?*

A: I did not.

Q: Do you know of anyone who did any of those things?

A: No.

Q: Did you ask Justice Manuel to write a separate dissent to help slow down the processing of the Tanner *case?*

A: I did not, emphatically.

Q: Did you ask him to write a separate dissent for any purpose?

A: I did not. I never discussed it with Justice Manuel prior to the time he wrote his dissent.

Q: Do you know of anyone else who asked Justice Manuel to write a separate dissent?

A: I do not.

Q: Did the Caudillo *case citation in the Clark dissent delay the processing of* Tanner *in any way?*

A: It did not delay the process in any way.

The last answer was obviously debatable, indeed unlikely.

Tobriner's testimony on the *Fox* case was not informative. Bird had consulted him about *Fox*, and Tobriner had thought at the time that it would be better if Newman's opinion were modified to meet the criticisms in Clark's dissent. If he had ever seen any difference between Clark's dissent and Bird's desire to decide the case on multiple grounds, Tobriner had forgotten what issues divided them by the time he testified, and he told the commission, quite wrongly, that the case had been argued on state rather than federal constitutional grounds.

The Press on Tobriner

The stories reporters filed about Tobriner's testimony generally recounted the day's testimony in a straightforward way. The early stories featured Tobriner's assertion that he never once considered the election in thinking about *Tanner*. Most accounts simply repeated Tobriner's assertion, but the skepticism of some reporters was evident. The *Los Angeles Herald Examiner*, for example, noted that Tobriner's record included

the Northern California Campaign chairmanship for the senate bids of Helen Gahagen Douglas in 1950 and Richard Richards in 1956; being a delegate to the 1956 Democratic National Convention, and being a member of the Executive Committee of the 1958 Edmund G. Brown, Sr. campaign for Governor.

Other stories noted that Hufstedler and Chodos appeared skeptical that Tobriner could have been as unaware of the election climate as he described himself.

Nearly all accounts featured Tobriner's charge that Clark had suggested delaying the release of *Tanner*, calling this development "shocking" or a "surprise" and it made headlines as "Chief Justice's Accuser Stands Accused." Some observed that there was a possible innocuous explanation for Clark's suggestion. Several noted that Clark was in the audience but refused to comment on Tobriner's testimony. Lee Fremstad, capitol bureau chief of the *Sacramento Bee*, wrote a long analytical article over the weekend framed by Tobriner's testimony that was, perhaps, a little harsher than most, but he directly made some points that others only hinted at:

We have now seen the state's highest court with its robes off: mere humans bickering, worrying, defending their reputations, criticizing one another's scholarship and integrity, dawdling on cases, worried about what the press is saying about them and, yes, trying to do a workmanlike job of law throughout it all.

Last week we saw Tobriner perspiring under cross-examination, changing his testimony, misremembering conversations, describing plans to protect himself and the Court before this Commission on Judicial Performance.

Fremstad also noted:

Hufstedler, unfailingly polite, is nonetheless dogged in establishing what he seeks to put into the hearing record. It is a chore that is made harder by Tobriner's reluctance to admit anything that he thinks will hurt him.

BIRD

There was some dramatic flow to Bird's testimony, which stretched out over five days (four half days and one full day). She began as a very aggressive witness, making a number of long speeches that were barely responsive to the questions asked. Perhaps unconsciously, Bird was imitating Governor Jerry Brown, a master of the art of the long answer that changes the subject without answering the question. But Hufstedler did not forget his questions, and Chairman Janes at one point interrupted the chief justice to suggest that "we . . . return to the question." Nonetheless, Bird's first day of testimony was quite effective in presenting her as a strong but not unreasonable human being, particularly to the public reading quotes taken from answers that did not answer.

Bird's testimony on the second, third, and fourth days was often tediously repetitive, through no fault of hers, but it was enlivened by periodic disclosures about her personality that were startling mostly because she apparently did not realize how much she was telling about herself. Unlike Tobriner and Richardson, who at times seemed less than forthright, Bird clearly was being candid. It became obvious that the clash between her and Clark was a major contributing cause of the delay in processing *Tanner* and that her rigid and suspicious character fueled the conflict and made its prompt resolution nearly impossible. It also became increasingly obvious that neither she nor anyone else had delayed the release of *Tanner* for the purpose of improving her chances in the election. To put it another way, Bird showed herself temperamentally ill-suited to be chief justice but, equally clearly, innocent of deliberate delay—the charge the commission was investigating.

Bird's fifth and final day of testimony ended in a public relations disaster that completely undid whatever she had accomplished by her speeches on the first day. On the instruction of counsel, Bird refused to answer questions put to her by Hufstedler. The clips on the nightly news were the first and only good theater to come out of the hearings:

Q: Have any members of your staff delivered to you any documents bearing upon the possible sources of leaks of confidential information from your court which you have not delivered to us?
A: I have no comment.
Q: Well, I would like to ask for an answer to that question.

A: I have no comment to the question.

Q: I'm not asking for comment. I am asking for an answer, Mr. Chairman. . . .

Chairman Janes: Answer the question, Justice Bird.

Mr. Delizonna: I'm instructing her not to answer on my direction. I still believe it invades the attorney-client and work product privilege, and I am instructing her not to answer.

Several days later Bird submitted written replies under oath to the question she earlier had refused to answer, but only a relative few in the public audience outside the hearing room could have noticed either that she had answered the questions or that she had not relied on the privilege against self-incrimination. Why Bird needlessly chose to assert a right she probably did not have, thereby irretrievably alienating the outside public, cannot be answered here, if ever. Probably fatigue, muddled thinking, and confused communications between client and counsel all contributed to the most memorable moment of the hearings.

The dramatic climax apart, the impression that Bird made as a witness is difficult to communicate. Bird did not often use imagery in her answers, but when she did speak metaphorically her images were oddly inapt. For example, in one of her speeches on the first day, widely clipped for use on evening news programs, she said:

This is a very delicate mechanism. I think Mr. Hufstedler at the beginning of this hearing indicated that we are the most fragile branch, and that is true. We are dealing with delicate china here and in some ways I feel we have thrown very delicate china into a laundromat.

Tobriner had referred to a cabinet in his office where he kept the boxes of cases awaiting his attention as a "kennel of barking dogs." Bird expanded on Tobriner's image at one point:

I know Justice Tobriner used the analogy that we were sort of the keeper of hounds and what you have to appreciate is that we don't have a little scottie coming into our office and we pet it for a little while and look at it and then a little scottie goes down to the next office and in comes a beautiful foxhound, we admire it and maybe feed it a little bit and let it go down.

We have a group of hounddogs coming in usually all at the same time and they all want out and the other wants to be fed and the other wants to be groomed and the other one wants to go outside. And so at any time, you have to constantly be on top of a flow almost—and I hesitate to use the words although I have done it in terms of sensitizing people to the problems that the trial courts have in our state—you have an assembly line and we have to avoid the problem of producing all little scotties and all little dachshunds and appreciate each is different. But they are all competing for your time and effort.

Bird also had trouble with figures of speech from the world of sports or games. At one point she told the commission that she thought the time had come to "call" Clark on his behavior toward her and she was asked:

Q: You have used the phrase "call him" or "call him on it." By that do you mean that you thought you should sit down face-to-face and discuss the problem with him?
A: I meant . . . that I should simply let him know that if he were playing another game that I was aware of it and I would call him as you would in the game of bridge or cards.
Mr. Chodos: Poker, Chief Justice Bird.
A: Thank you. I am not aware of that in poker.

With respect to a suggestion from Clark that *Tanner* might be held up until after the election, Bird described her reaction as follows: "I simply felt it was a ball that was coming by just to see how it slid over the base." And later, with respect to the same conversation: "My basic recollection is he just threw out the idea and watched it go across the baseline."

Bird also had a tendency to insist on a special definition for some words and was incapable of seeing that others could use the same words in a different sense without intending to disagree with her substantively. For example, she gave pejorative content to the word "backlog" in connection with the court's docket and got quite testy with Commissioner Chodos even after he explained that he was using the word simply to describe the number of cases pending between the grant of a hearing and argument. The most important of these definitional problems arose over press descriptions of the result in *Tanner* as "overturning" the "use a gun, go to prison" law. Bird regarded that usage as wholly inaccurate and a "political act" designed to arouse public hostility to the court because, apart from herself, the Supreme Court had not held the statute unconstitutional. The distinction between holding a statute ineffective to achieve its purpose and holding it unconstitutional is a legal distinction of importance—the legislature can do something about the former only—but reporters were not wrong to think that "overturn" or "nullify" encompassed both alternatives. Bird, however, built a considerable structure of suspicion on the foundation that press descriptions of *Tanner* as overturning the statute were consciously misleading, as if no other explanation for their word choice were possible.

Bird on Newman and Fox

As they were with all the justices, the commissioners and Hufstedler were consistently deferential to the chief justice, especially in asking questions based on legal points raised by the content of the opinions she had written. As a consequence, Bird was never asked the critical question about her *Fox* opinion: why did she insist upon doing all that original research to write a concurring opinion resting on four independent constitutional grounds when one would have sufficed?* An answer to that question can be inferred from the way she handled what she described as a "very delicate problem [of] one justice indicat[ing] to another justice that perhaps an opinion ought to be written in a different fashion or approach or style."

Bird described to the commission the source of the problem she had had with Newman's opinion in *Fox:*

Justice Newman was new to the court. He had very firm views about how we ought to reform the way we write opinions, and I suspect many people would be in agreement, that our opinions are much too incongruous [probably a transcription error] and much too long. His view was that instead of writing in the grand style we needed to add a more modern style of writing and I think he was working out that style when he came on the court.

In the early days and during this period of time he had a number of cases that circulated in the court for a long time without receiving signatures of other justices, and I think part of the problem was a natural resistance in a conservative body to a different way of approaching something as traditional as opinion writing. [Newman] was . . . attempting to come up with some new ideas. I looked at the record before I came and I think of his early opinions he had about five of the first eleven or twelve opinions that took more than fourteen months to proceed through the court and that was basically because he was writing in a little different way than had been traditional.

Rather than Newman's untraditional *Fox* opinion, Bird "felt that on such a basic issue we needed really a much more fundamental opinion and much more in the tradition of First Amendment and Bill of Rights opinions." That was at best a superficial analysis of the problem with Newman's opinion in *Fox*. Newman did have a tendency to be cryptic at

---

* Compare Bird's explanation for her inability to persuade Tobriner to join her opinion in *Tanner:* "He did not have to reach [the constitutional issue] in his opinion. And in fact, it is better form, and he was correct in not reaching the issue, because you should not reach out to discuss fundamental constitutional issues unless it is absolutely necessary. And if he had done so it would simply be an advisory [opinion] . . . or dictum. It would not be part of the holding of the case for his opinion [to discuss the constitutional issue.]"

critical junctures in his opinions—we have seen an example in his *Tanner II* opinion—but a desire for brevity did not explain Newman's failure to treat the federal constitutional issues Bird wanted him to discuss in *Fox*. Newman's decision to rest his opinion solely on the "preference" language in the California constitution was a deliberate maneuver taken for the purpose of not deciding a close issue of federal law.

Bird sent her schoolmarmish memorandum to Newman about *Fox*, quoted in Chapter V, without first talking with him. Given the uncompromisingly direct, almost rude, tone of her memorandum ("in fact, there is no clear holding at all except that the trial court is affirmed."), a diplomatic overture to soften the blow might have been in order. Bird's explanation for not first speaking to Newman was time and efficiency:

We had some very specific problems with the opinion itself. I thought probably the most efficient way to let him know what the problems were was to draft a memo outlining in specific detail where we had problems and passing the box back to him so that he had some explanation as to why I did not sign his opinion.

Bird said that passing the box was intended to be "an invitation to him to encourage him that perhaps if he'd make some changes I might be able to sign his opinion. And it is a way in which to say it without sounding harsh."

If so intended—Newman can be forgiven if he found the message garbled—her memo failed. Newman responded after a month with a memorandum of his own, never made public, and after a brief conversation with Newman, Bird determined that she would have to write on her own.

At about the same time, however, Bird spoke to Tobriner about her problem with Newman's *Fox* opinion to enlist his aid in attempting to persuade Newman to change his opinion. Bird explained that she

used both Justice Tobriner and Justice Sullivan when he was there, as senior advisors, so to speak. When I had problems in terms of understanding procedures, when I had difficulties understanding some of the prickly personalities that are on the courts, I often went to both Justice Tobriner and Justice Sullivan, who remained physically at the court for a year after he left the court, and sought their advice on how to handle particular problems.

Bird thought Tobriner might be helpful on this particular problem because she believed Newman "knew Tobriner before [Newman's] appointment to the bench, and I think Justice Newman had great respect for

[Tobriner]." Bird also indicated that she was reluctant to speak to New-man herself because

I had been a student at Boalt Hall at the time Justice Newman was dean of the law school, and it was more difficult, I think because I was a good deal younger, to go in and ask him to rethink in some ways the approach that he was using in opinion writing.

Tobriner talked to Newman as Bird had requested without success. Tobriner told the commission:

I felt that his opinion didn't cover the federal questions involved in this constitutional issue. . . . I felt that that should be treated and suggested he might get into and develop his opinion more. Justice Newman was not on the court very long when this case was given to him, a difficult case. It was obvious that he didn't get into [the case] sufficiently thoroughly in my opinion. Since that time he has developed his cases very beautifully, but at this particular point he, I thought, needed to elaborate that propo-sition.

Meanwhile Bird instructed one of her senior research attorneys, John Schulz, to start research on the issues in *Fox*. Schulz indicated that he confined his work to the state constitution because he found the First Amendment "extremely ambiguous . . . in historical perspective." He prepared two drafts before he left the chief justice to join the staff of the Administrative Office of the Courts in August, and Bird then assigned the case to a new staff member, Jeffrey Abramson. Abramson was the one who decided that the federal issues should be explored. As he testi-fied:

I am quite certain that I never received an instruction to delve into the federal cases. The opinion as it came to me was solely on the state consti-tution. At some point, I had a conversation with [Bird] in which we talked about adding the federal into it, and I made my best pitch for doing that, [and she] accepted that.

Bird testified that she originally hoped she would not have to write a separate opinion and that Newman would incorporate into his opinion some of her research and analysis. Later she may have hoped to persuade him to substitute her opinion for his own. But she did not show him drafts as they were developed or even give him a copy of her opinion before circulating it to the whole court as a separate opinion on October 3. As she explained to the commission:

I felt that it was important that the opinion be in as final a shape as possible when it circulated to him because I thought we probably had the best possibility of having him adopt it if it were in final form and very close to being a quality product. That's why I didn't have it circulated to him until I was totally satisfied that we had covered all of the issues.

During much of the time Schulz and Abramson were working on her opinion, the box remained with Justice Tobriner, all told for eighty-six days. Bird testified that leaving the box with Tobriner was intended to pressure Newman:

I thought Justice Tobriner, being a senior justice on the court, could probably bring more pressure to bear on Justice Newman in terms of hold-ing the box and knowing that there was dissatisfaction both in my office and in Justice Tobriner's office with the opinion. I used it as a peer group pressure point.

There is a human if not very noble explanation for Bird's curiously insensitive behavior with respect to Newman and *Fox.* First, Bird char-acteristically shied away from direct personal confrontation. It was much easier for her to write a memorandum to Newman, even a nasty one, than to speak with him. Second, Bird was on top of a bureaucratic pyramid and so long as she could keep the paper off her desk, she was, at least for the moment, ahead. By parceling out work to Schulz and Abramson, Bird could maintain the illusion of motion. The difficulty was that by the time her staff finished an opinion, she was committed to their product. She could have thrown away the bulk of their work in an effort to persuade Newman to make a few additions to his opinion, but that would have hurt morale within her staff and Bird was not indifferent to the feelings of her immediate staff. This explanation for Bird's behavior is unsupported by direct testimony and can be put forward only as a plausible hypothesis inferred from conduct otherwise inadequately ex-plained. It will to some extent be supported by her behavior with Clark in *Tanner.* But assuming the hypothesis is correct, it answers the ques-tion of why Bird spent six months writing an opinion in *Fox* on four separate constitutional grounds when one would have sufficed.

The hypothesis also suggests some other conclusions. First, there was an enormous amount of waste motion in Bird's chambers on *Fox.* If she had spent ten minutes thinking hard and perhaps talking out her problem with Newman she could probably have persuaded him to ex-pand somewhat his preference argument and to dispose of the proce-dural problems in *Fox* more adequately than he had, thereby saving six months of effort and perhaps prompting Clark to withdraw his separate dissent. Second, Bird was ill served by her staff. Schulz was proud of having "discovered" the second state constitutional ground; he should have been ashamed of suggesting that as a basis for her decision. Abramson apparently led Bird into the federal cases; there was no good reason to make that pitch. Bird was responsible for accepting their suggestions, but her staff was not making it easier for her to be a good judge. Third, and most important, her senior advisor, Tobriner, was not performing his counseling function well. He gladly ran errands for her, but he was not, apparently, questioning her judgment or analysis very closely. Tobriner would have been much more useful to Bird if he had tried to interpret Newman to her and specifically if he had encouraged her to talk to Newman herself. If he did any of those, there is no hint of it in the testimony.

Bird on Clark and Tanner

The box in *Tanner* first came to Bird's chambers on May 30. Shortly thereafter, Bird instructed Richard Neuhoff, her staff attorney principally charged with criminal matters, to speak with Clark's staff. Bird and Neuhoff were at the time skeptical of Tobriner's conclusion that the legislature did not intend robbers who used guns to go to prison and therefore they were disposed to agree with Clark on that point. Thus, Bird, unlike Tobriner, would have to confront the constitutional issue if she were going to affirm Judge Regan's conclusion that Tanner could be put on probation. Bird wanted Neuhoff to find out what answer, if any, Clark would have to a constitutional argument based on *Tenorio*. At that time, of course, Clark's dissent did not discuss that case or the constitutional issue. Neuhoff spoke to Richard Morris, one of Clark's senior research attorneys, and Morris after a few weeks gave Neuhoff a brief memorandum discussing *Tenorio*, *Cortez*, and *Ruiz*. The memorandum was unpersuasive to Bird and Neuhoff, and on July 11 the chief justice circulated her concurring opinion. Bird herself had a conversation with Morris about the boxes that had accumulated in Clark's office as Clark was leaving for Europe, urging Morris to pass on those boxes Clark's staff was not working on. Morris told Bird that he thought Clark would wish to revise his dissent in *Tanner* to meet her opinion by discussing the constitutional issue Clark had not covered.

Clark's new dissent, citing *Caudillo* in a footnote, circulated on August 15, shortly after his return. Neuhoff was the first to call the *Caudillo* citation in Clark's dissent to Bird's attention and they discussed it, "trying to understand," in Bird's words, "what legal theory they were trying to use to indicate that we were inconsistent [in *Tanner*] with the position we had taken in *Caudillo*." Bird and Neuhoff agreed that there was no inconsistency. Bird gave the commission two reasons for this conclusion. First, the decision in *Caudillo* dealt with the question of legislative intent—did rape constitute great bodily injury for purposes of enhancing the punishment for burglary? *Tanner*, on the other hand, involved the issue of whether the legislature could constitutionally prohibit a judge from striking an allegation that a robber had used a gun. Since the cases involved different issues, legislative intent versus constitutional power, they could not be inconsistent. Although an accurate description of a difference between the cases, this analysis overlooked entirely Bird's assertion in *Caudillo* that the legislature alone was authorized to define what conduct constituted criminal misbehavior. That language was what Clark found inconsistent.

Bird's second basis for thinking that her *Caudillo* opinion was irrelevant to *Tanner* is much harder to grasp. Bird described it as the adjudication as opposed to sentencing distinction. As she explained to the commission:

A: In Tanner, *the court was dealing with an adjudication, the question of whether or not the court had the power to strike a use finding. We had to reach that issue because we had come to the conclusion that the legislature intended to take away from the trial court the power to strike a use finding. So then the question became one of adjudication. Do the courts and the trial courts in this state have the power under the constitution in an adjudication as opposed to simply a sentencing? The sentencing comes after you make the determination on the use finding.*

Q: *And conversely in* Caudillo *you were dealing with a sentencing problem. Now, that was different in what respect?*

A: In Caudillo *you were simply dealing with [whether] rape was its own great bodily injury. The legislature had determined it was not, so you never reach the issues as to whether or not you can strike the use finding.*

Q: *And you were dealing with the extent of enhancement or whether or not it would be enhanced in* Caudillo, *that is, of the sentence?*

A: *Well, you don't reach that because the legislature indicated it was not its own great bodily injury, so the use enhancement is simply struck at the beginning rather than at the end of the process in* Tanner, *where we concluded that the legislature intended to take away the power of the trial court to strike the use finding.*

None of Bird's research attorneys referred to this distinction between adjudication and sentencing as an additional ground for thinking *Caudillo* irrelevant to *Tanner*. It is possible that there is something there that Bird failed to express clearly—she later referred to it as a fairly subtle argument—but, if so, it, like some foreign words or phrases, defies ready translation into English.

Bird also had a conversation about *Tanner* with Scott Sugarman, her other senior research attorney. Sugarman had not heretofore worked on the *Tanner* case because he was principally assigned to civil matters.

Bird's purpose was, she testified, "to test, as I had with [Neuhoff], whether or not I was perhaps missing an argument or an issue." Sugarman testified that he had had two conversations with Bird, during the first of which she explained to him why she thought *Caudillo* irrelevant; before the second conversation he read or reread the opinions in *Tanner* to familiarize himself with the problem. Like Neuhoff, Sugarman agreed with Bird's analysis, and Bird instructed him to talk with Morris about the problem and, if he were unsatisfied with Morris's response, to ask him whether the citation of *Caudillo* was "politically motivated." Sugarman said he had had no clear understanding of what Bird meant by "politically motivated" and did not ask for clarification. The commission pressed Bird as to what she meant by the phrase and she responded: "I don't believe I thought about it in terms of my own election. I thought that [the citation of *Caudillo*] was done to personally embarrass me." Commissioner Willoughby asked her:

Q: Is there a particular reason you chose the phrase "politically motivated" rather than, say, "personally motivated"?

A: Well, I guess what I was trying to get across is that I thought it was done not to personally just bother me within the court but to demean me in the eyes of the public. We had had two other occasions where there had been a problem, and I just felt this was the third one and perhaps I should not let it go by.

Willoughby was careful not to ask about the other instances, but Bird volunteered the answer "as the most graphic way I can illustrate":

A: Justice Clark publicly and often to the Court of Appeal justices, I think on more than one occasion, made comments concerning the ninety-day rule and an interpretation of the ninety-day rule that would require our court to interpret it to mean that a case should be filed within ninety days after the oral argument. I felt that this was an unfair comment in that if we were to do that as a collegial body, he would be one of the first people who would have to reform his own habits to live within the ninety-day rule, and . . . he knew full well that we on the court would not publicly comment on that fact. So that when he publicly made statements concerning the ability of our court to live within the ninety days, he knew full well that I as chief justice would not come out and say, "That would be fine if Justice Clark would live by his own prescription."

The second issue involved the appointment of Justice Auerbach, who is a municipal court judge, to sit at the Supreme Court. When I first came on the court, I felt that our trial courts had been overlooked, and I felt especially the tremendous contribution that the municipal courts made to our system. And one way that I thought we could acknowledge that would be by the appointment of a municipal court judge to sit for the very first time with the California Supreme Court. I made that assignment. And it happened to be in a case in which Justice Clark himself was disqualified.

A press release was made up indicating that Judge Auerbach would be sitting with the Supreme Court; for the first time a municipal court judge would be sitting with the California Supreme Court. The press release also indicated that Judge Auerbach would be taking the place of Justice Clark. As a courtesy I sent the press release down to Justice Clark's office, and we received back word that Justice Clark wanted his name deleted and did not want any mention that he was the judge who was disqualified in the case. So we deleted the reference. When the press called, we indicated that they would be informed as to who the justice was who Judge Auerbach would be replacing at the time the calendar was called.

As a result, a number of articles came out indicating my arrogance in being unwilling to indicate who the judge was who was not going to be sitting for this particular case. An editorial came out in the San Francisco Chronicle *speaking in terms of their hope that it was my inexperience and not my callousness toward the public generally that caused me not to give out the information as to who was sitting on this particular case. I later learned that when Justice Clark was called on the matter, he indicated to the press that he was the justice who was disqualified on the particular case. . . . I waited for Justice Clark to correct the record on that, and it never came.*

Mr. Willoughby: Did you suggest to him that he do so?

A: I was in Los Angeles at the calendar. And I informed him of the editorial in the Chronicle, *that it had been critical. I did not ask him to correct the record. I assumed that he would, as a gentleman, correct it. It did not happen. I simply felt by the time this happened that in terms of our own personal relationship . . . we would be on a better footing if perhaps I cleared the air and called him on what he was doing this time since I had not called him previously on the other occasions.*

Q: You're not suggesting, are you, that he was in some way responsible for the press calls and the newspaper editorial that followed?

A: I'm not suggesting that he manipulated the press. No.

Q: You are saying, however, that when all this occurred . . . you expected that he would . . . step forward and correct the record? You are suggesting that?

A: . . . I did not expect any kind of retraction from the newspapers, and I was not asking him to do any of that. I simply felt that is was unfair to leave the impression that it was due to my callousness that we had not given out his name as the person who was disqualified in this particular case. I had hoped that he would simply pick up the telephone, call the editor, and correct the record. Just for the future, not that I expected any retractions in the newspapers at all.

This glimpse inside Bird's mind was not asked for by the commission. Clark later testified that he was unaware that Bird was irritated at him over the Auerbach incident until he heard her testimony. Bird's reaction, taking the facts as she gave them, was excessive but characteristic. She invented a rule as to how a person ought to behave and without communicating that rule to the person involved she interpreted a failure to follow her rule as proof of an intention to hurt her, as if that were the only possible explanation for Clark's conduct.

Sugarman chatted briefly with Morris about the *Caudillo* citation. Sugarman described his talk:

I told Mr. Morris that the chief justice had asked me to come down and speak with him about Justice Clark's reference to Caudillo *in the dissenting opinion in* Tanner. *I told him that it was her opinion that the two cases, that is, her opinion in* Caudillo *and her opinion in* Tanner, *were not fairly compared in Justice Clark's opinion, that it was like comparing apples and oranges. I explained that the sole issue in the majority opinion in* Caudillo, *as well as her concurring opinion, was one of statutory interpretation and that her opinion in* Tanner *was solely directed to the constitutional question, which was never reached in* Caudillo. *And therefore, we saw no way in which they were fairly compared. I told him the chief justice wanted me to ask him why the reference was there and to ask him if the reference was politically motivated. I believe I sort of spoke this prologue probably relatively uninterrupted. Mr. Morris denied it was politically motivated, and the bulk of our conversation was a discussion, essentially of the merits, that is, [whether] the two cases [were] fairly compared.*

Morris asked Sugarman "at least three times" whether the chief justice wanted the citation deleted, to which Sugarman said no. However, Sugarman admitted that deletion was the logical end result of Bird's analysis, telling Morris:

"Even if I haven't convinced you that they're not fairly compared, that is, even if you're standing entirely on your challenge to the chief justice's constitutional argument, it seems to me your point is made in the text and in the first line of the footnote and that the reference to Caudillo *is gratuitous." What I was trying to do was say there's several arguments being made in the dissent and my coming down here was to point out one [that] made no sense.*

Morris denied any political motivation and, according to Sugarman, added that he "wouldn't want to provide ammunition to the chief's detractors."

Sugarman reported back to Bird. Soon thereafter Morris had another conversation with Sugarman, which Bird understood as follows:

> Sugarman reported that Mr. Morris had come to his office and indicated that he had spoken with Justice Clark and that both he and Justice Clark had indicated that there was no political motivation at all in the reference and that because the issue had been raised they felt it was necessary to elevate the footnote into the body of the opinion, but that if I would . . . withdraw my concurring opinion that they would withdraw any reference at all to Caudillo.

Shortly before Clark circulated his revised dissent on August 25, he called Bird. She testified about their phone conversation:

> A: Justice Clark indicated that he was upset by the reference that I had made to political motivation, and I indicated to him that my problem was that I was interested from a personal point of view as to . . . what his reasoning was for putting the citation of People v. Caudillo into the opinion. We commenced a brief discussion in which I attempted to illustrate to him that he was comparing apples and oranges, that he did not have an analogous situation in Caudillo. He indicated to me that he felt he did. And we got into a discussion in which I made clear to him that I was not . . . asking him to remove anything from his opinion. I was merely interested in what his motivation was in putting it in and what his legal analysis had been. . . . I don't know whether he said he was "hurt" or "disturbed" by the fact that I would indicate that I thought there might be some political motivation, and I indicated that I thought if there were not a legal basis for it it may have been done to personally embarrass me, that I wasn't asking for the removal of anything. I simply wanted to know why he was doing it.
> Q: And what reaction did you get from Justice Clark, if any?
> A: Basically Justice Clark was disturbed at my reference to political motivation. And he attempted to try to explain to me his legal reasoning. I kept saying to him, "You're comparing apples and oranges, Bill. I am trying to show you the distinctions because there are distinctions to be made here." He indicated to me he could not see them and as a result he felt it would be necessary to elevate the footnote into the body of the opinion. I said, "Fine, you do whatever you think is proper in this case."

Bird became, as she put it, "pretty annoyed" when the green sheet accompanying Clark's revised dissent came around. In it Clark said:

The staff to the Chief Justice has requested that our citation to People v. Caudillo *in footnote 8 of the opinion be deleted. The reasons given for deletion are that* Caudillo *is inapposite and that its use is "politically motivated."*

I reject both the request and the unfortunate reasoning. Rather, I now expand the discussion of Caudillo *to show that it is clearly apposite, moving it from footnote to body.*

Bird was "raw" for two reasons:

He misrepresented my position in terms of the green sheet. He knew from speaking to me on the telephone that I had not asked that the reference be deleted, and I was extremely annoyed that he misrepresented and put something that was inaccurate on the green sheet to the court. Secondarily, I felt that this was an issue between Justice Clark and myself. It was not an issue for the entire court. I had approached it by approaching his staff first, who had written the footnote, and then spoken to him. I felt that he was needlessly escalating the matter and misrepresenting it to the entire court. It was a personal issue between Justice Clark and myself and how we dealt with each other.

Hufstedler pointed out to Bird that the green sheet said that staff to the chief justice, not she, had requested the deletion, to which Bird responded:

Yes, I realize that, and I took greater offense . . . because I thought it was deliberate in the sense that it indicated staff and did not indicate myself, when he had spoken to me personally and he knew my personal feelings about it. And he knew full well from knowing my own personality that my staff didn't speak for me, that I spoke for myself and they didn't overrule me on something like this. . . . I could not understand why he didn't represent what my viewpoint was since he knew it quite clearly.

The affair had all the wisdom and detachment of a lover's quarrel between eighth-graders, and, like an eighth-grader, Bird discussed it with all her friends.

I think I may have had a conversation with Justice Tobriner asking him if perhaps I had missed some legal point in the allusions to the Caudillo *case, attempting to test whether or not there had been some significant point or some issue that I was just unable to see or comprehend. And he indicated to me that he did not see any reason for the reference to Caudillo. I believe I also had a conversation with Justice Manuel at some point in which I may have indicated that I thought this was unfortunate, that it had been escalated to the entire court. . . . It's possible I may have said something to Justice Newman about my annoyance. I was pretty annoyed.*

Manuel and Newman probably were not consulted by Bird about the relevance of the *Caudillo* citation. Tobriner, however, was, and that was a critical moment in the *Tanner* affair. At the very least, Tobriner could have told Bird what he told the commission later: the citation of *Caudillo* was of trifling importance and not worth getting upset about. Neuhoff and Sugarman could also have told Bird that Clark's citation was rational, at worst a cheap shot, but they were her subordinates, and although she testified that she was testing her analysis with Neuhoff and Sugarman there was no question what she wanted to hear. Tobriner, however, was uniquely situated to bring her to her senses. His failure to do so has to be ranked as a major cause of the controversy.

Tobriner had a second chance to make peace when Clark visited him late in September or early in October. Tobriner's account of the conversation, quoted in the previous section, makes it clear that Clark was hoping that Tobriner would play the role of mediator, but Tobriner's only advice to Clark was to delete the citation of *Caudillo* because it was legally illogical and improper.

The box in *Tanner* was with Tobriner from August 25 to September 21. Tobriner himself carried the *Tanner* box to the secretary of the court's office on September 21, stating that he understood that Manuel wanted to work on the case. Much of the testimony before the commission focused on why Tobriner did that (he had no clear recollection) and in particular whether either Tobriner or Bird had urged Manuel to write a dissent. Both Bird and Tobriner denied urging Manuel to write separately and the commission never heard publicly from Manuel on the issue, but some things about Manuel's role seem reasonably plain nonetheless.

Bird told Neuhoff when Clark's dissent citing *Caudillo* first appeared that she hoped neither Manuel nor Richardson would sign Clark's dissent. So far as known, she never discussed the subject with Richardson, but she did have a conversation with Manuel on the subject. The triggering event was Attorney General Younger's October 9 and 10 campaign speeches, in which he charged that the Supreme Court had finished work on some death penalty cases and *Tanner* and was withholding their release until after the election. Manuel's entire career before his appointment to the superior court had been in the attorney general's office, and according to Bird he respected and admired Younger. Bird testified that Manuel was "upset" by Younger's accusations and told her that he thought Younger's charge was "unfortunate and inaccurate." Bird was uncertain whether she learned then or earlier that Manuel was contemplating a separate dissent in *Tanner*, but they agreed that the processing of *Tanner* should not be influenced by extraneous events such as Younger's speech. Bird recalled saying to him,, "If you feel you need the time, you should take the time. If you feel you can do it quickly, you should do it quickly." Manuel told her that Clark "had indicated to him to hold off on writing a dissent in the hopes that [Clark] could bring some kind of accommodation between himself and [Bird]." Manuel must have been aware of Bird's strong feeling about Clark's dissent—indeed, she recalled telling him that she was sorry the matter had been escalated —and he could have understood from their conversation that Bird would be gratified if he would not sign Clark's opinion and write separately. Bird denied having thought of the fact that if Manuel dissented separately it would almost certainly mean that the opinion would not be filed before the election. On balance, Bird's answers to the ultimate questions seem accurate:

Q: Did you seek in any way to encourage Justice Manuel to file a dissent in the Tanner *case?*

A: I don't believe I did, unless you could say that my indicating to him that I felt the footnote unfortunate and not relevant was by implication a suggestion that he not stay on the opinion.

Q: And further, to the extent that you said in effect, "Take whatever time you need, don't be pressured," did you intend by that to imply that he should therefore not make any special efforts to move Tanner?

A: No, quite the contrary. He should do whatever he would normally do.

During the state bar convention in mid-September, Clark and Newman appeared on a panel before a newly formed association of staff lawyers for the courts, composed of research attorneys for the Courts of Appeal and the Supreme Court. Clark testified that he was unaware that Kang was in the audience, but she wrote a story for the *San Francisco Examiner* on September 13 under the headline "Logjam at the High Court Corral," which offended Bird. Kang said Clark had disclosed that "an unprecedented backlog of 248 cases are pending before the high court" and he "took issue" with the court's policy of "not abiding by the so-called ninety-day rule."

The court heard oral argument October 3–5 in Sacramento. At that point Clark told Bird he would like to speak with her; she put him off. As she phrased it, she had been "cool but correct" at least since the Kang article, and their epochal meeting did not take place until October 16 or 17. (Clark thought the meeting was a week earlier.) Buehl was present at Bird's request to take notes of the conversation. Buehl did not take short-hand but he reconstructed his notes as best he could some months later for Hufstedler. Although obviously incomplete, Buehl's notes nonetheless give a flavor of the conversation. The brackets indicate where Buehl inserted material.

CLARK: *Oh, did Younger call Wiley?*

BIRD: *Younger's assertion that* Tanner *is being held has been in the papers.*

CLARK: *I can recall an article by Nicholson a few months ago.*

BIRD: *We're getting calls from the press on Younger's assertion.*

CLARK: *I did not see Younger. Did Wiley see you?*

BIRD: *Yes. I told him to take his time and not be intimidated.*

CLARK: *Two weeks ago, I suggested it be shelved if something could be made out of the* Caudillo *citation [in my dissent in* Tanner*], but I cannot in conscience leave it out.*

BIRD: *[Regarding the green sheet attached to latest revision of your dissent in* Tanner,*] I only asked "why" you put [the reference to Caudillo] in your opinion, not that the reference be removed.*

CLARK: *That's not an issue.*

BIRD: *It is an issue because no one asked that anything be removed.*

CLARK: *Dick Morris says that Dick Neuhoff and someone else from your staff asked that it be removed.*

BIRD: *No one asked that anything be removed, only for an explanation as to why the reference to* Caudillo *was placed in your dissent. Not even in [McGaughran and (a pending case)] where you used language referring to "subhuman" misfits were you asked to remove anything.*

CLARK: *It's not unusual for someone to ask for removal.*

BIRD: *It never happened. You had the last word from me. I simply was curious as to why. In the future, represent me, not what someone told you.*

CLARK: *Morris was told that* Caudillo *did not belong there, that [its inclusion in my* Tanner *dissent] was politically motivated, and that it should be removed.*

BIRD: *We have no difference of opinion regarding what I said to you.*

CLARK: *I have notes.*

BIRD: *I never asked you to remove anything.*

CLARK: *No, you did not. But this really is not important.*

BIRD: *It's important to me.*

CLARK: *[The phrase] "politically motivated" greatly disturbed me. There have been a number of [?—notes unfinished here]. If we could set that aside for a moment, I'd like to do whatever we can to get cases moving and clear the backlog.*

BIRD: *You really do not do any service when you go out and make statements about a backlog. I can't as Chief Justice say you're wrong in public. I have made every effort to accommodate all views, including yours. I was [?—notes unfinished here].*

I don't care what you feel regarding me and my election, but I do ask that you do not undercut the institution at a time like this of heavy attack. The figures do not show a huge backlog. In fact, the conference load is up 10%, and yet the number of grants is similar to past years. Only [?—notes unfinished here].

CLARK: *I have had calls from the press. I had a call in the last hour from a woman reporter in San Diego asking about cases being held. [She wanted me to comment] on or off the record. I spoke on the record. [She asked me,] are you aware of cases having seven signatures but not filed. I said that was not true.*

I've felt your chill for three weeks now. I felt it was Tanner, but it may be something deeper. I did not use the term "huge backlog" but gave the number of cases pending, saying it was too large in my estimation if we try to correct all errors. [At the same panel discussion,] Justice Newman called for more staff.

BIRD: *But the problem is it gets called a backlog. The court is busier now than it has been in some time. Also, you are assigned a lot more cases now than you were under Wright.*

CLARK: *I liked [being assigned the (name of pending case).] Frank, Wiley, and I seem to have been fingered, especially by the national press. A number [of those publications,] such as the Wall Street Journal, seem very sympathetic to the court's side and your side. I would hope you might [?—notes unfinished here]. I feel you're overly sensitive to the press.*

BIRD: *Nonsense. If I were, I'd be dead by now.*

CLARK: *I feel our relationship has been good, but I am concerned by your coolness of the last few weeks. I felt it was Tanner, but I would hope you would pick up the phone and call me.*

BIRD: *Fine, but I do not want to see it in the press the next morning.*

CLARK: *The purpose of the green sheet is to get it off our chest in here, or by phone, or nose-to-nose. [Do you feel something has happened along those lines?] I judge from your smile that it has.*

BIRD: *I'll let you know after the election.*

CLARK: *I'd rather know on an ongoing basis about any area where you feel a wrong has been done that [?—notes unfinished here].*

BIRD: *I do feel that you've done the court harm in the backlog article ["Logjam in the High Court Corral" by K. Connie Kang, in the*

September 13, 1978, edition of the San Francisco Examiner]. *If you feel I'm a bad administrator and am the cause of the backlog, come to me and tell me. [But press statements of this sort] play into the hands of those who want to find a backlog.*

CLARK: *I don't know if I ever used the phrase backlog or logjam. I wasn't expecting the press [to be covering the panel discussion]. The Kang article uses the phrase "unprecedented backlog."*

BIRD: *If that's so, then in the future you might indicate that what you're talking about is a heavier-than-ever workload. Did you call Kang to say that's not what you said?*

CLARK: *No. If I started doing that [I'd have no time for anything else.]*

BIRD: *[What is stated in the] headlines becomes accepted as the truth and then that leads to further inquiries. But I don't say that you're in error in the press. [The Chief Justice then gave an example of an unfavorable article and editorial in the San Francisco* Chronicle *which arose out of a news release which the Administrative Office of the Courts had issued to announce the assignment of Los Angeles Municipal Court Judge Eric Auerbach to sit with the Supreme Court in June 1977 on a case in which Justice Clark had disqualified himself. . . .]*

CLARK: *I've never been very active in the Republican Party, but I felt very badly about [their coming out against you.] I hope you will not find me guilty by association.*

BIRD: *I've never found anyone guilty by association.*

CLARK: *I think I can understand your feelings about the backlog story.*

BIRD: *I wouldn't mind as much if I hadn't knocked myself out to get cases moving.*

CLARK: *They're moving. What should I do with* Tanner?

BIRD: *I think you should allow him [Justice Manuel] the time to write his opinion. I also want to answer some things. But that has nothing to do with holding up cases. If I'd wanted to do that, we wouldn't have gotten out Proposition 13 or busing, or I would have joined you and Richardson in* Caudillo *because I knew my decision was going to put me out on a limb.*

[At this point, I (Buehl) was called out of the room for approximately 30 seconds.]

CLARK: *Maybe the* Tanner *case should not be gotten out until after November lest there be any suggestion that Younger's statement influenced the court.*

BIRD: *No, it goes out when it's ready to be filed—no earlier and no later.*

CLARK: *If you were to withdraw your concurrence out of that opinion altogether (and I'm not anymore telling you what to do than you were telling me [to remove the reference to* Caudillo *from my opinion) and join the majority, I would remove the* Caudillo *reference from my dissent.*]

BIRD: [*That would not be intellectually honest of me.*] *I do not dodge any political brickbats.*

CLARK: *I noticed.*

BIRD: *We'll file* Tanner *when it's ready to be filed, whether that's before the election or after.*

[*At this point, Justice Clark and the Chief Justice exchanged a few pleasantries and shook hands. Justice Clark then left the Chief Justice's chambers.*]

The Buehl notes, although far from a verbatim record, were as close as the commission came to the Watergate tapes and in one respect they had a comparable impact: it was impossible thereafter to maintain the belief that high judicial office necessarily ennobles its holder. Bird's and Clark's pettiness and preoccupation with the press were at war with the image that judges are above politics, indifferent to public opinion, and responsive only to the professional and impartial discipline of the law. Unfortunately, the commission's attention tended to focus on what was, at bottom, a bootless inquiry—who was the more petty, Bird or Clark? —as if the answer to that question would somehow lead to a determination of innocence or guilt. As a consequence, some aspects of the Buehl notes were downplayed, if not overlooked entirely. In particular, the notes demonstrated that Bird and Clark were obsessed with how the press was covering them.

Bird's extreme irritation at Clark's "misrepresenting" her as requesting the deletion of the *Caudillo* citation obviously baffled Clark and is indeed inexplicable. There was nothing wrong with asking for a deletion and, despite her protestations, that was the obvious and only plausible purpose for the charge, which Bird never withdrew, that Clark was politically motivated. Neither Bird nor Clark suggested the simple resolution of their contretemps: if she would withdraw the charge of political motivation, Clark would delete the citation. Despite intense interrogation over the fine points of this squabble, no one on the commission asked whether that possible resolution ever entered the mind of either participant.

Bird's testimony before the commission amplified what she meant by not wanting to see her comments "in the press the next morning" and "I'll let you know after the election."

Clark was talking about the green sheet, [that it] should be used to get things off your [chest], * *and the rest sort of implying, "What's wrong with*

---

* Bird said "back" but she probably meant "chest." Clark certainly did.

you? Why are you raising these issues to me?" And *my response basically
was that I felt uncomfortable discussing them at that point because I felt
that things were seeping out of the court and I prefer simply to talk about
that later. Now, he may not have been aware that I was talking about
leaks, although I think at one point I said I didn't care to read about these
things in the morning paper the next day. Sometimes in conversations
people don't communicate directly, and what he had in mind may be
different from what I had in mind at that time. . . .*

Bird was quite explicit in her testimony that she then thought Clark may
have been responsible for some leaks:

> *I had some suspicions in my own mind at that time that he or
> someone on his staff might be releasing some information. I think that is
> what I was alluding to. I am not sure I made it very clear to him, however.
> It was [a] veiled reference, I think.*

The puzzling aspect of this testimony was the leaks Bird had in mind. As
of October 16 or 17, no leaks of accurate inside information had surfaced
in the papers. Clark's conversation with the San Diego reporter suggested that reporters may have been fed some information, but Bird
could not have known about this call before then. Only Younger's largely
erroneous charge about death penalty cases and *Tanner* had been
printed, prompting reporters to call the court and Buehl's response that
Younger's charges were unfounded, but this incident would not appear
to justify Bird's sense that "things were seeping out of the court."
    Unfortunately, no one asked what she was talking about, but her
charge of leaks probably related to something else Bird told the commission. She said it was not until the Younger statement that she began to
see a "pattern," connecting it up with her election:

> *A: The focus at that period [August] was on this personalized prob-
> lem between Justice Clark and myself. It wasn't in reference to the elec-
> tion. Later I began to see perhaps a pattern might be there as to why this
> was done.*
> *Q: At what point did you perceive such a pattern?*
> *A: When Mr. Younger began charging the court with delaying this
> case.*
> *Q: That would have been October 10 or thereabouts?*
> *A: Yes.*
> *Q: At that point did you believe that there may have been some
> connection between the Caudillo citation and your upcoming election?*
> *A: I think the possibility crossed my mind.*

Bird apparently meant that she "was being involved in General Younger's campaign as an issue to attack in the last days of the election." She was not asked to describe the pieces in the mosaic that made up the pattern in her mind but some are obvious. One was the Kang "Logjam at the High Court Corral" article, which came from Clark; another was the Younger charge of delay, which Bird tied to Clark through Edwin Meese, Jr:

Around that time I made some connection with the [Los Angeles Daily Journal] article that came out in which Mr. Meese was one of the co-authors, and someone had informed me or I learned in some way that he was connected with General Younger's campaign for the governorship or had some role in it.

Meese had succeeded Clark as Reagan's executive secretary and they had remained friends after Clark went on the bench. Bird evidently believed Clark either had fed or would give Meese derogatory information from inside the court to be used in the campaign.

Bird was right in one respect the commission rather overlooked. Her election and the gubernatorial campaign were inextricably intertwined so that any attack on her or the court was simultaneously a blow to Brown and a boost for Younger. Undoubtedly, Bird was supporting Brown and Clark, Younger. Furthermore, Clark could have been asked by his former political associates for any information about the court or Bird that might be helpful in the gubernatorial campaign. Under the circumstances, Bird did well to exercise caution in talking with Clark, though she may have been overly suspicious, but the Clark-Meese-Younger connection was pure speculation. If Bird had hard evidence, it was never revealed, and Clark denied discussing court matters with Meese before the election.*

Fox and *Tanner* came together in Bird's testimony concerning what was said at the Wednesday conferences in October. Mosk was concerned about the *Fox* case. In the spring he had suggested that the case not be filed on Christmas Eve. (He was sometimes reported to have said, "We shouldn't shoot Santa Claus on Christmas Eve.") He raised the subject again in October, after Bird's opinion had circulated. Bird described the discussion:

Justice Mosk was very agitated. He felt that the Fox case should get out. He was concerned that it was going to be filed right at Christmastime,

---

* He did consult Meese after the *Tanner* investigation was in prospect and offered to disclose the content of their conversation. However, Bird's lawyers, having earlier relied upon the attorney-client privilege, thought it impolitic to ask for disclosure because Clark testified that he had consulted with Meese for his advice as a lawyer.

and that politically that was the worst time for a court to file a sensitive opinion involving church-state issues, and that politically we should be a little more astute, and that we should attempt to get the opinion out sooner. He was quite agitated about it. It's my remembrance . . . that Justice Tobriner leaned over and tried to calm him down. I suspect I added fuel rather than calming the situation. I indicated I thought we ought to be able to discuss it as mature adults. He was very much concerned that the opinion go out, and I indicated to him—he said something about, "well—" sarcastically, I believe, and he felt that was legitimate. I am not being critical of him in saying that. He felt that the opinion was probably going to go out on Christmas Eve, and said so. I indicated to him that the opinion was not going to go out on Christmas Eve. It was not going to go out on Christmas Day. It was not going to go out on New Year's Eve. It was not going to go out on New Year's Day. It was not going to go out on Easter Sunday. It was not going to go out on Eastern Orthodox [Easter]. It was going out no sooner and no later than when it was ready. *

The tastelessness of Bird telling Mosk to behave like a "mature adult" was startling. Bird justified her strong reaction as follows:

My very strong feeling was that the court was under tremendous pressure at this time and we were slowly being drawn into the political whirlwind. And I was very much concerned for the institution that it not be, and I was trying to indicate that we had to process cases based on the case and not based on some idea of . . . what was smart politically and that we were trying to balance that. I may have been a little more emphatic because I thought it was an unfair criticism in terms of the Fox case. It was a very difficult case. I had somebody that entire summer working on the case. I put tremendous pressure on my own staff and I suspect that in my comments to Justice Mosk I reflected that vehemence.

---

* Clark presented a considerably different picture of Mosk's concern: "I got the clear understanding that [Mosk] was not concerned about either the religious or the political aspects of the [Fox] case; rather, he was troubled by the constant reference to this case. One Christmas had already come and gone. It did not seem to concern anyone, including Justice Mosk, that this was filed on Christmas or Easter or any other religious holiday. The context of "Let's not do it on Christmas Eve" was more in jest, and he smiled when he said it. Rather the concern, and I believe I share the concern, was the constant push to get out cases, and yet this of all cases seemed to be moving nowhere and the answers when given as to what was happening were non-answers. It had become, shall we say in the words of Snoopy, just curiouser and curiouser and that there were no answers on it, and so he was rather firm in this particular conversation. But the religious-political [concern], in my recall, never arose from him or from anyone else other than in the jesting remark earlier that year." It was Alice, not Snoopy, who said "Curiouser and curioser."

Clark at the same conference raised the *Tanner* matter, urging that the case be filed as soon as possible. Bird responded:

It's my memory that I made a sarcastic statement, something to the effect that I thought it strange that the only two cases that the newspapers were specifically raising were two cases in which there was a dissent by a particular judge on the court and it was the same judge.

Putting these remarks together, it seems that what may have begun as a suspicion in Bird's mind had by October become a conviction that Clark was trying to embarrass her publicly. Whether she thought Clark's goal was to unseat her or simply to help Younger is insignificant.

Bird exhibited poor legal judgment and inefficient bureaucratic management in *Fox*, flaws that doubtless could be found somewhere in the record of any chief justice. Her behavior toward Clark in *Tanner* was qualitatively different. Consider the matters she mentioned as forming a pattern that proved Clark's intent to embarrass her:

1. Clark's citation of *Caudillo* in his *Tanner* dissent. Whether relevant or not, the citation was at most of trifling consequence; more important, it was apposite.

2. Clark's telling Court of Appeal justices that the ninety-day rule should be extended to the Supreme Court when Clark regularly violated the rule himself. Clark, like every other Supreme Court justice, would have to reform his work habits if the court were to start complying with the ninety-day rule, but that should not bar him from advocating a change.

3. The Auerbach incident. Clark was under no duty to correct the record. Bird could easily have avoided the *Chronicle* editorial either by telling reporters off the record that Clark was the disqualified judge or, better, by requesting Clark's permission to use his name in response to a direct question from reporters.

4. Clark's backlog statement to the state bar convention panel of research attorneys. Clark had no reason to think his remarks would be quoted in the press and denied having called the backlog unprecedented; in any event, for a period after Bird's arrival the court had been granting hearings faster than it had been deciding cases.

5. Younger's charge that *Tanner* had been delayed. Bird linked the allegation to Clark because Clark knew Meese and Meese was involved with Younger's campaign.

6. The press calls in October asking about *Fox* and *Tanner*. Clark's responsibility for those calls was based on the fact that he was dissenting in both cases.

Bird's testimony prompted some reporters and maybe some commissioners to think that the commission was perhaps investigating the wrong issue. Bird's testimony suggested that her grasp of reality with respect to Clark before the election was quite tenuous. For the most part the pattern she found was woven out of thin air. Should that line of inquiry be pursued? A public probe of her emotional stability in addition to being tasteless was plainly not authorized by Rule 902.5. But how could the genie be kept in the bottle when the justices as witnesses persisted in displaying their weaknesses?

The Press on Bird

Providing balanced coverage of Bird's testimony was difficult, especially as it was spread over five days. The first and last days were relatively easy for reporters to cover. They generally emphasized Bird's opening day speeches, particularly her claim that the proceedings were the result of "faceless, nameless, anonymous accusers" and a "powerful newspaper" and her throwing "china into a laundromat" remark. Most reporters reminded their readers that Bird had requested the investigation.

Cartoon by Steve Greenberg, Editorial Cartoonist for the *Daily News of Los Angeles*. © *Daily News of Los Angeles*.

Many also noted that Bird was granted permission, because of a "nagging back problem," to speak from a podium rather than the witness chair and that her speeches were frequently unresponsive to Hufstedler's questions. Stories from the last day featured, as they had to, Bird's refusal to answer and speculation as to whether the commission might initiate contempt proceedings.

The hard stories to write dealt with the middle days. The daily articles could not do much more than report what Bird said. A number quoted more or less verbatim Bird's litany of Clark misdeeds, hoping perhaps that readers would evaluate the basis for her complaints.

The more important stories were the weekend wrap-ups and the articles for the Monday morning papers. After four days of Bird's testimony a number of reporters had decided that a smoking gun proving any justice guilty of delay was not going to be found. As Margaret Warner, of the *San Diego Union*, put it: "The unprecedented public investigation now playing before the Commission on Judicial Performance is closer to a family saga novel than a whodunit mystery. . . . Unravelling before the commissioners is a story about loyalty and suspicion, confidence and fear."

Similarly, Lou Cannon's Sunday account for the *Washington Post* said:

Behind a facade of judicial order and decorum, the California Supreme Court during the 1978 election campaign became a seething cauldron of fear, suspicion, political hostility and petty jealousy. . . . So far, the investigation . . . has proved much less, and revealed much more, than critics have alleged. . . . Nothing has emerged to confirm the accusation . . . that decisions were delayed to influence voter confirmation of controversial Chief Justice Rose Bird. On the other hand, testimony has shattered the Court's favorite depiction of itself as a "collegial" body moved only by consideration of law. . . . What has been exposed instead of ethical misconduct is a seige mentality in which everyone on the Court talked about "collegiality" but few practiced it.

In one sense, Hufstedler had by this point achieved his goal. The press was persuaded that his investigation had been thorough and that politically motivated delay in *Tanner* could not be proven. The focus was now the personalities of the justices. Who was responsible for the change in direction? Tobriner was the first to broaden the issues. As Warner noted:

Bird was credible in a key area in which the 75-year old Tobriner was not credible the previous week. The feisty Tobriner, who is alleged to have stalled the Tanner *decision on her behalf, so downplayed his awareness last fall of the impending election that several commissioners privately confessed incredulity.*

Bird was worse. She volunteered her vision of a pattern mostly as examples to illustrate answers that required no elaboration. Her examples gave verisimilitude to her denials of wrongdoing while simultaneously exposing her personality in ways that were unnecessary. Some of the commissioners, notably Chodos and Willoughby, did not help, but once the personality issue was out, the hearings were out of control. They had, as it were, a life of their own, and would have to run their course without the benefit of the discipline of relevance.

CLARK

Bird and Clark were similar in some respects: both were relatively young in 1979 (Bird, forty-one; Clark, forty-seven) and both came to the Supreme Court solely because of their close connection to a governor. Considering their youth, it is not surprising that neither had achieved a distinguished record as a judge or lawyer before being appointed. Both also lacked family connections or other linkages to an establishment, even a political one. They rose from obscurity, however, by different routes. Bird used public education in the traditional way whereas Clark had risen despite academic failure. As Clark told the commission:

I grew up on cattle and sheep ranches in both southern and northern California. I attended rural schools, primarily in Tehama and Shasta counties. I was admitted to Stanford in 1949. I spent two years there. I did not obtain a degree. I went on to Loyola Law School. Following my first year there, during the Korean War, I was drafted. I served in military service in Europe, where I met my wife. . . . We returned following discharge from the army to Los Angeles, where we both found employment.

I reentered Loyola night school. My third year, the dean, Father Donovan, approached me and suggested that I consider some other profession. So I did not graduate from Loyola. I did, however, continue my legal study on my own and on the second try passed the bar.

I then returned to the town of my birth, Oxnard [Ventura County], and opened my own firm and waited for the phone to ring. In 1965, my wife and I purchased a grain and cattle ranch in northern San Luis Obispo County. That still is [our] home.

Clark left his practice in Ventura County in 1966 to join the Reagan administration, working first on the transition team, then briefly as cabinet secretary, and finally as executive secretary and chief of staff in the governor's office. His political involvement before then was minimal; he testified that his first political experience was when Reagan asked him to be Ventura county campaign chairman in 1966.

Clark was probably most comfortable among others of a rural background. He obviously enjoyed the role of chef at cattle-branding barbeques in San Luis Obispo county. Unlike Bird, Clark was well liked by the court family—bailiffs, secretaries, and legal staff; he knew their names and bantered with them in the halls with genuine interest in their welfare. He was considerably less at ease with his colleagues. In Wright's time the justices frequently lunched together; Clark rarely joined them. And rather than move his family to the Bay Area, Clark rented a small apartment near the court in San Francisco; thus, he and his wife were largely unavailable for weekend social events.

Reagan gave Clark some judicial experience—two years as a superior court judge in San Luis Obispo County and two years on the Court of Appeal in Los Angeles—before elevating him to the Supreme Court in 1973. Clark was rumored to have been the only justice on the court to send a congratulatory note to Bird at the time of her appointment, and he testified that in general he thought his relations with Bird initially were cordial despite their frequent disagreement in opinions.

Clark was candid to the commission about his dependence on staff. He rarely did anything without consulting them and he evidently saw himself as a team leader rather than a sole decisionmaker with assistants whose role was quite subordinate and relatively inconsequential.

Clark was on the stand longer than any other witness, almost five full days. His testimony reads better than it sounded largely because he was a ponderously slow witness, choosing his words carefully and frequently pausing. He had one strange mannerism: as if he were standing outside himself, he would occasionally refer to himself by name and title. For example, in response to a question about what was happening at a particular time, Clark responded: "Staff and Judge Clark were working on an opinion." The questioning from the commissioners was sometimes hostile. In particular, Commissioner Pacht, who had thrown nothing but softballs at Richardson, Tobriner, and Bird, was at times antagonistic, thereby suggesting a pro-Bird bias that offended some observers. Nevertheless, Clark emerged from the hearings pretty much what he purported to be: a plain man who did his best to express a conservative viewpoint and who was startled to find himself in the middle of a brouhaha he did not know how to escape. Unlike Tobriner and Bird, Clark had no secondary level of meaning in his testimony. His reasons for various actions sometimes were unsatisfactory, but he made no unwitting self-revelations.

By the time Clark took the stand, the commission had heard two full weeks of testimony and the commissioners had a firm grasp of the prin-

cipal events in the *Tanner* and *Fox* chronicles. Thus far, all the testimony
had come from one side of the controversy. Clark was the key witness to
present a different view. Hufstedler had an obvious set of questions to
explore: was Clark's purpose in citing *Caudillo* political, to embarrass
Bird publicly? Why did Clark elevate the citation from the footnote to
the text? Was Clark trying to trap Bird by suggesting that *Tanner's* release
be delayed until after the election? Did Clark believe that the release of
Tanner was delayed for political reasons? If so, on what evidence? Had
Clark been directly or indirectly responsible for any leaks to the press?
Clark's response to the last question has already been discussed. The
most troublesome aspect of Clark's testimony was the suspicion he had
as early as October that *Tanner* could and should have been filed before
the election. Clark continued to believe that when he testified before the
commission, but he had no evidence to support an improper purpose.
Before discussing this puzzle, it is necessary to cover Clark's responses
to the first questions.

The Citation of Caudillo

Clark learned about Bird's separate opinion in *Tanner* in a telephone
conversation with his research attorney, Richard Morris, that took place
while Clark was in Europe. Morris told him that he had re-called Clark's
opinion, and by the time Clark returned to San Francisco on August 6
Morris had drafted an expanded version of the Clark dissent for the
justice to consider.

Morris and Clark soon conferred about *Tanner*. The draft that Morris had prepared did not include a citation to *Caudillo*, but Clark remembered that Morris had raised the possibility:

Morris said . . . that People v. Caudillo *would have to be mentioned in
our modification for the reason that it appeared that the chief had . . .
different feelings on the question of constitutional power from what she
had referred to in the* Caudillo *case. He went on to say that, however, in
my absence the* Caudillo *case had caused some . . . "unfair criticism,"
perhaps of the chief justice, and he felt it a sensitive matter on the one
hand and yet on the other that we had to make reference to* People v.
Caudillo *in any consideration that we were giving the constitutional
issue.*

Clark did not believe that he had read Kirsch's article in *New West* at
that point, which is likely since he was in Europe when it came out,
although he admitted to reading the story sometime. Clark testified that
after more discussion with Morris "I made the decision that *Caudillo*
had to be cited; that, however, we would relegate it to a footnote and he
went back, as I recall, and did some more work drafting and came for-

ward with essentially [the new dissent in *Tanner*]." Clark was required by the commission to go over this conversation many times; he never changed its substance although at one point he reported saying to Morris: "All right, I am relying on you; early in my first week back, we'll put [the *Caudillo* citation] in. But we are going to relegate it to a footnote; we are not going to discuss it."

Morris confirmed Clark's testimony about their conversation and expanded somewhat on their reasoning for citing *Caudillo* and citing it in a footnote:

Well, let's start with the proposition that we thought it belonged in the body of the opinion and should be given good display. And our reason for that is that in our opinion we first deal with each case that the chief justice relied upon in her constitutional development. We attempt to distinguish these cases and show that they are not applicable. And then we rely on other cases that she did not refer to in her opinion, showing this is the true constitutional law, that it is in fact the legislature and not the court which has the authority to define crimes and fix the penalty, including penalty enhancing factors. And we thought that these were persuasive constitutional arguments.

We realized, too, however, that the chief justice in her research and the research of her staff . . . probably [had] come across these same cases . . . and had in fact rejected them because in their opinion they make no reference to the ones that we relied upon. So we thought that when she sees these cases cited, she will give them little heed and again ignore them.

The most telling authority that would be acceptable to her would be her own, her own authoritative statements to what the constitutional law was. And that one statement, her own statement and the more recent statement, was contained in People v. Caudillo. *So this was the logical and the proper thing to cite to her to persuade her that she was going off on her own track. So we would have put it in the body of the opinion was the thing we thought we should end up with. This is the thing that finally breaks the camel's back. You develop an argument along the way. So that was one reason for putting it in. The reason for not putting it in was the fact that she was getting some bad press on it. She was taking a lot of flak that we felt she did not deserve. That was the reason for taking it out. In all of these kinds of things, I think the courts constantly have to weigh one thing against another thing. There are always ways to go on each side of a balance, and you finally come up with a decision because there is more weight on one side than the other.*

The thing that made the difference to us and caused us to conclude that we should use the reference to Caudillo *was the fact that the damage to the chief justice on* People v. Caudillo *had already been done. It had* been in the press for a long time. It was going to continue to be in the press merely because of People v. Caudillo. Not because of People v. Tanner *but because of* People v. Caudillo *it was going to be spread out and continue to be used against her. The mere citation* of Caudillo *in our* Tanner *case, if it became within the public knowledge before the election, was going to have almost absolutely no effect at all. They have already, the impact* of Caudillo, *had already been out. To cite it again would be like pouring a cup of water into San Francisco Bay, insofar as its impact was concerned. That was the thing that persuaded us that we should use* Caudillo.

But we took it out of where it belonged really, and we put it in the footnote. And we used one sentence: "Besides, the Chief Justice agrees with us in her earlier expression, see People v. Caudillo." We don't even say that she is being inconsistent as has been claimed by others here. . . . We merely say that she agreed with us in People v. Caudillo. We don't quote language in People v. Caudillo to show that. That was the mildest comment we could have made.

The next event was the meeting between Morris and Sugarman, when, according to Bird, Sugarman was to ask whether Clark was politically motivated. Morris and Sugarman differed as to who was present and what was said at that meeting, but on essentials they were in substantial accord. Morris testified about the meeting as follows:

A: Well, [Sugarman's] concern was that it was inapposite, that it didn't belong there, that it had no valid legal reason for being there. We discussed that at some length.

Q: He gave the arguments why it was inapposite and you gave the opposite argument?

A: That's correct.

Q: I gather at the conclusion of that conversation . . . as far as you could tell you had not persuaded him?

A: Yes, it was an impasse.

Q: What happened next?

A: He then said, "Well, we have also concluded that it's politically motivated."

Q: Any alternative language that might have occurred? . . . Now, did he put it as strongly as that?

A: Oh, yes.

Q: He didn't say, "We wonder why it's there"?

A: My recollection is he said it was politically motivated.

Q: He didn't ask, "We want to ask whether it's politically motivated"?

A: No, he did not make that inquiry.

Mr. Chodos [takes over the questioning]: Did you ask him what he meant by that?

A: No, it didn't occur to me that it needed explanation. It occurred to me that . . . the politics was apparent at that time, at least to me. . . .

Q: You connected it with the chief justice's campaign for confirmation?

A: Yes, without inquiring further I did so connect it.

Q: What did you tell him when he said, "We have concluded it's politically motivated"?

A: I then attempted to explain how we had downgraded it and that they were making accusations that were false, that I was upset because we had made a conscientious effort to downgrade it and now we are accused of doing just the opposite. It did upset me. If he had watched carefully, as the chief justice had requested him to do, he would have seen the reaction, I am sure. The reaction being that the adrenalin began to flow. But yes, I was very upset and that's when I made an effort to determine whether or not the chief justice had in fact been involved in their judgment [of political motivation]. . . .

Q: Did you deny that it was politically motivated?

A: Oh, yes, firmly and often.

Q: Did Mr. Sugarman tell you he wasn't asking you to delete it?

A: No. In fact, he asked me to delete it.

Morris immediately reported his conversation to Clark, who "could not believe" that Bird thought he was so motivated. Clark thought the appropriate thing to do was to speak with Bird personally and he talked with her on the phone within the hour. Clark's recollection of the conversation did not differ significantly from Bird's:

A: After she realized why I was calling, as I recall she said, "Bill, those cases are apples and oranges." And I said, "Rose, that's not my concern on this call to you so much as is the allegation of political motivation." And I added, "If I were so motivated certainly I would be doing something beyond placing a citation in a footnote at the end of an opinion." And she confirmed, first of all, that her staff felt that this was placed there in political motivation. I think she may have told me then, "Bill, I am not asking you to remove the citation." And I said, "Rose, that is not my concern. That does not offend me. What does is the political motivation charge." I may have asked her, I know it was certainly on my mind after she told me about her staff's concern, I believe I asked her if she felt that way. I don't know that I got a direct answer of yes, but I came away with the impression at the conclusion of the call that there was no question but she, too, felt that the citation was, quote, politically motivated.

Q: Did you discuss the legal issues, that is, whether or not the Cau-dillo case was really . . . relevant?

A: Not beyond her statement of apples and oranges. I didn't feel it appropriate to go into the merits of the case on the telephone. I felt this would follow.

Q: Did you have any discussion with regard to how you and she might resolve this problem?

A: Not at that point.

Q: Was there any mention of your getting together to talk about it further or explaining memoranda or anything of that sort?

A: I recall stating that I regretted that she did not understand the reference to Caudillo and that I would probably have to expand my reasons because of it.

Clark then conferred with Morris to consider what they should do next. Clark and Morris assumed that Bird's sensitivity was related to her election and the "inordinate publicity" given to *Caudillo.* Clark con-cluded that they had three "options":

One, we could leave the footnote in and allow circulation to continue. Another option would be to remove the reference to Caudillo altogether. The third, as I viewed it, would be, as I had suggested to the chief justice on the phone, to explain why Caudillo is being referred to because appar-ently it was not clear. Not only unclear, it caused the allegation that concerned us deeply.

Clark was never asked to explain why they rejected his first option. Mor-ris, however, testified:

We felt that the chief's staff had drawn some implications of political motivation—evidently, that had not occurred to us before—but they had drawn those implications. If we left it in the footnote in no greater detail than it appeared . . . perhaps some reader of the opinion, not being aware of what was said in Caudillo, might think, "Well, what did she say in Caudillo? . . . Maybe it's just a way of getting in a cheap shot by citing Caudillo."

The option that Clark and Morris evidently considered most seriously was to remove the citation altogether. Morris admitted that the chief justice's separate opinion in *Caudillo* was not the only citation available for the point of law being asserted:

We could have probably cited fifteen cases to that point of law. No one of them was necessary to develop the legal theory. We could have eliminated any one of them, including Caudillo, *and still made the same intellectual point that we were trying to make.*

Nonetheless, they rejected this alternative. Clark explained:

I felt that that would, to use a term of the chief last week, not be intellectually honest. It would certainly indicate [that] maybe Clark was taking a cheap shot by that reference, had been called on it in the allegation of political motivation, and he took his toys and went home.

Morris's testimony was similar:

[Removing the citation] was not a comfortable [option] for us. It indicated, by removing [it] after being scolded by the chief justice's staff, that we were in fact guilty of the accusations that had been made when we were not guilty at all of that accusation. And . . . so we necessarily had to reject that one.

Morris revised the dissent to include in the text the discussion of *Caudillo*, quoting the relevant passages from Bird's opinion. Clark then wrote the green sheet, circulated with the revised dissent, in which he said that staff to the chief justice had asserted that the citation of *Caudillo* was politically motivated and requested its deletion. Clark testified that he "was careful not to say that the chief justice has requested [the deletion] because she did not ask me to remove the cite." Clark recalled that in their telephone call Bird had said, "I am not asking you to remove your citation," but he thought that unimportant because "I think that she was telling me that it's politically motivated, ergo it doesn't belong there, which is, essentially, 'take it out.' " Nevertheless, the green sheet told the entire court of the political motivation charge. Why did Clark do that? "Well, for one, I understood that term [political motivation] was pretty well around the court already. And I felt it should be very clear that those are words of concern. And I felt that they had to be met." Clark's staff had told him by then that "the word was somewhat around that there [had been] a conversation between Clark and Bird."

We received, should we say, rather heavy communication that Caudillo *belonged in this case. They would hope that it would remain, that Clark wouldn't back out of this in the face of the suggestion that there was bad motivation, because the cite had merit in the opinion.*

Bird considered the green sheet and the elevation of the *Caudillo* citation from the footnote to the text an escalation of their conflict. Her reaction was predictable, but Clark steadfastly maintained that his purpose had been merely to clarify his position. No one apparently advised Clark that his actions were likely to make things worse although he discussed the subject with Richardson and probably also with Manuel shortly after talking with Bird on the phone.

With the benefit of hindsight, there were courses of action open to Clark other than the three options he considered. Perhaps the most obvious was further private communication with Bird, either written or face-to-face. Clark never doubted that Bird endorsed the charge of political motivation, but she had not said that to him directly and their telephone conversation never went beyond "apples and oranges." Clark could thus reasonably have proposed that he would withdraw the citation if she would withdraw the charge. Such a maneuver in the interests of peace would have required both justices to repudiate to some extent their staffs, which may explain why Clark did not entertain this solution.

A fair assessment of Clark's failure to speak privately to Bird requires a knowledge of the way the justices related to each other generally. The commission's exclusive focus on the issues of delay and leaks deprived it of any such general picture but one glimpse outside that narrow framework was provided, oddly enough, by counsel for Tobriner, who introduced a memorandum sent to the entire court by Tobriner in response to a dissent by Clark in another case. The memorandum, dated July 12, 1978, read:

Though replete with eye-catching rhetoric, Justice Clark's dissenting opinion is woefully deficient in one rather critical attribute—accuracy. Indeed, apart from the dissent's caption, it would be difficult to determine to which circulating opinion the present dissent is actually directed. . . .

If Justice Clark views such a holding as documenting a doctrine of absolute liability, it is clear that he has seized the prerogative once claimed by the eminent Humpty Dumpty. . . .*

In sum, I believe the inaccuracies and defects in the dissenting opinion are so numerous and so self-evident that no response within the body of the majority opinion is necessary.

* In *Through the Looking Glass*, Humpty Dumpty informed Alice, "When I use a word, it means just what I choose it to mean, neither more nor less."

It is hard to know what to make of this document. The commission was not told how often communications of comparable sophomoric wit were circulated around the court, but it obviously happened sometimes. There was a reason of sorts for Tobriner to advise his colleagues why he was not responding to Clark's dissent, but that limited objective could certainly have been achieved with more dignity. Given a context of, as

Chodos put it, "spitball throwing," it is hard to call Clark's telling the entire court about his quarrel with Bird a serious breach of decorum.

From August 25 to Election Day

Clark evidently had no clear expectations as to what would happen after he circulated his revised dissent on August 25. He told the commission that it had not occurred to him then that *Tanner* might not be filed before the election, and he indicated that he had some hope that Bird would explain, presumably in a revision of her opinion, what she meant by apples and oranges. Clark was, however, aware of Manuel's feelings, and he testified that he was concerned about what he assumed to be Manuel's distress at being in the middle of an intracourt feud.

I knew that Justice Manuel by personality [is] a very sensitive person, very sincere, and I could tell from conferences that he didn't particularly enjoy, at least in the beginning [of his time on] the court, the give-and-take between judges when, shall we say, our conferences became at all heated.

There is no reason to doubt the genuineness of Clark's concern for Manuel's sensitivity to internecine quarrels, but it also seems likely that Clark, as well as Bird, was hoping hard to gain Manuel's support in the squabble. On the merits of the *Tanner* case Manuel had already voted with Clark and it would be too much to expect him to change his vote, but Bird hoped that Manuel would not sign Clark's opinion but rather dissent separately. A difficulty was that Manuel was not the kind of person who would respond to direct lobbying on a point of this sort; indeed, such a tactic might be counterproductive and offend him. Although neither Bird nor Clark admitted it, the testimony of both was fully consistent with serious but restrained solicitation of Manuel's support.

As noted previously, Bird dated her "cool but correct" behavior toward Clark to Kang's September 13 "Logjam at the High Court Corral" article. Clark thought something was amiss somewhat sooner. According to Clark, he and Bird did not speak between their mid-August telephone call and their October 10 meeting (as Clark had it; October 16 or 17 according to Bird and Buehl). As a practical matter, from Clark's point of view, cool but correct meant:

The relationship was such that when I went into her chambers for Wednesday conferences, there was no acknowledgment. And in other situations where we came together, my attempts to even get into pleasantries failed. More concern to me, however, was the same treatment to my staff, which they were upset over. . . .

It may seem petty now. It seemed awfully important to us all at that time. My staff is primarily career staff on the court, representing some seventy years of service among the secretary, Miss Wong, and the clerks. Mr. Morris, I think, first indicated that he had seen the chief justice on the elevator and had said good morning, and she had turned in the opposite direction without acknowledging his presence. . . . [M]y secretary referred to the same slighting.

Another incident, I recall, which upset her most, and did not concern me all that much at the time. The chief justice had her carpeting replaced in her chambers. Bessie [Wong] had been promised part of the used carpeting for her own office, which is linoleum. She came in and said, "What have you done to the chief justice? My carpeting has been given to others." And, as I say, this may sound petty now, but it seemed rather important to us at that time.

Clark talked to Mosk about his problem with Bird at some point: "I do recall talking to Justice Mosk and the thing that prompts my recollection is, again, the attitude of the chief, her treatment of both myself and my staff. Justice Mosk had had a similar experience in which the chief refused to acknowledge him." Whether Mosk suggested that Clark discuss the subject with Tobriner is not known, but that was Clark's next move. Clark described his interview with Tobriner as follows:

A: It was a brief meeting. I phoned in advance to determine if I could speak with him. I went in and, as I can best recollect, said, "Matt, I have a problem that I would like you to help . . . me on." To explain my presence, because I wasn't there all that often prior to that appointment, I said, "It must be obvious to all that Rose and I have a personal problem that has reached a point that I feel must be resolved." His response was, "They're doing just terrible things to her, just terrible." He explained what he meant by "they." He seemed to be referring to the [Senator] Richardson campaign against her confirmation. I think that I acknowledged sympathy with what he was saying in this regard. However, I brought him back to, I thought, the . . . reasons for my presence to meet with him. I mentioned Tanner and the Caudillo controversy, whereupon he said, "Bill, Caudillo doesn't belong in your opinion. And I agree with Rose in that regard." I said, "Matt, that is not the question at this moment, whether it does or does not belong there." I may have even mentioned no one has indicated why it doesn't, I'm not sure. But I pointed up . . . what was on my mind, my concern for both my staff and myself and the treatment that must be obvious to him, and [asked whether] he might assist me in approaching the chief justice to help resolve it. At that point, I believe I said, "If she removes the reason for the reference to Caudillo, obviously Caudillo will be removed." I'm not sure that he responded to that. I got into the allegation of political motivation. I am not sure whether he brought that up or whether I did, but it arose.

Q: And what was said about political motivation?

A: I said, "Matt, clearly, if Rose feels there are political implications to the citation of Caudillo, she obviously has the power to not file the opinion until after her confirmation"—in an attempt to show that this was not a political motivation.

Q: And what, if anything, did he say?

A: I recall his response well. It was unusual. He said nothing. . . .

And in stating that, I do not mean to be personal, but rather I recall distinctly that he did not say, "Justice Clark, that would be a dastardly thing to do," or anything else. He just said nothing. And about that time, he went to a cabinet, which would be approaching his door to the right side of his door, opened the top cabinet—each office has the same wooden setup cabinet-wise—and took the box out, which I presumed to be Tanner. I didn't look at the little label to see that it was. I think it looked familiar, however, by size. I brought up Justice Manuel's name in particular, suggesting that I felt that from my conversations with Judge Manuel, and as I knew him, he was very concerned about the controversy between the chief and myself. He was close to us both in a personal way. And I felt it a little unfair for Justice Manuel to be caught in this crossfire between Clark and Bird. I don't recall any response to that. I felt that the purpose of my being there had been expressed and I didn't sit down during the conversation. I went out the door and on back to my own office.

Clark and Tobriner dated the conversation somewhat differently, but the principal point of divergence between their recollections concerned Tobriner's reaction to what Tobriner told the commission was Clark's highly improper suggestion that *Tanner* be held until after the election. Questioned by Chodos, Clark amplified for the commission what he had intended:

A: Clearly, it is the chief justice who files the submittal order which leads to the filing of the opinion. And I was merely recognizing the power to file or not file in the face of the allegation that there was political motivation on my part. I was hoping to show that the suggestion of political motivation is a rather hollow one, in the realization that Clark sure can't run down the hallway and file an opinion at will. In fact, I'm not so sure that four votes on the court can do that. This lies, as we all recognize, in the hands of the chief. And my state of mind was that by recognizing the obvious, that it must be clear that Clark has no political motivation in mind.

Q: Well, Justice Clark, didn't you recognize in making that suggestion that if Justice Tobriner or the chief justice were to rise to that bait, *they might be stepping into the very trap that Meese and Nicholson and James had articulated in the article published ten days earlier, which came to your attention?*

A: Well, of course, rising to the bait certainly was not the situation, Mr. Chodos. The only bait that Clark had in mind was to resolve what was obviously the court's number one crisis in a long time. At that time Clark couldn't care less whether the opinion called People v. Tanner was filed before or after election day.

Q: *Did you ever come to care about that before election day?*

A: I don't think so. My concern was resolving the Caudillo issue inside the halls of the courthouse, and not what might be the concern outside.

Clark talked with Manuel sometime during the week of September 25, when he knew that the box in *Tanner* was with Manuel. He reported his unproductive conversation with Tobriner and told Manuel that he planned to talk with the chief justice about "the impasse on the *Caudillo* problem." He told Manuel that he hoped that his conversation with Bird would resolve the controversy, thus enabling Manuel to remain on Clark's dissent. Up to that point, Manuel had not decided, so far as Clark knew, whether he would write separately. Manuel told Clark that he hoped he would be successful.

Bird admitted that she put Clark off when, early in October, he first requested a meeting with her about *Tanner* when the court was hearing arguments in Sacramento. Clark testified that instead of going directly to San Luis Obispo for the weekend as he normally did, he returned instead to San Francisco, expecting to meet with the chief justice on Friday, October 6. Clark said he asked Bird's secretary for an appointment on Friday morning and ran into Buehl in the hall sometime Friday who told him he would let Clark know, but no word came. The next step, according to Clark, was:

As I recall, I saw Mr. Buehl in the hallway again on the morning, I believe, of Tuesday, October 10.

Q: *What did you and Mr. Buehl say on that occasion?*

A: I told Mr. Buehl that I expect to see the chief justice today and I said that I suggest that you see that it happens.

Q: *Did he or she subsequently get back in touch with you?*

A: Yes.

Q: *On that day?*

A: Within the hour.*

---

* Buehl had no recollection of either conversation. He also dated the conversation a week later because he and Bird were visiting the editorial board of the *San Francisco Chronicle* on October 10 when they first heard of Younger's charges.

With some relatively minor cavils, Clark did not dispute the essential accuracy of the Buehl notes of their conversation. Clark had essentially two things he wanted to say: first that he was not politically motivated in citing *Caudillo,* and second that he wanted to relieve Manuel's distress by finding some way out of the *Caudillo* citation impasse. To the first point he gave as proof of his apolitical purpose the fact that Bird, not he, controlled when *Tanner* would be filed and that the decision could be released after the election. He was rigorously cross-examined on this point but never retreated. To resolve the impasse, Clark suggested that Bird either sign Tobriner's opinion or concur without an opinion, in which event he, Clark, would withdraw the *Caudillo* citation since it would no longer be relevant. Neither suggestion was taken up by Bird, who seemed interested primarily in listing her grievances against Clark.

The Buehl notes show that both Bird and Clark had an agenda for their meeting, and that both were more interested in saying their set pieces than in trying to come to some accommodation. Clark, however, listened at least to the extent of conceding that he understood why Bird was upset about the "Logjam at the High Court Corral" article. Clark did not succeed in communicating to Bird his outrage at what he thought was a very serious and unfair charge that he was politically motivated. His failure to communicate may be attributed partly to Bird's unwillingness to hear, but also may be explained partially by Clark's somewhat laconic way of speaking. The evidence he presented to her to demonstrate his nonpolitical intent—that if he were politically motivated he would do something more substantial than a footnote citation in a dissenting opinion, and Bird's capacity to delay the filing of *Tanner* until after the election—were the sort of evidence that would persuade someone who already believed in his bona fides; they were far less forceful for someone who doubted his motives. Clark might well have been more effective if he simply asserted his innocence and pushed her to tell him how he could prove that his motives were pure. Clark could also have offered to withdraw the citation without being intellectually dishonest or violating any moral code. But magnanimity in the face of a challenge was not Clark's style, and, as is so often the case, it was much easier to retreat to high moral principle than to find an acceptable middle ground.

Immediately after his talk with Bird, Clark reported to Manuel that he had "struck out." Clark assumed that Manuel would write separately, as indeed he did. Clark said that about this time the thought first entered his mind that *Tanner* might well not be filed before the election, but he decided there was nothing further that he could do and he "sort of gave up." Clark told his staff about his talk with Bird and raised the *Tanner* case at least twice in Wednesday conferences during October, but he did nothing else before the election.

Both Clark and Morris indicated in their testimony that they were far more interested in resolving the controversy with Bird than in getting *Tanner* filed before the election. Getting *Tanner* filed was to them shorthand for putting the *Caudillo* controversy behind them. When Manuel's separate dissent circulated on October 24, they passed without consideration the possibility of withdrawing Clark's opinion altogether and signing Manuel's instead. Realistically, that was the last possible chance of getting *Tanner* filed before the election. Had they thought of it, signing Manuel's opinion and withdrawing Clark's would have been an elegant maneuver that might have induced Bird and Tobriner to polish up their opinions before the election.

Clark and Morris never doubted that Bird had in mind her own election when she charged Clark with being politically motivated. Clark and his staff were either much more candid in their testimony before the commission or much more aware of the political realities of the situation than anyone else. Maury Koblick, one of Clark's senior research attorneys, for example, told the commission that he saw political implications in *Tanner* from the time he read Clark's first dissent (before there was any citation to *Caudillo*):

[Tanner] *had significant political implications. I guess all cases might, but this one had significant political implications. If you read Justice Clark's dissent you'd see it yourself because it points towards the governor; and if the governor was issuing statements on signing the bill, enthusiastic statements, I think almost anyone could assume that there was political sensitivity.*

Furthermore, Koblick thought it obvious that *Tanner* would become "acutely politically sensitive" when Bird issued her separate dissent because of what he called the "lesson of *Caudillo*."

While the media started out by attacking the court for the Caudillo *opinion, it quickly became apparent that the chief justice's concurring opinion was functioning like a lightning rod and that all the flak was being directed towards her. When I saw the chief justice's opinion in* Tanner *come out as a concurring opinion, I sort of had the feeling, "Here we go again." When it came I guess I was thinking then that, short of withdrawing that opinion, it could be quite a bit of harm to her election campaign unless the opinion was not issued before the election.*

Morris phrased much the same thoughts differently:

If Tanner *were not filed before the election it was bound to be an embarrassment for the court [because of the Younger charges]. I perhaps had discussions with Justice Clark that it would be an embarrassment mainly for certain justices if filed before, and it would be an embarrassment for the court if filed after.*

The commission treated these observations with the utmost circumspection, demanding evidence that the thoughts were communicated to a justice before they would regard them as relevant. This response converted their observations into political predictions of unusual sagacity and probably was a mistake. In fact, Morris and Koblick were simply stating what should have been and, despite testimony to the contrary, probably was apparent to everyone on the court: *what was politically damaging to Bird in* Tanner *was not Clark's citation of* Caudillo *but the court's decision and especially Bird's concurrence.* In addition to the lightning rod effect, her opinion was likely to be offensive because of the ground she took. As Koblick phrased it:

The content also affected that because the "use a gun" statute I thought had two effects. Basically it was a symbolic statute because most people who committed those enumerated felonies and used guns were going to prison already. All opinions tended to recognize that or at least the lead opinion did. So it was primarily somewhat symbolic in the sense that we will make it automatic. That will deter people. And that was the effect of the statute. It was more a popular statute than a statute designed to put a large number of people in prison. Secondly, it was also doing something else, of course. It was an implied recognition that judges haven't properly been doing their job and we were going to clip their wings. And the chief justice's opinion, of course, went right against that policy or purpose. Because it was saying you can't clip any wings in the legislature.

If *Tanner* had been filed during the summer, even as late as September, its impact on the election of Bird or anyone else probably would not have been great because *Tanner* would have been just one more issue for Younger and Duekmejian to scream about as proof of their charge about liberals being soft on crime. By October, however, its potential was volcanic. By then the polls made it obvious that Bird was in serious trouble, that there was an enormous undecided vote on her still pending, and *Tanner* would have given Senator Richardson the issue and publicity he was hoping would emerge to revive his failing campaign against her. Furthermore, the governor would have a hard time defending Bird on *Tanner*. He could only have responded, as he later did, by promising vigorous and prompt action to overturn the result when the legislature reassembled.

Justices Richardson and Tobriner denied awareness of any political implications of *Tanner* and were never pressed as to whether they thought the case might be more politically sensitive in October than it had been in June or July. Bird was never asked. Clark, however, knew from the outset that *Tanner* was politically potent, and he doubtless also knew that its explosive power increased as election day approached. Thoughts about *Tanner* and the election of Bird were certainly common coinage among the court staff. Although the commission paid little attention to it, the reality of the politics of *Tanner* must have been an important part of the context for Clark of the charge against him that he was politically motivated. To him that charge must have seemed to have all the logic of the Southern position that Lincoln provoked war because the South fired on Fort Sumter. Had Clark been political, as Bird thought he was, it would have been in his interest to get *Tanner* filed before the election, so much so that he would have been glad to remove the *Caudillo* citation and done anything else to push the case out as quickly as possible. That he did not remove the citation is not strong evidence that Clark had no political purpose in citing *Caudillo*—it is dangerous to draw inferences about a person's intentions from his failure to do something he may never have considered—but his awareness of the political reality in which the court was living is important in evaluating his conduct.

Clark's behavior up to the election was not beyond criticism, especially his answers to Fairbanks, which led to the November 7 story, but compared to Bird he looked good. Perhaps he overreacted to the political motivation charge, but once the controversy got going he tried to resolve it. He made three separate overtures: the telephone call to Bird as soon as he heard the charge, the talk with Tobriner in late September or early October, and the meeting with Bird recorded in the Buehl notes. He was rebuffed each time, and no gestures were made in his direction. To the contrary, he and his staff were subjected to a kind of retributive abuse normally associated with petulant opera stars. Clark could have been magnanimous and withdrawn the *Caudillo* citation; he also could have been clever, withdrawn his opinion, and signed Manuel's. But these possibilities seem most obvious in hindsight.

Clark after Election Day

Clark was involved in three incidents just before and following the election that already have been discussed, but a full evaluation of his behavior requires a review of those incidents in the light of what has been covered since the discussion in Chapter IV. First, Clark knew that Fairbanks was relying on his equivocal responses on November 6 but did nothing to prevent Fairbanks from drawing inferences of wrongdoing broader than Clark later claimed to have intended. Second, although it would have been hard to face down Tobriner's need for reassurance, Clark should have insisted on developing a formula for the Tobriner

Use a gun, go to pieces. Cartoon by Steve Greenberg, Editorial Cartoonist for the *Daily News of Los Angeles.* © *Daily News of Los Angeles.*

statement that he could sign rather than run the risk of public uproar over this episode. Finally, the "decisive reasons" remark about failing to sign the Tobriner statement was unnecessary and inevitably was misinterpreted by Cannon and others.

Bird probably assumed that Clark's intention in each of these instances was to force an investigation of the Supreme Court and to humiliate her. Clark's testimony before the commission suggests, however, that Clark rather drifted into each of these incidents. Toward the end of his questioning, Clark himself referred to a memorandum concerning the filing of *Tanner I* as accurately expressing his belief at the time of the commission hearings as well as in November. He said in that memorandum, dated December 20: "In conscience, it must be clear to all on the Court that the *Tanner* case was signed up and ready for filing well in advance of November. The question remaining appears to be why it was not filed?" Clark reluctantly conceded that as a technical matter the case was not ready for filing on election day but asserted that his statement meant that *Tanner* could and should have been filed before the election. In other words, Clark believed that *Tanner* had been delayed for political reasons but could not prove it. Assuming such was his state of mind, what evidence did Clark have of wrongdoing?

The strongest reason for suspecting wrongdoing was that it was very much in Bird's interest that *Tanner* not be filed, especially in late September and October, when the decision would revive the faltering campaign against her. But, as every reader of detective fiction knows, the presence of a motive is not proof of wrongdoing. Facts known to Clark were inconclusive. Tobriner did nothing on the case from August 15 to September 21, when, except for two days, the box was with him. Some of that time Tobriner was on vacation; moreover, in that period Proposition 13 was a major preoccupation of the court. Tobriner had twice okayed his majority opinion in *Tanner* without change, once before and once after Bird circulated her concurrence. The first okay took Tobriner three days; the second, two weeks. Since the last okay by Tobriner, Clark had revised his dissent and to some extent had toned down his comments insofar as they related to Tobriner's opinion. Clark asked his clerks whether they knew what was going on in Tobriner's chambers during this period but they reported nothing; he could not have known whether Tobriner was perhaps, for example, trying to work out an accommodation with Bird to get a four-vote majority on his opinion. Furthermore, Tobriner frequently dawdled over boxes in his office. Clark could have suspected an illicit delay, but Tobriner's nonaction was at most suggestive and far from proof.

Clark might have suspected that Manuel had been lobbied by Bird or Tobriner to write separately in *Tanner* but he apparently never asked Manuel whether any pressure had been put on him. Clark himself was partially responsible for the month that it took Manuel to write his separate dissent since Clark had asked Manuel to hold off doing anything on the case until after Clark had tried to resolve his problems with Bird. The period between circulation of Manuel's dissent and the election (from October 24 to November 7) was too brief to expect the opinion to be filed, especially since the court was hearing arguments in Los Angeles during one of those weeks.

There remained the distant possibility that Bird had created the brouhaha over Clark's citation of *Caudillo* with the object of slowing down the filing of *Tanner* by provoking the very controversy that developed. Clark's testimony never suggested consideration of such a Machiavellian scheme.

The sum of the matter is that Clark could not prove wrongdoing, but his suspicions were not irrational. It must be emphasized that Clark never directly asserted that he suspected wrongdoing, but assuming that he did, he was in a difficult position on election day. Once the *Los Angeles Times* story was out, there would obviously be considerable pressure for more information about *Tanner*, and it was possible that someone else within the court had the hard evidence of wrongdoing, the smoking gun, that Clark lacked. For Clark to join in a sweeping denial of wrongdoing presented the risk of becoming a participant in a cover-up, and in November 1978 the lesson of Watergate was very fresh. The reluctance of Clark and Richardson to join the Tobriner statement is thus easily understood. But it should also have been clear to Clark that once the *Times* story was printed, how he reacted after November 7 could shape subsequent events. Seemingly, Clark never thought through a coherent course of action.

One thing he could have done was to consult more broadly with his colleagues. He spoke with Richardson and Manuel on election day, but we know only that they talked about dealing with press calls. Clark did not speak with either Mosk or Newman. Those two were relatively uninvolved in the *Tanner* controversy and if Clark had candidly laid his suspicions before them they might have provided the evidence he lacked or persuaded him that his suspicions were unfounded. He also could have confronted Bird and Tobriner and insisted on a conference discussion of his suspicions. Clark may have thought such a discussion would result from his response to the Tobriner statement, but he should have demanded it earlier, even before the Thursday conference on November 9.

Both Bird and Clark have been criticized here for failing to consult with all of their colleagues on or immediately after election day. It is important to recognize that every member of the court could have insisted upon such a meeting, and each therefore shares a degree of responsibility for not having done so. How seriously that default should be regarded depends heavily upon an imponderable: how obvious was it on election day that the court was confronting a major crisis calling for a coordinated response and full and candid discussion? In retrospect it may seem obvious that the *Los Angeles Times* story would result ultimately in an investigation, but perhaps that result was not obvious at the time. Clark evidently thought the appropriate response was silence, and he may well have been right. A Tobriner type statement was another possibility. Properly executed either strategy might have quieted public anxiety about the court. But these things should have been talked about, not left to individual decision made privately by each justice and discussed only in regularly scheduled formal conferences, especially since the discussion there seemed never to get very far beyond fault finding. Events occasionally create a situation in which it becomes important to depart from the normal course of behavior, to speak more fully than usual and to insist upon saying things normally left unspoken out of respect for the sensitivities of others, or even fear. It takes wisdom and courage to see those moments and to seize them. Not one of the seven justices exhibited those characteristics on or after election day.

Another course of action open to Clark was to lay his suspicions before the commission. Such an aggressive and hostile action against Bird and Tobriner would have irretrievably damaged his already strained relations with them, making the remaining years of his service on the court very difficult. You do not shoot at the King except to kill, and Clark was a very long way from proof of wrongdoing. If Clark considered laying his problem before the commission, which seems unlikely, nothing in his testimony suggests it.

Perhaps there were other things that Clark might have done. What he did was indefensible: made ambiguous statements that implied wrongdoing but did not assert it. Although deplorable, it does not follow that his behavior was part of a conscious plan to provoke an investigation.

Clark's Report of a Mosk–Tobriner Conversation

Toward the end of the third day of his testimony, Clark described a conversation he had had with Mosk:

> At the time of the January [1979] calendar in Los Angeles, Justice Mosk in a discussion of the hearings that were either scheduled or would be scheduled said, "Bill, before election day, I told Matt that it was obvious that cases were being held for filing after [the] election and I told him it was obvious and if it were later revealed he would have to pay the consequences."

Hufstedler and the commission made Clark go over this conversation several times, but Clark could add nothing of importance, such as when the Mosk-Tobriner discussion took place, what cases Mosk was referring to, or how Tobriner had responded.

Testifying about this conversation apparently was difficult for Clark, particularly since he had not mentioned it in any of the interviews he had had with Hufstedler or in any of his depositions. When pressed as to why he had not mentioned the conversation earlier, Clark explained:

> I think I can state that deep down [I hoped] that at least I wouldn't be the first one asked about it. If I can be honest with you, I kind of hoped that it would go away, and if it didn't go away, that it would not be asked of Clark, Clark not having been a part of the conversation referred to.

Clark had, however, reported the conversation to Morris, and Morris had mentioned it to Hufstedler when Clark began his public testimony.

Counsel for the chief justice and Tobriner, while recognizing that hearsay was not, as such, inadmissible in this investigatory proceeding, requested the commission to permit them to move to strike this evidence should Mosk ultimately not testify. The possibility that Mosk might not testify was suggested by press reports that Mosk was contemplating filing a lawsuit challenging the commission's power to hold public hearings and, indeed, on the next day, Friday June 6, Hufstedler announced that Mosk had filed an action in the superior court in Los Angeles that would be heard the following Wednesday, June 10. Was Clark's report of his conversation with Mosk in some way connected to the *Mosk* suit? Clark denied this possibility categorically.

No, I assure you that there is no connection. I knew no more yesterday about the probability that he would or would not testify than I did at least a month ago, maybe more than that. I think that at the time of the depositions, we discussed his thinking that he might not even have his deposition taken.

The incident put Clark in an unfavorable light. He offered no adequate excuse for failing to mention the conversation when he was interviewed by Hufstedler, and though no question in Clark's deposition squarely required disclosure of the Mosk conversation, its relevance was obvious. Probably, if Hufstedler had known of this conversation, he would have asked Tobriner and Mosk about it first; knowledge of the conversation might even have influenced Hufstedler's ordering of the witnesses. Clark made the situation worse by reporting a second conversation with Mosk just a week before Clark testified in which he told Mosk that he might have to testify about their January conversation. Mosk confirmed Clark's recollection and told him, " 'Yes, Bill, that is correct.' And he added . . . 'I had two such conversations with Matt.' "

Up to this point, Mosk's testimony looked important on only one issue: what he had said to Endicott or Fairbanks on November 6. Mosk's involvement in *Fox* and *Tanner* was minimal; he was known to have encouraged the prompt processing of *Fox* and he had held the box in either case only once for more than a day. The sole open issue on which Mosk's testimony was needed was the matter of the incomplete citations in *Hawkins* and *Levins*. By this point, no one was very interested in that matter. But Clark's testimony suddenly made Mosk a critical witness. It was entirely possible, perhaps even likely, that Mosk when he spoke to Tobriner meant no more than that it would look terrible if a flood of controversial cases came down after the election. If that happened, Bird and Tobriner as her supporter would be under heavy suspicion. Mosk needed no evidence of wrongdoing to make this prediction. However, unless Mosk testified, his meaning would remain in doubt.

Clark Tries to Take an Adversary Position

Clark and Richardson were the only justices who had not hired lawyers to represent them in the commission proceedings. Although

Clark dispatched his research attorney, Morris, to the commission proceedings to serve as an observer, he tried to convey the impression that
he was no more than a disinterested witness in an investigation in which
he had no personal stake. However, at the conclusion of his testimony,
Clark began publicly to shift to a more aggressive posture. Two questions
arose at this point: to what extent were counsel for the other justices,
principally Bird and Tobriner, going to be permitted to cross-examine
Clark and would they have access to the deposition Hufstedler had taken
of Clark to prepare themselves for cross-examination? All the justices
except Clark had long before exchanged copies of their depositions;
Clark, refusing to participate in the exchange, did offer counsel for his
colleagues an opportunity to interview him.

Counsel for Bird, particularly Delizonna, made a rather impassioned plea to the commission for access to Clark's deposition. Delizonna asserted that Clark's disclosures to the press were part of a
campaign to discredit Bird, to put her in a "false light," so that the voters
would reject her. If this argument were true, Hufstedler had the responsibility of investigating the matter. It was hard to see how proving Clark
guilty of wrongdoing would help the legal defense of Bird before the
commission, although it would obviously help Bird in the court of public
opinion if her adversary, Clark, were discredited.

Nonetheless, the commission decided to permit counsel for Bird and
Tobriner to see Clark's deposition to assist them in showing "good cause"
to cross-examine Clark. In exchange, Clark was offered access to the
depositions of Bird and Tobriner, an offer he initially rejected but on
reflection decided to accept. Counsel for Bird were given a few days to
study the deposition before laying before the commission the issues on
which they wished to cross-examine Clark.

The cross-examination request was heard by the commission in the
afternoon of July 18 (that morning Hufstedler was in Long Beach arguing
the *Mosk* suit before superior court Judge Robert Wenke). Clark made a
motion at the outset, which he introduced with the following statement:

*Mr. Chairman and members of the commission, I have a motion to make.
It's my first motion before the commission and hopefully my last. And I
make it most reluctantly.*

*I hope that it is clear that following the chief justice's request to the
Commission on Judicial Performance last year to investigate the Supreme
Court, my staff and I cooperated fully with your special counsel, Mr.
Hufstedler, . . . in spite of my very grave reservations concerning the con-
stitutionality of the unprecedented public hearing that is now going on.
In the same vein, my staff and I have proceeded without representation
by outside counsel, without preparation of any self-serving statement,
without conducting our own independent probe of the court and its per-*

*sonnel, and without refusing to answer questions or to deliver documents
concerning these matters.*

*We consider ourselves witnesses, not litigants or adversaries toward
any other member of the court. However, ladies and gentlemen, events of
the past few days compel me to conclude that another member of the
court, or at least her lawyers, are attempting to convert this hearing into
an adversary proceeding and, therefore, in preparation for their examination of me or members of my staff, if any examination is to be allowed, I
make the following five-point motion at this time.*

The first four parts of Clark's motion sought access to the depositions of Bird's staff and a twenty-page statement Bird had given Hufstedler at the outset of his investigation. The fifth portion of his motion asked
that

*special counsel examine the chief justice's lawyers and staff concerning
their knowledge, if any, of the document I described during my testimony
and missing from my files, comprising approximately two pages prepared
by Mr. Fairbanks.*

Clark explained the last point more fully:

*I believe my testimony was to the effect that in February or very early
March Mr. Fairbanks dropped by my office to state that he was interviewing judges in preparation for a rather massive article covering the entire
Tanner matter. This was after, of course, the filing of Tanner. He stated
that he desired to include in his article in the* Los Angeles Times *a
description of the coffee cup incident. I said fine. He said, "Well, then, I
am going to hand you," and did hand me, his proposed script in that
matter. I read through to the third conversation and said, "Mr. Fairbanks,
that part is inaccurate." He took it back. He said, "I guess you are right.
I probably won't use it." He left the document on my desk and I recall
placing that in my file. It was not there when I went through that file in
preparation for my testimony in this hearing.*

Counsel for Bird promptly denied any knowledge concerning the disap-
pearance of the pages Fairbanks had given Clark, saying that they knew
as much about it as they knew about the "eighteen-minute gap on the
Nixon tape."

It took a whole afternoon to hear argument on the scope of cross-
examination and a request of special counsel that the commission receive in evidence a statistical comparison of the time elapsed between
argument and decision in the U.S. Supreme Court as opposed to the
California Supreme Court. The arguments were quite intense: seem-

ingly, the lawyers had been frustrated at their limited role, and a lot of impassioned rhetoric came pouring out on issues that were not very important.

The next day the chairman prefaced his announcement of the commission's rulings with a little speech addressed principally to Bird's counsel and Clark saying, among other things:

Although each justice will be given full opportunity to defend and vindicate himself or herself against any charge that has been made, this is not a platform from which justices may take to the public their charges and claims against their colleagues.

Consistent with that admonition, the commission restricted the cross-examination of Clark by counsel for Bird and Tobriner to minor incidentals, denied Clark access to the depositions of Bird's staff, and refused to receive the comparative figures Hufstedler had prepared.

Reporters had been looking forward to cross-examination of Clark by Bird's counsel, particularly since Clark announced that he would not answer questions from Delizonna although he had no objection if Bird's other counsel, Jerome Falk, was the interrogator. That announcement was patently out-of-bounds. Hufstedler quickly sought to defuse Clark's bomb by telling the commission:

I should indicate to you that this morning I talked both with Justice Clark and with Mr. Delizonna, suggesting from the point of view of the commission and special counsel and the court, as well as the parties, that it would be helpful if we can all cooperate to minimize the personal differences that may exist between the justices except and to the extent that they are relevant to this precise controversy. I should report to you that Justice Clark and Mr. Delizonna both agreed enthusiastically with that position.

In fact, the cross-examination that took place a few days later was dull. The commission's rulings had so confined its scope that nothing dramatic could happen, and Clark—having been told that Hufstedler would not tolerate his attempt to control who questioned him—docilely accepted cross-examination by Delizonna.

The Press After Clark's Testimony

Clark began testifying on the afternoon of July 2. In the morning of that day, Bird had refused to answer some of Hufstedler's questions, and her refusal was the obvious lead for all the press accounts of the hearings for that and the next day, when Chairman Janes instructed Hufstedler to advise the commission by Thursday, July 5, what course of action he would recommend the commission follow in obtaining answers from Bird. The stories for the July 4 papers were mostly speculation as to what Hufstedler might suggest—would California be treated to the spectacle of a chief justice held in contempt?—and the press accounts of the proceedings on July 5 reported, as they had to, Bird's written replies to the questions she had refused to answer three days earlier. Finally, press coverage of Clark's testimony on July 6 was somewhat preempted by the filing of Mosk's suit to close the hearings on that day. As a result of these events extraneous to his evidence, Clark's testimony was not given the same intense coverage as Tobriner's and Bird's before him, especially in the daily stories.

Clark's name appeared in column heads only with his revelation of the Mosk-Tobriner conversation, usually with the word "stuns" or "staggers" or "surprises," and several accounts overplayed the importance of this testimony. For example, the *Los Angeles Herald Examiner* reported:

Clark's version of his conversations with Mosk directly contradicted Tobriner's sworn testimony of last week. . . . Asked last week whether before the election it had "entered your conscious mind" that Tanner was being withheld, Tobriner replied, "It did not."

The *Herald Examiner* warned that Clark's testimony, if true, "could result in the censure or removal from the high court of Justice Tobriner."

The weekend stories were generally shorter and less complete than they had been in earlier weeks; except for the *Los Angeles Times*, editors apparently felt that their readers were losing interest in the saga. Myrna Oliver, for the *Los Angeles Times*, wrote an article that focused principally on Bird. Oliver described the hearings in general as a "very public and unprecedented washing of the Court's dirty linen" and concluded:

While the hearings have failed to establish the truth, they have produced insight into the Court's inner workings, particularly in relation to Ms. Bird's dealings with other justices. It is clear Ms. Bird reacts in highly personal ways to anything she sees as a slight from the other justices, and that she views many things as slights.

Oliver also charged Bird with hypocrisy in her relations with the press:

She frequently criticized the news media for purported inaccuracies in reporting Supreme Court decisions. Yet her testimony made clear what every reporter in California has learned: the Chief Justice rarely talks to the news media, deferring all questions to her aide, Stephen Buehl. She testified she never returned a call from Endicott seeking her side of the story for the election day article she considered inaccurate. The 42-year old Chief Justice also lamented that the Court is perhaps too secret and wished the public could better understand its processes. She "endorsed" conducting the current hearings in public. Yet she lost no time on her first day of testimony in scolding the Commission for publicly scrutinizing "the most fragile branch" of government.

The *San Francisco Examiner* ran a long Sunday article examining a related issue: the quality of Brown's appointments to the bench generally, including but not limited to the Supreme Court. The story reported that former Chief Justice Wright approved of some of Brown's appellate court appointments but not of his appointments to the Supreme Court, which Wright thought had demoralized the justices on the Courts of Appeal. This article also picked up the theme of an editorial in the *San Diego Union* under the head "A Discredited Court":

One conclusion is already inescapable. These shenanigans, involving appointees of the last two governors of California, discredit the executive branch as well as the judicial. Governor Brown, whose three appointees had no prior experience on an appellate court, is particularly culpable.

Clark was the only witness to admit having talked with the press before the election day story, and most accounts of his testimony gave full treatment to his recollections of his conversations with Fairbanks. Only one story made an explicit judgment as to whether the *Times* had been justified in running its story. The *Los Angeles Herald Examiner* stated unequivocally that "a confirmation occurs when someone tells a reporter that a story is substantially correct, or refuses to say that a story is substantially wrong." Under this standard, the *Times* was justified. There were no editorials or other commentary that discussed the issue of journalistic ethics.

Although it was competing with stories about the *Mosk* suit, Clark's implied charge in his July 18 motion that Bird's lawyers had stolen a document from his file was well covered by the press. "Rose Bird, Clark Draw Battle Lines" was the theme of several headlines and some accounts emphasized the hostile atmosphere of the proceedings.

Bella Stumbo, a reporter for the *Los Angeles Times* who had not earlier written any of the daily articles on the hearings, wrote an article for the Sunday *Times* that was mocking and harshly critical: The article opened with some "atmosphere" paragraphs:

Inside the auditorium at Golden Gate University, Supreme Court justices and their attorneys and staffs continued, for the fifth straight week, to treat each other like liars and backstabbers and possible thieves.

Outside, at the information desk, sat four students from the law school which is hosting this event. They were discussing sports and the weather. Asked why they were not inside, witnessing history in the making, three looked surprised and one smirked.

"That crap?" asked the one with the smirk. "I'll read about it in the newspapers."

"Yeah, it's a drag," agreed another, a skinny young man in a T-shirt that read: "The Bird is the Word—drink Wild Turkey."

Having established a tone, Stumbo went on to develop her theme by noting that one commissioner had said to a reporter of Mosk's suit, "Stan [Mosk] doesn't want to testify because he doesn't want to have to lie." Stumbo also reported that

a couple [of commissioners] have even taken to writing limericks to each other during testimony, poking wry fun at whoever happens to be on the witness stand. They are very witty verses, and should be reprinted here, but the gifted Commissioners were afraid, as one said, "that the justices might not see the humor in them."

Stumbo's article was full of deplorable quotations. For example:

Delizonna's entire face lights up as he discusses possible removal from office of one or more of the justices. "One, or possibly two, of the justices of the California Supreme Court may be committing perjury in these hearings," says Delizonna, clearly believing that at least one already has. "Those justices should be thrown off the Court and disbarred. Forbidden to ever practice law again, in Paso Robles [Clark's hometown] or anyplace else." . . .

"It's McCarthyism, the way [Clark] has felt free, throughout these hearings to stand up and publicly point the finger at the Chief Justice, make wild, unsubstantiated charges that he knows are untrue," Delizonna rages, stopping just short of condemning the Commission too.

"Mr. Delizonna says a lot of strange things," said Clark with a smile of cool contempt. "And I wouldn't comment on any of them."

Not surprisingly, Stumbo's long article irritated nearly everyone. No other reporter had similarly dwelt on hostilities or tried to snitch on the commissioners, who by this time had been at it for four weeks and had become quite relaxed, perhaps too much so, about chitchat with reporters and observers. The picture Stumbo gave of the hearings was not one that most reporters shared. The chairman and Hufstedler were plainly trying to dampen anger and hostility among the justices, and reporters had cooperated by giving very little space to Delizonna or anyone else who attempted to pump up personality issues. The Stumbo article came out at a very inopportune time, the beginning of the week in which the *Mosk* case was heard in superior court, and may have influenced how the Court of Appeal reacted to his suit a week later.

Stumbo's article aside, in general Clark received little criticism. Nearly all papers reported his failure to correct Fairbanks's impression that he was actually confirming the election day story and his failure promptly to tell Hufstedler of the Mosk-Tobriner conversation—about the only points on which Clark was even implicitly criticized.

THE FACELESS STAFF: WHO WERE THEY?

Edward Lascher, once a member of the board of governors of the state bar and well known to California lawyers as the author of an amusing if opinionated column in the state bar journal, submitted an article to the *Los Angeles Times* that was printed on July 16. Lascher's principal point, nowhere made more clearly, was that the commission's hearings were exposing problems about the court far more important than the charges under investigation. Lascher was particularly disturbed about the court's workload—he called it "totally impossible"; at the same time he asserted that too much of the judging was

done by clerks (full-time employees of the Court, often newly out of law school, or persons who have never done anything but clerk for a court) and by externs (not even lawyers, but second- and third-year law students). It is these faceless folks, most of them novices and all of them antiseptically free of familiarity with the business of the legal world—let alone experience in judging—who play the principal role in determining what cases the Court hears and how it decides them. (The justices may decide which side wins, but the form and scope of their opinions are often far more important to society in the long run.) This is unconscionable.

Lascher's description of research attorneys as novices was inaccurate insofar as the court staff who testified before the commission were concerned, especially if Bird's staff were excluded. Two of Tobriner's three research attorneys testified, Harold Cohen and Michael Willemsen. Each had been with Tobriner for ten years, and Willemsen had had some experience in law practice. The two research attorneys from Clark's staff who testified were even more senior: Richard Morris had been with the court for twenty-seven years and Maury Koblick for twenty-three, considerably longer than the most senior justice, Tobriner. None of these men were novices, inexperienced in judging. By the time of the hearings, there was someone of substantial seniority on the staff of every justice except Bird.*

Bird's senior staff were not "newly out of law school." Richard Neuhoff had graduated from Stanford in 1972 and had worked in the public defender's office in Santa Clara County (where he had worked with Bird) until he joined Bird's staff in 1977. Scott Sugarman, Bird's other senior research attorney, had graduated from Stanford in 1975 where he had been a student of Bird, and had practiced law in Washington, D.C., until joining the chief justice's staff in 1977. He took over the research attorney position in 1978 from John Schulz, who left Bird's court staff to work for the Administrative Office of the Courts before the hearings started. Schulz had graduated from Yale in 1968; his somewhat eclectic career included working for Ralph Nader and later for Bird when she was agriculture secretary. Jeffrey Abramson, the fourth staff member of Bird's who testified, was the only one who fitted Lascher's description. His title was law clerk and his job was temporary (one year), but Abramson had a Ph.D. in political science from Harvard and had taught at Wellesley and Brandeis while he was going to Harvard Law School.

Tobriner's and Clark's staff were better witnesses than their bosses, and they were very impressive as knowledgeable and able lawyers. Perhaps because they were older and had worked for many years for justices other than Clark, Morris and Koblick particularly gave the impression of a high level of professionalism. They were clearly subordinate to the justice for whom they worked,† but they nonetheless felt a loyalty to the law as a discipline and to the court as an institution that to some extent transcended their immediate relationship with Clark. This aura of professionalism was less obvious with Cohen and Willemsen because they had worked with such dedication for Tobriner for so long that they seemed to have submerged their own personalities in his. They obviously identified with Tobriner and, at the time they testified, they were emotionally committed to him in a way that might make it difficult for them to transfer their allegiance to another justice, especially one with a view

---

* Newman at first avoided experienced help, but within a year added Guy Coburn to his staff. Coburn had worked for some years for Chief Justice Wright and came to the court an experienced lawyer.

† All of the staff who testified occasionally slipped into a form of speech that could be misunderstood, speaking about how "we decided" this as if the research attorney was a joint decision-maker with the justice. At one point the Chairman interrupted Morris to clarify the point: "To get things in some perspective here, the ultimate decision, for example, as to whether the *Caudillo* reference was to be removed, was for Justice Clark, not for Richard Morris, wasn't it?" A: "Absolutely, no question about it." Q: "He makes those decisions, he bears the responsibility?" A: "We discuss these matters; I make recommendations. The final judgment is always his, and I never question his final judgment on these matters, unless I think he is not fully aware of circumstances that he should be aware of, but once he is fully aware of these things, I never question his judgment."

of the judicial role that differed from Tobriner's. Still, their competence was obvious, and outside the contentious atmosphere of the commission's hearings, where loyalty was at a premium, they likely would have appeared less partisan and more professionally detached.

Neuhoff, Schulz, and Sugarman had either studied or worked with Bird before she became chief justice, and their testimony gave less of an impression of objective professionalism. Their nearly exclusive loyalty was to Bird. Neuhoff and Sugarman seemed to be competent young lawyers, less willing perhaps than their counterparts on Tobriner's or Clark's staff to challenge their boss but capable of executing her wishes reasonably well. However, Schulz, the first of Bird's staff to testify, tended to say much more than was necessary and to appear self-important:

> Q: Mr. Schulz, where did you get your legal education?
> A: I'm a graduate of the Yale Law School, where I graduated in 1968 in the top 5 percent of my class. . . .
> Q: By the time you left [Bird's] chambers had you completed a draft concurring opinion [in Fox] covering all these points you referred to?
> A: I had completed a second draft . . . based on a meticulous reading of sixteen hundred pages from the 1879 California constitution[al convention]. But that still focused exclusively on two provisions of the California constitution. My draft was approximately twenty-eight pages in length.
>
> I might say that in working on the second draft it has now occurred to me that I was preoccupied for a few weeks in that time by the birth of my first child. I went to birth classes and assisted my wife in the birth and found myself quite preoccupied with that, and at home, and taking care of the baby that was born. And that happened on June 28, 1978.

Although there were occasional discrepancies in their recollections of minor details, the staff, with one exception, invariably supported the testimony of their bosses. The exception to the rule of loyalty was Abramson.

Abramson worked on the Fox case after Schulz left. He and Bird had a conversation in October, after Bird's opinion had circulated, in which Abramson wondered aloud to Bird whether Newman was sitting on the case because he did not want the opinion to come out before the election. When his deposition was taken, Abramson told Hufstedler this had been rank speculation, but Bird's attorneys were present and they no doubt reported this evidence to her. Bird thus knew that Abramson's remark would come out, and she asked to be allowed to put her conversation with Abramson "in context," as follows:

A: Mr. Abramson had just come to my staff in August. This was the first time he had ever clerked for a court. He . . . came a little bit early and I asked him to do some independent research for me on the independence of the judiciary in anticipation of a speech that I was going to write. . . . I paid him independently out of my own funds for that. I, however, did not use his research in that particular instance.

He then worked on the Proposition 13 cases for me. And, again, I did not follow his recommendations. . . . And I suspect it was beginning to be a little discouraging for Jeffrey.

This was his third strike, so to speak. And I think he felt very uncomfortable about the fact that he had worked on the case for over a month, and I had put a great deal of pressure on him concerning the case. I think almost every time I saw him, I would nudge him and ask him what he was doing on it, how it was coming. I had some concerns because I had not agreed with his research in the past. . . .

It's in this context and also in the context that around the time that this discussion was going on the press was calling about . . . both Tanner and Fox. And I believe it was also after General Younger had made his attacks on the court.

And I think somehow Jeffrey felt responsible for the fact that the case didn't move more quickly from my office out into the circulation process. I tried to explain to him and to calm him down that he would not be held responsible for this, that the case was an important one, that we needed to give Justice Newman enough space to consider all the issues that were before us. And I also felt somewhat uncomfortable due to his newness on my staff to discuss another justice with him in this manner.

Also, I think you have to take into account what happens on a court when charges are brought about the holding up of cases or when charges are brought about leaks. You get almost a McCarthy type mentality . . . people begin to wonder about everyone else and things that were quite usual under other circumstances become unusual and suspect, and I think in that context that is why Jeffrey brought up the issue and that is why he had a feeling that somehow this case had to get out before the November election.

Q: As I understand, the question that he asked you was something to the effect, "Do you think Justice Newman doesn't want it to come out until after the election?"

A: I'm not certain of the exact framing of the question. I think the essence of it was his concern that it was not going to get out before the November election.

Q: I guess my question to you was, What did you respond?

A: *I told him that I thought it probably would in our circulation process, but I generally tried to calm him down is my recollection.**

Abramson was in the audience when Bird testified, and he overreacted to the significance of what she had said. He startled the commission by challenging her characterization of the context of his statement in very dramatic terms:

A: *I . . . sensed yesterday that I had walked into a piece of history in which I didn't belong as I sat here in kind of nightmarish disbelief while the chief justice recounted what our relationship was and what the fate of my work products before Fox had been as we met there on that day. I had the feeling that the commission was being told a very smart tale made of half cloth at my expense for reasons that I am not yet certain of. But up until the time of my deposition in this case, I believe that I had a close working relationship with the chief justice, that I enjoyed her respect, and that she enjoyed mine.*

The chief justice recounted our conversation in a way that I do not recall. And furthermore, she implied that she went into that meeting having been dissatisfied with my three previous work products at the court. Those three as identified by her were my work on the speech, my work on Proposition 13, and my work in Fox. The commission remembers she used the metaphor of three strikes. In fact, in each . . . of those examples, my work product found its way into print, and though I would not dispute or try to second-guess what her state of mind was about me, I feel as a small fly on the wall [it is] necessary to take at least this opportunity to speak in my own defense and at least to establish my credibility before going on to this conversation.

[First,] I was asked to provide her with quotations for a speech. I was not asked to write a speech; I was asked to provide quotations. I did so. Some of those quotations were used. . . .

In Proposition 13 it is true, as the chief justice testified, that I vehemently disagreed with her decision to dissent on equal protection grounds. However, what the chief justice did not say was that she had previous to that asked me as a person with constitutional background on the federal law to provide her with a memo on the equal protection grounds, making the best argument that I could. I . . . provided her with a memo on the equal protection argument. Much of that memo was reworked by the chief justice [and] as rearranged and rewritten [it] is, in fact, in print. So that I never viewed that as a second strike, although I felt it necessary to

---

* In testifying about Abramson, Bird several times called him by his first name, Jeffrey. Never in her testimony did she similarly refer to any other staff member by his first name without also using his last. She usually referred to her staff as Mr. Buehl or Mr. Sugarman or Mr. Neuhoff.

tell her that having made that argument on paper, I did not think it worked.

And the third strike evidently is supposed to be Fox v. City of Los Angeles. *And as the chief justice herself, I think, had to say, she does view that not as a third strike but as a good work product. She told me so at the time, and she gave me a copy of the opinion, sending it to me with her autograph on it, which is not something that she has ever done on any other case to me, although it may be a regular habit of hers to others. I don't know.*

I go into all this just because—far from [having a] McCarthy-like attitude myself, looking under the table as I talked to her for delayers—I was surprised to find that after I've talked to her so many times about McCarthy and what he did . . . I could walk blindly into this piece of history and as a person of no reputation be swatted against the wall in order to distance herself from whatever she thinks is damaging in my testimony. And I don't think, in fact, there is much damaging [to her] in my testimony.

Q: What did occur in that conversation? What did you say and what did the chief justice say?

A: I believe this conversation took place in my office rather than in hers. She walked in. I'm not sure what she said although . . . my memory is that she asked me what I felt was happening with Fox. *I then volunteered a question, which was a speculation on my part and which I had no grounds for making and I'm sorry I made. But I asked her whether she thought Justice Newman might not want it to come out before the election. That's all that I said. And it was entirely groundless speculation on my part. She just said she didn't know, shrugged her shoulders, something like that. I don't remember getting a positive response. I do remember that her recollection yesterday at this commission that she comforted me and she wanted to calm me down [was incorrect].*

Perhaps the most important thing about Abramson's testimony was the way the press reported it. Despite the obvious potential for headlines, most stories did not mention Abramson's charges at all and those that did generally minimized the importance of the incident. Such restraint showed that reporters were trying hard not to sensationalize the hearings. Abramson vastly overstated the importance of Bird's characterization of her relationship with him, but he was right that there was little, if anything, damaging to her in his testimony. If the Abramson episode had any significance at all, it was in the way Bird reached out to attempt to defuse it. As Warner of the *San Diego Union* said:

Observers had been struck . . . by the eagerness with which Bird, when asked about the conversation, had insisted . . . on characterizing Abram-

son as an easily discomfited young man who was "discouraged" because she had found his previous work unsatisfactory.

Except for Abramson, the staff who testified were not only indians, they were also subordinate chiefs. The staff of each justice included in addition to the three permanent research attorneys four or more externs. Externs were second or third year law students who typically spent about half a year (one semester plus a vacation) working for a justice. Externs were supervised by the research attorneys who assigned them cases to work on and reviewed their work product. The use of externs started in Wright's time, but it evolved in less than ten years from an experiment in legal education into a regular practice that the court depended upon heavily. Presumably much of the work of externs was relatively insignificant, preparing, for example, the memoranda on petitions for hearing that were obviously destined to be denied. Nonetheless, there is something unconscionable, as Lascher said, about using half-trained students to perform an essential government service. Apart from the psychic rewards of working for the Supreme Court, externs were unpaid, and their rapid turnover could only be inefficient. Although no particular point was made of it in the hearings, the use of externs also vastly increased the problem of maintaining security of confidential information. Roughly sixty externs passed through the court annually, and all of them had access to some inside information.

THE DIVISION OF LABOR BETWEEN JUSTICES AND STAFF

The justices organized the work in their chambers according to their own preferences, but in broad outline there was a pattern common to all. The commission learned most about how Tobriner's chambers worked because Tobriner had an interest in showing how much work he was doing during the critical period of late August and September and also because one of his research attorneys, Willemsen, was the first staff member to testify and he was used to explain the role of staff in general.

In very large part, the work was organized around the regular Wednesday conferences at which the court considered petitions for hearing. Tobriner described the process as follows:

First, we must be ready with the cases that we were assigned to do ourselves. Each of the justices gets a proportionate amount of these cases to work up a memorandum for presentation to the conference. We usually get about seven or eight cases a week. That requires that I assign the case to a law clerk. The law clerk discusses the petition with me, studies it, and I must be prepared to write a memorandum. That requires not only [that I read] the petition but [also] that I read the Court of Appeal opinion. And then I read the memorandum, of course, or work on the memorandum itself. I have sometimes written the memorandum myself and other times used the clerk's memorandum with additions and corrections and supplementation.

Willemsen described the work from his perspective:

The cases come before the court on petition for hearing or extraordinary writ. One-sixth of the civil cases are assigned to Justice Tobriner. I divide these up and assign them to various members of the staff, including myself, for preparation of conference memoranda. So I write some memoranda myself and supervise the externs in the memoranda that they will write. Then, in addition, we divide all of the conference memos written by other staffs among the seven of us; prepare a short notice to Justice Tobriner, explaining the crucial facts and issues of those cases; and have a weekly meeting, which is usually lunchtime on Tuesdays, in which we discuss all of the cases on the A list, that is, all of the cases whose recommendations indicate that they are difficult cases that the court should seriously consider granting. And we also discuss such B list cases as the people on the staff have selected out as being cases which possibly have been misclassified and deserve treatment.

After we have our staff conference on Tuesday, we have a meeting of the entire staff with Justice Tobriner Tuesday afternoon. And this runs about two hours and we discuss again all of the A list cases plus any select B list cases of importance at that conference. We are looking there for the court conference the following Wednesday morning and the discussion concerns what Justice Tobriner's reviews of the cases are or sometimes he will ask us for advice on a case; sometimes he may have arguments he wants to try out to see if we have a way of answering them.

As a practicing lawyer Commissioner Chodos had an understandable interest in how the decision was made to put a case on either the A or the B list and what happened after that. The extern who prepared the conference memorandum would make a recommendation for A or B list treatment, which would be reviewed first by Cohen or Willemsen, then by Tobriner. Assuming Tobriner agreed, that recommendation would go forward to all the other justices. With respect to B list cases for which conference memorandums were prepared in other chambers or by the central staff, Willemsen described Tobriner's review of them as relatively superficial:

I think [Tobriner] does make a brief review of those B list cases. It's not, I'm sure, as intensive as the review he makes of the A list cases. I doubt that he reads the petition [or] the Court of Appeal opinion with any depth in the B list cases.

This practice could be regarded as a deplorable delegation of decision-making to people who had not even graduated from law school since many of the conference memos were prepared by externs. On the other hand, these memorandums were presumably reviewed closely by senior staff and, given a weekly agenda of eighty cases plus the important other work that a justice must do, any time a justice spent reviewing B list cases with care could as well be regarded as an irresponsible waste of a limited resource.

When Tobriner described his workload he said that four days a week were devoted largely to preparing for and participating in the Wednesday conference (except during the weeks when the court was hearing oral arguments). That left one day a week and weekends for work on calendar memorandums and opinions and no doubt somewhat exaggerated Tobriner's personal involvement in the petition for hearing process. Richardson indicated that "more than 50 percent of my time is spent in preparing for Wednesday conferences." His estimate, if accurate, would seem a disproportionate investment of judicial energy in deciding what to decide. Obviously, docket strategy is important, but overlooking a worthy case or deciding a relatively unimportant matter are ephemeral mistakes with far less significant consequences than a wrong decision or a sloppily drafted opinion.

Willemsen described the staff involvement in the preparation of calendar memorandums for cases to be heard in oral argument:

A: When a case has been granted a hearing it is assigned to a justice to [prepare] a calendar and roughly once a month Hal Cohen and I and Justice Tobriner will meet and we'll talk about which person on the Tobriner staff will research and draft the calendar memoranda in cases that are coming up that have been assigned to him. And so I will draft calendar memoranda six, seven, eight times a year on cases assigned to Justice Tobriner, and I'll work with other persons on his staff who may have been assigned calendar memoranda on cases.

Q: Does Justice Tobriner review these memoranda before [they are] distributed to other chambers?

A: Yes. Early in this stage, before it is drafted, we will discuss the issues with him in some depth. Sometimes he will request outlines of memoranda devoted to particular issues. Then when a draft is submitted, he goes through it carefully; we discuss various points. He will want things drafted differently, additional issues mentioned, make changes in wording. We go through two, maybe three, drafts before it is distributed to the court.

Willemsen indicated that much the same process was followed when calendar memos were converted into opinions but with the justice involving himself more in the process:

A: We will have a conference and decide who is going to work opinions. Often, if the calendar was also written by Justice Tobriner and the calendar is acceptable to the court, whoever wrote it will work on turning it into an opinion. There will be cases where the calendar maybe [was] written by somebody who has since left and someone else has to turn [the calendar into] an opinion, and a good part of my job is the researching and drafting of opinions for him.

Q: And does Justice Tobriner review these draft opinions before they are circulated to other justices?

A: Yes, it's the same process as the calendar, except perhaps two differences: with the opinions, he is much more meticulous and goes over [them] much more in wording and is much more likely to write additional matter. . . . The calendars that are up against a deadline, the cases already set for oral arguments, sometimes they have to be rushed out, are not really in a polished state—but the opinions we can take the time and polish them.

Q: Would it be fair to say that Justice Tobriner has a heavy pen when it comes to your draft of opinions?

A: Yes, definitely on opinions.

Tobriner's description was a little different; like Richardson, he was reluctant to be fully candid about the role of staff. Commissioner Schwartz questioned him:

Q: Do the staff actually prepare calendar memoranda and opinions for your review and modification? In other words, do they generate a product which you then review and modify, rather than you actually generating it from the beginning?

A: That depends upon the case. In most instances, the staff will work up the memorandum on the petitions for hearing for conference. The staff performs a large role in that respect. At times I will write them myself, but ordinarily I get that from the staff, work it over with them, correct it if I have to, or add to it if I have to. On a calendar memorandum, I like to participate almost from the beginning. I discuss the case with the clerk. The clerk will try to embody in the calendar memorandum what we have discussed, or at times I might even do it myself. If the clerk gives me a calendar memorandum, I will carefully go over it, make many changes to it, add to it, edit.

Tobriner avoided a direct answer to Chodos's question:

Q: With respect to the matters that other justices have worked up, as opposed to your own, is it fair to say that by and large the tendency is to rely on the other justices' conference or calendar memo as generated by staff instead of your trying to read all the briefs and records of the other justices' cases?

A: With respect to calendars prepared by the other justices, I will very often disagree and want to write a supplemental one myself. So I will not depend on the other justices in that regard, Mr. Chodos.

Q: But on the conference list?

A: Conference memos we will very often go along with the justice who writes it but very often [we] come up with a supplemental memo ourselves. And we disagree. Part of the process is we have seven justices and we don't always agree. So that means I have to write a supplemental conference memo if I don't like what the justice has written to whom it has been assigned, and[that] happens quite frequently.

It may have been inadvertent, but neither Tobriner nor Willemsen nor anyone else mentioned as a major component of their work a close review of opinions or calendar memorandums from other justices. Willemsen mentioned almost as an aside that "[we also] review calendars and draft opinions prepared by other staffs and we will counsel with Justice Tobriner and on occasion write memos to him respecting those opinions."

To the extent that the calendar memorandum was a final draft of an opinion, its text would be available for discussion at the postargument conference, but dissenting or separate opinions could not be thrashed out collectively without a special meeting, and the same lack of a forum for collaborative effort on the language of opinions was present if the circulated opinion differed to any significant degree from the calendar memo, as, for example, in *Fox*. Although no one else so testified, all the justices probably shared Richardson's view that it was unseemly to criticize in any detail the opinions that emerged from a colleague's chambers. Thus, with the aid of staff, each justice prepared the opinions assigned to his or her chambers, working in substantial isolation from colleagues, and expected them either to sign or not to sign a circulating opinion without making suggestions for changes. Only if a majority were not obtained, as in *Hawkins*, was much attention paid to the content of opinions from other justices.

That at least some justices spent very little time in close study of the

work of their colleagues was suggested by the charts Hufstedler prepared
showing the passage of the *Tanner* and *Fox* boxes through the chambers
of the various justices. The box in *Tanner* never spent more than a day
in Mosk's office, and the same was true of *Fox* with one four-day exception (the four days included a weekend). Other justices were less consistently speedy, but unless a justice were preparing an opinion the box
would usually go through an office in less than a week. Staff involvement
in reviewing opinions from other justices was presumably relatively minimal, but it may have been more important than communications among
the justices. Indeed, there was hardly any substantive discussion of cases
among the justices after the postargument conference, and outside of
conferences the justices communicated almost entirely by memorandums.

Staff level negotiation about opinions was apparently common and
quite important. Morris, for example, had been told by people from
Manuel's staff that Manuel probably would be uncomfortable with the
strong language in Clark's first dissent in *Tanner*. Morris assured Manuel's staff that there would be no difficulty in toning down that language,
as was ultimately done. There was no direct communication on this
problem between Manuel and Clark until after Clark's opinion had been
altered. Morris also testified that staff communication between the
chambers of some of the justices—notably Clark and Richardson—was
extremely good and frequent. Commissioner Schwartz asked:

*Q: Is it a common practice in your office or for you to discuss verbally
or through a memo the inconsistency that you are going to point out in
an opinion with the staff of the justice who wrote the majority opinion
prior to actually circulating the dissenting opinion with the inconsistency
in it?*

*A: On occasion, yes. I think it must be apparent that one of the
troubles with our Supreme Court is a lack of good intercommunications
between staffs. I think there are good communications between particular
staffs. I don't think any one staff necessarily has good communications
with every staff, and I think that's probably true of each staff on the court.
We communicate well with particular staffs.*

*I could tell you what I would do, for instance, [if] the Richardson
staff had a matter come up similar to what had come up with the* Tanner
*case. Of course, we are often on the same side of an issue with Richardson,
but not always. We dissent to Richardson's opinions; and I can think of
three recent cases where I have prepared dissents for Justice Clark to majority opinions by Justice Richardson. Had a matter come up like this
involving our disagreement with Justice Richardson and [if I] thought
that we had some inconsistent statement with something that Justice
Richardson had said on a prior occasion, I feel sure I would have gone to*

Justice Richardson's senior research attorney and said something like, "Are you crazy? If this is the position you're going to take, we're going to throw back at you your statement in such and such a case and we're going to make you look real silly." Our conversation probably would have gone on from there, and we might well have resolved the whole difficulty. But we weren't doing that with the Chief Justice's staff and perhaps not with Justice Tobriner's staff as much as we should have, and perhaps they weren't doing it with our staff as much as they should have.

I'm not trying to fix fault for the failure of communication. I tell you it exists, and I am sure that the Clark staff contributes to it, but so do others.

SOME TENTATIVE CONCLUSIONS ABOUT STAFF AND COLLEAGUESHIP

The commission had no jurisdiction to make recommendations about how the justices organized their work or the role of staff. As a consequence, the evidence the commission heard about such matters was introduced only as background and was never developed systematically. Accordingly, only tentative conclusions can be offered.

It was obvious from the testimony at the hearings that all of the justices on the court in 1978 worked very hard. They did not need to. The McComb affair showed that it was possible for a justice to function with a minimum of personal effort by relying almost entirely on staff and colleagues. But even with the most diligent effort there was far too much to be done for the justices themselves to do it all or even very much of it. Two things follow: first, heavy reliance on staff is inevitable; second, how the justices allocate their scarce time is crucial because whatever they choose not to do themselves will be done more or less adequately by staff. The first may be regrettable,* but the second is more important. The second involves basically a management problem; each justice is of necessity the manager of a bureaucratic team. Administrative ability, particularly as measured by the capacity to maximize productivity and maintain high standards among subordinates, is not normally regarded as an important qualification for judicial office, but that was perhaps the preeminent skill needed for a justice of the California Supreme Court.

---

* Those who yearn for a time when public servants wrote their own opinions or speeches tend to forget that although staff work may have a tendency to even out quality, the leveling can be up as well as down. No doubt Holmes wrote better opinions than his law clerks could have. But the quality of opinions produced by Clark and Tobriner with aid of staff was undoubtedly much better than what they would have been able to produce had they been obliged to write their opinions from scratch by themselves.

The justices obviously varied somewhat in their practices. Clark probably left a good deal more of the opinion writing to his staff than did Tobriner, but both justices confined themselves largely to refining drafts written by others. More important, both Tobriner and Clark had done very well in staff development; Bird, on the other hand, had done relatively poorly. The difference was plainly visible in her opinions as opposed to theirs.

The courtwide allocation of work between staff and justices had apparently evolved without much self-conscious attention. No witness evidenced concern about the process, but to an outsider such as Lascher the justices were clearly spending too much time evaluating petitions for hearing. Any number of screening devices could be imagined to assist the justices in reducing that burden, from subdividing the work among themselves to more extensive use of senior and central staff operating under more explicit guidelines and policy direction than the Rules of Court provided.

A second practice, plain to outsiders, that aggravated the justices' workload problem was the production of separate or dissenting opinions. In addition to burdening the justices, that also made work for their staffs, but there seemed scarcely any recognition that each dissent or separate opinion was consuming a limited resource that might have been conserved by reaching agreement. Bird acknowledged that she wrote separately too often, but she evidently considered this practice unfortunate not because it was wasteful but because it contributed to the image of a divided court. That is a reason, but not the best one, for the justices to become more involved in preparing opinions and especially in reviewing the work of their colleagues.

The best reason for close collaboration on opinions has to do with the essential nature of an appellate court. A consensus is desirable because the court's decisions are supposed to reflect the jointly developed views of the whole. The great dissenters, Holmes and Brandeis, hardly ever did so; they dissented only on points of unusual importance; typically they submerged their views in those of their colleagues although often after fighting hard for language changes and the like.

By Bird's time, the California Supreme Court was operating under a different conception of colleagueship, closer in many ways to a legislative than a judicial model. Apparently the justices conceived their most important responsibility as voting, and they spent the bulk of their time deciding results, first on petitions for hearing and then on opinions. But opinions were voted up or down as presented with strikingly little attention paid to their content. If a justice did not like the result, a dissent would be prepared. If there was something distasteful about an opinion, a separate concurring or dissenting opinion would be written. Bridging differences—say, muting language to appease others even if that altered somewhat the meaning—was a relatively low priority concern for the justices themselves. It was seemingly more important to the justices to maintain the purity of their personal positions than to work towards a general view. The tendency toward individualism was evident before Bird joined the court. The inclination to work as seven autonomous chambers could be overcome only by a substantial and self-conscious reorganization of the court's processes to give the justices more time to focus on collaborative opinion preparation. Bird may not have been responsible for the decline of cooperation but by 1978 she had shown herself wholly unsuited by temperament to lead the court into greater joint effort on opinions.

THE END OF THE PUBLIC HEARINGS

Hufstedler was nearly through his witness list when Manuel took the witness chair at eleven on Tuesday, July 17. After Manuel, only Newman and Mosk remained. Everyone was eager to get the proceedings over: the commission had by then been hearing evidence for sixteen days.

The commission recessed at noon for lunch, and when it reconvened Hufstedler announced that he had received a telecopy of the Court of Appeal's summary opinion reversing Judge Wenke and ordering, as Mosk had requested, the commission's subpoena directing Mosk to testify in public quashed. Although technically not required to cease his questioning of Manuel, Hufstedler suggested that the commission might wish to consider whether it wanted to continue in view of the broad constitutional ground of the court's opinion. The commission accepted his suggestion and temporarily adjourned. Later that afternoon the commission reassembled but only to state that no decision had been reached and to adjourn until the following morning.

The next morning the commission announced that it had requested the Supreme Court to transfer the *Mosk* suit to itself and to convene immediately an impartial court to decide the case authoritatively. The commission hoped that the court would consider the matter that day at its normal Wednesday conference and the commission accordingly adjourned until three. At three, however, Chairman Janes reported that word had been received that no decision from the court would be available that afternoon; the commission again adjourned.

On Thursday July 19 the chairman stated that the court had denied the commission's request to treat the case on an emergency basis and that no final disposition of the lawfulness of its proceeding in public was possible for some weeks. The commission thereupon adjourned the public hearings. Although it later received additional evidence from the justices in private, the commission never again met in public.

SEVEN

The *Mosk* Suit and Newman's Disqualification

The story of what happened to the California Supreme Court in 1979 abruptly changed direction with the end of the commission's public hearings. The forum was shifted and the mode of discourse changed from testimony to formal legal papers—mainly pleadings, briefs, and opinions—and, surprisingly, statements to the press. Hufstedler's role became unambiguously adversary to the two justices who up to this point had been only names: Mosk and Newman. Very little new about the internal processes of the court was learned but some things emerged, especially about the characters of Mosk and Newman from the controversies they initiated.

MOSK AND HIS LAWSUIT

In 1979, Mosk was sixty-seven, in excellent health, and generally regarded as perhaps the ablest of the four justices left after Wright and Sullivan retired. Almost all of Mosk's career had been in public life. With only a few years in private practice in Los Angeles after attending the University of Chicago Law School, Mosk involved himself in the gubernatorial campaign in 1938, and he first came to public attention when

Governor Culbert Olson appointed Mosk his executive secretary. Shortly before Olson left office, he put Mosk on the superior court in Los Angeles (at the time Mosk was the youngest superior court judge in the state), but Mosk kept his finger in Democratic politics and remained active as a speaker for various worthy causes.

Mosk found the work of a trial court judge rather confining since he had broad interests in public affairs, ranging from foreign policy to municipal reform. Like his mentor, Olson, Mosk was essentially a progressive with a strong concern for civil liberties. When Pat Brown decided in 1958 to attempt to follow Earl Warren by moving up from attorney general to governor, Mosk determined to try to succeed Brown as attorney general. He got some support from old friends from Olson's time, as well as considerable financial help from politically active Jewish sources, and he beat an old-line northern California Democrat in the primary.

Nineteen fifty-eight was a good year for Democrats in California; both Pat Brown and Mosk won easily. Brown and Mosk made an interesting contrast. Although they were very similar in ideology (if highly pragmatic politicians can be said to have ideologies), they were quite different in temperament. Pat Brown was a San Francisco Irish Catholic with all that that background implies: warm, outgoing, loyal to friends, emotionally committed to helping the weak and underprivileged. Brown's concern, for example, for the mentally ill was genuine and rooted in nothing more complex than compassion for the unfortunate. Mosk, in contrast, was far more cerebral. He was not a cold man, but his nature was analytical and he won friends through the force of his mind and his wit; Mosk was the first prominent politician to use the phrase "little old ladies in tennis shoes." Mosk and Brown, not surprisingly, were never personally close, and Mosk's 1958 campaign was run rather independently of Brown's. They cooperated as governor and attorney general during their first terms and in their successful reelection campaigns in 1962. When U.S. Senator Claire Engel suffered a disabling stroke, Mosk seriously considered running to succeed him in 1964. Brown, however, declined to support that ambition and Mosk ultimately withdrew before entering the primary.

That same year, 1964, Brown put Mosk on the Supreme Court when Gibson resigned and Brown made Traynor chief justice. Mosk worked reasonably well with Traynor, and he greatly admired Wright after the latter was appointed chief justice in 1970. Mosk was a consistently liberal judge with a voting record not unlike Tobriner's. As a former attorney general, Mosk might have been expected to be sympathetic to the law enforcement point of view, but over time it became clear that the civil libertarian strain was stronger; Mosk had little sympathy for what he regarded as abusive police practices. He was, in general, a very capable judge with a sometimes astringent pen. He was reputed to be the only member of the court consistently on top of his work and with enough free time to maintain an active social life.

The *Bakke* case, decided late in Wright's tenure, was a major event for Mosk. Liberals generally favored affirmative action programs for racial and ethnic minorities, such as the special admissions program for the University of California's medical school at Davis, at dispute in *Bakke.* Mosk wrote a powerful opinion holding the program unconstitutional under the equal protection clause of the Fourteenth Amendment.* He carried with him all his colleagues but Tobriner, who wrote a deeply felt and bitter dissent. Although the result Mosk reached was affirmed by the U.S. Supreme Court, that Court was sharply divided (4-1-4) and, contrary to Mosk, approved the concept of preferences based on race. The whole experience must have been an emotionally searing one for Mosk, who was publicly and unfairly assaulted as a racist and reviled by many who had once been his supporters. At the time of the appointments of Bird, Manuel, and Newman, the *Bakke* case was pending in the U.S. Supreme Court and it was widely supposed that on the issue of preferences for minorities the three new appointees would vote with Tobriner rather than Mosk.† The press reported that Mosk was furious when Bird, rather than he, was appointed chief justice by Jerry Brown in 1977. It was also widely supposed that Mosk transferred his disappointment at not being made chief justice into personal hostility toward Bird.‡ Mosk was the logical choice for chief justice if someone on the court were to be promoted since Tobriner was past retirement age and Clark and Richardson were Republicans. The assumption that Mosk's antagonism toward Bird was based on the frustration of his personal ambition probably did him an injustice—it would have been out of character for Mosk for blame the messenger for the message—but rumors of unvarnished hostility were common from the time of Bird's appointment. A few echoes were heard in the commission's hearings: Clark testified that he consulted Mosk at one point because Mosk had

---

* Bakke v. Regents of the University of California, 18 C.3d 34 (1976); in the U.S. Supreme Court, 438 U.S. 265 (1978).

† As indeed they did on the next racial preference case, Price v. Civil Serv. Comm'n, 26 C.3d 257 (1980).

‡ Mosk wrote a memorandum to Bird on November 24, 1978, of possible relevance. Mosk was reacting to an article by Endicott printed on November 23 in which it was said: "[Mosk] was bitterly disappointed at not being elevated to Chief Justice when Wright retired and was even more displeased with the Governor's choice of Ms. Bird and actively tried to head it off. He told friends recently she is 'not offering leadership and has cut herself off from the Court.' " Mosk's memo said of this: "I have read with dismay the article in Thursday's *Los Angeles Times.* I categorically deny having made the quotation attributed to me, either to Endicott or the unnamed 'friends,' and I intend to communicate my displeasure to him. The alleged quotation was made up out of whole cloth. Indeed, since the post-election controversy arose, I have absolutely refused to utter any words except 'no comment' to all press inquiries. The only explanation I can conceive for the error is that Endicott must have misread his own notes and attributed to me statements made by someone else."

earlier suffered "cool but correct" treatment from Bird; perhaps more significant, Bird never mentioned talking with Mosk outside of conference on any point. Despite apparent mutual antagonism, Mosk and Bird voted together much of the time and their hostility toward each other had not apparently caused either to move toward the Clark-Richardson camp.*

Mosk was abroad some of the time when the Judicial Council was considering Rule 902.5 authorizing public hearings. Later he wrote a letter to Chairman Janes on February 15, 1979:

I was out of the country from mid-December until early January, and learned upon my return of the adoption of Rule 902.5 by the Judicial Council. I am concerned not only with the substantive rule, but with the second Whereas clause which declares that "no opposition to such an inquiry has been expressed by members of [the Supreme] Court."

Indeed I do have personal reservations about such an inquiry.

First, the inquiry was requested by one member of the Supreme Court, not by the Court. No prior approval of the Court was sought and I doubt that it would have been forthcoming.

Second, the proposal calls for a "public inquiry into the actions of the Supreme Court." Absent specific and articulable accusations against an identified judge or justice, I know of no authority in the Commission to inquire into actions of the Court.

Third, the Commission has no authority to proceed with any inquiry except in confidence. Such authority to conduct hearings in public cannot be conferred by the Judicial Council, which under the Constitution, "shall make rules implementing this section and providing for confidentiality of proceedings." [Citation deleted.] The section is in the conjunctive, requiring both rules and confidentiality. Simple language is tortured with Orwellian technique when it is claimed that confidentiality is provided by the device of eliminating confidentiality.†

Mosk's dates do not support the implication that but for his foreign travel Mosk would have protested earlier the public investigation: Mosk did not leave until mid-December whereas Bird's request came on Thanksgiving weekend; Mosk returned early in January, which suggests that he was back before the Judicial Council acted on the commission's proposal to conduct an inquiry (January 16); and he certainly had returned by January 29, when the council modified its earlier action at Hufstedler's re-

---

* *Tanner II* and *Caudillo II* could be regarded as exceptions. In both cases Mosk voted with Clark, and his opinion in *Caudillo II* was sharp.

† This letter was included as an exhibit to Mosk's complaint in the superior court and is thus a public record. Technically its disclosure may have violated the very confidentiality rules Mosk was contending the commission was violating by holding hearings in public.

quest. Thus, Mosk could have dissociated himself from Bird's call for an investigation, and he could also have protested any relaxation of confidentiality while the matter was pending before the Judicial Council.

The basis for Mosk's lawsuit was the third point in his letter, but the issue of how Mosk should behave was narrower than whether he thought the commission could lawfully hold public hearings. Every justice who testified publicly did so under protest, and insofar as possible each made a record that would render the public nature of the commission's investigation a nonprecedent for the future. The question for Mosk was whether he would take the ultimate step of a suit testing the legality of public proceedings despite the facts that the public hearings had been mandated by the Judicial Council, so that the commission had no choice but to proceed in public, and all his colleagues had appeared and testified "under protest."* Two obvious questions were presented by Mosk's decision to file suit: why was he breaking ranks with his colleagues and why did he wait until July 9 to do so?

The question about timing is relatively easy to answer. An affidavit filed by Richard Mosk, the justice's son, who acted as his counsel, disclosed that conversations between Richard Mosk and Hufstedler on the matter came to a head about June 12, the day after Hufstedler made his opening statement. On June 12, Richard Mosk sent Hufstedler a copy of proposed papers in a lawsuit to quash the subpoena and they then agreed that when the commission made a final decision that Mosk's testimony would be needed his counsel would be given sufficient notice to be able to file a lawsuit. A subpoena had been issued to Mosk on May 25, and on June 27 Hufstedler informed Richard Mosk that the justice's testimony would be required.† They agreed that since a judicial determination of the lawfulness of public hearings was apparently needed, they would find a mutually convenient date for prompt disposition of the case, which turned out to be a hearing before superior court Judge Robert A. Wenke in Long Beach on July 11.

Hufstedler was thus partially responsible for the delay in filing the suit (June 12 to July 9). It is not hard to imagine why as of June 12 Hufstedler was anxious to postpone as long as possible a judicial determination of whether public hearings were lawful: the evidentiary hearings were scheduled for June 18. Mosk's lawsuit might well force a postponement—to the considerable inconvenience of Hufstedler's clients, the commissioners, who had cleared their calendars for two weeks starting June 18. Perhaps more important, by placing Mosk last on the witness list Hufstedler hoped that Mosk would feel pressured to aban-

* Newman did not appear in public, but he later publicly said that he would have had not Mosk's suit intervened.
† This was a week before Clark disclosed the Mosk-Tobriner conversation, which Clark had not mentioned in his deposition.

don his action. In short, Hufstedler suspected that Mosk was bluffing and ultimately would agree to testify under protest.

Mosk could have sought an injunction against public hearings as soon as the Commission on Judicial Performance made clear its intention to hold proceedings in public (April 25). Why did he wait until June to bring his lawsuit? First, he did not know what would happen and there is understandable reluctance to exercise any strategic option until necessary. More important, a lawsuit commenced before the hearings started would make Mosk look like an obstructionist with something to hide; the press and public response almost certainly would have been strongly adverse. To the extent that courts respond to public pressure, Mosk's chances of winning could only be improved by waiting. Hufstedler could have forced Mosk's hand by scheduling Mosk as his first witness, but that would have been inconsistent with Hufstedler's basic strategy of trying to get the investigation over so that the court could proceed free in one way or another of the cloud that it had manipulated the release of cases for political reasons.

Hufstedler was criticized after the fact for not having sought a judicial resolution of the public hearings issue before the proceedings started. To go forward with a constitutional cloud hanging over the commission invited the very disaster that occurred. Hufstedler's decision not to attempt any such action was based on his fear of getting bogged down in legally interesting but, at least to the public, irrelevant issues. In his view, getting the matter over with was paramount. He was undoubtedly correct in supposing that public confidence in the judiciary would not be promoted by dilatory lawsuits on issues collateral to the charge that the justices had delayed *Tanner* for improper reasons.

Mosk's decision to file his lawsuit appeared at the time to be a stunning repudiation of his colleagues and an insulting gesture as well. His brief to the superior court recited that Mosk

is not seeking to halt the proceedings or even to prevent violations of law by or as to others. Petitioner is only seeking relief as to himself so that he does not violate his oath of office by participating in what he believes to be an illegal proceeding.

Implicit in that assertion was the proposition that Mosk alone of the justices understood the full import of his oath. The appearance of deserting his colleagues was somewhat misleading, however. Mosk was not the first, but rather the fourth, justice to do something profoundly disrespectful of the others: by June, when Mosk acted, Bird had requested the commission's investigation without consulting her colleagues (except possibly Tobriner); Clark had refused to exchange depositions with the others; and Newman had refused to answer some of Hufstedler's questions on the ground of judicial privilege. Each of those actions was, in its way, at least as dramatic an example of "going it alone" as Mosk's lawsuit. Together these actions indicate that the justices failed almost totally to develop a coordinated strategy as to how they should relate to the commission; in this context, Mosk's decision to take a separate path seems less startling. *

How much of an effort the justices put into presenting a united front is largely unknown. There were occasional references in the commission's hearings to memoranda on legal points developed by court staff that were circulated to all chambers, but how much time was spent in conference or otherwise discussing how they should react is unknown. As Mosk's letter noted, the commission was limited to investigating wrongdoing by individual justices as opposed to probing the Supreme Court as an institution; this focus on individual wrongdoing undoubtedly contributed to the tendency of the justices to go their separate ways. Hufstedler at the outset of his investigation encouraged each justice to retain counsel, and each justice must at times have felt a tension between loyalty to the institution and a sense that the time may have come to save his or her own skin. There was both arrogance and irony in Mosk's and Newman's insistence, as each marched off to his own drummer, that they were acting to protect not themselves but institutional values; that each had nothing to hide, but neither could in conscience cooperate with Hufstedler, as his colleagues had, because an important principle essential to the court's proper functioning was at stake.

The common assumption that Mosk's suit indicated that he had something to hide was probably wrong. For one thing, Mosk did not escape testifying by winning his lawsuit; to the contrary, he testified before the commission in private and perjury was as possible there as in public. Second, it was not likely that Mosk had much to say that would be personally damaging. He was most vulnerable on the issue of leaks, especially on what he had said to Endicott or Fairbanks on November 6, but if his testimony were anything like Clark's it would have been at worst ambiguous and he need not have feared contradiction from the reporters. Nevertheless, Tobriner was anxious to have public testimony from Mosk on the Mosk-Tobriner conversation that Clark had reported,

---

* Less significant but also indicative of a willingness to part company with colleagues were: Manuel's decision (perhaps made by his counsel) to accept Clark's invitation to be interviewed by counsel in lieu of exchanging depositions (counsel for Bird, Tobriner, Mosk and Newman declined), Richardson's decision not to hire a lawyer, Mosk's decision not to dignify the commission's proceedings by the presence of his counsel—who never appeared before the commission in its public proceedings—and Newman's filing a claim for reimbursement for counsel fees before the hearings started. Later, and most spectacularly, Newman went his own way by refusing to disqualify himself from participating in the decision on the appeal of Mosk's suit. So far as known, only Bird and Tobriner consistently confronted the commission together.

so much so that Tobriner's counsel later told reporters: "I have a confidential deposition from Mosk. I know what is in it. But I have given my word. I'd be very happy to tell you if I were authorized to talk. All I can say is I wish it were public." Presumably, Bird was equally anxious to have Mosk testify publicly. Delizonna was quoted as saying: "To be accused anonymously but in public and then to be exonerated in private isn't much of an exoneration." If Mosk had an ignoble motive, and he may not have, it more likely related to showing up Bird as an incompetent leader rather than concealing the truth. In any event, there is no reason to doubt his sincere belief that public proceedings were unconstitutional.

THE *MOSK* SUIT IN THE SUPERIOR COURT AND THE COURT OF APPEAL

Hufstedler and Richard Mosk arranged the hearing of the *Mosk* suit to take place on Wednesday, July 11, because the commission had agreed to excuse any justice from testifying on Wednesday mornings to permit the court to hold its regular conferences. Observers were startled, therefore, to find Newman seated in the audience at the hearing in Long Beach. The world learned that justices could leave their votes and need not be physically present at the Wednesday conferences to participate.

The briefs prepared by Richard Mosk and Hufstedler were quite full, unusually so for a trial court presentation, but both sides had been preparing for quite a while; in truth, there was not much crucially relevant material to be presented. Hufstedler and Mosk agreed that time was important and Judge Wenke promised to give them a ruling early the following day. On Thursday morning he handed down a two-page opinion, finding in favor of Hufstedler.

Hufstedler hoped Mosk would not appeal Wenke's ruling. Appeal could have been unattractive to Mosk for two reasons: first, it would be time-consuming and could potentially drag out even further the commission's already unduly prolonged process; and second, there was no logical stopping place before the top rung of the appellate ladder, which was, in this instance, the same court whose justices were under investigation. If Mosk's concern was fear of breaching his oath, a trial court decision could well have sufficed to permit him to testify publicly in good conscience. Hufstedler's hopes were quickly dashed, however, when Richard Mosk immediately filed an appeal (technically, a writ of mandate) with the Court of Appeal in Los Angeles. Simultaneously he sought a stay of the subpoena ordering Mosk to testify pending the appellate court's decision.

Hufstedler rightly anticipated that the stay request would be granted (as it was on July 16), but the stay would not prevent the commission from continuing to take testimony from its remaining witnesses other than Mosk. And it was reasonable to expect that the Court of Appeal would take a week or more to consider the matter, by which time Hufstedler would be done with Manuel and Newman, especially if Newman did not make questioning difficult by continuing to insist on his theory of judicial privilege.

By lot, the *Mosk* case was assigned to division two of the Los Angeles Court of Appeal, composed of Justices Roth, Beach, Compton, and Fleming (the same panel that had issued the stay in the school busing case just before school was to start in the fall of 1978). The press described the panel as conservative; erratic, especially on civil matters of high public visibility, might have been more accurate. Even with division two, observers were surprised when, without the benefit of oral argument, that court on Tuesday, July 17, issued a final opinion reversing Wenke and holding the commission's public hearings unconstitutional. The court expressed not a shred of doubt as to its conclusion, which it reached on the basis of the papers earlier filed before Wenke in the superior court. Not giving Hufstedler a chance to argue was at the very least an insult to the Judicial Council, which had passed Rule 902.5, to the commission, which had labored long and hard at considerable public expense pursuant to the rule, and especially to the Supreme Court justices who had already testified.

The initiative shifted at this point to the commission and Hufstedler. Theoretically they could have sought a rehearing from division two (unlikely to be productive); accepted the decision (unthinkable in view of the investment of energy and prestige in the matter); or sought to overturn division two in the Supreme Court. They promptly chose the last course.

Time was critically important to the commission. A two-week public hearing had dragged on for more than a month, the welcome at Golden Gate University Law School was running out (school was to start in about a month), and the end was tantalizingly close particularly since the press, a little bored with the whole matter by now, was prepared to accept without cavil the inevitable conclusion that no probable cause to warrant formal proceedings would be found. Consequently, the commission acted quickly: Hufstedler prepared and delivered that afternoon a letter requesting the Supreme Court to transfer the case on an emergency basis to itself immediately, suggesting that thereafter seven replacement judges could be selected (perhaps by lot) to hear the case on the merits and urging that the case be scheduled for argument two days later. Hufstedler explained the need for haste:

This matter is urgent, since the proceedings were interrupted today upon receipt of information of the ruling of the Court of Appeal and the proceedings are in recess pending a response from this Court. In view of the public importance of these proceedings, as well as their great importance, the substantial expense to the State and the parties in holding the proceedings in abeyance and then restarting them, and the need for an early resolution of the pending questions, we would urge that the matter be set for argument this coming Friday, July 20.

On Wednesday morning, Hufstedler filed a formal emergency petition for extraordinary relief.

Hufstedler and the commission were asking for a lot, but extraordinary speed was consistent with what Hufstedler had been trying to do from the beginning—get the affair over with. If the court would treat this matter with the same urgency it had earlier given the Proposition 13 cases, the result would impressively demonstrate the capacity of the judiciary to act with dispatch on matters of public importance, as well as reveal the justices suitably willing to cooperate in an investigation of themselves.

On Thursday afternoon the Supreme Court sent a letter to Hufstedler and Richard Mosk requesting their views on a series of technical questions relating to whether the justices should disqualify themselves and setting forth a schedule as to when answers were to be supplied.

1. *Is the qualification of a Supreme Court justice to sit or participate in the consideration of issues raised by the emergency petition affected by the fact that (a) a fellow justice is a party to the proceeding; (b) the sitting or participating justice has been served with a similar subpoena; (c) the Commission, which has caused the issuance of the subpoena pursuant to the investigation of the Supreme Court, is the petitioner; or (d) the sitting or participating justice may previously before petitioner itself have raised objections or reservations during the course of the investigation?*

2. *Assuming a justice intends to disqualify from participating in the consideration of the issue of the merits of the underlying petition as it bears on the obligation to respond to a subpoena, may he or she, nevertheless, participate in a decision relative to the grant of the requested relief or the transfer of the cause to the Supreme Court on its own motion? [Citations deleted.]*

3. *How, if at all, would the answers to the above questions be altered by the "rule of necessity"? [Citations deleted.]*

4. *Does the California Constitution authorize the exercise of judicial power by a Supreme Court composed entirely of assigned pro tem justices, or is a minimum number of regularly sitting justices constitutionally required? [Citations deleted.]*

5. *If all or a substantial number of justices disqualify themselves,* *what procedure should be followed in the selection of their replacements?*

Hufstedler and Mosk were to file answers by July 25 and comment on each other's responses by July 30. The clerk was instructed to deliver the following message as an addendum to the questions: "Gentlemen: Let the record show that Justice William P. Clark deems it unnecessary and inappropriate for the parties to respond to questions posed by the Court in this proceeding."

To the commission the most important part of the court's letter was the schedule it set forth, as was made clear by the chairman's remarks to reporters at the final public session of the commission:

From the letter, it is apparent that it will be on the order of at least two *weeks before we know what judges will act upon the emergency petition,* *that is, the request of this Commission for review of the decision of the* *Court of Appeal. Thereafter it would be necessary for those judges to* *determine whether the Supreme Court will, in fact, hear the matter. If at* *some future date such judges should decide to grant the petition to review* *this matter, additional time would then be required for a decision on the* *merits, thus the contemplated procedure will require, at a minimum,* *several more weeks.*

To the commissioners and Hufstedler, the delay was a breathtaking repudiation of everything they had been trying to do from the outset. Although the legal issues raised by the court's letter were interesting, they could easily have been finessed if the court had shared even a small part of the commission's sense of urgency. No one could have criticized the justices for granting Hufstedler's request for an immediate transfer of the case to the Supreme Court, particularly since such an action appeared to run counter to their personal interests. The justices could then have disqualified themselves from further participation and created a publicly credible, impartial tribunal to decide the case on its merits by following Hufstedler's suggestion that an ad hoc Supreme Court be selected by lot from justices on the Courts of Appeal.*

The commissioners and Hufstedler were more than disappointed by the imposed delay; they felt ill used by the justices. The commissioners had not asked to investigate the Supreme Court justices; they had not

---

* The constitution provided for such a selection by lot of a Special Tribunal to review the recommendation of the commission if the subject of the commission's recommendation were a justice of the Supreme Court. That provision was, however, not in terms applicable to the *Mosk* suit because the issue in his case was not a commission recommendation for discipline. Although literally inapplicable, the constitutional provision for a Special Tribunal was an obvious analogy.

sought the public hearings; but they had loyally tried to do their duty, in some instances at considerable personal sacrifice. Chairman Janes, for example, had postponed his retirement, others had given up vacations, and all had, to a greater or lesser degree, imposed on colleagues, clients and family to help the justices who, for no obvious good reason, now seemed determined to frustrate the commissioners' earnest desire to get it over with.

Furthermore, the commission confronted a difficult choice: what was it to do for the month or more needed to resolve the *Mosk* suit? One possibility was to stop cold and wait. The commission could resume the hearings in public if it won, in private if it lost. But after a month's delay the evidence would be stale in the commissioners' memories and the logistical problems of starting all over—clearing calendars, finding a hearing room, and so on—were formidable. Alternatively, the commission could go immediately into private session and complete taking the testimony of Manuel, Newman, Mosk, and any witnesses they felt it necessary to recall. Presumably, the evidentiary process could be finished in a week or less. In the event the commission won the *Mosk* suit, either it could reopen public proceedings and repeat the testimony it had heard in private or perhaps it could avoid that redundancy by publishing the transcript of the private hearings.

The commission decided to take evidence in secret during the week of July 23–27. What was revealed in those sessions was never made public since the commission ultimately lost the *Mosk* suit. It seems highly likely that Newman persisted in his claim of judicial privilege and refused to answer questions relating to the substance of positions he and other justices (and staff) took concerning the *Tanner* and *Fox* cases. Assuming Newman asserted a privilege, he thereby created a major problem for the commission. The public hearing issue presented by the *Mosk* suit was unique to this proceeding and unlikely to recur. In contrast, Newman's assertion of judicial privilege posed a serious threat to the authority of the commission to search out and discipline judicial misconduct. Newman's theory did not depend on whether the commission proceeded in public or private. He was claiming that in the absence of a stronger showing than had been made to date about wrongful delay in *Tanner* and *Fox*, a judge could not be compelled to answer questions or reveal documents concerning communications between judges (or their staffs) as to the substance of cases. Not only could the commission not compel answers; presumably, the judges were enjoined by the canons of judicial conduct from replying. The assertion of such a privilege in proceedings by the commission would thus seriously hamper the commission in its general disciplinary work, especially with respect to misconduct on appellate courts.

Newman's position on this point was not supported by any obviously controlling precedent and his argument was not likely to generate much support outside the judiciary, if there. If, as here supposed, Newman refused to answer questions, the commission was authorized by statute to initiate an action to compel him to answer in the superior court, a possibility the commission earlier had considered when Bird temporarily refused to answer questions. The chances were good that Hufstedler would win such a lawsuit against Newman, especially since no other justice had refused to answer questions on that ground. (A number of justices had said that they were queasy testifying about conference discussions and the like, but all answered and none made even a formal objection for the record.)

But should the commission bring suit against Newman? Several factors probably influenced the commission to refrain. First, the commission might lose and thereby create an adverse precedent. Second, and probably more important, a suit against Newman would create yet one more diversion from the central question of improper delay and thereby further postpone a conclusion. Finally, it did not seem likely that Newman's testimony would add much. There was one question left open that only Newman could answer—why he had done nothing in the *Fox* case from October 4 to November 15—but the chances were good that the election had little to do with his delay if for no other reason than that *Fox* was, relative to *Tanner*, of minor political significance.

For whatever reasons, the commission decided not to bring suit against Newman, at least while Mosk's suit was pending. Thus, Newman was a principal beneficiary of the *Mosk* suit. Moreover, had division two waited but a day or two, Newman would have been forced to decide in public whether to continue refusing to answer questions on the ground of judicial privilege. And had Newman refused to answer questions in public testimony, the commission's decision not to sue him probably would have been different because the commission could not have tolerated such a notorious threat to its authority.

NEWMAN'S DISQUALIFICATION

Newman was the central figure in the next scene in this saga, an interlude, as it were, of theater of the absurd in the midst of an already somewhat surrealistic drama.

Newman was sixty-two in 1979 and, except for a brief period during World War II, he had spent his entire legal career as a law professor at the University of California at Berkeley (Boalt Hall), which he had attended as a student. He had been at Berkeley during the two most traumatic periods in the University's history: the loyalty oath fight of the 50's as a young law professor, and the "Free Speech" movement and student

Cartoon by Steve Greenberg, Editorial Cartoonist for the *Daily News of Los Angeles.* © *Daily News of Los Angeles.*

unrest that followed in the Viet Nam era, as Dean of the Law School. Newman was publicly identified as an important supporter of the professors who refused to sign the oath, and was, in general, sympathetic to the students who were rebelling in the 60's although his position was less visible to outsiders. Although not particularly active in partisan politics, Newman had always been involved in public affairs. His principal academic specialty for many years had been administrative law, and he had chaired the administrative law section of the American Bar Association. President Kennedy appointed him to a term on the Federal Home Loan Bank Board and Newman had also served on the California Constitutional Law Revision Commission. Dean of Boalt Hall from 1961 to 1966, Newman chose after he left the deanship to focus his academic interest on international human rights. He quickly became an internationally recognized authority on the subject, very active in Washington and in the United Nations in trying to bring pressure on repressive regimes to cease using torture.

Newman's decision to specialize in human rights in 1966 was characteristically a little ahead of its time, somewhat out of fashion when he did it, but nonetheless well within the mainstream of advanced liberal thought. Newman was an almost made-to-order appointment for Jerry Brown. Who could attack a sixty-year-old former dean of one of the nation's major law schools whose resumé made him appear to be a citadel of the establishment? The impression, however, was misleading: Newman combined brilliance with an almost instinctive anti-establishment attitude, and he could be relied on to support, if not lead, progressive assaults on entrenched legal doctrine. His flaw, if he had one, was not vision but an occasional lapse of balance or judgment. As one of seven justices, however, that defect was unlikely to present a serious risk.

Newman's weakness of judgment was made spectacularly obvious when the court considered the responses Hufstedler and Richard Mosk had made to its questions. On Wednesday, July 31, the court filed an order announcing that six of the justices, all but Newman, had disqualified themselves from even considering whether to decide the *Mosk* case on its merits. The court ordered the clerk to select by lot six replacement justices that afternoon. The clerk did so, and Bird signed an order appointing six Court of Appeal justices, including Bernard Jefferson, to hear the case.*

Counsel for Mosk immediately wrote Newman and his temporary colleagues requesting Jefferson to recuse himself since he had participated as a member of the Judicial Council in the issuance of Rule 902.5. This move irritated Hufstedler, perhaps excessively, who responded by writing a letter objecting to

the apparent partisan judge-shopping by counsel for Justice Mosk. Justice Newman is, we believe, clearly disqualified in this proceeding as a matter of law, pursuant to the provisions of subdivisions 1, 4 and 5 of the Code of Civil Procedure section 170. . . . Yet counsel for Justice Mosk did not . . . suggest that the status of Justice Newman should be reviewed. Fairness is a two-way street. Justice Newman's obvious disqualification is ignored by Justice Mosk because he apparently believes that Justice Newman will favor his position.

* By signing the order, Bird undercut (intentionally or not) an argument that might have justified Newman's failure to disqualify himself. In the past, whenever a chief justice disqualified himself or herself, the selection of the replacement was left to an acting chief justice on the theory that a disqualified justice ought not take any action in a matter in which he or she was disqualified. Under the constitution only an associate justice could be an acting chief justice. Thus, if all the justices disqualified themselves there would be no one to appoint their replacements. Newman was the logical choice for acting chief because Mosk was plainly disqualified from considering his own case and all the other justices, except Newman, had testified before the commission in public, conduct that could easily be thought to compromise their ability to judge impartially Mosk's assertion that it would violate his oath to uphold the constitution if he testified publicly.

This letter was written August 6, the day the ad hoc Supreme Court was to meet in conference for the first time; later that day Hufstedler filed a formal motion for the disqualification of Newman. Attached to this motion was an exhibit under seal, which was explained as follows:

Justice Newman has [before the commission] asserted as a party a position on the merits of a substantive issue that is central to these proceedings in the Supreme Court. The substance of Justice Newman's position has not been publicly released by the Commission. The Commission believes public disclosure of Justice Newman's position before the Commission is appropriate in the context of this motion. However, due to uncertainty as to the scope of the decision of the Court of Appeal [in Mosk's suit], the Commission file[s] under seal an exhibit setting forth Justice Newman's position and incorporates said exhibit herein by this reference.

On August 6 the ad hoc Supreme Court issued a string of orders. Most important, the court granted Hufstedler's petition for hearing, but it also stayed the subpoena to Mosk pending a decision on the merits, announced Jefferson's recusal ("I have no desire or wish to sit on this case in which a party thereto has expressed a belief that I will not be able to objectively, fairly and impartially determine the issues involved"), directed the clerk to select by lot a replacement, ordered the exhibit filed under seal to be kept under seal, and denied the request that Newman be disqualified. The following day, the case was scheduled for argument on September 20. Except for the order granting a hearing, which was signed by all the justices (excluding Jefferson), all the orders, including those appointing Jefferson's replacement and denying the motion to disqualify Newman, were signed "Newman, Acting Chief Justice."

On August 9, the clerk of the Supreme Court sent to counsel a letter asking a series of questions, including some relating to Newman's disqualification. The letter asked, in substance, for further briefing on certain issues presented by Mosk's suit. The question about Newman's disqualification was a surprise and suggested that his participation was still in doubt. Indeed, Newman told reporters on August 9, "I consider the question of disqualifying myself still pending before the Court." Asked his reaction, Hufstedler said, "I see nothing in the order that suggests it's an interim order."

Newman's refusal to disqualify himself and the court's scheduling oral argument six weeks later angered and frustrated the commissioners, who increasingly felt that they were being given a runaround by the judges, especially Newman. The commission met on August 13 to consider its next move. Before then, Larry Stammer of the *Los Angeles Times* reported on August 10 that the legal papers for a renewed challenge to Newman's participation had been drafted, citing "sources," presumably within the commission or its staff. The article went on to discuss a more ominous possibility:

In a related matter, sources said Newman had claimed a judicial privilege during his closed-door testimony before the Commission and refused to answer questions that went directly to the heart of the Commission's inquiry—whether the Court delayed decisions for political purposes.

Newman intimated to the Times that he did, in fact, refuse to answer certain questions.

Newman said he would answer questions dealing with Court procedures. But he said the "content of communications among the judges, or among the judges and staff that affects substantive matters," fell under judicial privilege.

Several months before the hearings began, Newman and aides took the same approach when depositions were taken by Hufstedler.

There is some sentiment among those associated with the investigation that a Superior Court order should be obtained to force Newman to answer the questions.

Hufstedler would not comment on that.

Whether the commission in fact reconsidered its earlier decision against seeking a superior court order against Newman is not known; if it did, a majority must have concluded not to change the earlier decision.

The commission, however, authorized Hufstedler to file a three-part motion with the ad hoc Supreme Court requesting the court, without the participation of Newman, to prohibit Newman from participating further in the proceedings, reconsider his disqualification, and advance the date for oral argument. The brief Hufstedler filed with this motion contained some very strong language:

The disqualification of Justice Newman is absolutely essential to the integrity of the Court, and to its ability to render a valid and binding judgment. On August 6, 1979, the Commission filed a verified Statement of Disqualification as to Justice Newman. The mandatory provisions of Code of Civil Procedure Section 170 provide that after a verified statement of disqualification is filed, the challenged judge is immediately suspended from further participation in the proceedings. The matter of disqualification must then be determined by a judge or judges other than the judge whose disqualification is sought. . . .

The parties and the people of California are entitled to a Court consisting of judges who are not interested in the outcome of the case, and who have not prejudged the issue. They are entitled to a Court consisting of seven justices who are, and who appear to be, independent and unprejudiced on the issue before them. It is impossible to explain to anyone—

judge, lawyer, or anyone else—that Justice Newman can be, or can appear to be, independent in these proceedings. He is a party to the underlying action; he will be directly affected by the outcome of these proceedings; he may be directly affected by the testimony under subpoena; and he has previously, as a party and advocate, asserted a position upon the constitutional issue before the Court. . . .

There is no apparent reason why the argument cannot be set at an earlier date. There are many pressing reasons for an early argument and resolution of these proceedings. It was public interest and necessity that initially prompted the investigation by the Commission, and that same public interest and necessity requires that the matter be concluded without delay. In addition, where appropriate, the justices, who are subjects of the investigation, have a right to a prompt removal of any cloud surrounding their performance, caused by the public allegations of wrongdoing. The Court as an institution will remain unable to restore public confidence in its integrity and ability to function until the proceedings are concluded. And finally, the members of the Commission have pressing personal and professional responsibilities which make it impossible to delay conclusion of the proceedings indefinitely.

Hufstedler's strong language probably reflected his difficulty holding his clients, the commissioners, together; indeed, Commissioner Gehrels resigned on August 13 and Commissioner Chodos, eleven days later. Hufstedler may have hoped to keep the commissioners on board with rhetoric that conveyed some of their extreme frustration and anger.

The other side of the coin, however, was that the court was acting with what, to the justices, seemed exceptional dispatch. Benfell reported in the *Los Angeles Daily Journal*, citing a source "in a position to know," that

the argument was deliberately placed six weeks ahead in order to allow thorough briefing and "a good calendar memorandum." The timing of the hearing date "shows the Court is giving special attention" to the case and is not seeking to delay it. "This is like the Proposition 13 cases" where the petition was filed in June, heard in August and a decision rendered on September 20, the source said. The Court "might even get this case out sooner" than the six weeks taken in deliberating the Proposition 13 cases, the source said.

How much reporters were simply putting together logical inferences from what was publicly known and probing for confirmation of plausible hypotheses versus how much they were being fed information from internal sources is not known. The general impression was that the commission and Newman were trying to take their case to the public through the press. The most dramatic leak, widely assumed to have been planted by the commission, was the publication by Stammer in the August 9 *Los Angeles Times* of a passage from the document Hufstedler had filed under seal with the court on August 6. The sealed exhibit, it turned out, was a letter written by Newman on May 9 to the commission, presumably in connection with the rules the commission had announced in April. Stammer quoted Newman's letter as asserting:

Article VI, Section 18(f) [of the California constitution] authorizes neither the relaxing of confidentiality that Rule 902.5 contemplates, nor the permitting of the kind of inquiry that the Commission unfortunately has undertaken. *

The impression that Stammer's article had its source in the commission was furthered by the fact that Stammer made too much out of Newman's signature on the ad hoc court's orders:

On Monday, Newman issued a two-sentence order denying without explanation a petition by the Commission that he disqualify himself from the case. . . .
Newman rejected the Commission's appeal that he make the letter public. On Tuesday, he issued an order as acting Supreme Court Chief Justice which declared that his letter was not part of the Court record.

The implication that the orders reflected unilateral decisions made by Newman alone was inaccurate, although there was no way Stammer or anyone else could have known that. Later the ad hoc court on Newman's behalf announced that Newman had urged that the sealed document be released but had been outvoted. At the same time, the court announced that the order refusing the commission's request that Newman disqualify himself had been made without Newman's participation, although the order he signed had said nothing so to indicate.

The most surprising instance of taking the *Mosk* case to the newspapers came from Mosk himself. At the American Bar Association convention in Dallas, Mosk was scheduled to appear on a panel discussing government and the courts and he used the occasion to level a blast at the commission. By chance his speech came on the same day, August 14, that Hufstedler filed his three-part motion, getting the commission

---

* That statement, if Newman continued to believe it, was a direct comment on the point of law in issue in the *Mosk* suit. That alone was not sufficient to show Newman's disqualification. A judge is not disqualified from ruling on a case simply because he has earlier formed a view on a point of law involved in the case since otherwise it would be almost impossible for a judge of any experience to rule on almost any question. The difficulty here was not that Newman had taken a position on the legal issue presented in Mosk's suit, but rather that he had done so as a participant in the underlying proceeding.

banner headlines on page one of the *Los Angeles Times:* "Harsh Charges in Court Probe."

Mosk's speech was full of carefully crafted, colorful phrases designed for easy quotation:

Such open proceedings [by the commission] appear to be contrary to state constitutional requirements of confidentiality, but reason was swept aside by fear and emotion. From that point on, the media had a field day. The Commission decreed that it was not bound by rules of evidence. Thus it permitted reports of corridor gossip among law clerks, inquiries into intent, motivation, speculation and the rankest type of hearsay. . . .

The entire investigation became a media event that replaced daytime soap operas, and, not surprisingly, the press reveled with prurient interest in every juicy morsel relating to internal Court personality conflicts. . . .

There is no more pathetic sight than learned judges cringing in fear of an aggressive investigative commission which is in turn pandering to an assaultive press.

Commission members obviously relish their role on center stage. . . . Humiliating the Court in public appeared to be a barrel of laughs to the Commission. *

Given the questionable propriety of Mosk's comments on a pending matter, there was something out of place about his statement that "while purporting to investigate leaks to the press from Court sources, Commission members themselves constantly leaked information and admissions to the press." Mosk apparently felt no compunction about discussing his own case while it was pending,† and implied that he had brought suit only because the commission had behaved badly:

I became so alarmed at this bizarre proceeding that conscience compelled me to bring a lawsuit to enforce our constitutional requirement of confidentiality in the mere preliminary investigation into alleged improper judicial conduct. Our intermediate appellate court, in which the matter was heard, unanimously agreed with me that such inquiries should be conducted confidentially.

---

* Mosk later published his speech, eliminating the last paragraph quoted above and the next quoted paragraph. Mosk, When the Supreme Court of California Became Exhibit A, 18 JUDGES J. #4 at 40 (1979).

† The much-discussed canon 3(A)(6) provides: "A judge should refrain from public comment about a pending or impending proceeding in any court. . . ." Whether a judge who is a litigant is bound by that is open to some question under the First Amendment, but as a matter of taste or decorum there is not much doubt that Mosk's speech was at least as inappropriate as the Duekmejian-Nolan debate in the *Times* before the reargument of *Tanner.*

To further compound judicial humiliation, however, and to titillate the public with resultant judicial impotence, the Commission on Judicial Performance pursued its appeal to the very Supreme Court it was investigating.

Reporters knew what was going on, and Jim Mann of the *Los Angeles Times* tried to put Mosk's comments in context. He sought out Hufstedler for comment and reported:

Tuesday night Hufstedler called Mosk's charges "either substantially overblown or overstated, or downright frivolous or in some instances inaccurate or incomplete. I would challenge Justice Mosk or anyone else to present evidence of leaks to the press," he said.

Mann did not report, as some others did, that Mosk left out of his speech a few sentences that were in his prepared text. Steven Pressman in the *Los Angeles Daily Journal* noted:

While Mosk made no references to other members of the Supreme Court in his remarks, his written text distributed afterwards to reporters contained two scratched out references to Chief Justice Bird.

At one point he mentioned that Bird had requested the Commission to investigate charges of withholding opinions for political reasons. But Mosk omitted saying, as his text mentioned, that Bird acted "unilaterally without discussing the matter with the Court—and in my opinion improvidently."

At another point in his remarks, while Mosk was discussing various matters that came up during testimony by Court employees and justices, he left out a reference to discussion of "why the Chief Justice gave the 'silent treatment' to a justice."

The next day at his press conference the newly installed president of the American Bar Association, Leonard Janofsky, came to the defense of his close personal friend, saying, "I don't think you could find a more competent and fairer lawyer to conduct those proceedings than Seth Hufstedler." Janofsky carefully did not accuse Mosk of improper or unethical conduct but he did say: "There is a real question [in my mind] as to whether the justices should be speaking in public on this matter."

Meanwhile, back in San Francisco, the ad hoc Supreme Court was considering what to do with Hufstedler's three-part motion. On August 22 it announced that certain questions presented by the motion required oral argument to be held the next week (August 29). As framed by the court the questions follow:

*May a justice of the Supreme Court be disqualified for cause if he declines
to recuse himself when the claimed cause is asserted by a party? If so,
what procedure is to be followed in determining whether he is disqualified
for cause? Specifically, is the procedure prescribed in Code of Civil Procedure Section 170, subdivision 5, to be followed? If so, with what varia-
tions, if any? If that procedure is not applicable, or if it may not be
pursued, what is the procedure to be followed and who shall determine
whether the affected justice is disqualified for cause?*

The order recited that Newman had not participated in the decision to
issue it but that he expected to be present at oral argument although he
would neither participate in the discussion nor preside. Before argument
was heard, however, the commission came close to dissolution through
two resignations.

THE DEPARTURE OF GEHRELS
AND CHODOS

Although there were obvious differences in attitudes toward the
court and the justices among the commissioners, they managed to present to the public a single view and to speak without dissent through the
chairman whenever the commission was obliged to act in any formal
way—issuing procedural rules or ruling on evidence points. The pressure on the commissioners was mounting, however, fueled no doubt in
significant part by the delay Mosk's suit imposed on their concluding the
investigation.

Commissioner Gehrels was the first to break away. She resigned on
August 13, saying only that "as a matter of conscience, I cannot participate in further deliberations of the Commission." Commissioner Chodos
left on August 24 but he did not follow Gehrels's precedent in two respects. First, he did not resign from the commission; rather, he announced that he would not "continue to participate" in the investigation
of the justices of the Supreme Court. Second, he made public a three-
page letter to Chairman Janes explaining his action.

Chodos was a favorite of observers of the public hearings. An enormous man with something of a theatrical manner, Chodos enjoyed turning a smart phrase in public, and he was often the source of the little
humor the proceedings held. His letter to Janes asserted that he was on
the commission as the "representative" of the bar, a dubious proposition
at best. Chodos was on the commission because he had been appointed
by the board of governors of the state bar, but as a commissioner he had
no special duty to represent lawyers as opposed to the public generally.

Nonetheless, he used his supposed representative status as the predicate for his withdrawal from the commission's proceedings:

In my judgment, it is basic to the role of the Bar in an adversary system that its members should only be called upon, and should only permit themselves, to argue or submit their causes to impartial tribunals. When a judge refuses to disqualify himself from sitting in a case in which his own interests are engaged, and where he has prejudged the issues, his refusal reflects upon himself. But if a lawyer submits himself and his cause to such a judge, and plays the advocate's part even though the result is foreordained and his arguments can have no actual bearing on the outcome, his participation reflects dishonorably on the lawyer and violates the principle of the independence of the bar.

Justice Newman has refused to disqualify himself despite the Commission's repeated challenges and requests; and he continues to insist on sitting as a member of the Court which will determine the rights and duties of the Commission with respect to further proceedings. . . .

I am aware that on August 22, oral arguments were scheduled for August 29 by the six Justices assigned to the Court, to consider, among other things, the Commission's renewed suggestion that they prohibit Justice Newman from participating further in our pending case. However, the questions posed in the order of August 22 strongly suggest that at least four of the other six members have grave doubts whether they have any legal power to remove Justice Newman if he refuses to recuse himself. From a technical standpoint, these doubts may or may not be well founded. But in my view, debate over such technical questions is beside the main point, and can only obfuscate the question of principle which now confronts me as a member of the Bar. . . .

The Commission has already spent more than five weeks in fruitless efforts to obtain a prompt, impartial, and final decision on the merits of an alleged constitutional question raised by Justice Mosk, which is itself procedural, rather than substantive. It has been prevented from doing so by an apparently endless succession of procedural technicalities and delays totally unrelated even to the merits of Justice Mosk's procedural objection. Meanwhile, Justice Newman continues to sit. The Commission is therefore unable to resume and complete the performance of its constitutional duty to investigate and deal with allegations of judicial misconduct by members of the Supreme Court.

The letter was passable rhetoric, not as quotable as Mosk's speech, but it made very little sense: no principle implicating the independence of the bar was involved and the commission had not yet lost the motion to compel Newman's disqualification (indeed, the commission ultimately prevailed on this point). Furthermore, the letter appeared to be, like Mosk's Dallas speech, an inappropriate attempt to influence the ad hoc court on Newman's disqualification and the merits of Mosk's suit, a criticism that could also be made of the statement Chairman Janes issued concerning the departure of Chodos:

> Mr. Chodos' withdrawal from the pending investigation is a deep loss to the Commission and an even graver loss to the public interest in prompt completion of the investigation and disposition of the matters under scrutiny. Mr. Chodos is expressing an understandable unwillingness to abide the apparently interminable procedural quagmire into which the Commission has been drawn. We will sorely miss his keen intellect, boundless energy and sound advice.

What was perhaps most troubling was Chodos's refusal to resign from the commission while withdrawing from the matter of the Supreme Court justices. There was precedent for this decision: Justice John Racanelli at the very outset of the commission's investigation had similarly recused himself from this case but had not resigned. Nevertheless, Chodos and Racanelli probably had no authority to follow this course. Their action was at bottom unfair since there was no mechanism for replacing a commissioner who refused to participate in a particular matter. But the commission needed a vote of five to resolve any proceeding, even by the dismissal of charges. Thus, as we saw earlier, each justice now had to get five votes out of seven, instead of five out of nine; realistically, the difficulty of replacing Gehrels changed the odds to five out of six votes.

Kang asked and got answers to the obvious question in an article printed in the *San Francisco Examiner* on August 28:

> At the moment at least, more resignations do not appear to be forthcoming. Five out of the six commissioners queried yesterday said they had no intention at this time to step down, however frustrated some of them feel about the present situation. But it appears that what happens next at the Commission could depend a lot on how the ad hoc Court resolves the issue of Newman's disqualification. If the Commission loses this battle, some of the Commission members may seriously reconsider their decision, highly placed judicial sources speculated. A mass resignation is one option, they said.

THE DEPARTURE OF NEWMAN

The ad hoc Supreme Court met in public for the first time in the court's San Francisco courtroom for the oral argument scheduled on

August 29. The senior Court of Appeal justice, James Cobey, presided, with Newman seated on the bench at Cobey's extreme left, Newman's usual seat as the most junior justice on the court. Cobey established a relaxed tone for the argument, noting during the argument that his son had remarked about Cobey's selection to sit on the ad hoc court, "Gee, Dad, another merit appointment." The occasion was a reunion for the audience, which included some of the research attorneys who had testified before the commission, as well as reporters and others who had not seen each other since the commission had recessed its public hearings on July 17.

Although he requested only forty-five minutes, Hufstedler was on his feet for nearly two hours. The points involved were intricate and no useful purpose would be served by discussing them here in detail. Canon 3(C)(1) of the code of judicial conduct provided: "A judge should disqualify himself in a proceeding in which his disqualification is required by law, or his impartiality might reasonably be questioned." The last clause was Hufstedler's strongest point. It was obvious to everyone, except Newman, that Newman's impartiality was reasonably questionable. Hufstedler's problem was that §170 of the code of civil procedure defining disqualifications required by law did not include the appearance of impartiality, as the canon did, but only bias or prejudice in fact. Section 170 thus provided no mechanism for the forced disqualification of a judge who only appeared to be biased or prejudiced. Furthermore, the § 170 mechanism for forced disqualification was designed with trial judges, not appellate justices, in mind.

For trial judges, the §170 mechanism was cumbersome but workable. A lawyer who believed a trial judge disqualified was to file a sworn statement setting forth the facts suggesting bias and the judge could either recuse himself at that point or within ten days file a response to the factual assertions. The disqualification matter would then be heard by another judge selected by agreement between the lawyers for both sides in the lawsuit or, if they were unable to agree, by a judge designated by the chief justice. Hufstedler presented a neat solution to ad hoc court's problem: since Newman had never responded to his formal statement of disqualification, Newman's failure to answer should be regarded as an admission of bias and Newman should therefore be ruled disqualified. The difficulty with this strategy was the doubtful applicability of the section to appellate justices; under such circumstances, it seemed harsh and unfair to treat Newman's failure to answer as a forfeiture of his position.

As oral argument or debate between opposing sides, the hearing was a failure because Richard Mosk made no effort to defend Newman's position; he essentially refused to respond to the questions the court had put to counsel. Mosk opened with a denunciation of the commission and with charges that commissioners had been making inappropriate statements, presumably a reference to Chodos's resignation letter of the previous week and oddly out of place in view of his client's speech to the American Bar Association two weeks earlier. His principal point was that the ad hoc court was invalidly constituted, an argument that was, at best, premature. At one point, one of the justices snapped at him, "If you are not going to answer my questions, I don't want to listen to speeches, you should sit down." Cobey quickly restored a more temperate atmosphere, and when Hufstedler concluded his brief rejoinder, Cobey closed the argument with a compliment to him, "It is always a privilege to watch an artist at work."

Two days later, the ad hoc Supreme Court issued a long, complex order that opened with the statement "Newman, J., did not participate." Without deciding whether the §170 mechanism was applicable to appellate court justices, the order decreed that the procedure there set forth should be followed "insofar as possible." The court gave Newman until September 7 to file, if he wished, a response to Hufstedler's statement of disqualification. If he did not, he would be disqualified; if he did, the parties (Hufstedler and Mosk) would have until September 12 either to agree on another judge or to refer the matter to the ad hoc Supreme Court to resolve the issue of Newman's disqualification. If Hufstedler and Mosk failed to agree, Chief Justice Bird was to designate a judge to decide the matter by September 14; if she did not, the matter would automatically be referred to the ad hoc court for resolution. Thus, in one way or another, Newman's disqualification would be resolved in time for the oral argument on September 20.

The next move was Newman's, and on September 7 he filed an "answer regarding disqualification" with an accompanying statement. This was the first time anyone had come forward with something approaching a legal justification for Newman's puzzling behavior. In addition to a very technical, though quite possibly correct, reading of §170,* Newman's principal point was that a judge has as strong a duty to sit unless disqualified as he has not to sit when disqualified:

[A] judge may not refuse to hear a case because he is squeamish about the facts, or thinks he is too busy, or wants to get off the hot seat, or is fearful that his rulings may inspire criticism or scorn. On the contrary, the oath of office requires that he "well and faithfully discharge the duties" of judging.

---

* Newman asserted, for example, that since the commission's hearings were at the investigatory stage he was no more than a witness, not a party, and the hearings were not an action or proceeding within the meaning of §170. Furthermore, he had no interest within the meaning of that section in whether Mosk testified publicly or privately since the Mosk testimony would presumably be the same in either circumstance.

Newman was implicitly criticizing the frequency with which Bird and others had been disqualifying themselves from cases, as Bird had done, for example, in *Caudillo II*. The point was by no means a foolish one, but this was surely an odd occasion for Newman to take a stand on it. Furthermore, although Newman asserted that his "mind was no more set in this case than it has been in countless cases where in many ways I have had prior exposure to and preliminarily discussed other complex and challenging legal questions," his statement never addressed the issue of whether people might not reasonably question his impartiality, as stated in the canon.

Newman's filing of an answer forced Hufstedler and Mosk under the court's order to decide whether they wanted the ad hoc court itself or some judge they could agree upon to rule on Newman's disqualification. Somewhat reluctantly, retired Chief Justice Wright agreed to perform this unexpected public service, and a hearing was scheduled for Monday, September 17, in a courtroom in Pasadena. Mosk and Hufstedler filed a stipulation reciting that Wright would act "upon appropriate designation." That phrase may well have been unnecessary, but it appeared to call upon Bird to "activate" Wright, who was then formally on retired status.

On September 13, Bird balked. In a letter to the ad hoc Supreme Court, Bird explained:

Justice Cobey has requested that I issue an assignment to former Chief Justice Donald R. Wright for the sole purpose of hearing and determining whether "Justice Newman is disqualified. . . ."

As much as I would like to cooperate in the resolution of this matter, I deeply regret that I cannot issue the requested assignment. Attorney General's Opinion Number 79-419 states unequivocally that "The parties may not agree upon a retired judge or justice." The only exception is when that judge or justice "is actually functioning under an assignment by the Chairperson of the Judicial Counsel at the time *he or she is agreed upon by the parties." (Emphasis added). Such is not the case here. I am certain that you would not want further questions raised as to the legality and/or validity of this important proceeding. . . . I appreciate your understanding that apparently the law precludes the issuance of the assignment you request. Should you wish, you may feel free to release this letter to the public.*

Bird's refusal was more laughable than anything else. A few weeks later, Ralph Kleps wrote about it in the *Los Angeles Daily Journal*:

The [attorney general's] opinion, rendered to the Administrative Director of the Courts in another context, concluded that stipulations under Sec-

tion 170(5) could not be made unless a retired judge was already under assignment. The assertion that a Chief Justice is bound by a deputy attorney general's opinion in this situation raised a number of challenging questions about judicial assignments.

—Why would the judicial system of the state ask the legal adviser for the executive branch to rule on a constitutional power of judicial administration vested in the Chief Justice?

—Where a special order of the substitute Supreme Court authorizes the procedure, why would one rely upon the Attorney General's interpretation of an inapplicable statute rendered in a different context?

—Even if the assignment to duty must precede the stipulation, why not make the assignment and give the parties a chance to stipulate again?

Ralph Gampell, Kleps's successor as director of the Administrative Office of the Courts, gave reporters an answer to the last question. "That would have been like the stuff that went on in Watergate,"Gampell told Phillip Hager of the Los Angeles Times. Not being able to distinguish between facilitating the prompt disposition of a pending matter and backdating a deed to gain an otherwise unavailable tax advantage was itself revealing.

The wisdom of making the ad hoc court's order of August 31 self-executing now became clear. Since the parties' stipulation that Wright would decide had been frustrated and Bird did not appoint another judge, the issue of Newman's disqualification automatically came before the ad hoc Supreme Court. The court held a brief hearing on September 18 to give Newman an opportunity to speak but on the following day, by a four–two vote, ordered Newman disqualified.* Pursuant to the ad hoc court's August 31 order, another Court of Appeal justice was selected by lot and Bird signed the appointment order. With no time to spare, a full court was finally ready to hear the merits of the Mosk suit as scheduled on September 20.

MOSK'S SUIT BEFORE THE AD HOC SUPREME COURT

The ad hoc Supreme Court heard argument on the merits in the Mosk suit on September 20; less than a month later, on October 18, three

---

* The majority wrote no opinion. Justice Miller dissented on the ground that "no legal authority for the disqualification" of Newman had been given. Justice Hopper, although saying that "considering all of the circumstances, Justice Newman should disqualify himself so that the Court may maintain the appearance of impartiality and to avoid any suspicion of unfairness," also dissented. He agreed with Miller but added the ground that a majority of the court had no power to disqualify any members who refused to do so themselves. Both dissenting opinions were published as an appendix to Newman's dissent in Olson v. Cory, 27 C. 3d 532, 597–603 (1980).

months to the day after Hufstedler first sought emergency relief from the Supreme Court, the court handed down a "by the court" opinion in favor of Mosk holding the Judicial Council's Rule 902.5 unconstitutional because it called for public hearings.* The opinion was full, dealing at some length with the factual background, as well as the two principal contentions urged by Richard Mosk.

Mosk's first argument was the same one he had prematurely attempted to lay before the court at the hearing on Newman's disqualification: the ad hoc Supreme Court was not a court because it was composed entirely of pro tem justices. If the ad hoc court were illegally constituted, it had no choice but to dismiss the action before it. A dismissal would have the effect of resurrecting the decision of division two of the Los Angeles Court of Appeal in favor of Mosk. The ad hoc court rejected this argument, relying in part on decisions from other states where the same problem had been presented.

Mosk's second argument was based on article VI, section 18, creating the commission, subsection (f) of which provides: "The Judicial Council shall make rules implementing this section and providing for confidentiality of proceedings." Subsection (f) is a shorter version of what had been in the constitution when Gibson proposed the creation of the Commission on Judicial Performance in 1960. According to the 1960 constitution: [A]ll papers filed with and proceedings before the Commission . . . shall be confidential [until filed with the Supreme Court in the event discipline is recommended].† Mosk argued that the shortening was part of a general effort by the Constitutional Revision Commission to reduce the length of the constitution and that no substantive changes were intended; therefore, the Judicial Council had no authority to open up any commission proceedings.

Hufstedler conceded that the 1960 version of the constitution would have prohibited the public hearings. His argument was that the revision of the constitution gave the Judicial Council discretion to relax confidentiality in some circumstances. Hufstedler pointed out that the Judicial Council had authorized some publicity in five situations before the cur-

---

* Mosk v. Superior Court, 25 C. 3d 474 (1979).

† The 1960 provision in full was: "All papers filed with and proceedings before the Commission on Judicial Qualifications [the Commission's earlier name] or masters appointed by the Supreme Court, pursuant to this section, shall be confidential and the filing of papers with and the giving of testimony before the commission or the masters shall be privileged; but no other publication of such papers or proceedings shall be privileged in any action for defamation except that (a) the record filed by the commission in the Supreme Court continues privileged and upon such filing loses its confidential character and (b) a writing which was privileged prior to its filing with the commission or masters does not lose such privilege by filing. The Judicial Council shall by rule provide for procedure under this section before the Commission on Judicial Qualifications, the masters, and the Supreme Court. A justice or judge who is a member of the commission or Supreme Court shall not participate in any proceedings involving his own removal or retirement."

rent controversy all of which would also have been prohibited under the 1960 constitution. The existing Rule 902(b) permitted the commission to release information about a proceeding

At the request of the judge being investigated, to the extent of making a "short statement of clarification and correction,"

   If the commission concluded that no proceedings or discipline was warranted, it could issue "a short explanatory statement,"

   Where a formal hearing had been ordered, in the interests of "confidence in the administration of justice" the commission could issue "one or more short announcements confirming the hearing, clarifying the procedural aspects, and defending the right of judge to a fair hearing,"

   If a judge aborted a commission proceeding by resigning or retiring, the commission could "release information" to a public entity (presumably a district attorney), and

   The commission could advise the person who filed a complaint with the commission about the disposition of complaints.

Under Mosk's interpretation, none of these disclosures by the commission would be permissible although they were sensible and consistent with the general objective of conducting the commission's proceedings in private. Hufstedler argued that Rule 902.5, a similar exception to the general rule of confidentiality, was made necessary by the extraordinary circumstances presented by the public accusations of wrongdoing by several members of the Supreme Court.

   In the course of the argument Justice Cobey suggested there was a difference between the narrow exceptions to confidentiality permitted under the existing rule and the broad mandate for public hearings embodied in Rule 902.5: "Admittedly [the exceptions] are relaxations of the rule of complete confidentiality, but in terms of a light meter, they introduce a little dusk, whereas 902.5 lets in a blinding light." "They certainly introduced a little pregnancy," Hufstedler replied. That was the core of his argument.

   The ad hoc court's opinion, however, did not rest in any way on a distinction between dusk and blinding light. The opinion spent considerable time reviewing the evolution of the new language in the Constitutional Revision Commission, a point that had not been thoroughly briefed by either side. This original research, presumably done within the court, was largely unhelpful: it did not show that the Judicial Council was deliberately vested with discretion to relax confidentiality; on the other hand, it did not very clearly show the opposite. The opinion listed several policy reasons for confidentiality of commission proceedings. Confidentiality, the court said, protects judges from injury from unwarranted complaints by disgruntled litigants and promotes public confidence by avoiding premature disclosure of groundless claims of judicial misconduct. Neither reason was relevant in the context of Mosk's suit, nor was the idea that judges would be more likely to resign or retire voluntarily if they had not been charged publicly with wrongdoing. Two other policies the opinion discussed, however, were somewhat germane: first, confidentiality protects witnesses against possible retaliation; and second, confidentiality is essential to the commission's least damaging sanction, private admonishment. Justice Mosk was not obviously within the class of witnesses intended to be protected by confidentiality from retaliation. Furthermore, by the time he filed his suit, the risk of retaliation against people like court staff had already been taken. The private admonishment policy was much more clearly involved and had been a basic flaw in Rule 902.5 from the very outset. But Mosk was an odd person to be claiming what the ad hoc court's opinion curiously called the "judge's constitutional right to a private admonishment."

The California Newspaper Publishers Association and some individual newspaper companies filed an amicus brief urging, among other things, that Mosk had waived any right to complain about the public hearings by postponing the filing of his suit until July. The ad hoc court's opinion dealt with this contention by pointing out that the delay from June 12 to July 9 was at the request of Hufstedler—scarcely a complete answer. It would have been difficult to find authority supporting the assertion that Mosk had waived his right to object to the public hearings by failing to bring suit before the hearings commenced, but the amicus brief raised a valid point: stopping the public hearings within days of the end and thereby preventing the commission from filing a detailed public report was "fundamentally unfair . . . to the members of the Court who did testify in public." It would have been possible to write an opinion favorable to Hufstedler that rested in part on that unfairness and in part on the fact that by this time no policy promoted by confidentiality would be furthered by closing the hearings down. The opinion need not have endorsed Rule 902.5's constitutionality, it could, indeed, have intimated that had the issue been presented earlier the conclusion would have been otherwise.

The court's opinion evaded Hufstedler's strongest argument by refusing to consider the constitutionality of the existing relaxations of confidentialtity.

The narrow issue decided by this Court is whether article VI, section 18, subdivision (f) of the Constitution precludes the Judicial Council from adopting rules, such as rule 902.5, which authorize public investigations and hearings by the Commission. The constitutionality of Rule 902(b) is not an issue before this Court, and we decline to express our views on the constitutionality of all the provisions of that section.

Despite that statement, the court ended by saying that the commission could report the "results" or "status" of its investigation to the public since the fact of the investigation was already widely known.

The court's opinion was thus a little pregnant with unanswered contentions, but at least it was written promptly and the case was over.

THE COMMISSION'S WHIMPERING CONCLUSION

Because Commissioner Pacht was abroad at the time only five commissioners were present for the final meetings on the investigation of the Supreme Court. The first matter before them was whether to frame formal charges on any of the issues they had started to investigate in public: improper delays in *Tanner* or *Fox* and leaks of confidential information.

As to *Tanner*, the commission's conclusion should not have been difficult. There arguably was probable cause to believe that one or more of the justices, notably Tobriner and Bird, had slowed down the processing of *Tanner* at the very end because of the election, but it was plain

Cartoon by Steve Greenberg, Editorial Cartoonist for the *Daily News of Los Angeles*. © *Daily News of Los Angeles*.

that clear and convincing evidence of wrongdoing could not be found. Accordingly, even viewing the evidence least favorably to Bird and Tobriner, there was not "sufficient cause to warrant further proceedings," as the commission's rules stated.

Fox was harder because there was a gaping hole in the evidence caused by Newman's claim of privilege and his refusal to respond to questions relating to why he had done nothing on the case from October 4 to November 15. The commission could have brought suit in superior court to compel answers; it could also have filed formal charges to see whether that action might produce answers. But the chance of uncovering any consequential evidence was slight. Furthermore, the commission would probably be seen as being vengeful rather than dispassionately diligent if it pursued Newman. The commissioners decided to drop *Fox.*

On the leaks issue, Clark could properly be regarded as having been foolish, but speaking ambiguously to the press was not an impropriety within the commission's power to discipline. Mosk presumably was guilty of no more. Unless the commission wanted to take on his speech before the bar association in Dallas, which would also look vengeful, there was nothing in the leaks issue substantial enough to justify formal charges.

The commissioners next had to cope with a set of problems created in large part by the structure of Rule 902.5. This rule had authorized the commission to investigate the justices publicly on specific kinds of possible wrongdoing. In the course of hearing evidence on the prescribed issues, the commission had learned a little about a number of other matters that, if fully developed, might well justify private admonishment if not public censure or removal from office. The commission and Hufstedler had tried with mixed success to keep evidence concerning possible uncharged misconduct out of the record during the public hearings, but there was good reason to suspect judicial misconduct on the part of Bird and Clark for having allowed their personality conflict to develop to the point where their antagonism was unduly interfering with the efficient dispatch of the court's business. Even though the evidence concerning that possible misconduct was relatively full, the commission could not proceed on it without first developing the evidence more fully and giving the justices a chance to explain their conduct. A whole string of other matters might similarly be developed into charges worthy of private admonishment; for example, there had apparently also been a disabling quarrel of unknown origins between Bird and Mosk, Newman's refusal to disqualify himself in the *Mosk* suit (and, conversely, Bird's too quick recusal in *Caudillo II* and other cases), Tobriner's perhaps unintentional threat to Clark of commission proceedings if he did not sign Tobriner's exculpatory statement; and possibly even Bird's failure to consult with her colleagues before calling for the commission investigation.

More basic, and perhaps clearer as a ground for discipline, was a generalized attitude of the justices that seemed to place the prompt disposition
of cases near the bottom of the things the justices thought truly important. A charge on that basis could be framed in terms of the ninety-day
rule; it could also have been framed in terms of attitude as measured, for
example, by the frequency with which Bird and others wrote separate
opinions that advanced no clear public purpose and seemed to serve only
their private interest in maintaining a personally consistent position.

If the commission wanted to pursue any of these possible grounds
for discipline, it would have to start over, formulate new charges, and,
unless the justices conceded the error of their ways, begin again with
hearings in confidence. Moreover, this litany of possible misdeeds was
subject at most to the commission's weakest sanction, private admonishment. If private admonishment was all that could emerge, it probably
seemed to the commissioners not worth the effort. Surely the justices
could have learned from the hearings that their behavior was not altogether commendable. If they had not, a private letter of admonishment
from the commission would be unlikely to reform them.

Bird and Tobriner had both publicly requested that the commission
exonerate them. According to press reports, several commissioners were
unwilling to do so, presumably because they found the evidence of
wrongdoing, albeit not perhaps sufficient to justify formal charges, at
least troublesome. Since the commission's rules required five votes to
act, one suspicious commissioner could have blocked an exoneration. A
number of reporters called the commission's final report a compromise
carefully crafted to say the minimum. The report read:

*At the outset of [this] proceeding, the Commission felt it inadvisable to
undertake an investigation of an issue of such general interest and public
importance unless a full public report could be filed at the conclusion of
the investigation. The Commission, therefore, requested of the Judicial
Council a rule change which would permit the Commission to waive the
requirements of confidentiality, under appropriate circumstances. However, the rule which was ultimately adopted by the Judicial Council, Rule
902.5, went beyond the Commission's request and mandated a public
hearing during the investigation, with all segments of the media present,
and a public report of its conclusions, which conclusions were required to
be based only on evidence taken at the public hearing.*

*In the judgment of the Commission, it remains vitally important
that all of the evidence relative to the issues in this proceeding be thoroughly examined and analyzed, and the reasons for any determinations
be clearly and openly stated.*

However, under the compulsion of the decision in Mosk v. Superior
Court, *the Commission is not only prohibited from concluding the hear-*

ings in public but also is prohibited from reviewing or commenting upon the testimony and other evidence, and from public dissemination of the analysis and reasoning employed in arriving at a determination and disposition of the proceedings. We are by that decision confined to a "status report" or an announcement of the "results" of the investigation. The Commission regrets this limitation but is bound to follow the law as announced by the Court.

Therefore, in accordance with its limited power under the decision in Mosk v. Superior Court, *the Commission hereby reports that the status of the investigation is that it is now terminated and the result hereby announced is that no formal charges will be filed against any Supreme Court justice.*

The Commission wishes to make clear that its role under Article VI, section 18, of the California Constitution is limited to determining whether a judge has violated the standards of conduct set forth therein and imposing or recommending discipline where appropriate. It is not a general investigative body to review the procedures and functioning of courts nor to recommend improvements in the courts; it has not so functioned in these proceedings.

The report was issued on November 5, 1979, almost a year after the *Los Angeles Times* story on election day 1978. Bird told reporters that she was "pleased that a long and difficult ordeal for the Court is now over." Tobriner issued a statement through the press officer of the court:

I am pleased that after the most careful investigation and thorough probing of the claims of alleged misconduct by justices of the Supreme Court, the Commission has unanimously decided to terminate and to conclude the proceedings and to file no formal charges, and that charges were not warranted.

Commissioners, insofar as they said anything, were a good deal less enthusiastic. Commissioner Willoughby, perhaps in reaction to Tobriner's curious syntax, told Fairbanks, "It's not an exoneration just because we did not vote to bring charges." He explained:

The Court would have looked better [if the commission could have filed an explanatory report]. It would have been protected against charges of a whitewash. Because we were not able to explain our action, several questions were left open. Did some Commissioners feel like bringing charges? Why was there no exoneration? I see no reason why the public should accept the result (of the investigation) because we did not explain it.

Willoughby's statement provoked the final oddity, fittingly revealed by Kang in the *San Francisco Examiner* a month later. Mosk, it appeared, wrote a brief letter to the governor concerning Willoughby's remarks:

Mr. Willoughby reported information on internal proceedings before the Commission, despite the constitutional requirement that all proceedings be confidential and despite an unequivocal holding by the ad hoc Supreme Court that the constitutional provisions are controlling.

While this is but the last of a disturbing series of leaks from the Commission to the media, it is particularly egregious because it purports to expand upon the public report. I hope you will bear this grave irresponsibility of Mr. Willoughby's in mind at the time his reappointment to the Commission is considered.

Chairman Janes wrote the governor a few weeks later:

I am authorized to state to you on behalf of a unanimous Commission and after Commission review of the subject article, that Mr. Willoughby's statements did not in any way report "information on internal proceedings before the Commission," or violate the confidentiality placed upon the Commission proceedings by the California Rules of Court or the decision of the ad hoc Court in Mosk v. Superior Court.

Wholly apart from the Commission view, I wish to add my own opinion and impression of Mr. Willoughby's conduct and his performance as a member of the Commission. . . . I can emphatically assure you that in my 11-year tenure the Commission has never been blessed with a more competent, conscientious and dedicated member as Tom, and in very few instances his equal.

And so, trading fusilades of insults to the end, the Commission on Judicial Performance and the Supreme Court retired from the battlefield of the daily press, for the time being, at least, no longer of interest to reporters.

WHO WON?

Large conclusions about the commission, the court, and the media must wait for more years than have yet passed, but some comments from observers offered at the time are worth noting.

Hufstedler correctly felt that he and the commission had done what they had set out to do—dispose of the charge of improper delay. How quickly the court could regenerate itself as a cohesive institution was up to the justices. Knowing what had been learned about them, Hufstedler was not particularly sanguine for the near future, but at least one matter essential to justices' credibility was behind them and they could, if they would, look forward rather than backward.

Jonathan Kirsch, author of the *New West* piece on *Caudillo*, took a much dimmer view:

What started out last June as a perilous but promising experiment in opening the judiciary to public scrutiny has degenerated into a disgraceful display of arrogance, pettifoggery and obstructionism on the part of several justices of the high court. By challenging the authority of the Commission to conduct open hearings—and by delaying the final resolution of that challenge through self-serving tactical maneuvers—these justices have inflicted grave injury on a court whose moral authority was already in question. . . .

Indeed, the only redeeming aspect of the whole sorry affair has been the conduct of the lawyers and judges who serve on the Commission. . . . They asked the hard questions and they insisted on honest answers. . . .

Public confidence, after all, is what the fight is all about. The public hearings offered an unprecedented opportunity—at a time of unprecedented crisis in the judicial system—to prove that our courts are not just a paper charade. The public needed to see justice done—swiftly, surely, straight-forwardly. Instead, the public is witnessing a shameful spectacle that only confirms the worst stereotypes of lawyers and the law. And even if the underlying questions of misconduct are answered someday—in public or behind closed doors—the unhappy headlines of the last few weeks (Legal Morass in Court Probe Grows Deeper) will never be erased from the public's memory.

The *Los Angeles Times* editorial writers were a little more hopeful:

No one will be satisfied with the outcome of the investigation into charges that members of the California Supreme Court deliberately withheld controversial decisions to help insure the confirmation of Chief Justice Rose Elizabeth Bird in last fall's election. [The commission's] verdict, arrived at in secrecy and without explanation, will most certainly be unacceptable to those who want to believe that certain justices were playing politics. Similarly, those who were hopeful that the proceedings would exonerate the Chief Justice and others on the Court are left with nothing tangible to sustain their belief. . . .

The most that Californians can now hope for is that the justices, the propriety of their actions still in question, will set aside their personal animosities and try to work together—if not in a spirit of mutual trust, at least with a common commitment to get on with the people's work.

Guy Wright, editorial columnist in the *San Francisco Examiner*, obviously enjoyed the role of viewing with alarm:

The question is why anyone should ever again take the Court seriously, having seen what it's really like. The backstage peek has been devastating —not highminded jurists in scholarly consultation, but peevish adolescents indulging in snits, refusing to speak to each other for weeks, sending aides back and forth with spite messages. In fact, the Tanner *delay got started when Chief Justice Rose Bird got mad over a footnote. The unhappy course of the investigation illustrates what's wrong with the courts. Instead of fast, full disclosure of the facts, we've been given a demonstration of footdragging. . . .*

Somewhere in all this, Seth Hufstedler, the investigation counsel, said, 'Our judicial system is on trial.' The public may already have reached a verdict and gone fishing.

In terms of molding opinion nationally, probably the most important contemporary commentary came from Laurence Tribe, a professor at the Harvard Law School.* His article in the American Bar Association Journal, written before Mosk's speech in Dallas, was published afterward and seemed to confirm Mosk's highly colored characterization of the proceedings. In "Trying California's Judges on Television: Open Government or Judicial Intimidation?" Tribe consistently referred to the inquiry as televised, as if masses of people had been watching; in fact, hardly anyone saw more than an occasional clip on the evening news. His analysis was premised on the belief that the origins of the inquiry were purely political, for example:

Sensing that they had come close to victory with the electorate Chief Justice Bird's critics [who had campaigned against her] began to call for an official probe into the charge that her allies on the Court had delayed one or more opinions to protect her from the voter's wrath.

This argument overlooked the nonsigning of the Tobriner statement by two justices; once that was public, the call for an investigation was universal and irresistible—Bird, Clark, and mostly Tobriner must be given credit here. Thus, Tribe's implication that the investigation was instigated by and was in the control of Bird's political opponents was false. Tribe ended by urging that confidentiality is essential to judicial independence: the wall of secrecy should never be breached.

Edward Lascher disagreed with Tribe's central point that confiden-

---

* A footnote to the article noted that Tribe had served as a law clerk to Tobriner.

tiality of the court's deliberative process is essential to the judiciary's independence:

[A]*nother astonishing product of the hearings* [*is*] *the almost religiously zealous passion for secrecy manifested by the justices. At least one (as of this time) has opined that secrecy is indispensable, the single most important aspect of the Supreme Court's functioning. . . . There was a bone chilling indication of a more real reason for that secrecy mania, one I suspect none of the justices consciously perceived, but that nevertheless oozed subliminally from their words. If one is contemptuous of one's colleagues and of their mental and ethical processes, but one still wants an aura of divine infallibility to cloak the group, then secrecy is the sine qua non. It won't do to let Dorothy see who is pumping the Wizard of Oz machine behind the screen.*

Seemingly, Lascher and Tribe had sharply different views on policy, but the source of their difference may very well have been rooted in matters of fact. Tribe saw the commission proceedings as instigated and run by political opponents of the Supreme Court, which implied a witch-hunt; hence the threat to judicial independence. Lascher, to the contrary, thought the commission investigation was caused by

the clumsy wagon circling, affidavit brandishing, memo writing and stonewalling with which the Magnificent Seven met the charges. [*That was what*] *rendered it inescapable that somebody would look into the matter. That being so, it seemed to me that the Commission was the utterly appropriate body to perform this task—and, indeed, that we are fortunate to have such a body available.*

One thing was clear. Jack Frankel, the Commission's executive officer, told reporters that the out-of-pocket cost of the affair to the state, which, of course, did not include counsel fees for the justices, was over $510,000.*

---

* Whether the state would have to pay the substantial fees of lawyers for the justices was still pending late in 1980.

EIGHT

Some Observations about Accountability

This description of what happened to Rose Bird and the other justices of the California Supreme Court in 1979 could be taken as nothing more than the story of an unusual event. So viewed, it is a sad account of institutions under stress and people who behaved for the most part rather badly, albeit with good intentions. This episode however, should also be viewed in a different perspective, one that tries to put aside questions about the wisdom of peoples' behavior to ask why the system needed to call upon the commission (or any other body) to conduct an inquiry into the court.

The critical point is that legal mechanisms of accountability, like the Commission on Judicial Performance, work best when they need not be resorted to. Nothing better illustrates this truism than Watergate: impeachment is a clumsy instrument to make a president law-abiding. Far more subtle and indirect devices served until Nixon to constrain presidential power; the Congress, the White House staff, the press, and the bureaucracy all operated to hold the president in check without resort to the blunderbuss of impeachment. Likewise, a properly functioning court is held in check by an elaborate set of informal constraints that function outside legal mechanisms of accountability such as judicial elections or the Commission on Judicial Performance. These indirect devices depend on the court's attentiveness to various dialogues that are constantly going on between the court and assorted audiences that read the court's opinions. Lawyers, politicians, the press, and others sometimes deplore, sometimes approve, and sometimes ignore what the justices write. The justices in turn respond to external criticism by altering their behavior to attract praise and to deflect harsh evaluations. This barely perceptible process should make unnecessary the use of formal mechanisms of accountability such as impeachment or recall.

The fact that Bird nearly lost the election in 1978 signaled a serious breakdown in these indirect mechanisms of accountability. Conceivably the break could have been caused by a personality defect in Bird, the way Watergate may be said to have had its roots in Nixon's criminality. This hypothesis has to be rejected: Bird was guilty of no aberrant behavior comparable to Nixon's. Her personality no doubt contributed to the court's crisis in 1978 and 1979, and a more adroit chief justice could have avoided the commission's investigation and all the difficulties that followed. But Bird's behavior up to the election was almost entirely unknown to the general public, and her opinions and votes that were known were unexceptional. Since the public was largely ignorant of aspects of the Bird record that might have justified a negative vote, her near defeat likely reflected broad public distrust of the court as an institution—the result of a long history that had relatively little to do with Bird.

The commission's investigation was not designed to uncover the roots of this popular dissatisfaction with the administration of justice; to the contrary, the commission was charged to investigate very narrow and specific charges of possible wrongdoing. But one effect of the hearings was to reinforce what the results of the Bird election suggested—a widespread recognition of basic weaknesses in the Supreme Court as an institution. The thesis here is that these popular misgivings about the court were based on a number of factors only some of which could fairly be blamed on the behavior of the justices. Because the commission's investigation was aimed in a different direction, the evidence the commission heard cannot prove this proposition. Nonetheless, illustrative traces of problems external to the court can be found in some of the matters discussed in this account.

The Supreme Court is one of many institutions involved in the administration of justice and governance, and the court's success depends on a constructive relationship between it and its surrounding institutions or publics such as the bar, the law schools, the executive branch, the lower courts, and the press. Over the years between Gibson and Bird the quantity and quality of the conversations between the court and these other institutions gradually deteriorated. What follows here is an attempt to explain this decline. As will be seen, the dissonance in the dialogue between the court and some of its publics frequently was caused less by the court than by subtle shifts in these related institutions, shifts that were often beyond the court's influence.

In sum, the justices experienced a crisis in 1978 and 1979 that viewed broadly was only in part a product of their own behavior. But as with any traumatic event, the commission's hearings were also an occasion for a reassessment of position. That presents the final issue; what lesson should the justices take from their experience and how should they modify their behavior?

LAWYERS AND THE COURT

Counsel in the Case

In theory a court responds only to the arguments that are presented to it. The advocates for each side are supposed to present the strongest, most persuasive arguments in support of their client's cause. In an ideal world, the task of an appellate judge would be to pick the best of the competing contentions of counsel and parrot back these arguments as conclusions in a judicial opinion.

One practical impediment to this relatively passive role for the bench is the inescapable reality that counsel, often for good reason, make weak or inadequate arguments. What is a court to do when a case raises an issue not discussed at all or only poorly by counsel? The *Fox* case is an example: quite understandably, neither Leichter nor the city attorney's office discussed in any detail the lawfulness of the display of the cross as a matter of state constitutional law. One possible response for a court, which the California Supreme Court has used increasingly, is to ask counsel for supplemental briefing. That was done in *Tanner II* on the issue of the relevance of after-the-event statements by legislators as evidence of an earlier legislative intent. Another possibility is to refuse to decide an issue unless and until it is adequately presented by counsel. Newman took this approach in *Tanner II* because he found the answers of counsel to the court's request for supplemental briefing so shallow. A third possibility is to decide the issue the court thinks important regardless of whether it has been argued well or at all. That is what Bird and Newman did in *Fox*, and in general the California Supreme Court has not hesitated to frame and decide issues without the help of prior argument by counsel. The court's internal process invites this sort of dissociation of judicial opinions from counsel's arguments because the justices for the most part work from the opinion of the Court of Appeal and staff generated documents—the conference and calendar memorandums—rather than from the parties' briefs. Counsel can try to state the issues for decision in their briefs, but their success depends heavily on the willingness of the Court of Appeal and the Supreme Court staff to accept counsel's framework.

There are several major consequences of persistent disconnection between counsel's arguments and judicial opinions. Once the court stops thinking of counsel as a primary audience to be addressed, it feels less and less obliged to respond to all the arguments presented. Perhaps the easiest way to reach a conclusion in an opinion is not to discuss good arguments in the way of the desired result, as the ad hoc court did to Hufstedler in the *Mosk* suit (the justices ducked around and never met his strongest argument). The same thing happened in large part in *Tanner I*; Tobriner never laid a glove on the Manuel-Clark argument that Tobriner's construction of the statutes rendered the "use a gun, go to prison" law purposeless. Over time this kind of judicial behavior will have an impact on the bar. If the court refuses to deal with good arguments, it becomes less important to make them.

The message that counsel's argument is irrelevant also emerges from the court's willingness to decide cases on issues not argued. This judicial penchant raises a more fundamental problem. One major operational distinction between a court and the political or democratic branches of government—the executive and the legislature—is that in theory a court had no control over its agenda. As noted earlier, the California and U.S. Supreme Courts, particularly during the 1970s, began crowding the agenda of politicians. But the California court during the same period sought increasingly to control its own agenda as well.* The grant of discretionary jurisdiction to the Supreme Court—the petition for hearing process—came, of course, from outside the court and gave the justices some control over what they would decide. However, the power to decide what to decide does not authorize the court to resolve issues not presented or to avoid legitimate arguments squarely raised in cases the court chooses to hear on the merits.

These ideal constructs—to deal only with argued issues and to answer all legitimate arguments presented—should not be viewed as inviolable. Some of the most important of the "great" decisions of the U.S. Supreme Court flagrantly went outside the issues argued by coun-

---

* People v. Drew, 22 C. 3d 333 (1978), the insanity case decided shortly before the election in which the court substituted the American Law Institute "test" for insanity for the historic M'Naughten test, is an example. In footnote 4 of the majority opinion, Tobriner noted: "Neither Drew's briefs in the Court of Appeal nor his petition for hearing attacked the court's instruction [based on the M'Naughten test]. The question whether we should continue to adhere to the M'Naughten rule, however, had been well briefed and argued this court in an earlier case, in re Ramon M.. . . . Finding that the evidentiary record in the present case presented a more suitable vehicle for resolution of that issue, we granted a hearing and requested counsel by letter to submit briefs and present argument on the M'Naughten issue."

sel.* Ultimately, how often and under what circumstances a court should disregard counsel's arguments is largely a matter of style or attitude—the degree of judicial self-confidence or, to be pejorative, judicial arrogance. But a self-confident court, like the California Supreme Court, willing to decide cases on its own grounds with only nominal attention to what the parties have urged is also likely to be a court that thinks about cases in broad policy terms rather than in terms of the factual merits of the particular case. Thus, in *Caudillo I* the court's revulsion at long sentences in general perhaps led the justices to undervalue the significance of the reality that Daniel Caudillo was a vicious criminal undeserving of their compassion.

The Bar in General

The state bar is another audience for the California Supreme Court. Opinions are written, so it is said, for the "guidance of the bar." The California bar grew at an astounding rate in the years between Gibson and Bird. When Gibson became chief justice in 1940 there were 12,500 active members of the California bar. When Traynor succeeded Gibson in 1964 the membership had grown to 24,300. By 1970, when Wright took over, the number was 31,500, and in 1978 it had jumped to 59,000. The reasons for the proliferation of lawyers are beyond this account, but as this audience has grown the nature of the dialogue between the bar and the court has, not surprisingly, changed.

Even in a state as large as California, the bar had a fair measure of shared values up to and during much of Gibson's time. There was a consensus of sorts about who were the leading lawyers, and distinction at the bar was not measured exclusively by financial success. Seth Hufstedler may be among the last of the breed of generally acknowledged leading lawyers. Lawyers have become increasingly specialized and both unfamiliar with and uninterested in vast chunks, if not the whole, of the court's workload. For example, criminal lawyers have stopped reading or caring about tort decisions. Perhaps more important, the business practice of many lawyers is increasingly apt to keep them out of the courts altogether, with the consequence that many lawyers have stopped reading decisions as they come down, looking at opinions only if they have reason to research a point of law.

This fracturing of the bar has had several consequences. For one thing, although the total number of lawyers has grown amazingly, the absolute number of lawyers who read the bulk of the court's opinions may well have gone down. Furthermore, the people who read opinions

---

* Marbury v. Madison, 5 U.S. (1 Cranch), 137 (1803) (Marshall); and Erie R.R. v. Tompkins, 304 U.S. 64 (1938) (Brandeis), are two famous examples.

are apt to read only the decisions in their specialty and frequently from the perspective of a partisan within that specialty. Two of the partisan specialty bars were politically self-conscious by 1978: the plaintiff's personal injury bar (the California Trial Lawyers Association) and the criminal prosecutors. It is noteworthy and possibly ominous that although neither group played a leading role, both made tentative, rather fumbling efforts to assert an institutional position in Bird's confirmation election.

The State Bar, which all California lawyers are required to join, lost its sense of identity as its membership exploded. Adding public members to the board of governors no doubt worsened this institutional problem of self-perception.* But for present purposes, what is more important is that the court lost what was, in Gibson's time, an organized constituency with a recognized leadership informed about the court that could speak with some authority for the bar as a whole. In sum, by Bird's time, if not earlier, there was no important professional audience of generalists. In their stead, small portions of the court's decisions were being watched closely by lawyers whose attitudes were shaped by their speciality. This partisan perspective puts most stress on winning or losing rather than the persuasiveness of the reasoning in an opinion.

If winning or losing is what matters to the audience, justices accordingly will tend to pay less attention to crafting their opinions. Perhaps the California court has yet to be influenced by this change in its audience. Nonetheless, the impression persists that the court's standards of craftsmanship declined during the seventies. Bird's opinion in *Tanner* and Jefferson's in *Caudillo* are examples of technically very weak opinions, but they entirely escaped criticism on grounds of craftsmanship. Perhaps the explanation is that these cases were seen as political; in that context, only the result matters. Interestingly, the only opinion discussed here in any detail that attracted criticism for its allegedly slipshod workmanship was Newman's opinion in *Fox*. Whether or not the criticism was justified, *Fox* was subjected to that sort of analysis possibly because the case lacked political consequence.

THE LAW SCHOOLS AND THE COURT

Traynor regarded scholars as an audience for his opinions,† and he was approvingly called a "law professor's judge."‡ Traynor followed the

---

* For an inside view from the board of governors, see Melchior, *Governing the State Bar*, 55 CAL. ST. B.J. 330 (1980).

† Traynor, *Law and Social Change in a Democratic Society*, 1956 U. ILL. L. FOR. 230.

‡ Kalven, *Torts: The Quest for Appropriate Standards*, 53 CALIF. L. REV. 189 (1965).

law review literature, incorporated in his opinions the views of scholars, and listened attentively to criticism from the law schools. His dissents often were aimed at the academic community in hopes that scholars would stimulate reform from outside the court. For the bulk of his thirty-year career, certainly in the early years, the scholarly community paid close attention to what Traynor and the California Supreme Court were doing. The dialogue, as it were, between the court, and the academy was constant and useful.

Unfortunately, in large part for reasons wholly extraneous to the court, the quantity and quality of attention paid to the court by the academic community declined markedly during the sixties and seventies. One contributing factor to the law schools' relative inattention to the California court was the increasing federalization of the law. Law professors tend to follow the frontiers, and the action was more and more in the U.S. Supreme Court, the Congress, and the federal administrative agencies. The post–World War II period also saw an upswing in the number of law professors engaged in policy formulation for government. Thus, although the California court became more innovative and creative, it lost some of its most critical audience to competitive institutions —the Congress and the executive.

The law schools also became more political and a good deal less certifiably impartial during the Vietnam era. In the wake of the civil rights struggles of the fifties and sixties, some of the more vocal law faculty frankly approached legal problems predominantly from a liberal point of view; others, whatever their bias, were less candidly partisan in print. Some judges, notably Rehnquist on the U.S. Supreme Court and Clark on the California court, became so suspicious of unstated bias in the law review literature that they stopped citing it altogether in their opinions. Other justices, no more helpful, indiscriminately cited law review articles that supported their conclusions, as if all academic writing were detached and impartial. The problem of political bias in the academic literature was of course accentuated by the increasing number of cases with heavy political overtones that the courts were deciding. Neutral commentary about abortion or the death penalty is hard to write.

The sum of the matter is that by the time Bird became chief justice, the quality of the conversation between the court and the law schools had deteriorated significantly. The audience that had once listened most closely and provided some of the most sophisticated commentary on the court's work had grown smaller, and some of its members had become, like the bar generally, partisan. Though it is not possible to prove that this shift in the academic audience made any difference in the quality of the court's opinions, the influence of this change could scarcely be constructive.

THE JUSTICES AND THE JUDGES: JUDICIAL NULLIFICATION

Supreme court decisions are supposed to be authoritative statements of law that control the rulings of the lower courts. In theory, whenever a trial or intermediate appellate court departs from the law as announced by the highest court, the decision can and should be reversed through the process of appeal. In fact, appellate review is an inefficient system for correcting error. Misapplications of law can be shielded from review, deliberately or otherwise, in any number of ways, and the sheer volume of cases makes it unrealistic to suppose that a supreme court itself, even with the willing aid of the intermediate appellate courts, can reach any significant percentage of what litigants think are possible mistakes by the trial courts.*

The California Supreme Court is dependent on the willingness of the lower courts to follow the law as the court announces it; the court cannot compel obedience. An obvious prerequisite to compliance is a reasonably intelligent lower court bench capable of understanding and alert to follow the Supreme Court's opinions. With one thousand two hundred overworked judges that is not easily come by. In addition, the lower courts must be possessed of an attitude of willing and ready compliance even with decisions that some judges consider wrong or repugnant. Nurturing a supportive and cooperative attitude throughout the judiciary is an important function of the court and particularly of the chief justice, who has a special role as symbolic leader of the whole system. This task is difficult because, apart from reversing decisions, the court has no power to remove or discipline an insubordinate judge and no way to reward the faithful.

Bird's symbolic attack on the hierarchical structure of the court system by assigning trial court judges to the appellate bench yielded an ambiguous message in this context. It is one thing to say, as Bird probably meant, that municipal courts are an important part of the system of justice; it is another to suggest that municipal judges and Supreme Court justices are fungible commodities by assigning a municipal judge to sit pro tem on the Supreme Court. The imperatives of the system require that municipal court judges not be encouraged to think that they have the same function as appellate judges at the highest level.

The style of judicial opinions, especially the language of dissenting opinions, is also important. Justice Clark was the worst offender; almost routinely, his dissents charged his colleagues with incompetence. But

---

* The numbers alone compel this conclusion. There were 65,000 contested dispositions in the California Superior Courts in 1979; 5,750 cases were decided in the Courts of Appeal, and 123 cases by the Supreme Court. This leaves out of account possible errors by Municipal Courts and administrative agencies.

Tobriner and Bird were scarcely restrained in their dissents in *Tanner II*, and Mosk was contemptuous in *Caudillo II*. If Supreme Court justices persistently talk about their colleagues as if they were unprincipled fools, the message eventually will trickle down the judicial hierarchy.

It is exceedingly difficult to measure the extent of lower court subversion of the Supreme Court's rulings. No doubt it exists to some extent in every court system as it does in the army and in every other large hierarchical structure. Trial court nullification, to the extent that it is successful, will necessarily be largely hidden from view. Intransigence rather than eagerness to follow the court can occasionally be detected in the published opinions of intermediate appellate courts. There was, for example, evidence of reluctance in the Courts of Appeal to implement a series of Supreme Court decisions concerning the use of prior convictions to impeach a witness.* More vividly, there have been some frankly disrespectful Court of Appeal opinions since Bird took office.† The decision of division two of the Los Angeles Court of Appeal in the school busing case may have been an intentional taunt to the Supreme Court, as perhaps was division one's order that Caudillo be released. Similar incidents could no doubt be found with respect to decisions of the court during the tenures of Gibson, Traynor, and Wright. In the end, it comes down to a question of how often and how serious these matters are, and particularly how widespread the attitude of disrespect is. The commission's hearings doubtless encouraged a contemptuous view by lower court judges of the justices and thus of the Supreme Court's decisions. Whether the commission was at fault here is less clear. As Chairman Janes remarked, "We ask the questions—we don't answer them."

THE COURT AND THE BUREAUCRACY: THE DECLINE OF PROFESSIONALISM

Starting with the progressivism of Governor Hiram Johnson (1910–1916), California had developed by Pat Brown's time a state civil service that was perhaps the best in the nation. Ralph Kleps, who resigned as director of the Administrative Office of the Courts shortly after Bird took office, embodied the high quality of nonpartisan professionalism that

* The chain of decisions started in Wright's time with People v. Beagle, 6 C. 3d 441 (1972). That decision was expanded (and the use of prior convictions for impeachment purposes greatly restricted) by two decisions in 1979, People v. Fries, 24 C. 3d 222 (1979) (per Bird, C.J.), and People v. Spearman, 25 C. 3d 107 (1979) (per Bird, C.J.). Illustrative of the difficulty in the Courts of Appeal in applying these decisions are People v. Harris, 105 C.A. 3d 204 (1980), and People v. Lassel, 108 C.A. 3d 720 (1980).

† See, for example, People v. Remiro, 89 C.A. 3d 809, 822 (1979); People v. Musante, 102 C.A. 3d 156, 159 (1980); DeRonde v. Regents, 102 C.A. 3d 221 (1980) (officially depublished).

could be found just below the elected and appointed leadership in nearly all state agencies. Before his appointment to the bench, Wiley Manuel had been such a person in the attorney general's office. Morris and Koblick, Clark's research attorneys, and Cohen and Willemsen, who worked for Tobriner, were similarly highly motivated civil servants of exceptional competence, as were many others among the court's senior staff.

Detached professionalism as a value had been encouraged by the state's political leadership. Governors Warren, Knight, and Pat Brown respected the views of experienced government servants, and they promoted many bureaucrats into leadership positions. The legislature was the least professional arm of government, but its quality was significantly improved under the leadership of Speaker Jesse Unruh and his successors in the sixties. California's became the best-staffed and most open state legislature in the country. Commissioner Willoughby was a good example of the high quality staff available to California legislators.

As Unruh's reforms were professionalizing the legislature, professionalism was being devalued in the executive by Reagan. Reagan's rhetoric was ahead of his accomplishments, but he persistently talked about government as if it were a disease and he apparently thought skill in governance could be found almost anywhere in the private sector more readily than among experienced civil servants. Jerry Brown was more like Reagan than his father in this respect. Like Reagan, Brown ran on an antigovernment platform, and he built his largely negative program, especially in the early years, chiefly around challenging the conventional wisdom of venerable establishments.

Of the three branches of government, the judiciary was probably the most committed to professionalism or, to put it the other way around, the branch most sensitive to charges of cronyism, partisanship, and ideological bias. The Judicial Council had been run since Gibson's time on the premise that policy issues of concern to the judiciary could be solved most effectively with single-minded attention to the merits of the issues as presented by well-qualified experts who approached all questions as if they were naked of any political dimension. Especially after Gibson's retirement, if politics or partisanship emerged on any issue the Judicial Council would promptly make its report and leave the field. The appointments of Clark by Reagan and Bird by Jerry Brown deeply offended many judges who thought the wrong people were being preferred for the wrong reasons. Bird's behavior when she assumed office—quarreling with Kleps and not using the experienced staff available to her— confirmed their belief that she, too, cared very little about professionalism.

The decline in detached expertise was visible in areas beyond Bird's influence. It could be measured, for example, in the gradual withering away of some kinds of law reform. In Pat Brown's time, the Law Revision Commission was an important agency of government. It totally revised numerous codes and statutes in much the way that the Constitutional Law Revision Commission rewrote California's constitution. Reform efforts of this nature require a high degree of consensus about goals and a broad willingness to defer to the judgment of experts with a record of impartiality. During the seventies, law reform of this type became extraordinarily difficult throughout the nation. For example, the California legislature created a special advisory panel to help it revise the penal code, but the effort fell apart when prosecutors began to suspect, rightly or wrongly, that the new body had a hidden agenda. A similar kind of distrust, although from a different source, delayed criminal code revision in the Congress for more than a decade.

The decline of professionalism in state government represents another shift in audience that will in time have an impact on the institutional success of the Supreme Court. Much of the business of the court concerns the actions of other arms of government. Some of this is constitutional law but the bulk requires the court to resolve ambiguities in the directives of other institutions of government—statutes, regulations, ordinances, executive orders and the like. Frequently, this responsibility entails articulating unstated premises of governmental programs and thereby resolving politically sensitive issues. How successful the court is in arbitrating controversies of this nature depends heavily on the attitude of people in the other branches of government. One aspect of the nonpartisan professionalism of the state civil service was its exceptional law-abidingness. People like Kleps and Manuel and hundreds of others throughout the government rigidly refused to consider maneuvers to avoid judicial decisions; to the contrary, they willingly implemented the spirit of the court's decisions to the extent that they understood them even though they were on the losing side of a particular case and thought the decision wrong. To the extent that professionalism declines within the bureaucracy, this audience will be less likely in the future to cooperate with the court's decisions.* Disrespect toward the Supreme Court's rulings will be nurtured by a belief within the government that the court itself is something less than perfectly nonpartisan and professional.

Hufstedler alluded to this problem in his opening speech to the commission when he spoke of the fragility of the court as an institution. Bird's "china in the laundromat" remark presumably expressed a similar concern. Probably, the court as an institution is a good deal more resilient than the word "fragile" suggests. The courts and the law survived

---

* Some think a hostile, uncooperative attitude has already emerged, not just in California but nationwide, with some elements of law enforcement. It was clearly visible in the attitude of the Los Angeles school board following the recall of its chairman, Howard Miller, in 1979.

widespread subversion of the decision in *Brown* v. *Board of Education* and many other assaults during the Vietnam era. But the prestige of the California court, which was once very high, was in decline by Bird's time.

There was a splendid irony in the commission's playing a role in the decline of the court's prestige. The Commission on Judicial Performance was conceived by people like Gibson who believed that government institutions could be impartial and professional, and the commission's success depended almost totally on public faith in detached expertise. For the commission to be an instrument in lowering the reputation of the court would seem as unlikely as the president of the League of Women Voters taking a bribe for a political endorsement. Certainly the commissioners and Hufstedler did not enter into the hearings with the intent of damaging the Supreme Court. Whether they, rather than the justices, were responsible for the court's lessened prestige after the hearings depends again on whether the questions they asked or the answers they received did the damage.

THE COURT AND ITS STAFF

The commission's hearings showed that the justices sometimes thought about an audience for the court's opinions that most external observers had probably never considered—the court's own staff. Clark acknowledged that he did not back down on the *Caudillo* citation partly because he felt that removing the citation would be seen as a craven retreat by staff elsewhere in the courthouse. Although Bird did not so testify explicitly, her commitment to her staff was probably the reason behind much of what was unfortunate in her *Tanner* and *Fox* opinions. Presumably, a similar impulse to support staff could be found in the chambers of the other justices.

The growth of the court's workload undoubtedly contributed to the tendency to use opinions as a mechanism to reward staff. In truth, the justices have practically nothing to give staff other than the psychic satisfaction staff attorneys may get by seeing their words and ideas in the official reports of the California Supreme Court. As the justices increasingly rely on staff, the natural inclination would be to reward staff more frequently. A tendency to write opinions to and for staff may also be accentuated by the use of career research attorneys whose need for reinforcement is greater than that of temporary law clerks.

How staff members perceive the justices is also important. If the staff see their role as keeping each justice consistent with himself or herself, what the staff think is animating the justices will tend to become a self-reinforcing truth. If a research attorney thinks of his or her job as primarily insuring the justice's consistency in doctrine, there will tend to be, as there was, a proliferation of separate opinions. On the other hand, if staff conceive of their role as helping the court announce competent decisions according to professionally derived standards external to any particular judge, the tendency will be toward unanimity. Both ideals are, of course, always present and not always in conflict. But there will occasionally be tension between them, and where that is the case, the issue becomes which ideal is stronger.

Bird's desire for a staff loyal primarily to her and her inclination to distance herself from other staff, including the central staff, nurtured individual consistency as the primary goal. The distance Clark felt from Tobriner and Bird, which may have had its beginnings in Wright's time, no doubt made it harder for Clark's staff to feel a part of a team effort and tended to make them relatively unresponsive to professional values external to Clark's. Some of Clark's more extreme rhetoric in dissent might have been toned down through his staff if they had been in better communication with the staffs in other offices.

Nourishing the spirit and the professionalism of staff, as well as the staff's identification with the court as a whole, was intuitive with Gibson, Traynor, and Wright. Not so with Bird. And as she devalued the importance of professionalism in the staff, the importance of staff as audience increased.

THE COURT AND LEGAL THEORY: THE INHERITANCE OF THE REALISTS

A contributing factor to the deterioration in the quality of all the conversations noted above might be described as a failure of ideas. It is hard to be professional, it is hard even to appear nonpolitical, if there is no clear standard against which to measure the court's performance. The absence of consensus on standards, especially in constitutional cases, surfaced during the seventies although the problem had its roots much earlier. The difficulty can be seen by contrasting two current but inconsistent versions of the judicial role: the variety taught in eighth-grade civics classes and the competing and insistent vision of the legal realists of the 1920s and thirties.

The eighth-grade model is easily stated: the legislature makes the laws, the courts apply them; all disputes can be solved by reference to a body of law already written down either in statutes or in case law. Case law is constant because of the doctrine of *stare decisis*; however, the rules as laid down in the precedents are subject to revision by the legislature. Since judges impartially apply a known body of law, any two judges will always come to the same result on identical facts. Because judges are duty-bound to apply the law as written by others who are democratically elected, it is not necessary that the power of judges be similarly legitimated through some democratic mechanism. Indeed, because judges must apply the law and certain decisions will be unpopular, the independence of judges should be encouraged through legal mechanisms that protect them from the whim of fleeting majorities.

There is an enormous amount of myth in this conception of law and judges. One accomplishment of the legal realists was to expose various facets of the mythology, if not for eighth graders at least for law students: the common law does not provide clear answers to all questions; statutes are often ambiguous; judges have a creative role to play both in the evolution of case law and in the interpretation of statutes; and judges are human beings who wear robes to help them be impartial but they necessarily see the world and the law through eyes that distort because of who they are and where they came from. Candid discussion of ideas of this nature by people like Karl Llewellyn and Jerome Frank in the twenties and thirties coincided with the tenure of the Nine Old Men and contributed powerfully to the liberal outrage at the court's obstruction of New Deal reform measures.

It was never easy to fit the judicial power to hold a statute unconstitutional into the concept of a government "of the people, by the people, and for the people." Judicial review could be forced into the eighth-grade syllabus by treating the Constitution as a self-executing instrument, although many phrases of the Founding Fathers were plainly little more than vague aspirations. In a famous passage, Justice Roberts invoked an ostensibly self-executing Constitution:

There should be no misunderstanding as to the function of this court in such a case. It is sometimes said that the court assumes a power to overrule or control the action of the people's representatives. This is a misconception. The Constitution is the supreme law of the land ordained and established by the people. All legislation must conform to the principles it lays down. When an act of Congress is appropriately challenged in the courts as not conforming to the constitutional mandate the judicial branch of the Government has only one duty—to lay the article of the Constitution which is invoked beside the statute which is challenged and to decide whether the latter squares with the former. All the court does, or can do, is announce its considered judgment upon the question. . . . This court neither approves nor condemns any legislative policy. Its delicate and difficult office is to ascertain and declare whether the legislation is in accordance with, or in contravention of, the provisions of the Constitution; and, having done that, its duty ends. *

* United States v. Butler, 297 U.S. 1, 62–63 (1935).

The hypocrisy of this statement infuriated those who accepted the realists' perception of what judges in fact do. At the time the liberals were outraged at Roberts's self-righteous protestations of neutrality. Bird's opinions in *Tanner* and the Proposition 13 cases invoked precisely the same mechanical conception of the judicial function that Roberts employed forty years earlier. But this time the right rather than the left cried out. (Perhaps others were also offended by the insincerity of Bird's claim that she was driven to her conclusions by unambiguous imperatives of legal doctrine.)

Although they never resolved it, the realists undeniably exposed for the profession generally a profound problem of American governance that had been troublesome at least since Jefferson became angry at some of Marshall's decisions—how to square judicial supremacy with democratic theory. In modern times the issue came to a crisis when Roosevelt tried to pack the Court. The fight was resolved politically by the "switch in time that saved nine" (Roberts was the one who switched in 1936) and in theory by notions of judicial self-restraint.

Judicial self-restraint never marked very clear boundaries, and it came under enormous pressure, especially from racial minorities, during the fifties. Indeed, judicial self-restraint seemed to work only as long as the memory of the Nine Old Men remained vivid. No doubt judges like Gibson and Traynor felt limits, but neither they nor anyone else succeeded in articulating these boundaries clearly (Learned Hand and Herbert Wechsler tried). In the hands of later generations of judges, the felt limits fell back and almost vanished whenever they were confronted with strongly held convictions by judges as to what was wise and good. In California, the death penalty case in 1972 perhaps best marks the collapse of judicial self-restraint as a significant leash on judicial power.

The sum of the matter is that during the seventies there was a serious gap in legal thought. Theology suggested that the power of judges was so confined that its exercise need not be legitimated through democratic mechanisms. Reality taught that this argument was tenable only if there was agreement about limits generally understood and routinely respected by judges. The realist assault on the mythology of formalism defined no such limits, and the absence of any widely shared set of ideas to confine judicial power became increasingly obvious.* As a consequence, it was sometimes impossible to fault a judge for having overstepped an unmarked boundary in a particular case and simultaneously impossible to defend the decision as plausibly compelled by the discipline

---

* Llewellyn foresaw the problem in the fifties: "The last thirty-five years of jurisprudence have made clear the quantum of leeway to too many lawyers who will become judges. The last thirty-five years have not, in Law School, made clear the narrow limits of the leeway." W. TWINING, KARL LLEWELLYN AND THE REALIST MOVEMENT 116 (1973).

of the law. The result was tyranny or justice, depending on one's political attitude.

THE COURT AND THE PRESS

Reporters

Press coverage of the court has improved appreciably over the years since Gibson's tenure, and the trend toward better reporting is likely to continue. Until the late 1950s, even decisions of the U.S. Supreme Court were covered quite superficially by reporters, with only occasional commentary from editorial writers and columnists, commentary that was often notably ill-informed. Anthony Lewis of the *New York Times* was the first reporter given the assignment to cover the U.S. Supreme Court and no more. He established a pattern of well-informed, detailed reporting about the Court and its decisions that became obligatory for any newspaper with pretensions toward national distinction, including the *Washington Post* and the *Los Angeles Times*. Better reporting sometimes brought better commentary. The California Supreme Court has yet to get comprehensive and rigorous attention from any newspaper, but the national trend suggests that sooner or later some paper, probably the *Los Angeles Times*, will make the court a principal assignment of one or more reporters.

Chief Justice Wright worried about the quality of press coverage and tried to improve it by making himself available to reporters and by expanding the issuance of press releases to include all of the court's decisions. The utility of these efforts, commendable in themselves, was sharply curtailed because the canons prevented Wright from explaining the substance of decisions (as opposed to procedure and terminology) and because the public information officer was limited to describing what was in the opinions. Harassed reporters with major other responsibilities based their stories on the court on quick readings of the opinions and occasionally on reactions to decisions from people who had an obvious interest in particular cases, for example, law enforcement figures. Reporters did not have time to think much about cases before decisions were filed and took as the whole truth statements made by the justices in the opinions and by partisan observers.

Bird dismantled what little Wright had been able to accomplish by refusing to talk with reporters and by reducing to a trickle the number of press releases concerning decisions. These actions had a predictably adverse impact on the attitude of reporters toward her. Reporters may well have misunderstood this behavior, dictated more by shyness or fear than arrogance. Bird certainly was not indifferent to what the papers said about her. The Buehl memorandum revealed her (and Clark's) extraordinary sensitivity to press coverage.

All the justices seemingly had a rather naive understanding of the way newspapers work. Apparently, they thought of newspapers as monolithic organizations, with reporters subject to a chain of command that could and would dictate the way the court was covered. The best indication of this view was Tobriner's letter to Reg Murphy, the editor of the *San Francisco Examiner,* in response to Kang's questions to Bird. Similarly, Bird's visits to the editorial boards of the major newspapers before the election suggested a belief on her part that if she could impress a few critical executives she could thereby influence how reporters covered her. According to the ethic of the profession today, it is the reporter on a story, not the editors, who determines in large part what will and will not be reported.

Endicott and Fairbanks, for example, did not consult with the editorial board of the *Times* before deciding to develop what turned out to be the November 7 story. They received information from unknown sources that *Tanner* was signed up but unfiled and made a decision for themselves that the story was worth some effort to verify. Their sources were almost certainly multiple, and it is safe to assume that neither Senator Richardson nor anyone in the Younger campaign was an important source since neither Richardson nor Younger could have known from the inside whether anything was untoward in the handling of *Tanner.* Endicott and Fairbanks were not the first reporters to get the lead, but they received from at least three justices, as apparently no one had before them, a nondenial of wrongdoing. They interpreted the nondenial as confirmation. Once the story reached that point, the editors in Los Angeles had no realistic alternative but to print the story on election day. For the *Times* not to publish the story would have been interpreted as a cover-up dictated by editorial policy. No newspaper of any pretension to public service could engage in such behavior.

Essentially the same bottom-upward structure was behind Kang's adverse stories in the *San Francisco Examiner.* During the spring and summer of 1978, Kang began to doubt Bird's reputation as a skillful administrator, and she investigated Bird's performance as head of the court system. No one told Kang to pursue this topic and she reported what she found as accurately as she could. Tobriner's letter to Murphy may have succeeded in slowing down somewhat the publication of Kang's October 6 article,* but pressure from high places to kill a story of

---

* Kang's October 6 story was based on information she had developed by late July or early August. Why publication was delayed until October is a mystery. Hufstedler asked Tobriner whether he had sought to prevent the story's publication and got a firm no. It is unlikely that Hufstedler would have asked the question without some clue that something fishy had taken place.

obvious importance that represents a reporter's best effort to report the truth is strongly resisted under the present ethic of the profession.

In general, the quality of press coverage is a function primarily of how much reporters know in general about their subject, which in turn depends mainly on how much time they can spend on a story. The point is well illustrated by the coverage reporters gave to the commission's proceedings. Fremstad, Kang, and Warner, among others, were assigned to the commission hearings from the beginning to the end, and they gave their readers very accurate, often insightful, accounts. For some reason, the beat was handed around to several reporters for the *Los Angeles Times*, and as a consequence the *Times* coverage, although often longer, was less perceptive. Unquestionably the most misleading article written about the commission was Stumbo's piece in the *Los Angeles Times*; the reason was probably her brief attendance at the hearings.

The principle that the quality of coverage depends mainly upon the amount of time reporters can spend learning about the subject matter explains the superficiality of press coverage of the substance of the court's decisions. In 1979 the *Los Angeles Times*, undoubtedly the California paper with the most reportorial resources, had two reporters (Endicott and Hager) in the San Francisco bureau whose responsibilities included coverage of the court's decisions when they were filed as well as everything else going on in the Bay Area. Kang covered all the local courts, state and federal, trial and appellate, in San Francisco for the *Examiner*. Many papers relied entirely on the wire services for their coverage of the Supreme Court. Considering the extent of their other responsibilities, reporters did a surprisingly good job of reporting what were stated to be the facts and law in the opinions, but that was about all. Colorful phrases in a dissent were likely to be quoted regardless of their fairness or accuracy, and some of Clark's more extravagant language seemed at times to be have been aimed directly at reporters.

Yet, the most important aspect of a decision often is not what the opinion says but rather the issues or arguments left out. This superficial coverage left the court exposed to unfair attack. Reporters will not print assertions they know to be inaccurate or foolish, but in order to exercise good judgment reporters have to be reasonably well informed. The claims that *Tanner I* gave "renewed hope to the armed robbers in this state" or that Bird was "soft on rape" ought never to have been printed. Once reporters have some confidence about their command of the subject, they will not print extreme statements of this nature. An illustration of selectivity based on knowledge is what happened to Jeffrey Abramson's overwrought assertion that Bird's testimony was "a very smart tale made of half cloth."

The public and the court were also ill served by an unconfident press corps in the Los Angeles school busing case in fall 1978. The grant of a stay by division two of the Los Angeles Court of Appeal was an arrogant and untimely assertion of power motivated either by an inappropriate vision of social policy or by a desire to embarrass politicians and a higher court, but there was not a word of criticism of division two in the press. Instead, the Supreme Court was unfairly left to play the role of the heavy. Only a reporter knowledgeable about law and courts could have put the blame in the right place.

Commentary for the General Public

Coverage of the court's opinions as they are handed down is only a portion of the problem in court-media relations. To help it evaluate the court, the public also needs perspective articles that assess the stream of the court's decisions and interpret trends and events in a larger context. Very little good writing of this nature about the California court was done despite obvious stimuli such as the occasion of Wright's retirement and later Bird's confirmation election. There was a major gap between academic commentary (found mostly in law reviews) for a professional readership and daily stories for the public written by reporters doing their best to cover the court along with other duties.

The U.S. Supreme Court gets considerable attention on the op-ed page in major newspapers, in national news magazines, and in articles in journals of opinion such as the *New Republic* and *Commentary*. The absence of good regular coverage, typically the basis for perspective pieces, probably goes a long way toward explaining why there was so little thoughtful work done by the media about the California Supreme Court during Bird's election. But there was also a puzzling problem of attitude in the media that seemed to reflect naiveté and ignorance more than anything else.

First, the media tended to treat the California Supreme Court as if it had the same freedom of action that a governor or legislator enjoys. For example, editorial writers for the *Los Angeles Times* thought the court should decide the *Tanner* case on the basis that any system of mandatory sentencing needs a safety valve. Thinking of the court that way is analytically indistinguishable from Senator Richardson's position that *Caudillo* proved Bird to be soft on rape; both presuppose that the court is free to decide any case according to policy criteria. There may be considerable leeway in the system, but commentators disserve both their readers and the court by treating the justices as if they had complete freedom of choice.

Second, the media viewed the California Supreme Court as if it were a baby U.S. Supreme Court with final authority over very little of consequence. Some of the California court's decisions are reviewable in Washington, but many are not because no federal question is presented;

in cases where the California court is the ultimate decisionmaker its decisions are most important and deserve the most critical attention, especially to California readers. Lay readers cannot be expected to understand the importance of the California court if they have never been told it. Similarly, the quality of governance in California depends significantly on the relationship between the legislature and the court. A cooperative relationship built on mutual respect leads to the rapid and efficient resolution of problems; hostility and disrespect produce prolonged and wasteful controversy. These matters are not beyond the comprehension of laymen. Certainly the relations between a governor and the legislature are regularly discussed by editorial writers and columnists; if these matters can be understood, there is no obvious reason why relations between the California Supreme Court and the California legislature should be disregarded.

THE COURT AND THE GOVERNOR: LOYALTY TO THE APPOINTING POWER

Governors and presidents tend to appoint people to the supreme court who reflect in a general way their own attitudes and values. Some observers accordingly consider the power to replace departing justices a democratic check on judicial power,* an idea with enough truth to threaten the way appointing powers view appointments and the way judges see themselves.

If a governor or president wants to appoint justices to perpetuate his or her own way of thinking, two criteria have major importance: youth (so the appointee will be around for a long time) and political ideology. Appointees will tend to be young people who are true believers rather than independent thinkers. Clark and Bird could be viewed as examples of this kind of appointment, although other appointments by Reagan and Jerry Brown (notably Wright and Manuel) suggested that these governors were not concerned exclusively with seeing their ideas implemented after they had left office.

Concern about the appointment power was visible in the immediate legislative reaction to the commission's investigation. A number of measures were proposed featuring constitutional amendments that would make all future appointments to the bench subject to confirmation in the state senate, the way presidential nominations are subject to confir-

---

* Even over a long period of time the check does not work very well. In the forty years between Olson and the end of Jerry Brown's first term, there was a Republican in the governor's office for six terms and a Democrat for only four. Nonetheless, Democrats appointed fourteen Supreme Court justices during that period whereas Republicans appointed only five.

mation in the U.S. Senate. These measures were defeated but they reflected a sense that the power of appointment has a political dimension that warrants a form of political review now lacking in California government. Ironically, in this sense the proposals reinforced rather than challenged the concept that the purpose of judicial appointments is to perpetuate on the bench the political thought of a governor.

How the justices view themselves is also significant. If they conceive of themselves as policymakers continuing the program of the person who appointed them, they are encouraged to implement their vision of the governor's ideas by attempting to get a majority of their colleagues to agree with them. Furthermore, given the nature of their mandate, they should act as quickly as possible because they can anticipate that appointees of later governors may well have a different set of priorities. In this framework, respect for the decisions of earlier justices declines to the same level that a cabinet officer feels for the decisions of predecessors appointed by an earlier executive. Bird as secretary for agriculture and services was free to depart from the policies of Reagan's agriculture secretary; her opinion in *Tanner* suggests that as chief justice she felt no more constrained by the decisions of Wright or Traynor or any other majority of the justices.

Bird's behavior suggests another ominous implication of the view that justices are spokesmen for the appointing power. If the justices think that way, there is very little reason why they should feel inhibited in communicating with the executive who appointed them so long as he or she is still in office and they avoid discussing pending or impending cases. This impulse overlooks the roots of the concept of an independent judiciary. Independence once meant freedom from excessive executive influence; that is why the English Act of Settlement gave judges tenure "during good behavior," the very language the Founding Fathers used to give federal judges life tenure. Judges were to be different from cabinet officers and other policymakers because they would not be subject to summary discharge if they deviated from the executive's wishes.

Over time California appears to have become complacent about this aspect of the separation of powers; consider the lack of discussion concerning Bird's relations with and dependence on Brown. Bird's influence over judicial appointments and promotions was readily visible but unremarked outside the judiciary; indeed, it could be said that she used her influence with the governor as a substitute for persuasion as a mechanism to achieve leadership of the court system. The implied threat of a gubernatorial veto was also used to discourage the introduction of bills in the legislature that would have weakened in one way or another the powers of the chief justice. Using influence with a governor as a tool of administration erodes the independence of the judiciary because it is not possible in the world of politics to ask for favors without incurring obligations. Bird's quickness to disqualify herself from cases in which the prestige of the Brown administration was involved perhaps reflected her degree of dependence on him. The only important case the governor can be said to have lost in the Supreme Court since Bird's appointment was one in which both Bird and Tobriner disqualified themselves.*

THE GOVERNOR AND THE COURT: STANDARDS FOR JUDICIAL APPOINTMENTS

There was a little noticed ambiguity in the issue to be decided in Bird's confirmation election: were the voters simply to veto or approve the governor's appointment or were they to pass judgment on Bird's performance between her appointment and the election.† Perhaps the issues were so entangled that trying to separate them is pointless. Nonetheless, the former was easier to decide than the latter because less than two years was too short an interval for Bird to have demonstrated her talents as an appellate justice, whereas the appointment itself was a completed act the day Bird took the oath of office.

Unfortunately, the standards for a good judicial appointment to the Supreme Court are no easier to formulate or apply than the standards for evaluating a judge's performance once on the bench. The "Hufstedler formula," used by the state bar in commenting on candidates to the Commission on Judicial Appointments—the candidate must possess "qualities and attributes considered to be worthy of special note as indicative of superior fitness to perform the judicial function with a high degree of skill and effectiveness"—is so opaque as to be nearly meaningless. There is frequent talk about "judicial temperament," which presumably has something to do with the appearance of impartiality and open-mindedness but is not easily measured. Disqualifying rigidity can occasionally be identified, but most lawyers are reasonably open to competing points of view, at least on most issues. The result of exclusive attention to judicial temperament is to sift out only a few and to qualify far too many for that to be a very helpful screening standard.

The commission's investigation suggested an array of attributes not

---

* Olson v. Cory, 27 C. 3d 532 (1980), involving a cap on increases in judicial salaries. The opinion was written by Clark; only Newman dissented.

† The theory of the 1934 initiative was probably that the voters would act much the way U.S. Senators act in voting to confirm a presidential appointment to the bench. The voters' pamphlet in support of the initiative spoke of the people exercising a "veto" on the governor's choice, and the original measure provided that the appointee would appear on the next general election ballot which could not be more than two years away from the appointment. The measure was amended in 1966 (by the Constitutional Law Revision Commission) to make the nominee appear on the ballot at the next gubernatorial election.

normally considered that could well be regarded as important in evaluating Supreme Court appointments. The evidence presented to the commission showed that as of 1978 a successful Supreme Court justice must have the following personality traits: a genuine respect for the views of others, combined with an instinct for finding the core issue that divides; a capacity to find solutions that accommodate seemingly conflicting principles; a desire to participate in the give-and-take of controversy without accumulating grudges; and, finally, the ability to lead and inspire a small bureaucratic team. The California Supreme Court in 1978 lacked enough people with these characteristics, and those traits are far more important than profound learning in the law or skill as a writer of opinions, both of which needs can be supplied by staff. Several other things are notable about this list. First, although the traits are themselves politically neutral, they are also the marks of a good politician. Second, experience on a trial court neither tests nor develops these traits, mostly because a trial judge works alone and has no need to develop consensus among equals.

Unhappily, these traits are only marginally more easy to measure than judicial temperament. The standard for appointment most likely to be extracted from the Supreme Court's troubles in 1978 and 1979 is that prior judicial experience is essential. It is factually accurate that none of Brown's appointees in 1977 had significant experience as a judge, whereas all of the appointees since Earl Warren's time had had some experience—mostly on the Court of Appeal. But reasoning backward from that to the conclusion that judicial experience should be a prerequisite for appointment to the Supreme Court overlooks entirely the equally significant fact that the justices who made the greatest contribution to the distinction of the California Supreme Court during the same period were Gibson and Traynor, neither of whom had been on a bench before their appointment to the Supreme Court.

The commission's investigation also suggested that a governor or a president ought to think about filling vacancies on a supreme court in terms of trying to build a balanced team of justices with varying talents, personality traits, and experiences. A court composed exclusively of scholars or politicians or experienced trial judges will be weaker than one composed of people with diverse backgrounds. Mosk was the only justice on the court in 1978 to have held nonjudicial elective public office; he was also the only justice to have had significant experience as a trial court judge. Seen in this light, Jerry Brown's three appointments in 1977 put the court woefully out of balance, with too many justices lacking relevant background and experience; Bird's sex and Manuel's race added nothing toward making the court's collective product stronger.

There are other useful ways of assessing appointments. For example, it could be asked whether an appointee is likely to be influential with colleagues, even those who might be predisposed to have a somewhat different outlook on issues. One might also consider whether the appointee's participation in a judgment would add weight to the result simply by his or her having endorsed it, as Hufstedler's participation added credibility to the commission's process. People with such stature are uncommon but they do exist—for example, Charles Evans Hughes, Harlan Fiske Stone, and Earl Warren.

Jerry Brown's penchant for twisting the tail of establishments made it unlikely that he would look for a Californian with credentials like those of a Warren or a Stone or a Hughes.* But it is troublesome that Brown felt free to depart so far from what might be thought of as the establishment's ideal appointment. Brown could get away with this strategy partly because California, as well as the nation, had come to accept as routine the idea that appointments to a high court are in part a political act. Governors are expected to make appointments that will be attractive to some constituencies that care more who the appointee is than how well he or she performs. Jerry Brown did not start this process. For many years there was a "Jewish seat" on the U.S. Supreme Court, there is now a "black seat," and it seems clear that there will soon be a "female seat." Once religious, ethnic, racial, and sexual factors become determinative, it is more difficult to hold a governor or president accountable for judicial appointments.

The point can be easily seen in the utterly garbled message that emerged from the 1978 election in which Bird's appointment was in fact an issue. Senator Richardson persuaded an indeterminate number of voters that her appointment was a reason to vote against Brown. But an equally unknown number voted for Brown (and Bird) because she was a woman; the women's movement tried to make the Bird appointment an asset for Brown, and the governor boasted about his appointment of women, blacks and Chicanos to the bench. Some voters no doubt reacted favorably to Brown's appointment practices; others, equally clearly, held it against him because they were bigots or antifeminists. Lost in the noise over the appointment of minorities and women were some voters whose main concern was either whether Bird was a qualified appointee or whether she had performed adequately.

THE CHOICE BEFORE THE JUSTICES

There remains the problem of how the justices should interpret this history of which they were a part. There are at least two ways of reading

---

* Warren Christopher, appointed deputy secretary of state in the Carter administration in 1977, was probably as close as Brown could have come to the Hughes-Stone-Warren standard.

the meaning of those events, with different consequences on how the justices should behave in the future.

One way starts from the premise that Bird's near defeat and the commission's hearings were bizarre events unlikely to be repeated in California or anywhere else. This interpretation presupposes that these events were primarily the product of small-minded people who seized the occasion to exploit antifeminism, racial bigotry, and fear of crime for narrow political gain. But this backlash failed: Bird won confirmation and the justices emerged from the hearings vindicated, the court's powers undiminished. Such an interpretation encourages the court to continue as before, its course unaltered by experience.

A quite different interpretation is also possible, one that takes as its starting point an observation by Tocqueville nearly a century and a half ago:

I am aware that a secret tendency to diminish the judicial power exists in the United States; and by most of the constitutions of the several states, the government can, upon the demand of the two houses of the legislature, remove judges from their station. Some other state constitutions make the members of the judiciary elective, and they are even subject to frequent re-elections. I venture to predict that these innovations will sooner or later be attended with fatal consequences; and that it will be found out at some future period that by thus lessening the independence of the judiciary they have attacked not only the judicial power, but the democratic republic itself. *

Tocqueville's prediction of the triumph of majority rule over judicial power has yet to be proven correct, but he was not wrong in anticipating that conflicts would emerge between judicial power and majority rule. The Court packing fight of the 1930s was the most famous instance in modern times, but there have been numerous skirmishes involving the U.S. Supreme Court and some state supreme courts. Typically such crises have been settled inconclusively, with the resolution combining a strategic retreat by the court with the soothing passage of time. In the larger sense, Tocqueville's prediction of the destruction of judicial powe. has been outflanked by judicial recognition that in any prolonged conflict between judicial power and majority rule, the popular will must ultimately prevail.

Starting from this premise, there is cause for concern in the gradual erosion of public confidence in the California court. The decline is plainly visible in the election results on the justices. They were confirmed in the early sixties by majorities of 90 percent; the percentage had

---

* 1 A. De Tocqueville, Democracy in America 289 (P. Bradley ed. 1945).

sunk by 1978 to 65 percent and in Bird's instance to a bare 52 percent. The ultimate weapon of majority rule, recall, has never been used against any California justice, but there was talk of recalling Bird in 1979 and 1980. A new decision or two by the court that arouses deeply felt animosities and thereby creates new anticourt constituencies might easily stimulate a successful drive to place her recall on the ballot.

In the mid-1960s, Wisconsin went through an instructive experience with judicial elections.* Unlike California, Wisconsin permits a challenger to Supreme Court justices on the ballot, and a man named Boyle violated the traditional norm of lawyerlike behavior by twice challenging incumbent justices for reasons that were plainly political and not unlike Senator Richardson's. In both instances Boyle was defeated, largely because the middle perceived his candidacy as an attack on the core values of impartiality and expertise presumed to animate the courts. The question in California is whether that same moderate middle will similarly rise to the defense of the justices the next time around. That could come as soon as a successful recall drive is mounted or at some later date when a justice's name automatically appears on the ballot. The issue could also be presented by placing on the ballot a constitutional amendment significantly reducing the powers of the chief justice or otherwise altering the method of selection or terms of justices of the Supreme Court.

The choice before the justices thus depends ultimately upon the combination of an answer to a historical question and a prediction. One analysis starts from the premise that what happened in 1978 and 1979 was a fortuitous event without antecedents and without predictable consequences. The other, which I favor, regards those events as another skirmish reflective of the tension inherent in the American judicial role. Another battle is certain to occur sooner or later in some form. Under this view, it is the highest duty of a judge to maintain for the future judicial power as part of our system of governance.

The preservation of judicial power is not easily accomplished if we put together some observations made earlier. First, as Clark's research attorney noted, many (if not most) of the court's decisions have a political dimension: politically active interest groups win and lose cases before the court (*Tanner*); ideas that are politically potent are furthered or diminished by the rhetoric of opinions (school busing); and popular policies are vindicated or demolished by court rulings (Proposition 13). Second, the legal mechanisms of accountability, although rarely utilized, are always in the wings, an ever present threat to overwhelm judicial power. Finally, there is not now, if there ever was, a broad and satisfactory consensus that reconciles judicial power with democratic theory.

* Ladinsky & Silver, *Popular Democracy and Judicial Independence*, 1967 WIS. L. REV. 128.

The combination of the inevitability of political decisions, the constant threat of superior power, and the absence of a theory that legitimates the judicial role would seem to put the justices in an intolerably tenuous position. But that has been true since John Marshall. Americans have come over the years to believe deeply that judges have a useful if limited role in their governance. The key word is "limited." Our most honored judges of the past have willingly accepted the proposition that continued judicial power depends upon the confidence of the moderate middle—the same group that rescued the Wisconsin court in the 1960s. Some great judges, like Marshall and Warren, were spectacularly adroit political statesmen; others, like Traynor and Cardozo, were fabulously skillful craftsmen but relatively humble as political operators. Most judges have not been that great, but nearly all share a belief that confidence in judicial power can best be cultivated by staying close to the ideal of the moderate middle that judges are professionals who care deeply about impartiality and who see themselves as neutral interpreters of policies principally declared through the political arms of government.

The California justices may find it useful to think of what has here been called audiences—the bar, the press, the civil service—not only as people who read and react to the court's opinions but also as leaders who shape the attitudes of the broader public toward the court. It matters what the bar, the law schools and others think about the justices because the attitudes of those audiences will be influential far beyond their numbers. Craftsmanship, for example, is important not only because a sense of craft operates to constrain the process of decision but also because a technically persuasive analysis builds credibility in mediating audiences that are looked to for leadership at critical moments.

Recognizing that judicial power is always threatened by some exercise of majoritarian power is debilitating only if the justices believe they have a mandate to govern by virtue of their office. Phrased differently, trimming is a problem only if there is a program to be diluted. If the court has no program beyond fair process and if its fundamental principle is to do its best to understand, articulate, and promote the policy preferences of others, then judicial power should endure despite the ambiguities inherent in the justices' high office.

Ultimately the issue is whether the California justices are willing to accept this limited vision of their function.

APPENDIX
Chronology

February 12, 1977. Governor Edmund G. (Jerry) Brown, Jr., announces the selection of forty-year-old Rose Elizabeth Bird, his secretary of agriculture and services, to replace Donald Wright, who retired as chief justice of California on February 1. Brown simultaneously announces the appointment of Wiley Manuel to the Supreme Court. Bird is the first woman and Manuel the first black ever appointed to California's highest court.

March 11, 1977. The Commission on Judicial Appointments, composed of acting Chief Justice Mathew O. Tobriner, Attorney General Evelle Younger, and the senior presiding justice of the Court of Appeal, Parker Wood, after two days of hearing evidence, votes to confirm Brown's selection of Bird and Manuel. Wood votes not to confirm Bird.

May 2, 1977. A special tribunal, composed of seven randomly selected Court of Appeal justices, agrees with the recommendation of the Commission on Judicial Performance to retire Associate Justice Marshall McComb for senility. He is thereby retired and a vacancy on the court created.

July 16, 1977. The third Jerry Brown appointment to the court, Frank C. Newman, is approved by the Commission on Judicial Appointments and is sworn in.

June 1, 1978. State Senator H. L. (Bill) Richardson, a Republican from the Los Angeles area, announces that the Law and Order Campaign Committee he chairs will mount a $1 million campaign to defeat Bird in November.

June 6, 1978: Primary Day. Jerry Brown wins renomination as the Democratic candidate for governor. The Republicans select Attorney General Younger as their candidate. The voters also overwhelmingly approve Proposition 13.

June 23, 1978. The Supreme Court hands down the decision in *People* v. *Caudillo*. Bird concurs in the opinion but also writes a brief separate opinion. Justices Frank Richardson and William Clark dissent.

September 1, 1978. The Court of Appeal in Los Angeles stays the order of superior court Judge Paul Egly requiring busing in Los Angeles to combat racial segregation in the schools.

September 6, 1978. The Supreme Court overturns the stay order of the Court of Appeal with the effect that school busing will commence as planned on September 12. Clark and Richardson dissent without opinion.

September 22, 1978. The Supreme Court sustains the constitutionality of Proposition 13 against all challenges. Bird dissents in part. Caudillo is released on parole.

November 1, 1978. The Los Angeles Court of Appeal orders Caudillo, rearrested at the request of prison authorities on October 24, released again on parole.

November 3, 1978. Before Caudillo's release order can be executed, Tobriner as acting chief justice stays the order with the effect that Caudillo remains in custody.

November 7, 1978: Election Day. The *Los Angeles Times*, in a front-page story under the by-line of William Endicott and Robert Fairbanks, reports that the Supreme Court has decided to overturn the "use a gun, go to prison" law in *People* v. *Tanner* but has not made the decision public.

Bird wins confirmation by 51.7 percent. Manuel, Newman, and Richardson win confirmation by wider margins. Earlier in the day Bird issues a statement denying that the release of any decision has been delayed for political reasons.

November 9, 1978. The Supreme Court releases the opinions in *Hawkins v. Superior Court* and *People v. Levins.*

November 15, 1978. The same *Los Angeles Times* reporters publish a story suggesting that the reason for the delay in announcing the *Tanner* case may have been a caustic dissent by Clark, which charged Bird with being inconsistent in her opinions in *Caudillo* and *Tanner.*

November 16, 1978. Tobriner is reported to have circulated a statement among his colleagues stating that "neither the final determination nor the filing of the decision [in *Tanner*] has been delayed for a political or any other improper purpose." At least one justice is reported to have refused to sign Tobriner's statement.

November 19, 1978. K. Connie Kang, a reporter for the *San Francisco Examiner,* writes a story containing the full history of the *Tanner* case.

November 23, 1978: Thanksgiving Day. Lou Cannon, West Coast correspondent for the *Washington Post,* writes an article reporting that court sources anticipate a formal inquiry into the *Tanner* matter by the Commission on Judicial Performance.

November 24, 1978. Bird releases to the press a letter to Justice Bertram Janes, chairman of the Commission on Judicial Performance, requesting that the commission undertake an investigation into the delay in filing the *Tanner* opinion.

December 1, 1978. The Commission on Judicial Performance announces that it is commencing a full inquiry into allegations of "improprieties in the processing of cases—and related matters—by the Supreme Court."

December 15, 1978. The Supreme Court files its decision in *Fox v. City of Los Angeles.* Newman, joined by Tobriner, Stanley H. Mosk, and Manuel, upholds an injunction against placing a lighted cross on the Los Angeles city hall during Christmas and Easter. Bird, joined by Tobriner, writes a concurring opinion. Richardson's dissent is joined by Clark, but Clark also writes a separate dissent criticizing Newman's opinion for failing to state a holding or a rationale.

December 18, 1978. The Commission on Judicial Performance requests the Judicial Council to amend the rules to permit it, after conducting a preliminary investigation, to conduct proceedings in public or to disclose its findings publicly.

December 22, 1978. The decision in *People* v. *Tanner* is announced. Bird concurs in the result but not the reasoning. Clark dissents in an opinion joined by Richardson. Clark's opinion cites Bird's opinion in *Caudillo* as supporting his view. Manuel dissents in a brief separate opinion.

December 29, 1978. The Commission on Judicial Performance announces the selection of Seth Hufstedler as its special counsel in the investigation of the Supreme Court.

January 10, 1979. The executive committee of the Judicial Council recommends to the full council a rejection of the commission's request for a relaxation of the confidentiality rules applicable to the commission.

January 16, 1979. Contrary to its executive committee, the Judicial Council adopts Rule 902.5, requiring that the preliminary investigation of the Supreme Court be conducted in public.

January 29, 1979. The Judicial Council amends Rule 902.5 to permit television stations to cover the proceedings.

February 9, 1979. The court decides to rehear the *Tanner* case and vacates its decision (announced December 22). Mosk joins the *Tanner* dissenters to make up the four votes necessary to order a rehearing.

March 7, 1979. Tanner is re-argued before the Supreme Court.

April 25, 1979. The commission announces that public hearings on the justices of the Supreme Court will commence on June 11 and states the procedural rules that will govern the preliminary stage of the proceedings.

June 11, 1979. The commission's public hearings start with Hufstedler's opening statement and introduction of his written report. The commission adjourns for a week to study Hufstedler's report and exhibits.

June 14, 1979. The Supreme Court announces the decision in *Tanner II.* Clark writes for a majority of himself, Mosk, Richardson, and Manuel. Bird, Tobriner, and Newman each file a separate opinion.

June 18, 1979. The commission's evidentiary hearings start. Richardson is the first witness.

June 19, 1979. Richardson concludes his testimony. He is followed by two witnesses from the staff of the Supreme Court.

June 20–22, 1979. Tobriner testifies.

June 25, 1979. Tobriner concludes his testimony. One of his research attorneys, Michael Willemsen, begins testifying in the afternoon.

June 26, 1979. Willemsen concludes. Bird testifies in the afternoon.

June 27–29, 1979. Bird testifies.

July 2, 1979. Bird continues to testify. She refuses to answer questions (on instructions from counsel) relating to information communicated by her staff to her counsel. In the afternoon Justice Clark takes the stand.

July 3, 5, and 6, 1979. Clark testifies.

July 9, 1979. Clark concludes his direct testimony. Steven Buehl, Bird's executive assistant, begins testifying. Mosk files a lawsuit in the Long Beach branch of the Los Angeles superior court to quash the subpoena requiring him to testify before the commission in public session.

July 10, 1979. Buehl concludes and is followed by two research attorneys on Bird's staff and one on Tobriner's staff.

July 11, 1979. Superior court Judge Robert Wenke hears arguments in the *Mosk* suit.

July 12, 1979. Wenke holds Rule 902.5 constitutional and refuses Mosk's petition to quash the subpoena. Mosk appeals to the Los Angeles Court of Appeal. Hal Cohen, Tobriner's research attorney, who started testifying on July 10, concludes his testimony.

July 13, 1979. Maury Koplick, one of Clark's research attorneys, testifies in the morning. Richard Morris, another Clark research attorney, starts his testimony in the afternoon.

July 16, 1979. Clark is cross-examined by counsel for Tobriner and Bird in the morning. Morris continues testifying in the afternoon. The Court of Appeal issues a temporary stay of Wenke's ruling.

July 17, 1979. Morris's testimony is concluded. Manuel takes the stand. Following the luncheon recess, Hufstedler announces that the Los Angeles Court of Appeal has directed the superior court in Los Angeles to quash the subpoena requiring Mosk to testify on the ground that Rule 902.5 requiring public proceedings by the commission is unconstitutional. The commission recesses until the next day.

July 18, 1979. Hufstedler files an emergency appeal in the *Mosk* suit to the Supreme Court. He asks the court to grant a hearing in the *Mosk* case and to select a panel of uninvolved judges to hear the case on the merits.

July 19, 1979. The Supreme Court asks counsel in the *Mosk* case a series of questions and sets a briefing schedule that will end on July 30. Since no final Supreme Court decision will be possible for several weeks, Chairman Janes indicates that the commission will reconvene in confidential session the next day. The commission never again meets in public session.

July 23–27, 1979. The commission hears evidence in seven new proceedings (one against each justice) in secret.

July 30, 1979. All the justices except Newman disqualify themselves from considering whether to hear the appeal in the *Mosk* case. Bird appoints six Court of Appeal justices selected by lot to sit on the case pro tem. Newman does not explain his refusal to disqualify himself.

August 7, 1979. The ad hoc Supreme Court* grants Hufstedler's petition for hearing and schedules argument on the merits for September 20. The ad hoc court refuses to disqualify Newman but requests further briefing on his participation. The court orders a document filed by Hufstedler as an exhibit sealed.

August 9, 1979. The *Los Angeles Times* publishes portions of the sealed document.

August 13, 1979. Kathryn Gehrels resigns from the commission.

August 14, 1979. Mosk denounces the commission in a speech at the American Bar Association convention in Dallas.

---

* Properly speaking this body is as much the Supreme Court as the "regular" court, but the phrase "ad hoc Supreme Court" is used here for convenience.

August 22, 1979. The ad hoc Supreme Court orders argument on the Newman disqualification for August 29.

August 24, 1979. In protest over Newman's failure to disqualify himself, commission member Hillel Chodos refuses to participate further in the investigation of Supreme Court justices, but he does not resign from the commission.

August 29, 1979. The ad hoc Supreme Court hears argument on the issue of Newman's disqualification.

August 31, 1979. The ad hoc Supreme Court, Newman not participating, rules that Newman has until September 7 to file a response to the commission's request that he be disqualified.

September 7, 1979. Newman files an answer and statement of explanation.

September 13, 1979. Hufstedler and counsel for Mosk agree that retired Chief Justice Wright should decide the Newman disqualification issue. Wright schedules argument for September 17.

September 14, 1979. Bird announces that Wright is legally unauthorized to sit on the Newman disqualification matter.

September 16, 1979. Newman and Hufstedler briefly argue Newman's disqualification before the ad hoc Supreme Court.

September 19, 1979. The ad hoc Supreme Court, Newman not participating, orders Newman disqualified by a four–two vote. Bird designates another Court of Appeal justice selected by lot to sit in Newman's place.

September 20, 1979. The ad hoc Supreme Court hears argument on the merits of the *Mosk* suit.

October 18, 1979. The ad hoc Supreme Court unanimously decides that Rule 902.5 unconstitutionally calls for public hearings. Under the ruling, the commission may only issue a report of the result of any investigation.

November 5, 1979. In a brief announcement the commission states that "the investigation [of justices of the Supreme Court] is . . . now terminated, and the result hereby announced is that no formal charges will be filed against any Supreme Court justice." Tobriner releases a statement expressing pleasure that the commission found "that charges were not warranted."

November 6, 1979: Election Day. Bird issues a statement that she is "pleased . . . that the long and difficult ordeal of the Court is now over." Commission member Thomas Willoughby tells reporters in Sacramento that the commission's report should not be viewed as an exoneration of the justices.

Index